DAX For Humans

The No CALCULATE Guide that Makes DAX Easy

Greg Deckler

DAX For Humans

© 2025 Gregory J. Deckler

Cover Art: Alexandre P, https://www.fiverr.com/alerrandre

Interior Art Editor: Rocket "Alex" Deckler

Interior Art Credits. These works are edited:

- Chapter 1: Frank R. Paul, Amazing Stories, April 1929
- Chapter 2: Frank R. Paul, Amazing Stories, June 1926
- Chapter 3: Frank R. Paul, Amazing Stories, July 1926
- Chapter 4: Frank R. Paul, Amazing Stories, August 1926
- Chapter 5: Frank R. Paul, Amazing Stories, August 1927
- Chapter 6: Frank R. Paul, Amazing Stories, July 1929
- Chapter 7: Frank R. Paul, Amazing Stories, January 1927
- Chapter 8: Frank R. Paul, Amazing Stories, May 1926
- Chapter 9: Frank R. Paul, Amazing Stories, July 1927
- Chapter 10: Frank R. Paul, Amazing Stories, August 1928
- Chapter 11: Frank R. Paul, Amazing Stories, March 1929
- Chapter 12: Frank R. Paul, Amazing Stories, April 1928
- Chapter 13: Frank R. Paul, Amazing Stories, November 1928
- Chapter 14: Unknown/Uncredited, Amazing Stories Quarterly, Summer 1929. Interior artwork for "Venus Liberated" credited to Hugh MacKay.
- Chapter 15: Frank R. Paul, Amazing Stories, June 1929
- Chapter 16: Frank R. Paul, Amazing Stories, March 1927

First published: July 2025

ISBN: 9781806699957

gdeckler@gmail.com

About the Author

Greg Deckler is a prolific writer and respected authority in the field of business intelligence, particularly known for his expertise in Microsoft Power BI and DAX. With over 30 years of experience in technology consulting, Greg currently serves as Vice President at a global technology consulting services firm.

Greg's literary contributions include several influential books aimed at both beginners and advanced users of Power BI including Learn Power BI 1st, 2nd and 3rd editions, DAX Cookbook, Power BI Cookbook 2nd and 3rd editions, Mastering Power BI 2nd edition, and The Definitive Guide to Power Query (M).

Greg is also an active Power BI community member, having authored more than 7,500 solutions on the Power BI community forums and nearly 200 entries to the community's Quick Measure Gallery. In addition, Greg often blogs, has founded Power BI user groups, presents at various conferences, and is a seven-time Microsoft MVP for Data Platform.

Beyond writing and community involvement, Greg also runs the YouTube channels Microsoft Hates Greg and DAX For Humans. In addition, Greg is the author of numerous external tools for Power BI including Microsoft Hates Greg's Quick Measures (MSHGQM).

Through his extensive work, Greg Deckler continues to be a pivotal figure in advancing the use and understanding of Power BI in the business intelligence landscape.

Dedication

This book is dedicated to my wonderful patrons who have supported the creation of this book and to whom I am forever grateful. Listed in order of joining my Patreon page.

1. **Brian Julius**
2. **Bryon Smedley**
3. **Deron Huskey**
4. John Dages
5. **Aske Laustsen**
6. **Tim Osborn**
7. **Rafiullah Shaheedullah**
8. **Henk-Jan van Well**
9. **Henrik Vestergaard**
10. **Hamish Maxwell**
11. **Jasmin Simader**
12. **Diana Ackermann**
13. **Aaron McVay**
14. John Howard
15. **Jacco**
16. **Alexis Olson**
17. Phillip Lind
18. Winston
19. **Tamer (Juma)**
20. Richard Burnett
21. **Garvin 5.0**
22. Catherine Palmer
23. Mark Cunningham
24. Bip
25. Jonathan Vandervort
26. Paul Wyatt
27. Micah Harner
28. Sadiq
29. Jan
30. **Christopher Aragao**
31. Mateusz Mossakowski
32. **Pawel Wrona**
33. Jason Richter
34. Nelson Mwangi
35. Henry Partner
36. Simon
37. **Rafael Ayres**
38. Rich McMullen
39. Greg Hamper
40. Chris
41. Nazmul Islam Jobair
42. Alexandru Badiu
43. Fernando Lopez
44. **Julliette Carignan**
45. **Matthew Floyd**
46. D-Lloyd Agencies
47. Kirill Perian
48. **Zachi Shefer**
49. **Rasmus Ludvigsen**
50. **Darran**
51. Paul
52. Carlo Romanelli
53. Abubakar Alvi
54. Lukasz Wrobel
55. Mark Brookes
56. TO
57. Adam
58. **Antti Rask**
59. Kev
60. Dean Kuhn
61. Tony
62. Susan Bayes
63. JAJ Snyman
64. Dennis Priester
65. DURAND
66. Inan Bhulyan
67. Qadim A

Additional Thanks

Special thanks to these additional Patreon followers:

- Aleksander
- D-Lloyed Agencies
- Nazmul Islam Jobair
- Nauris Ozols
- Lisa Sheehy
- kalyan kumar
- Maria Tynan
- Kamal
- mikhail stotskiy
- Manuel Barahona Gandia
- James Whitehead
- Peter
- Jedless
- Jim Titus
- Wale
- Achmad Farizky
- K
- Eric Laforce
- Morten Lillevik
- gianivo
- Stephanie
- Eliezer Kanevski
- philkhana aparna
- Jacobus Snyman
- Osama
- Khurram Sheikh
- David Johnson
- John Griffiths
- **Abraham Karmel**
- **Thomas Garvin**
- Mohammed
- Bartłomiej Jaskólski
- Rin Mai
- BC
- Gaurav Guliani
- valapo
- kjstvr
- Joanna Hryniewicz
- Douglas Cory
- Patrick JACQUART
- MSkovronsky
- amitmend
- Phillip Poole
- Jørgen
- Sathish
- Burkhard BrÃ¤kling
- Sarah Krusleski
- AJAY KUMAR
- Yann
- Gaetan Mourmant
- **Lionel Sheikboudhou**

Important Links

GitHub Repository

https://github.com/gdeckler/DAX-For-Humans/tree/main/book

DAX For Humans YouTube Channel

https://www.youtube.com/@daxforhumans

Microsoft Hates Greg YouTube Channel

https://www.youtube.com/@microsofthatesgreg

Table of Contents

Foreword

The fact that you are even holding this book in your hand or reading it on your screen is something of a miracle.

To understand why, let's set the Wayback Machine to July 23, 2020.

I am certain that if you'd conducted a survey on that day asking every single DAX user to name the most important DAX function, the unanimous answer would have been "CALCULATE".

Well, actually unanimous minus one, but I'm getting a little ahead of myself…

At that time, here's what the two top DAX books said about CALCULATE:

"CALCULATE( ) is the most important and powerful function in the DAX language. It is important because it is the only function that has the ability to modify the natural filtering behavior of visuals."

"CALCULATE is the most important, useful, and complex function in DAX, so it deserves a full chapter."

We all accepted this as if it was handed down to us on stone tablets, and CALCULATE was the cornerstone of every book, video, and course you could use to learn DAX.

Then on July 24, 2020 at 11:13am, Greg Deckler took the slingshot out of his back pocket and hurled a rock straight at this cornerstone, in the form of an article he posted on the Microsoft Community forum entitled *"CALCUHATE - Why I Don't Use DAX's CALCULATE Function"*. In this article, Greg laid out a very detailed argument why CALCULATE is not only inessential to DAX, but in fact makes it more difficult to write, debug, and maintain.

I wish I could tell you that upon reading that article, the scales immediately fell from my eyes and I recognized it as a better and easier way to write DAX. However, I did not. I'm not sure whether it was an insufficient understanding of the nuances of DAX necessary to fully grasp Greg's arguments, or intellectual laziness, or most likely some combination of both. Regardless, I kept writing DAX as I always had - with CALCULATE in the lead role.

However, that CALCUHATE article continued to nag at me, and two years later I found myself responsible for assembling the speakers for a large conference on DAX and Power BI. In that intervening period, I had gotten to know Greg a bit, bonding over our shared hatred of the DAX time intelligence functions.

He enthusiastically accepted my invitation to speak at the conference, delivering a masterful presentation entitled *"DAX Counterculture: Alternative Perspectives on DAX"* in which he clearly and systematically walked through his arguments against the use of CALCULATE and DAX time intelligence functions.

Unlike two years prior, I now found myself unable to ignore the incompatibility of the views that *"CALCULATE is the most important function in DAX"* and *"CALCULATE is wholly unnecessary, and actually makes DAX harder"*.

As the son of a biochemist who, from the time I was eight years old used to sneak me into the lab on weekends to conduct scientific experiments together, I publicly committed to performing an experiment of my own – for the entire month of September I would attempt not to use a single CALCULATE in any of the DAX I was writing, and would publish my results at the end of the month.

At that time, I was building Power BI reports on a daily basis and honestly expected that somewhere within those 30 days, I would encounter a situation that could not be resolved without the use of CALCULATE.

Much to my surprise, that day never came, and at the end of the 30-days, I found that DAX without CALCULATE **was** far easier to write, understand, and debug.

However, when I posted these results, many of the comments I received confidently stated that even if that were true, measures constructed without CALCULATE would perform much worse than those written in the accepted style.

So, back to the "lab" where I took reports from highly accomplished Power BI developers, reconstructed their measures in the "No CALCULATE" style, tested the performance of each pair of measures, and found no evidence of a statistical difference in performance between the two approaches.

I also ran these tests on increasingly large data sets, up to 20 million records, to counter the argument that the No CALCULATE approach would break down at large scale, and again found no evidence to support that contention.

Recognizing that CALCULATE is miles from being the most important function in DAX has profound implications for the way we should be teaching DAX. This revelation allows us to put CALCULATE in its proper context – a very advanced function (along the lines of CROSSFILTER or TREATAS) that should be one of the **last** ones taught, useful for "fine tuning" in very limited and specific use cases.

Now, the idea of teaching DAX beginners by building upon a foundation of CALCULATE makes no more sense to me than teaching a toddler to walk by taking them out to the track and shouting at them to run the 400m hurdles, or teaching a teenager to drive by strapping them into a racecar at the 24 Hours of Le Mans.

However, coming to that revelation presented me with an entirely new problem. By then I had become a very loud public proponent of Greg's approach to learning and writing DAX. DAX unquestionably remains the largest hurdle to learning Power BI, and many users struggling with it asked me the best way to learn the No CALCULATE approach.

Until this moment, my answer always felt largely unsatisfactory, pointing them to a scattered collection of articles (including CALCUHATE, of course...) videos, and presentations explaining it.

However, with the publication of this book, there now is an integrated and comprehensive resource for learning DAX in an easier and better way. Far from being a dry, theoretical tome it is a plain language treasure trove - packed with highly practical uses across a wide range of domains and applications. I sincerely hope you find it as enlightening and enjoyable as I have.

To me, it also stands as a valuable reminder that the truth of a statement is not always determined by the number of people repeating it. Occasionally, that lone dissenting voice with the insight and courage to tell the rest of us "you're wrong" ends up being right on target...

Brian Julius,

Power BI expert and instructor

CHAPTER 1

1

Introducing DAX

Data Analysis eXpressions (**DAX**) is a formula language that many might recognize as being similar to Excel's formula language. While this similarity is perhaps rather superficial, it is sufficient for our purposes that similar to how users can create formulas in Excel using Excel's formula language, so too can **Power BI Desktop** users create calculations in Power BI using DAX. While DAX can also be used in Excel with the **Power Pivot** add-in as well as in Analysis Services, this book focuses on the use of DAX within Power BI Desktop, which is Microsoft's premier business intelligence and reporting software and service.

Historically, DAX has a reputation of being difficult to learn and master. One might find this surprising considering that there are almost 200 functions in DAX that share the same name and functionality as Excel's formula language. Considering that DAX has just over 250 functions in total, these nearly 200 functions represent the majority of the DAX language and yet Excel's formula language has never been classified as "difficult to learn".

This seeming contradiction has its roots in the fundamental differences between how Excel's formula language "thinks" and how DAX "thinks". However, a larger issue is the traditional method by which DAX is taught, which centers on DAX's **CALCULATE** function. DAX's **CALCULATE** function is one of, if not the most, complex and difficult to understand functions in the DAX language. Attempting to learn DAX by first learning **CALCULATE** is like trying to learn physics by starting with quantum mechanics.

Therefore, this book takes a fundamentally different approach to learning DAX. In fact, by the end of this chapter, you will have already learned many of the functions required to create most common DAX calculations as well as learned a single, fundamental DAX formula pattern that will help you create just about any DAX calculation you can conceive of.

First, however, you will need to download and install the software where you will be writing your DAX formulas, so let's start by getting Power BI Desktop installed on our computer.

Getting Power BI Desktop

As mentioned, Power BI Desktop is Microsoft's premier business intelligence and reporting application. Power BI Desktop is designed to connect to data, mash up that data into a model and then analyze and visualize that data interactively in the form of bar charts, line charts, waterfall charts, etc.

To install Power BI Desktop, you must have a Windows PC running Windows 8, 8.1, 10 or 11. It is also recommended that you have at least 10 GB of disk storage space available.

The easiest way to install Power BI Desktop is to enter the following link into any browser window, https://aka.ms/pbidesktop. When prompted to open the **Microsoft Store**, click the **Open** button as shown in *Figure 1.1*:

Figure 1.1: Microsoft Store open prompt

Within the Microsoft Store application, click the **Install** button to install Power BI Desktop as shown in *Figure 1.2*:

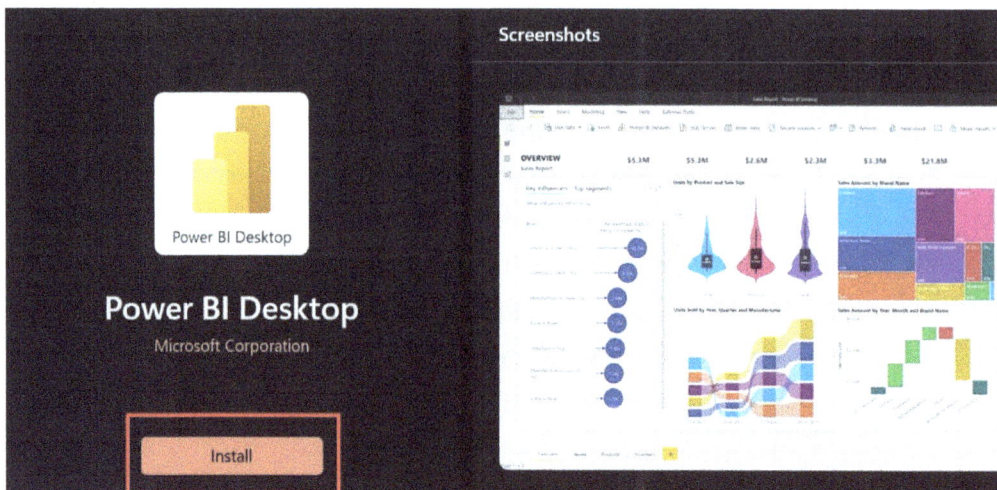

Figure 1.2: Installing Power BI Desktop from the Microsoft Store

Alternatively, you can type the word **"store"** into the Windows search bar and open the Microsoft Store directly as shown in *Figure 1.3*:

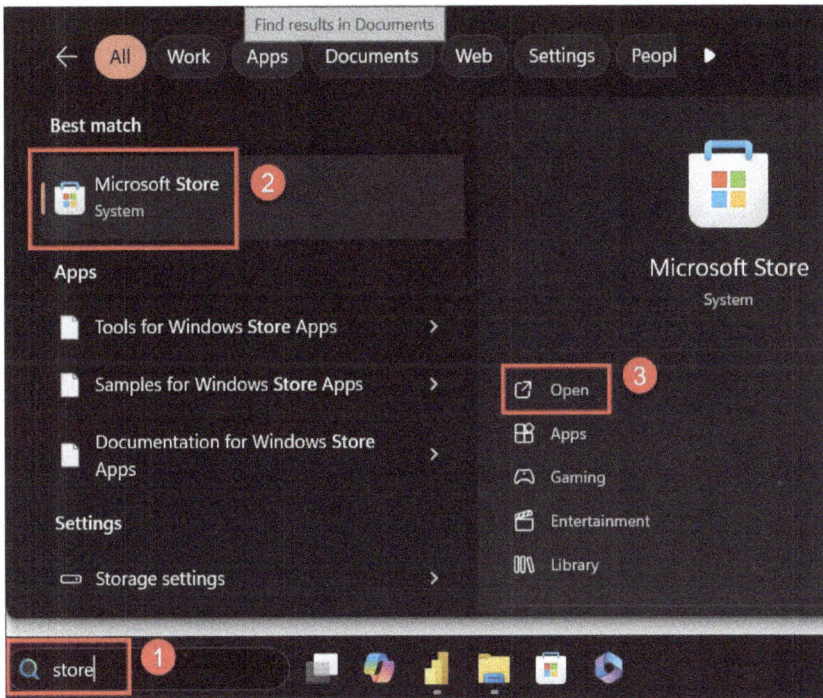

Figure 1.3: Opening the Microsoft Store from the Windows search bar.

In the Microsoft Store search bar, type **"power bi desktop"** and click on the suggested app:

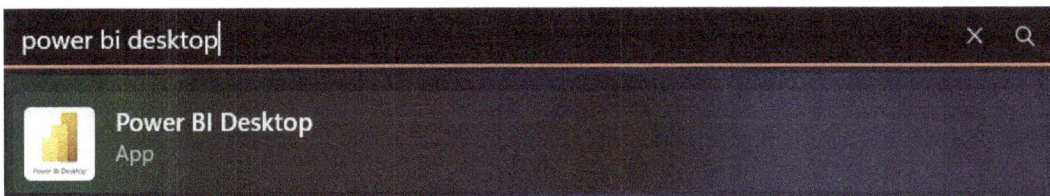

Figure 1.4: Power BI Desktop app in the Microsoft Store.

You can now click on the **Install** button as shown in *Figure 1.2*.

Watch the **Install** button to keep track of installation status. The app download is approximately 730 MB. Once downloaded and installed, the **Install** button will now have the text **"Open"**. Click the **Open** button to open Power BI Desktop.

It is recommended that you right-click the Power BI Desktop icon in the Windows taskbar and select **"Pin to taskbar"**. This pins Power BI Desktop to the taskbar for easy access. Next, close any splash screen that might appear for Power BI Desktop. Finally, on the Power BI **Home** page, select **Blank report**:

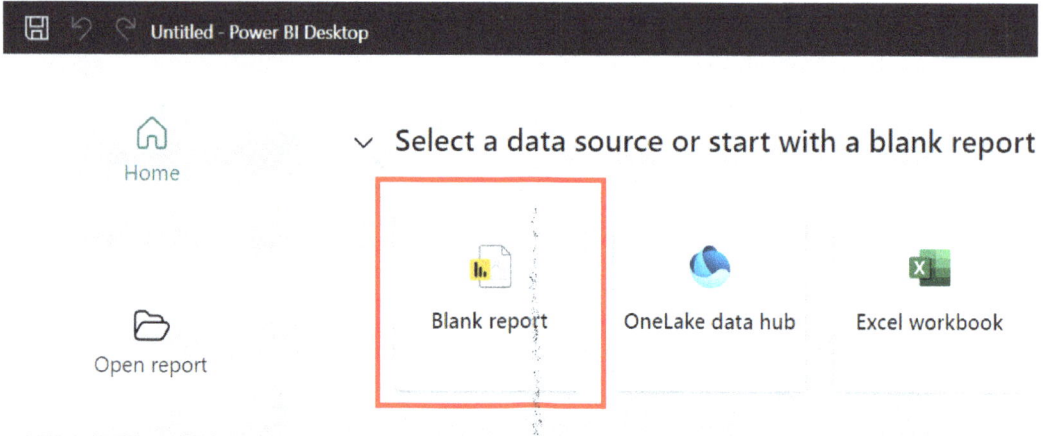

Figure 1.5: Power BI Desktop Home page.

We are now ready to briefly tour Power BI Desktop.

Touring Power BI Desktop

As shown in *Figure 1.6*, the Power BI Desktop user interface is generally analogous to other Microsoft Office applications, such as Microsoft Excel, with a **Header**, **Ribbon**, and central area, in this case known as the **Canvas**.

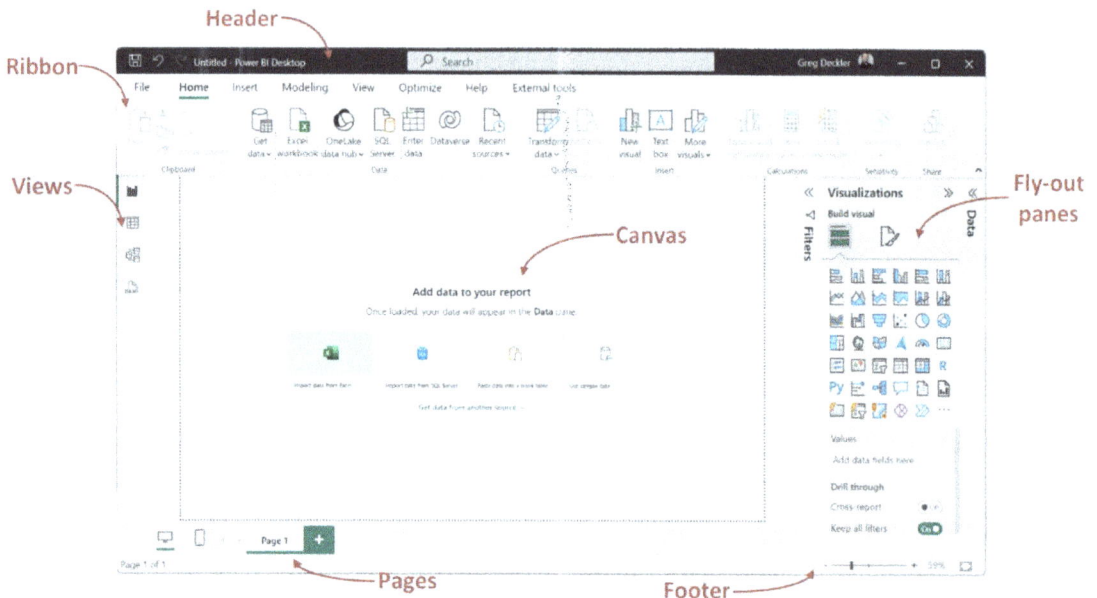

Figure 1.6: Power BI Desktop.

Header

As with other Microsoft Office applications, the **Header** area provides the ability to quickly save the file using the far-left icon as well as the name of the file, in this case "**Untitled**", a **Search** bar and standard minimize, maximize and close icons on the far right.

Ribbon

Below the **Header** is the **Ribbon** which provides access to various actions that can be performed across a number of tabs such as **File**, **Home**, **Insert**, **Modeling**, **View**, **Optimize**, and **Help**. Some of these tabs are conditional, such as the **External tools** tab shown in *Figure 1.6*. The **External tools** tab only appears if external (third-party) tools are installed such as Tabular Editor or DAX Studio.

Views

Below the ribbon on the far left is the **Views** pane. The **Views** pane contains four different views listed from the top to the bottom:

- **Report view** – Used for building interactive reports consisting of one or more visualizations.
- **Table view** – Used for viewing the underlying table data.
- **Model view** – Used for viewing and editing the semantic model (relationships between tables).
- **DAX Query view** – Used for writing and debugging DAX queries.

You will become familiar with these views as you progress in this book.

Canvas

To the right of the **Views** pane is the **Canvas**. The **Canvas** is actually different depending upon the view selected. In **Report** view, the **Canvas** is the central area where you place visuals as shown in *Figure 1.6*.

However, in **Table** view, the **Canvas** presents the report data in a manner similar to an Excel file as columns and rows as shown in *Figure 1.7*:

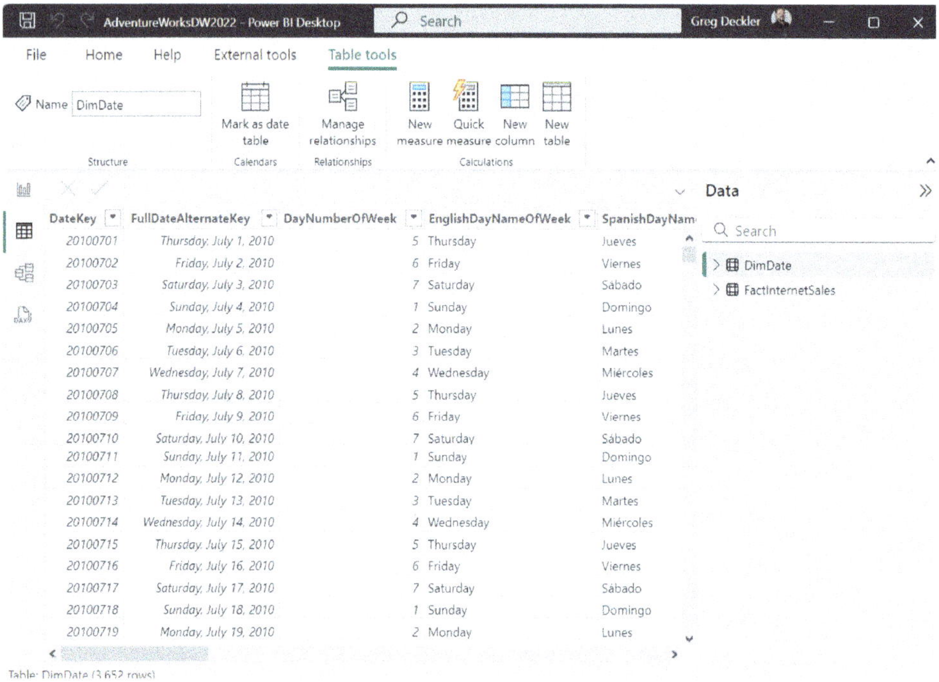

Figure 1.7: Table view.

Additionally, as shown in *Figure 1.7*, only certain ribbon tabs are available while in **Table view**.

In the **Model view**, the **Canvas** is again different and displays the various tables of the model as well as any relationships between those tables.

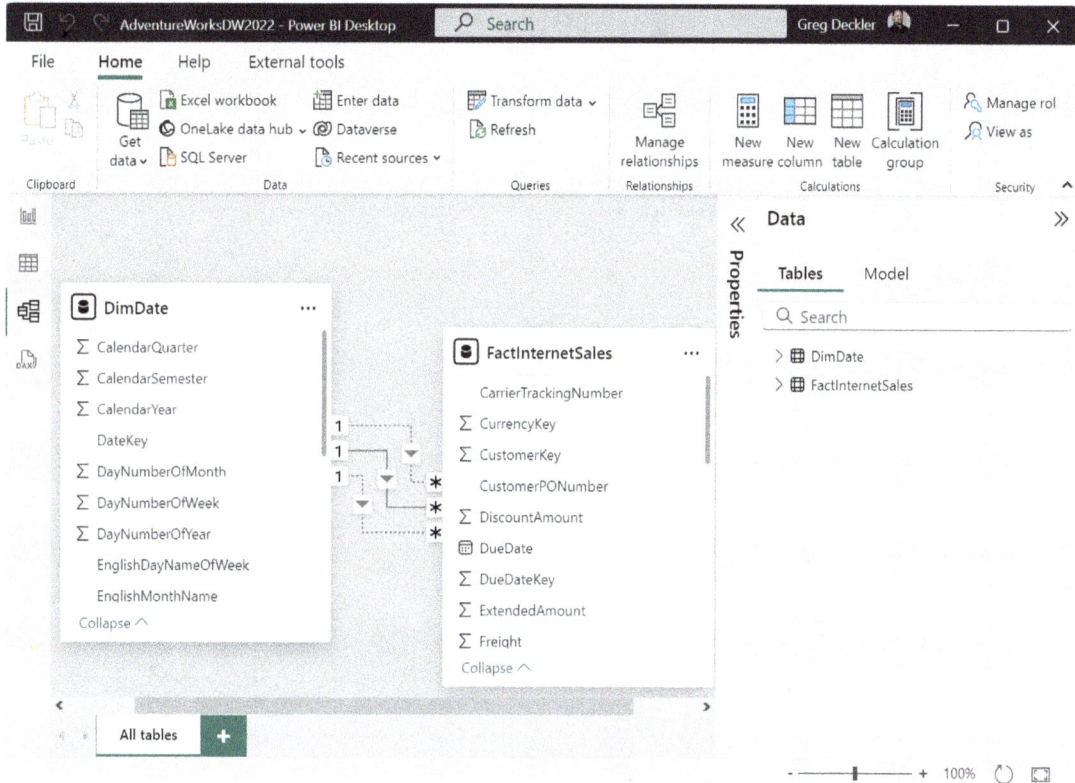

Figure 1.8: Model view.

Finally, in **DAX Query view**, the **Canvas** serves as an area for entering DAX queries and viewing results.

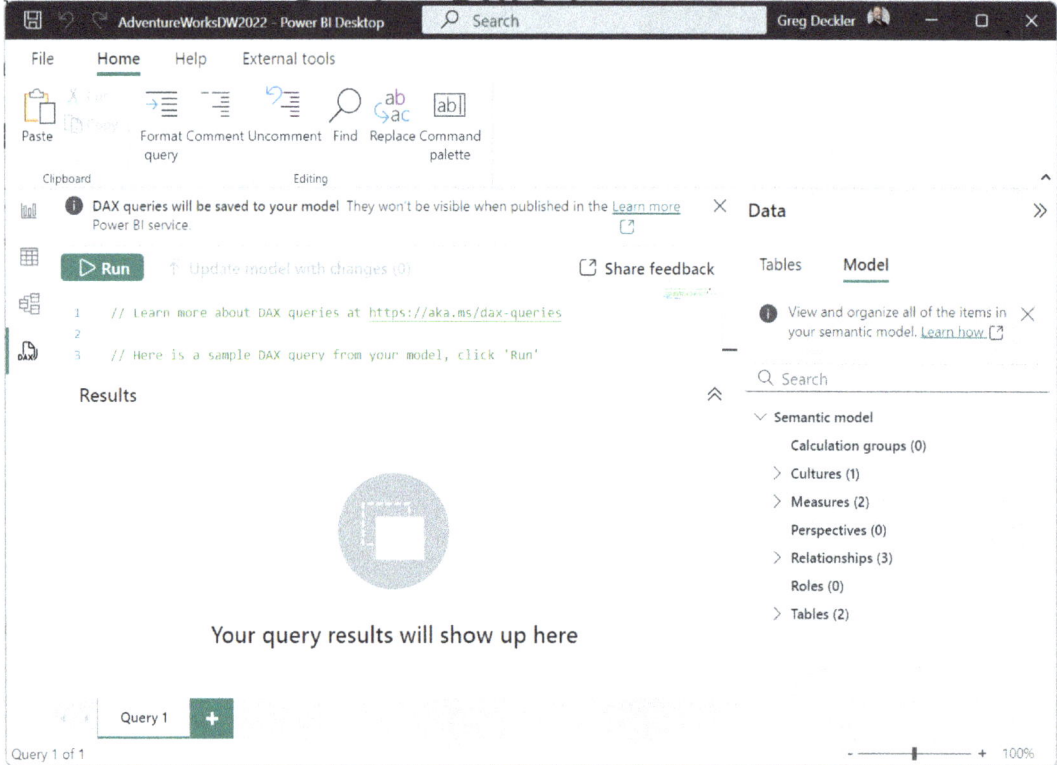

Figure 1.9: DAX Query view.

We will explore the purpose and function of the **Canvas** in each of these views throughout the rest of the book but let's now move on to **Fly-out panes**.

Fly-out panes

Similar to **Ribbon** tabs, the **Fly-out panes** are conditional depending upon which **View** you are in. These fly-out panes provide access to various functionalities including:

- **Data** – Enables you to select data as well as edit the properties of the data and edit the semantic model.
- **Visualizations** – Provides the ability to build and modify visuals
- **Filter** – Allows you to filter the entire report, individual pages or individual visuals.

These are not the only fly-out panes available but are the three primary fly-out panes used within this book. Other fly-out panes will be introduced as necessary throughout the rest of the book.

The fly-out panes can be expanded and collapsed by clicking on the double chevron icons (>> to collapse, << to expand) in the upper-right corner of each fly-out pane.

Pages

Pages in Power BI Desktop are similar to tabs in Microsoft Excel. Just as an Excel workbook can have multiple tabs of data, so too can a Power BI Desktop file have multiple report pages.

The **Pages** area also has different functions depending upon the particular **View** you are in. For example, in the **Model view**, the **Pages** area is used to present multiple views of the semantic model as shown in *Figure 1.8*, while in **DAX Query view**, the **Pages** area is used to create multiple DAX queries as shown in *Figure 1.9*.

Footer

The **Footer** area also varies depending upon your current **View**. However, in general, the **Footer** area provides additional controls and information such as a zoom slicer, the current page of a report and the number of total pages in the report.

Do not feel alarmed if all of this looks a bit overwhelming or be concerned that you do not understand some of the terms being used. This section is merely meant to quickly orientate you to the major components of the user interface versus providing a comprehensive, in-depth treatment of everything Power BI Desktop is capable of. You will become much more familiar with Power BI Desktop as we progress within this chapter and the rest of the book.

Entering and Importing Data

Power BI Desktop is a business intelligence, analytics and reporting tool that deals with data. As such, you can't really do anything in Power BI Desktop without first having some data to work with. Therefore, our first priority is to get some data that we can work with throughout the rest of this chapter. While there are a variety of methods of connecting to data, we will focus on two methods, **Enter data queries** and **import queries**.

> You can choose to follow the directions in this section to enter and import data into Power BI Desktop or, alternatively, you can download the files for this book from the GitHub repository located here:
> https://github.com/gdeckler/DAX-For-Humans/tree/main/book
>
> Open the file **EnteringAndImportingData.pbix** in the **Chapter1** folder and then skip to the next section, **Creating a Visual**.

Enter data queries

Enter data queries are the quickest, easiest way to get a small amount of ad hoc data into Power BI Desktop. To use an **Enter data** query, ensure that you are in **Report** view and on the **Home** tab of the ribbon. Click the **Enter data** option in the ribbon as shown in *Figure 1.10*:

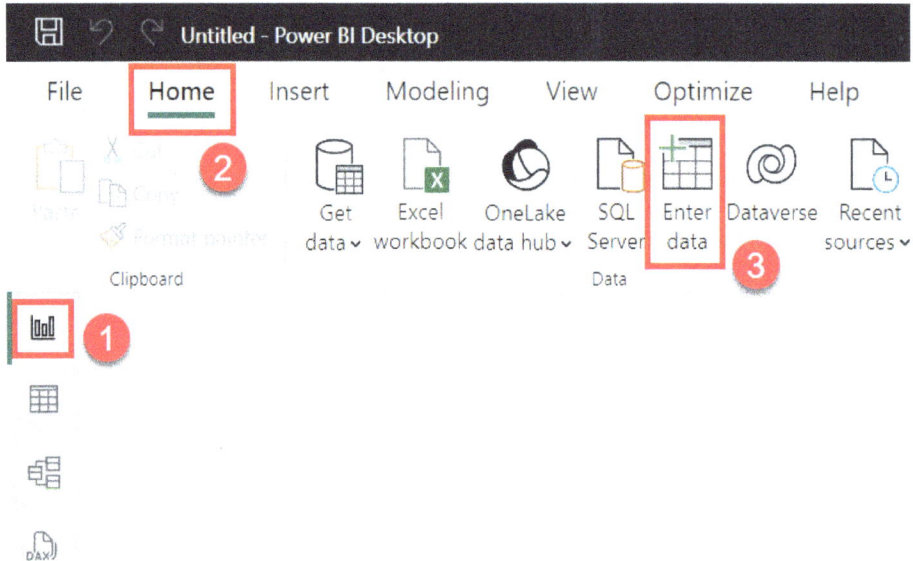

Figure 1.10: Enter data query.

The **Create Table** dialog appears as shown in *Figure 1.11*:

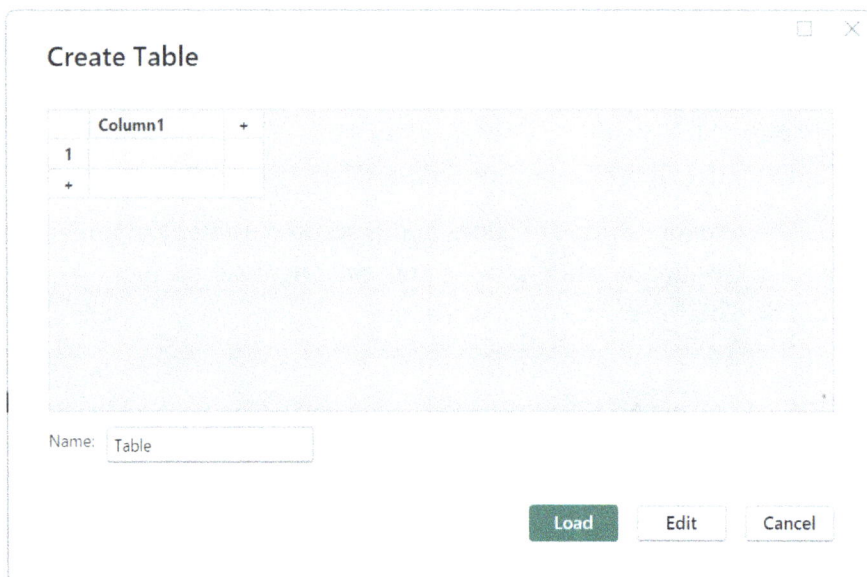

Figure 1.11: Create Table dialog.

First, click the **+** icon in the column header row to the right of **Column1** in order to add a new column called **Column2**. Repeat this procedure to add a **Column3** and **Column4**. Double-click the **Column1** header text and rename the column to **Item**. Repeat this procedure renaming **Column2** to **Price**, **Column3** to **Quantity** and **Column4** to **Date**.

Double-click the empty cell under the **Item** column in the row labeled with a **1**. Enter the word **Pickle** and then click the **Tab** key to navigate to the next empty cell to the right. Enter **3.99**. Click tab again and enter **2**. Click tab again and enter **1/2/2023**. Now click the **Enter** key to navigate to the next row.

Repeat this procedure to enter the information in *Table 1.1*.

Item	Price	Quantity	Date
Pickle	3.99	2	1/2/2023
Banana	2.99	3	1/2/2023
Pickle	3.99	4	1/10/2023
Banana	2.99	5	1/11/2023
Grapefruit	4.99	3	1/14/2023

Table 1.1: Enter data query data.

Once all of the data is entered, simply click the **Load** button shown in *Figure 1.11*. This closes the **Create Table** dialog and loads the data into Power BI Desktop.

Use the **File** menu to save your file or click the **Save** icon in the far left of the **Header**.

Import queries

As noted previously, **Enter data** queries are useful for quickly entering small amounts of ad hoc data. However, for larger amounts of data it is recommended to use import queries. Import queries can connect to hundreds, if not thousands, of different data sources including SQL databases, OData feeds, comma-separated files, SharePoint lists, and so on. To demonstrate the basics of how this is done, we will use an Excel file.

The Excel file to use can be found in the **Chapter 1** folder of the GitHub repository for this book: https://github.com/gdeckler/DAX-For-Humans/tree/main/book. The Excel file is called **EnteringAndImportingData.xlsx**. Download this file to your computer then follow these instructions.

Ensure that you are in **Report** view and on the **Home** tab of the ribbon. Click the **Excel workbook** option in the ribbon as shown in *Figure 1.12*:

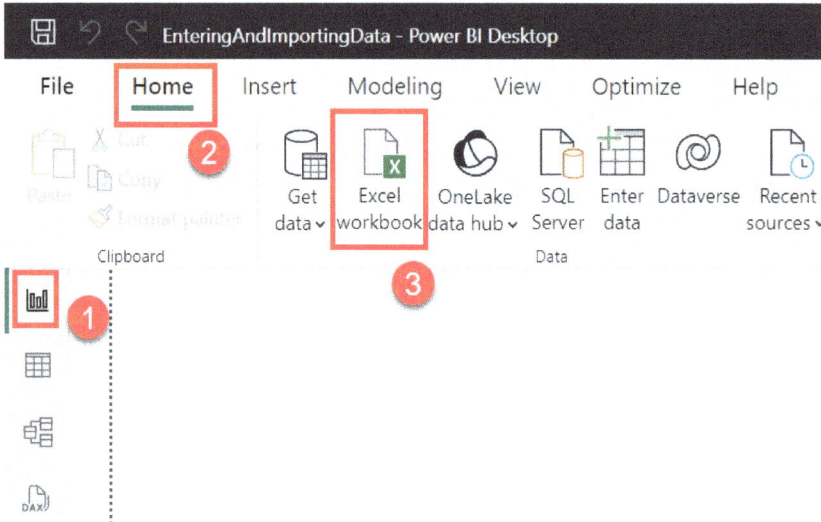

Figure 1.12: Import an Excel workbook.

Use the **Open** file dialog to navigate to and **Open** the downloaded file, **EnteringAndImportingData.xlsx**.

In the **Navigator** dialog, check the box next to **Sheet1** and then click the **Load** button as shown in *Figure 1.13*:

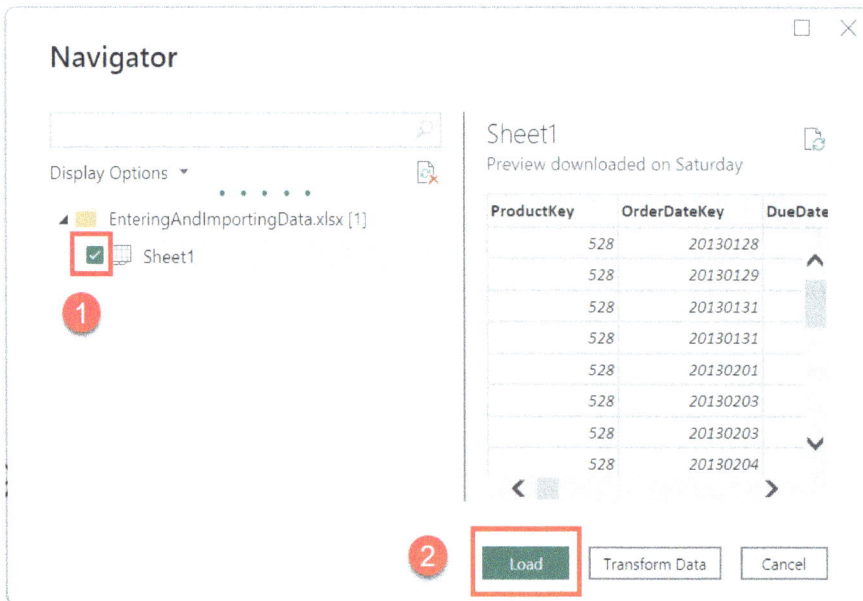

Figure 1.13: Navigator dialog for an Excel workbook.

The data within the Excel workbook is now imported into Power BI Desktop. Let's next look at how we can view and interact with the data.

Viewing and Interacting with the Data

Once data is entered or imported into Power BI Desktop, we can view and interact with the data. The first thing that you should notice is that the tables and columns for the entered/imported data now show up in the **Data** fly-out pane as shown in *Figure 1.14*:

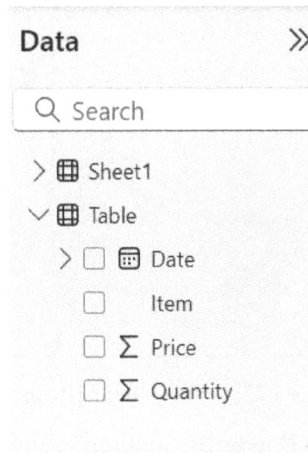

Figure 1.14: Data fly-out pane.

Notice the icons next to the column names. The calendar icon next to the **Date** column signifies that the column is a **Date** data type while the sigma icon denotes that the **Price** and **Quantity** columns are numeric. You can check and even change the data type for a column by clicking on the column name and using the contextual **Column tools** ribbon tab as shown in *Figure 1.15*:

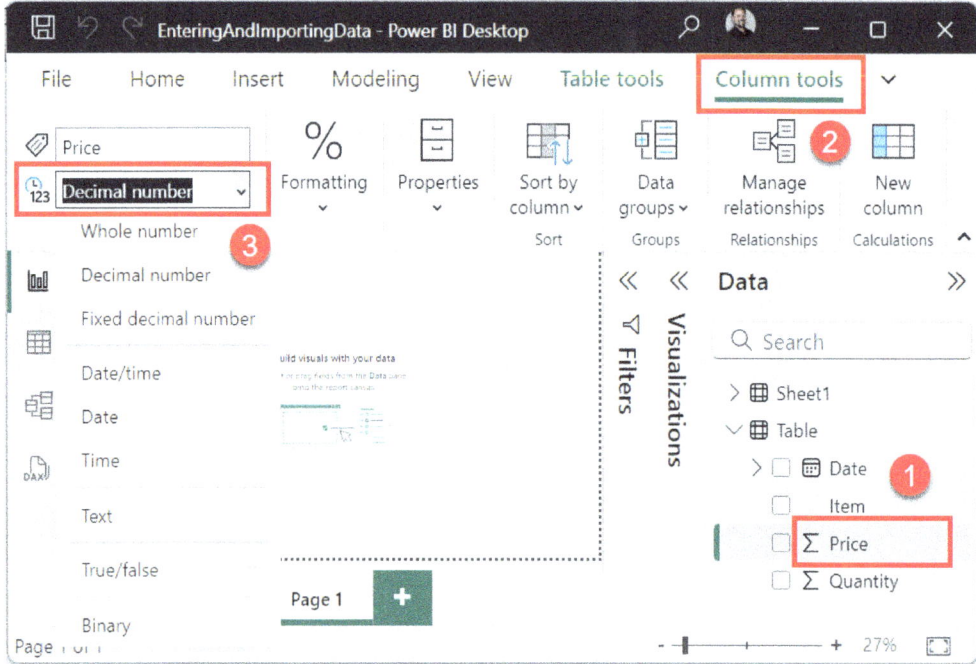

Figure 1.15: Column tools ribbon tab.

To view data entered/imported into Power BI Desktop, you can use the **Table view** as shown in *Figure 1.16*:

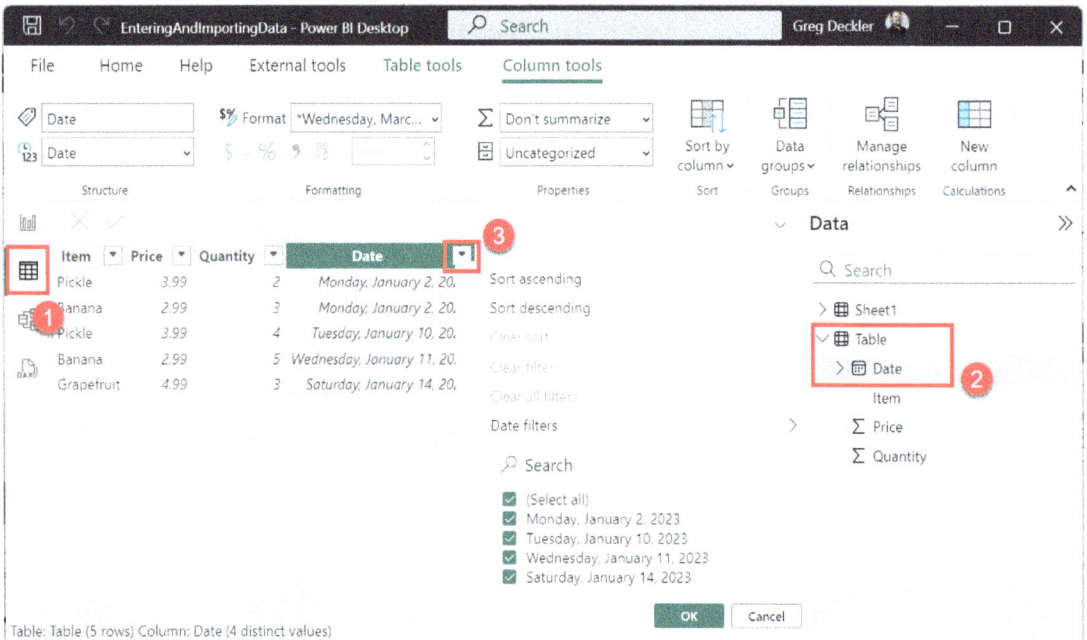

Figure 1.16: Table view.

As shown in *Figure 1.16*, you can sort or filter the data while in the **Table view** by clicking on the dropdown arrow for a column. It should be noted that this filtering and sorting only affects the **Table view** and not other views such as the **Report view**.

Let's next look at editing data queries.

Editing Queries

One final topic that must be covered when discussing entering and importing data is that of editing your queries once they are created. To do this, make sure that you are on the **Home** tab of the ribbon in either **Report**, **Table**, or **Model view** and then click **Transform data** as shown in *Figure 1.17*:

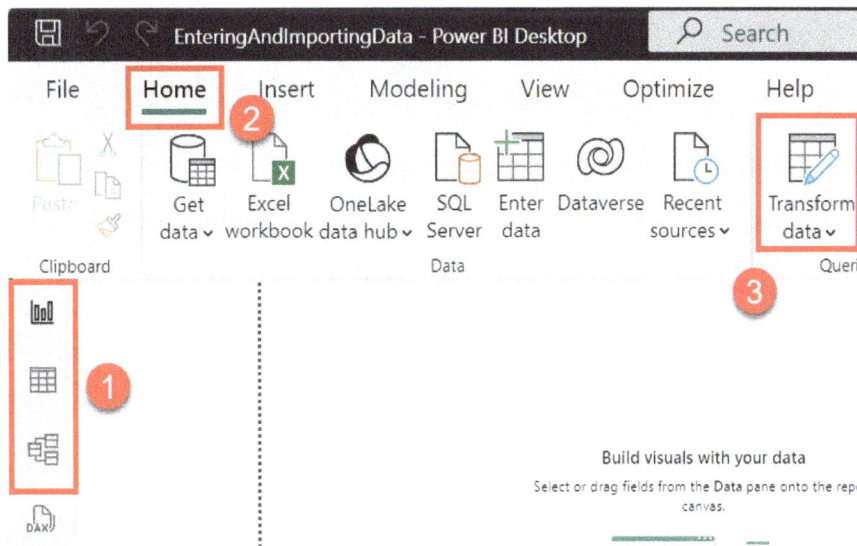

Figure 1.17: Transform data.

Clicking **Transform data** opens the **Power Query Editor** sub-application as shown in *Figure 1.18*.

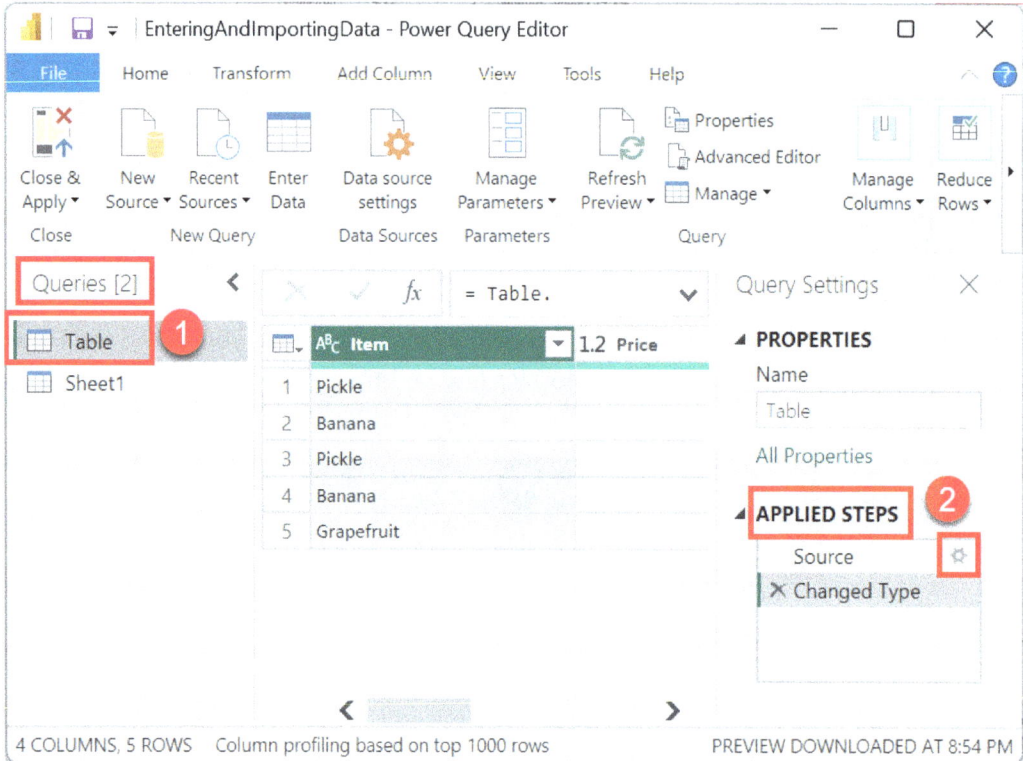

Figure 1.18: Power Query Editor.

Power Query Editor is a powerful tool for transforming data. Beneath the ribbon on the left-hand side are listed the **Queries** we created in this section, the **Table** query created using an enter data query and the **Sheet1** query created using an import query.

Each query is actually a series of applied transformation steps that are tracked under the **APPLIED STEPS** area as highlighted in *Figure 1.18*. By selecting a query, such as **Table** beneath **Queries** on the left-hand side, the two steps that comprise that query, **Source** and **Changed Type** are displayed beneath **APPLIED STEPS** on the right-hand side of the window. Clicking the **gear** icon highlighted in *Figure 1.18* displays the **Create Table** dialog, allowing you to edit the original data.

Now click on the **Changed Type** step and note how the icons next to the column names change. When the **Source** step is selected, all of the icons to the left of the column names display **ABC**. However, with the **Change Type** step selected, the icons change for the **Price**, **Quantity**, and **Date** columns to denote a change from a text data type to decimal, whole number and date respectively.

This is simply a brief introduction to the Power Query Editor and not meant to cover the vast capabilities of that tool. For now, simply close the Power Query Editor by clicking the **X** icon in the upper right corner of the window. If you have made any changes or edits, instead click the **Close & Apply** button on the far left of the ribbon's **Home** tab.

Once back in Power BI Desktop, save your work. Let's now tackle creating a visual.

Creating a Visual

Now that we have data in Power BI Desktop, it is time to create our first visual. This process is quite easy to do by following these instructions:

1. These instructions continue from the previous section, *Entering and Importing Data*. If you have not completed that section, simply download and open **EnteringAndImportingData.pbix** from the **Chapter 1** folder of the following GitHub repository: https://github.com/gdeckler/DAX-For-Humans/tree/main/book

2. Ensure that you are in Power BI Desktop in **Report view**.

3. Ensure that the **Data** fly-out pane is expanded by clicking the double chevron icon (<<) if necessary.

Figure 1.19: Collapsed Data pane.

4. Expand the table named **Table** by clicking the single chevron to the left of the name of the table (>).

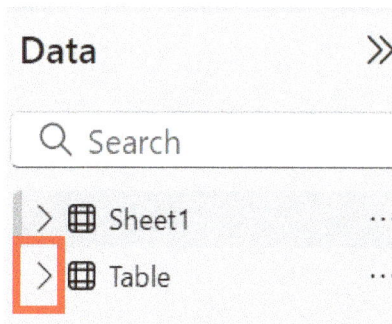

Figure 1.20: Collapsed table.

5. Now check the boxes next to the **Item**, **Price**, and **Quantity** columns in that order and note the **Table** visual created as shown in *Figure 1.21*:

Item	Sum of Price	Sum of Quantity
Banana	5.98	8
Grapefruit	4.99	3
Pickle	7.98	6
Total	**18.95**	**17**

Figure 1.21: Table visual.

Congratulations! You have created your first simple visual in Power BI. Note that while items such as **Banana** and **Pickle** appear multiple times within the source data, the **Table** visual only displays each **Item** once. Also, as denoted in the column headers of the **Table** visual, the **Price** and **Quantity** columns are being aggregated by summing the source data. The difference in behavior between the **Item** column and the **Price** and **Quantity** columns is because the **Item** column is text, and the **Price** and **Quantity** columns are numeric.

We can control the behavior of automatically aggregated columns. To do so, start by expanding the **Visualizations** fly-out pane. Next, ensure that you are on the **Build visual** sub-pane and then under **Columns**, click the downward chevron icon for the **Sum of Price** column and choose **Don't summarize** as shown in *Figure 1.22*:

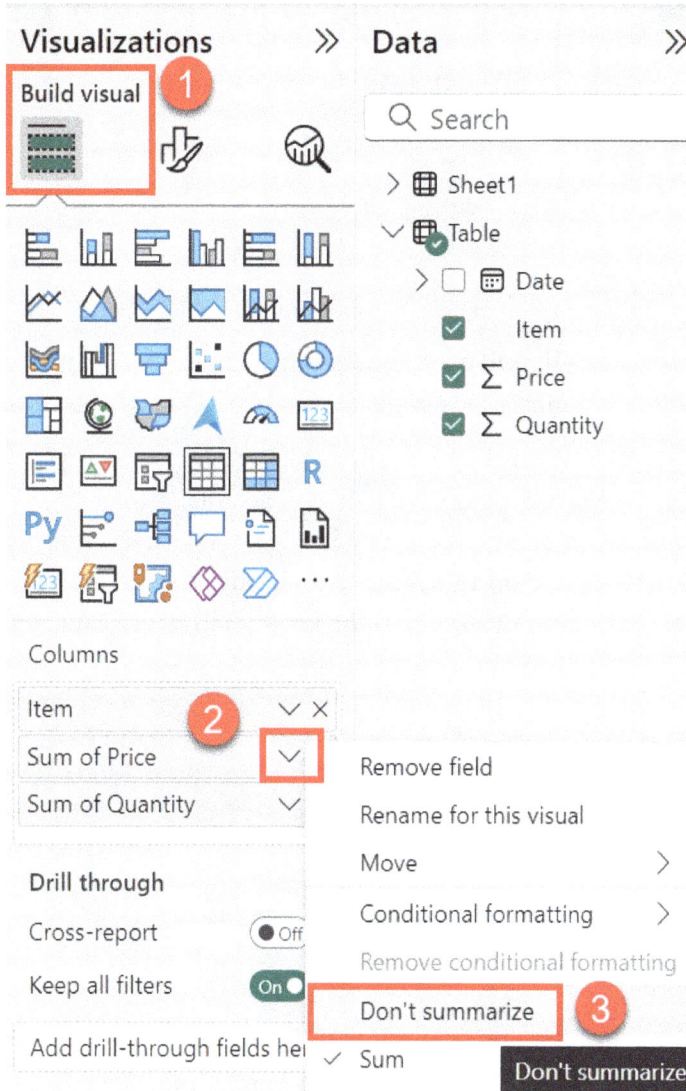

Figure 1.22: Controlling column aggregation.

The table now changes to show the unaggregated **Price** of each Item. However, since the **Price** is the same for each distinct **Item**, the table still only shows three rows of data. Now, repeat the same procedure for the **Sum of Quantity** column. This time, the table visual expands the rows to a total of five rows as shown in *Figure 1.23*:

Item	Price	Quantity
Banana	2.99	3
Banana	2.99	5
Grapefruit	4.99	3
Pickle	3.99	2
Pickle	3.99	4

Figure 1.23: Expanded table visual.

Unlike the **Price** column, the **Quantity** column has different values per row per **Item** within the source data. Thus, by not summarizing (aggregating) the **Quantity** column forces the **Table** visual to display each individual row.

We can easily switch between different visuals. To do this, ensure that the **Table** visual is selected on the **Canvas**. You know the visual is selected if the visual is framed by a thin line with sizing handles at the corners and mid-sections of each side of the visual. Once selected, simply select a different visual within the **Visualizations** pane, such as the **Clustered column chart**.

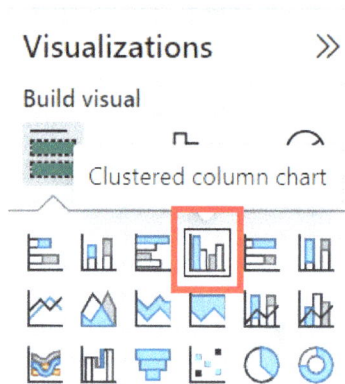

Figure 1.24: Clustered column chart.

Next, remove the **Quantity** column from the **Small multiples** field well by clicking the **X** icon:

Figure 1.25: Removing Quantity column from Small multiples field well.

Now, drag and drop the **Price** column from the **Legend** field well to the **Y-axis** field well to create the clustered column chart shown in *Figure 1.26*.

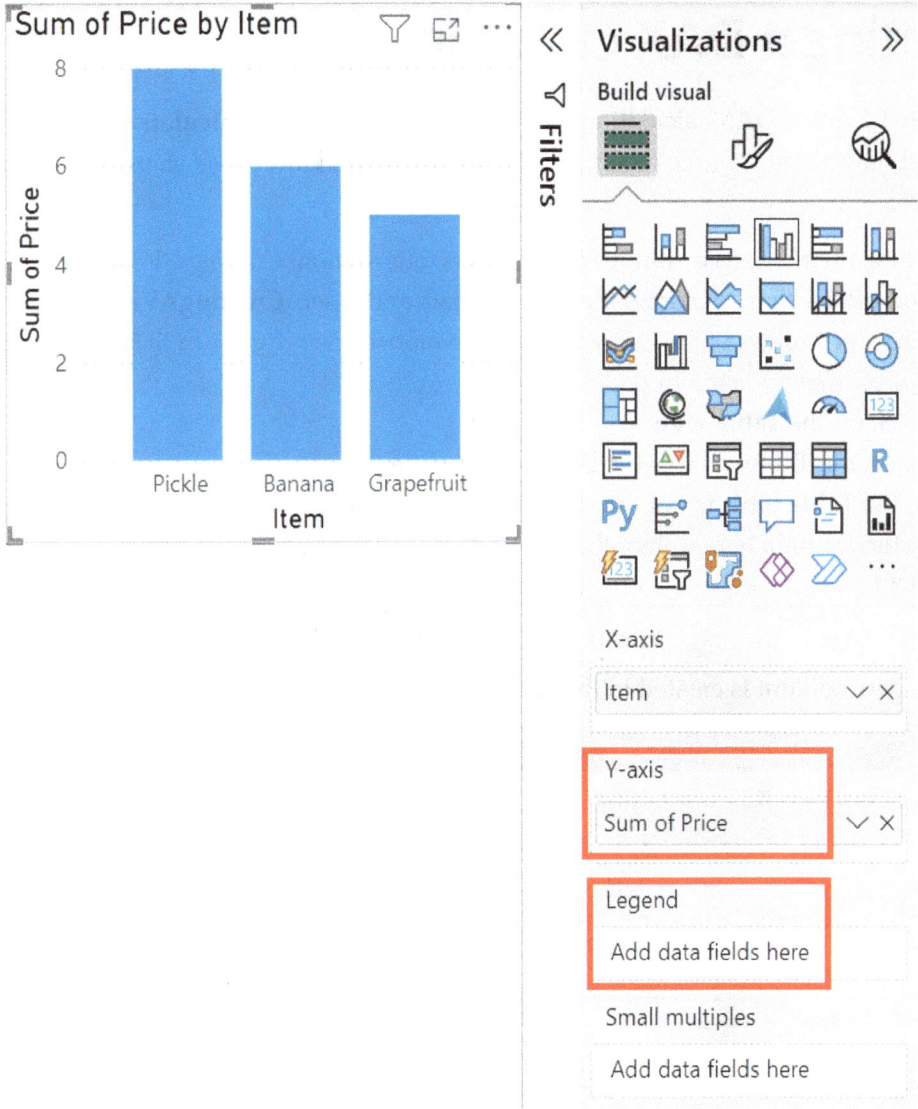

Figure 1.26: Moving Sum of Price from Legend field well to Y-axis field well.

Note that the **Y-axis** says **Sum of Price**. Change this aggregation to **Average** using the dropdown chevron icon.

This provides you with the basics regarding creating visuals in Power BI. The automatic aggregations that occur within the visuals for the numeric fields such as the **Price** and **Quantity** columns are actually implicit DAX calculations that employ simple aggregations for sum, average, minimum, maximum, etc. However, as you will see in the following sections and throughout this book, we can create explicit DAX calculations as well.

Let's create an explicit DAX calculation by creating a new column within the semantic model.

Creating a DAX Column

For our first explicit DAX calculation, we will create a new DAX **calculated column** that adds additional data to our source table. To accomplish this, follow these steps while referring to *Figure 1.27*:

1. These instructions continue from the previous section, *Creating a Visual*. If you have not completed that section, simply download and open **CreatingAVisual.pbix** from the **Chapter 1** folder of the following GitHub repository: https://github.com/gdeckler/DAX-For-Humans/tree/main/book

2. Click on the **Table view**.

3. Select the **Table** table in the **Data** fly-out pane.

4. In the **Table tools** tab of the ribbon, select **New column**.

5. In the formula bar, replace the text with the following formula and then press the **Enter** key:

$$\text{Total Cost} = [\text{Price}] * [\text{Quantity}]$$

6. A new column is created in the table called **Total Cost**.

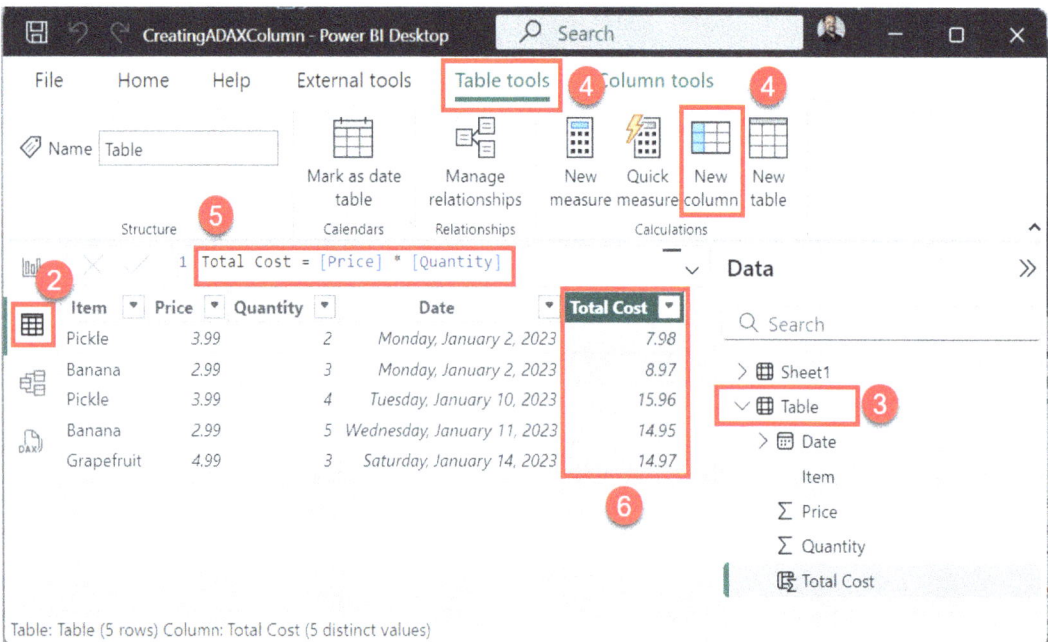

Figure 1.27: Creating a DAX column.

This simple DAX column multiplies the **Price** and **Quantity** columns for each row in the data using the multiplication operator (*) and referencing the columns between square brackets ([ ]).

Congratulations on creating your first explicit DAX calculation. While the creation of DAX calculated columns can generally be avoided by creating such columns in the source data or within Power Query Editor, DAX calculated columns can be useful for quickly adding additional data, for experimentation, and other purposes.

It is important to note that DAX columns are only calculated at the time of creation or when refreshing data. Thus, they are for all intents and purposes static and not dynamic such as with DAX measures.

To understand this difference between DAX calculated columns and measures, let's create a measure next.

Creating a DAX Measure

Another type of explicit DAX calculations are **measures**. Unlike DAX columns which are only calculated at the time of creation or when source data is refreshed, measures are dynamic and respond to user interactions. To demonstrate the creation and use of measures, follow these steps while referring to *Figure 1.28*:

1. These instructions continue from the previous section, *Creating a DAX Column*. If you have not completed that section, simply download and open **CreatingADAXColumn.pbix** from the **Chapter 1** folder of the following GitHub repository: https://github.com/gdeckler/DAX-For-Humans/tree/main/book
2. Click on the **Report view**.
3. Select the **Table** table in the **Data** fly-out pane.
4. In the **Modeling** tab of the ribbon, select **New measure**.
5. In the formula bar, replace the text with the following formula and then press the **Enter** key:

```
Average Total Cost = AVERAGE( 'Table'[Total Cost] )
```

A new measure is created in the table called **Average Total Cost**.

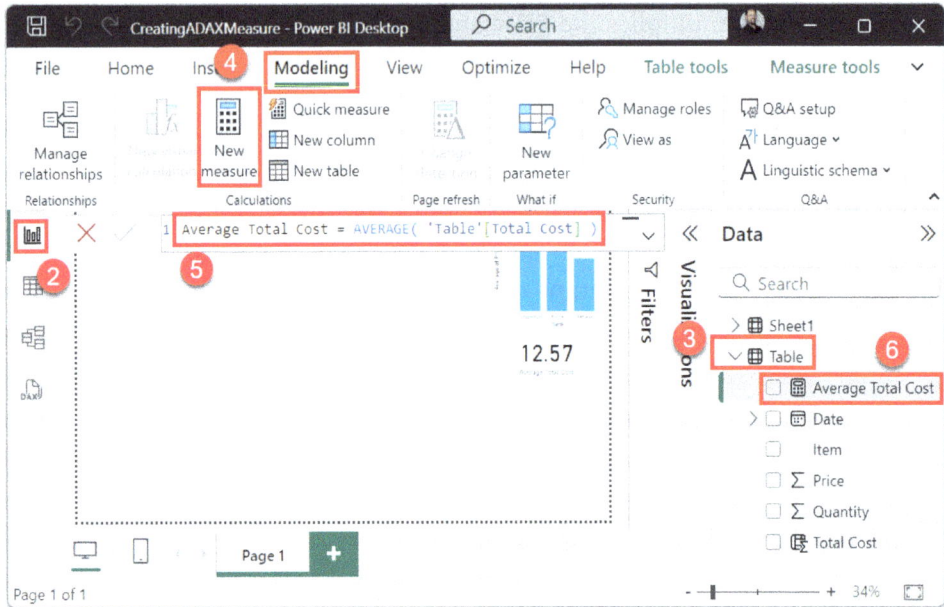

Figure 1.28: Creating a DAX measure.

This measure calculates the average of the **Total Cost** column. To see this measure in action, click on a blank area of the **Canvas**. Now, expand the **Visualizations** pane and ensure that the **Build visual** sub-pane is selected. Select the **Card** visual and then drag and drop the **Average Total Cost** measure from the **Data** fly-out pane into the **Fields** field well for the **Card** visual:

Figure 1.29: Creating a Card visual.

The card visual displays the number **12.57**, which is the average of the **Total Cost** column.

Measures differ from columns in several important ways. First, when referencing a column in a measure, you must use an aggregation function such as **AVERAGE, SUM, COUNT, MIN, MAX**, etc. It is a good idea to explicitly reference the table for the column as a prefix to the column reference enclosed in square brackets. In addition, when referencing a table, you should enclose the table name in single quote characters (').

The second difference between columns and measures is that columns must be created within a particular table. Conversely, measures can technically be created in any table. For example, we could have created the **Average Total Cost** measure in the **Sheet1** table, and the measure would work perfectly fine. However, the same cannot be said for the **Total Cost** column. We could not have created the **Total Cost** column in the **Sheet1** table because the formula refers to columns that are only found in **Table**.

The final and most significant difference between columns and measures however is that while columns are only calculated at the time of creation or immediately after the refresh of the source data, measures are dynamic and can respond to user interaction.

To see the dynamic nature of measures in action, click the **Pickle** column in the **Clustered column chart** visual. Note that the value in the **Card** visual changes from **12.57** to **11.97**. This is the average of the **Total Cost** column for just the **Pickle** rows in the data. By selecting the **Pickle** bar in the **Clustered column chart**, we filtered the rows available to the **Card** visual to just the **Pickle** rows.

Selecting the **Banana** column in the **Clustered column chart** returns the number **11.96** in the **Card** visual, the average of the **Total Cost** column for just the **Banana** rows and selecting the **Grapefruit** column in the **Clustered column chart** returns the number **14.97** in the **Card** visual, the average of the **Total Cost** column for the single **Grapefruit** row.

To fully understand what is going on, we need to talk about the concept of context.

Let's Talk About Context

Many people cite **context** as being something that makes DAX difficult to learn. However, there is nothing truly difficult about the concept of context. In fact, if you completed the previous section *Creating a DAX Measure*, you have already been introduced to context when you clicked on the individual columns within the **Clustered column chart** which, in turn, changed the number displayed by the **Average Total Cost** measure in the **Card** visual. That's context. In other words, context is simply the filters that affect a calculation in DAX.

For DAX columns, when referencing individual columns such as with the **Total Cost** column created in *Creating a DAX Column*, row context is in effect. In other words, the calculation is filtered to only the current row. Therefore, referencing **[Price]** returns the value of the **Price** column for the current row. Refer to *Figure 1.30* for a visual representation of row context:

Figure 1.30: Row context.

However, if you instead created a column in **Table** that included an aggregation of a column, such as the following:

$$\text{Average Price} = \text{AVERAGE}(\text{ [Price] })$$

Then the same number, **3.79** is displayed for all rows for the **Average Price** column. This is because when using aggregations in DAX calculated columns, the entire table is in context. In other words, there are no filters. Refer to *Figure 1.31* for clarification:

Figure 1.31: Aggregators in DAX columns breaks row context.

With an understanding of context for DAX columns, we now turn our attention to context for DAX measures. To better understand how context or filters affect DAX measures, create a table visual with the **Item** column and the measure, **Average Total Cost**. If necessary, refer to the previous section in this chapter, *Creating a Visual*.

If you have not completed *Creating a DAX Measure*, simply download and open **CreatingADAXMeasure.pbix** from the **Chapter 1** folder of the following GitHub repository: https://github.com/gdeckler/DAX-For-Humans/tree/main/book

Note that the **Average Total Cost** measure returns individual values for each row in the **Table** visual. This is because each row of the table visual has a different context or filters. The **Banana** row filters the data to just the **Banana** rows in the data. There are two **Banana** rows in the source data with **Total Costs** of **8.97** and **14.95** respectively. Thus, the average is (*8.97 + 14.95*) / *2 = 23.92 / 2 = 11.96*. This is perhaps better explained in *Figure 1.32*:

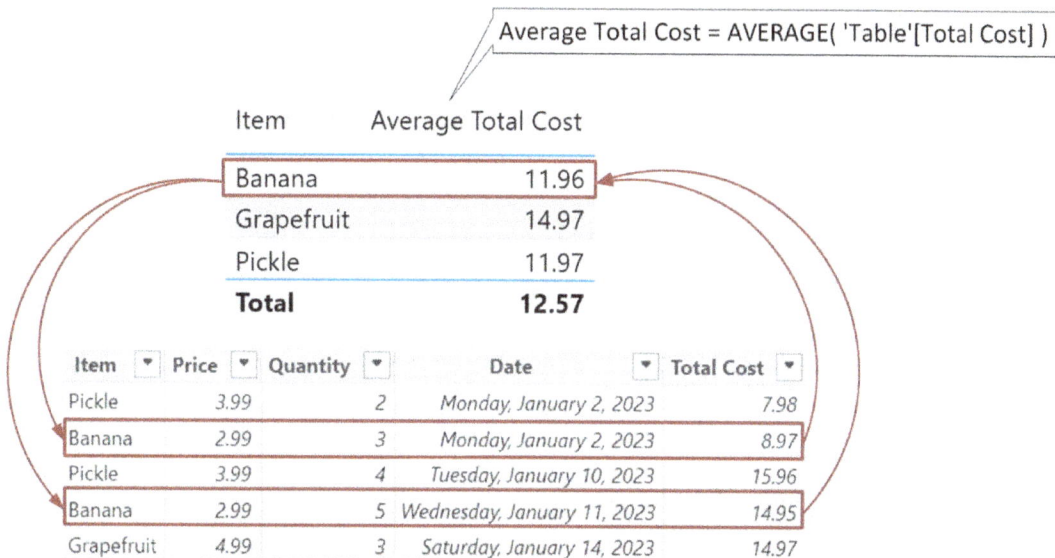

Figure 1.32: Visual's internal filter context for a measure.

As shown in *Figure 1.32*, the value of the **Item** column for a row in the **Table** visual filters the underlying data table to just the rows that match the same value for **Item** (in this case "Banana"). Thus, only the **Banana** rows are in context (filtered) for the measure calculation.

The same is true for the **Grapefruit** row. The **Grapefruit** row in the table visual filters the source data to the single **Grapefruit** row which has a **Total Cost** of **14.97** and thus the average of that single row is also **14.97**.

This same pattern holds for the **Pickle** row as well. However, the **Total** row does not filter the data at all and thus the **12.57** number displayed is the average of all of the **Total Cost** rows within the source data.

DAX measure context can also be affected by filters coming from outside of a visual as well as inside a visual such as with the **Table** visual just discussed. This can be seen when selecting an individual column within the **Clustered column chart** visual which filters the data available to the **Card** visual and thus the **Average Total Cost** measure within that **Card** visual. This process is similar to filters internal to a visual and can be seen visually in *Figure 1.33*:

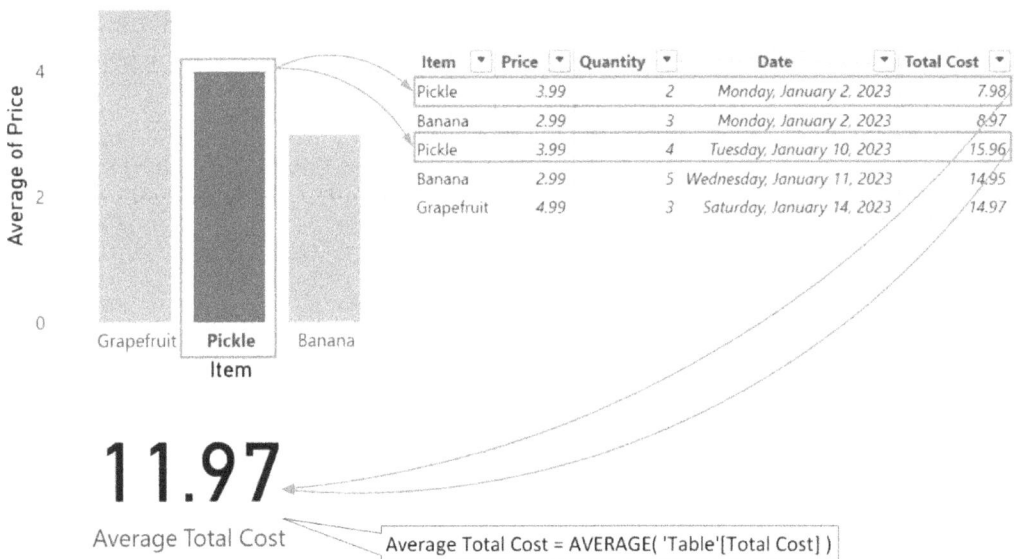

Figure 1.33: Visual's external filter context for a measure.

In fact, the external filters affecting a visual can be viewed by clicking the funnel icon that appears when hovering over a visual as shown in *Figure 1.34*:

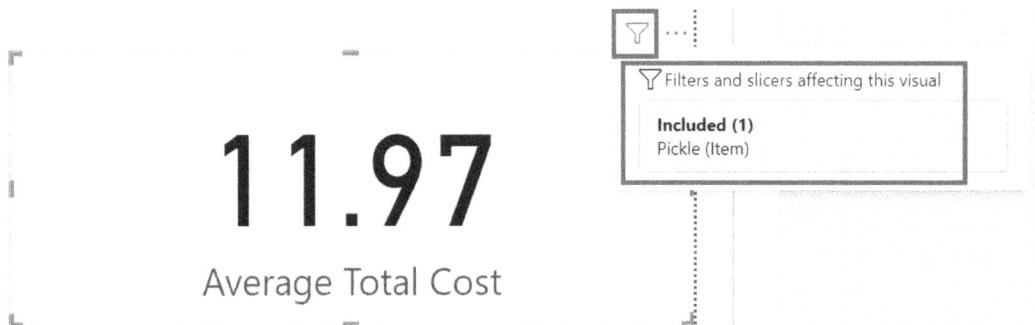

Figure 1.34: Filter context for a measure.

Thus, the context for a DAX measure can come from filters internal to a visual as well as external to a visual, such as selections in other visuals or filters propagated from the **Filters** fly-out pane. Finally, as we will see shortly, context (filters) can also come from within the DAX calculation itself (see *Filtering* section in this chapter).

For complex scenarios, tracking down the exact context affecting a DAX measure calculation can be tricky so we will explore more about this topic throughout this book. For now, let's first learn how to "think" in DAX.

Thinking in DAX

When learning any programming or formula language, it is critically important to understand how that language "thinks". In many cases this involves understanding the smallest unit that one can manipulate or how elements are stored internally. Take Excel for example. Excel "thinks" in terms of cell references and cell ranges. For an example of this, download **ThinkingInDAX.xlsx** from the **Chapter 1** folder of the GitHub repository for this book, https://github.com/gdeckler/DAX-For-Humans/tree/main/book

This file presents the same basic information as the data contained in the table named **Table** within our data. We can create an equivalent **Total Cost** column in this Excel file by editing cell **E3** to contain the following formula:

```
=B2*C2
```

We can then copy and paste this formula into cells **E3** through **E6,** and the cell references change to **B3*C3**, **B4*C4**, **B5*C5**, and **B6*C6** respectively.

Furthermore, we can edit **B7** to sum the **Price** values in cells **B2** through **B6** with the following formula:

```
=SUM(B2:B6)
```

Thus, it is clear that the Excel formula language "thinks" in terms of cells and cell ranges. However, DAX "thinks" differently than Excel. DAX "thinks" in terms of tables and by proxy rows and columns. One cannot simply reference a particular "cell" in a table with DAX, instead, one must filter a table down to a specific row and then select a column from that filtered set of rows.

This focus on tables, rows and columns is fundamental to how you must approach formulas when writing DAX. If you approach DAX with this in mind your learning process will be far easier. Luckily, this is exactly how this book approaches DAX and the No CALCULATE approach highlights this fundamental concept of DAX thinking.

Now that you understand the basics of how to think in DAX, lets' next take a look at a critically important topic, filtering.

Filtering

As mentioned in the previous section, *Thinking In DAX*, to be effective with DAX, one must think in terms of tables, rows and columns. Fundamental to DAX is the concept of filtering. You have already seen in the sections *Creating a DAX Measure* and *Let's Talk About Context* how visuals can filter the rows available to a DAX measure. However, DAX also includes the ability to explicitly define filters as well. This is done primarily via the **FILTER** function. To learn how to use the **FILTER** function, follow these steps while referring to *Figure 1.35*:

1. These instructions continue from the previous section, *Thinking in DAX*. If you have not completed that section, simply download and open **ThinkingInDAX.pbix** from the **Chapter 1** folder of the following GitHub repository: https://github.com/gdeckler/DAX-For-Humans/tree/main/book

2. Click on the **Table view**.

3. Select the **Table** table in the **Data** fly-out pane.

4. In the **Table tools** tab of the ribbon, select **New table**.

5. In the formula bar, replace the text with the following formula and then press the **Enter** key:

```
Table 2 = FILTER( 'Table', 'Table'[Item] = "Banana" )
```

6. A new table is created in the table called **Table 2**.

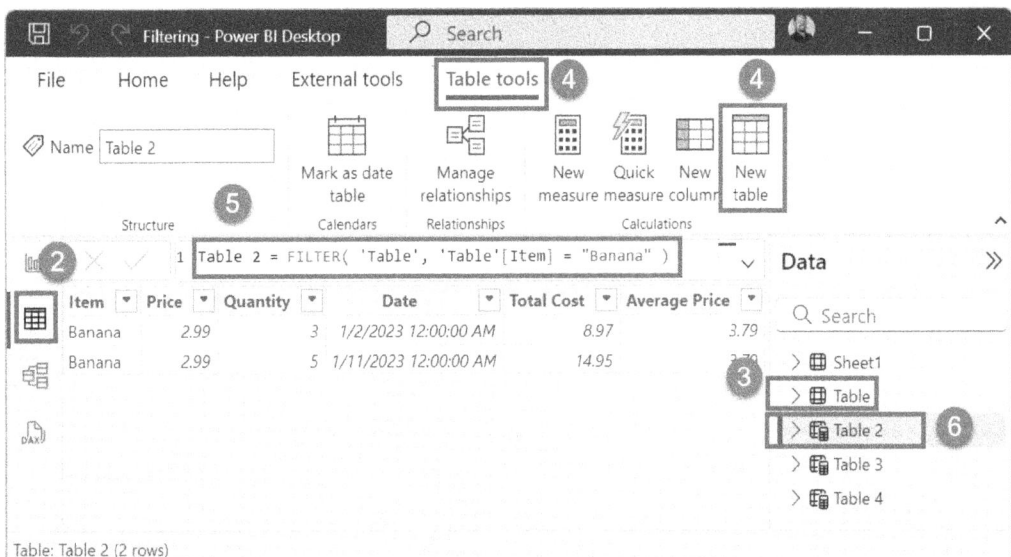

Figure 1.35: Creating a new table using FILTER.

You have created a DAX calculated table. This new table, **Table 2**, only contains the **Banana** rows from the **Table** thanks to the use of the **FILTER** function.

The **FILTER** function supports logical operators such as **&&** for "and", **||** for "or" and **<>** for "not". For example, the following formula would return a table with both the **Banana** and **Pickle** rows:

```
Table 3 =

    FILTER(

        'Table',

        'Table'[Item] = "Banana" || 'Table'[Item] = "Pickle"

    )
```

Conversely, the following formula only returns the **Banana** and **Grapefruit** rows:

```
Table 4 = FILTER( 'Table', 'Table'[Item] <> "Pickle" )
```

You now understand the basics of filtering in DAX, which is a core concept central to "thinking in DAX". Next up are X aggregators.

Using X Aggregators

In the section, *Creating a DAX Measure*, we briefly discussed the concept of DAX aggregation functions such as **AVERAGE, SUM, COUNT, MIN, MAX**, etc. Each of these DAX aggregations functions has an equivalent "X" version, **AVERAGEX, SUMX, COUNTX, MINX, MAXX**, etc.

The difference between these functions is that the basic aggregation functions only accept a column reference as a single parameter. The "X" versions, however, require two parameters. The first parameter can be a table reference or DAX expression that returns a table. The second parameter is any DAX expression resulting in a scalar (single value).

Therefore, the following two DAX formulas are equivalent to one another:

```
SUM( 'Table'[Price] )
```

```
SUMX( 'Table', 'Table'[Price] )
```

In fact, the DAX **SUM** function is actually just sugar syntax for the DAX **SUMX** function. And, in general, the X aggregation functions are much more flexible than their non-X counterparts. For example, if we wish to create a measure that returns the minimum **Total Cost** for items that are not **Pickle**, we can create the following measure:

```
Min Total Cost Not Pickle =

    MINX(
```

```
    FILTER( 'Table', 'Table'[Item] <> "Pickle" ),

    [Total Cost]

)
```

Note, to format your DAX formula as shown, use **Shift+Enter** keys to move to a new line and use the **Tab** key to indent.

To see this measure in action, follow these steps:

1. These instructions continue from the previous section, *Filtering*. If you have not completed that section, simply download and open **Filtering.pbix** from the **Chapter 1** folder of the following GitHub repository:

   https://github.com/gdeckler/DAX-For-Humans/tree/main/book

2. Click on the **Report view**.
3. Click on the **Card** visual.
4. Replace the **Average Total Cost** measure in the **Fields** field well with the **Min Total Cost Not Pickle** measure by dragging and dropping the measure from the **Data** fly-out pane into the **Fields** field well.

Note that the **Card** visual displays **8.97**, which is the minimum **Total Cost** for rows that are not **Pickle** in the data.

We have now learned a second critical component regarding thinking in DAX, column selection. The X aggregation functions allow us to filter the rows of a table and then select a particular column over which to aggregate values. We have one last DAX concept to introduce before presenting a DAX pattern that can solve most problems and that concept is variables.

Leveraging Variables

Variables are an important DAX concept that fundamentally changed how DAX was written when they were introduced to the DAX language. Prior to variables, DAX had to be written as a series of nested functions, similar to our **Min Total Cost Not Pickle** measure from the previous section, *Using X Aggregators*.

To demonstrate the utility of variables, consider if we wanted to create a new measure, **Min Plus Max Total Cost Not Pickle** with the following formula:

```
Min Plus Max Total Cost Not Pickle =

    MINX(

        FILTER( 'Table', 'Table'[Item] <> "Pickle" ),

        [Total Cost]
```

```
    )

    +

    MAXX(

        FILTER( 'Table', 'Table'[Item] <> "Pickle" ),

        [Total Cost]

    )
```

This code works perfectly fine, but notice that we have the same code repeated twice within the DAX expression, namely:

```
            FILTER( 'Table', 'Table'[Item] <> "Pickle" )
```

We can use variables to avoid this redundancy which helps with the readability of the code. In addition, variables can help performance and also aid in debugging, as we will see in the next chapter. In DAX, variables are invoked by using **VAR** and **RETURN** statements as follows:

```
Min Plus Max Total Cost No Pickle VAR =

    VAR __Table = FILTER( 'Table', 'Table'[Item] <> "Pickle" )

    VAR __Min = MINX( __Table, [Total Cost] )

    VAR __Max = MAXX( __Table, [Total Cost] )

    VAR __Result = __Min + __Max

RETURN

    __Result
```

This DAX code results in the same value as the previous DAX code that does not use **VAR/RETURN** statements. However, the use of **VAR** statements has several advantages.

First, the DAX code is potentially more efficient since the same table expression does not have to be evaluated twice. Second, the code is more compact and generally easier to read and follow since it is broken into a series of steps using multiple **VAR** statements. Finally, as we will see in the next chapter, the DAX code is far easier to debug and troubleshoot when each step of the calculation is a **VAR** statement.

A couple notes about best practices when using **VAR/RETURN** statements. First, it is general convention to precede the name of a variable with one or two underscore character(s). This helps avoid reserved words. For example, "Table" cannot be used as the name of a **VAR** because it is a reserved word. However, "_Table" and "__Table" are both acceptable.

Note that the double underscore convention actually comes from how Microsoft implemented DAX query statements internally within Power BI. If using the **Performance analyzer** fly-out pane (accessible via the **View** tab of the ribbon) and refreshing visuals, one can copy the internal query created. For the table visual, this results in the following DAX query:

```
// DAX Query

DEFINE

    VAR __DS0Core =

        SUMMARIZECOLUMNS(

            ROLLUPADDISSUBTOTAL('Table'[Item], "IsGrandTotalRowTotal"),

            "Average_Total_Cost", 'Table'[Average Total Cost]

        )


    VAR __DS0PrimaryWindowed =

        TOPN(502, __DS0Core, [IsGrandTotalRowTotal], 0, 'Table'[Item], 1)


EVALUATE

    __DS0PrimaryWindowed


ORDER BY

    [IsGrandTotalRowTotal] DESC, 'Table'[Item]
```

Don't worry if this DAX looks confusing, simply note the double underscore characters that prefix the variable names. We will cover more about DAX queries in later chapters.

Finally, it is also generally accepted convention to not include any DAX functions after the **RETURN** statement but instead to refer to a variable which is most often named "__Result" or "_Result". While not required, this, again, aids in debugging and troubleshooting.

Variables are the last major concept required to truly think in DAX. We now have all of the tools and understanding at our disposal to present a single DAX pattern that is able to solve most problems that you may encounter when creating your own calculations with DAX. It is this pattern that you will see repeated again and again throughout this book.

A DAX Pattern to Solve Most Problems

With the concepts of filtering, X aggregators and variables understood, we are now equipped to present a single pattern that can be used for most DAX calculations. In fact, you were already introduced to this pattern in the previous section *Leveraging Variables*. However, we will formally introduce and explain the pattern here.

To demonstrate this pattern, we will create a measure that sums the **Total Cost** column for all rows except rows where the **Item** is **Pickle**. To implement this measure, follow these steps:

1. These instructions continue from the previous section, *Leveraging Variables*. If you have not completed that section, simply download and open **LeveragingVariables.pbix** from the **Chapter** **1** folder of the following GitHub repository: https://github.com/gdeckler/DAX-For-Humans/tree/main/book

2. Click on the **Report view**.

3. In the **Data** fly-out pane, right-click the **Table** table and choose **New measure**.

4. In the formula bar, replace the text with the following formula and then press the **Enter** key:

```
Sum Total Cost No Pickle =

    VAR __ExcludeItem = "Pickle"

    VAR __Table = FILTER( 'Table', 'Table'[Item] <> __ExcludeItem )

    VAR __Result = SUMX( __Table, [Total Cost] )

RETURN

    __Result
```

5. Replace the measure in the **Fields** field well of the **Card** visual with the new **Sum Total Cost No Pickle** measure. The result should be **38.89**.

The DAX pattern can be described thusly:

1. Create one or more **VAR**'s depending upon the requirements of the calculation. In this case, we wish to exclude **Pickle** rows, so we create a variable that consists of the text "Pickle".

2. Create a table **VAR** that filters and potentially groups the rows as required by the calculation. In this case, we wish to exclude rows where the item is "Pickle", so we construct a simple DAX expression using the **FILTER** function.

3. Use an X aggregator to perform a calculation over the rows of the table variable. In this case we wish to sum the **Total Cost** column, so we use the **SUMX** function with the table variable __**Table** as the first parameter and the **Total Cost** column as the second parameter.

It must be stressed that this is the basic, simple form of the No CALCUALTE DAX pattern. However, this basic pattern can be extended to dozens of lines of DAX code to solve complex problems as we will see throughout the rest of this book.

Summary

In this chapter you have learned the basics of Power BI Desktop including how to install Power BI Desktop, a brief tour of its major components, and how to create basic visuals. You have also learned the basics of the DAX language, including how to create columns, measures and tables using DAX. In addition, you have learned how to think in DAX using filtering, x aggregators, and variables. Finally, you have learned a basic DAX pattern that can be used to solve most DAX calculations. This pattern will be used throughout the remainder of this book.

In the next chapter, we continue to explore some additional core concepts that we will need as a foundation for solving more complex problems in DAX.

2

More Core Concepts

In the last chapter, you installed and toured Power BI Desktop. You also learned how to enter and import data as well as create visuals. Additionally, you were introduced to the DAX language by creating columns, measures, and tables using DAX. Finally, you learned how to "think" in DAX and were presented a single DAX pattern that can solve most problems, the No CALCULATE pattern.

In this chapter, we expand your knowledge of basic DAX with topics that will be useful throughout the more complex scenarios presented in this book. This includes how to debug your DAX, lookup values, group rows, add columns, etc. First, however, let's explain what is meant by No CALCULATE vs. **CALCULATE**.

No CALCULATE vs. CALCULATE

In the last chapter, you learned about the basic No CALCULATE pattern for performing DAX calculations. In addition, we have discussed how we believe that a No CALCULATE approach to writing DAX is a better, easier method of learning the fundamentals of DAX versus the traditional approach of learning the **CALCULATE** function.

All of this No CALCULATE vs. **CALCULATE** discussion may be confusing to you if you are not familiar with the **CALCULATE** function. Therefore, in this section, we present both **CALCULATE** and No CALCULATE methods of performing the same DAX calculation and compare the two approaches so that you can understand the potential pitfalls of the **CALCULATE** function.

To complete the exercises in this section, download and open **Chapter2_Start.pbix** from the **Chapter 2** folder of the following GitHub repository: https://github.com/gdeckler/DAX-For-Humans/tree/main/book

At the end of the last chapter, we created a measure called **Sum Total Cost No Pickle** that presented the basic No CALCULATE pattern and had the following formula:

```
Sum Total Cost No Pickle =

    VAR __ExcludeItem = "Pickle"
```

```
VAR __Table = FILTER( 'Table', 'Table'[Item] <> __ExcludeItem )

VAR __Result = SUMX( __Table, [Total Cost] )

RETURN

    __Result
```

The same calculation can be created using the **CALCULATE** function and would traditionally be written as follows:

```
Sum Total Cost No Pickle C =

    CALCULATE(

        SUM( 'Table'[Total Cost] ),

        'Table'[Item] <> "Pickle"

    )
```

Placing this measure into a **Card** visualization returns the same result as the No CALCULATE version of the measure, **38.89**. You can think of the **CALCULATE** function as a fancy **FILTER** function. The **CALCULATE** function has two arguments. The first is any DAX expression that results in a single value (scalar). The second is a filter clause.

Instead of first filtering the table using the **FILTER** function and then aggregating across that filtered table using an X aggregator like **SUMX**, **CALCULATE** allows us to change the context (filters) while performing a calculation.

While the **CALCULATE** function can be thought of as a fancy **FILTER** function, it is actually a devilishly complex function with many different quirks and even deeper issues such as the ability to troubleshoot and debug calculations. We cover these quirks and issues in *Chapter 16, AI, Debugging, and CALCULATE.*

Visualizing Your DAX

Troubleshooting and debugging are common topics when discussing any language and DAX is no different. There are times, especially with more complex calculations, that the results of a DAX formula may not make sense and you will need to determine the cause of the incorrect results. This is where the No CALCULATE method shines as opposed to using the **CALCULATE** function.

Create the following measure and place it into a **Card** visual:

```
Sum Total Cost Grapefruit and also Pickle =

    VAR __Item1 = "Grapefruit"
```

```
VAR __Item2 = "Pickle"

VAR __Table = FILTER( 'Table', 'Table'[Item] = __Item1 )

VAR __Table1 = FILTER( __Table, 'Table'[Item] = __Item2 )

VAR __Result = SUMX( __Table1, [Total Cost] )

RETURN

    __Result
```

For this measure, if we want to understand the **BLANK** value being displayed in the **Card** visual, we can troubleshoot the measure by modifying the **RETURN** statement. For example, instead of returning __**Result**, we could instead return the following:

```
COUNTROWS( __Table )
```

The **COUNTROWS** function simply counts the number of rows in a table. In this case the result is **1**. Subsequently, we could again modify the **RETURN** statement to the following:

```
COUNTROWS( __Table1 )
```

Now the **Card** visual displays **(Blank)**. Thus, we know that there are no rows present in the __**Table1** variable.

We can take this troubleshooting a step further by actually visualizing the underlying data within our table variables. This can be done using the **TOCSV** function. This time, modify the **RETURN** statement to the following:

```
TOCSV( __Table )
```

Now the **Card** visual displays the following:

'Table'[Item],'Table'[Price],'Table'[Quantity],'Table'[Date],'Table'[Total Cost],'Table'[Average Price]
Grapefruit,4.99,3,1/14/2023,14.97,3.79

Sum Total Cost Grapefruit and also Pickle

Figure 2.1: Card visual produced by using TOCSV.

Here we can clearly see that the __**Table** variable contains a single row for the Item **"Grapefruit"**.

Note that you may have to reduce the font size for the **Callout value** and resize the **Card** visual. To adjust the **Callout value**, select the **Card** visual and then follow the steps in *Figure 2.2*:

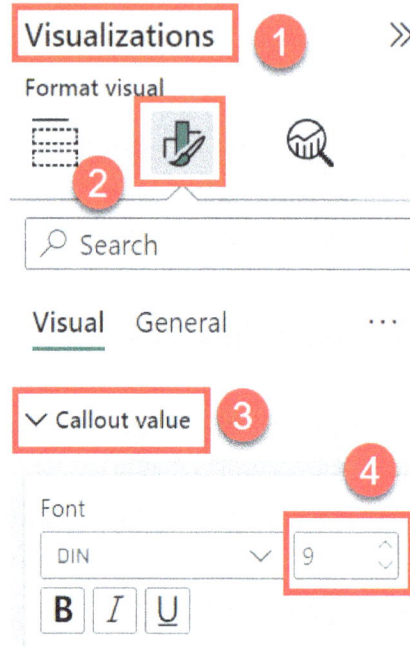

Figure 2.2: Formatting the Callout value.

The **TOCSV** function takes a table and returns it as text in **Comma Separated Value** (CSV) format. The **TOCSV** function takes up to four parameters:

1. **Table** – (Required) A table, table variable (VAR) or table expression
2. **MaxRows** – (Optional whole number) The maximum number of rows to return. The default is 10 rows.
3. **Delimiter** – (Optional text string) The column delimiter. The default is a comma (",").
4. **IncludeHeaders** – (Optional logical true/false) Whether column headers are included. The default is **true** or **TRUE()**.

Patron Recommendation

Henrik Vestergaard suggests using a **Table** visual instead of a **Card** visual when troubleshooting as the **Table** visual left-aligns text. In addition, using the **Consolas** font can be advantageous since that font is monospaced.

Now consider a similar **CALCULATE** formula:

```
Sum Total Cost Grapefruit and also Pickle C =

    CALCULATE(

        CALCULATE(

            SUM( 'Table'[Total Cost] ),
```

```
            'Table'[Item] = "Grapefruit"

    ),

    'Table'[Item] = "Pickle"

)
```

Because the formula is written in a single step, there is no native way to analyze the individual components of the formula. Attempting to modify the formula to be two separate **CALCULATE** statements would fundamentally alter the calculation and return different results. Instead, third party tools are required to analyze the individual aspects of the formula. This essentially makes the **CALCULATE** function a "black box" where you simply have to "know" how it works. But that is far easier said than done as you will see in *Chapter 16, AI, Debugging, and CALCULATE*.

Now that you understand basic DAX debugging, we move on to exploring additional core DAX concepts, starting with looking up values.

Looking up Values

In the section *Thinking in DAX* from *Chapter 1*, it was pointed out that while Excel "thinks" in terms of cells and cell ranges, DAX instead "thinks" in terms of tables, rows and columns. However, it is possible in DAX to look up individual "cell" values within a table by using a combination of filters and X aggregators.

To see how this works, follow these steps:

1. These instructions continue from the previous section, *Visualizing Your DAX*. If you have not completed that section, simply download and open **VisualizingYourDAX.pbix** from the **Chapter 2** folder of the following GitHub repository: https://github.com/gdeckler/DAX-For-Humans/tree/main/book
2. Select and delete all visuals on the page by pressing **Ctrl+A** keys and then the **Del** (delete) key.
3. Create a **Table** visual by placing the **Item**, **Price**, **Quantity**, **Date**, and **Total Cost** columns from the table called **Table** in the visual.
4. Set the **Date** column to display just the **Date** instead of the **Date Hierarchy** as shown in *Figure 2.3*:

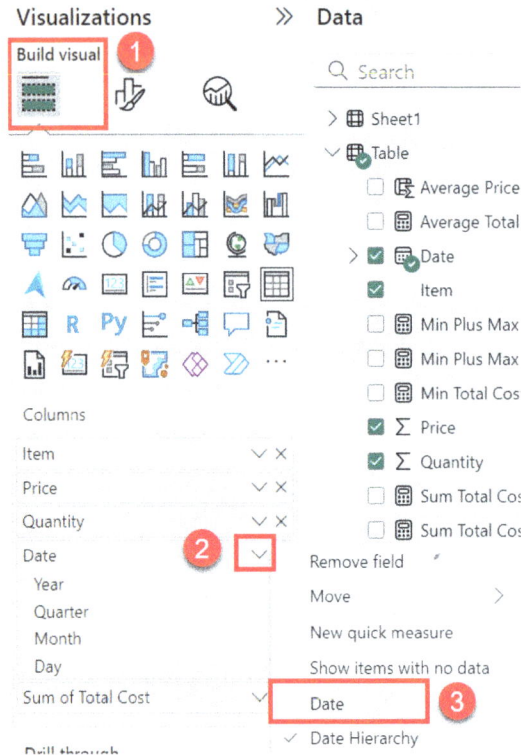

Figure 2.3: Setting a visual's column to Date instead of Date Hierarchy.

5.   When you are finished, your table should look like *Figure 2.4*:

Item	Sum of Price	Sum of Quantity	Date	Sum of Total Cost
Banana	2.99	3	Monday, January 02, 2023	8.97
Banana	2.99	5	Wednesday, January 11, 2023	14.95
Grapefruit	4.99	3	Saturday, January 14, 2023	14.97
Pickle	3.99	2	Monday, January 02, 2023	7.98
Pickle	3.99	4	Tuesday, January 10, 2023	15.96
Total	**18.95**	**17**		**62.83**

Figure 2.4: Table visual reflecting the underlying rows in the table called Table.

6.   Copy and paste this visual using **Ctrl+C** and then **Ctrl+V** keys, drag the new visual such that it does not overlap the original visual, and remove the **Date** column from the new visual. This is done by clicking the X next to the column name in the **Columns** field well as shown in *Figure 2.5*:

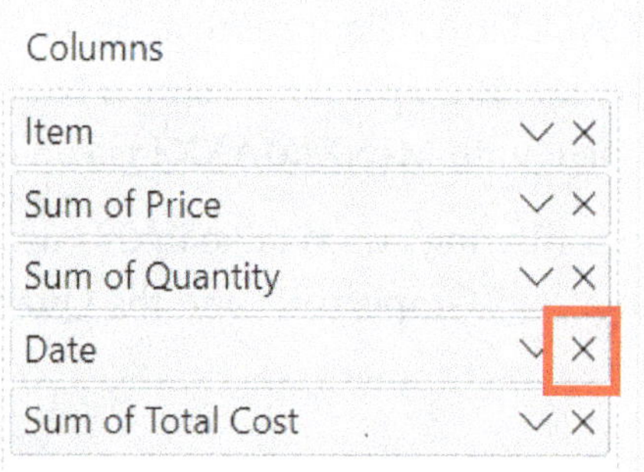

Columns

Item	∨	✕
Sum of Price	∨	✕
Sum of Quantity	∨	✕
Date	∨	✕
Sum of Total Cost	∨	✕

Figure 2.5: Removing a column from a visual.

We will use these two visuals as aids in helping us learn how to look up particular values using DAX. The first visual created represents the underlying rows of the table called **Table** and is primarily for quick reference without having to flip back and forth between **Report** view and **Table** view.

With the prep work complete, let's explore how to look up values using DAX. For our first example, we can use the basic No CALCULATE pattern to look up the minimum and maximum total costs for particular items. To this end, create the following measure:

```
Pickle Total Cost Min/Max =
    VAR __Item = "Pickle"
    VAR __Table = FILTER( 'Table', 'Table'[Item] = __Item )
    VAR __Result = MINX( __Table, [Total Cost] )
RETURN
    __Result
```

Placing this measure into a **Card** visual returns the number **7.98**, which corresponds to the lower value for the **Total Cost** for rows where the **Item** is "**Pickle**". We can instead return the maximum **Total Cost** for rows where the **Item** is "**Pickle**" by simply changing the **MINX** in the formula to **MAXX** which returns **15.96**.

Note that DAX includes a function called **LOOKUPVALUE**. However, this function only works if a single distinct value can be determined based upon the specified search criteria. Therefore, the behavior of **LOOKUPVALUE** can be duplicated by using the **FILTER** function combined with a **MINX/MAXX** function. Consider that if you filter down to a single distinct value based upon the specified filter criteria then the **MINX/MAXX** aggregators will return that distinct value.

One of the tenets of the No CALCULATE approach is to use the smallest number of base functions as possible. Therefore, looking up values using a No CALCULATE approach favors using the **FILTER** function coupled with **MINX/MAXX** instead of **LOOKUPVALUE**.

We can get very specific with our filtering criteria like in this next measure that filters for rows where the **Item** is either "**Banana**" or "**Grapefruit**" and the **Quantity** is **3**.

```
Banana or Grapefruit Qty 3 =
    VAR __Table =
        FILTER(
            'Table',
            ( 'Table'[Item] = "Banana" || 'Table'[Item] = "Grapefruit" )
            &&
            'Table'[Quantity] = 3
        )
    VAR __Result = MAXX( __Table, [Total Cost] )
RETURN
    __Result
```

Here, parenthesis are used to separate the first logical filter criteria (**Item** equals "**Banana**" or "**Pickle**" from the second filter criteria, **Quantity** equals **3.** Placing this measure into a visual returns **14.97**, the highest **Total Cost** for rows where the **Item** column is either "**Banana**" or "**Pickle**" and the **Quantity** is **3**.

One final example, we can perform a "double look up" using the following measure:

```
Double Lookup =
    VAR __MaxDate = MAX( 'Table'[Date] )
    VAR __Table = FILTER( 'Table', 'Table'[Date] = __MaxDate )
    VAR __Result = MAXX( __Table, [Total Cost] )
RETURN
    __Result
```

This measure first "looks up" the maximum **Date** in context (current filters). Then, a table variable (VAR) is created that filters the current rows down to just those rows where the **Date** equals this maximum date. Finally, the maximum **Total Cost** is returned for this filtered set of rows.

Place this measure into the **Table** visual created in *Step 6* of the preparation work performed earlier in this chapter. For the **Banana** row, this measure returns **14.95**, for **Grapefruit 14.97**, and for **Pickle 15.96**. *Figure 2.6* shows a graphical breakdown of the measure:

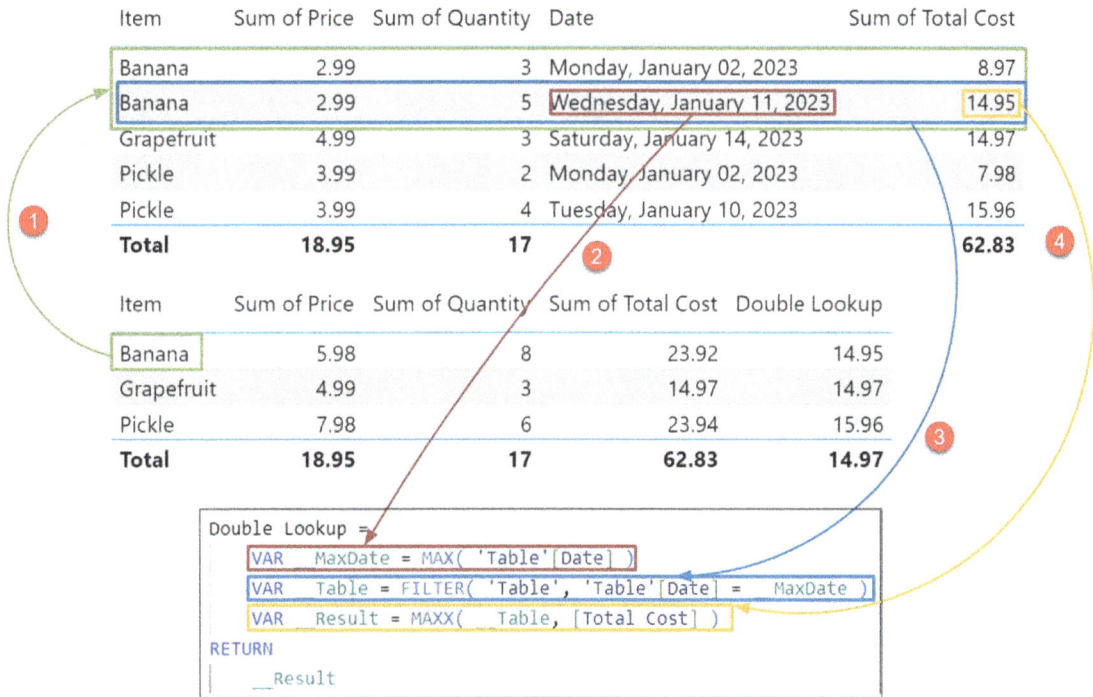

Figure 2.6: Graphical representation of the Double Lookup measure.

Looking up values for something on the first or last date is a common DAX calculation.

Now that you understand how to look up values in DAX, another important concept in DAX is the use of the **ALL** function.

All Functions

DAX includes two functions that allow us to remove filters within a DAX calculation. These functions are **ALL** and **ALLSELECTED**. As preparation for exploring these functions, perform the following steps:

1. These instructions continue from the previous section, *Looking up Values*. If you have not completed that section, simply download and open **LookingUpValues.pbix** from the **Chapter 2** folder of the following GitHub repository: https://github.com/gdeckler/DAX-For-Humans/tree/main/book

2. Select and delete all visuals on the page except the **Table** visualization that includes the **Date** column. You can do this by selecting each visual with your mouse and then pressing the **Del** (delete) key.

With this preparation complete, create the following measure:

```
Max Total Cost All Rows =

    VAR __Table = ALL( 'Table' )

    VAR __Result = MAXX( __Table, 'Table'[Total Cost] )

RETURN

    __Result
```

Place this measure into the remaining **Table** visualization and note that for all rows, the number **15.96** is returned which is the maximum value for the **Total Cost** column.

The **ALL** function does what its name implies, removes all filters (both internal to the visual as well as external to the visual) such that all rows are now in context for the calculation. Thus, for each row in the visual, the __**Table** variable contains all of the rows in the underlying table and thus returns the overall maximum **Total Cost** for each row in the visual.

The **ALLSELECTED** function differs from the **ALL** function in that it removes filters internal to the visual but not external to the visual. This is a bit of a simplification but suffices in most situations. Review the *Let's Talk About Context* section from *Chapter 1* to review how this is different from "normal" behavior and what is meant by internal filters and external filters for a visual.

Using what we have now learned about the **ALL** function as well as what we previously learned about looking up values using DAX from the section *Looking up Values*, we can perform some common, interesting DAX calculations. The first of these calculations is a running total.

To create a running total, create the following measure:

```
Running Total Cost =

    VAR __MaxDate = MAX( 'Table'[Date] )

    VAR __Table = FILTER( ALL( 'Table' ), 'Table'[Date] <= __MaxDate )

    VAR __Result = SUMX( __Table, [Total Cost] )

RETURN

    __Result
```

Create a **Line chart** with **Date** (not **Date Hierarchy**) in the **X-axis** and the **Running Total Cost** measure in the **Y-axis**. The visual should look like *Figure 2.7*:

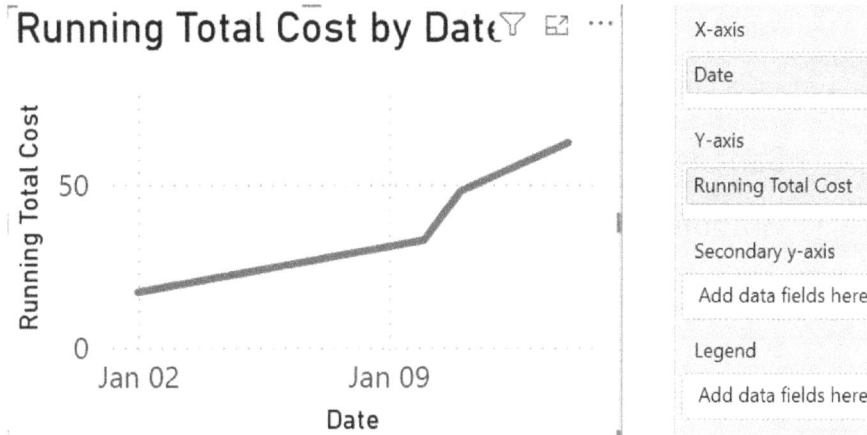

Figure 2.7: Running total visualization.

To observe the difference between **ALL** and **ALLSELECTED**, create the following measure:

```
Running Total Cost Selected =

    VAR __MaxDate = MAX( 'Table'[Date] )

    VAR __Table =

        FILTER(

            ALLSELECTED( 'Table' ),

            'Table'[Date] <= __MaxDate

        )

    VAR __Result = SUMX( __Table, [Total Cost] )

RETURN

    __Result
```

The only difference between this measure and the **Running Total Cost** measure is that the **ALL** function has been replaced with **ALLSELECTED**. Add this measure to the **Y-axis** field well for the **Line chart**. Notice that both lines overlap.

Now add a **Slicer** visual to the page and place the **Item** column from the table **Table** into the **Field** field well as shown in *Figure 2.8*:

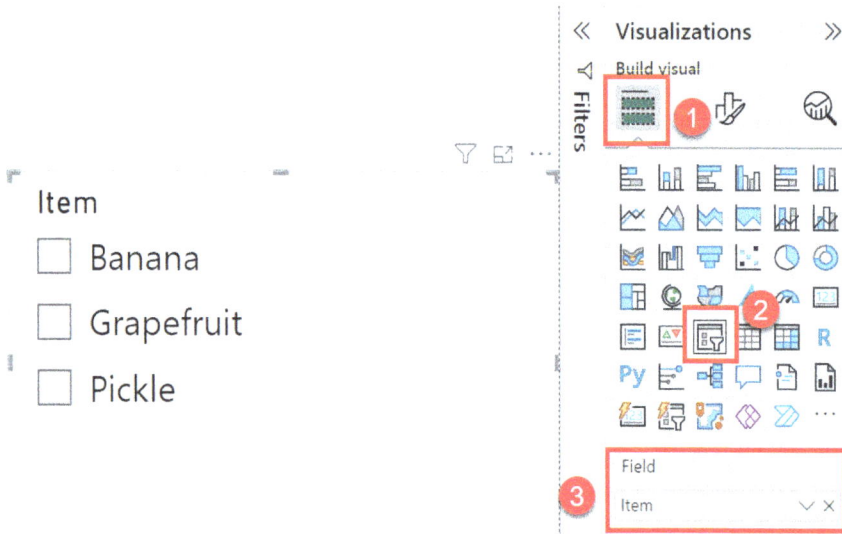

Figure 2.8: Adding a Slicer visualization.

Now select either **Banana** or **Pickle** in the **Slicer**. Notice that the lines no longer overlap. This is because the **Running Total Cost** measure includes all items while the **Running Total Cost Selected** measure only includes the items selected in the **Slicer**.

> Note that when selecting an item in the slicer visual that the number of dates change to only include the dates for the selected item. This may seem surprising since we used the **ALL** function in the first measure. Why then is that measure only returning values for the dates of the selected item? This is due to a "feature" of Power BI Desktop informally called **auto-exist**.
>
> In short, if Power BI Desktop determines that there are two or more filters active for the same table, then Power BI only calculates values for the intersection of those filters. This behavior is called **auto-exist**. Since the **Item** column in the slicer and the **Date** column in the **Line chart** are from the same table, **auto-exist** determines that values should only be calculated on the intersection of those filters. Microsoft has recently released the ability to control this behavior called the **Value Filter Behavior** for the semantic model but "auto-exist" is still currently the default behavior.

Another common DAX calculation is comparing the value of a current row with that of a previous row. This too is made possible by the **ALL** and **ALLSELECTED** functions. To retrieve the value of a previous row, you can create a measure such as the following:

```
Previous Total Cost =

    VAR __Item = MAX( 'Table'[Item] )

    VAR __Date = MAX( 'Table'[Date] )
```

```
VAR __Table =

    FILTER(

        ALL( 'Table' ),

        'Table'[Item] = __Item && 'Table'[Date] < __Date

    )

VAR __PreviousDate = MAxx( __Table, [Date] )

VAR __Result =

    MAXX(

        FILTER(

            __Table,

            [Date] = __PreviousDate

        ),

        [Total Cost]

    )

RETURN

    __Result
```

This DAX formula creates a table variable called **__Table** that filters **ALL** the underlying data to just the rows for the current **Item** (**__Item**) and where the **Date** is less than the current row's **Date** (**__Date**). The formula then looks up the latest previous date using the **MAXX** function and stores this date in the variable **__PreviousDate**. Finally, the **__Result** variable looks up the **Total Cost** for the **__PreviousDate**. You should recognize this pattern as the "double look up" presented at the end of the section *Looking up Values*.

Make sure that this measure is formatted as a **Decimal number** with **2** decimal places and place this measure in the **Table** visual. The results should look similar to *Figure 2.9*:

Item	Date	Sum of Total Cost	Previous Total Cost
Banana	Monday, January 02, 2023	8.97	
Banana	Wednesday, January 11, 2023	14.95	8.97
Grapefruit	Saturday, January 14, 2023	14.97	
Pickle	Monday, January 02, 2023	7.98	
Pickle	Tuesday, January 10, 2023	15.96	7.98
Total		**62.83**	**15.96**

Figure 2.9: Previous Total Cost measure.

Only **Banana** and **Pickle** return a **Previous Total Cost** because only those items have more than a single row with different dates. In addition, even those items do not return a **Previous Total Cost** value on their earliest dates because there is no previous row (as defined by the **Date** column).

This completes our exploration of the **ALL** and **ALLSELECTED** functions. Next, we take a look at another core concept in DAX, how to group rows.

Grouping Rows

Power BI visuals generally group rows for us depending on the data. For example, we can demonstrate this behavior by following these steps:

1. These instructions continue from the previous section, *All Functions*. If you have not completed that section, simply download and open **AllFunctions.pbix** from the **Chapter 2** folder of the following GitHub repository: https://github.com/gdeckler/DAX-For-Humans/tree/main/book

2. Select and delete all visuals on the page by pressing **Ctrl+A** keys and then the **Del** (delete) key.

3. Create a **Table** visual by placing the **Item** and **Total Cost** columns from the table called **Table** in the visual. The resulting visual is displayed in *Figure 2.10*:

Item	Sum of Total Cost
Banana	23.92
Grapefruit	14.97
Pickle	23.94
Total	**62.83**

Columns

Item   ∨ ×
Sum of Total Cost   ∨ ×

Drill through

Cross-report   ● Off
Keep all filters   On ●

Add drill-through fields here

Figure 2.10: Simple table visual.

As you can see, the default behavior of the visual is to only show each **Item** once even though there are multiple rows for "**Banana**" and "**Pickle**" and to aggregate the numeric columns such as **Total Cost**. In this case, the default aggregation is to sum the column amounts.

We can emulate this behavior in DAX by creating a calculated **Table** such as that shown in *Figure 2.11*:

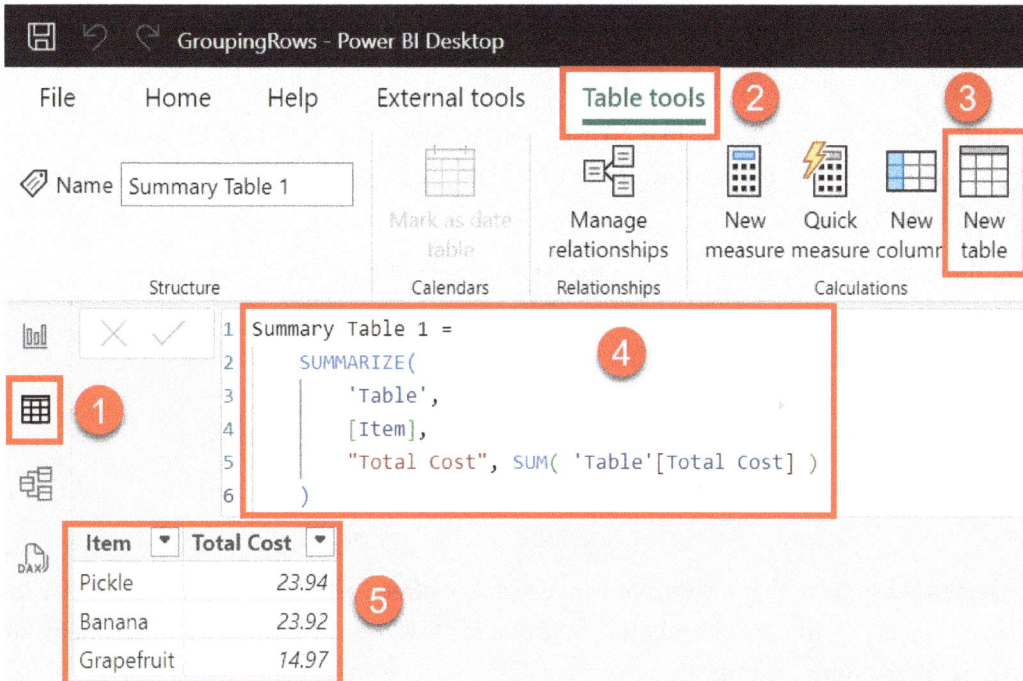

Figure 2.11: Using SUMMARIZE to create a table.

For ease of reference, here is the DAX code used:

```
Summary Table 1 =
    SUMMARIZE(
        'Table',
        [Item],
        "Total Cost", SUM( 'Table'[Total Cost] )
    )
```

In this DAX code, the **SUMMARIZE** function is used to create a summary table of '**Table**' where the table is grouped by the **Item** column and the **Total Cost** column is summed. Notice that this exactly mirrors the behavior of our **Table** visual other than the **Total** row. Another similar function for grouping rows in DAX is the **GROUPBY** function. The same table can be returned using this DAX code:

```
Summary Table 2 =
    GROUPBY(
```

```
    'Table',

    [Item],

    "Total Cost", SUMX( CURRENTGROUP(), 'Table'[Total Cost] )

)
```

You must use an X aggregator like **SUMX** when using the **GROUPBY** function to create aggregated columns and the first argument to the X aggregator must be the special function, **CURRENTGROUP**.

A third alternative for grouping rows is the **SUMMARIZECOLUMNS** function:

```
Summary Table 3 =

    SUMMARIZECOLUMNS(

        'Table'[Item],

        "Total Cost", SUM( 'Table'[Total Cost] )

    )
```

It may seem odd to have three different functions that effectively do the same or similar things. There are a variety of historical and other reasons for this, but in some ways, this speaks to the importance of grouping rows in DAX.

These simple scenarios can be expanded upon, such as in the case of this next example:

```
Summary Table 4 =

    SUMMARIZECOLUMNS(

        'Table'[Item],

        'Table'[Price],

        "Avg Qty", AVERAGE( 'Table'[Quantity] ),

        "Max Date", MAX( 'Table'[Date] ),

        "Total Cost", SUM( 'Table'[Total Cost] )

    )
```

Here, the **SUMMARIZECOLUMNS** function is used to return a table consisting of five columns. The original table, **Table**, is grouped by both **Item** and **Price** columns. The three other columns return the average of the **Quantity** column, maximum of the **Date** column and sum of the **Total Cost** column respectively.

Let's now move on to the concept of adding columns in DAX.

Adding Columns

In the *Grouping Rows* section, we explored how to group rows using DAX. This included adding columns such as **Total Cost** directly inside the **SUMMARIZE**, **GROUPBY**, and **SUMMARIZECOLUMNS** functions.

In our last example, we created a summarized table with five columns which included the **Item**, **Price**, average **Quantity** (**Avg Qty**), maximum **Date** (**Max Date**), and summed **Total Cost**. However, what if we wanted to add an average cost column by multiplying our **Price** column by our **Avg Qty** column? Unfortunately, if we attempt to do so within the **SUMMARIZECOLUMNS** function with the code below, we receive an error:

```
Summary Table 5 =
    SUMMARIZECOLUMNS(
        'Table'[Item],
        'Table'[Price],
        "Avg Qty", AVERAGE( 'Table'[Quantity] ),
        "Max Date", MAX( 'Table'[Date] ),
        "Total Cost", SUM( 'Table'[Total Cost] ),
        "Avg Price", [Price] * [Avg Qty]
    )
```

The error returned indicates that the value for '**Price**' cannot be determined. The same would be true in attempting to identify a value for the **Avg Qty** column. This is because these columns aren't available for reference *inside* of the **SUMMARIZECOLUMNS** function.

To get around this, we can use the **ADDCOLUMNS** function as follows:

```
Add Columns 1 =
    ADDCOLUMNS(
        SUMMARIZECOLUMNS(
            'Table'[Item],
            'Table'[Price],
            "Avg Qty", AVERAGE( 'Table'[Quantity] ),
            "Max Date", MAX( 'Table'[Date] ),
            "Total Cost", SUM( 'Table'[Total Cost] )
```

```
    ),

    "Avg Price", [Price] * [Avg Qty]

)
```

This example uses nested DAX functions. However, we can rewrite this formula to more closely follow the No CALCULATE philosophy of leveraging variables as follows:

```
Add Columns 2 =

    VAR __SummaryTable =

        SUMMARIZECOLUMNS(

            'Table'[Item],

            'Table'[Price],

            "Avg Qty", AVERAGE( 'Table'[Quantity] ),

            "Max Date", MAX( 'Table'[Date] ),

            "Total Cost", SUM( 'Table'[Total Cost] )

        )

    VAR __AddColumnTable =

        ADDCOLUMNS(

            __SummaryTable,

            "Avg Price", [Price] * [Avg Qty]

        )

RETURN

    __AddColumnTable
```

Now that we understand how to use the **ADDCOLUMNS** function, the next core concept we want to cover is the concept of logical DAX functions.

Logical Functions

DAX includes a number of logical functions with the most important being the **IF** and **SWITCH** functions which return results based on the passing or failing of logical tests. To demonstrate the utility of these functions, perform the following steps:

1. These instructions continue from the previous section, *Adding Columns*. If you have not completed that section, simply download and open **AddingColumns.pbix** from the

Chapter 2 folder of the following GitHub repository: https://github.com/gdeckler/DAX-For-Humans/tree/main/book

2. Add the **Date** column (not the **Date Hierarchy**) from the table **Table** into the **Table** visualization.

Next, create the following simple measure and add the measure to the **Table** visualization:

```
Color =
    VAR __Item = MAX( 'Table'[Item] )
    VAR __Result = IF( __Item = "Pickle", "Green", "Yellow" )
RETURN
    __Result
```

This measure performs a simple logical test to determine if the **Item** in the current row is "**Pickle**" and if so return "**Green**", otherwise returning "**Yellow**". As you can see in the **Table** visual, the **Banana** and **Grapefruit** rows display "**Yellow**" while the **Pickle** rows display "**Green**".

IF statements are a simple way to return different results based on a logical test. However, they can be a bit messy when the logical tests become more complex. For example, consider if we want to return **Green** for **Pickle**, **Yellow** for **Banana** and **Orange Red** for **Grapefruit**. We could use the following DAX code:

```
Color 1 =
    VAR __Item = MAX( 'Table'[Item] )
    VAR __Result =
        IF(
            __Item = "Pickle",
            "Green",
            IF(
                __Item = "Grapefruit",
                "Orange Red",
                "Yellow"
            )
        )
RETURN
    __Result
```

Adding this measure to the Table visual indeed returns the desired color for the desired items. However, the nesting makes the code messy and hard to follow. Thus, we could instead use the **SWITCH** statement as follows:

```
Color 2 =
    VAR __Item = MAX( 'Table'[Item] )
    VAR __Result =
        SWITCH( __Item,
            "Pickle", "Green",
            "Grapefruit", "Orange Red",
            "Banana", "Yellow",
            "Unknown"
        )
RETURN
    __Result
```

This is the standard version of the DAX **SWITCH** statement. The standard version evaluates a single value, in this case the **__Item** variable which represents the value of the **Item** column in the current row. The rest of the parameters in the **SWITCH** statement are pairs such that if the value being evaluated by the **SWITCH** statement matches the left side of the pair, then the value on the right side of the pair is returned. An optional final value can be provided, in this case "**Unknown**", if no matches are found.

We can now use our knowledge of logical functions in DAX to explore the concept of the Complex Selector. A Complex Selector is a DAX formula that embeds complex selection logic into the formula itself and can then be used via the **Filters** pane to filter down to specific rows within a visualization. To demonstrate how this works, create the following DAX formula:

```
Selector 1 =
    VAR __Item = MAX( 'Table'[Item] )
    VAR __Cost = SUM( 'Table'[Total Cost] )
    VAR __Result =
        IF(
            ( __Item = "Pickle" || __Item = "Grapefruit" )
                &&
```

```
        __Cost > 10,

    1,

    0

  )
```

RETURN

```
  __Result
```

Adding this measure to the **Table** visualization returns **1** for the **Grapefruit** row and **1** for the **Pickle** row where the **Total Cost** is greater than **10**. For the other rows, **0** is returned.

Here the logical test consists of a logical OR test as well as a logical AND test. The double pipe characters (||) represent the logical OR while the double ampersand characters (&&) represent the logical AND. Thus, the statement first tests whether the **Item** (**__Item**) is **Pickle** or **Grapefruit**. Second, the statement tests if the **Total Cost** is greater than **10**. If these logical tests are successful, **1** is returned. Otherwise, **0** is returned.

As mentioned, the **Filters** pane can be used to filter this measure to just the instances where the measure returns 1 as shown in *Figure 2.12*:

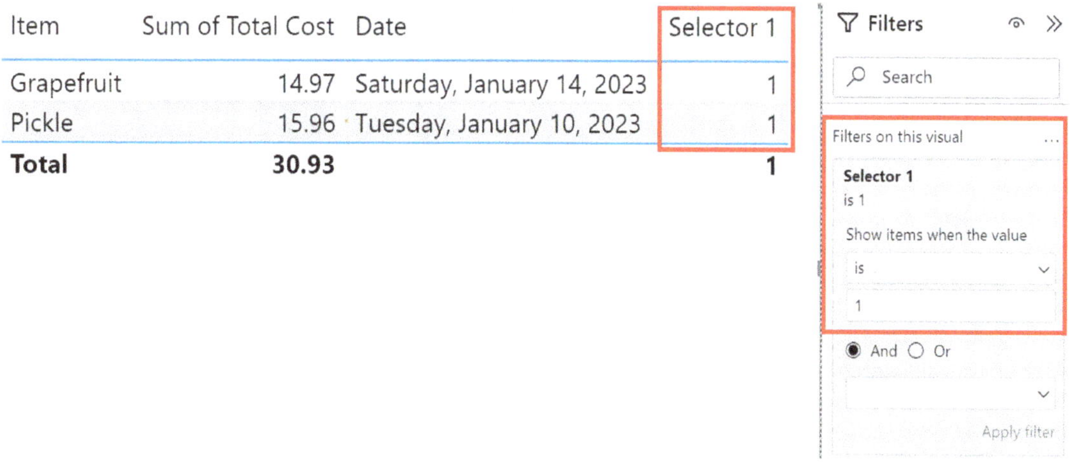

Item	Sum of Total Cost	Date	Selector 1
Grapefruit	14.97	Saturday, January 14, 2023	1
Pickle	15.96	Tuesday, January 10, 2023	1
Total	**30.93**		**1**

Filters

Search

Filters on this visual   ...

Selector 1
is 1

Show items when the value

is   ⌄

1

● And ○ Or

⌄

Apply filter

Figure 2.12: Using a Complex Selector.

Note that the same **IF** statement can be written using additional logical functions such as **OR** and **AND**:

```
Selector 2 =

    VAR __Item = MAX( 'Table'[Item] )

    VAR __Cost = SUM( 'Table'[Total Cost] )
```

```
VAR __Result =

    IF(

        AND(

            OR( __Item = "Pickle", __Item = "Grapefruit" ),

            __Cost > 10

        ),

        1,

        0

    )

RETURN

    __Result
```

However, using the || and **&&** operators tends to be preferable and fits more naturally into reading and writing DAX.

Finally, there is a special version of the **SWITCH** statement, known as a **SWITCH TRUE** statement, that allows us to perform logical tests as the left-hand sides of each pair. For example:

```
Selector 3 =

    VAR __Item = MAX( 'Table'[Item] )

    VAR __Cost = SUM( 'Table'[Total Cost] )

    VAR __Result =

        SWITCH( true,

            ( __Item = "Pickle" || __Item = "Grapefruit" ) &&

                __Cost > 10, 1,

            0

        )

RETURN

    __Result
```

Here, the first argument for the **SWITCH** statement is simply the **TRUE** function or **true** keyword. Now, the left-hand side of the pairs can be any logical statement that evaluates to true or false. If evaluated to true, the corresponding right-hand side of the pair is returned. While not much is added in the way of clarity in this particular case, the **SWITCH TRUE** statement is a powerful construct that allows us to create a series of complex logical tests while maintaining readability.

This completes our discussion of logical functions in DAX. Next, we move on to information functions.

Information Functions

While there are numerous information functions in DAX, the two we cover in this section are **HASONEVALUE** and **ISINSCOPE**. To explore these functions, we have slightly modified the base data we have used thus far. Specifically, we have added a **Cucumber** row to the data in the table **Table** as well as added an **Item Color** column using DAX's **SWITCH** function as shown in *Figure 2.13*:

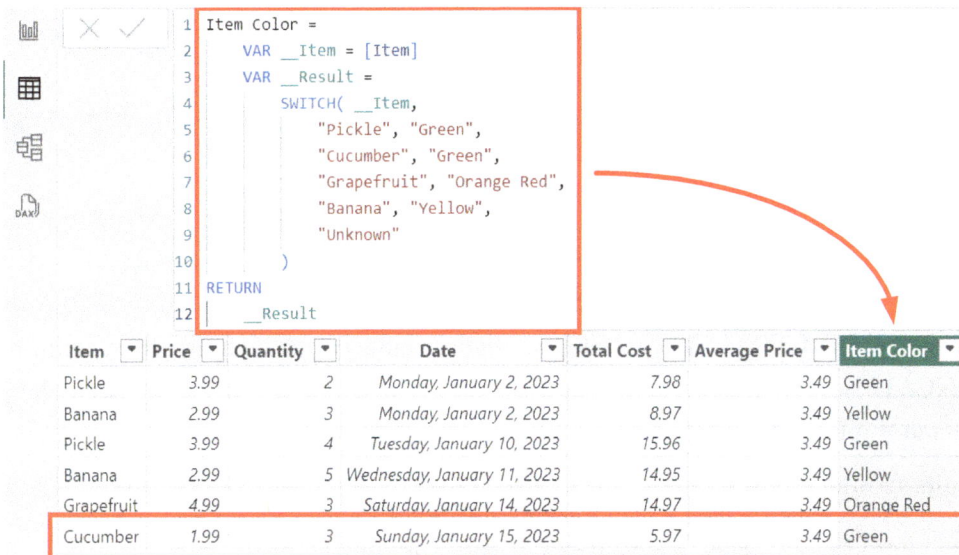

Figure 2.13: Modified data.

To complete this section, download and open **InformationFunctions_Start.pbix** from the **Chapter 2** folder of the following GitHub repository: https://github.com/gdeckler/DAX-For-Humans/tree/main/book.

Create the following measure:

```
Has One Value =

    VAR __Result = HASONEVALUE( 'Table'[Item] )

RETURN

    __Result
```

Create a **Table** visual with the **Item** column from the table **Table** and the measure **Has One Value**. Observe that all rows return **True** for the **Has One Value** measure except the **Total** row which returns **False**. This is because of the inherent grouping performed by the **Table** visual. Even though the underlying data has multiple **Banana** and **Pickle** rows, within the visual, each row contains only one distinct value. Thus, the **HASONEVALUE** function returns **True** for each row except the **Total** row where all items are in context and thus the **Item** column has more than one distinct value.

Create a second **Table** visualization but this time use the **Item Color** column from the table **Table** and the **Has One Value** measure. Here both the **Green** and **Total** rows display **False** while the **Yellow** and **Orange Red** rows display **True**. This is because there is only one distinct item with an **Item Color** of **Yellow** (**Banana**) and **Orange Red** (**Grapefruit**).

To more clearly demonstrate this, create the following measure and add it to this latest **Table** visualization.

```
Has One Value Text =
    VAR __Table = SUMMARIZE( 'Table', [Item] )
    VAR __Result = CONCATENATEX( __Table, [Item], ", " )
RETURN
    __Result
```

This formula uses **SUMMARIZE** to return a distinct table of values in the **Item** column. Then, the **CONCATENATEX** function is used to append each of these values to a single text string with a separator (delimiter) of a comma with a space after it.

The results should look like *Figure 2.14*:

Item Color	Has One Value	Has One Value Text
Green	False	Pickle, Cucumber
Orange Red	True	Grapefruit
Yellow	True	Banana
Total	**False**	**Pickle, Banana, Grapefruit, Cucumber**

Figure 2.14: Has One Value table visual.

Here you can clearly see the different items that are included in each row and why the **HASONEVALUE** function returns **True** and **False** for each row.

Let's now turn our attention to the **ISINSCOPE** function. To explore this function, first create a **Matrix** visual by following the steps in *Figure 2.15*:

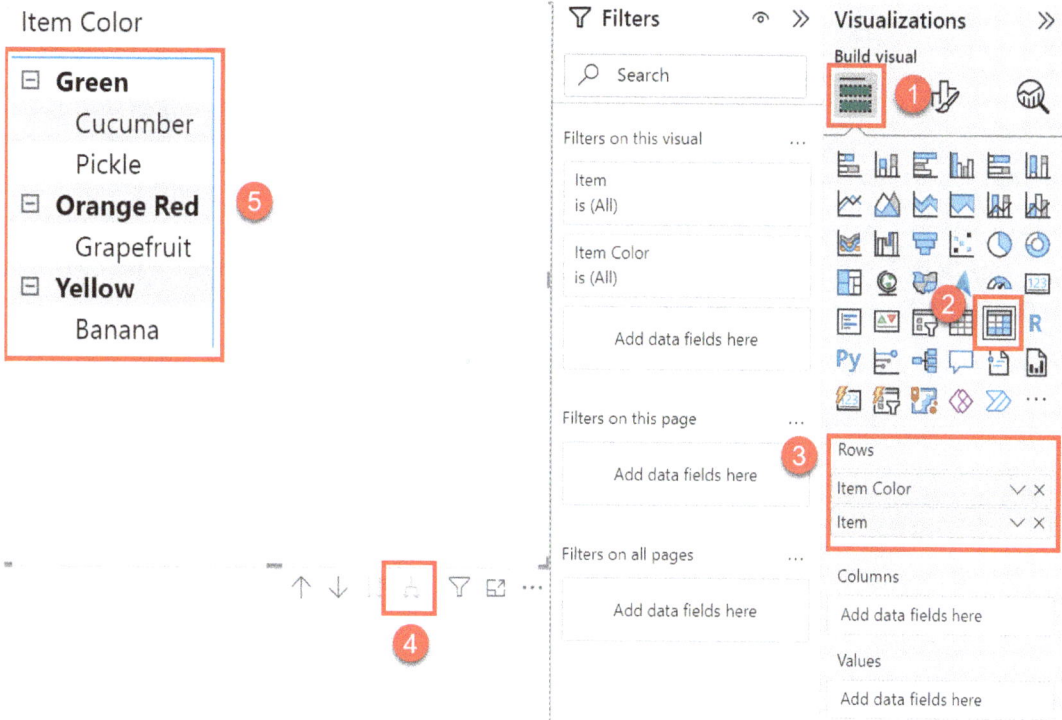

Figure 2.15: Matrix visual.

Next, create the following measure and add the measure to the **Matrix** visual in the **Values** field well.

```
Is In Scope = ISINSCOPE( 'Table'[Item] )
```

Note that the **Is In Scope** measure returns **True** for all of the rows where the **Item** is displayed but returns **False** for rows where the **Item Color** is displayed as well as the **Total** row. According to Microsoft, the **ISINSCOPE** function returns **TRUE** when the specified column is the level in a hierarchy of columns. By placing multiple columns in the **Rows** field well, we have created an ad-hoc column hierarchy.

Let's explore the **ISINSCOPE** function further by creating this next measure and adding the measure to the **Matrix** visualization in the **Values** field well.

```
Is In Scope 2 =
    VAR __Result =
        SWITCH( TRUE(),
            ISINSCOPE( 'Table'[Item] ), 1,
            ISINSCOPE( 'Table'[Item Color] ) , 2,
```

```
            0

        )
```

RETURN

```
    __Result
```

The **Is In Scope 2** measure displays **2** for the rows where the **Item Color** is displayed, **1** for rows where the **Item** is displayed and **0** for the **Total** row. This follows the logic specified in the **SWITCH TRUE** statement.

However, one must be careful with the **ISINSCOPE** function. For example, consider the following measure where we simply change the order of our two logical tests:

```
Is In Scope 3 =

    VAR __Result =

        SWITCH( TRUE(),

            ISINSCOPE( 'Table'[Item Color] ) , 2,

            ISINSCOPE( 'Table'[Item] ), 1,

            0

        )
```

RETURN

```
    __Result
```

Adding this measure to our **Matrix** visual in the **Values** field well returns **2** for every row except the **Total** row. The reason for this is two-fold. First, the way a **SWITCH TRUE** statement works is that once a condition is found to evaluate to **TRUE**, the **SWITCH** statement stops processing and returns the corresponding value. Second, because **Item Color** is higher in the column hierarchy than **Item**, the **Item Color** column is technically "in scope" at both levels of the hierarchy. Thus, it is advisable to structure any logical tests regarding **ISINSCOPE** in reverse order from the bottom of the hierarchy to the top of the hierarchy.

Finally, **ISINSCOPE** cannot be used for columns that are not included in a visual. For example, the following measure returns **False** for all rows in the **Matrix** visual.

```
Is In Scope 4 = ISINSCOPE( 'Table'[Total Cost] )
```

This completes our exploration of DAX information functions. We next take a look at how to select columns in DAX.

Selecting Columns

There are times in DAX where we only need a subset of the columns in a table. In fact, it is often advisable from a performance perspective to only select and work with the specific columns that you need rather than the entire table. Luckily, this is easily accomplished using the **SELECTCOLUMNS** function. To demonstrate how this works, create a new table by following *Figure 2.16*:

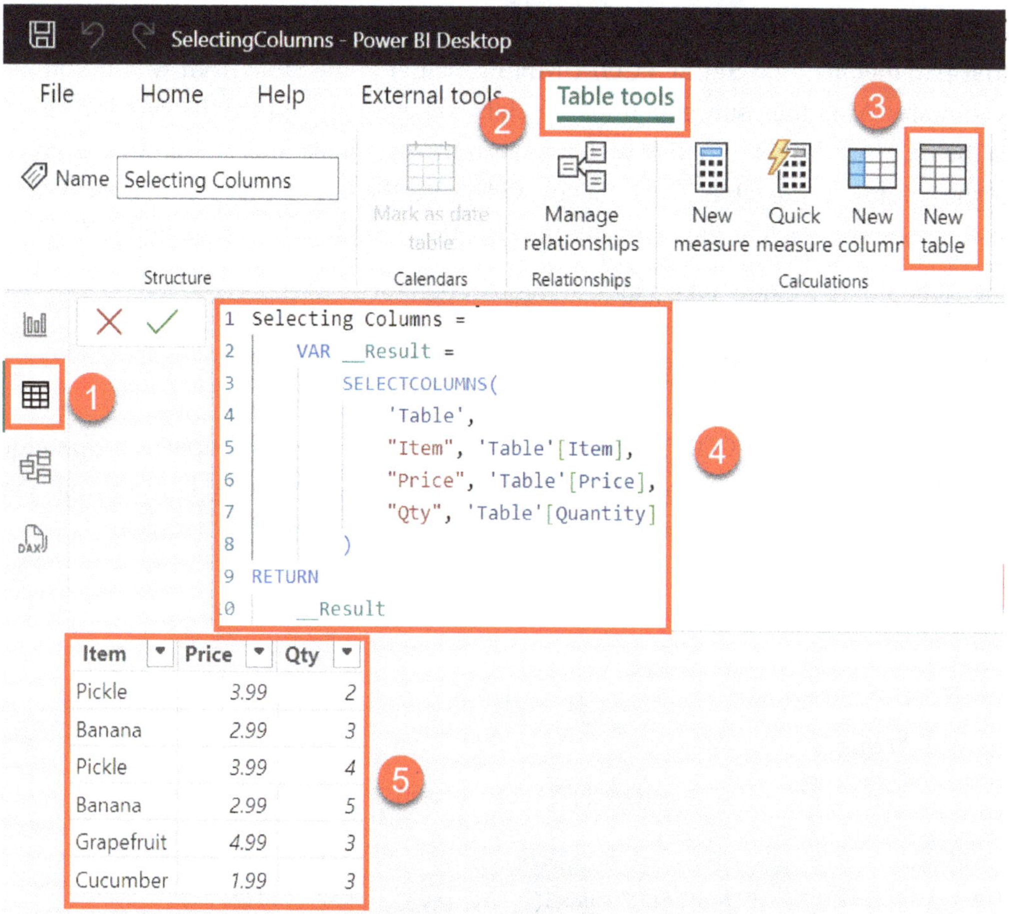

Figure 2.16: Using SELECTCOLUMNS to create a table.

The DAX code used is reprinted here for convenience.

```
Selecting Columns =
    VAR __Result =
        SELECTCOLUMNS(
```

```
            'Table',

            "Item", 'Table'[Item],

            "Price", 'Table'[Price],

            "Qty", 'Table'[Quantity]

        )

RETURN

    __Result
```

The first parameter to the **SELECTCOLUMNS** function is the table from which you wish to select columns. After that, subsequent parameters come in pairs where the lefthand side of the pair is the name of the column as it will appear in the new table and the righthand side of the pair is the column in the table. Thus, this provides you the opportunity to rename columns in the destination table such as the case with the **Quantity** column being renamed to **Qty**.

Moving right along, we now take a look at the **IN** operator.

The IN Operator

The DAX **IN** operator, or **CONTAINSROW** function, is a useful comparison operator that returns **TRUE** if a value or row of values exists within a specified table. For example, create a table using the following DAX formula.

```
IN Operator =

    VAR __Table =

        FILTER(

            'Table',

            'Table'[Item] = "Banana" || 'Table'[Item] = "Pickle"

        )

    VAR __SelectedColumns = SELECTCOLUMNS( __Table, "__Item", [Item] )

    VAR __Values = DISTINCT( __SelectedColumns )

    VAR __Result = FILTER( 'Table', [Item] IN __Values )

RETURN

    __Result
```

Refer to *Figure 2.15* if necessary for steps on creating a table in Power BI Desktop and simply replace the fourth step with the specified DAX code. This DAX formula returns a table of just the rows where the **Item** is "**Banana**" or "**Pickle**". This is done by first filtering the table using **FILTER**, then selecting just the **Item** column using **SELECTCOLUMNS**, and finally only returning the distinct values in the column using the **DISTINCT** function. This means that both __**Table** and __**SelectedColumns** have four rows (2 **Banana** rows and 2 **Pickle** rows) while __**Values** only has 2 rows (1 **Banana** row and 1 **Pickle** row). We can then use this table as input to the **IN** operator.

We could also have written the formula as follows:

```
IN Operator 2 =
    VAR __Table = { "Banana", "Pickle" }
    VAR __Result = FILTER( 'Table', CONTAINSROW( __Table, [Item] ) )
RETURN
    __Result
```

Here we have used the table constructor ({ }) to create a single column table containing the rows "**Banana**" and "**Pickle**" and have replaced the **IN** operator with its equivalent, the **CONTAINSROW** function.

Let's now move on and briefly cover multiple table functions such as **UNION**, **EXCEPT**, **INTERSECT** and **CROSSJOIN**.

Multiple Table Functions

DAX includes several interesting functions that have multiple tables as parameters. To investigate these functions, create the following calculated tables, referring to *Figure 2.15* for the steps if necessary.

```
Union Table = UNION( 'Table', 'Table' )
```

The DAX **UNION** function appends two tables together. Each table must have the same number of columns.

The DAX **EXCEPT** function returns all of the rows from the first table parameter that do not appear in the second table parameter. For example, the following formula returns only the rows in the table **Table** where the **Item** column does not have a value of "**Banana**".

```
Except Table =
    VAR __Table = FILTER( 'Table', [Item] = "Banana" )
    VAR __Result = EXCEPT( 'Table', __Table )
RETURN
    __Result
```

The **INTERSECT** function is the exact opposite of the **EXCEPT** function and thus the following DAX formula only returns rows where the **Item** column equals "**Banana**" because those are the only rows contained in both tables.

```
Intersect Table =
    VAR __Table = FILTER( 'Table', [Item] = "Banana" )
    VAR __Result = INTERSECT( 'Table', __Table )
RETURN
    __Result
```

Finally, the **CROSSJOIN** function creates a **Cartesian product** of two tables. In other words, the resulting table has as many rows as there are possible combinations of values between the two tables. To understand this, create the following DAX table.

```
Crossjoin Table =
    VAR __Items = DISTINCT( 'Table'[Item] )
    VAR __Colors = DISTINCT( 'Table'[Item Color] )
    VAR __Result = CROSSJOIN( __Items, __Colors )
RETURN
    __Result
```

This formula creates a table where there is a row for every **Item** and **Color** combination as shown in *Figure 2.17*:

Item		Item Color	
Pickle		Green	
Banana		Green	
Grapefruit		Green	
Cucumber		Green	
Pickle		Yellow	
Banana		Yellow	
Grapefruit		Yellow	
Cucumber		Yellow	
Pickle		Orange Red	
Banana		Orange Red	
Grapefruit		Orange Red	
Cucumber		Orange Red	

Figure 2.17: Table resulting from a CROSSJOIN operation.

We have finished exploring most of the core concepts in DAX and thus end the chapter with a common DAX issue and a standard pattern on how to solve it.

Measure Totals

Without getting into long winded explanations about additive, non-additive, and semi-additive measures, suffice to say that there are some measures that do not total correctly in table and matrix visuals. That is to say, the total does not sum the rows as one might expect or desire. To understand this behavior, follow these steps to prepare your environment:

1. These instructions continue from the previous section, *Multiple Table Functions*. If you have not completed that section, simply download and open **MultipleTableFunctions.pbix** from the **Chapter 2** folder of the following GitHub repository: https://github.com/gdeckler/DAX-For-Humans/tree/main/book

2. Select and delete all visuals on the page by pressing **Ctrl+A** keys and then the **Del** (delete) key.

3. Create a **Table** visual by placing the **Item** column from the table **Table** into the **Columns** field well.

4. Create the following measure and add this measure to the **Columns** field well of the **Table** visual.

```
Sum Total Cost = SUM( 'Table'[Total Cost] )
```

5. Create the following measure and add this measure to the **Columns** field well of the **Table** visual.

```
Sum Total Cost 2 = SUM( 'Table'[Total Cost] ) - 2
```

Following these steps produces a **Table** visual as shown in *Figure 2.18*:

Item	Sum Total Cost	Sum Total Cost 2
Banana	23.92	21.92
Cucumber	5.97	3.97
Grapefruit	14.97	12.97
Pickle	23.94	21.94
Total	**68.80**	**66.80**

Figure 2.18: Table visual with an odd Total.

In this sample scenario, the minus 2 can be thought of as overhead costs. Thus, in our fictional grocery store, in order to stock an item, there is overhead cost related to sourcing the item, etc.

For the measure **Sum Total Cost**, adding up the rows of the table results in a grand total of **68.80** which is correct. However, comparing **Sum Total Cost 2** to **Sum Total Cost** shows that **Sum Total Cost 2** is always 2 less than **Sum Total Cost**, which makes sense given the math. However, this also means that the individual rows for **Sum Total Cost 2** do NOT add up to **66.80** but rather **60.80**.

This difference between the displayed value and the expected value is commonly known as "The Measure Totals Problem" or, in some circles, "Banana Pickle Math" after this rather infamous image:

Item	Measure
Banana	2
Pickle	5
Total	**11,000,000**

Figure 2.19: Banana Pickle Math meme.

What is happening is that in the **Total** row the measure is evaluated such that the **Total Column** row is summed and then 2 is subtracted from this value, which results in the **Total** row only being 2 less than the **Sum Total Cost** measure instead of 8 less as one might expect.

This problem is effectively relegated to the default **Table** and **Matrix** visuals since other visuals such as stacked column visuals and waterfall charts do not exhibit this behavior. Luckily there is a standard pattern for fixing these types of issues that leverages much of the knowledge we have gained in this chapter.

Create the following measure and add the measure to the **Column** field well for the **Table** visualization.

```
Total Sum Cost 2 =
    VAR __Table =
        SUMMARIZECOLUMNS(
            'Table'[Item],
            "__TotalCost", [Sum Total Cost 2]
        )
    VAR __Result = SUMX( __Table, [__TotalCost] )
RETURN
    __Result
```

Here we can observe that the individual row results for **Total Sum Cost 2** match that of the **Sum Total Cost 2** measure and that the **Total** row returns **60.80** as expected.

To explain this pattern, we begin with the premise that we have a measure, in this case **Sum Total Cost 2** that returns the correct results for the individual row but not the **Total** row.

Next, we construct a table variable (__**Table**) that summarizes the data in exactly the same way as the visual, in this case grouping only on the **Item** column. We also include an additional column that returns the measure for our individual row, in this case **Sum Total Cost 2**.

Finally, we simply perform a **SUMX** across our summarized table variable, __**Table** and return the result. To see what is happening behind-the-scenes, you can alternatively change the **RETURN** statement to TOCSV(__Table) to observe the rows of the table variable __**Table** that comprise the final calculation.

Matrix visuals exhibit the same issue. Create a **Matrix** visual with **Item Color** and **Item** columns from the table **Table** in an ad hoc hierarchy in the **Rows** field well. Refer to *Figure 2.14* for the steps if necessary. Add the **Sum Total Cost**, **Sum Total Cost 2**, and **Total Sum Cost 2** measures to the **Values** field well of the **Matrix** visual.

Observe that for the **Sum Total Cost 2** measure that the **Total** row is incorrect and that the **Green** row is incorrect as shown in *Figure 2.20*. However, these corrections are fixed in the **Total Sum Cost 2** measure.

Item Color	Sum Total Cost	Sum Total Cost 2	Total Sum Cost 2
⊟ **Green**	**29.91**	X **27.91**	**25.91**
Cucumber	5.97	3.97	3.97
Pickle	23.94	21.94	21.94
⊟ **Orange Red**	**14.97**	**12.97**	**12.97**
Grapefruit	14.97	12.97	12.97
⊟ **Yellow**	**23.92**	**21.92**	**21.92**
Banana	23.92	21.92	21.92
Total	**68.80**	X **66.80**	**60.80**

Figure 2.20: Incorrect and fixed totals in a Matrix visual.

This concludes our exploration of more core concepts in DAX.

Summary

This chapter built upon the previous chapter and expanded our knowledge of the DAX language as well as core DAX concepts. We learned about the differences between the No CALCULATE and CALCULATE approaches and explored basic debugging techniques that are central to the No CALCULATE approach to DAX. We learned numerous techniques such as the ability to look up values, group rows, add columns, select columns, and logically control the flow of our DAX formulas using functions such as **IF** and **SWITCH**.

Along the way we learned a number of useful DAX formulas and patterns such the "double look up", "running totals", "previous value" and "measure totals" as well as expanded our DAX function knowledge to information functions such as **HASONEVALUE** and **ISINSCOPE**, the ability to select columns using the **SELECTCOLUMNS** function as well as the **IN** operator and multiple table functions such as **UNION**, **EXCEPT**, **INTERSECT**, and **CROSSJOIN**. In the next chapter we continue to expand our DAX knowledge by looking at dates and calendars.

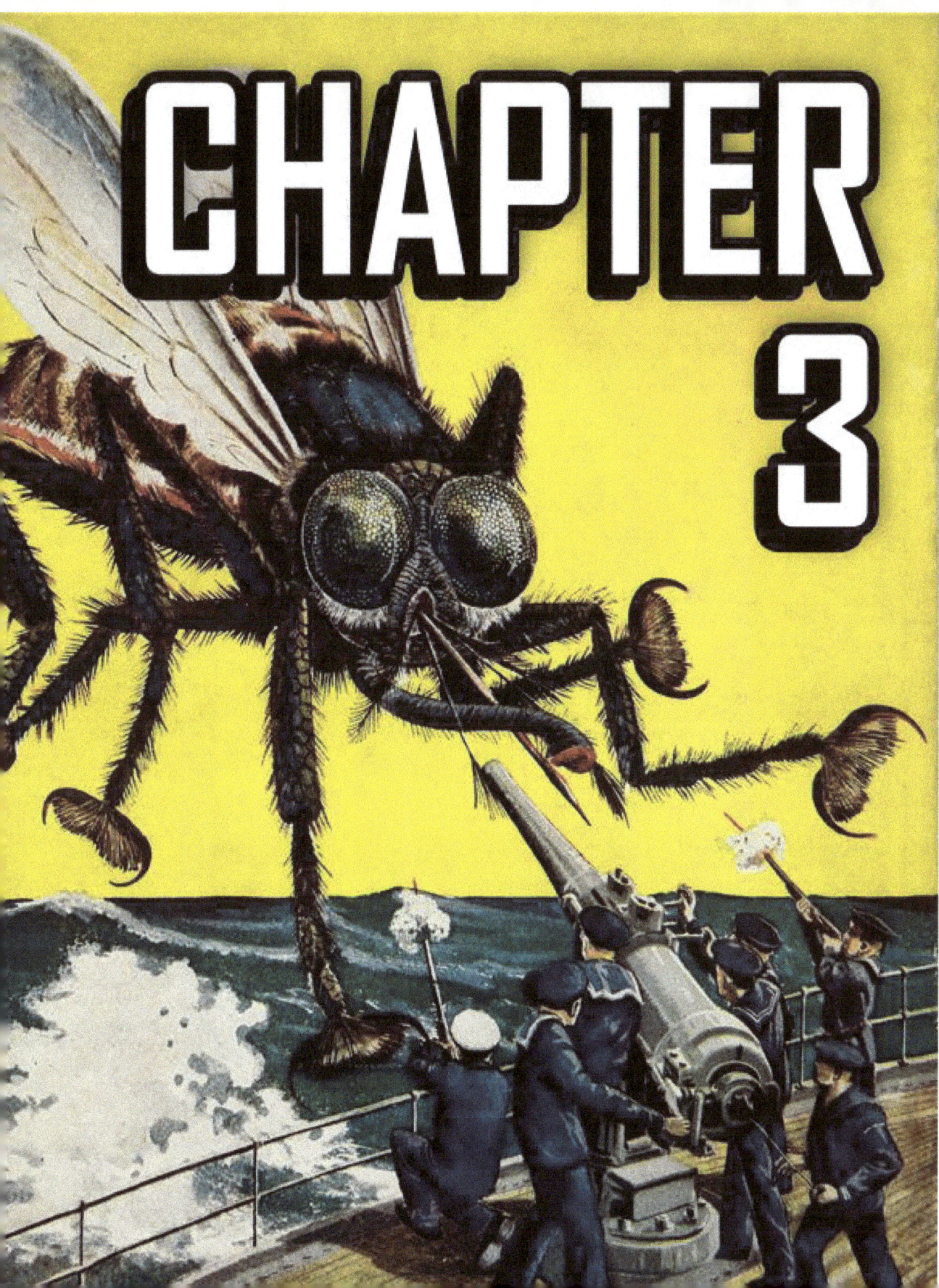

CHAPTER 3

3

Dates and Calendars

In just the first two chapters, you are already familiar with the majority of the functions that you will find useful when writing DAX. You will use those basic DAX functions as we explore more complex scenarios and calculations. However, an additional core area remains to be explored, and that subject is dates and calendars.

Dates and calendars are fundamental to nearly all Power BI semantic models. Being so fundamental, it should be no surprise that DAX has over 30 so called "time intelligence" functions designed to make complex date calculations "easy". Unfortunately, DAX's "time intelligence" functions are fundamentally flawed for a variety of reasons that will be made clear in this chapter. Instead, the No CALCULATE approach advocates using standard, core DAX functions coupled with the use of offsets to make complex date intelligence calculations.

In this chapter, we start with the basics of dates and calendars in DAX and then proceed to explore more complex calculations involving dates and calendars. However, before we explore dates and calendars, let's first learn about measure tables.

Measure Tables

Before we delve into dates and calendars, we need a place to store and organize our measures. In the first two chapters, we simply created measures within the various tables within our semantic model. However, it is a common practice to create a central table in which to store measures, a measure table. While there are competing views on this topic, with some advocating for measures to be placed within fact tables, we use a central measure table throughout this book.

To this end, start with a blank Power BI Desktop file and then perform the following steps:

1. From the **Home** tab of the ribbon, select **Get data** from the **Data** area.
2. Choose **Blank query**.

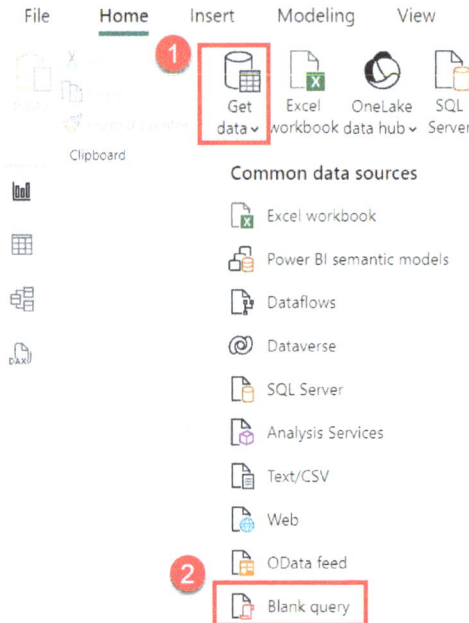

Figure 3.1: Create a Blank query.

3. In **Power Query Editor**, rename the query, **Query1**, to **Calculations** by changing the **Name** field under **PROPERTIES** in the **Query Settings** pane.

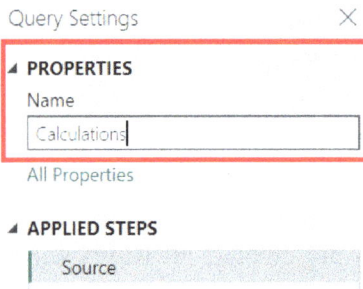

Figure 3.2: Rename query.

4. Select the **Close & Apply** button in the ribbon of the **Home** tab.

There are other methods for creating a central measure table including these patron recommendations:

Patron Recommendations

Jacco suggests using an empty **Enter data** query to create an empty measure table.

Alexis Olson suggests creating a DAX calculated table using a simple table constructor,
```
Calculations = { "" }
```

Both of these methods are also acceptable ways of creating a measure table. Now, let's turn our attention to dates.

Date Basics

Dates can be created using the **DATE** function. For example, a measure can be created that returns November 11, 2024, by doing the following:

1. Right-click the **Calculations** table and choose **New measure**.
2. In the formula bar, use the following formula:

```
Date Measure = DATE( 2024, 11, 4 )
```

3. Press the **Enter** key to create the measure.
4. In the **Data** pane, expand the **Calculations** table.
5. Right-click the **Calculations** column and choose **Hide**. If you created your measure table using an **Enter data** query, you would hide the **Column1** column. If you used a calculated table using the table constructor, you would hide the **Value** column.

   Note that the icon for the **Calculations** table changes to a calculator. This table is now designated as a measures table and will remain at the top of the tables in the **Data** pane.

6. Place **Date Measure** into a **Card** visual and note that **11/4/2024 12:00:00 AM** is displayed.
7. Select the **Date Measure** in the **Data** pane by clicking on **Date Measure** (not the checkbox).
8. In the **Measure tools** tab of the ribbon, select the **Format** dropdown in the **Formatting** area of the ribbon and note the wide array of different date, date/time, and time formats available.

All the different date, date/time, and time formats are actually implemented as annotations within the Power BI semantic model. Dates are, in fact, simply whole numbers, the number of days since midnight, **December 30th, 1899**. You can observe this by changing **Date Measure** to the following:

```
Date Measure = DATE( 1899, 12, 30 ) * 1
```

Observe that the **Card** visual now displays **0.00**. Multiplying the date by **1** forces the date to reveal its true nature. Now change **Date Measure** to the following:

```
Date Measure = DATE( 1899, 12, 30 ) + 1
```

The **Card** visual now displays **12/31/1899 12:00:00 AM**. Since dates are numbers, you can use simple whole number arithmetic to add and subtract days. You can even add and subtract dates. Change the **Date Measure** to the following:

```
Date Measure = ( DATE( 1900, 1, 1 ) - DATE( 1899, 12, 30 ) ) * 1
```

Here we first subtract two dates, enclosed within parenthesis, and then multiply by **1** to reveal that there are **2** days between the two dates.

Now that you understand the basics of dates, let's move on to calendars.

Creating a Calendar

Many Power BI semantic models include a calendar table which, in its simplest form, is just a list of dates. In fact, if a semantic model is more complex than a single table, the next table added is likely a calendar or dates table. Calendar tables are not usually created using DAX but rather in a SQL data warehouse or via Power Query (M). However, we will use DAX to create a calendar table so that you can become familiar with some of the basic date functions within DAX. That said, DAX calendar/date tables are not generally a good idea for a variety of reasons.

To create a basic calendar, do the following:

1. Select the **Modeling** tab of the ribbon and then choose **New table** from the **Calculations** section.
2. Enter the following DAX code in the formula bar:

```
Dates = CALENDAR( DATE( 2020, 1, 1 ), DATE( 2030, 12, 31 ) )
```

3. Press the **Enter** key to create the table.
4. Switch to the **Table view** in Power BI Desktop and note that the **Dates** table contains a single column of dates called **Date**.
5. Right-click the **Date** column header and choose **New column**.
6. Use the following DAX code in the formula bar and press the **Enter** key to create the column:

```
Year = YEAR( [Date] )
```

7. Create the following six additional columns:

```
Month = FORMAT( [Date], "mmmm" )

MonthSort = MONTH( [Date] )

Weekday = FORMAT( [Date], "dddd" )

WeekdaySort = WEEKDAY( [Date], 2 )
```

```
Weeknum = WEEKNUM( [Date], 2 )

Day = DAY( [Date] )
```

The **FORMAT** function has a variety of different format strings that can return different portions of a date as text, such as the month name and the weekday name for date as done here with "**mmmm**" and "**dddd**" respectively. Additional format strings can be found here: https://learn.microsoft.com/en-us/dax/format-function-dax.

The **MONTH** function simply returns the month number of a year (1 – 12) for the specified date. The **WEEKDAY** and **WEEKNUM** functions return the weekday number (1 – 7) and week number of the year (1 – 53) respectively. The second parameter, in this case **2**, determines the day the week starts on. 2 indicates that the week starts on Monday (1) and ends on Sunday (7).

8. Select the **Month** column by clicking on the header for the column.
9. On the **Column tools** tab of the ribbon, select **Sort by column** in the **Sort** section.
10. Select the **MonthSort** column.

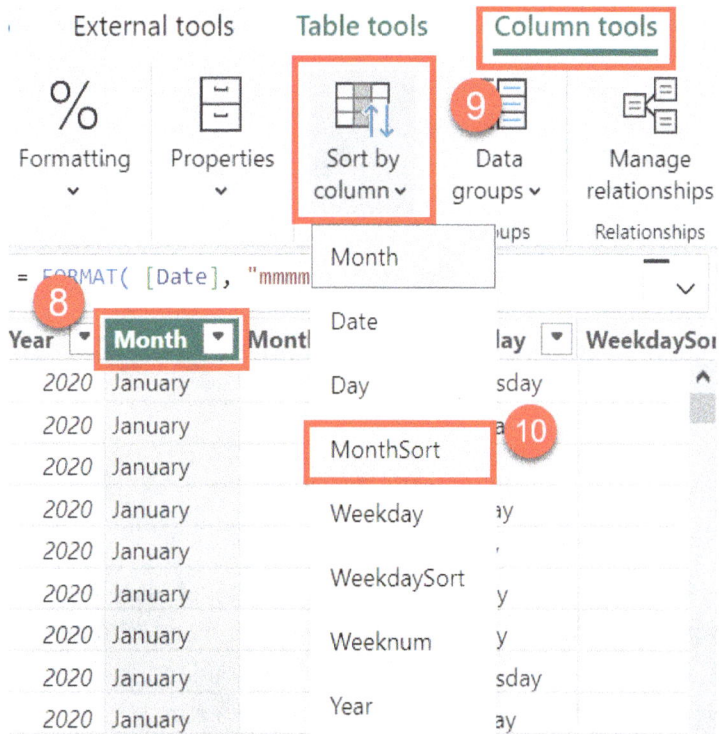

Figure 3.3: Sort by column.

11. Set the **Weekday** column to have a sort by column of **WeekdaySort**.

Setting the **Sort by column** for text columns overrides the default sorting behavior of Power BI, which is alphabetical, to ensure that text columns such as months are sorted correctly when displayed in visuals.

Patron Recommendations

Brian Julius notes that adding a custom **Sort by column** to a column brings that custom **Sort by column** into the filter context, and now in order to remove filters from that field you must remove the filters for the original column name as well as the **Sort by column**.

While not important for the No CACULATE approach, DAX "time intelligence" functions work best when the calendar table is marked as a date table. To do this, right-click the **Dates** table in the **Data** pane and choose **Mark as date table**. In the **Mark as date table** dialog box, toggle the **Mark as date table** setting to **On** and then for the **Choose the date column** setting, choose the **Date** column:

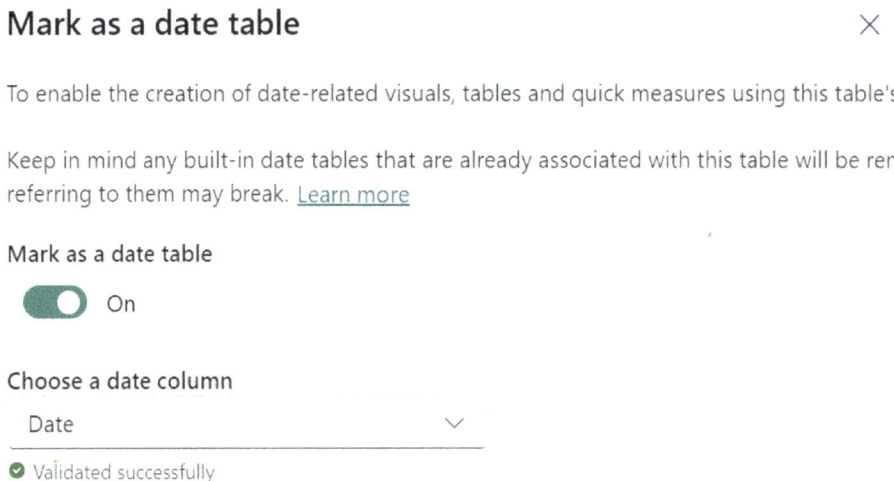

Mark as a date table   ✕

To enable the creation of date-related visuals, tables and quick measures using this table's

Keep in mind any built-in date tables that are already associated with this table will be ren referring to them may break. Learn more

Mark as a date table

⬤⚪ On

Choose a date column

Date   ⌄

✓ Validated successfully

Figure 3.4: Mark as date table dialog

When finished, click the **Save** button.

This completes the creation of a basic calendar table. However, note that, as we will see in the next section, calendar tables can be quite extensive with many additional columns. In addition, not all companies operate on a standard Gregorian calendar but often have custom fiscal calendars that start on June 1st, for example, and may also run 445 calendars where quarters have 13 weeks grouped into two 4-week months and one 5-week month.

In general, DAX's "time intelligence" functions, which are supposedly designed for complex date calculations, are generally incapable of dealing with custom fiscal calendars. For example, **PREVIOUSQUARTER** and similar DAX functions always assume a standard calendar. Therefore, the No CALCULATE approach to DAX eschews DAX's time intelligence functions for an alternative approach, offsets.

Offsets

Offsets are a superior method for performing complex DAX date calculations versus DAX's built-in "time intelligence" functions. The primary reason is that the use of offsets works with both standard calendars and custom fiscal calendars. But what are offsets? Simply stated, offsets work like a number line where the present period is 0, future periods are positive integers, and past periods are negative integers. Offsets can be visualized as follows:

Figure 3.5: Offsets.

To get a better understanding of offsets, create the following column in your **Dates** table:

```
Year Offset =
    VAR __Current = YEAR( TODAY() )
    VAR __Result = [Year] - __Current
RETURN
    __Result
```

Note that this column returns **-1** for dates in last year and **1** for dates in next year. The current year's dates return **0**. Thus, it should be obvious now that to perform a calculation such as a year-to-date total for the current year that the filter would simply be all rows where the **Year Offset** column is **0** and the **Date** column is less than today's date.

A more general version of DAX offsets is the following:

```
Month Offset =
    VAR __Today = TODAY()
    VAR __Current = YEAR( __Today ) * 100 + MONTH( __Today )
    VAR __Table =
        SUMMARIZE(
            ADDCOLUMNS(
```

```
            'Dates',

            "__Value", YEAR( [Date] ) * 100 + MONTH( [Date] )

        ),

        [__Value]

    )

    VAR __Row = YEAR( [Date] ) * 100 + MONTH( [Date] )

    VAR __Result =

        IF(

            __Row < __Current,

            COUNTROWS(

                FILTER(

                    __Table,

                    [__Value] >= __Row && [__Value] < __Current

                )

            ) * -1,

            COUNTROWS(

                FILTER(

                    __Table,

                    [__Value] <= __Row && [__Value] > __Current

                )

            ) + 0

        )

RETURN

    __Result
```

In this formula, the __**Current** variable is calculated such that the year value for today's date is multiplied by **100** and then added to the numeric month value for today's date producing a value such as **202503** for **March 2025**, for example.

Next a table variable (__**Table**) is created that adds the same type of column to the table and then summarizes the table by that column. Then, the same calculation is performed for the present row in the __**Row** variable.

Finally, the result is calculated simply by checking if the __Row value is less than the __Current value. If so, the __Table variable is filtered appropriately, the number of rows counted, and then the result multiplied by -1. If __Row is larger to or equal than __Current, the __Table variable is filtered appropriately, counted, and 0 is added.

This formula is a general version as it can also work with year offsets and week number offsets with minor changes. For example, to create a **Weeknum Offset** column, simply replace the **MONTH** functions in the formula with **WEEKNUM** functions using **2** as the second parameter.

While this is a book on DAX, as alluded to in the previous section, *Creating a Calendar*, it is not generally considered best practice to build date tables in DAX. Instead, such date tables are generally created in the data sources themselves using SQL, for example, or created in Power Query (M). Melissa de Korte has a robust Power Query (M) date table function. To demonstrate its use, do the following:

1. Navigate to the following link: https://forum.enterprisedna.co/t/extended-date-table-power-query-m-function/6390.
2. Copy the code for the **fnDateTable** function.
3. In Power BI Desktop, choose **Get data** from the **Home** tab of the ribbon in the **Data** section.
4. Choose **Blank query**.
5. In **Power Query Editor**, choose **Advanced Editor** from the **Query** section of the Home tab.
6. Use **Ctrl+A** to select all of the code.
7. Use **Ctrl+V** to paste the **fnDateTable** code.
8. Click the **Done** button.
9. Rename the query **fxCalendar**.
10. Select the **fxCalendar** query in the **Queries** pane.
11. Enter a **StartDate** of **1/1/2020** (January 1st, 2020), an **EndDate** of **12/31/2030** (December 31st, 2030), and a **FYStartMonthNum** of **6**:

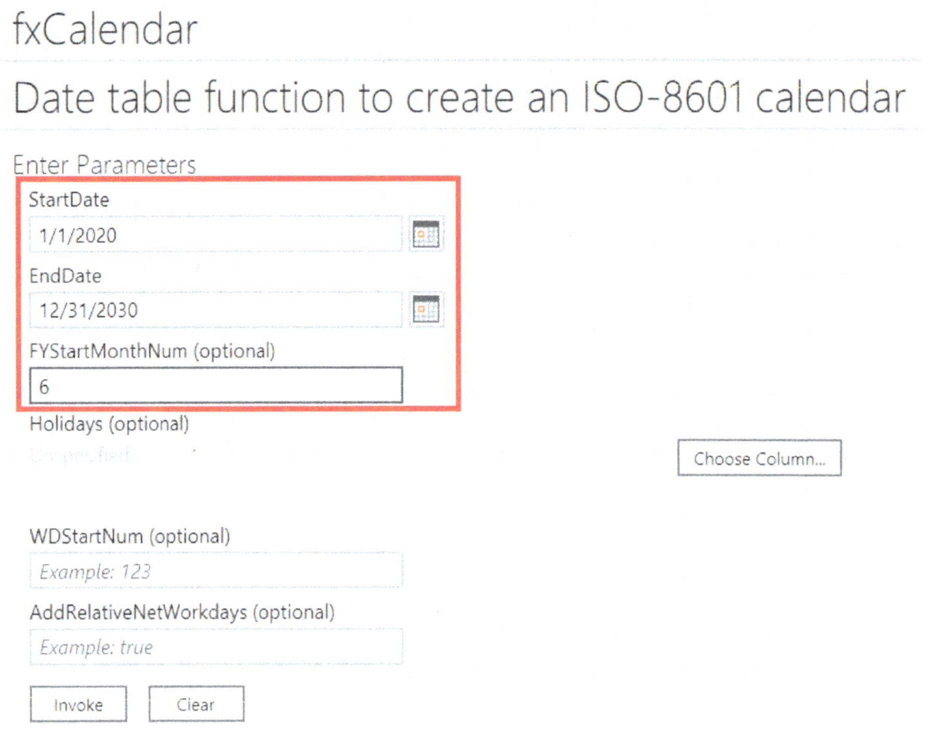

fxCalendar

Date table function to create an ISO-8601 calendar

Enter Parameters

StartDate

1/1/2020

EndDate

12/31/2030

FYStartMonthNum (optional)

6

Holidays (optional)

Choose Column...

WDStartNum (optional)

Example: 123

AddRelativeNetWorkdays (optional)

Example: true

Invoke   Clear

Figure 3.6: fxCalendar function.

12. Click the **Invoke** button.
13. Rename the **Invoked Function** query in the **Queries** pane to **Calendar**.
14. Click the **Close & Apply**.
15. In the **Table view**, set the sort by column for **Month Name** to **Month**.

In **Table view** back in Power BI Desktop, notice that this **Calendar** table has many more columns than our simple date table, **Dates**. In fact, there are 60 columns in total with many offset columns such as:

- **CurrYearOffset**
- **CurrQuarterOffset**
- **CurrMonthOffset**
- **CurrWeekOffset**
- **CurrDayOffset**

In addition, there are offset columns for ISO (International Organization for Standardization) dates and a **Fiscal CurrYearOffset** column as well. The ISO columns reference ISO 8601 which is an international standard for date and time-related data.

Now that you understand offsets, let's next move on to demonstrating how to use offsets in complex date calculations.

Period-to-Date

Period-to-date calculations such as year-to-date, quarter-to-date and month-to-date calculations are quite common. To explore these calculations, we first need some data in addition to our **Dates** and **Calendar** tables. To create this data, do the following:

1. Open the **Model view** in Power BI Desktop.
2. In the **Calculations** section of the **Home** tab, choose **New table**.
3. Enter the following formula in the formula bar and press **Enter** to create the table.

```
Table =
    VAR __Table =
        ADDCOLUMNS(
            CALENDAR( DATE( 2020, 1, 1 ), TODAY() ),
            "Value", RANDBETWEEN( 10, 100 )
        )
    VAR __Result = UNION( __Table, __Table, __Table )
RETURN
    __Result
```

This table is meant to simulate something like a table of daily sales transactions, in this case three transactions per day. The **RANDBETWEEN** function simply returns a random whole number between **10** and **100**. We use the **UNION** function to append the **__Table** variable three times meaning that each **Date** in the table will have the same **Value** repeated three times. Again, this is simply meant for the purposes of simulated data.

4. Create a relationship between the **Dates** table and the **Table** table based on the **Date** columns in each table. This can be done by dragging and dropping the columns or using the **Manage relationships** button in the **Relationships** section of the **Home** tab.
5. Make sure that the **Cardinality** of the relationship is **One to many** or **Many to one** depending on how the relationship is defined and that the **Cross-filter direction** is **Single**.

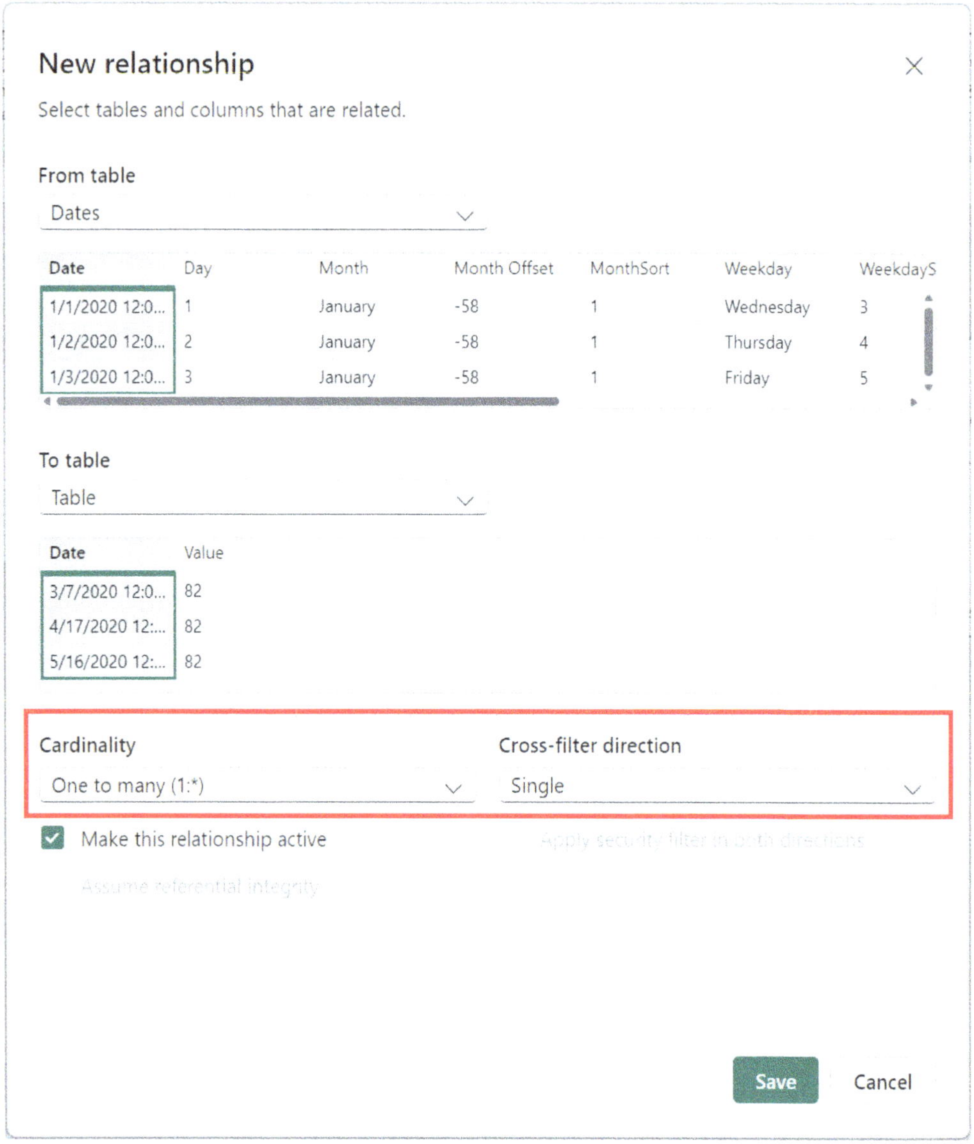

New relationship ✕

Select tables and columns that are related.

From table

Dates ⌄

Date	Day	Month	Month Offset	MonthSort	Weekday	WeekdayS
1/1/2020 12:0...	1	January	-58	1	Wednesday	3
1/2/2020 12:0...	2	January	-58	1	Thursday	4
1/3/2020 12:0...	3	January	-58	1	Friday	5

To table

Table ⌄

Date	Value
3/7/2020 12:0...	82
4/17/2020 12:...	82
5/16/2020 12:...	82

Cardinality   **Cross-filter direction**

One to many (1:*) ⌄   Single ⌄

☑ Make this relationship active   Apply security filter in both directions

Assume referential integrity

Save   Cancel

Figure 3.7: Creating a relationship.

6. Click the **Save** button.
7. Repeat steps **4-6** with the **Calendar** table and the **Table** table.

Your semantic model should now look as follows:

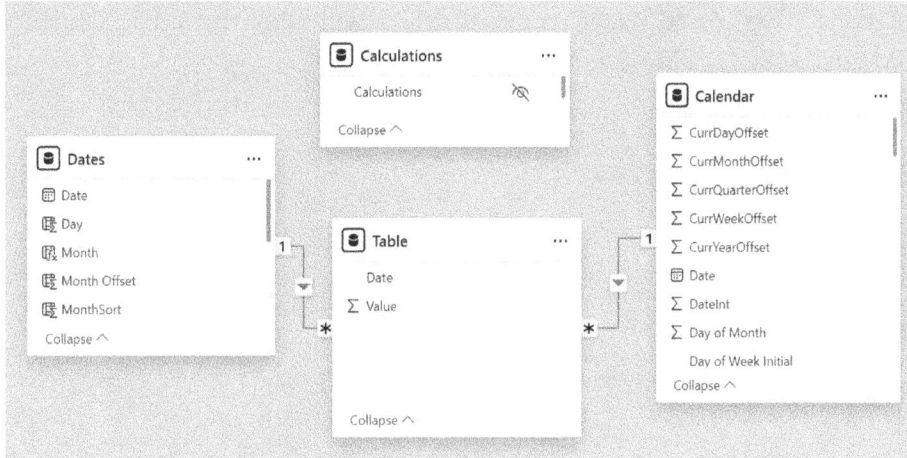

Figure 3.8: Semantic model.

Year-to-Date

Navigate to the **Report view** and remove any visuals. We can now create a simple period-to-date measures for year-to-date as follows:

1. Right-click the **Calculations** table and choose **New measure**.
2. Enter the following DAX code in the formula bar:

```
Year To Date =
    VAR __Today = TODAY()
    VAR __Table =
        SUMMARIZE(
            FILTER( 'Calendar', [Date] <= __Today && [CurrYearOffset] = 0 ),
            [Date],
            "__Value", SUM( 'Table'[Value] )
        )
    VAR __Result = SUMX( __Table, [__Value] )
RETURN
    __Result
```

Here we use the **SUMMARIZE** function to group the table by **Date** and **FILTER** the **Calendar** table for **Date** values that are less than or equal to **TODAY** and where the **CurrYearOffset** equals 0. We can then use **SUMX** across the __**Table** variable for the __**Value** column.

Note that we could have alternatively used this formula which uses the **SUMMARIZECOLUMNS** function instead:

```
Year To Date Alt =
    VAR __Today = TODAY()
    VAR __Table =
        SUMMARIZECOLUMNS(
            'Table'[Date],
            FILTER( 'Calendar', [Date] <= __Today && [CurrYearOffset] = 0 ),
            "__Value", SUM( 'Table'[Value] )
        )
    VAR __Result = SUMX( __Table, [__Value] )
RETURN
    __Result
```

3. Create a **Card** visual to display the **Year To Date** measure.
4. Navigate to the **Format visual** sub-pane of the **Visualization** pane, expand the **Callout value** section and set the **Display units** to **None**.

Figure 3.9: Set Display units to None.

Next, let's compare this to DAX's built-in function **TOTALYTD**. Create the following measure in the Calculations table:

```
YTD = TOTALYTD( SUM('Table'[Value]), 'Calendar'[Date] )
```

Note that after you create this measure that the **Card** visual for your **Year to Date** measure will change slightly. This is because the semantic model is updated when creating a measure and the random values generated by the **RANDBETWEEN** function change.

Now, do the following:

1. Create a **Table** visual.
2. Place the Year column from the **Calendar** table into **Columns** field well.
3. Change the summarization for the **Year** column to **Don't summarize**:

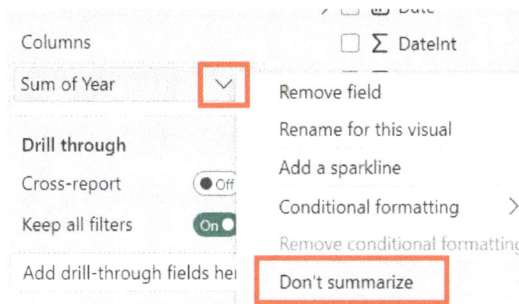

Figure 3.10: Set summarization to Don't summarize.

4. Place the **YTD** measure into the **Columns** field well.

Note that the values displayed by the **Year To Date** measure in the **Card** visual and **YTD** measure for the current year (2025) in the **Table** visual agree. However, consider that many year-to-date calculations do not include the current day of the year. This is often the case because the current day is not considered a fully completed day.

This is an easy change for our **Year To Date** measure, we simply change the comparison in our **FILTER** to < instead of <=. However, we cannot do this for the **YTD** measure. This highlights the inflexibility of DAX's "time intelligence" functions.

Now place the **Year To Date** measure into the **Table** visualization. Notice that a value is displayed for only the current year. We can modify this behavior by creating this alternate version of the **Year To Date** measure:

```
Year To Date 2 =

    VAR __Offset =

        IF(
```

```
            HASONEVALUE( 'Calendar'[Year] ),

            MAX( 'Calendar'[CurrYearOffset] ),

            0

        )

    VAR __Today = TODAY()

    VAR __MaxDate =

        DATE(

            YEAR( __Today ) + __Offset,

            MONTH( __Today ),

            DAY( __Today )

        )

    VAR __Table =

        SUMMARIZE(

            FILTER( 'Calendar', [Date] <= __MaxDate && [CurrYearOffset] = __Offset ),

            [Date],

            "__Value", SUM( 'Table'[Value] )

        )

    VAR __Result = SUMX( __Table, [__Value] )

RETURN

    __Result
```

This version is only slightly different than the previous version. We have simply added a check via the **__Offset** variable to determine if there are one or more years present. If a single year is present, we simply return the **CurrYearOffset** for that year. If multiple years are present, we calculate the offset to be **0**, the present year. We can then use this offset to determine the maximum date to display as well as in the **FILTER** clause to properly filter the table.

Adding this version of the measure to the **Table** visual displays values for all years but the values for the years other than the present year are different than the **YTD** measure. Adding the **Sum** of the **Value** column from the **Table** table exposes the fact that the **TOTALYTD** measure is simply returning the sum of the entire year for years other than the current year.

This may or may not make a lot of sense. Obviously, this behavior makes no sense if you are trying to compare a partial current year to a previous year for the same timeframe. Conversely, the **Year To Date 2** measure can be used for year-over-year comparisons.

We can make our year-to-date calculation work the same as DAX's **TOTALYTD** function by creating a third version as follows:

```
Year To Date 3 =

    VAR __Offset =

        IF(

            HASONEVALUE( 'Calendar'[Year] ),

            MAX( 'Calendar'[CurrYearOffset] ),

            0

        )

    VAR __Today = TODAY()

    VAR __MaxDate = IF( __Offset = 0, __Today, MAX( 'Calendar'[Date] ) )

    VAR __Table =

        SUMMARIZE(

            FILTER( 'Calendar', [Date] <= __MaxDate && [CurrYearOffset] = __Offset ),

            [Date],

            "__Value", SUM( 'Table'[Value] )

        )

    VAR __Result = SUMX( __Table, [__Value] )

RETURN

    __Result
```

In addition, this measure works in a **Card** visual as well. Displaying the **YTD** measure in a **Card** visual displays **(Blank)**. This highlights the inconsistency of DAX's "time intelligence" functions.

Finally, we can easily adapt our year-to-date measure to work with a fiscal calendar instead of a standard calendar. Recall that when we created the **Calendar** table, we specified a fiscal year start month (**FYStartMonthNum**) of **6** for June. Create the following measure:

```
FY To Date =

    VAR __Offset =
```

```
    IF(

        HASONEVALUE( 'Calendar'[Year] ),

        MAX( 'Calendar'[Fiscal CurrYearOffset] ),

        0

    )

VAR __Today = TODAY()

VAR __MaxDate =

    IF(

        __Offset = 0,

        __Today,

        MAXX( FILTER( ALL( 'Calendar'), [Fiscal CurrYearOffset] = __Offset ), [Date]
)

    )

VAR __Table =

    SUMMARIZE(

        FILTER(

            ALL('Calendar'),

            [Date] <= __MaxDate && [Fiscal CurrYearOffset] = __Offset ),

        [Date],

        "__Value", SUM( 'Table'[Value] )

    )

VAR __Result = SUMX( __Table, [__Value] )

RETURN

    __Result
```

In this version, we have swapped **CurrYearOffset** for **Fiscal CurrYearOffset**. In addition, we have slightly modified the **__MaxDate** variable and **__Table** variables to account for the fact that our fiscal years span the standard **Year** column we are using in our visual. This primarily involves introducing the **ALL** function.

Adding the **FY To Date** measure to our table visual produces slightly different results than previous measures because of the sliding time scale. It should be noted that the **TOTALYTD** function is one of the very few functions that includes the ability to account for a different starting date for a fiscal year other than January 1st.

You should now be starting to grasp some of the many issues with DAX's built-in "time intelligence" functions. Now that we have a relatively general solution for period-to-date calculations, let's apply the technique to different periods starting with quarters.

Quarter-to-Date

We now have a generalized period-to-date measure that can be easily adapted to other period-to-date calculations such as quarter-to-date. Start by creating a new table visual with un-summarized **Year** and **Quarter** columns from the **Calendar** table. Next, create the following measure:

```
Quarter To Date 3 =

    VAR __Offset =

        IF(

            HASONEVALUE( 'Calendar'[Year] ) && HASONEVALUE( 'Calendar'[Quarter] ),

            MAX( 'Calendar'[CurrQuarterOffset] ),

            0

        )

    VAR __Today = TODAY()

    VAR __MaxDate = IF( __Offset = 0, __Today, MAX( 'Calendar'[Date] ) )

    VAR __Table =

        SUMMARIZE(

            FILTER(

                'Calendar',

                [Date] <= __MaxDate && [CurrQuarterOffset] = __Offset

            ),

            [Date],

            "__Value", SUM( 'Table'[Value] )

        )

    VAR __Result = SUMX( __Table, [__Value] )

RETURN
```

```
__Result
```

Also create the following measure:

```
QTD = TOTALQTD( SUM( 'Table'[Value] ), 'Calendar'[Date] )
```

Place both measures in the new table visual and observe that they return the same results. However, it should be noted that, perhaps curiously, the **TOTALQTD** function lacks the fourth parameter of the **TOTALYTD** function and thus while the offset approach covered here can be easily adapted to work with any kind of fiscal calendar, DAX's quarter-based "time intelligence" functions are incapable of doing the same and only work if quarters align with standard calendar definitions.

Let's move on to month-to-date calculations.

Month-to-Date

We can use the same pattern for month-to-date calculations as follows:

```
Month To Date 3 =
    VAR __Offset =
        IF(
            HASONEVALUE( 'Calendar'[Year] ) && HASONEVALUE( 'Calendar'[Month] ),
            MAX( 'Calendar'[CurrMonthOffset] ),
            0
        )
    VAR __Today = TODAY()
    VAR __MaxDate = IF( __Offset = 0, __Today, MAX( 'Calendar'[Date] ) )
    VAR __Table =
        SUMMARIZE(
            FILTER(
                'Calendar',
                [Date] <= __MaxDate && [CurrMonthOffset] = __Offset
            ),
            [Date],
            "__Value", SUM( 'Table'[Value] )
        )
```

```
    VAR __Result = SUMX( __Table, [__Value] )

RETURN

    __Result
```

Also create the following measure:

```
        MTD = TOTALMTD( SUM( 'Table'[Value] ), 'Calendar'[Date] )
```

Place both measures into a **Table** visual along with un-summarized **Year** and **MonthName** columns from the **Calendar** table. Observe that both measures return the same values.

An interesting aspect of the offset approach is that it can work with single table data models as well. For example, add the following two columns to the **Table** table:

```
        Year = YEAR( [Date] )
```

```
        Month = FORMAT( [Date], "mmmm" )
```

Now create the following measure:

```
Month To Date =

    VAR __Offset =

        IF(

            HASONEVALUE( 'Table'[Year] ) && HASONEVALUE( 'Table'[Month] ),

            YEAR( MAX( 'Table'[Date] ) ) * 100 + MONTH( MAX( 'Table'[Date] ) ),

            YEAR( TODAY() ) * 100 + MONTH( TODAY() )

        )

    VAR __Table =

        SUMMARIZE(

            ADDCOLUMNS(

                'Table',

                "__Offset", YEAR( [Date] ) * 100 + MONTH( [Date] )

            ),

            [__Offset],

            "__Value", SUM( 'Table'[Value] )

        )

    VAR __Result =
```

```
   SUMX(

       FILTER(

           __Table,

           [__Offset] <= __Offset

       ),

       [__Value]

   )

RETURN

   __Result
```

Place this measure in a new table visualization along with un-summarized **Year** and **Month** columns from the **Table** table. Notice that the same results are returned in this table as in the table with the **Month to Date 3** and **MTD** measures. Thus, the offset method works with single table data models whereas DAX's "time intelligence" functions require a separate date table.

Also notice that this measure uses what are essentially dynamically created offsets. So, you do not even have to have offsets within your data table in order to use the offset method! This dynamic offset method can be used with any period-to-date calculation, not just month-to-date.

To round out this period-to-date section, let's finally look at week-to-date calculations.

Week-to-Date

It should come as no surprise that this same period-to-date pattern also works for weeks. To demonstrate, create the following measure:

```
Week To Date =

   VAR __Offset =

       IF(

           HASONEVALUE( 'Calendar'[Year] ) &&
               HASONEVALUE( 'Calendar'[Week Number] ),

           MAX( 'Calendar'[CurrWeekOffset] ),

           0

       )

   VAR __Today = TODAY()

   VAR __MaxDate = IF( __Offset = 0, __Today, MAX( 'Calendar'[Date] ) )
```

```
VAR __Table =

    SUMMARIZE(

        FILTER( 'Calendar', [Date] <= __MaxDate && [CurrWeekOffset] = __Offset ),

        [Date],

        "__Value", SUM( 'Table'[Value] )

    )

VAR __Result = SUMX( __Table, [__Value] )

RETURN

    __Result
```

Place this measure in a new table visual with un-summarized **Year** and **Weeknumber** columns from the **Calendar** table. We cannot compare these numbers to DAX's "time intelligence" functions because DAX's "time intelligence" functions do not support any kind of week calculations.

The advantages of the offset approach for complex DAX date calculations should now be obvious. The offset approach works for all semantic models, including single table semantic models, is far more flexible, more consistent, capable of handling both standard and fiscal calendars, works with all standard reporting periods including weeks, and can be easily debugged.

Before we move on to previous period calculations, rename **Page 1** to **Period to Date** and save your work.

Previous Period

Previous period calculations are common calculations that are useful for comparing one period with its immediately preceding period. Such calculations are critical to subsequently derived calculations like calculating growth percentages between periods.

Before we create the measures, create a new page using the **+** icon in the page tabs area and rename the page **Previous Periods**. Use the **Model view** to move all of the measures created thus far to a **Period to Date** folder by selecting the measure in the **Data** pane and then editing the **Display folder** property in the **Properties** pane.

Now create the following three standard DAX "time intelligence" measures in the **Calculations** table:

```
PY = CALCULATE( SUM( 'Table'[Value] ), PREVIOUSYEAR( 'Calendar'[Date] ) )
```

```
    PQ = CALCULATE( SUM( 'Table'[Value] ), PREVIOUSQUARTER( 'Calendar'[Date] ) )

    PM = CALCULATE( SUM( 'Table'[Value] ), PREVIOUSMONTH('Calendar'[Date] ) )
```

Next, create these offset measures:

Previous Year

```
Previous Year =
    VAR __Offset = MAX( 'Calendar'[CurrYearOffset] ) - 1
    VAR __Table =
        SUMMARIZE(
            FILTER( ALL( 'Calendar' ), [CurrYearOffset] = __Offset ),
            [Date],
            "__Value", SUM( 'Table'[Value] )
        )
    VAR __Result = SUMX( __Table, [__Value] )
RETURN
    __Result
```

Previous Quarter

```
Previous Quarter =
    VAR __Offset = MAX( 'Calendar'[CurrQuarterOffset] ) - 1
    VAR __Table =
        SUMMARIZE(
            FILTER( ALL( 'Calendar' ), [CurrQuarterOffset] = __Offset ),
            [Date],
            "__Value", SUM( 'Table'[Value] )
        )
    VAR __Result = SUMX( __Table, [__Value] )
RETURN
    __Result
```

Previous Month

```
Previous Month =
    VAR __Offset = MAX( 'Calendar'[CurrMonthOffset] ) - 1
    VAR __Table =
        SUMMARIZE(
            FILTER( ALL( 'Calendar' ), [CurrMonthOffset] = __Offset ),
            [Date],
            "__Value", SUM( 'Table'[Value] )
        )
    VAR __Result = SUMX( __Table, [__Value] )
RETURN
    __Result
```

Previous Week

```
Previous Week =
    VAR __Offset = MAX( 'Calendar'[CurrWeekOffset] ) - 1
    VAR __Table =
        SUMMARIZE(
            FILTER( ALL( 'Calendar' ), [CurrWeekOffset] = __Offset ),
            [Date],
            "__Value", SUM( 'Table'[Value] )
        )
    VAR __Result = SUMX( __Table, [__Value] )
RETURN
    __Result
```

All of these offset formulas work identically. The __Offset is simply the current respective offset in context minus one. The **ALL** function is used to override the current filters on the **Calendar** table and this filter context is replaced with a filter where the respective offset equals the __Offset variable.

On the **Previous Periods** page, create a table visual that includes the un-summarized **Year** column from the **Calendar** table along with the **YTD**, **PY**, and **Previous Year** measures.

Create a second table visual that includes the un-summarized **Year** and **Quarter** columns from the **Calendar** table along with the **QTD**, **PQ**, and **Previous Quarter** measures.

Create a third table visual that includes the un-summarized **Year** and **Month** columns from the **Calendar** table along with the **MTD**, **PM**, and **Previous Month** measures.

Create a fourth table visual that includes the un-summarized **Year** and **Week Number** columns from the **Calendar** table along with the **Week to Date** and **Previous Week** measures.

Observe how the offset measures return the same results as the standard DAX "time intelligence" versions. The exception is the **Previous Week** measure since it cannot be compared due to DAX "time intelligence" functions lacking any kind of week capabilities. However, one can easily see that the results are accurate by comparing the **Week to Date** measure for the preceding week.

Before continuing to the next section, move all of the measures created in this section to a **Previous Period** folder and save your work.

Previous Period to Date

The previous period calculations just covered are useful when dealing with entire periods of data. However, as was covered in the *Period-to-Date* section when discussing **Year to Date**, and specifically the **Year to Date 2** measure, it is often desirable to compare like partial periods. Before continuing, create a new page called **Previous Period to Date.**

In the **Calculations** table, create the following measures:

Previous Year-to-Date

```
Previous YTD =
    VAR __Offset = MAX( 'Calendar'[CurrYearOffset] ) - 1
    VAR __Today = TODAY()
    VAR __MaxDate = EDATE( __Today, __Offset * 12 )
    VAR __Table =
        SUMMARIZE(
            FILTER(
                ALL( 'Calendar' ),
```

```
                [Date] <= __MaxDate && [CurrYearOffset] = __Offset

        ),

        [Date],

        "__Value", SUM( 'Table'[Value] )

    )

  VAR __Result = SUMX( __Table, [__Value] )
RETURN

  __Result
```

This version is extremely similar to previous year-to-date calculations covered in the *Period-to-Date* section of this chapter. The main difference is using the **EDATE** function to calculate the **__MaxDate** variable. Also note that with the minor edit of removing the **-1** from the **__Offset** variable, this formula is yet another alternative formula for a year-to-date calculation.

The **EDATE** function takes a date as its first parameter and the number of months to move that date backwards or forwards in time as its second parameter. The **EDATE** function is incredibly useful in many different types of date intelligence calculations.

Prior to the **EDATE** function, the **EOMONTH** function was used instead. **EOMONTH** is similar to **EDATE** except that it returns the end of the month date. With this function it is also extremely easy to return the first of the month as well. For example, the following returns the first of the month from today six months ago:

```
        Six Months Ago = EOMONTH( TODAY(), -7 ) + 1
```

Previous Quarter-to-Date

```
Previous QTD =

  VAR __Offset = MAX( 'Calendar'[CurrQuarterOffset] ) - 1

  VAR __Today = TODAY()

  VAR __MinQuarterCurrent =

    MINX(

        FILTER(

            ALL( 'Calendar' ),

            [CurrQuarterOffset] = 0

        ),
```

```
            [Date]

        )

    VAR __MinQuarterDate =

        MINX(

            FILTER(

                ALL( 'Calendar' ),

                [CurrQuarterOffset] = __Offset

            ),

            [Date]

        )

    VAR __MaxDate =

        IF(

            __Offset = 0,

            __Today,

            __MinQuarterDate + ( __Today - __MinQuarterCurrent )

        )

    VAR __Table =

        SUMMARIZE(

            FILTER(

                ALL( 'Calendar' ),

                [Date] <= __MaxDate && [CurrQuarterOffset] = __Offset

            ),

            [Date],

            "__Value", SUM( 'Table'[Value] )

        )

    VAR __Result = SUMX( __Table, [__Value] )

RETURN

    __Result
```

Dropping the **-1** from the **__Offset** variable calculation creates a like period alternative for the quarter-to-date calculation covered in the *Period-to-Date* section of this chapter..

Previous Month-to-Date

```
Previous MTD =
    VAR __Offset = MAX( 'Calendar'[CurrMonthOffset] ) - 1
    VAR __Today = TODAY()
    VAR __MaxDate = EDATE( __Today, __Offset )
    VAR __Table =
        SUMMARIZE(
            FILTER(
                ALL( 'Calendar' ),
                [Date] <= __MaxDate && [CurrMonthOffset] = __Offset
            ),
            [Date],
            "__Value", SUM( 'Table'[Value] )
        )
    VAR __Result = SUMX( __Table, [__Value] )
RETURN
    __Result
```

Here again, the **EDATE** function is used to calculate the **__MaxDate** variable. Removing the **-1** from the **__Offset** variable calculation, creates an alternative month-to-date calculation that compares partial month periods versus full month periods.

Previous Week-to-Date

```
Previous WTD =
    VAR __Offset = MAX( 'Calendar'[CurrWeekOffset] ) - 1
    VAR __Today = TODAY()
    VAR __MiCurrent =
        MINX(
            FILTER(
                ALL( 'Calendar' ),
                [CurrWeekOffset] = 0
            ),
            [Date]
```

```
        )
    VAR __MinDate =
        MINX(
            FILTER(
                ALL( 'Calendar' ),
                [CurrWeekOffset] = __Offset
            ),
            [Date]
        )
    VAR __MaxDate =
        IF(
            __Offset = 0,
            __Today,
            __MinDate + ( __Today - __MiCurrent )
        )
    VAR __Table =
        SUMMARIZE(
            FILTER(
                ALL( 'Calendar' ),
                [Date] <= __MaxDate && [CurrWeekOffset] = __Offset
            ),
            [Date],
            "__Value", SUM( 'Table'[Value] )
        )
    VAR __Result = SUMX( __Table, [__Value] )
RETURN
    __Result
```

The formula for **Previous WTD** is extremely similar to **Previous QTD**. Here again, dropping the **-1** from the **__Offset** variable calculation creates a like period alternative for the week-to-date calculation covered in the *Period-to-Date* section of this chapter.

On the **Previous Period to Date** page, create a **Table** visual with the **Year** column from the **Calendar** table and the measures **Year To Date 2** and **Previous YTD**. Similarly, create another

Table visual with the **Year** and **Quarter** columns from the **Calendar** table along with the **Quarter To Date 3** and **Previous QTD** measures.

You can also create the alternative versions of the month-to-date and week-to-date measures as specified by dropping the **-1** from the calculation of the **__Offset** variable. Doing so allows you to confirm the function of the **Previous MTD** and **Previous WTD** measures using similar **Table** visuals.

Before moving on to another popular type of date intelligence calculation, rolling periods, save your work. Also, move the measures created in this section to a **Previous Period to Date** folder.

Rolling Periods

Rolling periods are a common date intelligence calculation that most often involve finding the average of a specified number of past periods. For example, the monthly average for the previous six months. Such a calculation is often referred to as a rolling average or moving average and can help organizations identify trends that might otherwise go unnoticed due to values that might fluctuate wildly over shorter periods of time.

Before proceeding, create a new page called **Rolling Periods**. Now, in the **Calculations** table, create the following measure:

```
Rolling 6 Month Average =
    VAR __MaxOffset = MAX( 'Calendar'[CurrMonthOffset] ) - 1
    VAR __MinOffset = MAX( 'Calendar'[CurrMonthOffset] ) - 6
    VAR __Table =
        SUMMARIZE(
            FILTER(
                ALL( 'Calendar' ),
                [CurrMonthOffset] >= __MinOffset && [CurrMonthOffset] <= __MaxOffset
            ),
            [Month],
            "__Value", SUM( 'Table'[Value] )
        )
    VAR __Result = AVERAGEX( __Table, [__Value] )
RETURN
    __Result
```

Create a **Table** visual with the **Year** and **Month Name** columns from the **Calendar** table. Add the **Value** column from the **Table** table with a default aggregation of **Sum**. Finally, add the **Rolling 6 Month Average** measure.

Note that for **February 2020** the **Rolling 6 Month Average** measure returns the same number as the **Sum of Value** for **January 2020**. This makes sense since there is only a single previous month. Starting with **July 2020**, the measure calculates the average **Sum of Value** for the previous six months.

This rolling period calculation can be easily adapted for similar, alternate calculations. For example, by simply adjusting the **__MinOffset** calculation, the previous nine or twelve month averages can be calculated.

Alternative rolling aggregations are possible simply by changing the **AVERAGEX** in the measure to **SUMX, MEDIANX**, etc. Finally, the formula is easily adaptable to alternate periods such as years, quarters, or weeks. For example, the following is a four-week rolling average:

```
Rolling 4 Week Average =
    VAR __MaxOffset = MAX( 'Calendar'[CurrWeekOffset] ) - 1
    VAR __MinOffset = MAX( 'Calendar'[CurrWeekOffset] ) - 4
    VAR __Table =
        SUMMARIZE(
            FILTER(
                ALL( 'Calendar' ),
                [CurrWeekOffset] >= __MinOffset && [CurrWeekOffset] <= __MaxOffset
            ),
            [Week Number],
            "__Value", SUM( 'Table'[Value] )
        )
    VAR __Result = AVERAGEX( __Table, [__Value] )
RETURN
    __Result
```

It is possible to also do rolling period to date calculations. However, such calculations can be somewhat tricky. Take, for example, the following DAX formula that calculates the average for the previous three years to date:

```
Rolling 3 YTD Average =
    VAR __MaxOffset = MAX( 'Calendar'[CurrYearOffset] ) - 1
```

```
    VAR __MinOffset = MAX( 'Calendar'[CurrYearOffset] ) - 3

    VAR __Today = TODAY()

    VAR __DayNumberOfYear = __Today - DATE( YEAR( __Today), 1, 1 )

    VAR __Table =
        SUMMARIZE(
            FILTER(
                ALL( 'Calendar' ),
                [CurrYearOffset] >= __MinOffset &&
                [CurrYearOffset] <= __MaxOffset &&
                [Date] - DATE( YEAR( [Date] ), 1, 1 ) <= __DayNumberOfYear
            ),
            [Year],
            "__Value", SUM( 'Table'[Value] )
        )
    VAR __Result = AVERAGEX( __Table, [__Value] )
RETURN
    __Result
```

The structure of this formula is essentially the same as the other rolling period to date calculations. However, an extra calculation and filter are added to ensure that we are comparing the same partial to-date periods versus full periods. In other words, if today is November 8th, then previous years are only summarized up until November 8th of each year.

If you create a table visual with an un-summarized **Year** column from the **Calendar** table, the **Year To Date 2** measure from the *Period-to-Date* section of this chapter and the **Rolling 3 YTD Average** measure, you will notice small discrepancies in the calculated averages. These discrepancies are caused by the existence of leap years such that November 8th in 2024 is the 313th day of the year but for non-leap years it is the 312th day of the year.

This discrepancy can be corrected by an improved year-to-date calculation as follows:

```
Year To Date 1 =
    VAR __Offset = MAX( 'Calendar'[CurrYearOffset] )

    VAR __Today = TODAY()

    VAR __MinYearCurrent =
        MINX(
            FILTER(
```

```
                ALL( 'Calendar' ),

                [CurrYearOffset] = 0

            ),

            [Date]

        )

    VAR __MinYearDate =

        MINX(

            FILTER(

                ALL( 'Calendar' ),

                [CurrYearOffset] = __Offset

            ),

            [Date]

        )

    VAR __MaxDate =

        IF(

            __Offset = 0,

            __Today,

            __MinYearDate + ( __Today - __MinYearCurrent )

        )

    VAR __Table =

        SUMMARIZE(

            FILTER(

                ALL( 'Calendar' ),

                [Date] <= __MaxDate && [CurrYearOffset] = __Offset

            ),

            [Date],

            "__Value", SUM( 'Table'[Value] )

        )

    VAR __Result = SUMX( __Table, [__Value] )

RETURN

    __Result
```

Notice that this version of the year-to-date calculation is effectively the same as the **Quarter To Date 3** and **Week To Date** measures from the *Period-to-Date* section.

Save your work and before continuing, move the measures created in this chapter to a **Rolling Periods** folder or another folder as appropriate. Let's now investigate leap years.

Leap Years

It can be handy to know if a year is a leap year or not. The following measure returns **TRUE** if a year is a leap year and **FALSE** otherwise.

```
IsLeapYear =
    VAR __Year = MAX('Calendar'[Year])
    VAR __Div4 = IF( MOD( __Year, 4 ) = 0, TRUE(), FALSE() )
    VAR __Div100 = IF( MOD( __Year, 100) = 0, TRUE(), FALSE() )
    VAR __Div400 = IF( MOD( __Year, 400) = 0, TRUE(), FALSE() )
    VAR __Result =
        SWITCH( TRUE(),
                __Div4 && NOT(__Div100), TRUE(),
                __Div4 && __Div100 && __Div400, TRUE(),
                FALSE()
            )
RETURN
    __Result
```

The **MOD** function is the standard modulo math function that returns the remainder of a division operation.

Let's explore the subject of Julian Days next.

Julian Days

Julian Days are a useful method of dates that are used in various scientific settings. Julian Days are a continuous count of whole solar days since a specified reference date and time of 0. The specified reference date and time is noon UTC, Monday January 1st, 4713 BC. Julian Days are used in a variety of different scientific and computing domains including astrology and software as the continues format and absence of leap years makes calculations easier and more consistent.

The following measure converts standard, Gregorian, calendar dates to Julian days.

```
Julian Day =

    // For converting from Gregorian dates

    // Adapted from Jean Meeus' Astrological Algorithms

    VAR __GregorianDate = MAX( 'Calendar'[Date] )

    VAR __GregorianYear = YEAR (__GregorianDate )

    VAR __GregorianMonth = MONTH( __GregorianDate )

    VAR __GregorianDay = DAY( __GregorianDate )

    VAR __Y = IF( __GregorianMonth > 2, __GregorianYear, __GregorianYear - 1 )

    VAR __M = IF( __GregorianMonth > 2, __GregorianMonth, __GregorianMonth + 12 )

    VAR __D = __GregorianDay

    VAR __A = INT( __Y/100 )

    VAR __B = 2 - __A + INT( __A/4 )

    VAR __Result =

        INT( 365.25 * (__Y + 4716) ) + INT( 30.6001 * (__M + 1) ) + __D + __B -1524.5

RETURN

    __Result
```

The **INT** function returns the integer portion of a number. When dealing with both positive and negative numbers, it is advisable to use **TRUNC** instead of **INT**. The reason is that INT(-2.1) returns -3 while TRUNC(-2.1) returns the desired result, -2.

This next measure converts a Julian Day date to a standard Gregorian calendar date:

```
Gregorian Date =

    // For converting from Julian Day

    // Adapted from Jean Meeus' Astrologial Algorithms

    VAR __JulianDay = [Julian Day]

    VAR __Z = INT( __JulianDay + .5 )

    VAR __F = __JulianDay + .5 - __Z

    VAR __A =

        IF(

            __Z < 2299161,
```

```
        __Z,

            VAR __alpha = INT( ( __Z - 1867216.25 ) / 36524.25 )

        RETURN

            __Z + 1 + __alpha - INT(__alpha/4)

    )

VAR __B = __A + 1524

VAR __C = INT( ( __B - 122.1 ) / 365.25 )

VAR __D = INT( 365.25 * __C )

VAR __E = INT( ( __B - __D ) / 30.6001 )

VAR __Day = __B - __D - INT( 30.6001 * __E )

VAR __Month = IF( __E < 14, __E - 1, __E - 13 )

VAR __Year = IF( __Month > 2, __C - 4716, __C - 4715 )

VAR __Result = DATE( __Year, __Month, __Day ) + __F

RETURN

    __Result
```

If you are paying attention, Julian Days are essentially offsets which, again, reenforces the fact that offsets are the proper way to do data calculations and not whatever black box wizardry goes on within DAX's "time intelligence" functions.

Let's now move on to calculations involving previous rows or occurrences.

Previous Row or Occurrence

In a variety of scenarios and calculations, it is often advantageous to understand the value from a previous row or occurrence. For example, if attempting to calculate the average time between events that might occur sporadically. To achieve this in DAX, one needs to have a method of identifying "previous". In most cases this is done using an index column or by using a date column.

The following is a general formula for calculating the previous value of a row or occurrence.

```
Previous Value =

    VAR __Current = MAX( 'Calendar'[Date] )

    VAR __Previous =
```

```
    MAXX(

        FILTER(

            ALL( 'Calendar' ),

            [Date] < __Current

        ),

        [Date]

    )

VAR __Result = SUMX( FILTER( ALL( 'Table' ), [Date] = __Previous ), [Value] )

RETURN

    __Result
```

Place this measure in a **Table** visual along with an un-summarized **Date** column from the **Calendar** table and the **Sum** of the **Value** column in the **Table** table.

The formula shown here may seem like overkill in this particular situation where every date is sequential, but its utility will be demonstrated in later chapters with more complex scenarios.

Summary

In this chapter we used a variety of the core, foundational DAX functions that we learned in the last two chapters coupled with the use of offsets to create a variety of standard date intelligence calculations. We demonstrated their accuracy by comparing them with equivalent measures created using the **CALCULATE** function and DAX's built-in "time intelligence" functions.

We also demonstrated the fundamental flaws of DAX's "time intelligence" functions such as their general inability to handle custom fiscal calendars, their inability to handle week periods, their inability to work with single-table semantic models, their inflexibility, their inconsistency, and their difficulty in debugging.

We finished the chapter by looking at some specialized date calculations including calculating leap years, Julian Days, and previous row/occurrence values. In the next chapter we cover both basic and advanced scenarios for working with text.

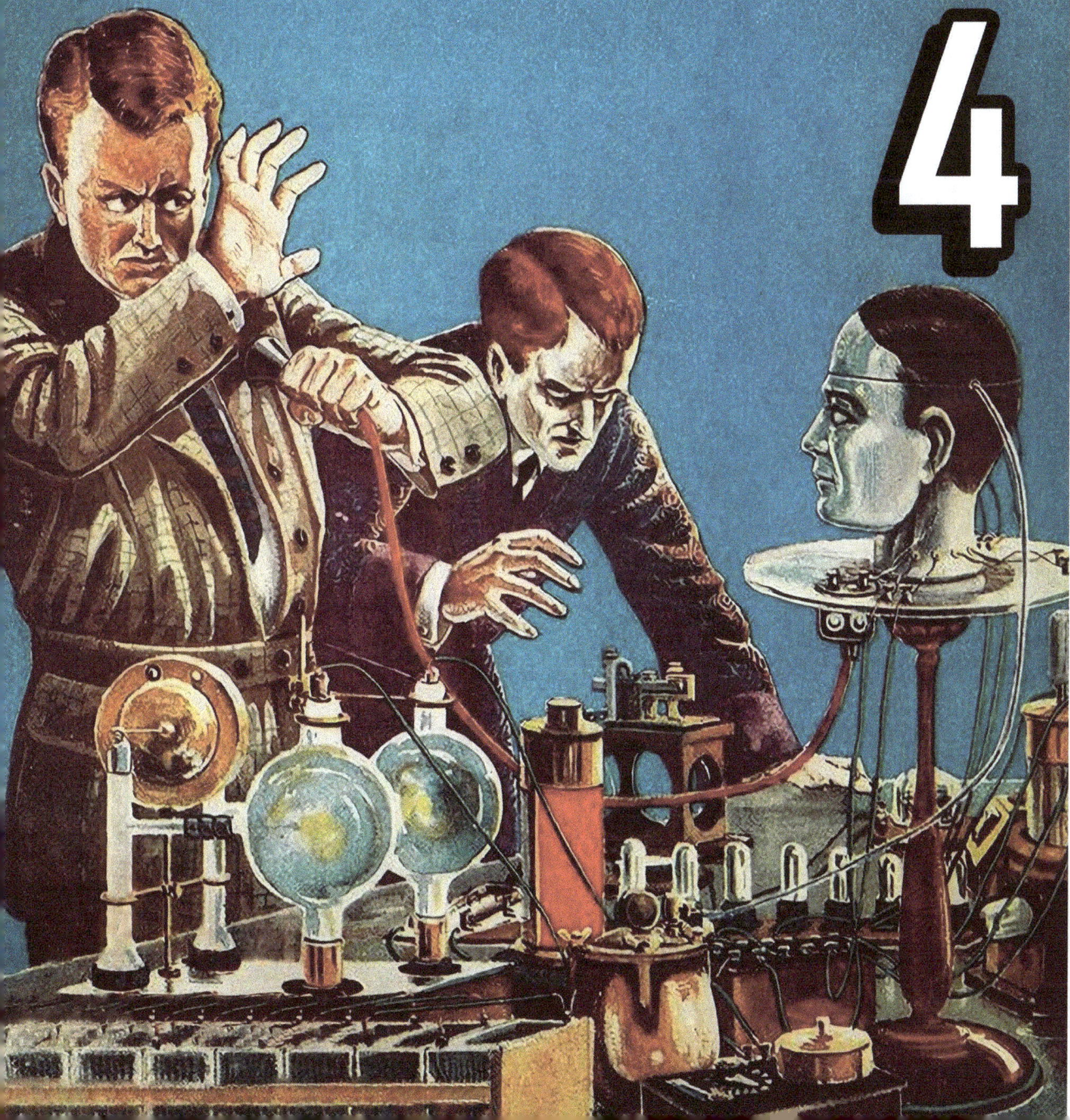

4

Text

The last chapter was all about dates, one of the core data types within the DAX language. In this chapter we seek to provide similar coverage of another core data type, text. Text is often overlooked in the world of business intelligence, but text plays a pivotal role in both data modeling and user experience. While numbers drive most calculations and visuals, it's the ability to clean, format, extract, and display text that brings polish and context to a report. This chapter dives deep into the DAX functions that enable text manipulation, starting with fundamental string functions. Through clear examples, we demonstrate how these tools can be combined to perform complex transformation and extraction logic that are crucial in real-world scenarios, such as parsing values from inconsistent formats or building dynamic titles and messages that adapt to filter context.

We also explore more advanced concepts such as how to convert text into tables, count specific character patterns, verify formats like phone numbers, and even preserve character casing despite Power BI's default collation behavior. From conditional formatting to anonymizing sensitive information, text in DAX becomes a powerful tool for enhancing both function and form in Power BI. Whether you're crafting personalized greetings or decoding poorly structured data, mastering these text techniques creates a wealth of practical and creative possibilities.

To explore dealing with text within the DAX language, we start with some of the core text functions. We then proceed to exploring how these core functions can be used to extract text and handle other more complex scenarios.

Core Text Functions

Let's start by exploring some basic text functions. First, however, we will need some sample data. Use an **Enter data** query to create a single column, single row table containing the words **"The quick brown fox jumps over the lazy dog."**. Leave the column name **Column1** and name the table **Pangram**.

A pangram is a sentence that contains every letter of the alphabet at least once and is generally used in typeface displays, testing, and the development of skills such as typing, handwriting, and calligraphy.

While in **Table view**, create the following eleven calculated columns:

```
Left = LEFT( [Column1], 6 )

Right = RIGHT( [Column1], 6 )

Mid = MID( [Column1], 7, 6 )

Len = LEN( [Column1] )

Find = FIND( "Quick", [Column1], 1, BLANK() )

Search = SEARCH( "Quick", [Column1], 1, BLANK() )

Contains = CONTAINSSTRING( [Column1], "Quick" )

Contains Exact = CONTAINSSTRINGEXACT( [Column1], "Quick" )

Replace = REPLACE( [Column1], 5, 5, "slow" )

Lower = LOWER( [Column1] )

Upper = UPPER( [Column1] )
```

By viewing the results, it should be obvious what each of these functions do. Text strings are made up of characters and each of those characters has a position within the text string starting with position **1**, the starting character of the text string.

Therefore, the **LEFT** function returns the specified number of characters starting at the beginning of the text string. The **RIGHT** function returns the specified number of characters starting at the end of the text string. The **MID** function returns the specified number of characters (third parameter) starting at the specified starting position (second parameter). The **LEN** function returns the total number of characters in the string. The pangram has 35 letters, 8 spaces, and a period for a total of **44**.

The **FIND** and **SEARCH** functions are identical in that they both return the first position of the specified search text (first parameter) from within the specified text string (second parameter) starting at the specified position within the text string (third parameter). The text string is searched from left-to-right. If the search text is found, the starting position of the found text is returned, otherwise, the value of the fourth parameter is returned. In this case, the value of the fourth parameter is specified as the **BLANK()** function, which simply returns **BLANK**, which can be thought of as *null*. The difference between **FIND** and **SEARCH** is that the **FIND** function is case-sensitive while the **SEARCH** function is not case-sensitive.

The **CONTAINSSTRING** and **CONTAINSSTRINGEXACT** functions return True or False depending on whether the search string (second parameter) is found within the text string (first parameter). **CONTAINSSTRING** is case insensitive while **CONTAINSTRINGEXACT** is case sensitive.

The **REPLACE** function replaces a portion of text within a text string (first parameter). In this case, the specified starting position is **5** (second parameter) and the number of characters to replace is also **5** (third parameter). The starting position is counted as the first character to replace. These characters are replaced by the specified text string (fourth parameter).

Finally, the **LOWER** and **UPPER** functions simply convert the text string to all lowercase and all uppercase respectively.

These basic text functions, as well as some additional text functions and operators, allow relatively efficient manipulation of text within DAX, such as the ability to extract text patterns from text strings which we look at next.

Extracting Text

To better demonstrate text extraction using a more complex example, enter the following data into an **Enter data** query. Call the table **Extraction**. Alternatively, import the **Extraction** sheet from the Excel spreadsheet, **Chapter4_Data.xlsx** which can be found in the GitHub repository for this book: https://github.com/gdeckler/DAX-For-Humans/tree/main/book.

Column1
Color: Yellow, Name: Brian, Number: 1
Number: 3, Name: Deron, Color: Red
number: 14, color: Blue, name: Diana
Name: Alexis
Color: Black
Number: 18

Table 4.1: Extraction table data.

Note that the different attributes; color, name, and number, can appear anywhere in the string and with different casing. Also, not all rows contain all the desired information.

To extract the **Name** from each string, create the following calculated column:

```
Name =
    VAR __Find = "Name: "
    VAR __Pos = SEARCH( __Find, [Column1], 1, BLANK() )
    VAR __CommaPos =
        IF(
            __Pos = BLANK(),
            BLANK(),
            SEARCH( ",", [Column1], __Pos, BLANK() )
        )
    VAR __CommaPos2 =
        IF(
            __CommaPos = BLANK(),
            LEN( [Column1] ) + 1,
            __CommaPos
        )
    VAR __Result =
        IF(
            __Pos = BLANK(),
            BLANK(),
                VAR __Len = LEN( __Find )
                VAR __Start = __Pos + __Len
                VAR __Result = MID( [Column1], __Start, __CommaPos2 - __Start )
            RETURN
                __Result
        )
RETURN
    __Result
```

Create two additional columns where only the first two lines are changed, a **Color** column:

```
Color =
    VAR __Find = "Color: "
```

A **Number** column:

```
Number =

    VAR __Find = "Number: "
```

The rest of each column formula is the exact same as the **Name** column.

Let's break this formula down. In doing so, refer to the following diagram:

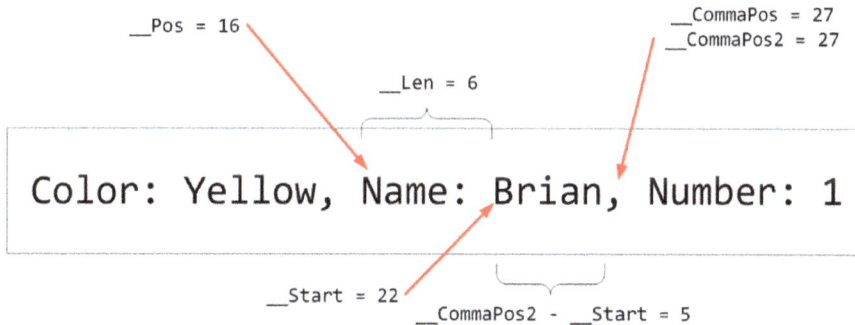

Figure 4.1: Extracting text from a text string.

The __**Find** variable specifies the attribute that we are attempting to extract from the text string. The next variable, __**Pos**, simply searches for the position of the __**Find** text within **Column1** starting at the beginning of the text string, position **1**. If the __**Find** text is not found, **BLANK** is returned.

The __**CommaPos** variable first checks if __**Pos** is **BLANK**, meaning that the __**Find** text was not found. If the __**Find** text was not found, __**CommaPos** is also assigned a **BLANK** value. Otherwise, **SEARCH** is again used to find the first comma after the position where the __**Find** text was found. If no comma is found, meaning that the attribute is at the end of the text string, then **BLANK** is assigned.

The __**CommaPos2** variable accounts for the attribute being at the end of the text string. There are two instances where __**CommaPos** is **BLANK**. The first is if __**Pos** is **BLANK** whereby the assigned value for __**CommaPos2** is irrelevant. The second is if the attribute is at the end of the text string. In that case, the length of the text string is returned plus 1. If __**CommaPos** is not **BLANK**, then the value of __**CommaPos** is assigned to __**CommaPos2** (no adjustment required).

To explain why the +1 is added in the case that the attribute is at the end of the text string, consider that when searching for the comma if the comma is found then the position returned is the next character after the text we wish to extract. However, with an attribute at the end of the text string, the length of the text string returns the position of the last character we wish to extract and thus we add 1 to that value to make it equivalent to the case where the comma is found. Interestingly, we could actually add 100 or even 1,000,000 and it would not matter but we most definitely have to at least add 1.

For the __Return variable, we introduce the concept of nested **VAR/RETURN** statements for efficiency reasons. First, we test if __Pos is **BLANK** and if so simply return **BLANK**. Otherwise, we calculate two **VAR**s, __Len, which is the length of the __Find text and __Start, which is the starting position at which to begin extracting text.

Naturally, __Start is the addition of the position of the first character of the __Find text found within the text string plus the number of characters for the __Find text. We then use **MID** to extract the text starting at the calculated starting character (__Start) and extracting the number of characters based on subtracting __Start from __CommaPos2. Note that **MID** is a very flexible function as it essentially serves as a **LEFT** and **RIGHT** function when the attribute is at the beginning or end of the text string.

Regarding nested **VAR/RETURN** statements, there is no real limit to the levels of nesting. In addition, observe that variables are scoped within each **VAR/RETURN** block. Notably, the __Return variable is used both within the outer **VAR/RETURN** block (**VAR** __Result) as well as the inner **VAR/RETURN** block starting with **VAR** __Len. This is a good reason why you should indent your **VAR**s statements as this makes the **VAR** statement blocks visually obvious in terms of their corresponding **RETURN** statements helping to visually define the various **VAR/RETURN** blocks within the code.

You might be wondering why __CommaPos and __CommaPos2 are not also inside the nested **VAR/RETURN** block. The answer is that they absolutely could be and would maximize the efficiency of the code. However, for the sake of walking through the code and explaining the code, it was decided to leave those two variables within the original **VAR/RETURN** block of code.

Obviously, each text pattern extraction is particular to the individual situation and data, however, this example provides a robust example and explanation of text extraction techniques that can apply to nearly limitless situations.

Let's next move on to counting the occurrence of characters or words within text strings.

Counting Occurrences

To demonstrate how to count occurrences of text strings within a text string, let's move back to using our **Pangram** table. If you do not have a Pangram table, complete the *Core Text Functions* section of this chapter prior to continuing with this section.

While in **Report view**, create a **Table** visual with **Column1** from the **Pangram** table. Now create the following measure to count the number of occurrences of the letter "o":

```
Count of o =

    VAR __Text = MAX( 'Pangram'[Column1] )

    VAR __Len = LEN( __Text )

    VAR __Substitute = SUBSTITUTE( __Text, "o", "" )

    VAR __NewLen = LEN( __Substitute )

    VAR __Result = __Len - __NewLen

RETURN

    __Result
```

Put the measure into the **Table** visual and note that the value displayed is **4**. The key to this measure is the **SUBSTITUTE** function. The **SUBSTITUTE** function replaces the old text (second parameter) with the new text (third parameter) within the specified text string (first parameter). There is also a fourth parameter that allows you to specify the instance number of the old text to replace. The default is to replace all instances.

In this case, we simply replace what we are trying to find, the letter "o" with null or blank "". This means that we simply need to get the length of the text string before the substitution and then subtract the length of the text string after the substitution, assuming that the text being replaced is a single character.

If the string being replaced is multiple characters, the formula changes slightly leading to a generalized solution:

```
Count of the =

    VAR __Replace = "the"

    VAR __ReplaceLen = LEN( __Replace )

    VAR __Text = MAX( 'Pangram'[Column1] )

    VAR __Len = LEN( __Text )

    VAR __Substitute = SUBSTITUTE( LOWER( __Text ), __Replace, "" )

    VAR __NewLen = LEN( __Substitute )

    VAR __Result = DIVIDE( __Len - __NewLen, __ReplaceLen )

RETURN

    __Result
```

Here we have changed the formula to count the occurrences of the word "**the**". We specify this text in the __**Replace** variable and calculate the number of characters in the __**ReplaceLen** variable.

Since **SUBSTITUTE** is case-sensitive and the word "**the**" appears with two different casings within our text string, we use the **LOWER** function to return the __**Text** variable as all lowercase prior to performing the **SUBSTITUTE**. We then simply need to **DIVIDE** the difference between our two lengths with the number of characters for the text being replaced, __**ReplaceLen**.

Finally, we can also use the same technique for counting the number of words in our sentence:

```
Count of Words =
    VAR __Replace = " "
    VAR __ReplaceLen = LEN( __Replace )
    VAR __Text = MAX( 'Pangram'[Column1] )
    VAR __Len = LEN( __Text )
    VAR __Substitute = SUBSTITUTE( LOWER( __Text ), __Replace, "" )
    VAR __NewLen = LEN( __Substitute )
    VAR __Result = DIVIDE( __Len - __NewLen, __ReplaceLen ) + 1
RETURN
    __Result
```

The only difference in this formula from the previous is the addition of **1** to the __**Result**. Since we are counting the separators, we need to account for the last item that has no subsequent separator. This last technique is quite useful for counting the number of items in a comma-separated list, for example.

We mentioned that the **SUBSTITUTE** function has a fourth parameter, let's see how we can use it to substitute or replace text counting from the right instead of the left.

Replace From Right

If you have not completed the *Core Text Functions* section of this chapter, please do so now.

When using the **SUBSTITUTE** function, there is a fourth parameter that controls what instance of the found text to replace. This instance is counted from left to right. For example, the following calculated column in the **Pangram** table replaces the third instance of the letter "o", the "o" in the word "over", with "O":

```
Replace from Left = SUBSTITUTE( [Column1], "o", "O", 3 )
```

However, what if we wanted to replace the third instance from the right? That can be done with this generalized formula as a calculated column:

```
Replace from Right =
    VAR __Replace = "o"
    VAR __Replacement = "O"
    VAR __Instance = 3
    VAR __Text = [Column1]
    VAR __Instances =
        DIVIDE(
            LEN( __Text ) - LEN( SUBSTITUTE( __Text, __Replace, "" ) ),
            LEN( __Replace )
        )
    VAR __Result =
        IF(
            __Instance > __Instances,
            __Text,
            SUBSTITUTE(
                __Text,
                __Replace,
                __Replacement,
                __Instances - __Instance + 1
            )
        )
RETURN
    __Result
```

This calculated column replaces the third instance of the letter "o" counting instances from the right instead of the left. As such, the letter "o" in the word "**fox**" is replaced. To explain how this works, consider that the first four variables simply configure what we wish to replace (**__Replace**), what we wish to replace it with (**__Replacement**), the instance to replace (**__Instance**), and the text string in which to perform the replacement (**__Text**).

The __**Instances** variable calculates how many instances of the replacement text exist within the text string. This is essentially our measure from the *Counting Occurrences* section of this chapter.

Finally, the __**Result** variable first checks if the specified instance number to replace (__**Instance**) is greater than the number of instances of the replace text (__**Instances**). If this logical check is true, then there are fewer instances of the replace text than the desired instance to replace and thus the original text string is returned (__**Text**). Otherwise, the **SUBSTITUTE** function is used where the instance to replace is converted to the instance as if counted from left-to-right.

That is, take the value of __**Instances**, subtract the desired __**Instance** and add **1**. Thus, in the example, since there are four instances of the letter "**o**", the third instance counted from the right is the second instance when counted from the left.

Let's next look at the many potential applications for dynamic text.

Dynamic Text

Dynamic text is useful in many types of scenarios and can greatly enhance the overall user experience when viewing and interacting with a report. Dynamic text can be particularly useful when using slicers or drill through report pages to help the user identify and keep track of filters.

If you have not already completed the *Extracting Text* section of this chapter, do so now.

To demonstrate dynamic text, create the following measure:

```
Dynamic Text 1 =

    VAR __Table = FILTER( 'Extraction', [Color] <> BLANK() )

    VAR __Result = CONCATENATEX( __Table, [Color], ", ", [Color] )

RETURN

    __Result
```

Place this measure into a **Card** visual. Now place a slicer on the page and put the **Color** column from the **Extraction** table in the slicer. Experiment with selecting different combinations of colors in the slicer and note how the text in the **Card** visual changes dynamically based on the selected colors. Hold down the **Ctrl** key to select multiple colors in the slicer.

The **Dynamic Text 1** measure first filters out **Color** values that are **BLANK()**. Then, the **CONCATENATEX** function is used to concatenate the different values of color in a comma-delimited string. The first parameter is the table over which to iterate. The second parameter is the value to extract for each iterated row, in this case the **Color** column. The third parameter is the delimiter or separator to use between extracted values. The fourth parameter specifies how to sort the values in the final string, in this case alphabetically based on the **Color** column. Technically, the fourth parameter is not needed in this case.

Note that if you select **(Blank)** in the slicer, the **Card** visual also displays **(Blank)**. We can fix this by modifying the code as follows:

```
Dynamic Text 2 =
    VAR __Table = FILTER( 'Extraction', [Color] <> BLANK() )
    VAR __Result =
        IF(
            COUNTROWS( __Table ) = 0,
            "None",
            CONCATENATEX( __Table, [Color], ", ", [Color] )
        )
RETURN
    __Result
```

Patron Note

Alexis Olson notes that you can also use `ISEMPTY( __Table )` instead of `COUNTROWS( __Table ) = 0`

There may be times when a **Card** visual may have limited space and cannot display all selections. In that case, you can do something like the following:

```
Dynamic Text 3 =
    VAR __Table = FILTER( 'Extraction', [Color] <> BLANK() )
    VAR __First = MINX( __Table, [Color] )
    VAR __Count = COUNTROWS( __Table )
    VAR __Result =
        SWITCH(
            __Count,
            0, "None",
            1, __First,
```

```
        __First & " +" & __Count - 1 & " more"

    )

RETURN

    __Result
```

In this version, when more than one **Color** is selected, the measure displays the first color and then " **+*n* more**", where *n* is the number of additional colors selected. The ampersand sign (**&**) is DAX's concatenation operator and is extremely useful for building dynamic text strings. As you can see in the formula, both text and numbers can be concatenated into a single string. This is because DAX automatically converts values such as numbers to text when needed.

There are nearly endless permutations of this concept such as the following:

```
Dynamic Text 4 =
    VAR __Table = FILTER( 'Extraction', [Color] <> BLANK() )

    VAR __Count = COUNTROWS( __Table )

    VAR __CountAll = COUNTROWS( FILTER( ALL( 'Extraction' ), [Color] <> BLANK() ) )

    VAR __Result =

        SWITCH(

            TRUE(),

            __Count = 0, "None",

            __Count = 1, MINX( __Table, [Color] ),

            __Count = __CountAll, "All",

            "Multiple"

        )

RETURN

    __Result
```

In this version, when all non-blank color values are selected, the measure returns "**All**" while if more than one color value is selected but not all, the measure returns "**Multiple**". A special form of **SWITCH** statement is used here in order to support conditional logic such as comparing the **__Count** to **__CountAll** in order to determine if all colors are selected.

Let's next use our new ability to create dynamic text to craft a simple greeting for users.

Simple Greeting

We can create a simple greeting to personalize reports to individual users viewing a report. To create a simple greeting, create the following measure:

```
Greeting =
    VAR __User = USERPRINCIPALNAME()
    VAR __Hour = HOUR( NOW() )
    VAR __Greeting =
        SWITCH(
            TRUE(),
            __Hour < 12, "Good morning ",
            __HOur < 17, "Good afternoon ",
            "Good evening "
        )
    VAR __Result = __Greeting & __User
RETURN
    __Result
```

This measure uses the **USERPRINCIPALNAME** function to return the username based on who is viewing the report. Locally, this will generally return the username in **Domain\Username** format while in the service this will generally be the user's email address.

The **HOUR** and **NOW** functions are used to retrieve the current hour in 24-hour format. This can then be used to personalize the greeting based on the time of day. More information about time-related functions is included in *Chapter 6, Time and Duration*.

An even better greeting can be created using a lookup table. For example, imagine that we had a table called **Users** that consisted of two columns, **UserPrincipalName** and **FriendlyName**. We could modify the greeting measure as follows:

```
Greeting 2 =
    VAR __User = USERPRINCIPALNAME()
    VAR __Name =
        MAXX(
            FILTER( 'Users', [UserPrincipalName] = __User ),
```

```
            [FriendlyName]

    )

VAR __Hour = HOUR( NOW() )

VAR __Greeting =

    SWITCH(

        TRUE(),

        __Hour < 12, "Good morning ",

        __HOur < 17, "Good afternoon ",

        "Good evening "

    )

VAR __Result = __Greeting & __Name & "!"

RETURN

    __Result
```

Here we resolve the user's friendly name by filtering the **Users** table based upon the **UserPrincipalName** column and returning the **FriendlyName** for that row.

Our next topic is conditional formatting.

Conditional Formatting

Conditional formatting can greatly enhance the user experience when viewing reports, especially for quickly ascertaining the state of key performance indicators. While Power BI Desktop includes a robust rules editor for defining conditional formatting, many argue that any rules-based conditional formatting should rather be done in DAX measures.

If you have not already completed the *Extracting Text* section of this chapter, do so now.

To demonstrate using measures for conditional formatting, do the following:

1. Create the following measure:

    ```
    CF 1 = MAX( 'Extraction'[Color] )
    ```

2. Place the **Name**, **Color**, and **Number** columns from the **Extraction** table into a **Table** visualization.
3. With the **Table** visual selected, in the **Columns** field well of the **Visualizations** pane, right-click the **Name** column.
4. Choose **Conditional formatting**.

5. Choose **Font color**.

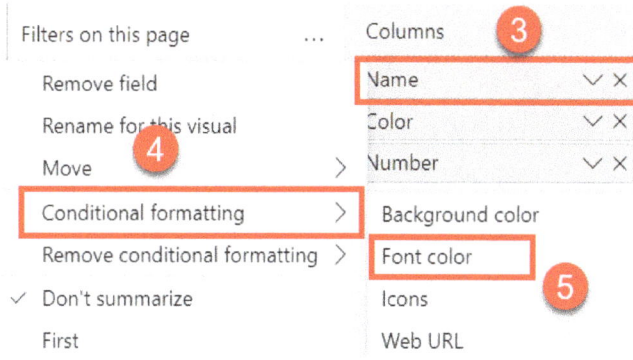

Figure 4.2: Conditional formatting.

6. In the conditional formatting dialog, choose **Field value** for **Format style**.
7. Select the **CF 1** measure for **What field should we base this on?**.

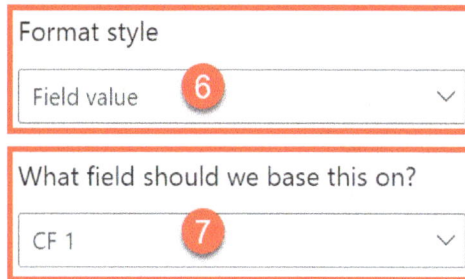

Figure 4.3: Field value conditional formatting.

8. Click the **OK** button.

Notice that the font colors for **Brian**, **Deron** and **Diana** all correspond to their corresponding **Color** values. Also note that **Alexis** is still the default font color. When basing conditional formatting on field values, common color names are recognized. These include all 141 default Microsoft Windows color names such as PapayaWhip, Lime, DarkSlateGray, DeepPink, etc.

Conditional formatting by field values also supports 3, 6, or 8 digit hexadecimal codes. To demonstrate this, create the following three measures:

```
CF 2 = "#0F0"
```

```
CF 3 =
    VAR __Number = MAX( 'Extraction'[Number] ) + 0
```

```
VAR __Result =

    SWITCH(

        TRUE(),

            __Number < 2, "#FF0000",

            __Number < 5, "#00FF00",

            "#0000FF"

    )

RETURN

    __Result

CF 4 =

    VAR __Number = MAX( 'Extraction'[Number] ) + 0

    VAR __Result =

        SWITCH(

            TRUE(),

                __Number < 2, "#FF000077",

                __Number < 5, "#00FF0077",

                "#0000FF77"

        )

RETURN

    __Result
```

Copy and paste the **Table** visual three times and modify each visual's conditional formatting to correspond to **CF 2**, **CF 3**, and **CF 4**.

For three-digit hexadecimal color codes, each hexadecimal digit (0 – F) corresponds to one of the primary color codes, red, green, blue (RGB) respectively. In this case, CF 2 colors everything green.

Six-digit hexadecimal color codes use two hexadecimal digits for each color while eight-digit hexadecimal color codes include two additional hexadecimal digits for transparency.

Patron Note

Diana Ackerman notes that for eight-digit hexadecimal codes using 00 for the seventh and eight digits is fully transparent while FF is no transparency.

Field value conditional formatting includes four additional methods of specifying colors. To demonstrate, create the following four additional measures:

```
CF 5 = "RGB( 0, 0, 255 )"

CF 6 = "RGBA( 0, 0, 255, .5 )"

CF 7 = "HSL( 360, 75%, 75% )"

CF 7 = "HSLA( 360, 75%, 75%, .5 )"
```

Make four more copies of the **Table** visual and apply these measures as conditional formatting.

The **RGB** and **RGBA** formats both specify red, green, and blue values in ranges from **0** to **255**. **RGBA** adds a fourth value for transparency that ranges from **0** to **1**.

The **HSL** and **HSLA** formats both specify hue, saturation, and lightness values with hue values ranging from **0** to **360** and saturation and lightness values from **0%** to **100%**. **HSLA** adds a fourth value for transparency that ranges from **0** to **1**.

This completes our exploration of conditional formatting. Let's next look at converting text to a table.

Text to Table

The ability to convert text into a table within a DAX measure is surprisingly useful. This is because of how central tables are to DAX. Thus, once a string of text is converted into a table, a multitude of powerful DAX operations can be applied to solve complex problems. If you have not already completed the *Counting Occurrences* section of this chapter, do so now.

A simple text to table in DAX looks like the following calculated table expression:

```
Text to Table =
    VAR __Text = MAX( 'Pangram'[Column1] )
    VAR __Path = SUBSTITUTE( __Text, " ", "|" )
    VAR __Length = PATHLENGTH( __Path )
    VAR __Table =
        ADDCOLUMNS(
            GENERATESERIES( 1, __Length, 1 ),
            "Word", PATHITEM( __Path, [Value] )
        )
RETURN
```

```
    __Table
```

Here we utilize the **PATH** family of functions to do the heavy lifting of converting a text string to a table. A path is simply a text string with a pipe character (|) as a separator between items in the path. Paths are typically used when dealing with hierarchies in DAX but also come in handy for converting text to tables. We convert the **__Text** variable to a path (**__Path**) by using the **SUBSTITUTE** function to replace the spaces with pipe characters. We can then calculate the length of the path using the **PATHLENGTH** function.

To create the table, we use **GENERATESERIES** to create a table of numeric values that ranges from our start number of **1** (first parameter) to the number of desired rows which is held by our **__Length** variable (second parameter) with an increment between numbers of **1** (third parameter).

Note, just as the **CALENDAR** function automatically creates a column called "**Date**", **GENERATESERIES** and similar functions default to using **Value** as the column name. It is worth keeping in mind that if a table with more than one column is created by similar functions or by such things as DAX's default table constructor, the columns are named **Value**# where # is the order number of the column starting at **1**.

Using **ADDCOLUMNS**, we add a "**Word**" column to this base table which uses the **PATHITEM** function to get the item in the path at the value specified by the **Value** column.

Using the **PATH** family of functions is not always required, as in this calculated table expression that turns each character into a separate row:

```
Text to Table 2 =
    VAR __Text = MAX( 'Pangram'[Column1] )
    VAR __Length = LEN( __Text )
    VAR __Table =
        ADDCOLUMNS(
            GENERATESERIES( 1, __Length, 1 ),
            "Word", MID( __Text, [Value], 1 )
        )
RETURN
    __Table
```

It was mentioned that using DAX to convert text to tables can have some surprising uses. For example, create the following DAX measure and place the measure into a **Card** visual. This measure uses the **Pangram** table so if you have not already done so, please complete the *Core Text Functions* section of this chapter prior to creating this measure.

```
Vowel Count =
    VAR __Vowels = { "a", "e", "i", "o", "u" }
    VAR __Text = MAX( 'Pangram'[Column1] )
    VAR __Length = LEN( __Text )
    VAR __Table =
        SELECTCOLUMNS(
            ADDCOLUMNS(
                GENERATESERIES( 1, __Length, 1 ),
                "Word", MID( __Text, [Value], 1 )
            ),
            "Word", [Word]
        )
    VAR __Intersect = INTERSECT( __Table, __Vowels )
    VAR __Result = COUNTROWS( __Intersect )
RETURN
    __Result
```

While used for something simple here, finding the number of vowels in the text (**__Text**), the same basic technique can be used to find keywords within columns of text or even modify or replace text as in the next two examples. This next example capitalizes the first character of every word in the sentence:

```
Caps =
    VAR __Text = MAX( 'Pangram'[Column1] )
    VAR __Path = SUBSTITUTE( __Text, " ", "|" )
    VAR __Length = PATHLENGTH( __Path )
    VAR __Table =
        ADDCOLUMNS(
            GENERATESERIES( 1, __Length, 1 ),
            "__Word",
```

```
            VAR __Word = PATHITEM( __Path, [Value] )

            VAR __Result =

                UPPER( LEFT( __Word, 1 ) ) &

                RIGHT ( __Word, LEN( __Word ) - 1 )

        RETURN

            __Result

    )

    VAR __Result = CONCATENATEX( __Table, [__Word], " " )

RETURN

    __Result
```

This time the standard table constructor is modified to manipulate the text such that the first letter of each word is capitalized. This is done using the **UPPER** function along with judicious use of the **LEFT**, **RIGHT**, and **LEN** functions. For the **__Result**, we simply use **CONCATENATEX** to convert the table back to text.

This last example uses a replacement table to replace words in the sentence:

```
The Replacements =

    VAR __Replacements =

        {

            ( "quick", "slow" ),

            ( "dog", "cat" )

        }

    VAR __Text = MAX( 'Pangram'[Column1] )

    VAR __Path = SUBSTITUTE( __Text, " ", "|" )

    VAR __Length = PATHLENGTH( __Path )

    VAR __Table =

        ADDCOLUMNS(

            ADDCOLUMNS(

                GENERATESERIES( 1, __Length, 1 ),

                "__Word", PATHITEM( __Path, [Value] )

            ),

            "__Replaced",
```

```
            VAR __Lookup =

                MAXX(

                    FILTER( __Replacements, [Value1] = [__Word] ),

                    [Value2]

                )

            VAR __Result = IF( __Lookup = BLANK(), [__Word], __Lookup )

        RETURN

            __Result

    )

    VAR __Result = CONCATENATEX( __Table, [__Replaced], " " )

RETURN

    __Result
```

This measure adds an additional column called __Replaced. This column looks up the word (__Word) in the __Replacements table and returns the replacement if found, otherwise it simply returns the original word.

If you are paying attention, you will note that both instances of the word "the" are capitalized. If you were really paying attention, you would have noticed the same phenomenon in the output from **Table to Text**.

This is not a bug in the DAX code but rather a consequence of perhaps "questionable" design decisions made regarding the storage mode for Power BI Desktop semantic models. Let's give this subject a deeper look.

Preserving Case

The problem of case sensitivity in DAX has to do with what is known as the **collation style** in Analysis Services. In Power BI Desktop, the Power BI service, and in Azure Analysis Services, the collation is set to case insensitive and cannot be changed. For Analysis Services on-premises, you can control the collation and configure case sensitivity if desired.

What this case insensitivity means is that all text strings with the exact same characters in the same order, regardless of case, inherit the casing of the first instance of that string. You can prove this to yourself by creating the following calculated table:

```
            Collation Woes = { "The", "the", "ThE", "tHe" }
```

Looking at the table in **Table view**, you will note that all of the rows are "**The**".

Now, if you are thinking, *"Gee, just what every business intelligence tool should do, immediately munge my data without asking me or letting me know."*, then you would not be the first individual to think this and/or smack yourself in the forehead with the palm of your hand. Be that as it may, this is an unfortunate fact of life in the Power BI world.

The good news is that there is a solution to this problem. The bad news is that it is not exactly an easy solution or necessarily worth the trouble. The trick lies in changing capitalized letters so that the resulting strings are different from their lowercase counterparts. This can be done with a non-printing character, specifically **Unicode** character **8203**. In DAX, we can specify Unicode characters using the **UNICHAR** function. Thus, we can modify our **Collation Woes** calculated table to the following:

```
Collation Woes =
    {
        "T" & UNICHAR( 8203 ) & "he",
        "the",
        "T" & UNICHAR( 8203 ) & "h" & "E" & UNICHAR( 8203 ),
        "t" & "H" & UNICHAR( 8203 ) & "e"
    }
```

This time, the casing is preserved for each row of the table. Applying similar logic to our **The Replacements** measure from the previous section, *Text to Table*, we can preserve the casing for both of our instances of the word "the" as follows:

```
The Replacements 2 =
    VAR __Replacements =
        {
            ( "quick", "slow" ),
            ( "dog", "cat" )
        }
    VAR __Text = MAX( 'Pangram'[Column1] )
    VAR __Substitute = SUBSTITUTE( __Text, "T", "T" & UNICHAR(8203) )
    VAR __Path = SUBSTITUTE( __Substitute, " ", "|" )
    VAR __Length = PATHLENGTH( __Path )
    VAR __Table =
```

```
        ADDCOLUMNS(

            ADDCOLUMNS(

                GENERATESERIES( 1, __Length, 1 ),

                "__Word", PATHITEM( __Path, [Value] )

            ),

            "__Replaced",

                VAR __Lookup =

                    MAXX(

                        FILTER( __Replacements, [Value1] = [__Word] ),

                        [Value2]

                    )

                VAR __Result = IF( __Lookup = BLANK(), [__Word], __Lookup )

            RETURN

                __Result

        )

    VAR __Result = CONCATENATEX( __Table, [__Replaced], " " )

RETURN

    __Result
```

Here we preserve the casing for capital "T" characters in the __**Substitute** variable. This works well since **SUBSTITUTE** is case sensitive. Obviously, for a generalized solution, there would need to be a total of 26 steps involving **SUBSTITUTE** but this is left as an exercise for the reader.

You should note that the **UNICHAR** function has a twin, the **UNICODE** function, which returns the decimal Unicode number for a text character. Let's next look at a use case for the **UNICODE** function.

Anonymous

There may be instances where you wish to anonymize data. This might be the case if presenting a report to a user group, for example. The **UNICODE** function provides a quick method of doing this.

If you have not already completed the *Extracting Text* section of this chapter, do so now.

Create the following measure and place this measure into a **Table** visual along with the **Name** column from the **Extraction** table:

```
Anonymous =

    VAR __Value = MAX( 'Extraction'[Name] )

    VAR __Result =

        IF(

            __Value = BLANK(),

            BLANK(),

                VAR __Table =

                    ADDCOLUMNS(

                        ADDCOLUMNS(

                            GENERATESERIES( 1, LEN( __Value ), 1 ),

                            "Char", MID( __Value, [Value], 1 )

                        ),

                        "Unicode", UNICODE( [Char] )

                    )

                VAR __Result = CONCATENATEX( __Table, [Unicode], , [Value] )

            RETURN

                __Result

        )

RETURN

    __Result
```

This is yet another use for our text to table technique. Here we convert the name to a table with one character per row. We can then determine the **UNICODE** for each character and then use **CONCATENATEX** to reconstruct a text string representation of the original text. Note that for even more obscurity, you can leave off the third and fourth parameters from the **CONCATENATEX** function to help scramble the letters.

Let's now take a look at using DAX to verify phone numbers.

Phone Number Verifier

Data validation is important to business intelligence endeavors. A common data validation need is to validate phone numbers. To demonstrate using DAX to verify phone numbers, create a table called "**Numbers**" using an **Enter data** query with the following data:

Phone#
--2580
614-559-3722
614-
614-555-777
614:555:7777
614-555-77778
1--2580
1-614-559-3722
1-614-
1-614-555-777
1-614:555:7777
1-614-555-77778
614-5A5-7777
1-61A-555-7777

Table 4.2: Numbers table data.

Alternatively, import the **Numbers** sheet from the Excel spreadsheet, **Chapter4_Data.xlsx** which can be found in the GitHub repository for this book: https://github.com/gdeckler/DAX-For-Humans/tree/main/book.

Create the following measure and place the measure into a **Table** visual along with the **Phone#** column from the **Numbers** table:

```
Phone Number Verifier =

    VAR __ValidLen = 12

    VAR __Sep = "-"

    VAR __PhoneNumber = MAX( 'Numbers'[Phone#] )

    VAR __First3 = LEFT( __PhoneNumber, 3 )

    VAR __FirstSep = MID( __PhoneNumber, 4, 1 )

    VAR __Second3 = MID( __PhoneNumber, 5, 3 )

    VAR __SecondSep = MID( __PhoneNumber, 8, 1 )

    VAR __Third4 = RIGHT( __PhoneNumber, 4 )

    VAR __First3Valid = ISERROR( VALUE( __First3 ) )

    VAR __Second3Valid = ISERROR( VALUE( __Second3 ) )

    VAR __Third4Valid = ISERROR( VALUE( __Third4 ) )

    VAR __Result =
        IF(
            LEN( __First3 ) = 3 && NOT( __First3Valid ) &&
            LEN( __Second3 )= 3 && NOT( __Second3Valid ) &&
            LEN( __Third4 ) = 4 && NOT( __Third4Valid ) &&
            __FirstSep = __Sep && __SecondSep = __Sep &&
            LEN( __PhoneNumber ) = __ValidLen,
            TRUE(),
            FALSE()
        )

RETURN

    __Result
```

The first two variables, **__ValidLen** and **__Sep** configure the basic format for phone numbers, **12** characters with a dash (-) as a separator. The next five variables simply parse out the components of the phone number using the **LEFT**, **MID**, and **RIGHT** functions.

The next three lines, starting with the **__First3Valid** variable attempt to convert the text string to a number and capture the operation using **ISERROR**. If the conversion is successful, then the value **False** is returned, otherwise, the error means that there are not 3 or 4 digits present but rather the text includes some other non-numeric character(s).

The **__Result** variable is simply a series of logical tests, all of which must be true. Each part of the phone number is checked to ensure that the part has the proper number of digits and does not include non-numeric characters. In addition, the two separators are checked to ensure that they are correct, and finally the overall length of the phone number is checked for good measure.

An international phone number verifier is similar:

```
International Phone Number Verifier =

    VAR __ValidLen = 14

    VAR __Sep = "-"

    VAR __PhoneNumber = MAX( 'Numbers'[Phone#] )

    VAR __CountryCode = LEFT( __PhoneNumber, 1 )

    VAR __CountrySep = MID( __PhoneNumber, 2, 1 )

    VAR __First3 = MID( __PhoneNumber, 3, 3 )

    VAR __FirstSep = MID( __PhoneNumber, 6, 1 )

    VAR __Second3 = MID( __PhoneNumber, 7, 3 )

    VAR __SecondSep = MID( __PhoneNumber, 10, 1 )

    VAR __Third4 = RIGHT( __PhoneNumber, 4 )

    VAR __First3Valid = ISERROR( VALUE( __First3 ) )

    VAR __Second3Valid = ISERROR( VALUE( __Second3 ) )

    VAR __Third4Valid = ISERROR( VALUE( __Third4 ) )

    VAR __CountryCodeValid = ISERROR( VALUE( __CountryCode ) )

    VAR __Result =
        SWITCH(TRUE(),
                LEN( __First3 ) = 3 &&  NOT( __First3Valid ) &&
                LEN( __Second3 )= 3 && NOT( __Second3Valid ) &&
                LEN( __Third4 ) = 4 && NOT( __Third4Valid ) &&
                LEN(__Third4) = 4 && NOT( __CountryCodeValid ) &&
```

```
        __FirstSep = __Sep && __SecondSep = __Sep && __CountrySep = __Sep &&

    LEN(__PhoneNumber) = __ValidLen,

    TRUE(),

    FALSE()

    )

RETURN

    __Result
```

Only a single phone number is valid for each measure.

As a final exercise, let's revisit extracting text with a particularly vexing example.

Extracting Text Revisited

As mentioned at the end of the *Extracting Text* section, the requirements for extracting text can be quite varied and are dependent on the specific situation. The example presented here is quite challenging.

To prepare for this exercise, create a table called "**Worst Extraction Ever**" using an **Enter data** query with the following data:

Column1
1002223 - 7003117328 - ID: 74526 - Attendance
1046890301 - 210438 1002515 - CW
2047074788 - 210525-1002834
1053847149 - 1016727- 212170 - cw upper
100001204040 - cp lower
1234567890 - cp

Table 4.3: Worst Extraction Ever table data.

Alternatively, import the **Worst Extraction Ever** sheet from the Excel spreadsheet, **Chapter4_Data.xlsx** which can be found in the GitHub repository for this book: https://github.com/gdeckler/DAX-For-Humans/tree/main/book.

The particulars of this data extraction are as follows:

- A number beginning with "1" appears anywhere in the text.
- Only numbers beginning with "1" that have exactly 7 continuous numbers are desired.
- Only one such number appears in each row.
- It is possible that no valid numbers exist.

Note that the desired number in the example data appears at the beginning of the row, at the end of the row and in the middle of the row. Also note that there is no standard "eighth" character like a space or hyphen, the number immediately following the 7-digit number can be any character. You can essentially think of this exercise as an example of some useful item of data surrounded by meaningless garbage.

The solution for this extraction is the following calculated column:

```
Extraction =

    VAR __Start = "1"

    VAR __Len = 7

    VAR __Len2 = __Len - 1

    VAR __Length = LEN( [Column1] )

    VAR __S1 = SEARCH( __Start, [Column1], 1, BLANK() )

    VAR __S2 = IF( __S1 <> BLANK(), SEARCH( __Start, [Column1], __S1+1, BLANK() ) )

    VAR __S3 = IF( __S2 <> BLANK(), SEARCH( __Start, [Column1], __S2+1, BLANK() ) )

    VAR __S4 = IF( __S3 <> BLANK(), SEARCH( __Start, [Column1], __S3+1, BLANK() ) )

    VAR __S5 = IF( __S4 <> BLANK(), SEARCH( __Start, [Column1], __S4+1, BLANK() ) )

    VAR __S6 = IF( __S5 <> BLANK(), SEARCH( __Start, [Column1], __S5+1, BLANK() ) )

    VAR __Table =

        ADDCOLUMNS(

            ADDCOLUMNS(

                FILTER(

                    UNION(

                        { __S1 }, { __S2 }, { __S3 }, { __S4 }, { __S5 }, { __S6 }
```

```
                    ),

                    [Value] <> BLANK()

                ),

            "__Extract",

                IF(

                    [Value] + __Len > __Length,

                    RIGHT( [Column1], __Len ),

                    MID( [Column1], [Value], __Len )

                ),

            "__Eighth",

                IF(

                    [Value] + __Len2 > __Length,

                    RIGHT( [Column1], 1 ),

                    MID( [Column1], [Value] + __Len, 1 )

                ),

            "__Pre",

                IF(

                    [Value] = 1,

                    BLANK(),

                    MID( [Column1], [Value] - 1, 1 )

                )

        ),

        "__Check1", ISERROR( VALUE( [__Extract] ) ),

        "__Check2", ISERROR( VALUE( [__Eighth] ) ),

        "__Check3", ISERROR( VALUE( [__Pre] ) ) || ISBLANK( [__Pre] )

    )

VAR __Result =

    MINX(

        FILTER(
```

```
            __Table,

        [__Check1] = FALSE() && [__Check2] = TRUE() &&

            [__Check3] = TRUE()

    ),

        [__Extract]

    )

RETURN

    __Result
```

The first four variables simply setup the overall parameters such as the desired number starting with "1" and being 7 characters long.

We then enter into the concept of "reasonable maximum". These are the variables __S1 though __S6. Each of these variables searches the text string (**Column1**) for the __Start variable and returns the character position if found and **BLANK()** if not found. Each of the subsequent searches starts its search at the previously found character plus 1 to ensure that no duplicates are found. Additional search variables could be introduced if deemed necessary.

The __Table variable starts with a base table constructed using the **UNION** function along with a somewhat novel use of DAX's table constructure ({}). Wrapping the single values of the search variables (__S1 through __S6) turns these single values into single row tables which can be appended together to form a single table. This table is then filtered to remove blank rows.

For each remaining row in the table, an __Extraction column is calculated based on knowing that only 7-character numbers are desired. In addition, the following character (__Eighth) and preceding character (__Pre) are also captured. Finally, three additional columns are added that check if the extracted number only has numeric characters in it and whether the following and preceding characters are numbers as well.

The __Result variable filters the table based on the three check columns and returns the extraction. Four rows in the table include a valid number while two rows do not.

Summary

This chapter was all about working with and manipulating text. We first looked at some of the core DAX text functions such as **LEFT**, **RIGHT**, **FIND**, **SEARCH**, etc. Next, we investigated methods of extracting relevant text from data. We then looked at how to count occurrences of text within data using the **SUBSTITUTE** function. Continuing our exploration of the **SUBSTITUTE** function, we demonstrated how to invert **SUBSTITUTE**'s functionality to replace from the right instead of the left. After that, we covered the creation of dynamic text for **Card** visuals for exposing filters and greeting report viewers. After that, we covered conditional formatting, converting text into tables, preserving case using the **UNICHAR 8203** character, using **UNICODE** to anonymize text, verifying phone numbers and finally presenting a rather vexing text extraction example. All these exercises should give you confidence when dealing with text within DAX.

In the next chapter, we look to provide similar coverage for numbers in DAX.

CHAPTER 5

5

Numbers

The last chapter was all about text, another of the core data types within the DAX language. In this chapter we seek to provide similar coverage of another core data type, numbers. Obviously, numbers are the foundation of nearly every business intelligence calculation, and understanding how to manipulate numbers effectively within DAX is essential for anyone building data models in Power BI. In this chapter, we take a comprehensive journey through the numeric capabilities of the DAX language, beginning with basic aggregation functions and progressing toward more nuanced operations such as standard deviation, variance, and median calculations. Along the way, we demystify quirks like rounding behavior, explore trigonometric functions, and discuss safe numerical practices, such as using the **DIVIDE** function to prevent divide-by-zero errors. Whether you're calculating simple metrics or managing complex numerical transformations, a strong grasp of DAX's number functions is key.

However, DAX's capabilities with numbers go far beyond basic math. This chapter also dives into more advanced techniques, such as implementing weighted averages, ranking, approximating values using linear interpolation, and regression analysis. You'll also learn how to overcome common pitfalls, such as "quirks" in the **MOD** and **MEDIAN** functions, and discover workarounds for missing functionality, like computing the statistical mode. Finally, we'll explore formatting techniques that help present numeric insights with precision and clarity. By the end of this chapter, you'll be well-equipped to tackle even the most sophisticated numerical scenarios in Power BI using DAX.

To explore dealing with numbers within the DAX language, we start with some of the core number functions.

Core Number Functions

Let's start by looking at some core number functions. To begin exploring core number functions, first create some sample data by selecting **New table** on the **Modeling** tab of the ribbon and entering the following formula:

```
Table = GENERATESERIES( 10, 100, 10 )
```

Create a **Calculations** table to store your measures and then create the following measures:

```
Sum = SUMX( 'Table', [Value] )

Average = AVERAGEX( 'Table', [Value] )

Minimum = MINX( 'Table', [Value] )

Maximum = MAXX( 'Table', [Value] )

Count = COUNTX( 'Table', [Value] )

Standard Deviation = STDEVX.P( 'Table', [Value] )

Variance = VARX.P( 'Table', [Value] )

Median = MEDIANX( 'Table', [Value] )
```

These calculations should be self-explanatory with a basic knowledge of math. There are two variations of both the **STDEVX** and **VARX** functions, the **.P** versions used here as well as **.S** versions, **STDEVX.S** and **VARX.S**. The **.P** versions assume that the column reference is the entire population while the **.S** versions assume that the column reference is for a sample of the entire population. Thus, the internal calculation is slightly different, and you will get different results. It is also worth remembering that the standard deviation is the square root of the variance.

In addition to these basic aggregation functions, there are also an entire collection of trigonometric functions including cosine (**COS, COSH**), sine (**SIN, SINH**), tangent (**TAN, TANH**), cotangent (**COT, COTH**), arccosine (**ACOS, ACOSH**), arcsine (**ASIN, ASINH**), arctangent (**ATAN, ATANH**), and arccotangent (**ACOT, ACOTH**). The **H** versions of these functions are the hyperbolic versions.

It is worth noting that for the standard **COS, SIN, TAN,** and **COT** functions the input number must be in radians. If you only know the degree of the angle, use the **RADIANS** function to convert from degrees to radians or simply multiply the number of degrees by **PI()/180**. There is an equivalent function called **DEGREES** to convert from radians to degrees.

Finally, numbers support numerous operators such as addition (**+**), subtraction (**-**), multiplication (*****), division (**/**), and exponentiation (**^**). For exponentiation you can also use the **POWER** function and the **SQRT** function. But, keep in mind that **SQRT(#)** is equivalent to **POWER(#, 0.5)**.

There are also standard comparison operators such as less than (**<**), less than or equal to (**<=**), greater than (**>**), and greater than or equal to (**>=**). There is also not equal to (**<>**) and two equal operators, equal to (**=**) and strict equal to (**==**). The most important difference between equal to and strict equal to is that **0 = BLANK()** is true while **0 == BLANK()** is not true. Knowing that 0 is equivalent to a blank or null value can help save hours of troubleshooting.

When dividing numbers, unless the divisor is a constant, it is generally advisable to use the **DIVIDE** function instead. This is because the **DIVIDE** function includes a third parameter that specifies a value to return in the event of an error such as division by zero. The **DIVIDE** function's first parameter is the numerator and its second parameter the divisor. There is also the **QUOTIENT** function which returns just the integer portion of division; however, it strangely does not have the same third parameter and thus it is safer to use this format instead:

INT(DIVIDE([numerator], [divisor], BLANK()))

This protects against divide-by-zero errors. If dealing with negative numbers, then the preferred version is:

TRUNC(DIVIDE([numerator], [divisor], BLANK()))

This is because **INT(-2.1)** is **-3** while **TRUNC(-2.1)** is **-2**.

This bit of information then leads nicely into our next subject, rounding.

Rounding

There are a surprising number of functions for rounding in DAX. These include:

- **INT**
- **TRUNC**
- **ROUND**
- **ROUNDDOWN**
- **ROUNDUP**
- **MROUND**
- **CEILING**
- **ISO.CEILING**
- **FLOOR**
- **EVEN**
- **ODD**
- **CURRENCY**

Let's explore the subtleties between these various functions.

We covered the basics of **INT** and **TRUNC** in the last section. These two functions work identically for positive numbers, returning just the integer portion of a number. However, for negative numbers, **INT** effectively rounds the number down to the next whole integer while **TRUNC** truncates the number to just the integer portion of the number.

To demonstrate this behavior, create the following table:

```
Decimals = GENERATESERIES( -15, 15.01, .01 )
```

Notice how, perhaps oddly, **15.01** is not included in the table. This is a "quirk" of **GENERATESERIES** when using a decimal value as an increment due to imprecision. Now create the following two columns:

```
Int = INT( [Value] )

Trunc = TRUNC( [Value] )
```

Notice that for 0 and all positive numbers that both **INT** and **TRUNC** return the same value. However, for negative numbers **TRUNC** always returns one more than **INT** unless the number is exactly an integer such as **-2** in our table.

Next, let's explore the next three functions, **ROUND, ROUNDDOWN**, and **ROUNDUP** by creating the following three columns:

```
Round = ROUND( [Value], 1 )

Round Down = ROUNDDOWN( [Value], 1 )

Round Up = ROUNDUP( [Value], 1 )
```

For each of these functions, the first parameter is the number to round, and the second parameter is the number of decimals to round the number to. You may be surprised at how these functions handle rounding negative numbers. For example, **ROUNDUP** rounds the negative numbers to be more negative and **ROUNDDOWN** rounds the negative numbers to be less negative which may strike you as odd. However, the proper way to consider the rounding performed is that **ROUNDUP** rounds numbers away from zero and **ROUNDDOWN** rounds numbers to be closer to zero.

The **ROUND** function acts the same way as well. The difference between **ROUND** and **ROUNDUP** is that the **ROUND** function rounds numbers away from zero based on whether the number to the right of the specified number of digits (second parameter) is **5** or more then the number is rounded up (away from zero) else the number is rounded down (towards zero). Conversely, **ROUNDUP** and **ROUNDDOWN** always round up or down respectively.

In all cases if **0** is specified for the number of digits, then the number is rounded to the appropriate integer. It is also possible to specify a negative number for the number of digits. For example, create the following column:

```
Round Negative = ROUND( [Value], -1 )
```

Specifying a negative number rounds the number to the left of the decimal point instead of the right of the decimal point.

Let's next look at **MROUND**. Create the following column:

```
MRound = IF( [Value] < 0, MROUND( [Value], -3 ), MROUND( [Value], 3 ) )
```

MROUND returns an error if the signs of the two parameters are not the same. The first parameter is the number to round, and the second parameter is a multiple. **MROUND** rounds a number to the nearest multiple of the specified number (second parameter). This is done by rounding away from zero if the remainder after dividing the first parameter by the second parameter is equal to or greater than half the second parameter. You can also specify a decimal for **MROUND**'s second parameter.

Let's now look at the **CEILING, ISO.CEILING,** and **FLOOR** functions by creating the following three columns:

```
Ceiling = IF( [Value] < 0, CEILING( [Value], -.05 ), CEILING( [Value], .05 ) )

ISO Ceiling = ISO.CEILING( [Value], -.05 )

Floor = IF( [Value] <= 0, FLOOR( [Value], -.05 ), FLOOR( [Value], .05 ) )
```

If necessary, increase the number of decimals displayed to two for these columns. All of these functions are similar to **MROUND** in that they round the specified number (first parameter) up to the nearest specified multiple (second parameter). However, unlike **MROUND**, the two numbers do not need to have the same sign. Both **CEILING** and **ISO.CEILING** work with both negative and positive numbers when the multiple is positive. **CEILING** generates an error if the multiple is negative and the value being rounded is positive while **ISO.CEILING** does not exhibit this behavior.

Both **CEILING** and **ISO.CEILING** act exactly the same when the multiple is zero or a positive number. In addition, both functions return the same number when the value being rounded is a positive number. The only difference between the two functions shows up when the value being rounded and the specified multiple are both negative. In this case, **CEILING** rounds numbers away from zero while **ISO.CEILING** rounds numbers towards zero.

The **FLOOR** function can be thought of as the opposite of the **CEILING** function in that it rounds numbers down instead of up. Otherwise, it has the same properties as the **CEILING** function.

Let's explore the last three functions, **EVEN**, **ODD**, and **CURRENCY** by creating the following three columns:

```
Even = EVEN( [Value] )

Odd = ODD( [Value] )

Currency = CURRENCY( [Value] )
```

EVEN and **ODD** round numbers away from zero to the nearest even or odd integer respectively. **CURRENCY** returns the value in currency format but also performs rounding up to the fifth significant decimal. In other words, this is akin to using the **ROUND** function with a second parameter of **4**.

This completes our coverage of the extensive rounding capabilities in DAX. Let's next take a closer look at the **MOD** function.

A Better MOD

If you have not already completed the previous section, **Rounding**, do so now.

You can think of the **MOD** function as the opposite of the **QUOTIENT** function. The **QUOTIENT** function returns the integer portion from a division while the **MOD** function returns the remainder of a division operation. Like the **QUOTIENT** function, **MOD** returns an error if the divisor is zero.

The **MOD** function actually has a bug or "quirk" in it when dividing by decimal numbers. To see this behavior in action, create the following column in the **Decimals** table:

```
Mod = MOD( [Value], .02 )
```

Set the number of decimals to two for this column. Notice that most of the numbers returned are either **.01** or **.02** and that they alternate. This is obviously incorrect. The root of the problem stems from the fact that in mathematics, the modulo function is only expressed in terms of integers (whole numbers) and not in terms of decimals. This is why many programming languages include a decimal or **floating-point mod** (**fmod**) function.

We can create our own "fmod" function in DAX that works with both integers and whole numbers as the following calculated column in the **Decimals** table:

```
Better MOD =

    VAR __Value = [Value]

    VAR __Divisor = .02

    VAR __Divide =
```

```
        ROUND(

            DIVIDE( __Value, __Divisor, 0 ),

            LEN( __Divisor & "" )

        )

    VAR __FMod = ( __Divide - TRUNC( __Divide ) ) * __Divisor

    VAR __Result =

        IF(

            TRUNC( __Divisor ) = __Divisor && TRUNC( __Value ) = __Value,

            MOD( __Value, __Divisor ),

            __FMod

        )

RETURN

    __Result
```

In effect, what this formula does is to compute a floating-point mod (__FMod) by dividing the two numbers, __Value and __Divisor, subtracting the truncation (TRUNC) of that division and then multiplying the result by the divisor (__Divisor)

Here, the key to avoiding floating point issues is to use the ROUND function. We specify the significant digit for rounding to be a function of the __Divisor. Essentially, we convert the __Divisor to text by appending a blank text value and return the length of the resulting text string.

In the __Result variable, we first test whether the __Divisor and __Value are integers and, if so, we simply use the MOD function. Otherwise, we use our __FMod calculation.

MOD is not the only buggy math function in DAX, the MEDIAN function can also cause problems so let's look at that next.

A Better MEDIAN

If you have not already completed the **Core Number Functions** and **Rounding** sections of this chapter, please do so now.

The DAX **MEDIAN** function takes a single parameter, a column reference and computes the median value of the numbers in that column. The median value is the number that has an equal number of items that are greater and less than itself. In mathematical terms, median is defined as follows:

For a data set x of n elements, ordered smallest to largest:

n is odd, median$(x) = x_{((n+1)/2)}$

n is even, median$(x) = \left(x_{(n/2)} + x_{((n/2)+1)} \right) / 2$

In most situations, the **MEDIAN** function works perfectly fine. However, **MEDIAN** can cause a problem when used in a column. To demonstrate this behavior, create the following column in the **Decimals** table:

```
Median = MEDIAN( 'Decimals'[Value] )
```

In this case, **MEDIAN** works correctly. Now create the following column in the **Table** table:

```
Median = MEDIAN( 'Table'[Value] )
```

Here **MEDIAN** returns the error, *Expressions that yield variant data-type cannot be used to define calculated columns*. Along with the poor grammar and unnecessary hyphenation, there is little about this error message that makes sense. Note that **MEDIAN** used in a measure works correctly in either case.

The **MEDIAN** function is not alone in behaving this way. **MEDIANX**, **PERCENTILE.EXC**, **PERCENTILE.INC**, **PERCENTILEX.EXC**, and **PERCENTILEX.INC**, all exhibit this bizarre behavior.

Luckily, there are several approaches we can use to fix this. The first is to implement the mathematical definition of median in DAX code. We can do this as follows in the **Table** table as a calculated column:

```
Better Median =
    VAR __Table = SELECTCOLUMNS( 'Table', "Value", [Value] )
    VAR __Path = CONCATENATEX( __Table, [Value], "|", [Value], ASC )
    VAR __Length = PATHLENGTH( __Path )
    VAR __IsOdd = ISODD( __Length )
    VAR __Result =
        IF(
            __IsOdd,
            PATHITEM( __Path, ( __Length + 1 ) / 2, TEXT) + 0,
```

```
        (

              PATHITEM( __Path, ( __Length / 2 ), TEXT ) +

              PATHITEM( __Path, ( ( __Length / 2 ) + 1 ), TEXT ) + 0

        ) / 2

    )

RETURN

    __Result
```

This formula implements the mathematical definition of median. We start by getting all of the values in the column into a single column table. We then turn this table into a path using **CONCATENATEX**. We specify the fourth and fifth parameters to ensure that the numbers are sorted from smallest to largest.

Next, we get the length of the path using **PATHLENGTH** and determine if that length is odd or even using the **ISODD** function. Finally, we can calculate the median in the **__Result** variable depending on whether the number of items in the column is odd or even. In both cases, we add zero to the result to force conversion from text to a number.

While this formula is a fun exercise that once again demonstrates the power of **CONCATENATEX** and the **PATH** family of functions, there is an easier method as well. Namely, forcing the conversion of the output of **MEDIAN** to be a particular data type such as this version:

```
Even Better Median = CONVERT( MEDIAN( 'Table'[Value] ), DOUBLE )
```

Note that **DOUBLE** in this case means a decimal number. You need to use **DOUBLE** and not **INTEGER** because the median of a set of numbers is often a decimal number.

Let's now move on to computing another common statistic, the mode of a set of numbers.

Computing the Mode

In mathematics and statistics, the mode of a set of numbers is the number that occurs the most frequently. Mode is also applicable to non-numeric values such as text. Perhaps strangely, while the DAX language has nearly 100 mathematical and statistical functions, a function to compute mode does not exist. Luckily, we can compute a simple mode relatively easily. Start by creating the following table:

```
Mode Table = { 1, 2, 2, 3, 4, 6, 7 }
```

We can create a mode calculated column or measure with the following formula:

```
Mode =
    VAR __Table = SELECTCOLUMNS( 'Mode Table', "__Value", [Value] )
    VAR __Summarized = SUMMARIZE( __Table, [__Value], "__Count", COUNTROWS( 'Mode Table'
) )
    VAR __Max = MAXX( __Summarized, [__Count] )
    VAR __Result = MAXX( FILTER( __Summarized, [__Count] = __Max ), [__Value] )
RETURN
    __Result
```

The concept behind this measure is rather simple to understand. After selecting all the values in the column using **SELECTCOLUMNS**, we use **SUMMARIZE** to group the table variable, **__Table**, by the values while also computing the number of rows for each value in a column called **__Count**. We can then get the maximum of **__Count** using **MAXX** and then effectively look up the row with the maximum count using **MAXX** and **FILTER** to return the corresponding value.

There are improvements that we can make to this simple version of the mode formula. Namely, we can add additional logic to account for when there might be more than one mode value:

```
Improved Mode =
    VAR __Table = SELECTCOLUMNS( 'Mode Table', "__Value", [Value] )
    VAR __Summarized = SUMMARIZE( __Table, [__Value], "__Count", COUNTROWS( 'Mode Table'
) )
    VAR __Max = MAXX( __Summarized, [__Count] )
    VAR __Modes = FILTER( __Summarized, [__Count] = __Max )
    VAR __ModeCount = COUNTROWS( __Modes )
    VAR __Result = IF( __ModeCount > 5, "Many", CONCATENATEX( __Modes, [__Value], "," )
)
RETURN
    __Result
```

Here we have added additional logic where we use the same **FILTER** as before to return a table that includes only the rows with the maximum **__Count**. This is the **__Modes** variable. We then count how many rows are in that table. Finally, we included an arbitrary cutoff of more than **5** values to simply return "**Many**", otherwise, we use **CONCATENATEX** to return a list of all the modes. Obviously, this logic can be adjusted as desired.

Let's move on and look at another common calculation that generally involves numbers, ranking.

Ranking

Ranking is a common activity within business intelligence and is useful for a variety of business scenarios such as:

- **Sales**: Identifying the top-performing sales representatives or regions to understand success factors.
- **Customers**: Ranking customers by purchase frequency or value to tailor marketing campaigns.
- **Suppliers**: Ranking suppliers based on delivery times, quality, and cost to optimize the supply chain.
- **Financial**: Ranking investment opportunities by potential return and risk profile.

To continue exploring ranking, we need some data. Use an **Enter data** query and create a table called **Ranking** with the following data. Alternatively, import the **Ranking** sheet from the Excel spreadsheet, **Chapter5_Data.xlsx** which can be found in the GitHub repository for this book: https://github.com/gdeckler/DAX-For-Humans/tree/main/book.

Item	Price	Quantity	Date
Pickle	3.99	2	1/2/2023
Banana	2.99	3	1/2/2023
Pickle	3.99	4	1/10/2023
Banana	2.99	5	1/11/2023
Grapefruit	4.99	3	1/14/2023
Orange	3.99	3	1/14/2023

Table 5.1: Enter data query data.

For years there was a single ranking function in DAX, **RANKX**. More recently, two additional ranking functions have been added, **RANK.EQ**, and **RANK**. We will briefly cover **RANKX** before covering the newer ranking functions.

RANKX is often cited as one of the most confusing and complex functions in all of DAX. We will avoid most of this confusion and complexity by using simple scenarios of calculated columns. Create the following three calculated columns in the **Ranking** table.

RANKX P*Q = RANKX('Ranking', [Price] * [Quantity])

RANKX P Skip = RANKX('Ranking', [Price], , DESC)

RANKX P Dense = RANKX('Ranking', [Price], , DESC, Dense)

The first example, **RANKX P*Q** is the simplest **RANKX** formula possible. Only two of the possible five parameters are used. The first parameter is the table for the **RANKX** function to iterate over. The second parameter is the expression that generates the values that are ranked. In this case, the value to be ranked is the product of the **Price** and **Quantity** columns. **RANKX** iterates over each row of the table, calculating the value of the expression for each row and returns the ranks of each value as a whole number starting at 1 for either the highest value or lowest value. In the case of **RANKX P*Q**, all of the rankings are unique because the expression evaluates to a unique value for each row of the table.

The sorting order for **RANKX** is controlled by the fourth parameter as can be seen in **RANKX P Skip**. The values for the fourth parameter are either **DESC** or **ASC** with the default being **DESC**. **DESC** sorts in descending order such that the highest value is assigned **1** as its rank. Note that there are only three distinct ranks for **RANKX P Skip**, **1**, **2**, and **5**. There is only a single row with the highest value, **4.99** and this row is assigned a rank of **1**. The next highest number in the table is **3.99** and the three rows with this value are assigned the rank of **2**. The lowest number in the table is **2.99** and the two rows with this value are assigned the rank of **5**. This rank of **5** comes from the fact that there are four higher ranked rows, one **1** and three **2**'s. Thus, the next rank is **5**.

The last column, **RANKX P Dense** changes the default behavior of "skipping" ranks by specifying the fifth parameter as **Dense**. This fifth parameter can also be **Skip**, the default. With the **Dense** ranking, the two rows with the smallest value, **2.99** are ranked **3** instead of **5** as in **RANKX P Skip**.

The third parameter of the **RANKX** function is seldom used. This third parameter specifies a value that should be ranked in relation to the other values returned by the second parameter.

The **RANK.EQ** function is a port of the same function from Excel. This function operates identically to how **RANKX** works with using **Skip** as the fifth parameter. You can observe this by creating the following calculated column:

```
Rank EQ = RANK.EQ( [Price], 'Ranking'[Price], DESC )
```

Here the three parameters are the expression to be ranked as the first parameter, a column reference against which ranks are determined as the second parameter, and the ranking order, either **DESC** or **ASC** as the third parameter.

DAX's latest ranking function, **RANK** is the function that you will likely want to learn and use for almost all your ranking in DAX. While the **RANK** function can appear confusing and daunting at first since there are no less than seven parameters, all of which are "optional", there is seldom a need to stray outside of the base patterns that are presented here. To demonstrate the simplest version of **RANK**, create the following column:

```
RANK P = RANK( DENSE, ORDERBY( 'Ranking'[Price], DESC ) )
```

The first parameter for the **RANK** function controls how ties are handled and can be either **DENSE** or the default, **SKIP**. The **ORDERBY** clause used as the second parameter is actually the third parameter. The second parameter is either a table expression over which ranks are determined for calculated columns and measures or an axis such as **ROWS** or **COLUMNS** when used in a visual calculation.

The **ORDERBY** function in DAX specifies pairs of expressions and sorting direction. In this case the **Price** column is specified with an order of descending (**DESC**). More than one pair can be specified. For example, the following DAX calculated column expression is valid and sorts the rows first by **Price** in a descending order and then by **Quantity** in an ascending order:

```
RANK P 2 = RANK(  DENSE, ORDERBY( 'Ranking'[Price], DESC, 'Ranking'[Quantity], ASC ) )
```

Let's move on to creating measures using **RANK**. To start, create a **Table** visual that includes the **Item** column from the **Ranking** table, the sum of the **Price** column, and the **Quantity** column set to **Do not summarize**. This creates a **Table** visual with all the rows from the **Ranking** table displayed.

Now create the following measure and then place the measure into the **Table** visual:

```
RANK P*Q = RANK( DENSE, ALL( 'Ranking' ), ORDERBY( [Price] * [Quantity], DESC ) )
```

Here we must use the **ALL** function in the second parameter in order to ensure that each row takes all of the rows of the table into account when ranking.

The **RANK** function also makes ranking grouped values extremely easy, something that is rather daunting to do with the **RANKX** function. To see how this works, create the following measure and then place the measure into the **Table** visual:

```
Rank Group =
    RANK(
        DENSE,
        ALL( 'Ranking' ),
        ORDERBY( 'Ranking'[Quantity], DESC ),
        PARTITIONBY( 'Ranking'[Item] )
    )
```

Here we have added a **PARTIONBY** clause to the **RANK** function. The **PARTIONBY** function specifies the columns containing the values that should partition the rows. By specifying the **Item** column, each individual value for **Item** is ranked as a group instead of ranked across all rows of the table.

Finally, to demonstrate using **RANK** in a **visual calculation**, you can create the following visual calculation:

```
Calculation = RANK( DENSE, ROWS, ORDERBY( [Sum of Price], DESC ) )
```

You may have to turn on the preview feature for visual calculations and restart Power BI Desktop. You can turn on preview features by navigating to **File** | **Options and settings** | **Options** and then selecting **Preview** features. Here, the main difference is that the axis, **ROWS**, is specified as the second parameter.

Finally, we should discuss a common complaint that has plagued ranking in DAX since the very beginning and that is the subject of unique ranks. Notice that neither **Dense** nor **Skip** prevent ties. There have been many that have wished for a third option such as **Unique**, that would force unique rankings. There are some convoluted formulas that can manage this but they are either extremely complex or require additional columns, such as how the **RANK P 2** column used both **Price** and **Quantity**.

Luckily, there is a rather straight-forward formula for returning unique ranks that leverages our knowledge from working with text in **Chapter 4**. Create the following measure and then add this measure to the **Table** visualization:

```
Rank Unique =
    VAR __Row = MAX( 'Ranking'[Item] ) & "^" &
```

```
                    MAX( 'Ranking'[Price] ) & "^" &

                    MAX( 'Ranking'[Quantity] )

VAR __Path =

    CONCATENATEX(

        ALL( 'Ranking' ),

        [Item] & "^" & [Price] & "^" & [Quantity],

        "|",

        [Price],

        DESC

    )

VAR __Table =

    ADDCOLUMNS(

        GENERATESERIES( 1, COUNTROWS( ALL( 'Ranking' ) ), 1 ),

        "__Row", PATHITEM( __Path, [Value] )

    )

VAR __Result = MAXX( FILTER( __Table, [__Row] = __Row ), [Value] )

RETURN

    __Result
```

This measure ranks items based on the **Price** column without using the **RANKX, RANK.EQ,** or **RANK** functions. Adding this measure to the **Table** visual displays a unique rank for each row even though multiple rows have the same price. We accomplish this by first creating a row identifier with the **__Row** variable. Here we simply concatenate the information that makes a row unique using the concatenation operator (**&**) and separating the individual values with a caret (**^**).

Next, we turn the same concatenation of values into a path (**__Path**) using **CONCATENATEX**. However, we use the fourth and fifth parameters of **CONCATENATEX** to specify how to sort the concatenated values. We specify sorting the values by the **Price** column in a descending manner (**DESC**).

We then use **GENERATESERIES** to create a table with a **Value** column that counts from 1 to the number of rows in the **Ranking** table incrementing by **1**. For each row, we grab the corresponding **PATHITEM** from our **__Path** variable.

Finally, we simply need to "lookup" our __**Row** within __**Table** and return the corresponding **Value** by using **MAXX** combined with **FILTER**.

While this approach may seem like a lot of work, it is relatively simple and straightforward to implement and uses a standard pattern. In addition, because none of DAX's ranking functions are used, this technique can be used against virtual tables as well as physical tables in the semantic model.

This concludes our exploration of ranking in DAX. We now move on to aggregating measures.

Aggregating Measures

While it is easy to aggregate columns, one cannot aggregate a measure the same way such as writing the following:

SUM([Measure])

This subject often comes up because one wishes to display some total in a **Table** or **Matrix** visual as a **Card** visual to highlight the metric within a report or dashboard.

To explore this concept, create the following measure and add it to the **Table** visual created in the previous section, **Ranking**. If you have not completed that section, do so now.

```
P*Q = SUM( 'Ranking'[Price] ) * SUM( 'Ranking'[Quantity] )
```

The first thing that you should notice is that this measure exhibits the infamous "Banana Pickle Math" problem covered at the end of **Chapter 2** but in a much more realistic way. The total is obviously wrong because adding up all of the prices and then multiplying by the sum of all of the quantities is not the same as computing the measure for each individual row and then summing those values.

If you are now thinking that aggregating measures is essentially the same as solving the measure totals problem, then you would be exactly correct. The solution is effectively the same. Create the following measure and place this measure into the **Table** visual as well as a **Card** visual:

```
P*Q Total =
    VAR __Table = SUMMARIZE( 'Ranking', [Item], [Price], [Quantity], "__Value", [P*Q] )
    VAR __Result = SUMX( __Table, [__Value] )
RETURN
    __Result
```

Let's now move on to weighted averages.

Weighted Averages

Weighted averages are incredibly common calculations used across almost every sector and industry such as finance, education, economics, supply chain, environmental science, life sciences, manufacturing, and insurance. Common scenarios include the following:

- **Finance**
  - **Portfolio Returns**: Investors calculate the average return of a portfolio by weighting each asset's return by its proportion in the portfolio.
  - **Weighted Average Cost of Capital (WACC)**: Companies use WACC to determine the average rate of return required by their investors, weighting the cost of equity and debt according to their proportions in the company's capital structure.
- **Education**
  - **Grade Point Averages (GPA)**: Schools often calculate GPAs by weighting course grades based on credit hours or course difficulty, giving more significance to more important or intensive courses.
  - **Assessment Scores**: Teachers may weigh different assignments or exams differently when calculating final grades, reflecting the varying importance of each assessment.
- **Economics**
  - **Consumer Price Index (CPI)**: CPI measures inflation by calculating a weighted average of prices of a basket of consumer goods and services, with weights based on their importance in household spending.
  - **Gross Domestic Product (GDP)**: Weighted averages are used to adjust GDP figures to account for price changes, providing real GDP values.
- **Supply Chain**
  - **Weighted Average Cost Method**: Businesses calculate the cost of goods sold and ending inventory by averaging the costs of all similar items in inventory, weighted by the number of units purchased at each cost.
  - **Demand Forecasting**: Weighted moving averages help in forecasting demand by giving more weight to recent data, improving prediction accuracy.
- **Environmental Science**
  - **Air Quality Index (AQI)**: AQI is calculated using weighted averages of various pollutant concentrations, with weights reflecting their health impacts.
- **Life Sciences**

   ◦ **Epidemiological Studies**: Weighted averages adjust statistical analyses to account for population differences, such as age or sex distributions.

   ◦ **Dosage Calculations**: Medication dosages may be determined using weighted averages based on patient factors like weight and age.

- **Insurance**
  - **Premium Calculations**: Insurers calculate premiums using weighted averages of risk factors, with higher weights assigned to factors that contribute more significantly to potential claims.
  - **Loss Ratios**: Weighted averages help assess the performance of different insurance products or customer segments.
- **Manufacturing**
  - **Defect Rates**: Manufacturing processes use weighted averages to calculate overall defect rates, weighting defects by severity or cost impact.
  - **Supplier Performance**: Companies assess suppliers using weighted criteria such as delivery time, quality, and cost.

In concept, weighted averages are easy to conceptualize. You have a set of values that you wish to multiply by a corresponding set of weights and then determine the average from the results of this multiplication. A more formal definition would be to multiply each value by its corresponding weight, add the individual rows and then divide by the sum of the weights. Here is a simple example that you can load using an **Enter data** query as a table called **Grades**:

Item	Grade	Weight	Grade * Weight
Homework	80	20%	16
Quizzes	90	30%	27
Final Exam	70	50%	35

Table 5.2: Weighted average calculation.

Alternatively, import the **Grades** sheet from the Excel spreadsheet, **Chapter5_Data.xlsx** which can be found in the GitHub repository for this book: https://github.com/gdeckler/DAX-For-Humans/tree/main/book.

Here the values in the **Weight** column add up to **1** and the values in the **Grade * Weight** column add up to **78** so the weighted average is **78** divided by **1** or just **78**.

If you think that this seems like a reasonably trivial and straightforward calculation, you would be correct. It is thus bizarre that the default Power BI Desktop quick measure **Weighted average by category** inexplicably returns something akin to this DAX monstrosity:

```
Grade weighted by Weight per Item =

VAR __CATEGORY_VALUES = VALUES('Grades'[Item])

RETURN

    DIVIDE(

        SUMX(

            KEEPFILTERS(__CATEGORY_VALUES),

            CALCULATE(SUM('Grades'[Grade]) * SUM('Grades'[Weight]))

        ),

        SUMX(

            KEEPFILTERS(__CATEGORY_VALUES),

            CALCULATE(SUM('Grades'[Weight]))

        )

    )
```

Fortunately, there is a much more straightforward solution that uses the No CALCULATE approach:

```
Weighted average =

    VAR __Numerator = SUMX( 'Grades', [Grade] * [Weight] )

    VAR __Denominator = SUMX( 'Grades', [Weight] )

    VAR __Result = DIVIDE( __Numerator, __Denominator, 0 )

RETURN

    __Result
```

If you were doubting the No CALCULATE approach to DAX, perhaps this comparison demonstrates the utility of the approach in making calculations much more straightforward and comprehendible.

Let's now move onto the subject of linear regression.

Linear Interpolation

Linear interpolation is a method used to estimate an unknown value that falls between two known values. This method assumes that the unknown value falls on a straight line or linear function between the two known values.

Linear interpolation can be visually represented as:

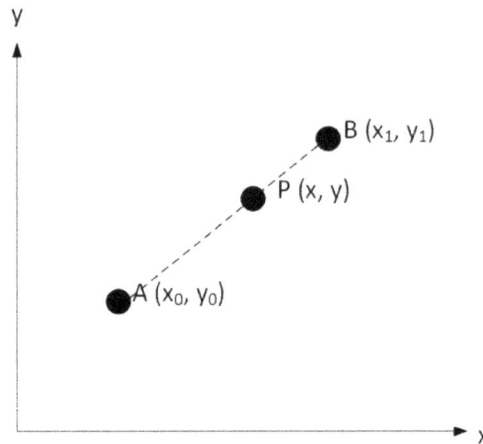

Figure 5.1: An unknown point P between two known points A and B.

Essentially, linear interpolation works by drawing a straight line between the two points and then finding the value of the function at a point along that line.

Mathematically, for two known points (x_0, y_0) and (x_1, y_1), the linear interpolation formula to estimate the value y at a point x is:

$$y = y_0 + (x - x_0)\left(\frac{y_1 - y_0}{x_1 - x_0}\right)$$

Interpolation is used heavily in mechanical engineering for subjects such as thermodynamics and fluid dynamics but is also used in computer graphics, finance, geosciences, economics and statistics, manufacturing, and navigation.

To demonstrate calculating linear interpolation in DAX, paste the following into a **Blank** query in Power Query Editor using the **Advanced Editor** to completely replace the contents of the query. Call the query **TempPressure**.

```
let

    Source =
Table.FromRows(Json.Document(Binary.Decompress(Binary.FromText("NZLLjUMxDAN7eefAMPW1agm2
/zb2RaJPQSa0PaLy/T57bTyf38feAeTz9/k+fslJiSbYRBA5Q24IuScjNyOqNeRmlBfrjZgYyY14yByym0k9PuRm
ymuIMwNRAkbgOTJxE8UjwYT4tgbJhELmOwN65obD3y0NAxjwPONeTOTGdFJMHAuwtolgYx4Fi4QpAVtD8VKwI8mt
A1iIBpzND7CMMQeHDRwCzpYlBD0Mfrvh9mqAuAuXN8DduDsMqJ0jJm0qS1Hctw7IyplW2lSXWtz9D6hrKm1qK0pm
OGlTX85hpUVjGYKPtGguM3asLXqWn5xHtEVrnfDR0BbFO9yZjrVFIes472hRvB6bR1oUsZx/Qm1RnBX00BaVt0Lj
pfnO9du3yNrxsr9/", BinaryEncoding.Base64), Compression.Deflate)), let _t = ((type
nullable text) meta [Serialized.Text = true]) in type table [#"Temp (C)" = _t,
#"Pressure (MPa)" = _t]),

    #"Changed Type" = Table.TransformColumnTypes(Source,{{"Temp (C)", Int64.Type},
{"Pressure (MPa)", type number}})

in

    #"Changed Type"
```

Alternatively, import the **TempPressure** sheet from the Excel spreadsheet, **Chapter5_Data.xlsx** which can be found in the GitHub repository for this book: https://github.com/gdeckler/DAX-For-Humans/tree/main/book.

This table includes temperature and pressure values of water from .01 degree Celsius to 373.95 degrees Celsius. Increments vary but are generally 5 or 10 degrees Celsius. We can construct a second interpolation table for all whole number degree values of Celsius between 1 and 373 degrees by doing the following:

Create a calculated table using this formula:

```
Interpolation =

    SELECTCOLUMNS(

        GENERATESERIES( 1, 373, 1 ),

        "Temp (C)", [Value]

    )
```

Now create a calculated column in the **Interpolation** table with this formula:

```
Pressure (MPa) =

    VAR __Temp = [Temp (C)]

    VAR __Pressure = MAXX( FILTER( 'TempPressure', [Temp (C)] = __Temp ), [Pressure
(MPa)] )
```

```
VAR __Result =

    IF(

        ISBLANK( __Pressure ),

            VAR __x0 = MAXX(FILTER('TempPressure',[Temp (C)]<__Temp ), [Temp (C)] )

            VAR __x1 = MINX(FILTER('TempPressure',[Temp (C)]>__Temp ), [Temp (C)] )

            VAR __y0=MAXX(FILTER('TempPressure',[Temp (C)]=__x0),[Pressure (MPa)] )

            VAR __y1=MAXX(FILTER('TempPressure',[Temp (C)]=__x1),[Pressure (MPa)] )

            VAR __Result = __y0+(__Temp - __x0) * DIVIDE(__y1 - __y0, __x1 - __x0 )

        RETURN

            __Result,

        __Pressure

    )

RETURN

    __Result
```

This formula first checks if there is a known value for __**Pressure**. If there is a known value, then the formula returns that value. Otherwise, the formula "looks up" the values of the closest temperature both greater than and less than the current row's temperature (__**Temp**). This is done in the __**x0** and __**x1** variables.

Once these values are known, the pressures at those temperatures can also be looked up, __**y0** and __**y1**. Finally, the linear interpolation function is used to determine the approximate value of the pressure at the current temperature.

Create a scatter plot using the **TempPressure** table with the **Temp (C)** column as the **X-axis** and the **Pressure (MPa)** as the **Y-Axis**. Set both columns to **Don't summarize**. Repeat this procedure with the **Interpolation** table.

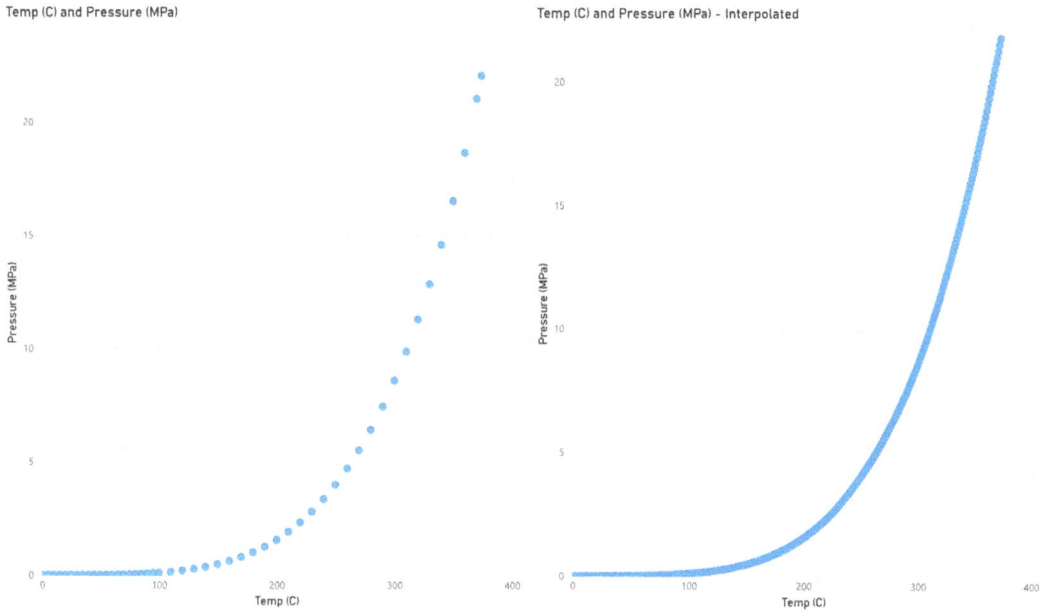

Figure 5.2: Non-interpolated (left) versus interpolated (right) data.

As you can see, the original table on the left has gaps between known values. The interpolated data on the right smooths out and fills in these gaps in the data. While the overall shape of the function is quadratic, the small gaps between known data points can be approximated as straight lines (linear).

This completes our exploration of linear interpolation. Let's next look at another mathematical method known as linear regression.

Simple Linear Regression

Simple linear regression is a statistical method used to model and analyze the relationship between two or more variables. One variable is the dependent variable while one or more variables are the independent variables. The goal is to create a linear equation that can predict the value of the dependent variable based on the values of the independent variables.

Visually, linear regression can be represented as follows:

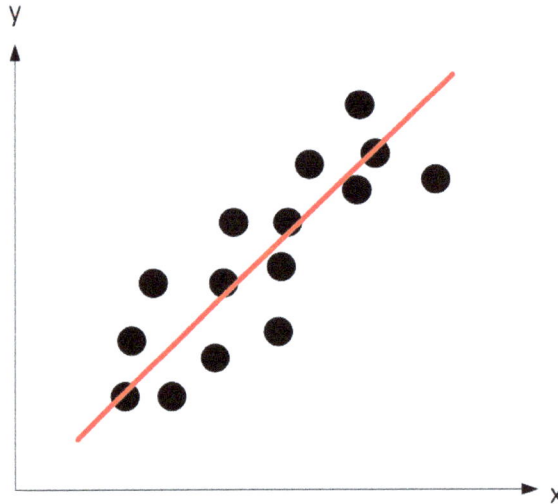

Figure 5.3: Linear regression.

Here, the red line represents a "best fit" line that minimizes the vertical distances between the known data points and the line. Generally, the ordinary least squares method is used to establish the relationship between the variables and calculate the equation of the line.

Luckily, DAX includes two functions that implement the least squares method, **LINEST** and **LINESTX**. Both functions can be used to return a single row table that includes the information about a regression line. To demonstrate, enter the following data into an **Enter data** query and save as a table called **Advertising**:

Advertising Spend ($ thousands)	Sales ($ thousands)	Index
10	25	1
15	30	2
20	45	3
25	55	4
30	65	5

Table 5.3: Advertising and Sales dollars.

Alternatively, import the **Advertising** sheet from the Excel spreadsheet, **Chapter5_Data.xlsx** which can be found in the GitHub repository for this book: https://github.com/gdeckler/DAX-For-Humans/tree/main/book.

Create a table using the following formula:

```
Regression =

    LINEST(

        'Advertising'[Sales ($ thousands)],

        'Advertising'[Advertising Spend ($ thousands)]

    )
```

A table is returned with ten columns, the most important of which are **Slope**, **Intercept**, and **CoefficientOfDetermination**. The **Slope** and **Intercept** define the equation of the line while **CoefficientOfDetermination** measures how correlated the two variables are. This value is between **0** and **1** with a value of **1** being perfect correlation and a value of **0** being no correlation.

Note that with both the **LINEST** and **LINESTX** functions that the y value (the dependent variable) is the first parameter while the second parameter is the x value (the independent variable). Also, you do not need to use a static calculated table when using these functions, these functions can also be used to create a table variable (**VAR**) within a measure such that the table is dynamic.

The equation of a line is generally expressed as the following formula:

$$y = mx + b$$

Where m is the slope and b is the intercept. We can therefore construct the following measure:

```
Regression Line =

    VAR __Slope = MAX( 'Regression'[Slope1] )

    VAR __Intercept = MAX( 'Regression'[Intercept] )

    VAR __x = MAX( 'Advertising'[Advertising Spend ($ thousands)] )

    VAR __Result = __Slope * __x + __Intercept

RETURN

    __Result
```

Note that if we were using a dynamic table variable for our **LINEST** function instead of a static, calculated table, we could use the **MAXX** function combined with **SELECTCOLUMNS** to retrieve our slope and intercept values.

With a bit of formatting magic, we can then visualize the results in a **Line** chart:

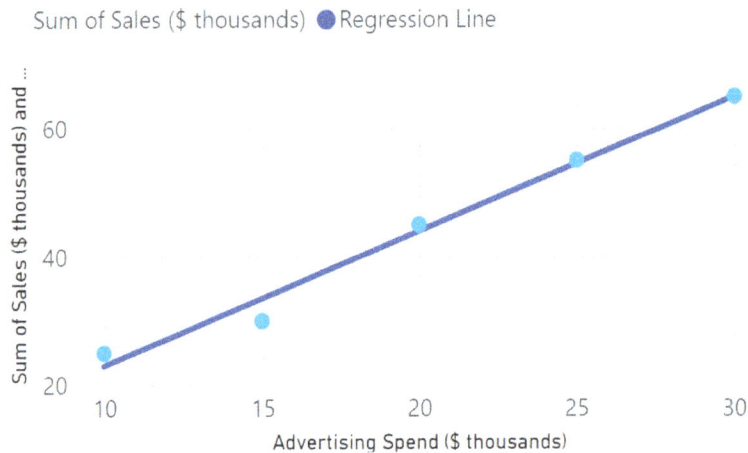

Figure 5.4: Linear regression line.

The dots represent the known values while the line is created by the **Regression Line** measure. This completes our exploration of linear regression for now. Let's next turn our attention to formatting numbers.

Formatting Numbers

Power BI Desktop has several predefined formats for numbers. These formats are found on the **Column Tools** and **Measure Tools** tab of the ribbon in the **Formatting** area. The predefined formats are the following:

- General
- Currency
- Decimal number
- Whole number
- Percentage
- Scientific

In addition, measures have one additional format option, **Dynamic** which we cover later in this section.

In addition to the standard, predefined formats, DAX also includes a function called **FORMAT** that provides additional options for formatting numbers with the caveat that the number is converted to text. The **FORMAT** function has the following form:

FORMAT(<value>, <format_string>[, <local_name>])

Here, **<value>** is the number, **<format_string>** is a predefined or custom format string and the optional **<local_name>** which is a language specifier such as "en-US", "en-GB", etc. A full list of language tags can be found here: https://learn.microsoft.com/en-us/windows-hardware/manufacture/desktop/available-language-packs-for-windows?view=windows-11.

The **FORMAT** function includes the following predefined formats:

Format	Description
"General Number"	Number is displayed without thousands separator
"Currency"	Number is displayed with thousands separators in the local currency format.
"Fixed"	Number is displayed with a decimal separator having at least one digit to the left and two digits to the right.
"Standard"	Number is displayed with thousands separators and decimal separator having at least one digit to the left and two digits to the right.
"Percent"	Number is multiplied by 100 and a decimal separator with two digits to the right. A percent sign (%) is displayed at the end.
"Scientific"	Number is displayed in standard scientific notation, with two significant digits.
"Yes/No"	If the number is 0, displays "No", otherwise displays "Yes".
"True/False"	If the number is 0, displays "False", otherwise displays "True".
"On/Off"	If the number is 0, displays "Off", otherwise displays "On".

Table 5.4: Predefined number formats.

It is also possible to construct custom format strings. These format strings can have up to three sections which are separated by semicolons. If two sections are specified, then the first section applies to zero and positive numbers while the second section applies to negative numbers. If three sections are specified then the first section applies to positive numbers, the second to negative numbers, and the third to zeros.

Custom format strings can have the following elements:

Character	Description
None	No formatting.
0	Displays a digit or a zero.
#	Displays a digit or nothing.
.	Decimal placeholder. In some locales, a comma is used as the decimal separator.
%	The expression is multiplied by 100 and the percent character (%) is displayed.
,	Thousand separator. In some locales, a period is used as a thousand separator.
:	Time separator. Some locals may have alternative time separator characters.
/	Date separator. Some locals may have alternative time separator characters.
E- E+ e- e+	Scientific format.
- + $ ( )	Displays the character.
\	The "escape" character. Displays the next character but not the backslash. Used to display characters that have special meaning. This character is often referred to as an "escape" character.
"ABC"	Displays the text inside the double quotation.

Table 5.5: Custom number format elements.

As mentioned, measures have an additional formatting option, **Dynamic**. **Dynamic** formatting allows you to enter a DAX formula for formatting the measure. This can be helpful in situations where a DAX measure might return a percentage or a whole number, for example. When constructing **Dynamic** formats, it is helpful to know the default format strings as shown in the following table:

Format	Format string
General	`" "`
Currency	`"\$#,0.##############;(\$#,0.##############);\$#,0.##############"`
Decimal number	`"0.00"`
Whole number	`"0"`
Percentage	`"0.00%;-0.00%;0.00%"`
Scientific	`"0.00E+000"`

Table 5.6: Format strings for standard formats.

Thus, in the case of a measure that might display both percentages and whole numbers, the dynamic format string might be:

```
IF( [Measure] >= 1, "0", "0.00%;-0.00%;0.00%" )
```

This concludes our discussion around formatting numbers.

Summary

This chapter was all about working with numbers. We first covered numerous core DAX functions for working with numbers including the standard aggregation functions, trigonometry functions, and basic operators for addition, subtraction, multiplication, division, and exponentiation. Next, we covered the surprising number of rounding functions in DAX. We then explored some problematic DAX number functions, MOD and MEDIAN as well as a "missing" DAX function, mode. After that we cover more advanced topics such as ranking, aggregating measures, computing weighted averages, linear interpolation, and linear regression, finishing off the chapter with a brief treatment of different methods of formatting numbers.

In the next chapter, we cover the last remaining core data types in DAX, time as well as the concept of duration.

CHAPTER

6

6

Time and Duration

In the last three chapters, we have covered dates, text and numbers. In this chapter, we cover the last notable data type in Power BI, time. While there are also types for **True/false**, **Blank**, and **Binary**, these data types are either relatively trivial or legacy (**Binary**). **True/false** stores **Boolean** values which are either true or false and **Blank** stores blank values.

While nearly all semantic models have dates, text, and numbers, not every semantic model deals with time. However, time is fundamental to many semantic models and business intelligence analysis. In addition, the concept of duration is vitally important to many aspects of business intelligence reporting. Unfortunately, unlike Power Query, which has a true duration data type, DAX does not have a duration data type.

In this chapter, we start with the basics of time and time tables and then proceed to explore more complex calculations involving time and duration. Let's start by explaining the basics of time within DAX.

Time Basics

Time values can be created using the **TIME** function. For example, a measure can be created that returns 5:21:36 PM by doing the following:

1. In a new Power BI file, create a measure table called **Calculations**. See the *Measure Tables* section of *Chapter 3, Dates and Calendars*.
2. Right-click the **Calculations** table and choose **New measure**.
3. In the formula bar, use the following formula:

```
Time Measure = TIME( 17, 21, 36 )
```

4. Press the **Enter** key to create the measure.
5. In the **Data** pane, expand the **Calculations** table.
6. Right-click the **Calculations** column and choose **Hide**.
7. Place the **Time Measure** measure into a **Card** visual and note that **12/30/1899 5:21:36 PM** is displayed. Recall that in regards to dates that 0 is 12/30/1899. Refer to *Chapter 3, Date*

and Calendars for more information. Note that the hour parameter is based on a 24-hour clock with 0 being midnight and 23 being 11 PM.

8. Select the **Time Measure** measure in the **Data** pane by clicking on **Time Measure** (not the checkbox).

9. In the **Measure tools** tab of the ribbon, select the **Format** dropdown in the **Formatting** area of the ribbon and note the wide array of different date, date/time, and time formats available. The time-only formats are at the bottom.

All the different date, date/time, and time formats are actually implemented as annotations within the Power BI semantic model. Times are, in fact, simply decimal numbers, the fraction of a day. You can observe this by changing the **Time Measure** to the following:

```
Time Measure = TIME( 17, 21, 36 ) * 1
```

Observe that the **Card** visual now displays **.72**. Multiplying the time by **1** forces the time to reveal its true nature. To understand how this fraction of a day works, create a new measure called **Measure** with the following formula:

```
Measure = 17/24 + 21/24/60 + 36/24/60/60
```

Here, **17** hours is divided by the number of hours in a day, **24**. **21** minutes is divided by **24** hours in a day and then by **60** minutes in an hour. Finally, **36** seconds is divided by **24** hours in a day then by **60** minutes in an hour and then by **60** seconds in a minute. Add this measure to a **Card** visual and notice that **.72** is displayed.

Since times are actually numbers, you can use simple arithmetic to add and subtract times. For example, change the time measure to the following:

```
Time Measure = ( TIME( 17, 21, 36 ) - TIME( 15, 21, 36 ) ) * 24 * 60 * 60
```

The **Card** visual now displays **7.20K** or **7,200**, which is the number of seconds in 2 hours.

The **TIME** function has some interesting aspects. For example, change the **Time Measure** measure to the following:

```
Time Measure = TIME( 17, 21, 66 )
```

The Card visual now displays **12/30/1899 5:22:06 PM**. Since the seconds are greater than **59**, the time value rolls over to the next minute. The same is true if the minutes parameter exceeds **59**, the time value rolls over to the next hour. However, if the hour parameter exceeds 23, the value does not roll over to the next day. Instead, the hour simply cycles around the clock. In fact, the following measure returns the exact same time value:

```
Time Measure = TIME( 41, 21, 66 )
```

There are only a few DAX functions related to time other than the **TIME** function itself. These include **HOUR, MINUTE,** and **SECOND**. Predictably, the **HOUR** function returns the hour portion of a time value while the **MINUTE** and **SECOND** functions do the same for minutes and seconds respectively.

The last time-related function is **TIMEVALUE,** which converts the string representation of time to a time value. For example, the following measure returns the same time value as our original **Time Measure** formula:

```
Time Value = TIMEVALUE( "05:21:36 PM" )
```

And so does this version, which uses the date time literal:

```
dt = TIMEVALUE( dt"2024-11-25 17:21:36" )
```

Now that you understand the basics of time, let's move on to building time tables.

Creating Time Tables

Just as date or calendar tables are useful for performing date calculations and analysis, so too can time tables assist with time calculations and analysis. Time tables can be easily created using DAX with the following formula:

```
Time Table =
    VAR __Hours = SELECTCOLUMNS( GENERATESERIES( 0, 23, 1 ), "Hour", [Value] )

    VAR __MinSec = GENERATESERIES( 0, 59, 1 )

    VAR __Minutes = SELECTCOLUMNS( __MinSec, "Minute", [Value] )

    VAR __Seconds = SELECTCOLUMNS( __MinSec, "Seconds", [Value] )

    VAR __Table =

        ADDCOLUMNS(

            CROSSJOIN( __Hours, __Minutes, __Seconds ),

            "Time", TIME( [Hour], [Minute], [Seconds] )

        )

RETURN

    __Table
```

This formula produces a table with **86,400** rows, which is the number of seconds in a day. The **__Hours** and **__MinSec** variables use the **GENERATESERIES** function to generate tables from **0** to **23** and **0** to **59** respectively. Since we use the **CROSSJOIN** function to create a Cartesian product, we just use **SELECTCOLUMNS** to rename the **Value** column for all three tables, **__Hours**, **__Minutes**, and __**Seconds**. We can then simply add a column called **Time** that uses the **TIME** function.

This table can be used in a similar manner to a date or calendar table. If you have date and time stamps coming from source systems, it is recommended that you separate out the date and time portions into two columns. Then, the date column can be related to a date/calendar table and the time column related to this time dimension table. In addition, separating date and time values into separate columns can help to reduce the cardinality of the original column and thus make columnar compression more efficient.

Let's now look at adding and subtracting time.

Time Addition and Subtraction

The **DATEDIFF** function can be used to find the difference between two time values. For example, placing the following measure into a **Card** visual returns   -121 or a difference of **121** minutes.

```
Time Diff = DATEDIFF( TIME( 15, 21, 36), TIME( 13, 20, 16 ), MINUTE )
```

This is the difference between 5:21:36 PM and 3:20:16 PM measured in minutes. This works because the **DATEDIFF** function includes options for **HOUR**, **MINUTE**, and **SECOND**.

Unfortunately, most other date-related functions, such as **DATEADD**, do not support time values. The **DATEADD** function only allows adding values in increments of **DAY**, **MONTH**, **QUARTER**, and **YEAR**. However, we can write a general-purpose DAX formula to mimic DAX's **DATEADD** functionality as follows:

```
Time Add =
    VAR __Time = TIME( 17, 21, 36 ) // Base time

    VAR __NumberOfIntervals = 5

    VAR __Interval = "MINUTE" // "HOUR", "MINUTE", "SECOND"

    VAR __Result =
        SWITCH( __Interval,
            "HOUR", __Time + __NumberOfIntervals/24,
            "MINUTE", __Time + __NumberOfIntervals/24/60,
            "SECOND", __Time + __NumberOfIntervals/24/60/60
        )
```

```
RETURN

    __Result
```

To use this measure, set the **__Time** variable to the base time. Set the **__NumberOfIntervals** variable to the number of intervals you wish to add or subtract to/from the base time, **__Time**. This value can be positive or negative. Set the **__Interval** variable to either **"HOUR"**, **"MINUTE"**, or **"SECOND"** to denote the desired interval to add.

Be sure to set the **Format** of the measure to a time format such as **1:30:55 (h:nn:ss AM/PM)**. This formula returns **5:26:36 PM** if placed in a **Card** visual.

A modified version allows us to add hours, minutes, and seconds simultaneously:

```
Time Add 2 =

    VAR __Time = TIME( 17, 21, 36 )

    VAR __HoursToAdd = 2

    VAR __MinutesToAdd = 5

    VAR __SecondsToAdd = 30

    VAR __Result =

        __Time + __HoursToAdd/24 +

        __MinutesToAdd/24/60 + __SecondsToAdd/24/60/60

RETURN

    __Result
```

This version allows you to set the base time, **__Time**, as well as the hours to add, **__HoursToAdd**, minutes to add, **__MinutesToAdd**, and seconds to add, **__SecondsToAdd**. This measure displays **7:27:06 PM** in a **Card** visual. Note that the addition of **30** seconds caused the time value to roll to the next minute just like when using the **TIME** function with seconds that exceed **59**!

Let's move on to calculating decimal duration.

Decimal Duration

You can calculate the duration between two date and time values by simply subtracting the two date and time values and then forcing the conversion to a decimal number. For example, the following formula returns **0.041666667**:

```
Measure = ( dt"2024-11-26 07:00:00" - dt"2024-11-26 06:00:00" ) * 1.
```

This value is simply 1 divided by 24 since there is a 1-hour difference between the two date and time values. The other way you can end up with decimal durations is if you set a column in **Power Query Editor** to be of type **Duration**.

Since Power BI does not have a true duration data type, we can convert this to a more standard duration format in one of two ways. To see how this is done, first create the following **Decimal Duration** table:

```
Decimal Duration = GENERATESERIES( 0, 5, .03 )
```

Now create the following column:

```
Duration =
    VAR __Value = [Value]
    VAR __Days = TRUNC( __Value )
    VAR __Decimal1 = __Value - __Days
    VAR __Hours = TRUNC ( ( __Decimal1 ) * 24 )
    VAR __Decimal2 = __Decimal1 - __Hours / 24
    VAR __Minutes = TRUNC ( ( __Decimal2 ) * 24 * 60 )
    VAR __Decimal3 = __Decimal2 - __Minutes / 24 / 60
    VAR __Seconds = TRUNC ( ( __Decimal3 ) * 24 * 60 * 60 )
    VAR __Result = __Days & ":" & __Hours &":" & __Minutes & ":" & __Seconds
RETURN
    __Result
```

The math involved here should be fairly obvious knowing that the days are the integer portion of a decimal number and the decimal portion is the fractions of a day. For the decimal portion, to retrieve the hours, we retrieve the integer portion using **TRUNC** after multiplying the decimal portion by **24**. The remainder is the number of minutes and seconds. We simply repeat that basic operation again for minutes and seconds. We can then stitch the component parts into a duration text string using the concatenation operator "**&**".

The disadvantage of this method is that the decimal duration is converted into a text string and thus cannot be used in many different visual charts within Power BI. We can solve this issue by using a technique I call **Chelsie Eiden's Duration**. This time, instead of a column, create a measure as follows:

```
Chelsie Eiden's Duration =
    VAR __Value = SUM( 'Decimal Duration'[Value] )
```

```
VAR __Days = TRUNC( __Value )

VAR __Decimal1 = __Value - __Days

VAR __Hours = TRUNC ( ( __Decimal1 ) * 24 )

VAR __Decimal2 = __Decimal1 - __Hours / 24

VAR __Minutes = TRUNC ( ( __Decimal2 ) * 24 * 60 )

VAR __Decimal3 = __Decimal2 - __Minutes / 24 / 60

VAR __Seconds = TRUNC ( ( __Decimal3 ) * 24 * 60 * 60 )

VAR __Result = __Days * 1000000 + __Hours * 10000 + __Minutes * 100 + __Seconds
RETURN
    __Result
```

Note that only the __**Value** and the __**Result** variables have changed. Since this is a measure, we must use an aggregation function like **SUM** when referencing the column. Also, instead of concatenating the duration parts together, we instead use different multipliers for each duration part and then add the parts together.

In **Report view**, create a **Table** visual with the **Sum of Value** column from the **Decimal Duration** table as well as the **Duration** column and the **Chelsie Eiden's Duration** measure. The result from the measure looks bizarre. Now switch to the **Model view** and select the **Chelsie Eiden's Duration** measure. In the **Properties** pane, expand the **Formatting** card and change the **Format** to **Custom** and the **Custom format** to **00:00:00:00** as shown in the following figure:

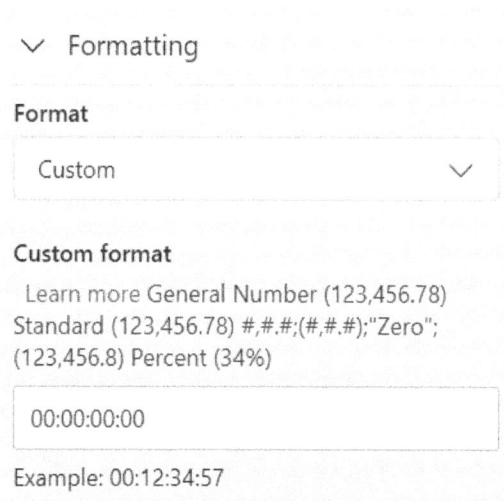

Figure 6.1: Custom format string.

Revisit the **Report view** and note that the **Chelsie Eiden's Duration** measure now mirrors the **Duration** column except that the total, for once, is calculated correctly versus being blank.

This technique is named after Chelsie Eiden who implemented custom format strings while an intern at Microsoft. Let's continue our exploration of durations by investigating how we can convert a duration into seconds.

Duration To Seconds

If you have not already completed the previous section, *Decimal Duration*, please do so now.

It is not uncommon for durations to appear as text within Power BI semantic models due to Power BI's lack of a true duration data type. We can convert such durations to seconds so that we can aggregate the durations or otherwise perform mathematical operations. To see how this is done, create the following column in the **Decimal Duration** table:

```
Duration to Seconds =

    VAR __Duration = [Duration]

    VAR __Path = SUBSTITUTE( __Duration, ":", "|" )

    VAR __Days = PATHITEM( __Path, 1 ) * 60 * 60 * 24

    VAR __Hours = PATHITEM( __Path, 2 ) * 60 * 60

    VAR __Minutes = PATHITEM( __Path, 3 ) * 60

    VAR __Seconds = PATHITEM( __Path, 4 )

    VAR __Result = __Days + __Hours + __Minutes + __Seconds

RETURN

    __Result
```

With the duration converted to seconds, we can perform mathematical operations such as adding durations (in seconds) together. We can then convert seconds back to duration using the following measure formula that leverages the Chelsie Eiden's Duration technique demonstrated in the previous section, *Decimal Duration*:

```
Seconds to Duration =

    VAR __SecInDay = 60 * 60 * 24

    VAR __SecInHours = 60 * 60

    VAR __SecInMin = 60

    VAR __Duration = SUM( 'Decimal Duration'[Duration to Seconds] )
```

```
    VAR __Days = TRUNC( __Duration / __SecInDay )

    VAR __DaysRemainder = MOD( __Duration - ( __Days * __SecInDay ), __SecInDay )

    VAR __Hours = TRUNC( __DaysRemainder / __SecInHours )

    VAR __HoursRemainder =

        MOD(

            __DaysRemainder - ( __Hours * __SecInHours ),

            __SecInHours

        )

    VAR __Minutes = TRUNC( __HoursRemainder / __SecInMin )

    VAR __Seconds = ROUNDUP( MOD( __HoursRemainder, __SecInMin ), 0 )

    VAR __Result = __Days * 1000000 + __Hours * 10000 + __Minutes * 100 + __Seconds

RETURN

    __Result
```

Setting a custom format string for this measure to **00:00:00:00** and adding this measure to the table visualization created in the previous section, *Decimal Duration*, notice that the **Seconds to Duration** measure returns the same values as the **Chelsie Eiden's Duration** measure and **Duration** column.

I am forever grateful to Konstantinos Ioannou for first teaching me about DAX variables after I created an early version of this formula without using variables (**VAR** statements). The knowledge of variables completely changed my approach to writing DAX and led directly to the No CALCULATE approach to DAX.

Let's now tackle another duration format, text durations.

Text Duration Conversion

Some systems use a text duration format such as **1 hour 6 minutes** or **1 day 8 hours 30 minutes 25 seconds**. These duration formats can be challenging to convert to either seconds or more standard duration formats.

To get started, import the **Text Duration** sheet from the Excel spreadsheet, **Chapter6_Data.xlsx** which can be found in the GitHub repository for this book: https://github.com/gdeckler/DAX-For-Humans/tree/main/book.

Now create the following measure:

```
Text Duration to Seconds =
    VAR __Separator = " "
    VAR __Text = MAX( 'Text Duration'[Text Duration] )
    VAR __Len = LEN( __Text )
    VAR __Count = __Len - LEN( SUBSTITUTE( __Text, __Separator, "" ) ) + 1
    VAR __Path = SUBSTITUTE( __Text, __Separator, "|" )
    VAR __Table =
        ADDCOLUMNS(
            ADDCOLUMNS(
                GENERATESERIES(1,__Count,1),
                "__Word", PATHITEM( __Path, [Value] )
            ),
            "__Key", LOWER( [__Word] )
        )
    VAR __DayPos = MAXX( FILTER( __Table, [__Key] = "day" ), [Value] ) - 1
    VAR __Days = MAXX( FILTER( __Table, [Value] = __DayPos ), [__Word] ) + 0
    VAR __HourPos = MAXX( FILTER( __Table, [__Key]= "hour"), [Value] ) - 1
    VAR __Hours = MAXX( FILTER( __Table, [Value] = __HourPos ), [__Word] ) + 0
    VAR __MinPos = MAXX( FILTER( __Table, [__Key] = "minute" ), [Value] ) - 1
    VAR __Minutes = MAXX( FILTER( __Table, [Value] = __MinPos ), [__Word] ) + 0
    VAR __SecPos = MAXX( FILTER( __Table, [__Key] = "second" ), [Value] ) - 1
    VAR __Seconds = MAXX( FILTER( __Table, [Value] = __SecPos ), [__Word] ) + 0
    VAR __Result =
        __Days * 60 * 60 * 24 + __Hours * 60 * 60 + __Minutes * 60 + __Seconds
RETURN
    __Result
```

This measure uses a variety of text processing techniques from *Chapter 4, Text*. Central to this measure is that a common separator, in this case a space, separates the numbers and words within the text duration string. We can use this to find out the number of elements within the string by calculating the length of the text and subtracting the length of the text with the separator removed.

Next, we turn the text into a path using the **SUBSTITUTE** function, replacing the separator with the pipe character (|). We then create a table using our text to table technique of using **GENERATESERIES** combined with **PATHITEM**. We add an additional column __**Key** to make filtering easier since the text duration may have mixed case or be plural or singular. If using **TOCSV** on the __**Table** variable, an individual result might look like the following:

[Value]	[__Word]	[__Key]
1	1	
2	Day	day
3	1	
4	hour	hour
5	51	
6	Minutes	minute

Table 6.1: Sample TOCSV output.

This represents a duration of 1 day, 1 hour, and 51 minutes. As you can see, the value for each duration part is in a row that is one less than where the __**Key** appears for that duration part. Thus, to find how many days, we simply filter the table to where the __**Key** equals "days". We then know that the number of days is in the previous row. Thus, we simply subtract 1 from the calculated **Value**. We can then use this __**DayPos** variable to "lookup" the number of days in the previous row in the __**Days** variable.

We simply need to repeat this process for hours, minutes, and seconds and then multiply and add these parts accordingly to obtain the __**Result**. Place this measure into a **Table** visual along with the **Text Duration** column from the **Text Duration** table.

Let's move on to exploring an additional duration topic, the concept of net work duration.

Net Work Duration

There is a DAX function called **NETWORKDAYS** that facilitates the calculation of the number of workdays (Monday through Friday) between two dates. Unfortunately, there is no equivalent function for calculating the number of working hours, minutes, or seconds between two date and time values.

The calculation of working hours can be useful in a variety of circumstances. For example, such as a ticketing system that tracks when a ticket was created and when a ticket ended. One might wish to determine how many working hours, minutes, or seconds that each ticket was open.

To explore the concept of working hours, import the **Working Hours** sheet from the Excel spreadsheet, **Chapter6_Data.xlsx** which can be found in the GitHub repository for this book: https://github.com/gdeckler/DAX-For-Humans/tree/main/book.

Now create the following measure:

```
Net Work Duration =

    VAR __startWorkTime = TIME( 7, 30, 0 )

    VAR __endWorkTime = TIME( 18, 0, 0 )

    VAR __startTime = [Start]

    VAR __endTime = [End]

    VAR __netWorkDays = NETWORKDAYS( __startTime, __endTime )

    VAR __weekdayStart = WEEKDAY( __startTime, 2 )

    VAR __weekdayEnd = WEEKDAY( __endTime, 2 )

    VAR __fullDays =

        SWITCH( TRUE(),

            __weekdayStart > 5 && __weekdayEnd > 5, __netWorkDays,

            __weekdayStart > 5 || __weekdayEnd > 5, __netWorkDays - 1,

            __netWorkDays < 2, 0,

            __netWorkDays - 2

        )

    VAR __fullDayMinutes = DATEDIFF( __startWorkTime, __endWorkTime, MINUTE )

    VAR __fullDayDuration = __fullDays * __fullDayMinutes

    VAR __startDayTime = __startTime - TRUNC( __startTime )

    VAR __startDayDuration = DATEDIFF( __startDayTime, __endWorkTime, MINUTE )

    VAR __endDayTime = __endTime - TRUNC( __endTime )

    VAR __endDayDuration = DATEDIFF( __startWorkTime, __endDayTime, MINUTE )
```

```
VAR __Result =

    IF(

        __netWorkDays = 1,

        DATEDIFF( __startTime, __endTime, MINUTE ),

        __fullDayDuration + __startDayDuration + __endDayDuration

    )

RETURN

    __Result
```

The first two variables, __**startWorkTime** and __**endWorkTime** set the start and end of working hours, in this case 7:30 AM to 6 PM. The next two variables __**startTime** and __**endTime** grab the appropriate values for the current row. Note, to turn this formula into a measure, you would simply need to wrap the column references in an aggregation function such as **MAX**.

The next four variables culminate in calculating the __**fullDays** variable which represents the number of full working days between the two dates and times. We start by calculating the number of working days using the **NETWORKDAYS** function. We then calculate the weekday of both the start date and time and end date and time.

Based on these results, we adjust the __**netWorkDays** result to calculate __**fullDays**. This is necessary because if the start and end days fall on a working day, then those days are not full working days. For example, for a start date of Monday and an end date of Wednesday, the **NETWORKDAYS** function would return **3**. However, only one of those days, Tuesday, is a full working day, the Monday and Wednesday are only partial working days.

We can now calculate the total number of minutes in a full working day, __**fullDayMinutes**, by using **DATEDIFF**, using __**startWorkTime** and __**endWorkTime**. The __**fullDayDuration** simply multiplies __**fullDays** by __**fullDayMinutes** to calculate the total minutes for full working days.

Next, we calculate the partial day for the start day. The __**startDayTime** variable calculates just the time portion of the date and time value for the start day, __**startTime**. This is done by removing the whole number portion of the value using **TRUNC**. Recall that a date and time value is simply a decimal number where the integer (whole number) portion represents the date and the decimal portion is the time. We can then determine the partial working day minutes using **DATEDIFF** once again in the __**startDayDuration** variable.

The next two variables, __**endDateTime** and __**endDayDuration** repeat the same calculation as __**startDayTime** and __**startDayDuration** but for the end partial working day. Finally, we check to see if **__netWorkDays** is equal to **1**. If it is, then the ticket was opened and closed on the same day and thus the total minutes are calculated using **DATEDIFF** for the **__startTime** and **__endTime**. Otherwise, we simply add up the values for **__fullDayDuration**, **__startDayDuration**, and **__endDayDuration**.

Note that this formula can be converted to hours or seconds simply by replacing all instances of **MINUTE** in the **DATEDIFF** functions with **HOUR** and **SECOND** respectively.

Let's next take a look at a breakdown of hours.

Hours Breakdown

Somewhat similar to net work duration, it is sometimes desirable to break down an event into its component parts, such as the minutes consumed in each hour of the day. We call this an hours breakdown.

To explore this topic, create a table called **Hours Breakdown**. There are two ways to create this table. The first is to copy and paste the following into an **Enter Data** query and name the table **Hours Breakdown**.

ID	Date	Start	End
1	Tuesday, January 1, 2019	8:00:00 AM	9:24:00 AM
1	Wednesday, January 2, 2019	5:24:00 AM	9:14:00 PM
2	Tuesday, January 1, 2019	9:59:00 AM	4:13:00 PM
2	Wednesday, January 2, 2019	3:31:00 AM	12:01:00 PM
3	Tuesday, January 1, 2019	8:24:00 AM	8:55:00 AM

Table 6.2: Hours Breakdown table data.

Alternatively, import the **Hours Breakdown** sheet from the Excel spreadsheet, **Chapter6_Data.xlsx** which can be found in the GitHub repository for this book: https://github.com/gdeckler/DAX-For-Humans/tree/main/book.

This table represents three different event IDs spanning multiple days and multiple hours within those days and we wish to understand the breakdown of these events across these days and hours.

Now create the following table using DAX:

```
Hours =

    VAR __Table =

        ADDCOLUMNS(

            GENERATESERIES( 0, 23, 1 ),

            "Hour", TIME( [Value], 0, 0 )

        )

RETURN

    __Table
```

Set the **Hours** column to have a short time format such as **1:30:55 PM (h:nn:ss AM/PM)**. Also, make certain that the **Hours** table and **Hours Breakdown** table are not related to one another.

Create the following measure:

```
Hours Breakdown =

    VAR __Hour = HOUR( MAX( 'Hours'[Hour] ) )

    VAR __Start = MAX( 'Hours Breakdown'[Start] )

    VAR __StartHour = HOUR( __Start )

    VAR __StartMinutes = MINUTE( __Start )

    VAR __End = MAX( 'Hours Breakdown'[End] )

    VAR __EndHour = HOUR( __End )

    VAR __EndMinutes = MINUTE( __End )

    VAR __Table =

        ADDCOLUMNS( GENERATESERIES( __StartHour, __EndHour, 1),

            "__minutes",

            SWITCH( TRUE(),

                __StartHour < __EndHour &&

                    [Value] <> __EndHour &&

                        [Value] <> __StartHour, 60 ,

                __StartHour < __EndHour &&

                    [Value] = __EndHour, __EndMinutes ,
```

```
            __StartHour < __EndHour &&

                [Value] = __StartHour, 60 - __StartMinutes ,

            __EndMinutes - __StartMinutes

        )

    )

VAR __Final = FILTER( __Table, [__minutes] > 0 )

VAR __Result = SUMX( FILTER( __Final, [Value] = __Hour ), [__minutes] )

RETURN

    __Result
```

Place this measure into the **Values** field well of a **Matrix** visualization. Add the **ID** column from the **Hours Breakdown** table to the **Columns** field well. Add the **Date** column (not the **Date hierarchy**) from the **Hours Breakdown** table to the **Rows** field well. Finally, under the **Date** column in the **Rows** field well, add the **Hour** column from the **Hours** table. Use the forked arrow icon to expand the hierarchy.

The result should be similar to the following image:

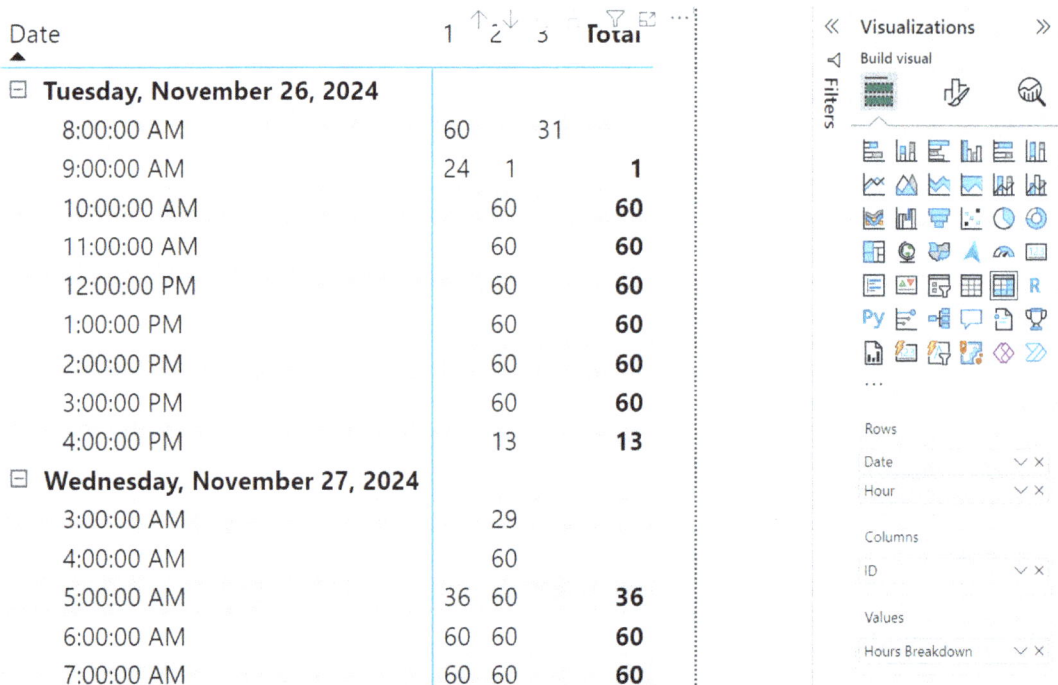

Figure 6.2: Hours breakdown matrix.

The measure works by forming the relationship between the unrelated tables, **Hours** and **Hours Breakdown**. The logic is similar to the logic for *Net Work Duration*. After collecting a variety of information, the real magic is in the creation of the __**Table** variable and, in particular, the __**minutes** column.

The **SWITCH** statement logic can be read thusly:

- If the __**StartHour** is less than the __**EndHour** and the current hour (**Value**) is neither the __**StartHour** or the __**EndHour**, then this is a full hour and thus 60 minutes.
- If the __**StartHour** is less than the __**EndHour** and the current hour (**Value**) is the __**EndHour**, then return __**EndMinutes**, the number of minutes in the last hour.
- If the __**StartHour** is less than the __**EndHour** and the current hour (**Value**) is __**StartHour** then return 60 - __**StartMinutes**, the number of minutes in the first hour.
- Otherwise, the two times fall within the same hour and thus we simply subtract __**StartMinutes** from __**EndMinutes**.

It must be noted that this formula only works for events that start and end on the same day.

You may notice that there are no totals for the rows and that, shockingly, the column totals are incorrect. To fix this, we can create the following measure:

```
Hours Breakdown Total =

    VAR __Table = SUMMARIZE( 'Hours Breakdown', [Date],[ID])

    VAR __Table1 = GENERATE( __Table, 'Hours' )

    VAR __Table2 = ADDCOLUMNS( __Table1, "__Duration", [Hours Breakdown])

    VAR __Result = SUMX(__Table2,[__Duration])

RETURN

    __Result
```

Replace the **Hours Breakdown** measure in the **Matrix** visual with the **Hours Breakdown Total** measure and notice that both row and column totals are now correct.

Let's now shift our attention to, well, shifts.

Shifts

If you have not completed the previous section, **Hours Breakdown**, please do so now.

Many organizations, especially in the manufacturing industry operate on a 24 by 7 basis using multiple shifts. A common format for this is three shifts that are 8 hours each. We can classify each hour of the day into its corresponding shift using the following calculated column in the **Hours** table:

```
Shift =
    VAR __1stBegin = 9        // 9 AM
    VAR __2ndBegin = 17       // 5 PM
    VAR __3rdBegin = 1        // 1 AM
    VAR __Time = [Hour]
    VAR __Hour = HOUR( __Time )
    VAR __Result =
        SWITCH( TRUE(),
            __Hour >= __1stBegin && __Hour < __2ndBegin, "First",
            __Hour >= __2ndBegin || __Hour < __3rdBegin, "Second",
            "Third"
        )
RETURN
    __Result
```

Here the shifts begin at 9 AM, 5 PM and 1 AM. For shifts that begin at other times, some adjustments may be necessary.

Let's now look at time zones.

Time Zones

Time zones, along with the concept of Daylight Savings Time have wreaked havoc on the world of software development and time calculations since their invention. There are no DAX functions that specifically address time zones. However, we can use our knowledge of time arithmetic and the concept of Coordinate Universal Time (UTC) offsets to convert times into other time zones.

In short, UTC divides the world into 24, more-or-less, equal degrees of longitude. This is a severe oversimplification as the actual UTC time zones look like they were gerrymandered by a corrupt politician.

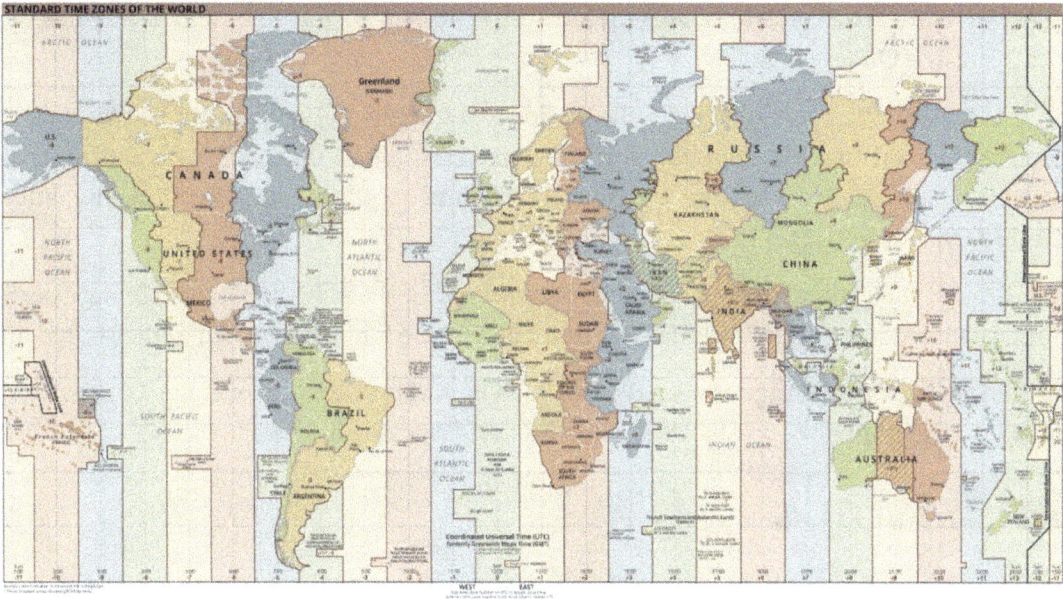

Figure 6.3: Time zones of the world (Wikipedia).

Regardless, to explore time zone calculations, start by importing the **Time Zones** sheet from the Excel spreadsheet, **Chapter6_Data.xlsx** which can be found in the GitHub repository for this book: https://github.com/gdeckler/DAX-For-Humans/tree/main/book.

Now create the following measure:

```
TZ Convert =
    VAR __SourceTime = TIME( 13, 0, 0 )
    VAR __SourceTZOffset = -5 / 24
    VAR __DestTZOffset = MAX( 'Time Zones'[UTC Offset] ) / 24
    VAR __UTCTime = __SourceTime - __SourceTZOffset
    VAR __Result = __UTCTime + __DestTZOffset
RETURN
    __Result
```

Create a **Table** visual that includes the **TZ Convert** measure along with the **Abbr.**, **Name**, and **UTC Offset** columns from the **Time Zones** table.

The **TZ Convert** measure is quite simple. The **__SourceTime** variable defines the time to be converted from one time zone to another. In this case the time is 1PM. The **__SourceTZOffset** defines the UTC time zone offset, in this case **-5** or EST and divides that number by **24**, the number of hours in day. Next, we look up the destination time zone offset and divide this by **24** in the **__DestTZOffset** variable.

The **__UTCTime** variable converts the **__SourceTime** to UTC time by subtracting the **__SourceTZOffset** variable. Note that for a negative UTC offset, this adds instead of subtracts. Finally, we simply need to convert from UTC time to the destination time by adding **__DestTZOffset** to **__UTCTime**.

In the **Table** visual, we can see which time zones are a day ahead by looking at the date portion returned. If the date is **12/31/1899** then the destination time is one day ahead of the source time.

Now that we understand time zone math, let's next look at how we can leverage this knowledge to create a timestamp for our reports that records the last refresh time.

Timestamps

We can use our newfound knowledge of time zone math to create a timestamp for our semantic models to denote when it was last refreshed. To do this, use an **Enter data** query to create a table with the following information:

UTC Offset
-5

Table 6.3: Timestamp table.

Name this table **Timestamp** and feel free to enter your own UTC offset for your local time zone. Now create the following calculated column:

```
Timestamp = UTCNOW() + [UTC Offset] / 24
```

Now, every time the semantic model refreshes, this calculated column gets recalculated and thus contains the timestamp of the last refresh. You can place this column in a **Card** visual on your report.

Let's next understand how to convert Unix times to UTC and back again!

Handling Unix Times

There are many systems that store time values in what is referred to as Unix time or Epoch time. According to Unix systems, the world began at midnight on January 1st, 1970, UTC 0. This date and time is referred to as the Unix epoch. A Unix timestamp is the number of non-leap seconds since the Unix epoch.

To demonstrate how we can convert Unix times to UTC dates and times, create a table called **Unix Times** using an **Enter data** query and copying and pasting the following data:

Unix Time
0
1400000000
1500000000
1600000000
-1400000000
-1500000000
-1600000000

Table 6.4: Unix time table.

Alternatively, import the **Unix Times** sheet from the Excel spreadsheet, **Chapter6_Data.xlsx** which can be found in the GitHub repository for this book: https://github.com/gdeckler/DAX-For-Humans/tree/main/book.

Next, create the following calculated column:

```
Unix 2 UTC =
    VAR __UnixTIme = [Unix Time]
    VAR __Time = DIVIDE( __UnixTIme, 60 * 60 * 24 )
    VAR __UnixEpoch = DATE( 1970, 1, 1 )
    VAR __Result = __UnixEpoch + __Time
RETURN
    __Result
```

Since Unix time is stored as the number of seconds since the Unix epoch, we simply need to convert these seconds into a decimal number by dividing the Unix time by the number of seconds in a day (**60 * 60 * 24**). We then simply need to add this to the decimal number returned from the **DATE** function for January 1st, 1970.

To convert back to Unix time from UTC, create the following calculated column:

```
UTC 2 Unix =
    VAR __UTC = [Unix 2 UTC]
    VAR __UnixEpoch = DATE( 1970, 1, 1 )
    VAR __Result = ( __UTC - __UnixEpoch ) * 60 * 60 * 24
RETURN
    __Result
```

This math simply reverses the operations performed to convert Unix time to UTC.

For our last section, let's return to the subject of duration and explore how to convert milliseconds to duration.

Milliseconds Duration

Converting milliseconds to duration is quite similar to converting seconds to duration, which was covered in the *Duration To Seconds* section of this chapter. The main difference is that we are converting milliseconds instead of seconds.

To demonstrate how to convert milliseconds to duration, start by creating a table called **Milliseconds**. This can be done using one of three different methods. The first is to use an Enter data query to create the table by copy and pasting the following data:

Milliseconds
25920
44999
12550
2456
175
1244999

Table 6.5: Milliseconds table.

Alternatively, import the **Milliseconds** sheet from the Excel spreadsheet, **Chapter6_Data.xlsx** which can be found in the GitHub repository for this book: https://github.com/gdeckler/DAX-For-Humans/tree/main/book.

Now create the following column in the **Milliseconds** table:

```
Milliseconds to Duration =
    VAR __MSecInDay = 60 * 60 * 24 * 1000
    VAR __MSecInHours = 60 * 60 * 1000
    VAR __MSecInMin = 60 * 1000
    VAR __MSecInSec = 1000
    VAR __Duration = [Milliseconds]
    VAR __Days = TRUNC( __Duration / __MSecInDay )
    VAR __DaysRemainder = MOD( __Duration - ( __Days * __MSecInDay ), __MSecInDay )
    VAR __Hours = TRUNC( __DaysRemainder / __MSecInHours )
    VAR __HoursRemainder = MOD( __DaysRemainder - ( __Hours * __MSecInHours ),
__MSecInHours )
    VAR __Minutes = TRUNC( __HoursRemainder / __MSecInMin )
    VAR __MinsRemainder = MOD( __HoursRemainder - ( __Minutes * __MSecInMin ),
__MSecInMin )
    VAR __Seconds = TRUNC( __MinsRemainder / __MSecInSec )
    VAR __MilliSeconds = ROUNDUP( MOD( __MinsRemainder, __MSecInSec ), 0 )
    VAR __Result = __Days & ":" & __Hours & ":" & __Minutes & ":" & __Seconds
                    & ":" & __MilliSeconds
RETURN
    __Result
```

This formula is extremely similar to the **Seconds to Duration** measure created in the section *Duration to Seconds*. It is effectively the same pattern with one additional level of calculations for milliseconds.

Summary

In this chapter, we explored the world of time and duration in DAX. While there are only a scant few functions related to time in DAX and none that deal with duration, we were able to construct a wide variety of different time calculations after mastering the basics of time in DAX. This included the creation of time tables, adding and subtracting time, working with decimal durations, converting durations to second and back, and converting text duration strings.

We also looked at some more advanced calculations such as computing net work duration and an hours breakdown. Next, we looked at calculating shifts with DAX and then covered times zones which then allowed us to demonstrate how to create a DAX timestamp for a report's last refreshed time. We then finished up with converting Unix times and creating a duration from milliseconds.

This chapter marks the end of the *Basics* segment of this book. The next chapter starts the *Scenarios* segment of this book and begins with looking at customer metrics.

CHAPTER 7

7

Customers

Thus far, we have covered the basics of the DAX language, which consists of working with core functions and data types. While some scenarios and techniques have been presented, these scenarios have all been in the context of dealing with specific types of data such as dates, text, numbers, times, and durations. This chapter is the start of more scenario-based content focused on core business topics important to most organizations and we begin with customers and customer KPIs.

Customers are critical to most businesses and organizations, since customers drive demand, shape brand reputation, and ultimately determine profitability. By closely monitoring customer KPIs such as satisfaction, retention rates, and engagement, companies can better understand how they are meeting customer needs. Tracking these metrics helps businesses identify emerging trends, improve product and service offerings, and create strategies and tactics to better serve their audience.

In this chapter, we cover a range of important customer KPIs that can help create a data-driven approach that fosters stronger relationships, encourages repeat business, and promotes sustained growth, helping organizations stay in tune with their customers and remain competitive in an ever-changing marketplace.

New, Lost, and Returning Customers

It is common for organizations to track when new customers are acquired, when customers are lost, and when lost customers return. These are important metrics that help determine whether the customer base is growing or shrinking as well as potentially measure the effectiveness of marketing campaigns and other initiatives.

To demonstrate some DAX calculations that identify new, lost, and returning customers, we first need some data. To this end, create the following five tables in a new Power BI Desktop file:

```
Calculations = { 0 }
```

Dates =

```
    VAR __Calendar =
        ADDCOLUMNS(
            CALENDAR( DATE( 2025, 1, 1 ), DATE( 2025, 12, 31 ) ),
            "Month", FORMAT( [Date], "mmmm" ),
            "MonthSort", MONTH( [Date] ),
            "Year", YEAR( [Date] )
        )
RETURN
    __Calendar

Base Customers =
    VAR __Calendar = 'Dates'
    VAR __Table =
        GENERATE(
            SUMMARIZE(
                __Calendar,
                [Month],[MonthSort],[Year],
                "Date",
                    VAR __Month = [Month]
                    VAR __Result =
                        MINX( FILTER( __Calendar, [Month]=__Month ), [Date] )
                RETURN
                    __Result
            ),
            SELECTCOLUMNS(
                GENERATESERIES( 1+INT( [MonthSort]/3 ), 24 + INT( [MonthSort]/2 ) ),
                "ID", [Value]
            )
        )
    VAR __Result =
```

```
        SELECTCOLUMNS(

            __Table,

            "Date", [Date],

            "Month", [Month],

            "MonthSort", [MonthSort],

            "Year", [Year],

            "ID", [ID]

        )

RETURN

    __Result

Returning Customers =

DATATABLE(

            "Date", DATETIME,

            "Month", STRING,

            "MonthSort", INTEGER,

            "Year", INTEGER,

            "ID", INTEGER,

            {

                { "5/1/2025", "May", 5, 2025, 1 },

                { "8/1/2025", "August",8, 2025, 2 },

                { "10/1/2025", "October", 10, 2025, 3 }

            }

        )

            Customers = UNION( 'Base Customers', 'Returning Customers' )
```

The **Calculations** table is a blank table for holding measures and the **Dates** table is a standard table of dates.

The **Base Customers** table creates a table of customers where a new customer is added every other month, and a customer is lost every third month. The **Returning Customers** table adds in some lost customers that returned in later months. The **Customers** table simply uses the **UNION** function to append these two tables together.

Patron Recommendation

Jasmin Simader notes that if you get an error in your **Customers** table, make certain that the column order for both **Base Customers** and **Returning Customers** is the same.

For the three customer tables, you can alternatively simply import the **Customers** sheet from the Excel spreadsheet, **Chapter7_Data.xlsx** which can be found in the GitHub repository for this book: https://github.com/gdeckler/DAX-For-Humans/tree/main/book.

Create a relationship between the **Dates** table and the **Customers** table based on the **Date** columns in both tables. No other relationships should exist between any other tables.

Now create the following measure in the **Calculations** table:

```
New Customers =

    VAR __Date = MIN( 'Dates'[Date] )

    VAR __Current = DISTINCT( 'Customers'[ID] )

    VAR __Previous =

        DISTINCT(

            SELECTCOLUMNS(

                FILTER(

                    ALL( 'Customers' ),

                    [Date] < __Date

                ),

                "ID", [ID]

            )

        )

    VAR __Table = EXCEPT( __Current, __Previous )

    VAR __Result = COUNTROWS( __Table ) + 0

RETURN

    __Result
```

Place this measure into a **Table** visual along with the **Month** column from the **Dates** table. Note that January has 24 new customers since there is no previous month. Also note that every even-numbered month adds a single new customer.

While there are different ways of identifying new customers, this version of the formula identifies new customers as customers that have never appeared in the data before. To accomplish this, we get the minimum date in context using the **MIN** function for the __Date variable. We then create a single column table of distinct customer **IDs** in the current context in the __Current variable.

The __Previous variable holds a similar single column table of distinct customer IDs that appeared in all prior months by using **ALL** to override the current filter context and filter to all rows with a **Date** less than the __Date variable. We then use the **EXCEPT** function to find customer IDs that are in the __Current variable but not in the __Previous table. Finally, we return the count of the customer IDs using the **COUNTROWS** function, adding **0** to ensure that a numeric value is returned.

Adding a zero to the result of a calculation is a quick way to ensure that a numeric value is returned instead of a blank value. This can be helpful but can also cause problems since the measure always returns a value, meaning that the measure may return values where you would instead want those values to be blank and thus be excluded from the visual entirely. In those situations, you can instead simply not add the zero.

Note that the **COUNTROWS** function could be replaced by a **CONCATENATEX** function to return a list of new customers added such as in this alternative formula:

```
New Customers Alt =
    VAR __Date = MIN( 'Dates'[Date] )
    VAR __Current = DISTINCT( 'Customers'[ID] )
    VAR __Previous =
        DISTINCT(
            SELECTCOLUMNS(
                FILTER(
                    ALL( 'Customers' ),
                    [Date] < __Date
                ),
                "ID", [ID]
            )
        )
    VAR __Table = EXCEPT( __Current, __Previous )
```

```
    VAR __Result = CONCATENATEX( __Table, [ID], "," )
RETURN

    __Result
```

Patron Recommendation

Jacco Maathius suggests that another useful calculation for the **__Result** is **SUMX(**
__Table, [Revenue]) to show the value of new customers.

We can also identify lost customers in almost the exact same way. The time frame of when a customer is considered lost can vary, however, we define lost customers as customers who purchased last month but not in the current month with the following formula:

```
Lost Customers =

    VAR __Date = MIN( 'Dates'[Date] )

    VAR __Current = DISTINCT( 'Customers'[ID] )

    VAR __Previous =

        DISTINCT(

            SELECTCOLUMNS(

                FILTER(

                    ALL( 'Customers' ),

                    [Date] > EOMONTH( __Date, -2 ) &&

                    [Date] < __Date

                ),

                "ID", [ID]

            )

        )

    VAR __Table = EXCEPT( __Previous, __Current )

    VAR __Result = COUNTROWS( __Table ) + 0

RETURN

    __Result
```

This formula is nearly identical to the original **New Customers** measure. However, note that the **FILTER** clause for the **__Previous** variable has been modified to only the previous month. This is done by filtering for dates that are greater than the end-of-the-month (**EOMONTH**) two months ago as well as dates less than the minimum current date in context which is the first of each month. The other difference is that the order of the tables in the **EXCEPT** function are reversed.

Finally, we can also identify returning customers. For our purposes, returning customers are customers who have bought in the current month as well as in a past month, but not in the immediately previous month. This formula is as follows:

```
Returning Customers =
    VAR __Date = MIN( 'Dates'[Date] )
    VAR __Current = DISTINCT( 'Customers'[ID] )
    VAR __PreviousMonth =
        DISTINCT(
            SELECTCOLUMNS(
                FILTER(
                    ALL( 'Customers' ),
                    [Date] > EOMONTH( __Date, -2 ) &&
                    [Date] <= __Date - 1
                ),
                "ID", [ID]
            )
        )
    VAR __Previous =
        DISTINCT(
            SELECTCOLUMNS(
                FILTER(
                    ALL('Customers'),
                    [Date] < __Date
                ),
                "ID", [ID]
            )
        )
```

```
    VAR __Table = EXCEPT( INTERSECT( __Current, __Previous ), __PreviousMonth )

    VAR __Result = COUNTROWS( __Table ) + 0

RETURN

    __Result
```

Here the __**Previous** variable from **Lost Customers** becomes the __**PreviousMonth** variable in this formula. The __**Previous** variable for this formula is the same as the __**Previous** formula from the **New Customers** measure. The __**Table** variable contains the returning customers and is calculated by first intersecting (**INTERSECT**) the __**Current** variable with the __**Previous** variable. This identifies customers that have purchased both in the previous month and in the past. The resulting table is then passed to the **EXCEPT** function along with the __**PreviousMonth** variable to exclude any customer IDs that purchased in the previous month.

Let's now look at crafting a Net Promoter Score (NPS®) measure.

Net Promoter Score

Net Promoter Score (NPS®) is a measure of how likely a customer is to recommend a company's products and/or services to others. Most often, the source data for this metric is some kind of survey that asks a question such as *"How likely are you to recommend our products/services to others?"*. The variations on the exact question are nearly endless but the important aspect is the recommendation and then a ranking, which is often on a scale of 0 to 10 with 0 being highly unlikely and 10 being highly likely.

Survey responses are categorized into three groups, detractors (0 – 6), passives (7 – 8), and promoters (9 – 10). NPS subtracts the percentage of detractors from the percentage of promoters to arrive at a final score between -100 and 100.

To create some data for our NPS measure, create the following table:

```
Promoters =

    SELECTCOLUMNS(

        ADDCOLUMNS(

            GENERATESERIES( 1, 10 ),

            "Score",

                SWITCH( TRUE(),

                    MOD( [Value], 2 ) = 0, 10,

                    [Value] = 3, 6,
```

```
                        [Value] = 5, 7,

                            9

                    )

            ),

            "Response", [Value],

            "Score", [Score]

        )
```

You can alternatively import the **Promoters** sheet from the Excel spreadsheet, **Chapter7_Data.xlsx** which can be found in the GitHub repository for this book: https://github.com/gdeckler/DAX-For-Humans/tree/main/book.

Now create the following **NPS** measure in the **Calculations** table:

```
NPS =

    VAR __Table = ALL( 'Promoters' )

    VAR __Total = COUNTROWS( __Table )

    VAR __Detractors = COUNTROWS( FILTER( __Table, [Score] < 7 ) )

    VAR __Promoters = COUNTROWS( FILTER( __Table, [Score] > 8 ) )

    VAR __PercDetractors = DIVIDE( __Detractors, __Total, 0 )

    VAR __PercPromoters = DIVIDE( __Promoters, __Total, 0 )

    VAR __Result = ( __PercPromoters - __PercDetractors ) * 100

RETURN

    __Result
```

The formula is fairly straightforward. We first ensure that we have all rows in context using the **ALL** function and store that table in the __**Table** variable. We get the total number of rows using **COUNTROWS** and store that in the __**Total** variable.

The __**Detractors** variable holds the count of responses that have a **Score** less than **7** while the __**Promoters** variable holds the count of responses that have a **Score** of greater than **8**. We then calculate the percentages of detractors and promoters in the __**PercDetractors** and __**PercPromoters** variables respectively. Finally, we simply subtract __**PercDetractors** and __**PercPromoters** and multiply the difference by **100**.

Placing the **NPS** measure into a **Card** visual returns a value of **70**.

Note that Net Promoter®, NPS®, NPS Prism®, and the NPS-related emoticons are registered trademarks of Bain & Company, Inc., NICE Systems, Inc., and Fred Reichheld. Net Promoter Score[SM] and Net Promoter System[SM] are service marks of Bain & Company, Inc., NICE Systems, Inc., and Fred Reichheld.

Let's now turn our attention to churn rate.

Churn Rate

Customer churn rate is a relatively straightforward concept. In short, churn rate measures how many customers leave within a given length of time. Tracking this metric over time helps identify if there are issues within the business or service being provided. Churn rate is often used with subscription services, such as software-as-a-service. In addition, churn rate is a required calculation for customer lifetime value (CLTV).

The following example uses a relatively simple methodology for calculating churn rate on a monthly basis. The previous month is considered the start period while the current month is considered the end period. We then simply need to compare the customers in the current period with the customers in the previous period to determine the churn rate.

To start, create the following table in the semantic model:

```
Churn =
    VAR __Jan15 = DATE( 2025, 1, 15 )
    VAR __Jan31 = DATE( 2025, 1, 31 )
    VAR __Feb14 = DATE( 2025, 2, 14 )
    VAR __Feb28 = DATE( 2025, 2, 28 )
    VAR __Mar16 = DATE( 2025, 3, 16 )
    VAR __Mar31 = DATE( 2025, 3, 31 )
    VAR __Cal1 = CALENDAR( __Jan15, __Mar31 )
    VAR __Cal2 = CALENDAR( __Jan15, __Feb14 )
    VAR __Cal3 = CALENDAR( __Jan15, __Jan31 )
    VAR __Cal4 = CALENDAR( __Feb14, __Mar31 )
    VAR __Cal5 = CALENDAR( __Mar16, __Mar31 )
    VAR __Cust1 = SELECTCOLUMNS( GENERATESERIES( 1, 6, 1 ), "Customer", [Value] )
    VAR __Cust2 = SELECTCOLUMNS( GENERATESERIES( 7, 9, 1 ), "Customer", [Value] )
```

```
VAR __Cust3 = SELECTCOLUMNS( { 10 }, "Customer", [Value] )

VAR __Cust4 = SELECTCOLUMNS( { 11 }, "Customer", [Value] )

VAR __Cust5 = SELECTCOLUMNS( { 12, 13 }, "Customer", [Value] )

VAR __Table1 = GENERATE( __Cal1, __Cust1 )

VAR __Table2 = GENERATE( __Cal2, __Cust2 )

VAR __Table3 = GENERATE( __Cal3, __Cust3 )

VAR __Table4 = GENERATE( __Cal4, __Cust4 )

VAR __Table5 = GENERATE( __Cal5, __Cust5 )

VAR __Result = UNION( __Table1, __Table2, __Table3, __Table4, __Table5 )

RETURN

    __Result
```

Alternatively, you can import the **Churn** sheet from the Excel spreadsheet, **Chapter7_Data.xlsx** which can be found in the GitHub repository for this book: https://github.com/gdeckler/DAX-For-Humans/tree/main/book.

If you have not already created the **Dates** table from *New, Lost, and Returning Customers* section, do so now. Create a relationship between the **Dates** table and the **Churn** table based upon the **Date** columns in each table.

To visualize what is going on, create the following measure:

```
CustomerList =

    CONCATENATEX(

        DISTINCT( 'Churn'[Customer] ), [Customer], ",", [Customer]

    )
```

Place this measure into a **Table** visual along with the **Month** column from the **Dates** table. This results in the visual shown here:

Month	CustomerList
January	1,2,3,4,5,6,7,8,9,10
February	1,2,3,4,5,6,7,8,9,11
March	1,2,3,4,5,6,11,12,13

Figure 7.1: Customer list.

As you can see, January and February both have customers 1 – 9 but January includes customer 10 while February includes customer 11. March adds customers 12 and 13 but removes customers 7, 8, and 9.

Now create the following measure for **Churn Rate**:

```
Churn Rate =
    VAR __MinDate = MIN( 'Dates'[Date] )
    VAR __PMStart = EOMONTH( __MinDate, -2 ) + 1
    VAR __PMEnd = EOMONTH( __MinDate, -1 )
    VAR __Customers = DISTINCT( 'Churn'[Customer] )
    VAR __PMCustomers =
        DISTINCT(
            SELECTCOLUMNS(
                FILTER(
                    ALL( 'Churn' ),
                    [Date] >= __PMStart && [Date] <= __PMEnd
                ),
                "Customer", [Customer]
            )
        )
    VAR __CMCustomers = INTERSECT( __Customers, __PMCustomers )
    VAR __PMCount = COUNTROWS( __PMCustomers )
    VAR __TotalLostCusotmers = __PMCount - COUNTROWS( __CMCustomers )
    VAR __Result = DIVIDE( __TotalLostCusotmers, __PMCount, BLANK() )
RETURN
    __Result
```

Adding this measure to the Table visual returns a **Churn Rate** of **10%** for **February**, **30%** for **March** and **100%** for **April** (since our data only includes January, February, and March.

The measure starts by getting the minimum date in context. Getting the maximum date in context would work just as well. Next, the previous period start and end dates are calculated and stored in **__PMStart** and **__PMEnd** respectively.

We then get the distinct list of customers in context and store these as a single column table in **__Customers**. To get the previous period's list of customers, we simply need to filter the base table by our **__PMStart** and **__PMEnd** dates. We use **SELECTCOLUMNS** and **DISTINCT** to ensure we have a single column table of customer IDs in the **__PMCustomers** variable.

We now need to exclude any new customers from the current period's list of customers, so we use **INTERSECT** to ensure that any new customers are excluded from the rest of the calculation. Now, we can calculate the total number of lost customers using simple subtraction and finally turn this into a percentage using the **DIVIDE** function.

Looking at the results returned, **January** has **10** unique customers. One of those customers (customer **10**) was lost in **February** while a new customer (customer **11**) was added. The churn rate is **10%** because **1** lost customer divided by **10** customers in **January** is **0.10**. Similarly, **February** also has **10** unique customers. In **March**, three customers were lost while two were added. Three divided by ten is **0.30** or **30%**.

We can use an extremely similar formula to calculate growth rate:

```
Growth Rate =
    VAR __MinDate = MIN( 'Dates'[Date] )
    VAR __PMStart = EOMONTH( __MinDate, -2 ) + 1
    VAR __PMEnd = EOMONTH( __MinDate, -1 )
    VAR __Customers = DISTINCT( 'Churn'[Customer] )
    VAR __PMCustomers =
        DISTINCT(
            SELECTCOLUMNS(
                FILTER(
                    ALL( 'Churn' ),
                    [Date] >= __PMStart && [Date] <= __PMEnd
                ),
                "Customer", [Customer]
            )
        )
    VAR __NewCustomers = EXCEPT( __Customers, __PMCustomers )
    VAR __PMCount = COUNTROWS( __PMCustomers )
```

```
    VAR __NewCount = COUNTROWS( __NewCustomers )

    VAR __Result = DIVIDE( __NewCount, __PMCount, BLANK() )

RETURN

    __Result
```

Here we use **EXCEPT** instead of **INTERSECT** in order to return a list of new customers in the **__NewCustomers** variable.

Let's now turn our attention to customer lifetime value or CLTV.

Lifetime Value

Introduced in the 1980's, lifetime value (LTV), has become an important customer KPI that is widely adopted within Fortune 500 firms and other organizations. This is because LTV provides the ability to segment customers into groups based upon their relative value to an organization as well as justify marketing and customer acquisition activities.

LTV is alternatively called lifetime customer value (LCV) and customer lifetime value (CLV/CLTV). While there is no universally accepted methodology for calculating LTV, the example used here provides the ability to identify the most valuable customers within an organization.

The goal of this example is to create an LTV measure that works on an individual customer level as well as in the aggregate. In addition, the measure needs to work across various time periods such as a single year or multiple years.

To get started with this example, create the following table:

```
Lifetime Value =

    DATATABLE(

        "Date", DATETIME,

        "Customer", INTEGER,

        "Value", INTEGER,

        {

            { "3/1/2021", 1, 500 },

            { "12/1/2021", 1, 300 },

            { "6/1/2023", 2, 200 },

            { "8/1/2023", 2, 600 },
```

```
        { "9/1/2023", 2, 800 },

        { "1/1/2024", 3, 200 },

        { "3/1/2024", 3, 250 },

        { "1/1/2023", 4, 1200 },

        { "3/1/2023", 5, 1100 },

        { "8/1/2024", 4, 1500 },

        { "9/1/2025", 1, 500 },

        { "9/1/2025", 2, 500 },

        { "9/1/2025", 3, 200 },

        { "9/1/2025", 4, 1500 },

        { "9/1/2025", 5, 1400 },

        { "9/1/2025", 6, 600 },

        { "9/1/2025", 6, 200 }

    }

)
```

Alternatively, you can import the **Lifetime Value** sheet from the Excel spreadsheet, **Chapter7_Data.xlsx** which can be found in the GitHub repository for this book: https://github.com/gdeckler/DAX-For-Humans/tree/main/book.

Now, create the following measure:

```
Yearly Churn Rate = .15
```

This measure hard codes the yearly churn rate to 15%. For an example of dynamically calculating a customer churn rate, see the *Churn Rate* section of this chapter.

Next, create the **LTV** measure:

```
LTV =
    VAR __Customers = COUNTROWS( DISTINCT( 'Lifetime Value'[Customer] ) )

    VAR __MinDate = MIN( 'Lifetime Value'[Date] )

    VAR __MaxDate = MAX( 'Lifetime Value'[Date] )

    VAR __Years =
        IF(
            ( __MaxDate - __MinDate ) < 366,
```

```
            1,

            YEAR( __MaxDate ) - YEAR( __MinDate ) + 1

        )

    VAR __AvgPurchaseFrequency =

        DIVIDE(

            COUNTROWS( 'Lifetime Value' ),

            __Years,

            BLANK()

        )

    VAR __AvgPurchaseValue = AVERAGE( 'Lifetime Value'[Value] )

    VAR __AvgCustomerValue = __AvgPurchaseValue * __AvgPurchaseFrequency

    VAR __AvgCustomerLifespan = 1 / [Yearly Churn Rate]

    VAR __Result =

        DIVIDE(

            __AvgCustomerValue * __AvgCustomerLifespan,

            __Customers,

            BLANK()

        )

RETURN

    __Result
```

Creating a **Card** visual and placing the **LTV** measure into the **Fields** well returns a value of **2.57K** meaning that each customer is expected generate a value of $2,570 over the lifespan with the business.

The measure works by first getting the distinct number of customers, minimum date, and maximum date and storing these values in **__Customers**, **__MinDate**, and **__MaxDate** respectively.

Patron Recommendation

Alexis Olson notes that you can use **DISTINCTCOUNT** to get the distinct number of customers instead of using the **COUNTROWS** and **DISTINCT** functions. This is absolutely true, however, one of the tenets of the No CALCULATE approach is to utilize the least number of functions possible. Less functions means less to learn and memorize. However, this is all ultimately left to personal preference.

The __**Years** variable holds the number of years over which the customer or customers have made purchases. Dividing the number of purchases by the number of years provides the average purchase frequency (__**AvgPurchaseFrequency**).

The average purchase value (__**AvgPurchaseValue**) is simply the average of the purchases. Multiplying __**AvgPurchaseValue** by __**AvgPurchaseFrequency** provides the average customer value (__**AvgCustomerValue**).

The average customer lifespan (__**AvgCustomerLifespan**) is simply the reciprocal of the **Yearly Churn Rate** measure. Finally, the lifetime value is calculated by multiplying __**AvgCustomerValue** by __**AvgCustomerLifespan** and dividing by the number of unique customers (__**Customers**).

Now that we understand how to calculate lifetime value, let's next look at acquisition costs.

Acquisition Cost

Acquisition cost, or customer acquisition cost (CAC), is the cost of marketing and other activities related to convincing a first-time customer to purchase goods and/or services. CAC is a useful metric for evaluating the overall effectiveness of marketing campaigns and other sales and marketing activities and can be particularly useful when coupled with other KPIs such as lifetime value.

To get started, consider a business that runs three different pay-per-click marketing campaigns using digital advertising on three different platforms. The campaigns can be summarized as follows:

Campaign	# of Clicks	Cost Per Click	New Customers
Click-ad Campaign 1	200	50	10
Click-ad Campaign 2	200	100	30
Click-ad Campaign 3	200	200	40

Table 7.1: Pay-per-click campaign results.

Use an **Enter data** query to enter this data, creating a table called **Acquisition Cost**. Alternatively, import the **Acquisition Cost** sheet from the Excel spreadsheet, **Chapter7_Data.xlsx** which can be found in the GitHub repository for this book: https://github.com/gdeckler/DAX-For-Humans/tree/main/book.

Now create a measure with the following formula:

```
AC =

    VAR __Table =

        ADDCOLUMNS(

            'Acquisition Cost',

            "__Cost", [# of Clicks] * [Cost Per Click]

        )

    VAR __Customers = SUMX( __Table, [New Customers] )

    VAR __Cost = SUMX( __Table, [__Cost] )

    VAR __Result = DIVIDE( __Cost, __Customers )

RETURN

    __Result
```

Create a **Table** visual adding all the columns from the **Acquisition Cost** table as well as the **AC** measure. The result should look like the following:

Campaign	Sum of # of Clicks	Sum of Cost Per Click	Sum of New Customers	AC
Click-ad Campaign 1	200	50	10	$1,000
Click-ad Campaign 2	200	100	30	$667
Click-ad Campaign 3	200	200	40	$1,000
Total	**600**	**350**	**80**	**$875**

Figure 7.2: Acquisition costs.

The **AC** measure works at the individual campaign level as well as in the aggregate at the total level. Here we can see that the **Click-ad Campaign 2** had the lowest customer acquisition cost and that the overall acquisition cost for customers over all three campaigns was **$875** per customer.

The **AC** measure works by first adding a column to the **Acquisition Cost** table called **__Cost** that multiplies the **# of Clicks** column by the **Cost Per Click** column. This is done per row such that the table variable **__Table** now holds the following information:

Campaign	# of Clicks	Cost Per Click	New Customers	__Cost
Click-ad Campaign 1	200	50	10	10000

| Click-ad Campaign 2 | 200 | 100 | 30 | 20000 |
| Click-ad Campaign 3 | 200 | 200 | 40 | 40000 |

Table 7.2: Data within the __Table variable.

It is important to perform this calculation for each individual row of the table versus multiplying the columns in the aggregate. This is because, the total of the __Cost column in this case is 70,000. However, if we multiply the **SUM** of the # **of Clicks** column (600) by the **SUM** of the **Cost Per Click** column (350), we get a total cost of 210,000 (600 * 350) which is obviously incorrect.

Once we have this revised table, we can then simply sum the number of customers acquired (**New Customers**) as well as sum the overall costs (__Cost . Finally, we simply **DIVIDE** the number of new customers acquired (__**Customers**) by the total cost of the campaigns, (__**Cost**).

This is a simple example of calculating acquisition cost. However, this example only considers the actual cost of the marketing campaign itself. Missing is the total cost of everything involved in the marketing campaign, such as the creation of the ad itself as well as other factors, such as salaries. To take these factors into account, use another **Enter data** query to enter the following information into a table called **Acquisition Cost Too**:

Item	Yearly Cost
Fully loaded marketing salaries	198000
Fully loaded sales salaries	230000
Agency fees	10000
Creative fees	20000
Sales commissions	30000
Payment processing fees for first time purchases	1000

Table 7.3: Overhead cost data.

Alternatively, import the **Acquisition Cost Too** sheet from the Excel spreadsheet, **Chapter7_Data.xlsx** which can be found in the GitHub repository for this book: https://github.com/gdeckler/DAX-For-Humans/tree/main/book.

We can now construct an additional measure as follows:

```
CAC =
    VAR __Customers = SUM( 'Acquisition Cost'[New Customers] )
    VAR __Costs = SUM( 'Acquisition Cost Too'[Yearly Cost] )
    VAR __CampaignCosts = [AC]
    VAR __Result = DIVIDE(__Costs, __Customers ) + __CampaignCosts
RETURN
    __Result
```

Placing this measure into a **Card** visual returns the number **$6.99K**, which is the per customer acquisition cost. The important aspect of this formula is that since the **AC** measure already calculates the acquisition cost per customer, we must add the **AC** measure after we calculate the cost of the overhead costs per customer.

Let's next look at a customer service topic by demonstrating how to calculate metrics for customer support tickets, such as the number of open tickets per day.

Open Tickets

Many organizations operate call centers that handle customer service and support requests. While there are a wide variety of KPIs that are tracked for these types of operations, one important metric is the number of open tickets per day or potentially per hour.

Use an **Enter data** query to create a table called **Open Tickets** with the following data:

Ticket Num	Opened Date	Closed Date
1	January 4, 2025	April 15, 2025
2	February 8, 2025	February 15, 2025
3	January 14, 2025	February 3, 2025
4	February 4, 2025	March 12, 2025
5	January 29, 2025	January 29, 2025
6	February 18, 2025	February 19, 2025

Ticket Num	Opened Date	Closed Date
7	January 5, 2025	February 24, 2025
8	January 5, 2025	March 2, 2025
9	March 3, 2025	March 15, 2025
10	March 6, 2025	April 13, 2025
11	April 1, 2025	

Table 7.4: Ticket data.

Alternatively, import the **Open Tickets** sheet from the Excel spreadsheet, **Chapter7_Data.xlsx** which can be found in the GitHub repository for this book: https://github.com/gdeckler/DAX-For-Humans/tree/main/book.

This table contains the bare minimum information for the scenario which includes a unique ID, the **Ticket Num** column, the date each ticket was created (**Opened Date**) and the date each ticket was closed (**Closed Date**). Ensure that the **Opened Date** and **Closed Date** columns have a date type of **Date**.

Ensure that you have created a **Dates** table as shown in the section, *New, Lost, and Returning Customers*, within this chapter. Also, ensure that no relationships exist between the **Dates** table and the **Open Tickets** table.

The main issue with this data is that a ticket can span multiple days, but not each of these days is tracked as a row in the table. Instead, the data only presents the date the ticket was created or opened and the date the ticket was closed. The intervening dates that the ticket was open are not present within the data and must be inferred given the **Opened Date** and **Closed Date** columns. To solve this problem, we must effectively "invent" the intermediary dates within a measure as follows:

```
Tickets Open =
    VAR __Tickets =
        ADDCOLUMNS(
            'Open Tickets',
            "__EffectiveDate",
            SWITCH( TRUE(),
```

```
                    [Closed Date] <> BLANK(), [Closed Date],

                    TODAY() >= [Opened Date], TODAY(),

                    [Opened Date] + 1

                )

            )

    VAR __Table =

        SELECTCOLUMNS(

            GENERATE(

                __Tickets,

                FILTER(

                    'Dates',

                    [Date] >= [Opened Date] &&

                    [Date] <= [__EffectiveDate]

                )

            ),

            "__ID",[Ticket Num]

        )

    VAR __Result = COUNTROWS( __Table )

RETURN

    __Result
```

The first step in this DAX measure is to deal with blank values within the data. It is quite typical for help desk software systems to leave a blank in the "Closed Date" column when a ticket is not yet closed. To deal with this, we add a column called __**EffectiveDate** to the ticket data. This __**EffectiveDate** column holds the following logic. If the **Closed Date** column is not blank, then use the **Closed Date**. Otherwise, if today's date (**TODAY**) is greater than or equal to the **Opened Date**, then use **TODAY**. In all other cases, simply use the **Opened Date** plus one day.

The next step is to "invent" the intermediate rows for each ticket. This is done by using the **GENERATE** function, which returns a Cartesian product between two tables. More specifically, the **GENERATE** function returns the Cartesian product between each row in a table (first parameter) and a second table that is evaluated within the context of each row of the first table. This is why we can compare the **Date** column from the **Dates** table to the **Opened Date** and __**EffectiveDate** columns within the __**Tickets** table.

The final step is to simply count the number of rows in the __Table variable to get the number of tickets open on any particular date. To visualize this data, create a **Clustered column chart** with the **Date** column from the **Dates** table as the **X-axis** and the **Tickets Open** measure as the **Y-axis**.

To better understand what is occurring, create a copy of the **Tickets Open** measure called **Tickets Open Debug**. This measure is identical to the **Tickets Open** measure with one small change. Change the **RETURN** statement from __**Result** to the following:

```
RETURN

    TOCSV( __Table )
```

Create a **Table** visual with the **Date** column from the **Dates** table and the **Tickets Open Debug** measure. Observe that the IDs for each ticket that was open on a particular date are displayed in a text table next to each date.

> **Patron Recommendation**
>
> Alexis Olson notes that there is an alternative form for this measure that replaces the __**Table** variable that uses **GENERATE** with the following two variables:
>
> ```
>     VAR __CurrDate = MAX ( Dates[Date] )
>
>     VAR __Table =
>
>         FILTER (
>
>             __Tickets,
>
>             __CurrDate >= [Opened Date] &&
>
>             __CurrDate <= [__EffectiveDate]
>
>         )
> ```

We can use this same data to calculate another important customer service KPI, average time to close. To calculate the average time to close customer support tickets use the following measure:

```
Average TTC =

    VAR __Tickets =

        ADDCOLUMNS(

            ADDCOLUMNS(

                'Open Tickets',

                "__EffectiveDate",

                SWITCH( TRUE(),
```

```
                      [Closed Date] <> BLANK(), [Closed Date],

                      TODAY() >= [Opened Date], TODAY(),

                      [Opened Date] + 1

                )

          ),

          "__Days", ( [__EffectiveDate] - [Opened Date] + 1 )

      )

   VAR __Result = AVERAGEX( __Tickets, [__Days] )
RETURN

   __Result
```

Placing this measure into a **Card** visual returns the number **30.27**, which is the average number of days to close tickets.

The **Average TTC** measure starts the same way as the **Tickets Open** measure with adding the **__EffectiveDate** column. An additional column is then added, **__Days**, which represents how many days each ticket is open. This is done by subtracting the **Opened Date** value from the **__EffectiveDate** value and adding **1** which makes the math correct and ensures a numeric value is returned. Recall that dates are really just numbers, with the integer portion being the number of days since December 30th, 1899. We then simply need to calculate the average using **AVERAGEX**.

It is fair to consider whether currently open tickets should be counted within the average time to close, and this is ultimately a judgement call. If you eliminate open tickets completely, this can significantly skew the metric as there may be tickets that are open for significantly long periods of time. That said, in other situations where there is a large volume of tickets opened each day, this could skew the metric the opposite way by including a large number of tickets closed in one or zero days. The right version of the metric therefore depends on your specific circumstances.

Let's now turn our attention to creating a customer funnel drop-off rate.

Funnel Drop-off Rate

Funnel drop-off rates are important customer metrics often used in e-commerce scenarios where customers purchase goods and services over the internet. This purchase process most often involves several steps such as the customer selecting a product, placing that product into their shopping cart, visiting the shopping cart, entering payment information, and finally confirming the purchase.

At any step within this purchase process, a customer may decide to abandon the purchase. Analyzing the drop-off rate for various steps along the process can help identify problematic steps in the process that are causing friction with customers. In addition, funnel drop-off rates can be combined with AB testing to help create conversion processes that enhance or maximize the potential for customers to complete purchases once initiated.

To see how this works, we will create some sample data in a table called **Funnel** using the following DAX code:

```
Funnel =
    VAR __Step1 =
        ADDCOLUMNS(
            GENERATESERIES( 1, 100000, 1 ),
            "Page", "Product",
            "Step", 1
        )
    VAR __Step2 =
        ADDCOLUMNS(
            GENERATESERIES( 1, 7000, 1 ),
            "Page", "Add to Shopping Cart",
            "Step", 2
        )
    VAR __Step3 =
        ADDCOLUMNS(
            GENERATESERIES( 1, 4000, 1 ),
            "Page", "Shopping Cart",
            "Step", 3
        )
    VAR __Step4 =
        ADDCOLUMNS(
```

```
            GENERATESERIES( 1, 2000, 1 ),

            "Page", "Confirmation",

            "Step", 4

        )

    VAR __Result = UNION( __Step1, __Step2, __Step3, __Step4 )
RETURN

    __Result
```

Alternatively, import the **Funnel** sheet from the Excel spreadsheet, **Chapter7_Data.xlsx** which can be found in the GitHub repository for this book: https://github.com/gdeckler/DAX-For-Humans/tree/main/book.

This table represents clicks on four separate pages. The first step is landing on a product page. The second step is adding the product to a shopping cart. The third step is visiting the shopping cart, and the final step is confirming the purchase.

To create a measure that analyzes the drop-off rate between steps, use the following formula:

```
Drop-off Rate =

    VAR __CurrStep = MAX( 'Funnel'[Step] )

    VAR __PrevStep = __CurrStep - 1

    VAR __CurrCount = COUNTROWS( 'Funnel' )

    VAR __PrevCount =

        IF(

            __CurrStep = 1, 0,

            COUNTROWS( FILTER( ALL( 'Funnel' ), [Step] = __PrevStep ) )

        )

    VAR __Result = DIVIDE( __PrevCount - __CurrCount, __PrevCount, 0 )
RETURN

    __Result
```

Format this measure as a percentage. Add the **Step** column from the **Funnel** table to a **Table** visual and set the column to **Don't summarize**. Add the **Drop-off Rate** measure to the table. Turn the total off for the table as it is meaningless.

Overall, the drop-off rate calculation is relatively straightforward. We get the current step (__**CurrStep**) in context using the **MAX** function. We could also have used the **MIN** function, assuming that there is only a single step in context.

We can then get the previous step (__**PrevStep**) by simply subtracting **1** from __**CurrStep**. Next, we get the current step's row count using **COUNTROWS** and store this in the __**CurrCount** variable.

The previous step's count (__**PrevCount**) is calculated by bringing the entire **Funnel** table back into context using **ALL**, filtering down to just the rows where the **Step** column equals the __**PrevStep** variable, and then counting the rows using the **COUNTROWS** function. Finally, we perform the necessary math to calculate the percentage drop-off rate by subtracting the current stage's count (__**CurrCount**) from the previous stage's count (__**PrevCount**) and then dividing that result by __**PrevCount**.

An alternative method of calculating drop-off rate is called **abandonment rate**. This method calculates the percentages of customers at the beginning of the process that do not make it to each subsequent step in the process. This version is calculated as follows:

```
Abandonment Rate =
    VAR __CurrStep = MAX( 'Funnel'[Step] )
    VAR __PrevStep = 1
    VAR __CurrCount = COUNTROWS( 'Funnel' )
    VAR __PrevCount =
        IF(
            __CurrStep = 1, 0,
            COUNTROWS( FILTER( ALL( 'Funnel' ), [Step] = __PrevStep ) )
        )
    VAR __Result = DIVIDE( __PrevCount - __CurrCount, __PrevCount, 0 )
RETURN
    __Result
```

The only difference between this version and the previous version is that the __**PrevStep** variable is hard coded to **1**. Placing this measure into the same table results in the following:

Step	Drop-off Rate	Abandonment Rate
1	0.00%	0.00%
2	93.00%	93.00%
3	42.86%	96.00%
4	50.00%	98.00%

Figure 7.3: Drop-off and abandonment rates.

This version makes it clear that only 2% of customers that start on the product page actually end up purchasing the product.

Let's now turn our attention to a different type of customer metric that analyzes which products customers purchase together.

Better Together

The goal of this calculation is to identify items that are ordered in conjunction with one another. Identifying items sold in the same order can assist with providing recommendations to future customers regarding what other items they may wish to purchase.

To get started with this calculation, create a table called **Better Together 1** using an **Enter data** query along with the following purchase data:

Order_ID	Item_Name	Item_Qty
1	Kettle	1
2	Kettle	1
2	Iron	1
3	Tomatoes	2
3	Cucumber	2
4	Kettle	1
4	Iron	1
4	Cucumber	2

Order_ID	Item_Name	Item_Qty
5	Cucumber	2
5	Kettle	1
5	Tomatoes	1
6	Kettle	2
6	Iron	1

Table 7.5: Purchase data.

Alternatively, import the **Better Together 1** sheet from the Excel spreadsheet, **Chapter7_Data.xlsx** which can be found in the GitHub repository for this book: https://github.com/gdeckler/DAX-For-Humans/tree/main/book.

This table provides the minimum details necessary regarding orders including an **Order_ID** column that tracks the ID of an order, an **Item_Name** column that identifies the product purchased, and an **Item_Qty** column that lists the quantity of product purchased.

To identify which items are sold together most frequently, create a table using the following formula:

```
Better Together 2 =
    VAR __Items = DISTINCT( 'Better Together 1'[Item_Name] )
    VAR __Table =
        FILTER(
            GENERATE(
                SELECTCOLUMNS( __Items, "__Item1", [Item_Name] ),
                SELECTCOLUMNS( __Items, "__Item2", [Item_Name] )
            ),
            [__Item1] < [__Item2]
        )
    VAR __Result =
        ADDCOLUMNS(
            __Table,
```

```
            "Bought Together",
                VAR __Table =
                    SUMMARIZE(
                        FILTER(
                            'Better Together 1',
                            [Item_Name] = [__Item1] ||
                            [Item_Name] = [__Item2]
                        ),
                        [Order_ID],
                        "__Count", COUNTROWS( 'Better Together 1' )
                    )
                VAR __Result = COUNTROWS( FILTER( __Table, [__Count] > 1 ) ) + 0
            RETURN
                __Result
    )


RETURN

    __Result
```

This formula may look somewhat daunting so let's break down how this formula works and why it is structured in this manner.

We start by getting a distinct list of items using the **DISTINCT** function and store the result in the __**Items** variable. Next, we need to get a Cartesian product such that we have every item listed with every other item. To do this, we use the **GENERATE** function and simply use the __**Items** variable as our base table. Since **GENERATE** would error if there were two columns with the same name, we use the **SELECTCOLUMNS** function to rename the **Item_Name** column to __**Item1** and __**Item2**. Finally, we filter out any rows where __**Item1** and __**Item2** are equal. This completes the creation of our base table, __**Table**.

The base table has an issue where the same item pairs appear twice but in reversed order. For example, **Iron** and **Kettle** appear twice in the rows of the table, one where **Iron** is __**Item1** and **Kettle** is __**Item2** and another row where the opposite is true.

To address this, we use a **FILTER** statement to compare the **Item1** and **Item2** columns, keeping only the rows where the value in the **Item1** column is less than the value in the **Item2** column. This has two primary effects. First, this removes rows where the values in the **Item1** and **Item2** columns are equal to one another. Second, this also removes duplicate rows where the values in the **Item1** and **Item2** columns are simply in reverse order.

We are now able to construct the final table, **_Result**. This formula uses the **ADDCOLUMN** function to add a column to **_Table1** called **Bought Together**. The **Bought Together** column is calculated by using the **FILTER** function to filter the original table, **Better Together 1** for rows where the **Item_Name** matches either **_Item1** or **_Item2**. The results are then grouped using the **SUMMARIZE** function on **Order_ID** and a **_Count** row is added that counts the rows in the **Better Together 1** table using the **COUNTROWS** function.

The final value for the **Bought Together** column is determined by counting the rows in the temporary table variable after filtering for a **_Count** greater than **1** and then adding **0**. This ensures that we are not counting rows where just one product was sold as part of an order, such as **Order_ID 1**.

The final result is shown here:

_Item1	_Item2	Bought Together
Iron	Kettle	3
Cucumber	Kettle	2
Cucumber	Iron	1
Kettle	Tomatoes	1
Iron	Tomatoes	0
Cucumber	Tomatoes	2

Figure 7.4: Items bought together frequency.

As you can see, six rows are returned, which also happens to be the same number of combinations possible given four items (n) and two samples (r) where order does not matter which is given by the following standard combinations formula:

$$C(n,r) = \binom{n}{r} = \frac{n!}{(r!\,(n-r)!)}$$

Let's next look at annual contract value or ACV.

Annual Contract Value

Annual Contract Value (ACV) is an important KPI that calculates the average revenue that customer contracts generate each year. This is an especially important metric for Software as a Service (SaaS) firms. However, ACV is often misunderstood or confused with similar metrics such as **Annual Recurring Revenue** (ARR) and **Total Contract Revenue** (TCR).

To understand the differences between these metrics, start by creating the following table of data using an **Enter data** query and name the table **Annual Contract Value**:

Customer	TCV	Years
1	$6,000	1
2	$25,000	5
3	$2,000	0.5

Table 7.6: Customer contract data.

Alternatively, import the **Annual Contract Value** sheet from the Excel spreadsheet, **Chapter7_Data.xlsx** which can be found in the GitHub repository for this book: https://github.com/gdeckler/DAX-For-Humans/tree/main/book.

ACV is straightforward to implement as a measure except for the fact that the total needs to be the average of the individual customer ACVs. To implement, create the following measure:

```
ACV =
    VAR __Table =
        ADDCOLUMNS(
            'Annual Contract Value',
            "__ACV", DIVIDE( [TCV], MAX( [Years], 1 ) )
        )
    VAR __Customers = COUNTROWS( 'Annual Contract Value' )
    VAR __ACV = SUMX( __Table, [__ACV] )
    VAR __Result = DIVIDE( __ACV, __Customers, 0 )
RETURN
    __Result
```

Create a **Table** visual like the following to visualize the results:

Customer	Sum of TCV	Sum of Years	ACV
1	$6,000	1.00	6,000.00
2	$25,000	5.00	5,000.00
3	$3,000	0.50	3,000.00
Total	**$34,000**	**6.50**	**4,666.67**

Figure 7.5: ACV for three customers.

The ACV measure starts by adding a column to the base **Annual Contract Value** table called **__ACV**. This is simply the **TCV** column value divided by the number of years of the contract with the exception that any contract that is less than a year is considered to be 1 year since ACV is an annual measure.

We do this using the alternative form of the **MAX** function which returns the maximum between two specified values. We can then proceed to calculate the ACV by counting the number of customers being evaluated, summing the **__ACV** column in the **__Table** variable and then dividing the **__ACV** variable by the number of customers (**__Customers**).

For individual rows in the **Table** visual, the **__Customers** variable is **1** and there is only a single row in the **__Table** variable. Thus, the end result is the same as if the formula was simply:

```
ACV Simple =
    VAR __Years = MAX( 'Annual Contract Value'[Years] )
    VAR __YearsFinal = IF( __Years < 1, 1, __Years )
    VAR __TCV = SUM( 'Annual Contract Value'[TCV] )
    VAR __Result = DIVIDE( __TCV, __YearsFinal )
RETURN
    __Result
```

However, the total in this case is **6,800**, which is incorrect.

Let's now turn our attention to calculating another customer metric, sales after event.

Sales After Event

In some cases, businesses may wish to track specific sales, such as any new sales that occur after specific events. These events may be a visit from a salesperson or the start of a particular marketing campaign. Such metrics can help organizations evaluate the overall effectiveness of various sales and marketing activities towards customers.

In the scenario presented here, a business wishes to report on sales for any new products sold at a store after a visit from a sales manager. To qualify, that item must not have been sold at that store for a certain period, in this scenario, 100 days. To prepare for this calculation, create a table called **Sales** using the following data in an **Enter data** query:

Date	Store	Product	Qty
Saturday, February 1, 2025	1	Alpha	1
Sunday, February 2, 2025	1	Bravo	1
Monday, February 3, 2025	1	Alpha	1
Tuesday, February 4, 2025	1	Bravo	1
Wednesday, February 5, 2025	1	Charlie	2
Thursday, February 6, 2025	1	Alpha	1
Friday, February 7, 2025	1	Bravo	1
Saturday, February 8, 2025	1	Charlie	1
Saturday, February 1, 2025	2	Charlie	1
Sunday, February 2, 2025	2	Bravo	1
Monday, February 3, 2025	2	Charlie	1
Tuesday, February 4, 2025	2	Bravo	1
Wednesday, February 5, 2025	2	Alpha	1

Date	Store	Product	Qty
Thursday, February 6, 2025	2	Alpha	3
Friday, February 7, 2025	2	Bravo	1
Saturday, February 8, 2025	2	Alpha	2

Table 7.7: Sales data for stores.

In addition, create a **Visits** table using the following data in an **Enter data** query:

Date	Store
Tuesday, February 4, 2025	1
Monday, February 3, 2025	2

Table 7.8: Visit data for stores.

Alternatively, import the **Sales** and **Visits** sheets from the Excel spreadsheet, **Chapter7_Data.xlsx** which can be found in the GitHub repository for this book: https://github.com/gdeckler/DAX-For-Humans/tree/main/book.

Create a relationship between the two tables based on the **Store** columns in each table:

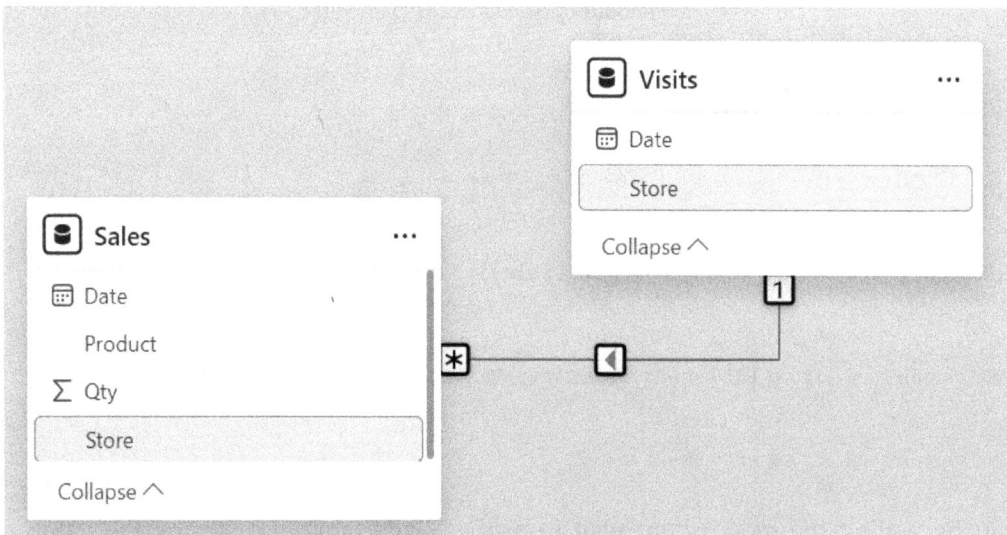

Figure 7.6: Relationship between Sales and Visits tables.

Now create the following measure:

```
Sales After Visit =
    VAR __MostRecentVisit = MAX( 'Visits'[Date] )
    VAR __SalesAfterVisit =
        ADDCOLUMNS(
            ADDCOLUMNS(
                SUMMARIZE(
                    FILTER('Sales', [Date] > __MostRecentVisit),
                    'Sales'[Product],
                    "__Qty", SUM( 'Sales'[Qty] ),
                    "__Date", MIN( 'Sales'[Date] )
                ),
                "__LastSale",
                    MAXX(
                        FILTER(
                            'Sales',
                            [Date] <= __MostRecentVisit &&
                                [Product] = EARLIER( [Product] )
                        ),
                        [Date]
                    )
            ),
            "__Diff",( [__Date] - [__LastSale]) * 1.
        )
    VAR __Result = SUMX( FILTER( __SalesAfterVisit, [__Diff] >= 100 ), [__Qty] )
RETURN
    __Result
```

We start by getting the most recent visit from the **Visits** table and storing the value in the **__MostRecentVisit** variable. Note that this assumes at least some context comes from the **Visits** table when calculating the measure since the relationship between the **Visits** table and **Sales** table is not bi-directional.

Next, we create our virtual table variable __**SalesAfterVisit** by first using **SUMMARIZE** along with **FILTER** to create a summarized table of **Sales** with just the rows after the __**MostRecentVisit** grouped by **Product** with two additional columns, __**Qty**, the **SUM** of the **Qty** column in the **Sales** table and __**Date**, the minimum (**MIN**) date within the **Sales** table for each **Product**. Note that this minimum date respects the **FILTER** clause and thus the minimum date here is the minimum date after the __**MostRecentVisit**.

We then add two additional columns to the table. The first column is __**LastSale**. This column holds the last sale of a product prior to __**MostRecentVisit**. This is done using **MAXX** coupled with the correct **FILTER** statement. In this case, the **FILTER** function filters out rows that are greater than the date stored in __**MostRecentVisit** as well as any rows that are not the current **Product**. The **EARLIER** function is used here for brevity instead of creating nested **VAR** statements.

The second column is the __**Diff** column which is simply the number of days between the __**Date** column (the minimum date for a product sale after __**MostRecentVisit**) and the __**LastSale** column. Finally, we calculate the __**Result** by filtering the __**SalesAfterVisit** table where the __**Diff** column is greater than or equal to **100** days and summing the __**Qty** column.

To visualize the data, create a **Table** visual with the **Store** column from the **Visits** table, the **Product** column from the **Sales** table and the **Sales After Visit** measure.

Store	Product	Sales After Visit
2	Alpha	6
1	Charlie	3
Total		

Figure 7.7: Sales After Visit measure.

Note that the **Total** line displays a blank value. This is easily correctable by creating the following measure:

```
Sales After Visit Total =

    VAR __Table =

        SUMMARIZE(
```

```
        'Sales',

        'Visits'[Store],

        'Sales'[Product],

        "__Value", [Sales After Visit]

    )

    VAR __Result = SUMX( __Table, [__Value] )
RETURN

    __Result
```

This code should look familiar as it is patterned after the *Measure Totals* section from *Chapter 2, More Core Concepts*.

This completes our exploration of customer metrics and KPIs.

Summary

In this chapter, we explored numerous scenarios dealing with customers. This included identifying new, lost, and returning customers as well as calculating net promoter score, churn rate, lifetime value, and acquisition costs. In addition, we explored support metrics such as open tickets and average time to close. Next, we calculated customer funnel drop-off rates and explored how to report on different products being ordered together. Finally, we wrapped up the chapter with calculations for annual contract value (ACV) as well as sales after an event.

Throughout this chapter, almost every calculation has essentially been a version of the *A DAX Pattern to Solve Most Problems* from *Chapter 1, Introducing DAX*. Most of the formulas use the basic pattern of creating virtual tables that group and/or filter the base data and then use X aggregators across those tables. This pattern continues as we explore human resource metrics and KPIs in the next chapter.

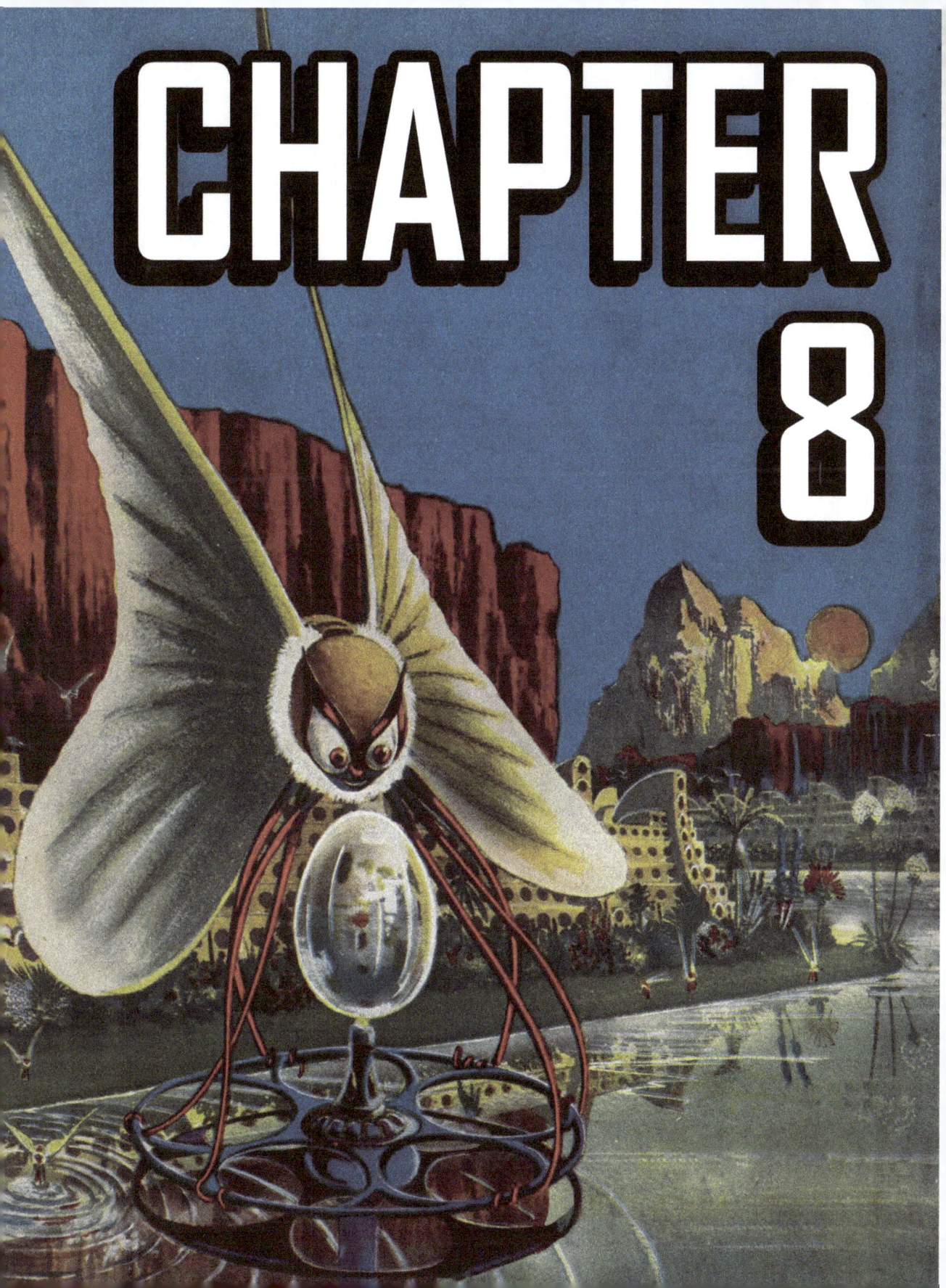

CHAPTER 8

8

Human Resources

Just as customers are critical to most businesses and organizations, so too are employees since employees are the driving force behind daily operations, innovation, and long-term growth. Employees bring diverse skills, knowledge, and experiences that shape company culture and productivity. When employees are engaged and motivated, they collaborate effectively, create value for stakeholders, and help build a competitive advantage. The insights and creativity of people employed within an organization often lead to process improvements, new product ideas, and customer relationship enhancements which are all critical to an organization's ability to thrive and adapt in a rapidly changing business landscape.

Tracking employee metrics and KPIs is crucial because it provides a clear, data-driven way to evaluate how well employees are contributing to organizational goals as well as how well the organization is treating its employees. By identifying specific, measurable metrics, companies can better understand strengths and weaknesses within their workforce as well as what can be done to enhance or improve employee engagement. Such tracking not only highlights areas requiring improvement but also helps managers recognize high performers and align resources effectively. Ultimately, well-structured KPI tracking promotes accountability, fosters a culture of continuous improvement, and helps organizations remain agile and competitive.

This chapter covers many different employee KPIs that can help organizations evaluate and track their workforce. We start with employee turnover rate.

Employee Turnover Rate

Employee turnover rate (ETR) is one of the most important employment KPIs to track since a high ETR has many negative impacts on an organization such as the loss of organizational knowledge, loss of productivity, and replacement costs.

The formula for calculating ETR is quite simple:

$$ETR = (\text{Employees leaving} / \text{Average employees}) * 100$$

Importantly, ETR is calculated for specific time periods such as annually or quarterly for example. Therefore, to get started, create the following **Dates** table:

```
Dates =

    VAR __Calendar =

        ADDCOLUMNS(

            CALENDAR( DATE( 2020, 1, 1 ), DATE( 2025, 12, 31 ) ),

            "Quarter", QUARTER( [Date] ),

            "Month", FORMAT( [Date], "mmmm" ),

            "MonthSort", MONTH( [Date] ),

            "Year", YEAR( [Date] )

        )

RETURN

    __Calendar
```

Be sure to set the **Sort by column** for the **Month** column to the **MonthSort** column.

Next, create the following table to hold measures:

$$Calculations = \{ 0 \}$$

Use an **Enter data** query to create an **Employees** table:

Employee	Hire Date	Term Date	Annual Salary
Greg	3/3/2020	12/31/9999	100000
Carl	12/4/2021	12/31/9999	150000
Sandy	6/17/2022	12/31/9999	120000
Laurie	8/5/2022	12/31/9999	75000
Dan	9/10/2022	2/17/2024	45000
Penny	1/12/2023	12/31/9999	110000
Julie	3/12/2023	12/31/9999	90000
Tammy	4/16/2023	12/31/9999	80000

Employee	Hire Date	Term Date	Annual Salary
Pam	8/7/2023	12/3/2023	70000
Mike	3/25/2024	12/31/9999	60000
Paul	3/25/2024	12/31/9999	100000
Lori	3/25/2024	12/31/9999	150000
Cayla	3/25/2024	12/31/9999	90000
Bob	3/25/2024	12/31/9999	100000
Pi-Jou	3/25/2024	12/31/9999	110000
David	3/25/2024	12/31/9999	80000

Table 8.1: Employee data.

Alternatively, import the **Employees** sheet from the Excel spreadsheet, **Chapter8_Data.xlsx** which can be found in the GitHub repository for this book: https://github.com/gdeckler/DAX-For-Humans/tree/main/book.

Some HR systems use a blank value or null value for the termination date of employees who are still actively employed. This approach signals that no termination event has taken place and prevents accidental processing of an end-of-employment record. Alternatively, other systems use a "dummy" or "sentinel" date such as 12/31/9999 as a placeholder in the termination date field. This method ensures that every record has a value in the date field, which can simplify certain standardized reporting and system logic. However, the specific practice often depends on the HR platform's data model, reporting requirements, and organizational preferences. Here we are using a sentinel date of **12/31/9999** for the **Term Date** column.

Ensure that the **Hire Date** and **Term Date** columns are of type **Date** and that there is no relationship between the **Dates** table and the **Employees** table.

Now, create the following measure in the **Calculations** table:

```
ETR =

    VAR __Start = MIN( 'Dates'[Date] )

    VAR __End = MAX( 'Dates'[Date] )
```

```
VAR __StartingEmployees =

    COUNTROWS(

        FILTER(

            ALL( 'Employees' ),

            [Hire Date] <= __Start && [Term Date] > __Start

        )

    )

VAR __EndingEmployees =

    COUNTROWS(

        FILTER(

            ALL( 'Employees' ),

            [Hire Date] <= __End && [Term Date] > __End

        )

    )

VAR __TermedEmployees =

    COUNTROWS(

        FILTER(

            ALL( 'Employees' ),

            [Term Date] >= __Start && [Term Date] <= __End

        )

    )

VAR __AverageEmployees = ( __StartingEmployees + __EndingEmployees ) / 2

VAR __Result = DIVIDE( __TermedEmployees, __AverageEmployees, 0 ) + 0

RETURN

    __Result
```

Format this measure as a percentage and hide the **Value** column in the **Calculations** table.

This measure starts with getting the minimum (**__Start**) and maximum (**__End**) dates within the current context. Next, the number of employees at the start of the period (**__StartingEmployees**) and at the end of the period (**__EndingEmployees**) are calculated using **COUNTROWS** along with the appropriate filters. In both cases, the **ALL** function is used to ensure that all employees employed at the time are counted since employees are likely to have hire and leave dates that do not fall within the current period. With the configuration of having no relationship between the **Dates** table and **Employees** table, this is technically unnecessary, but better safe than sorry.

Similarly, we next calculate the number of termed employees (**__TermedEmployees**) again using **COUNTROWS** and **FILTER**. We can then find the average number of employees (**__AverageEmployees**) employed during the period by adding **__StartingEmployees** and **__EndingEmployees** and then dividing by **2**. Using a simple average is generally sufficient for most normal scenarios although there may be extreme edge cases where this could skew the results. Finally, the **__Result** is calculated by dividing the **__TermedEmployees** by the **__AverageEmployees**.

It should be noted that using a sentinel date of 12/31/9999 simplifies the filtering required. If these values were blank or null, additional filtering would be required to account for these blank or null values.

Place the **Year** and **Quarter** columns from the **Dates** table into the **X-axis** field well of a **Line chart** visual as well as the **ETR** measure in the **Y-axis** field well to display a visualization such as the following:

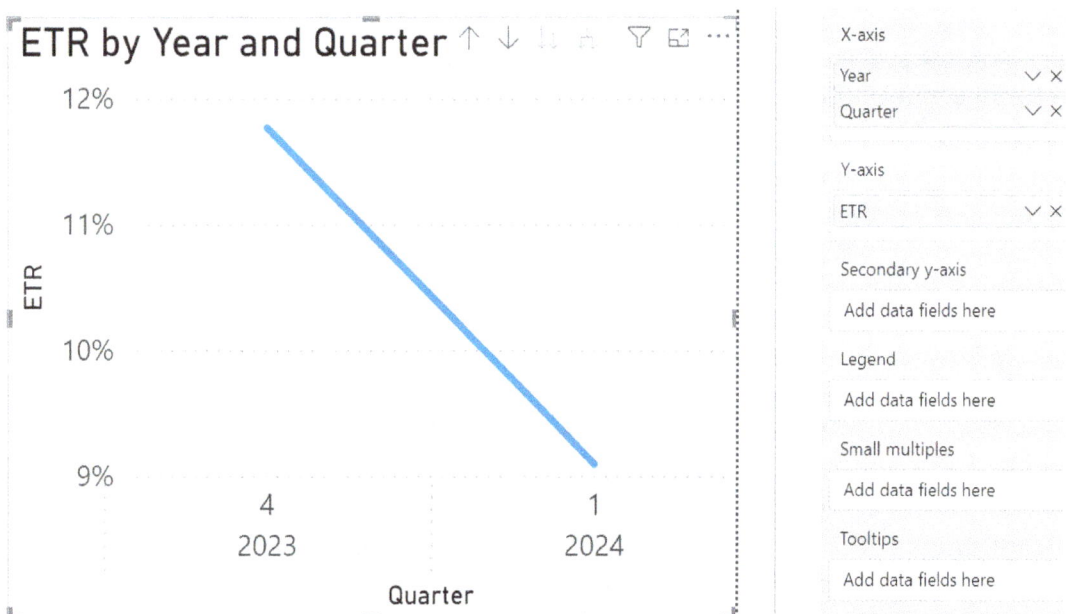

Figure 8.1: ETR measure in a line chart.

Note that the **ETR** measure only returns values for quarter 4 of 2023 and quarter 1 of 2024, the quarters when at least one employee was terminated. This is because if the **__TermedEmployees** variable in the DAX measure evaluates to **BLANK**, then the **ETR** measure returns **BLANK** and is not displayed in the line chart by default. To modify this behavior, you can add "**+ 0**" to either the **__TermedEmployees** variable or the **__Result** variable such as:

```
VAR __Result = DIVIDE( __TermedEmployees, __AverageEmployees, 0 ) + 0
```

You may think it odd that a function like **COUNTROWS** would return **BLANK** and not 0 but this is indeed the case. If the **FILTER** clause returns **BLANK** due to not holding any rows, then using **COUNTROWS** on that resulting table also returns **BLANK**.

Now that we have demonstrated employee turnover rate (ETR), let's next take a look at absenteeism.

Absenteeism

Absenteeism measures the amount of time employees are unexpectedly unavailable for work. It is used here to distinguish between planned absences such as personal time off (PTO), holidays, family leave, and long-term disability versus employees calling in sick or simply not showing up for work. Absenteeism is an important metric to track both at an individual level and a department level since chronic absenteeism is a drain on overall organizational productivity.

Absenteeism is generally measured in hours or days. The basic formula is to simply divide the number of hours or days absent by the total number of working hours or days within the same period. However, calculating absenteeism becomes more complex when calculating against a department or business unit since employees may be hired or leave during the period in question. In addition, absences may span different date periods, which also complicates the calculation.

To get started calculating absenteeism, first complete the setup for the previous section, *Employee Turnover Rate*, including the **Dates** table, **Calculations** table and **Employee** table. Next, create the following **Absences** table using an **Enter data** query:

Employee	Start Date	End Date
Dan	1/17/2024	1/19/2024
Mike	6/3/2024	6/4/2024
Mike	7/1/2024	7/3/2024

Employee	Start Date	End Date
David	3/4/2024	3/6/2024
David	4/3/2024	4/5/2024
David	5/6/2024	5/8/2024
David	6/3/2024	6/6/2024
David	7/3/2024	7/5/2024
David	12/30/2024	1/3/2025

Table 8.2: Absentee data.

Alternatively, import the **Absences** sheet from the Excel spreadsheet, **Chapter8_Data.xlsx** which can be found in the GitHub repository for this book: https://github.com/gdeckler/DAX-For-Humans/tree/main/book.

Create a one-to-many relationship between the **Employees** table and the **Absences** table. Your data model should look like the following:

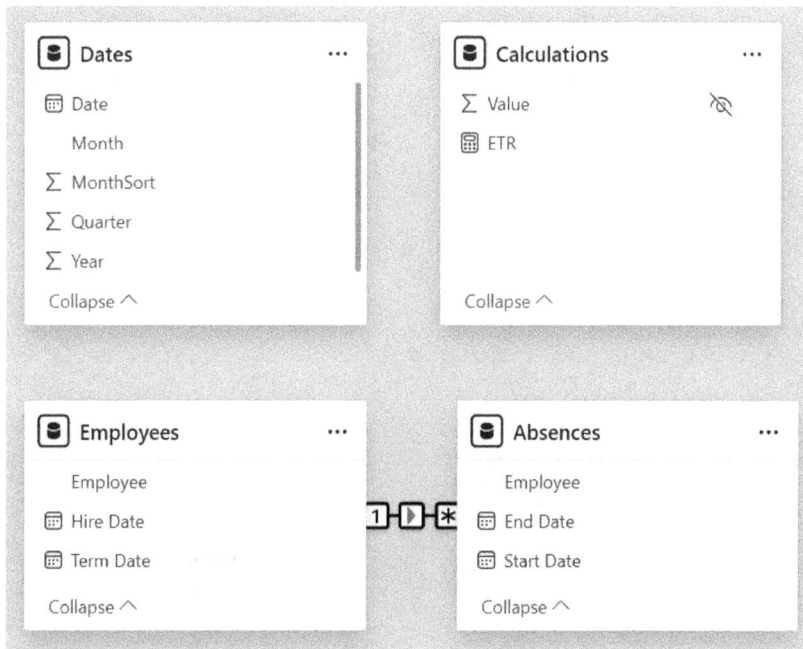

Figure 8.2: Absenteeism data model.

Next, create the following measure in the **Calculations** table:

```
Absenteeism =
    VAR __Start = MIN( 'Dates'[Date] )

    VAR __End = MAX( 'Dates'[Date] )

    VAR __EmployeeContext = SELECTCOLUMNS( 'Employees', "__Employee", [Employee] )

    VAR __Employees =
        ADDCOLUMNS(
            ADDCOLUMNS(
                FILTER(
                    ALL( 'Employees'),

                    [Employee] IN __EmployeeContext &&

                    [Hire Date] <= __End && [Term Date] >= __Start
                ),

                "__Min", IF( [Hire Date] > __Start, [Hire Date], __Start ),

                "__Max", IF( [Term Date] < __End, [Term Date], __End )
            ),

            "__WorkDays", NETWORKDAYS( [__Min], [__Max] )
        )

    VAR __TotalDays = SUMX( __Employees, [__WorkDays] )

    VAR __Absences =
        ADDCOLUMNS(
            ADDCOLUMNS(
                FILTER(
                    ALL( 'Absences'),

                    [Employee] IN __EmployeeContext &&

                    (
                        ( [Start Date] >= __Start && [End Date] <= __End )

                        ||

                        ( [Start Date] < __Start && [End Date] >= __Start &&
```

```
                              [End Date] <= __End

                        )

                        ||

                        ( [Start Date] >= __Start && [Start Date] <= __End

                              && [End Date] > __End

                        )

                        ||

                        ( [Start Date] <= __Start && [End Date] >= __End )

                    )

                ),

                "__Min", IF( [Start Date] < __Start, __Start, [Start Date] ),

                "__Max", IF( [End Date] > __End, __End, [End Date] )

            ),

            "__WorkDays", NETWORKDAYS( [__Min], [__Max] )

        )

    VAR __AbsentDays = SUMX( __Absences, [__WorkDays] )

    VAR __Result = DIVIDE( __AbsentDays, __TotalDays, 0 ) + 0

RETURN

    __Result
```

Format the **Absenteeism** measure as a percentage with two decimal places. Create a **Card** visualization and place the **Absenteeism** measure in the **Card** visual's **Fields** field well.

Next, create a **Matrix** visualization. Place the **Employee** column from the **Employees** table in the **Rows** field well, the **Absenteeism** measure in the **Values** field well, and the **Year** column from the **Dates** table in the **Columns** field well. As you can see, this **Absenteeism** measure functions at the individual level as well as at the group level and different date periods.

The complexity in this calculation comes from ensuring that only active employees are considered and only for the days that those employees are active within the period as well as covering the four different possible absence scenarios.

The four different absence scenarios can be visualized as follows where the green squares represent non-absent days and the red squares represent absent days:

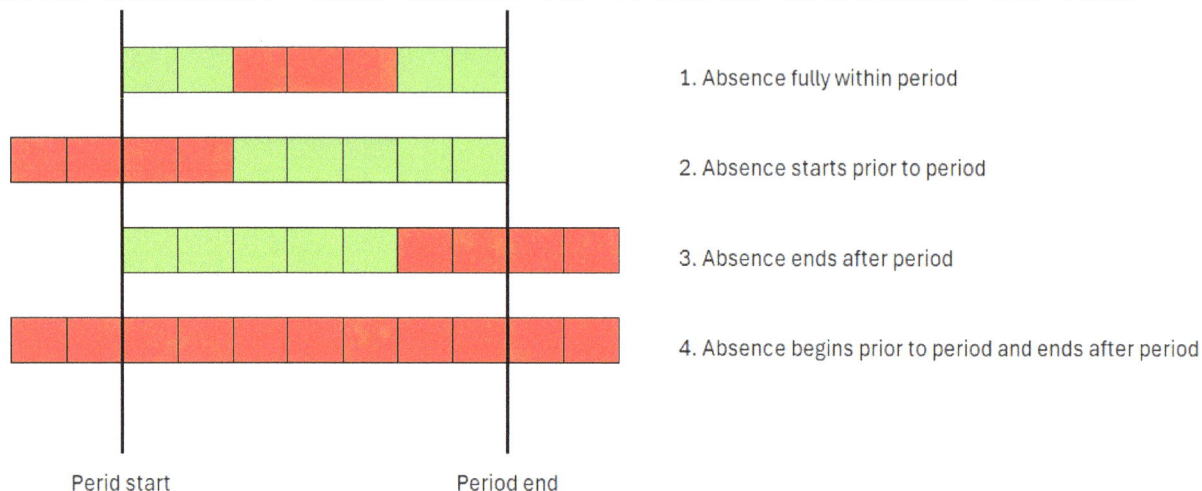

1. Absence fully within period

2. Absence starts prior to period

3. Absence ends after period

4. Absence begins prior to period and ends after period

Perid start   Period end

Figure 8.3: Four different types of absences.

For the calculation to work, each of these four scenarios must be accounted for within the measure's logic.

To tackle these challenges, we start by simply getting the minimum date in context (__Start) and the maximum date in context (__End). These dates represent the period's start and period's end.

Next, we must tackle only analyzing employees for the days they were active within the period. To do this, we first create a single column table, __EmployeeContext, which is simply a list of the employees currently in context. We get this table because we wish to preserve the filter context of employees but remove all other context when calculating the __Employees table variable. This is not strictly necessary since no other tables, such as the **Dates** table, have relationships with our **Employees** table, but this is done for illustrative purposes to account for more complex semantic models which may have such relationships.

Calculating the __Employees table variable involves three steps. First, we use **FILTER** and remove all filter contexts on the **Employees** table by using the **ALL** function. We reinsert the filter context from the **Employees** table by using a filter clause where we use the **IN** operator to ensure that we filter down to the rows in the **Employees** table where the value in the **Employee** column matches a row in our __EmployeeContext table. The second filter clause ensures that the employee was active during the period in question with a **Hire Date** that is less than or equal to the period end (__End) and a **Term Date** that is greater than or equal to the period start (__Start).

The second step is to calculate the correct minimum and maximum dates for each employee within the period. For example, if an employee was hired three days after the start of the period, then we want to use the employee's **Hire Date** as the minimum date since the two days at the start of the period should not be counted as days not absent.

Similarly, if an employee leaves the company four days prior to the end of the period, then we want to use the **Term Date** for that employee versus the period's end date. These are the calculations performed for the **__Min** and **__Max** columns within the first **ADDCOLUMNS** function that wraps our **FILTER** function.

The third step is using our two new **__Min** and **__Max** columns to calculate the total days the employee was active within the period. This is the **__WorkDays** column in the outer **ADDCOLUMNS** function. The **NETWORKDAYS** function is used to calculate this number. The **NETWORKDAYS** function is useful here as it excludes weekends (Saturday and Sunday) by default and can also exclude holiday dates.

While not used in this calculation, the fourth parameter of the **NETWORKDAYS** function controls excluded holiday dates. This parameter is simply a single column table of dates that should be excluded as holidays. The third parameter controls what is considered a weekend. There are many different possible values for this as shown in the following table:

Parameter Value	Days excluded as weekends
1 or omitted	Saturday, Sunday
2	Sunday, Monday
3	Monday, Tuesday
4	Tuesday, Wednesday
5	Wednesday, Thursday
6	Thursday, Friday
7	Friday, Saturday
11	Sunday only
12	Monday only
13	Tuesday only
14	Wednesday only

15	Thursday only
16	Friday only
17	Saturday only

Table 8.3: NETWORKDAYS fourth parameter settings.

Note that, unfortunately, there is no value that does not exclude at least one day. This means that businesses that operate seven days a week are unable to use the **NETWORKDAYS** function to calculate working days. Instead, the following calculation could be used in these circumstances:

$$([\_\_Max] - [\_\_Min]) * 1.$$

If you still need to exclude holiday dates, then the following could be used instead:

```
COUNTROWS(
    EXCEPT(
        GENERATESERIES( [__Min], [__Max], 1 ),
        {
            DATE( 2024, 12, 25 ),
            DATE( 2025, 1, 1 )
        }
    )
)
```

We can then total up all the working days for all employees in context within the period (__**TotalDays**) by simply using **SUMX** to sum the __**WorkDays** column within the __**Employees** table variable.

The calculations for the __**Absences** table variable and __**AbsentDays** variable follow a similar pattern as the __**Employees** table variable and __**TotalDays** variable. The main difference is the filter clauses are more complex to account for the four different absence types. These are the four filter clauses separated by OR logic (| |).

Once the __**AbsentDays** are calculated, we can then simply divide the __**AbsentDays** by the __**TotalDays** to arrive at our __**Result**. Note that the __**Result** calculation includes a **+0**. This ensures that a value is returned for every calculation. This **+0** can be excluded from the formula such that only employees with absences would be included in the **Matrix** visualization.

Bradford Factor

The Bradford Factor is another common metric used in relation to absenteeism. The Bradford Factor weighs the number of days absent based upon the frequency of absences. The assumption is that frequent unplanned absences, even if they are short, are more disruptive than more infrequent, longer unplanned absences. The equation for the Bradford Factor is the following:

$$\text{Bradford Factor} = \text{Instances}^2 * \text{Days Absent}$$

Here again, we still need the number of days absent so we can reuse much of our original absenteeism measure.

```
Bradford Factor =
    VAR __Start = MIN( 'Dates'[Date] )
    VAR __End = MAX( 'Dates'[Date] )
    VAR __EmployeeContext = DISTINCT( 'Employees'[Employee] )
    VAR __Absences =
        ADDCOLUMNS(
            ADDCOLUMNS(
                FILTER(
                    ALL( 'Absences'),
                    [Employee] IN __EmployeeContext &&
                        [Start Date] <= __End && [End Date] >= __Start
                ),
                "__Min", MAX( __Start, [Start Date] ),
                "__Max", MIN( __End, [End Date] )
            ),
            "__WorkDays", NETWORKDAYS( [__Min], [__Max] )
        )
    VAR __AbsentDays = SUMX( __Absences, [__WorkDays] )
    VAR __Instances = COUNTROWS( __Absences )
    VAR __Result = __Instances^2 * __AbsentDays
RETURN
    __Result
```

Here the __Start, __End, and __AbsentDays calculations are identical to the **Absenteeism** measure. The __**EmployeeContext** and __**Absences** variables use alternate DAX and logic suggested by patron **Alexis Olson**. This includes using **DISTINCT** instead of **SELECTEDCOLUMNS**, using the alternative forms of the **MIN** and **MAX** functions instead of using **IF** statements and finally a greatly simplified logic to identify relevant absences. This logic is that the absence should either begin before or when the period ends or ends after or when the period starts.

The calculation for the __**Instances** is simply a **COUNTROWS** over the __**Absences** virtual table. For the __**Result**, we use the exponentiation operator (^) to square the __**Instances** and then multiply by __**AbsentDays**. We could instead have used the **POWER** function such as:

```
VAR __Result = POWER( __Instances, 2 ) * __AbsentDays
```

This completes our exploration of absenteeism calculations. Let's now move on to employee engagement.

Employee Satisfaction

Employee satisfaction or engagement is an important metric for human capital management or human resource departments to regularly monitor and report on. Employees that are more satisfied at work tend to be more productive and less likely to quit.

There is no single, universal way of measuring employee satisfaction. Numerous different methods exist such as the Gallup Workplace Audit (GWA), Employee Satisfaction (ESAT), Employee Engagement Index (EEI), and Utrecht Work Engagement Scale (UWES). However, all these methods rely on employees answering a survey and ranking how satisfied they are for each survey question or area.

For our employee satisfaction calculation, we will use a generic survey system that has three questions numbered 1 to 3 and a ranking from 1 to 5 where 1 indicates low satisfaction and 5 indicates high satisfaction. Use an **Enter data** query to create a table called **Satisfaction** with the following data:

Employee	Question	Answer
Greg	1	5
Greg	2	5
Greg	3	5

Employee	Question	Answer
Carl	1	4
Carl	2	4
Carl	3	4
Sandy	1	3
Sandy	2	3
Sandy	3	3
Laurie	1	2
Laurie	2	2
Laurie	3	2
Dan	1	1
Dan	2	1
Dan	3	1
Penny	1	4
Penny	2	3
Penny	3	2
Julie	1	2
Julie	2	3
Julie	3	4
Tammy	1	3

Employee	Question	Answer
Tammy	2	2
Tammy	3	2
Pam	1	4
Pam	2	3
Mike	1	3
Mike	2	4

Table 8.4: Survey data.

Alternatively, import the **Satisfaction** sheet from the Excel spreadsheet, **Chapter8_Data.xlsx** which can be found in the GitHub repository for this book: https://github.com/gdeckler/DAX-For-Humans/tree/main/book.

Note that not all questions were answered by all survey respondents. If you have not already completed the *Employee Turnover Rate* section in this chapter, please do so now and create the **Employees** table. Create a relationship between the **Employee** column of the **Employees** table and the **Satisfaction** table. The relationship should be one (**Employees**) to many (**Satisfaction**).

Now create the following **Satisfaction** measure:

```
Satisfaction =

    VAR __TopRating = 5

    VAR __Count = COUNTROWS( 'Satisfaction' )

    VAR __MaxScore = __Count * __TopRating

    VAR __Score = SUMX( 'Satisfaction', [Answer] )

    VAR __Result = DIVIDE( __Score, __MaxScore, 0 )

RETURN

    __Result
```

This calculation is quite straightforward. The top rating is **5** so we store that in the **__TopRating** variable. Therefore, the maximum potential score would be if all survey questions were answered with the top rating of **5**. Thus, we simply need to count the rows in the **Satisfaction** table using **COUNTROWS** and multiply this by **__TopRating**. We can then sum the **Answer** column in the **Satisfaction** table and divide this number (**__Score**) by the maximum possible score, **__MaxScore**.

Create the following additional six measures as well:

```
Survey Response % =

    VAR __Employees = COUNTROWS( DISTINCT( 'Employees'[Employee] ) )

    VAR __Respondents = COUNTROWS( DISTINCT( 'Satisfaction'[Employee] ) )

    VAR __Result = DIVIDE( __Respondents, __Employees, 0 )
RETURN

    __Result

        Survey Respondent Count = COUNTROWS( DISTINCT( 'Satisfaction'[Employee] ) )


                    Survey Average = AVERAGE( 'Satisfaction'[Answer] )


                Survey Median = MEDIAN( 'Satisfaction'[Answer] )


            Survey Standard Deviation = STDEV.P( Satisfaction[Answer] )


                Survey Variance = VAR.P( Satisfaction[Answer] )
```

Format the **Satisfaction** and **Survey Response** % measures as percentages with two decimal places.

Create a **Table** visual with the **Employee** column from the **Employees** table and the **Satisfaction** measure. Create **Card** visuals for **Survey Respondent Count**, **Survey Response %**, **Survey Average**, **Survey Median**, **Survey Standard Deviation**, and **Survey Variance**. Finally, create a **Matrix** visual with **Question** in the **Rows** field well, **Answer** in the **Columns** field well, and **Survey Respondent Count** in the **Values** field well.

Employee ▲	Satisfaction
Carl	80.00%
Dan	20.00%
Greg	100.00%
Julie	60.00%
Laurie	40.00%
Mike	73.33%
Pam	66.67%
Penny	60.00%
Sandy	60.00%
Tammy	46.67%
Total	**60.67%**

10
Survey Respondent Count

62.50%
Survey Response %

3.03
Survey Average

3.00
Survey Median

Question	1	2	3	4	5	**Total**
1	1	2	3	3	1	**10**
2	1	2	4	2	1	**10**
3	1	3	2	3	1	**10**
Total	**1**	**4**	**6**	**5**	**1**	**10**

1.14
Survey Standard Deviation

1.30
Survey Variance

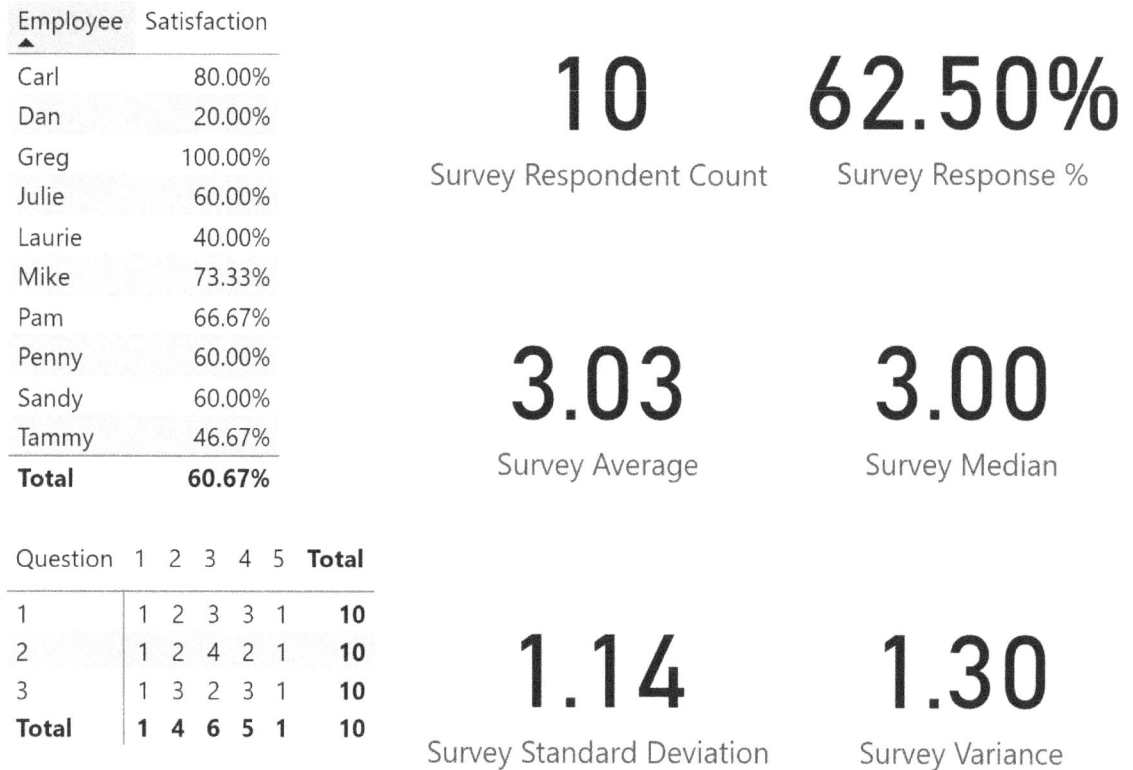

Figure 8.4: Employee satisfaction.

Another popular method of evaluating employee survey responses is to analyze the minimum scores for employee responses. This method is implemented using the following metric:

```
Satisfaction 2 =
    VAR __CurrentScore = MAX( 'Satisfaction'[Answer] )

    VAR __RespondentCount = COUNTROWS( DISTINCT( ALL( 'Satisfaction'[Employee]) ) )

    VAR __MinScores =
        SUMMARIZE(
            ALL( 'Satisfaction' ),
            [Employee],
            "__MinScore", MIN( 'Satisfaction'[Answer] )
        )

    VAR __ScoreCount = COUNTROWS( FILTER( __MinScores, [__MinScore] = __CurrentScore ) )

    VAR __Result = DIVIDE( __ScoreCount, __RespondentCount, 0 )
```

RETURN

    __Result

Format this measure as a percentage with 2 decimal places and place this measure in a **Table** visual along with an un-summarized **Answer** column from the **Satisfaction** table. Note that 50% of the survey respondents had a minimum score of 1 or 2. Also note that the total is incorrect so either turn the total off or you can fix it using the techniques demonstrated in *Chapter 2, Measure Totals*.

This measure starts by getting the current score in context, __**CurrentScore**. Next, we calculate the total respondent count using the **ALL** function to ensure that all survey respondents are counted. We can then create a table of minimum scores per respondent. This is the __**MinScores** table variable. **SUMMARIZE** is used across the entire **Satisfaction** table, grouped by the **Employee** column, and then the __**MinScore** column stores the minimum **Answer** for each employee.

We then calculate the number of employees that have a __**MinScore** that is equal to the __**CurrentScore**. This is done by using the **FILTER** function to filter the __**MinScores** table to the rows where __**MinScore** equals __**CurrentScore**. We then use **SELECTCOLUMNS** to select only the **Employee** column, retrieve the unique employees using **DISTINCT**, and then simply count the rows using **COUNTROWS**. Finally, we use the **DIVDE** function to divide the __**ScoreCount** by the total number of respondents, __**RespondentCount**.

This concludes our analysis of employee satisfaction. Next, we turn our attention to calculating full time equivalents.

Human Capital Value Added

Human Capital Value Added (HCVA) measures the average profit each employee contributes to an organization within a specific time period. This metric is distinct from Revenue Per Employee (RPE), which is the average amount of revenue per employee. HCVA is calculated using the following formula:

$$HCVA = \frac{(Revenue - (Total\ Cost - Employment\ Costs))}{FTE}$$

Revenue, Total Cost, and Employment costs would typically come from financial accounting and human capital management systems. **FTE** stands for **Full Time Equivalent**.

Organizations employing part-time employees often find it beneficial to understand how the hours worked by these part-time employees translate to an equivalent number of full-time employees or full-time equivalents (FTEs). The FTE metric is used in many KPIs, metrics, and business processes such as project scheduling, budget analysis, as well as the analysis of office square footage, revenues, and profits. However, the calculation of FTE is not only for part-time employees, but also for organizations that have individuals leave or join the organization somewhere within the period being evaluated.

The calculation for FTE is straightforward. The general formula is:

$$FTE = \frac{(\text{Part time hours } + \text{ Full time hours })}{\text{Maximum full time hours in period}}$$

One might note that while the part-time and full-time hours are separated in the formula, the formula can be simplified to just:

$$FTE = \frac{\text{Total Hours}}{\text{Maximum full time hours in period}}$$

The first step in calculating this metric is to determine the period being evaluated and the maximum full-time hours in that period. For example, one might use a year as the period and the maximum full-time hours in that period to be 2,080 hours, which is 40 hours per week for 52 weeks. However, this does not account for personal time off (PTO), sick time, and holidays. If we assume three weeks on average per employee for PTO and sick time per year and eight holiday days, then the 2,080 hours becomes 1,896 hours, for example.

Each organization has its own method of calculating the maximum full-time working hours for a year. For our calculations, we use a different method than hours for calculating FTE but since FTE is an important metric in many different calculations then it is important to keep the various methods of calculating FTE in mind.

To prepare for this calculation, if you have not already completed the *Employee Turnover Rate* section of this chapter, please do so now to create the **Employees**, **Dates**, and **Calculation** tables.

For our HCVA calculation, we have the following parameters, an organization with $4,000,000 in revenue and $3,900,000 in total cost for the year 2024. We also assume a benefits cost factor of 1.2. The benefits cost factor is simply a multiplier applied to annual salaries that factors in such things as health insurance, 401K benefits, and other non-wage compensation.

Some benefit cost factors include personal time off, however, that is not included in our cost factor since we are already accounting for that time in our maximum full-time hours. The benefits cost factor is often called the loaded cost factor, and the adjusted employment cost the "fully loaded cost".

With these assumptions, we can calculate HCVA as follows:

HCVA =

```
VAR __Revenue = 4000000

VAR __TotalCost = 3900000

VAR __LoadedCostFactor = 1.2

VAR __Start = DATE( 2024, 1, 1 )

VAR __End = DATE( 2024, 12, 31 )

VAR __TotalDays = ( __End - __Start ) * 1. + 1

VAR __Table =
    ADDCOLUMNS(
        ADDCOLUMNS(
            ADDCOLUMNS(
                ADDCOLUMNS(
                    'Employees',
                    "__Min", IF( [Hire Date] < __Start, __Start, [Hire Date] ),
                    "__Max", IF( [Term Date] > __End, __End, [Term Date] )
                ),
                "__Days", ( [__Max] - [__Min] ) + 1
            ),
            "__Percent", DIVIDE( [__Days], __TotalDays, 0 )
        ),
        "__FullyLoadedCost", [Annual Salary] * [__Percent] * __LoadedCostFactor,
        "__FTE", 1 * [__Percent]
    )

VAR __EmploymentCosts = SUMX( __Table, [__FullyLoadedCost] )

VAR __FTE = SUMX( __Table, [__FTE] )

VAR __Result = DIVIDE( ( __Revenue - ( __TotalCost - __EmploymentCosts ) ), __FTE, 0 )
)
RETURN

    __Result
```

The overall concept for the **HCVA** measure is that it spans an entire year and calculates the employment costs and FTEs by determining what percentage of the year each employee was employed. This percentage is used to adjust their employment costs and FTE amount. We use the annual salaries for each employee posted in the **Employees** table to calculate each employee's fully loaded cost (**__FullyLoadedCost**). For example, if an employee was employed for 50% of the year, then their employment cost would be 50% of their annual salary multiplied by the loaded cost factor of 1.2. Similarly, they would count as .5 FTE.

The heart of this measure is the **__Table** variable, which consists of four nested **ADDCOLUMNS** statements. The innermost **ADDCOLUMNS** calculates the **__Min** and **__Max** columns, which represent the time period in which the employee was employed during the year. Employees that were employed prior to the start of the period get **__Start** as their **__Min** while employees that hired in after the start of the period get their **Hire Date** as **__Min**. The **__Max** column is a similar calculation using **__End** and **Term Date**.

The next **ADDCOLUMNS** statement calculates the number of days between **__Min** and **__Max** as the **__Days** column using simple math since the integer portion of a date is the number of days since December 30th, 1899. The third **ADDCOLUMNS** calculates the percentage of the period worked by each employee using the **__Days** column and the **__TotalDays** variable. Finally, the fully loaded cost (**__FullyLoadedCost**) and FTE (**__FTE**) are calculated for each employee in the outermost **ADDCOLUMNS** function.

Once the **__Table** variable is created, it is a simple matter to use **SUMX** across this table to calculate **__EmploymentCosts** and **__FTE**. These are then used in the standard HCVA formula to calculate the **__Result**.

An alternative method of calculating employment costs and FTE is to calculate these metrics at the beginning and ending of the period and then take the average. This alternative version is as follows:

```
HCVA 2 =
    VAR __Revenue = 4000000
    VAR __TotalCost = 3900000
    VAR __LoadedCostFactor = 1.2
    VAR __Start = DATE( 2024, 1, 1 )
    VAR __End = DATE( 2024, 12, 31 )
    VAR __TableStart = FILTER( 'Employees', [Hire Date] <= __Start )
    VAR __TableEnd = FILTER( 'Employees', [Term Date] >= __End )
    VAR __StartCosts = SUMX( __TableStart, [Annual Salary] ) * __LoadedCostFactor
    VAR __EndCosts = SUMX( __TableEnd, [Annual Salary] ) * __LoadedCostFactor
```

```
    VAR __StartFTE = COUNTROWS( __TableStart )

    VAR __EndFTE = COUNTROWS( __TableEnd )

    VAR __AverageCosts = AVERAGEX( { __StartCosts, __EndCosts }, [Value] )

    VAR __AverageFTE = AVERAGEX( { __StartFTE, __EndFTE }, [Value] )

    VAR __Result = DIVIDE( ( __Revenue - ( __TotalCost - __AverageCosts ) ),
__AverageFTE, 0 )

RETURN

    __Result
```

This method is perhaps not quite as accurate as the previous method but is still generally sufficient overall. Note the table constructors used to compute **__AverageCosts** and **__AverageFTE**. This is a simple, compact way to compute such averages, although a **DIVIDE** statement could have been used as well.

Let's now turn our attention to computing utilization.

Utilization

For certain organizations, such as consulting and professional services firms, there is no more important metric than utilization. Utilization is calculated as a percentage and is simply the amount of billable time divided by the total amount of time possible within a given period. Most often, the inputs to utilization calculations are hours.

To prepare for this calculation, download the **Chapter8_Utilization.xlsx** file from the GitHub repository for this book: https://github.com/gdeckler/DAX-For-Humans/tree/main/book

Import the **Hours** tab from **Chapter8_Utilization.xlsx** as a table named **Hours** and the **Tasks** tab as a table named **Tasks**. For **Tasks**, you may need to edit the query to ensure that the first row is used as headers.

Create a relationship between the **Tasks** table and **Hours** table based upon the **TaskID** columns. If you have a **Dates** table, you can also create a relationship between your **Dates** table and **Hours** table based upon the **Date** columns.

Create the following measure in the **Calculations** table:

```
% Utilization =

    VAR __DailyWorkHours = 8

    VAR __Start = MIN( 'Hours'[Date] )

    VAR __End = MAX( 'Hours'[Date] )
```

```
    VAR __Employees = COUNTROWS( DISTINCT( 'Hours'[EmployeeID] ) )

    VAR __TotalHours = NETWORKDAYS( __Start, __End ) * __DailyWorkHours * __Employees

    VAR __BillableTasks =

        SELECTCOLUMNS(

            FILTER( 'Tasks', 'Tasks'[Category] = "Billable" ),

            "__TaskID", [TaskID]

        )

    VAR __BillableHours =

        SUMX(

            FILTER( 'Hours', [TaskID] IN __BillableTasks ),

            [Hours]

        )

    VAR __Result = DIVIDE( __BillableHours, __TotalHours, 0 ) + 0

RETURN

    __Result
```

Format this measure as a percentage with two decimal points. The **% Utilization** measure starts by defining **__DailyWorkHours** as **8** hours, the number of billable hours in a day. We also define the start and end of the period being evaluated in the **__Start** and **__End** variables respectively.

We now need to calculate the total billable hours within the period in question. We do this by first determining the number of unique employees in the **__Employees** variable using **COUNTROWS** and **DISTINCT**. We then calculate the number of working days in the period using **NETWORKDAYS** and multiply this by **__DailyWorkHours** and **__Employees** to calculate the total number of possible billable hours in the period, **__TotalHours**. For alternatives to the **NETWORKDAYS** function, see the *Absenteeism* section of this chapter.

To get the total amount of billable hours, we first need to get a list of the billable tasks. This is done with the **__BillableTasks** virtual table where we first filter the **Tasks** table for rows where the **Category** column equals "**Billable**" and then select a single column from the result, **TaskID**. We can now calculate the billable hours within the period (**__BillableHours**) using the **__BillableTasks** table as a filter to the **Hours** table using the **IN** operator to filter the **Hours** table to only those rows with a **TaskID** that is billable. Then we sum the **Hours** column using **SUMX**. Finally, we divide the **__BillableHours** by the **__TotalHours**.

Patron Recommendation

Alexis Olson suggests using **SUMMARIZE** instead of **SELECTCOLUMNS** for
__BillableTasks if there are multiple rows for each **TaskID**.

Create a **Card** visual to display the overall **% Utilization** measure. In addition, create a **Table** visual that displays the **Division** column from the **Hours** table along with **% Utilization**.

69.15%

% Utilization

Division	% Utilization
1001 Technology	72.41%
2001 Accounting	68.88%
3001 Management	52.24%
8001 Customer Management	26.50%
9001 Sales	82.22%
Marketing	0.00%
Quality	0.00%
Shared Services	0.00%
Total	**69.15%**

Figure 8.5: % Utilization

This completes our exploration of utilization, we now move on to using the Kaplan-Meier estimator.

Kaplan-Meier estimator

The Kaplan-Meier estimator measures the percentage chance of survival for a population over a specified period. The Kaplan-Meier estimator is a statistical measure also known as the product-limit estimator and is given by the following formula:

$$Survival(t) = \prod_{i:t_i \leq t}(1 - \frac{d_i}{n_i})$$

Here, d is the number of non-surviving entities while n is the number surviving entities. Thus, reading this formula in plain English, the survival is the product of 1 minus the number of non-surviving entities divided by the number of surviving entities calculated for all increments of time (t_i) that are less than or equal to the current time, t.

The best way to understand this formula is to think of it as a running product over time. Similar to a running total over time, the formula is calculated at a specified time interval, such as monthly, and then the individual results are multiplied together in a similar manner to how a running total calculates a total at specified time intervals and then adds the individual values together.

The Kaplan-Meier estimator is most often used in the clinical sciences to estimate the percentage chance of survival over time once a patient has received treatment for an affliction or been diagnosed with a condition. However, the Kaplan-Meier estimator also has applications in other areas. For example, the Kaplan-Meier estimator can be used to evaluate a population of manufacturing equipment and a historical record of machine failures to forecast when the next failure is likely.

One might reasonably question what this topic is doing in a chapter about, well, human resources. Well, for our application of the Kaplan-Meier estimator, we will evaluate the expected tenure of employees within an organization based upon the hire and termination dates of employees as our population.

To prepare for this calculation, if you have not already completed the *Employee Turnover Rate* section of this chapter, please do so now in order to create the **Employees** and **Calculations** tables. Next, create the following table:

```
Days =
    VAR __Start = MIN( 'Employees'[Hire Date] )
    VAR __End = TODAY()
    VAR __Days = ( __End - __Start ) * 1. + 1
    VAR __Table = GENERATESERIES( 1, __Days, 1 )
    VAR __Result = SELECTCOLUMNS( __Table, "Day", [Value] )
RETURN
    __Result
```

This table contains a single column of incrementing day numbers where 1 represents the earliest **Hire Date** from the **Employees** table. The number of days increments by one until the last day represents the current date, (**TODAY**). This table represents our time series where each day is an instance of *i* from our original Kaplan-Meier formula. Ensure that there is no relationship between this table and any other table in the semantic model.

Now, create the following measure:

```
KM Survival =
    VAR __Day = MAX( 'Days'[Day] )
    VAR __Employees =
```

```
        ADDCOLUMNS(

            'Employees',

            "__Days", ( [Term Date] - [Hire Date] ) * 1. + 1

        )

    VAR __KMTable =

        ADDCOLUMNS(

            ADDCOLUMNS(

                GENERATESERIES( 1, __Day ),

                "d(i)", COUNTROWS( FILTER( __Employees, [__Days] = [Value] ) ),

                "n(i)", COUNTROWS( FILTER( __Employees, [__Days] > [Value] ) )

            ),

            "1-d(i)/n(i)", 1 - DIVIDE( [d(i)], [n(i)], 0 )

        )

    VAR __Result = PRODUCTX( __KMTable, [1-d(i)/n(i)] )

RETURN

    __Result
```

This calculation starts by getting the current **Day** in context as the __**Days** variable. We then calculate the __**Employees** table variable by adding a column that calculates the number of days each employee is employed at the organization. Next, we calculate the Kaplan-Meier survival table, __**KMTable**. This table calculates the individual values for **d**, **n**, and finally **1 – d/n** for each day (*i*).

Recall that *d* represents the number of non-surviving entities for that particular value of *i* (day in our case). Therefore, we can calculate **d(i)** simply by counting the number of rows in the __**Employees** table variable with a __**Days** value that corresponds to the current day value, the column **Value** in our case created by our **GENERATESERIES** function. Similarly, the surviving entities, **n(i)**, are all rows in the __**Employees** table variable that have a __**Days** greater than the current day value.

With **d(i)** and **n(i)** calculated, we can now calculate *1* minus the quotient of dividing *d(i)* by *n(i)* in a column called **1-d(i)/n(i)** for each row of the table. Finally, for the __**Result**, we multiply the **1-d(i)/n(i)** column for all rows of the table to complete the calculation.

Format the **KM Survival** measure as a percentage with 2 decimal places. Create a **Line chart** with the **Day** column from the **Days** table as the **X-axis** and the **KM Survival** measure as the **Y-axis** to create a chart like the following:

KM Survival by Day

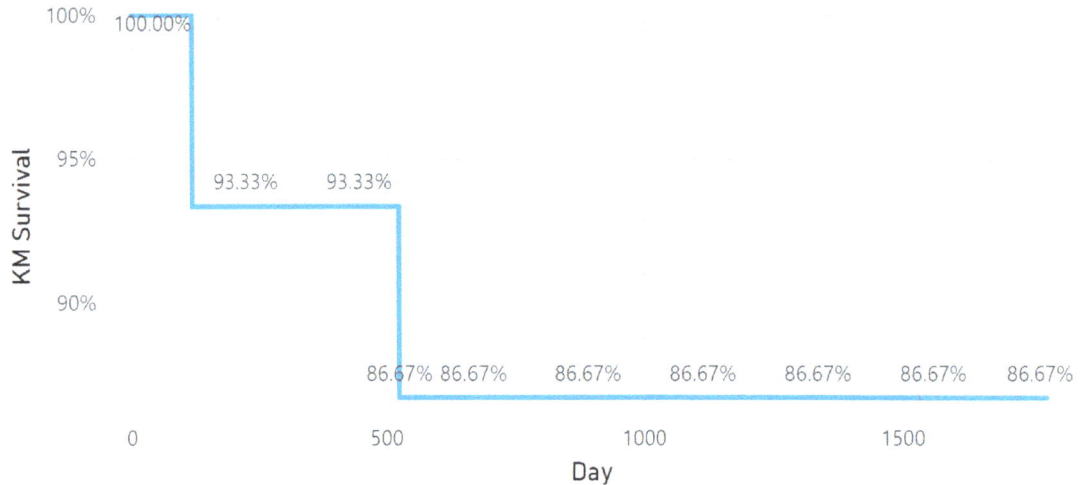

Figure 8.6: Kaplan-Meier survival curve

The chart represents the survivability percentage for the population in question for each time increment (day).

Let's now look at pay equality.

Pay Equality (Gini coefficient)

The **Gini coefficient** is an index that measures the degree of inequality within a distribution. The Gini coefficient is most often used to measure the wealth distribution of countries. However, the Gini coefficient can also be used to measure the equality or inequality of pay distributions within an organization.

To understand how the Gini coefficient is calculated, consider the following diagram:

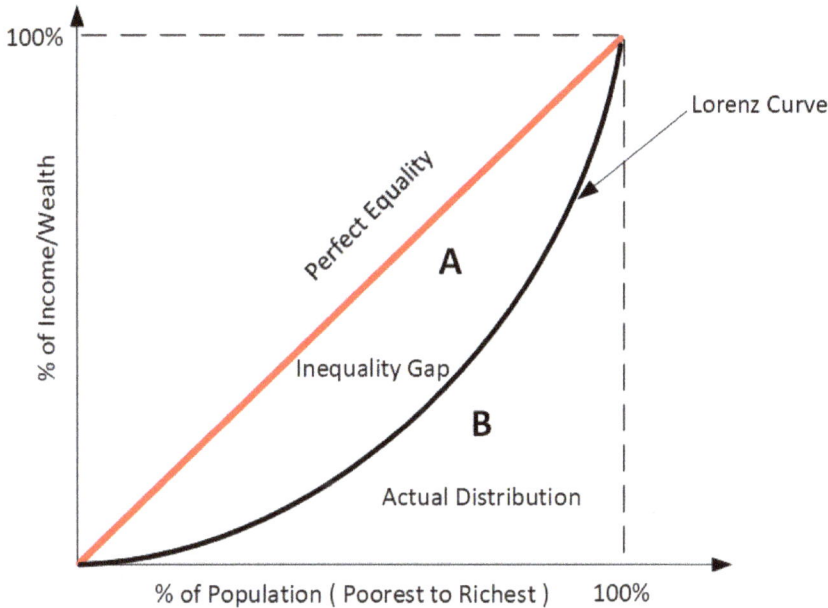

Figure 8.7: Gini coefficient

This diagram plots the % of the population on the x-axis and the % of income or wealth held by that population on the y-axis. The 45-degree line represents perfect income equality with regard to distribution while the **Lorenz curve** represents the actual income distribution. The area above the Lorenz curve is considered area A, the inequality gap, while the area below the Lorenz curve is area B, the actual distribution of income/wealth.

Considering the diagram, the formula for calculating the Gini coefficient is the following:

$$Gini\ coefficient = \frac{A}{(A+B)}$$

Thus, if there is perfect equality, then the area of A is zero and thus the Gini coefficient is also zero. Conversely, a Gini coefficient of 1 indicates perfect inequality.

To prepare for this calculation, please complete the *Employee Turnover Rate* section of this chapter to create the **Employees** and **Calculations** tables if you have not already done so. Next, create the following table and format the **Value** column as a percentage:

```
Population = GENERATESERIES( 0, 1.01, .01 )
```

This creates a single column table with 101 rows from 0% to 100% in 1% increments. We can now visualize the Gini coefficient for our **Employees** table with the following two measures:

```
Perfect Equality = MAX( Population[Value] )
```

```
Lorenz curve =
```

```
VAR __CurrentPercent = MAX( 'Population'[Value] )

VAR __AllEmployees = COUNTROWS( DISTINCT( ALL( 'Employees'[Employee] ) ) )

VAR __Table =

    ADDCOLUMNS(

        'Employees',

        "__Percent",

            VAR __Salary = [Annual Salary]

            VAR __Count =

                COUNTROWS(

                    FILTER( ALL( 'Employees' ), [Annual Salary] <= __Salary )

                )

            VAR __Result = DIVIDE( __Count, __AllEmployees )

        RETURN

            __Result

    )

VAR __AllIncome = SUMX( 'Employees', [Annual Salary] )

VAR __Employees =

    SELECTCOLUMNS(

        FILTER( __Table, [__Percent] <= __CurrentPercent ),

        "__Employee", [Employee]

    )

VAR __Income = SUMX( FILTER( __Table, [Employee] IN __Employees ), [Annual Salary] )

VAR __Result = DIVIDE( __Income, __AllIncome ) + 0

RETURN

    __Result
```

The **Lorenz curve** measure first gets the current percentage in context, **__CurrentPercent**. Next, we determine the total number of unique employees and store this in the **__AllEmployees** variable.

The **__Table** variable adds a column called **__Percent**. The **__Percent** column returns each employee's percentage in terms of where their income ranks within the population. In other words, the highest paid employee has a __**Percent** of 1 while the lowest paid employee has a __**Percent** of 1/16 or .0625, since there are 16 employees in the table. This is done by getting the current employee's salary, counting the rows in the **Employees** table that are equal to or less than that salary and then dividing this count by the total number of employees, **AllEmployees**.

We then need to determine the percentage of income. To do this we first store the sum of the **Annual Salary** column in the **Employees** table in the __**AllIncome** variable. Next, we create the __**Employees** table, which filters the __**Table** variable created earlier down to just the rows where the __**Percent** column is equal to or less than the current percent, __**CurrentPercent**.

We then sum of the **Annual Salary** column from the **Employees** table that are in our __**Employees** table variable. Finally, we calculate the __**Result** by dividing the __**Income** by __**AllIncome** to get the percentage of income for the current percentage of the population in context.

Visualize these two measures by creating a **Line chart** with the **Value** column from the **Population** table in the **X-axis** as well as the **Perfect Equality** and the **Lorenz curve** measures in the **Y-axis**.

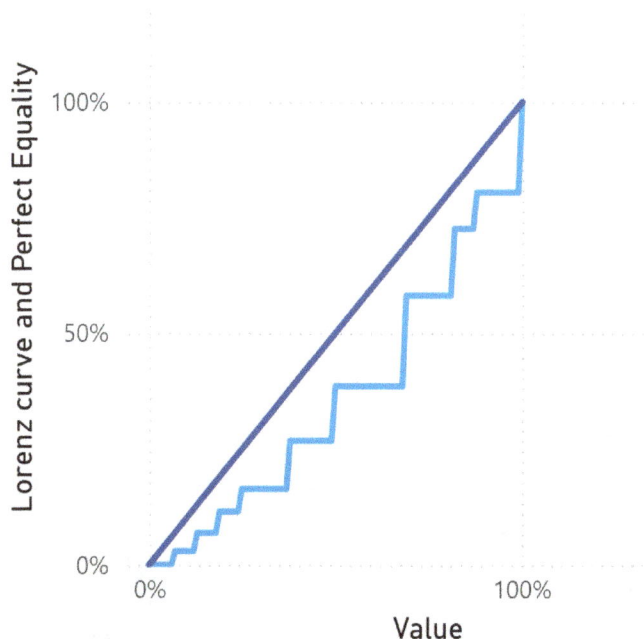

Figure 8.8: Lorenz curve and Perfect Equality

The calculation for the Gini coefficient is quite similar to the Lorenz curve measure:

```
Gini Coefficient =
    VAR __AllEmployees = COUNTROWS( DISTINCT( ALL( 'Employees'[Employee] ) ) )
    VAR __Table =
        ADDCOLUMNS(
            'Employees',
            "__Percent",
                VAR __Salary = [Annual Salary]
                VAR __Count =
                    COUNTROWS(
                        FILTER( ALL( 'Employees' ), [Annual Salary] <= __Salary )
                    )
                VAR __Result = DIVIDE( __Count, __AllEmployees )
            RETURN
                __Result
        )
    VAR __AllIncome = SUMX( 'Employees', [Annual Salary] )
    VAR __GiniTable =
        ADDCOLUMNS(
            GENERATESERIES( 0, 1.01, .01 ),
            "__Value",
                VAR __CurrentPercent = [Value]
                VAR __Employees =
                    SELECTCOLUMNS(
                        FILTER( __Table, [__Percent] <= __CurrentPercent ),
                        "__Employee", [Employee]
                    )
                VAR __Income = SUMX( FILTER( __Table, [Employee] IN __Employees ),
[Annual Salary] )
                VAR __Result = DIVIDE( __Income, __AllIncome ) + 0
```

```
        RETURN

            __Result

    )

  VAR __B = SUMX( __GiniTable, [__Value] * 100 )

  VAR __TotalArea = 1/2 * 100 * 100

  VAR __A = __TotalArea - __B

  VAR __Result = DIVIDE( __A, __A + __B, 0 )

RETURN

  __Result
```

The formula is largely the same up until the __GiniTable table variable. Here we create a table that is the same as our **Population** table created earlier. And, if you look closely, the same calculations are being performed inside of the __Value column that were being performed in the **Lorenz curve** measure. This is because we are calculating the Lorenz curve value for each percentage of the population in order to generate our __GiniTable.

We can now approximate the area of **B** from the original Gini coefficient formula by imagining each percent calculation as a 1-unit width rectangle with the other side being the value along the Lorenz curve. Therefore, the area under the Lorenz curve is simply the sum of the Lorenz curve values, otherwise known as a **Riemann's Sum**. We know from basic math that formula for the area of a triangle is $\frac{1}{2}$ * *base* * *height* and thus the area of __A is simply the __TotalArea minus the area of __B. And with that, we have the necessary information to calculate the Gini coefficient for the population for the __Result.

Creating a **Card** visual of the Gini coefficient measure provides a value of **0.27**. Note that this is an approximation considering that our Lorenze curve is stair-stepped. This could be fixed by figuring out the differential equation for the curve, but then you'd have to deal with differential equations so…hard pass.

Patron Recommendation

Alexis Olson suggests using an alternative area under the curve approximation approach, termed "half of the relative mean absolute difference":

```
Gini Alt =

    VAR __N = COUNTROWS ( Employees )

    VAR __TotalSalary = SUM ( Employees[Annual Salary] )

    VAR __SumPairDiffs =
```

```
            SUMX (

                Employees,

                SUMX (

                    Employees,

                    ABS (

                        Employees[Annual Salary] -

                        EARLIER ( Employees[Annual Salary] )

                    )

                )

            )

    VAR __Result = __SumPairDiffs / ( 2 * __N * __TotalSalary )

RETURN

    __Result
```

This concludes our exploration of human resources KPIs and metrics.

Summary

This chapter was all about the KPIs and metrics important to human resources or human capital management teams. We explored topics such as employee turnover rates, absenteeism, employee satisfaction and human capital value added (HCVA). In addition, we covered the utilization of employees, as well as using the Kaplan-Meier estimator to create a survival curve that reflects employee retention rates. Finally, we used the Gini coefficient to demonstrate how to evaluate the pay equality within an organization.

Again, while many of the calculations in this chapter are long and complex, they all still resemble in fundamental ways the base DAX pattern learned in the section *A DAX Pattern to Solve Most Problems* from *Chapter 1*. Again and again, basic pattern of creating virtual tables that group and/or filter the base data and then use X aggregators across those tables. This is the power of the technique presented throughout this book.

In the next chapter, we investigate project metrics.

CHAPTER 9

9

Projects

The concept of projects is effectively universal within organizations and businesses for all industries. Projects are how complex problems are solved and projects are essential to organizations because projects provide a structured, goal-oriented method for driving change, innovation, and improvement. Examples of projects include developing a new product, implementing technological upgrades, and streamlining internal processes. Such projects enable teams to focus on specific goals and objectives to deliver tangible outcomes. This targeted approach not only helps companies stay organized and efficiently allocate resources but also promotes collaboration among cross-functional teams.

Because projects are how organizations affect change and improve systems, organizations must marshal money and resources to fund such projects. Thus, it becomes imperative to track project metrics and Key Performance Indicators (KPIs) in order to track progress, performance, and overall impact on the organization. By carefully measuring factors such as budget adherence, timeline milestones, resource utilization, and quality standards, project managers and stakeholders can quickly identify risks or bottlenecks, adjust strategies, and maintain control over project outcomes. In addition, these metrics foster accountability within project teams and encourage continuous improvement. Ultimately, robust tracking of project KPIs ensures that resources are used efficiently, goals remain aligned with organizational priorities, and the final deliverables meet or exceed expectations.

This chapter explores numerous metrics that are important for effectively managing projects. Data and other files for this chapter are available in the GitHub repository for this book: https://github.com/gdeckler/DAX-For-Humans/tree/main/book. We start by creating a burndown chart.

Burndown Chart

Burndown charts provide a useful way to visualize the work being performed on a project compared to an idealized or expected work schedule. Burndown charts calculate the cumulative amount of work on a project and subtracts that amount from the total work for the entire project.

To demonstrate burndown charts, use an **Enter data** query to enter the following data into a table named **Project** or download **Chapter9_Data.xlsx** from the GitHub repository for this book and import the data on the **Project** sheet.

ID	Project	Phase	Name	Work	Start	Finish	%	PV	EV
3	Project	Phase 1	Task 1	24	1/13/2025	1/13/2025	1	2040	2040
4	Project	Phase 1	Task 2	160	1/14/2025	1/27/2025	1	14400	14400
5	Project	Phase 1	Task 3	40	1/28/2025	2/3/2025	1	3400	3400
7	Project	Phase 2	Task 4	240	2/4/2025	2/24/2025	0.75	21600	16200
8	Project	Phase 2	Task 5	200	2/25/2025	3/30/2025	0.5	19000	9500
9	Project	Phase 2	Task 6	160	3/31/2025	4/27/2025	0.25	13600	3400
11	Project	Phase 3	Task 7	120	4/28/2025	5/4/2025	0	9800	0
12	Project	Phase 3	Task 8	240	5/5/2025	5/25/2025	0	18000	0
13	Project	Phase 3	Task 9	80	5/26/2025	6/8/2025	0	6000	0

Table 9.1: Project data

In addition, create a **Dates** table using the following DAX code:

```
Dates = CALENDAR( DATE( 2024, 1, 1 ), DATE( 2025, 12, 31 ) )
```

Finally, import the **Hours** sheet from the **Chapter9_Data.xlsx** file available in the GitHub repository for this book into a table called **Hours**.

Create a relationship between the **ID** columns in both the **Project** table and the **Hours** table. Ensure that the **Dates** table is not connected to either table. Your semantic model should look like the following:

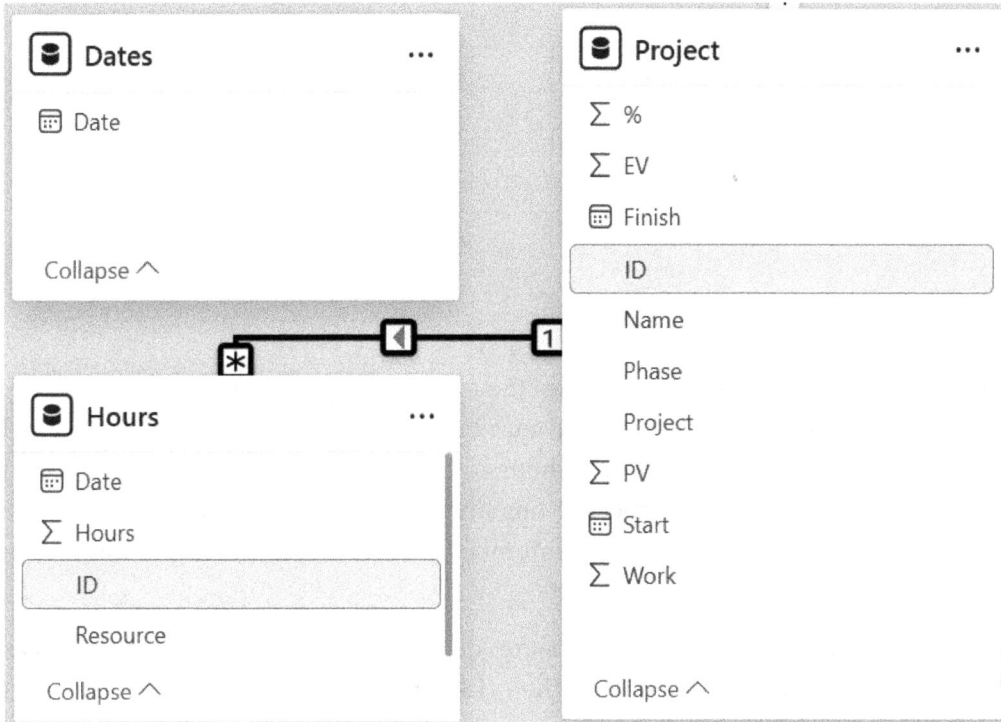

Figure 9.1: Semantic model relationships

Now create the following measure:

```
Idealized Burndown =

    VAR __Date = MAX( 'Dates'[Date] )

    VAR __StartDate = MINX( 'Project', 'Project'[Start] )

    VAR __FinishDate = MAXX( 'Project', 'Project'[Finish] )

    VAR __TotalProjectHours = SUMX( ALL( 'Project' ), 'Project'[Work] )

    VAR __IdealHoursPerDay =

        DIVIDE(

            __TotalProjectHours,

            ( __FinishDate - __StartDate ) + 1,

            0

        )

    VAR __IdealConsumedHours = __IdealHoursPerDay * ( ( __Date - __StartDate ) + 1 )

    VAR __Result =
```

```
    IF(

        __Date < __StartDate || __Date > __FinishDate,

        BLANK(),

        __TotalProjectHours - __IdealConsumedHours

    )

RETURN

    __Result
```

The **Idealized Burndown** measure calculates the total amount of hours of work for the project and then divides this number by the total number of days for the project. This calculation provides the expected average number of hours of work needed to be performed per day to complete the project within the expected timeline. Thus, for any given day, the idealized number of hours consumed is the average number of work hours per day multiplied by the number of days since the start of the project.

Note that the **Idealized Burndown** measure does not exclude weekends. You can use **NETWORKDAYS** in the denominator for the **__IdealHoursPerDay** variable to address this if necessary.

```
Burndown =

    VAR __ReportingDate = DATE( 2025, 4, 1 )

    VAR __Date = MAX( 'Dates'[Date] )

    VAR __StartDate = MINX( 'Project', 'Project'[Start] )

    VAR __FinishDate = MAXX( 'Project', 'Project'[Finish] )

    VAR __TotalProjectHours = SUMX( ALL( 'Project' ), 'Project'[Work] )

    VAR __TotalConsumedHours =

        SUMX(

            FILTER(

                ALL('Hours'),

                'Hours'[Date] <= __Date

            ),

            'Hours'[Hours])

    VAR __Result =

        IF(
```

```
            __Date < __StartDate || __Date > __ReportingDate,

        BLANK(),

        __TotalProjectHours - __TotalConsumedHours

    )

RETURN

    __Result
```

The **Burndown** measure is similar to the **Idealized Burndown** measure except for the calculation of the consumed hours, **__TotalConsumedHours**. Instead of calculating an idealized number of hours, we instead calculate the cumulative total number of hours worked up until the current date in context. This is done by using **FILTER** and **ALL** to return all rows within the **Hours** table where the **Date** column is less than or equal to the current **__Date** in context and then summing the **Hours** column using **SUMX**.

Once these two measures are created, create a **Line chart** using the **Date** column from the **Dates** table as the **X-axis** and the **Idealized Burndown** and **Burndown** measures as the **Y-axis**.

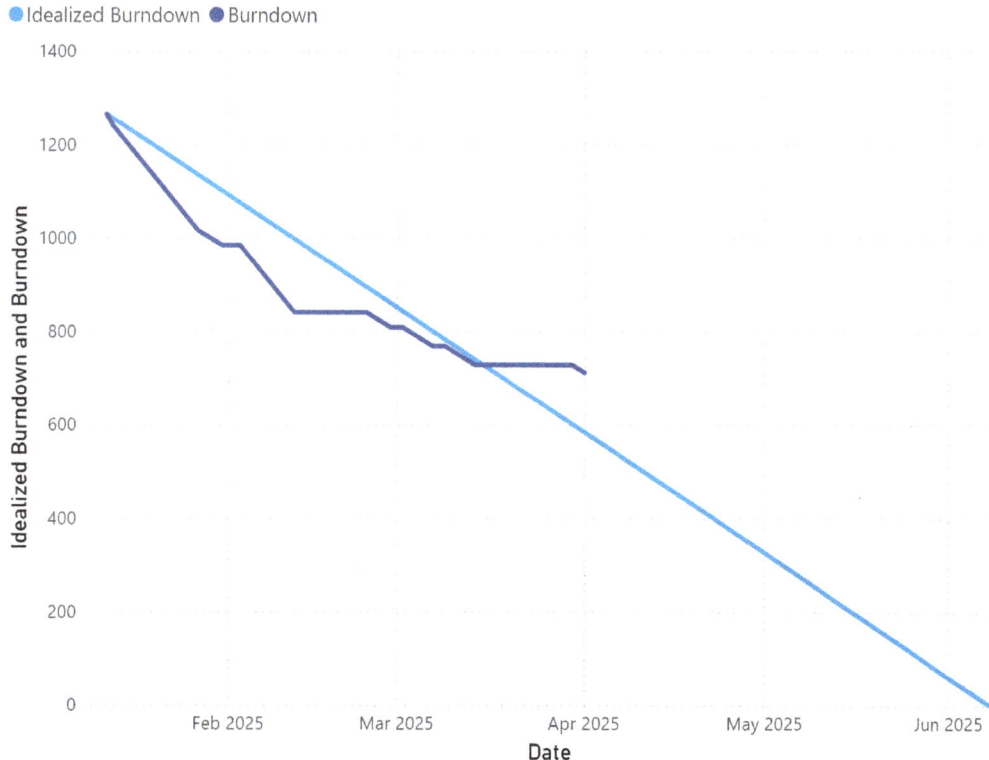

Figure 9.2: Burndown chart

Here we can see that initially, more work was being done on the project compared to what was expected. However, towards the end of March, project work stalled and now less work has been done compared to the expected consumption of work hours.

This completes our exploration of burndown charts. Next, we explore the topic of planned and earned value.

Planned and Earned Value

Planned and earned value are common metrics used within project management circles, particularly in relation to the **Earned Value Management** (**EVM**) methodology. **Planned value**, PV, is the baseline cost, or budget, for a project. Obviously, PV plays a key role in determining whether a project is completed within its original budget. PV is also known as **Budgeted Cost of Work Scheduled** (**BCWS**).

Earned value, EV, uses planned value as an input along with the percentage complete for the project, phase, or task to calculate the amount of budget that should have been consumed based upon what is and is not completed. Earned value is also known as **Budgeted Cost of Work Performed** (**BCWP**).

It must be noted that the budget for a project includes the cost of physical materials such as hardware or other supplies as well as the costs of salaries or hourly wages. The calculations presented here only factors in salary and wages for the budget and earned value.

If you have not already completed the section, *Burndown Chart* in this chapter, please do so now to create the **Project** and **Dates** tables. Next, use an **Enter data** query to enter the following data into a table named **Assignments** or download **Chapter9_Data.xlsx** from the GitHub repository for this book and import the data on the **Assignments** sheet.

ID	Work	Resource
3	8	Greg
3	8	Jennifer
3	8	Pam
4	80	Greg
4	80	Jennifer

ID	Work	Resource
5	40	Jennifer
7	120	Greg
7	120	Jennifer
8	200	Greg
9	160	Jennifer
11	40	Greg
11	40	Pam
11	40	Mike
12	120	Pam
12	120	Mike
13	80	Pam

Table 9.2: Assignments data

Use another **Enter data** query to create a **Costs** table with the following data. Alternatively, import the **Costs** sheet from **Chapter9_Data.xlsx**.

Hourly Cost	Resource
95	Greg
85	Jennifer
75	Pam
75	Mike

Table 9.3: Costs data

Create a relationship between the **ID** columns of the **Project** and **Assignments** tables. Create another relationship between the **Resource** columns of the **Costs** and **Assignments** tables and ensure that this relationship is bi-directional. Your semantic model should now look like the following:

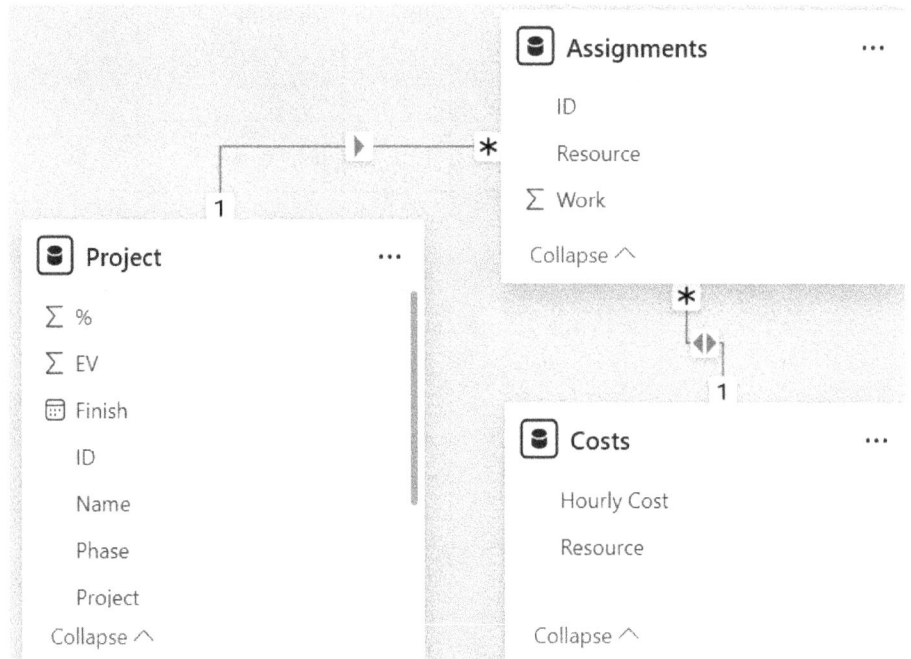

Figure 9.3: Semantic model relationships

Now, create the following measure:

```
PV =
    VAR __Table =
        ADDCOLUMNS(
            ADDCOLUMNS(
                'Assignments',
                "__HourlyCost", RELATED( 'Costs'[Hourly Cost] )
            ),
            "__PV", [Work] * [__HourlyCost]
        )
    VAR __Result = SUMX( __Table, [__PV] )
RETURN
    __Result
```

The **PV** measure calculates the planned value by multiplying the **Work** column from the **Assignments** table by the **Hourly Cost** column from the **Costs** table. This is done for each row of the **Assignments** table and then **SUMX** is used to compute the total planned value within the current context.

The **RELATED** function returns a value from a related table. This is used to retrieve the **Hourly Cost** from the **Costs** table for the associated resource in the **Assignments** table.

Now create a **Matrix** visualization and place the **Project**, **Phase**, and **Name** columns from the **Project** table into the **Rows** field well and the **PV** measure in the **Values** field well.

Project	PV
⊟ **Project**	**$107,840**
⊟ **Phase 1**	**$19,840**
Task 1	$2,040
Task 2	$14,400
Task 3	$3,400
⊟ **Phase 2**	**$54,200**
Task 4	$21,600
Task 5	$19,000
Task 6	$13,600
⊟ **Phase 3**	**$33,800**
Task 7	$9,800
Task 8	$18,000
Task 9	$6,000
Total	**$107,840**

Figure 9.4: Planned value

The matrix displays the planned value or budget for each task, phase, and the entire project. However, another way to visualize the budget for a project is the cumulative planned value over time. To demonstrate visualizing the cumulative planned value over time, create the following measure:

```
Cumulative PV =

    VAR __MaxDate = MAX( 'Project'[Finish] )

    VAR __Date = MAX( 'Dates'[Date] )

    VAR __Table =

        ADDCOLUMNS(

            ADDCOLUMNS(
```

```
                FILTER( 'Project', 'Project'[Start] < __Date ),

                "__TaskDays",

                ( [Finish] - [Start] ) + 1,

                "__Days",

                ( __Date - [Start] ) + 1

            ),

            "__PV",

            SWITCH( TRUE(),

                __Date > __MaxDate, BLANK(),

                [__Days] >= [__TaskDays], [PV],

                [__Days] / [__TaskDays] * [PV]

            )

        )

    VAR __Result = SUMX( __Table, [__PV] )
RETURN

    __Result
```

This measure calculates the planned value for each project task using the **PV** measure created earlier. The budget consumption is idealized such that all work is expected to be completed on time. Thus, the planned value for a task in progress is the current percentage of the overall days for a task multiplied by the total planned value (**PV**) for that task. This percentage calculation is handled by calculating the total number of days for a task (**__TaskDays**) and the current number of days since the start of the task, **__Days**.

Now create a **Line chart** with the **Date** column from the **Dates** table in the **X-axis** and the **Cumulative PV** measure as the **Y-axis**. Your chart should look like the following:

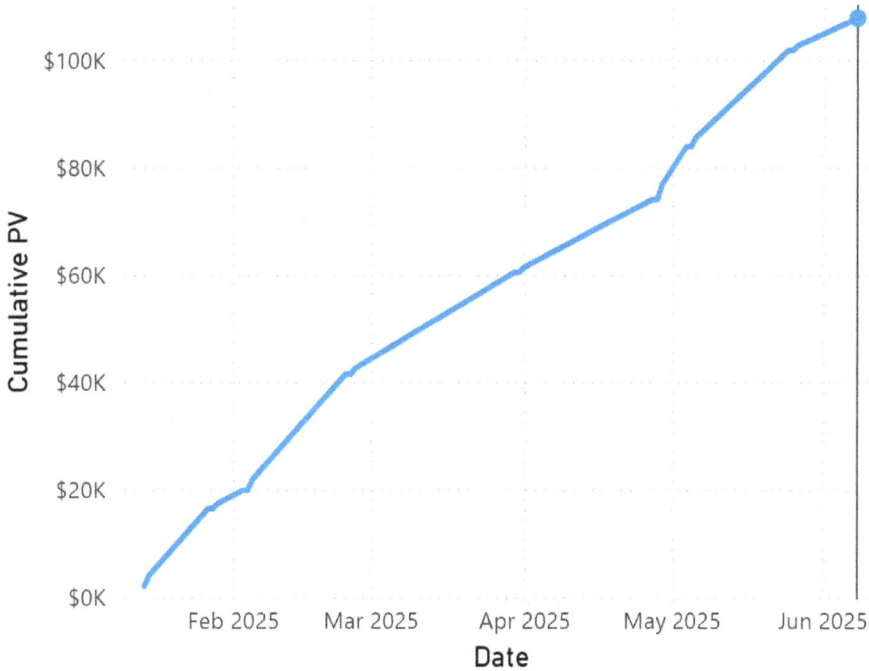

Figure 9.5: Cumulative planned value

We can use what we have learned about calculating planned value to calculate earned value. The following measure demonstrates how to calculate earned value without assuming the creation of a planned value measure.

```
EV =
    VAR __Table =
        ADDCOLUMNS(
            'Project',
            "__PV",
                VAR __Table =
                    ADDCOLUMNS(
                        ADDCOLUMNS(
                            RELATEDTABLE( 'Assignments' ),
                            "__HourlyCost", RELATED( 'Costs'[Hourly Cost] )
                        ),
```

```
                    "__PV", [Work] * [__HourlyCost]

                )

            VAR __Result = SUMX( __Table, [__PV] )

        RETURN

            __Result

    )

VAR __Result = SUMX( __Table, [%] * [__PV] )
RETURN

    __Result
```

The **EV** measure is like the **PV** measure created earlier. However, the difference is that the planned value is calculated as a calculated column added to the **Project** table. The earned value then is simply the percentage completion for the task, the % column from the **Project** table, multiplied by the planned value for the task, phase, or project.

If a PV measure has already been created, the formula can be simplified as follows:

```
EV Alt 1 =

    VAR __Table =

        ADDCOLUMNS(

            'Project',

            "__PV", [PV]

        )

    VAR __Result = SUMX( __Table, [%] * [__PV] )
RETURN

    __Result
```

It should be noted that there are different methods used to calculate earned value rather than simply multiplying the percent complete by the planned value. For example, some project management methodologies specify that tasks in progress have an earned value of 20% of planned value, regardless of the actual completion percentage. This version of earned value is demonstrated in the following measure:

```
EV Alt 2 =

    VAR __Table =

        ADDCOLUMNS(
```

```
        ADDCOLUMNS(

            'Project',

            "__PV", [PV]

        ),

        "__EV",

        SWITCH( TRUE(),

            [%] = 1, [__PV],

            [%] > 0, [__PV] * .2,

            0

        )

    )

    VAR __Result = SUMX( __Table, [__EV] )

RETURN

    __Result
```

Create a **Matrix** visualization and place the **Project, Phase,** and **Name** columns from the **Project** table into the **Rows** field well and the three **EV** measures in the **Values** field well.

Project	EV	EV Alt 1	EV Alt 2
⊟ **Project**	**$48,940**	**$48,940**	**$30,680**
⊟ **Phase 1**	**$19,840**	**$19,840**	**$19,840**
Task 1	$2,040	$2,040	$2,040
Task 2	$14,400	$14,400	$14,400
Task 3	$3,400	$3,400	$3,400
⊟ **Phase 2**	**$29,100**	**$29,100**	**$10,840**
Task 4	$16,200	$16,200	$4,320
Task 5	$9,500	$9,500	$3,800
Task 6	$3,400	$3,400	$2,720
⊟ **Phase 3**	**$0**	**$0**	**$0**
Task 7	$0	$0	$0
Task 8	$0	$0	$0
Task 9	$0	$0	$0
Total	**$48,940**	**$48,940**	**$30,680**

Figure 9.6: Earned value

We can also visualize the cumulative earned value over time in the same way as planned value with the following measure:

```
Cumulative EV =
    VAR __ReportingDate = DATE( 2025, 4, 1 )
    VAR __MaxDate = MAX( 'Project'[Finish] )
    VAR __Date = MAX( 'Dates'[Date] )
    VAR __Table =
        ADDCOLUMNS(
            ADDCOLUMNS(
                FILTER('Project','Project'[Start] < __Date),
                "__TaskDays",
                ( [Finish] - [Start] ) + 1,
                "__Days",
                ( __Date - [Start] ) + 1
            ),
            "__EV",
            SWITCH( TRUE(),
                __Date > __MaxDate, BLANK(),
                [__Days] >= [__TaskDays], [EV],
                [__Days] / [__TaskDays] * [EV]
            )
        )
    VAR __Result = IF( __Date > __ReportingDate, BLANK(), SUMX(__Table, [__EV]) )
RETURN
    __Result
```

Now create a **Line chart** with the **Date** column from the **Dates** table in the **X-axis** and the **Cumulative EV** measure as the **Y-axis**.

Cumulative EV and Cumulative EV Alt by Date

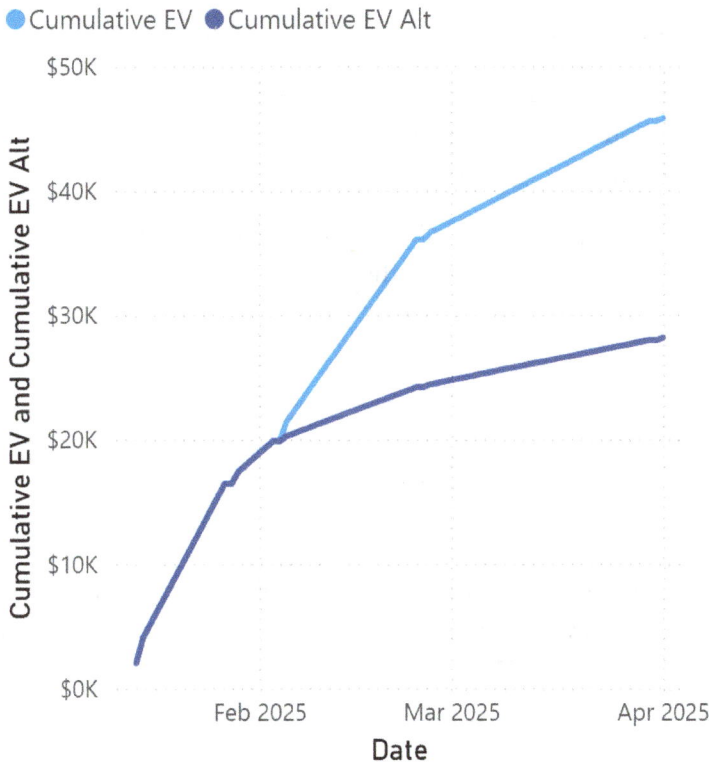

Figure 9.7: Cumulative earned value

Note that *Figure 9.7* shows the **Cumulative EV** measure as the light blue line and a **Cumulative EV Alt** measure as the dark blue line. The **Cumulative EV Alt** measure is the same as the **Cumulative EV** measure except that all references to the **EV** measure are replaced by the **EV Alt 2** measure. You can also add the **Cumulative PV** measure to the **Line chart** to analyze the current state of the project.

Now that we have established how to calculate the baseline metrics of planned value and earned value, let's next turn our attention to calculating variances.

Schedule Variance

Project schedule variance (**SV**) is the difference between the planned value for a project and the earned value for that same project. SV indicates whether a project is ahead of or behind its planned schedule at any given point in time.

If the SV for a project is positive, then this indicates that the project has completed more work than planned and is ahead of schedule. Conversely, a negative SV means that the project has completed less work than originally scheduled and is thus likely behind schedule.

By monitoring schedule variance, project managers can identify timing issues early, make informed decisions about resource allocation and schedule adjustments, and ultimately improve the chances of delivering the project on time.

If you have not already completed the sections, *Burndown Chart* and *Planned and Earned Value* in this chapter, please do so now. Next, create the following measure:

```
SV$ =

    IF( ISBLANK([Cumulative EV] ),

        BLANK(),

        [Cumulative EV] - [Cumulative PV]

    )
```

This is the basic SV metric which simply subtracts the **Cumulative PV** measure from the **Cumulative EV** measure. Since **Cumulative PV** and **Cumulative EV** are expressed in dollars, so too is SV. We can use this base **SV$** measure to calculate the current SV for the project:

```
Current SV$ =

    VAR __Table =

        ADDCOLUMNS(

            'Dates',

            "__SV$",

            [SV$]

        )

    VAR __CurrentDate = MAXX( FILTER( __Table, NOT( ISBLANK( [__SV$] ) ) ), [Date] )

    VAR __Result = MAXX( FILTER( __Table, [Date] = __CurrentDate), [__SV$] )

RETURN

    __Result
```

The **Current SV$** measure is calculated by calculating the base **SV$** measure for each date within the **Dates** table. The current date is the maximum date where **SV$** is not **BLANK**. Thus, the current SV is the **SV$** value for the **__CurrentDate** value.

We can also calculate the number of days ahead or behind schedule:

```
SV Days =
    VAR __Table =
        ADDCOLUMNS(
            'Dates',
            "__PV",
            [Cumulative PV],
            "__EV",
            [Cumulative EV]
        )
    VAR __EVDate = MAXX( FILTER( __Table, NOT( ISBLANK( [__EV] ) ) ), [Date] )
    VAR __CurrentEV = MAXX( __Table, [__EV] )
    VAR __Table1 =
        ADDCOLUMNS(
            FILTER( __Table, NOT( ISBLANK( [__EV]) ) ),
            "__Diff",
            ABS( [__PV] - __CurrentEV )
        )
    VAR __MinDiff = MINX( __Table1, [__Diff] )
    VAR __PVDate = MAXX( FILTER( __Table1, [__Diff] = __MinDiff ), [Date] )
    VAR __Result = ( __PVDate - __EVDate ) * 1. + 1
RETURN
    __Result
```

The **SV Days** measure expresses SV in terms of the number of days ahead or behind schedule. This is done by calculating the **Cumulative PV** and **Cumulative EV** for each date within the **Dates** table (__Table).

The current EV (__**CurrentEV)** is found similarly to the **Current SV$** measure. We then add a column to the __**Table** variable that calculates the absolute (**ABS**) difference between the planned value for each date and the current EV (__**CurrentEV**). The minimum difference between __**PV** and __**CurrentEV** indicates the date on which the original schedule would have reached the **__CurrentEV** for the project (**__PVDate**). We can then calculate the number of days ahead or behind based upon the current EV date (**__EVDate**) and **__PVDate**.

Create a **Line chart** to view the **Cumulative PV**, **Cumulative EV** and **SV$** measures. In addition, create **Card** visualizations to view the **Current SV$** and **SV Days** measures.

Figure 9.8: Schedule variance

We can clearly see that the project is behind schedule.

This completes our exploration of schedule variance. Next, we take a look at calculating the actual costs for a project.

Actual Cost

The **Actual Cost (AC)** of a project is the actual costs of goods and services consumed during the project. For salary or wages, the cost is the number of hours worked multiplied by the fully loaded hourly cost for the resource.

If you have not already completed the sections, *Burndown Chart* in this chapter, please do so now to create the **Project**, **Hours**, and **Dates** tables. Next, use an **Enter data** query to create a **Resources** table with the following data or alternatively, import the **Resources** sheet from **Chapter9_Data.xlsx**.

Hourly Cost	Resource
95	Greg

85	Jennifer
75	Pam
75	Mike

Table 9.4: Resources data

Create a relationship between the **ID** columns of the **Project** and **Hours** tables if there is not one created already. Create another relationship between the **Resource** columns of the **Hours** and **Resources** tables and ensure that this relationship is bi-directional. You semantic model should look like the following:

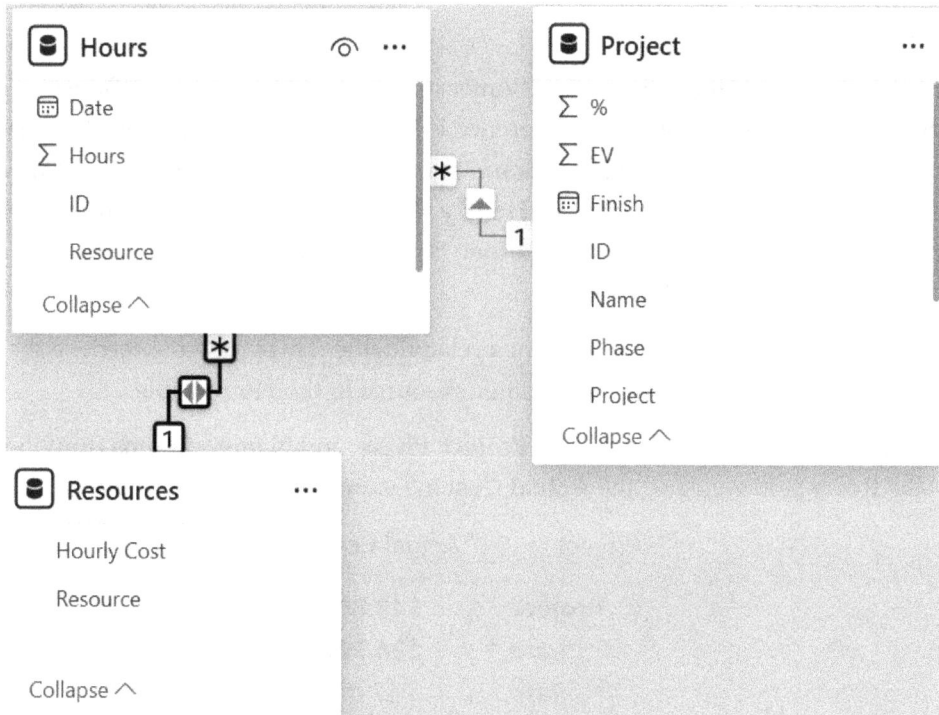

Figure 9.9: Semantic model relationships

Now create the following **Actual Cost** measure:

```
Actual Cost =
    VAR __Table =
        ADDCOLUMNS(
            ADDCOLUMNS(
```

```
            'Hours',

            "__HourlyCost",

            RELATED('Resources'[Hourly Cost])

        ),

        "__ActualCost",

        [Hours] * [__HourlyCost]

    )

VAR __Result = SUMX(__Table,[__ActualCost])

RETURN

    __Result
```

This measure is structured the same as the **PV** measure created in the section *Planned and Earned Value* section of this chapter. The main difference is that the **Hours** table is used instead of the **Assignments** table. The **Actual Cost** measure calculates the actual cost by multiplying the **Hours** column from the **Hours** table by the **Hourly Cost** column from the **Resources** table. This is done for each row of the **Hours** table and then **SUMX** is used to compute the total planned value within the current context.

The **RELATED** function returns a value from a related table. This is used to retrieve the **Hourly Cost** from the **Resources** table for the associated resource in the **Hours** table.

Create a **Matrix** visualization and place the **Project, Phase,** and **Name** columns from the **Project** table into the **Rows** field well and the **Actual Cost** measure in the **Values** field well.

Project	Actual Cost
⊟ **Project**	**$49,880**
⊟ **Phase 1**	**$24,920**
Task 1	$2,040
Task 2	$20,160
Task 3	$2,720
⊟ **Phase 2**	**$24,960**
Task 4	$12,960
Task 5	$10,640
Task 6	$1,360
Total	**$49,880**

Figure 9.10: Actual Cost

We can also create a cumulative version of actual cost such as the following:

```
Cumulative AC =
    VAR __ReportingDate = DATE( 2025, 4, 1 )
    VAR __Date = MAX('Dates'[Date])
    VAR __Table =
        ADDCOLUMNS(
            ADDCOLUMNS(
                FILTER('Hours', [Date] <= __Date),
                "__HourlyCost",
                RELATED('Resources'[Hourly Cost])
            ),
            "__AC",
            [Hours] * [__HourlyCost]
        )
    VAR __Result = IF( __Date > __ReportingDate, BLANK(), SUMX( __Table, [__AC] ) )
RETURN
    __Result
```

This measure calculates the actual cost for each row of the **Hours** table where the value of the **Date** column is less than the current date in context. Typically, the **__ReportingDate** would not be hard coded to a particular date but instead be set to the value of the **TODAY** function.

Create a **Line chart** with the **Date** column from the **Dates** table in the **X-axis** and the **Cumulative AC** measure as the **Y-axis**.

Cumulative AC by Date

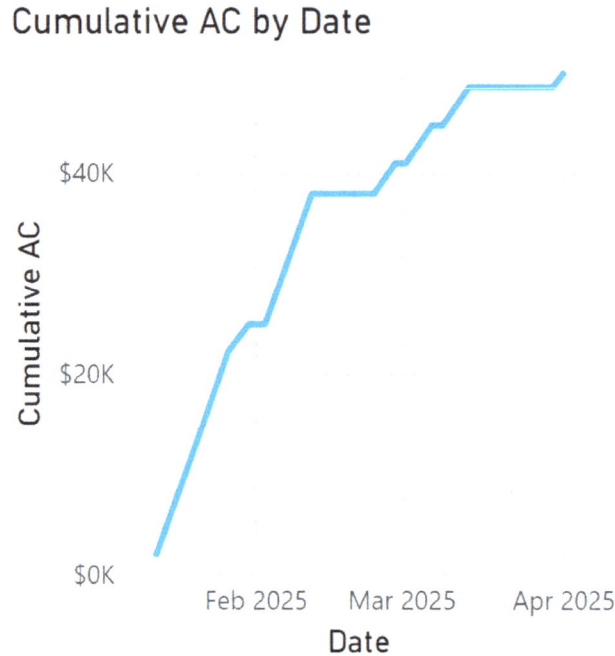

Figure 9.11: Cumulative actual cost

Now that we demonstrated how to create the actual cost for a project, we can next demonstrate how to calculate the cost variance for a project.

Cost Variance

Cost variance (CV) is the difference between the earned value of a project and the actual cost of that project. CV is a key metric that indicates whether a project is under or over budget at a specified point in time.

A positive value indicates the project's actual spending is less than the value of the work completed, in other words, the project is under budget. Conversely, a negative cost variance means the project's actual spending has exceeded the value of the completed work and thus the project is over budget. By regularly monitoring cost variance, project managers can quickly detect cost overruns or savings, enabling them to proactively adjust resources, manage budgets, and maintain tighter control over project finances.

If you have not already completed the sections, *Burndown Chart*, *Planned and Earned Value*, and *Actual Cost* in this chapter, please do so now. Next, create the following measure:

```
CV = [Cumulative EV] - [Cumulative AC]
```

This is the base **CV** measure which simply subtracts the **Cumulative AC** measure created in the *Actual Cost* section of this chapter from the **Cumulative EV** measure created in the *Planned and Earned Value* section of this chapter.

```
Current CV =
    VAR __Table =
        ADDCOLUMNS(
            'Dates',
            "__CV",
            [CV]
        )
    VAR __CurrentDate = MAXX( FILTER( __Table, NOT( ISBLANK( [CV] ) ) ), [Date] )
    VAR __Result = MAXX( FILTER( __Table, [Date] = __CurrentDate ), [__CV] )
RETURN
    __Result
```

The **Current CV** measure calculates the most recent **CV** value for the project. This is done by calculating the **CV** for each **Date** in the **Dates** table, filtering that table to remove **BLANK** values, retrieving the maximum date left in that table, and finally retrieving the **CV** for that maximum date.

Create a **Line chart** and **Card** visualization to display the **CV** and **Current CV** measures as well as the **Cumulative EV** measure:

Cumulative EV, Cumulative AC and CV by Date

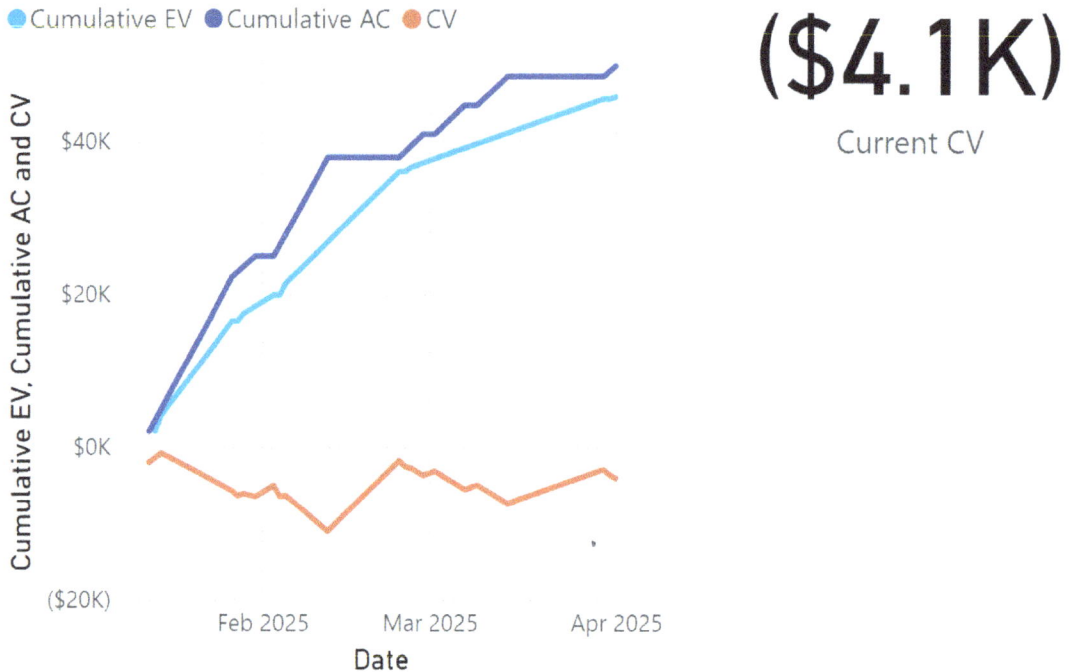

Figure 9.12: CV and Current CV

Here we can clearly see that the cumulative actual costs have exceeded the cumulative earned value during the entire project, resulting in a negative CV overall. This means that the project is over budget.

This concludes our exploration of cost variance and in general concludes our overall exploration of Earned Value Management metrics. We next look at overlapping meetings.

Overlap

Projects tend to create meetings. So much so that it is not uncommon for individuals to be involved in overlapping meetings. When meetings overlap, it can be difficult to calculate the actual amount of time spent in meetings since one cannot simply add the duration of the individual meetings together.

This calculation demonstrates one method of determining the actual amount of time spent in meetings even when meetings overlap one another.

Use an **Enter data** query to enter the following data into a table named **Meetings** or download **Chapter9_Data.xlsx** from the GitHub repository for this book and import the data on the **Meetings** sheet.

Index	Start	End
1	6/25/2024 11:00	6/25/2024 12:00
2	6/25/2024 12:00	6/25/2024 12:30
3	6/25/2024 12:30	6/25/2024 13:00
4	6/25/2024 13:00	6/25/2024 13:30
5	6/25/2024 13:00	6/25/2024 14:00
6	6/25/2024 11:00	6/25/2024 12:00
7	6/25/2024 13:00	6/25/2024 14:00
8	6/25/2024 11:30	6/25/2024 12:30
9	6/25/2024 14:30	6/25/2024 15:00

Table 9.5: Meetings data

Now create the following measure:

```
Overlap =
    VAR __Start = MIN( 'Meetings'[Start] )
    VAR __End = MAX( 'Meetings'[End] )
    VAR __Table =
        GROUPBY(
            ADDCOLUMNS(
                GENERATE(
                    GENERATESERIES( __Start, __End, 1/24/60 ),
                    ALL( 'Meetings' )
                ),
                "__Include", IF([Value] >= [Start] && [Value] <= [End], 1, 0 )
```

```
            ),

            [Value],

            "__Minute", MAXX( CURRENTGROUP(), [__Include] )

        )

    VAR __Result = SUMX( __Table, [__Minute] ) / 60
RETURN

    __Result
```

The **Overlap** measure creates a table, **__Table**, for every minute between the minimum **Start** date and time (**__Start**) and the maximum **End** date and time (**__End**) using **GENERATESERIES** with an increment of **1/24/60**. Remember that the decimal portion of a date and time value is the faction of a day which represents the time value. Thus, 1 divided by 24 divided by 60 returns the fraction of a day represented by a minute, .000694444.

The **GENERATE** function is used to evaluate every row from the **Meetings** table within the context of the table created by the **GENERATESERIES** function. For each minute, for each meeting, the **__Include** column determines if that minute is in the meeting, returning **1** if the minute is included and **0** if the meeting is not included.

We use **GROUPBY** to group the resulting table by the **Value** column (the decimal minute) and then the **__Minute** column determines once and for all whether each particular minute was included in one of the meetings being evaluated or not. We then simply need to sum the **__Minute** column from **__Table** and divide by **60** to get the number of hours.

We can also calculate the reverse, the minutes that are not included in the overlap using a similar measure:

```
Not Included =
    VAR __Start = MIN( 'Meetings'[Start] )

    VAR __End = MAX( 'Meetings'[End] )

    VAR __Table = GENERATESERIES( __Start, __End, 1/24/60)

    VAR __Table1 = ALL('Meetings')

    VAR __Table2 = GENERATE(__Table, __Table1)

    VAR __Table3 =

        ADDCOLUMNS(

            __Table2,
```

```
            "__Include",
        IF(
            COUNTROWS(
                FILTER( __Table1, [Value] >= [Start] && [Value] <= [End] )
            ) >= 1,
            0,
            1
        )
    )
VAR __Table4 =
    GROUPBY(
        __Table3,
        [Value],
        "__Minute", MAXX( CURRENTGROUP(), [__Include] )
    )
VAR __Result = SUMX( __Table4, [__Minute] ) / 60
RETURN
    __Result
```

The **Not Included** measure breaks the calculation down into multiple steps regarding the creation of the table variable. This is done to provide greater clarity and improved troubleshooting capabilities. However, the only actual difference between the **Not Included** and **Overlap** measures is in the calculation of the __Include column.

Create **Card** visuals for both measures. The **Overlap** measure returns a value of **3.5** hours even though the total duration of the meetings equals 7 hours. The **Not Included** measure returns .5 hours. Note that the **3.5** and .5 add up to the total of 4 hours, which corresponds to the minimum **Start** date and time, **6/25/2024 11:00** and the maximum **End** date and time, **6/25/2024 15:00**.

Let's now move on to another project management topic, the overallocation of resources.

Overworked

It is not uncommon for employees and other resources to be involved in multiple projects at the same time. In such situations, it is easy for those resources to be overallocated. Overallocation occurs when a resource is expected to work beyond their capacity in terms of available hours in a day or week.

To demonstrate how to visualize this overallocation we can start by using an **Enter data** query to enter the following data into a table named **Tasks** or download **Chapter9_Data.xlsx** from the GitHub repository for this book and import the data on the **Tasks** sheet.

Employee Id	Task Id	Project Id	Task Due	Hours	Week	Task Start
1	1	1	1/31/2025	8	5	1/31/2025
2	2	1	1/24/2025	32	4	1/21/2025
3	3	1	1/17/2025	16	3	1/16/2025
3	4	1	1/17/2025	8	3	1/17/2025
3	5	1	1/17/2025	8	3	1/17/2025
3	6	2	1/17/2025	8	3	1/17/2025
3	7	2	1/17/2025	8	3	1/17/2025
1	8	2	12/6/2024	8	49	12/6/2024
3	9	2	11/29/2024	40	48	11/25/2024
3	10	3	11/22/2024	16	47	11/21/2024
1	11	3	2/14/2025	24	7	2/12/2025
4	12	3	2/14/2025	32	7	2/11/2025

Table 9.6: Tasks data

This data represents four different employees working on three different projects. Each task is assigned to exactly one employee.

Now create the following calculated table:

```
Overworked =

    VAR __Weekdays =

        FILTER(

            CALENDAR( MIN( 'Tasks'[Task Start] ), MAX( 'Tasks'[Task Due] ) ),

            WEEKDAY( [Date], 2 ) < 6

        )

    VAR __Table =

        SELECTCOLUMNS(

            ADDCOLUMNS(

                GENERATE(

                    DISTINCT( 'Tasks'[Employee Id] ),

                    __Weekdays

                ),

                "__WorkHours", 8

            ),

            "__EmployeeId", [Employee Id],

            "__Date", [Date],

            "__WorkHours", [__WorkHours]

        )

    VAR __Result =

        SELECTCOLUMNS(

            ADDCOLUMNS(

                __Table,

                "Week", WEEKNUM( [__Date]),

                "Hours",

                    SUMX(

                        ADDCOLUMNS(

                            FILTER(
```

```
                                'Tasks',

                                'Tasks'[Employee Id] = [__EmployeeId]

                        ),

                        "Must Work",

                        IF( [__Date] >= [Task Start] && [__Date] <= [Task Due], 1 )

                    ),

                    [Must Work]

                ) * [__WorkHours]

            ),

        "Employee Id", [__EmployeeId],

        "Date", [__Date],

        "Work Hours", [__WorkHours],

        "Week", [Week],

        "Hours", [Hours]

    )

RETURN

    __Result
```

This table works similarly to the **Overlap** measure from the previous section of this chapter. However, instead of creating a table of every minute of every day for every meeting, the **Overworked** table creates a table of every day for every employee. This table is then filtered to only weekdays and a maximum of eight work hours are assigned to each day (__**WorkHours**).

It is important to note the use of **SELECTCOLUMNS** for the __**Table** variable. Once **SELECTCOLUMNS** is invoked, only the specified columns are included in the resulting table and all other columns are lost. Thus, for example, the __**Table** variable does not include an __**IsWeekDay** column.

One might wonder why it is necessary to use **SELECTCOLUMNS** and the answer is to rename the columns to avoid confusion by the DAX engine. Had we not renamed the **Employee ID** column specifically, the comparison made when calculating the __**Result** variable would have returned incorrect results.

Specifically, this line from the **Overworked** table:

```
                    'Tasks'[Employee Id] = [__EmployeeId]
```

Would have looked like the following without a rename:

```
'Tasks'[Employee Id] = [Employee Id]
```

In this case, the DAX engine would interpret the second **Employee ID** column specification to also come from the **Tasks** table, which is not what is desired.

The __**Result** variable performs the heavy lifting of calculating the actual hours that must be worked on each day by each employee. This is done by summing up the number of work hours for each task that the employee is assigned to each day. Finally, the __**Result** variable simply renames the columns from internal code names to friendly names.

Patron Recommendation

Alexis Olson created an alternative form for this table calculation:

```
Overworked Alt =
    VAR __Calendar =
        CALENDAR(
            MIN( Tasks[Task Start] ),
            MAX( Tasks[Task Due] )
        )
    VAR __Weekdays =
        FILTER(
            __Calendar,
            WEEKDAY( [Date], 3 ) < 5
        )
    VAR __WorkHours = 8
    VAR __Result =
        GENERATE(
            __Weekdays,
            SUMMARIZE(
                FILTER(
                    Tasks,
                    [Date] >= [Task Start]
                        && [Date] <= [Task Due]
```

```
            ),

            Tasks[Employee Id],

            "Work Hours", __WorkHours,

            "Week", WEEKNUM( [Date] ),

            "Hours", COUNTROWS( Tasks ) * __WorkHours

        )

    )

RETURN

    __Result
```

We can visualize the **Overworked** table by creating a **Clustered bar chart** visual with the **Employee ID**, and **Week** columns in the **Y-axis** field well and the **Sum of Hours** in the **X-axis** field well. Add an **X-axis** constant line of **40** hours.

Sum of Hours by Employee Id and Week

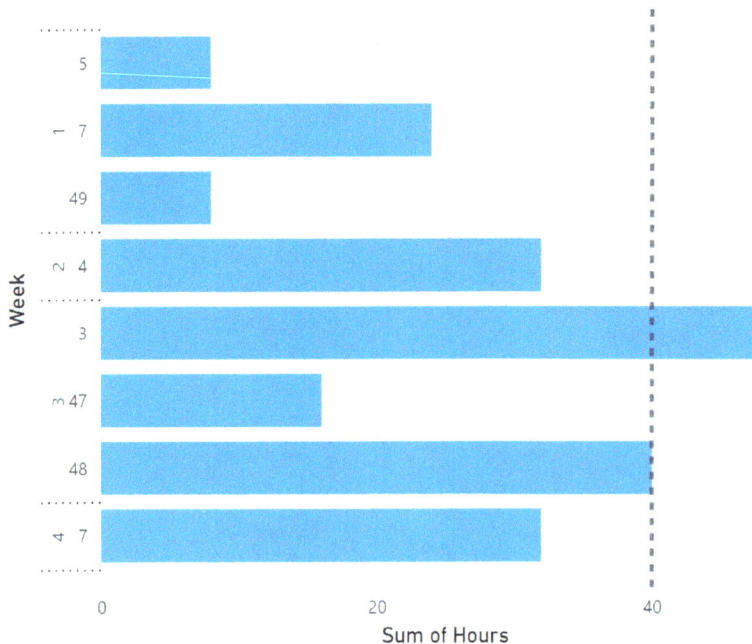

Figure 9.13: Overworked table viewed weekly

Here we can clearly see that **Employee ID 3** is overallocated for the 3rd week of the year. We can also view the data by day, creating the same chart but with **Employee ID** and **Date** in the **X-Axis**:

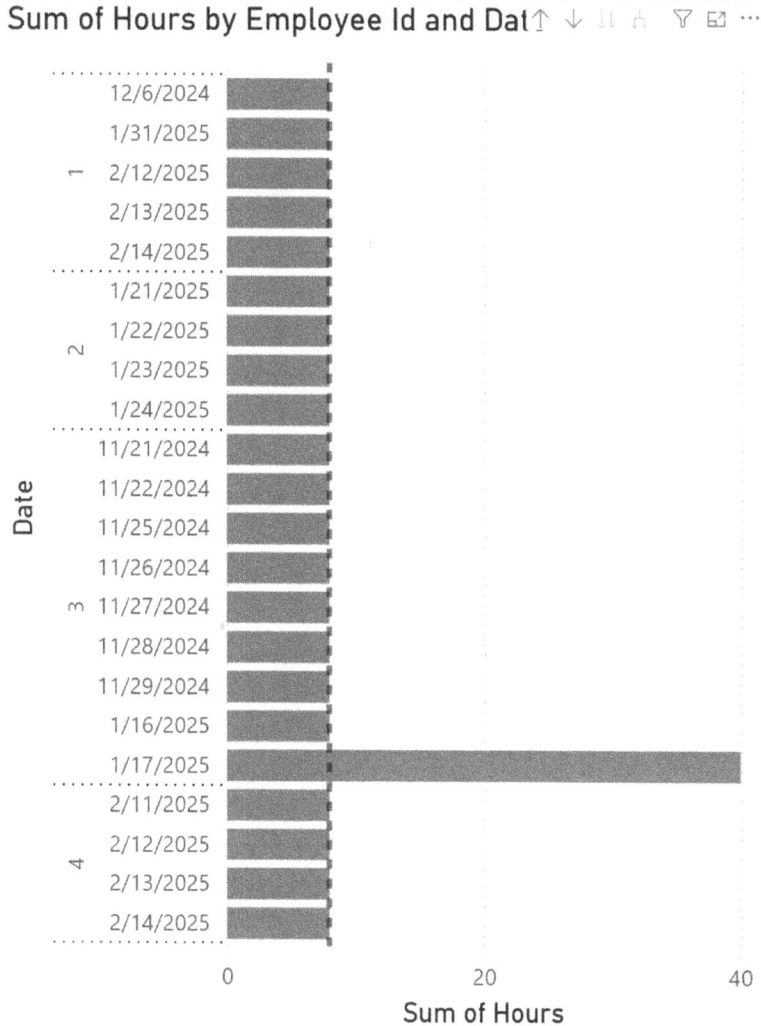

Figure 9.14: Overworked table viewed by date

Here we can clearly see that **Employee ID 3** is expected to work 40 hours in a single day, which is, of course, impossible.

This concludes our exploration of project management metrics and KPI's.

Summary

This chapter focused on project management KPIs and metrics with a strong emphasis on Earned Value Management (EVM) methodologies. We began by explaining the significance of projects within organizations as vehicles for change, innovation, and improvement. We then explored key EVM concepts such as Planned Value (PV), Earned Value (EV), Schedule Variance (SV), Actual Cost (AC), and Cost Variance (CV). Many of these topics included current value calculations as well as cumulative calculations.

In addition to EVM metrics, we also covered topics such as the creation of burndown charts, overlapping meetings and visualizing overallocated employees. The vast majority of all the calculations in this chapter again followed the typical No CALCULATE pattern of creating one or more virtual table variables and then performing X-aggregations across those tables. As a whole, this chapter presents an effective set of calculations that can assist in tracking and evaluating project performance.

In the next chapter, we delve into financial metrics and KPIs.

CHAPTER 10

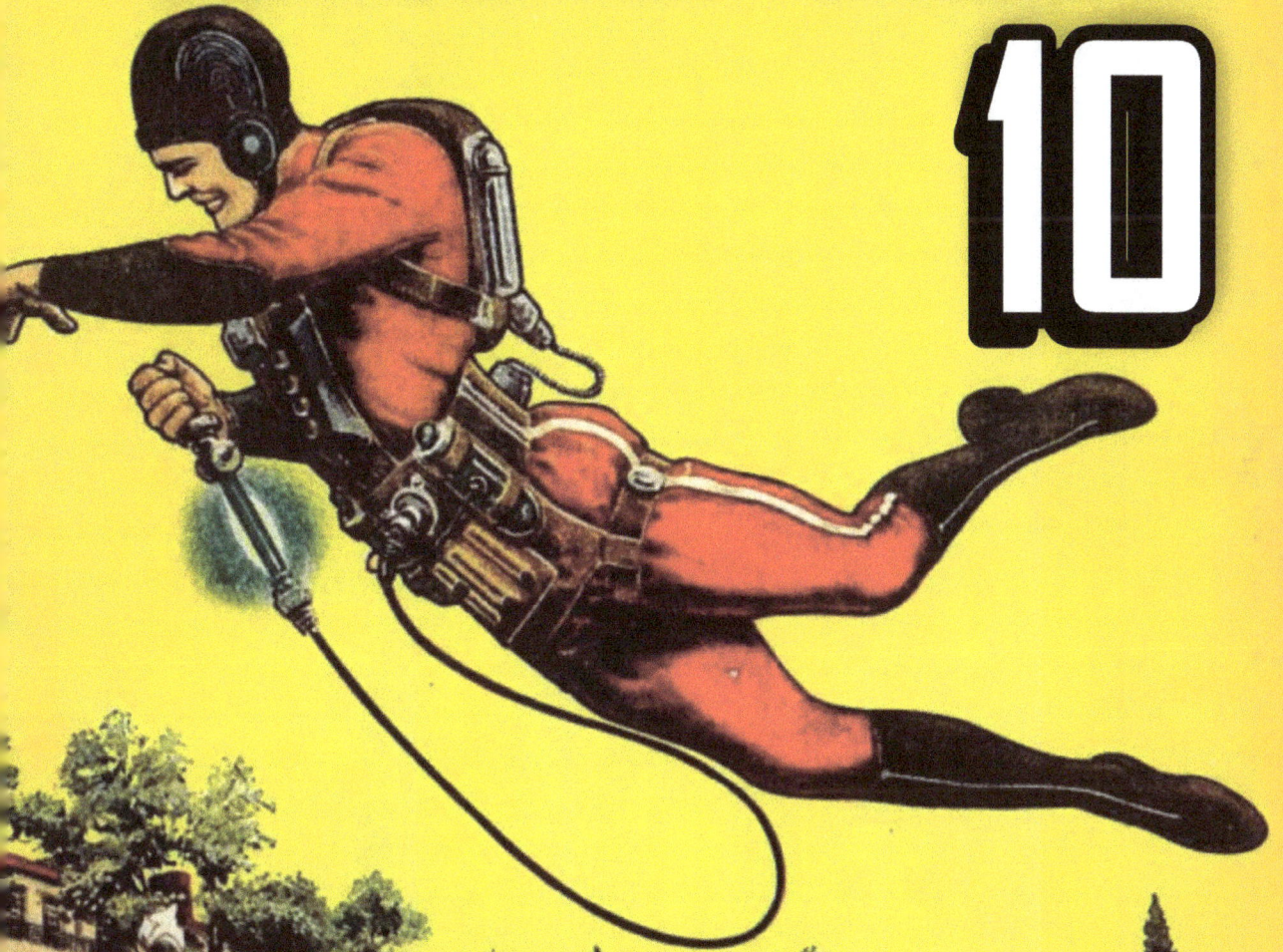

10

Finance

It goes without saying that finances are critical to any organization. Tracking financial metrics and Key Performance Indicators (KPIs) is critical because such measures are the best method of evaluating an organization's fiscal health and profitability. By measuring factors such as revenue growth, operating margins, and cash flow, organizations gain the ability to make data-driven decisions about such things as resource allocation, pricing strategies, and cost management, which ultimately leads to stability and enhanced profitability. In addition, monitoring financial metrics can assist in uncovering potential risks or inefficiencies allowing course corrections and other corrective actions.

In addition to the benefits mentioned thus far, the transparent reporting of financial KPIs fosters accountability and trust among stakeholders such as investors, creditors, and employees. Well-defined metrics and targets help individuals and departments align themselves with the broader financial objectives of an organization. For instance, a sales team might prioritize efforts to increase recurring revenue if **monthly recurring revenue (MRR)** is a priority of the organization. Similarly, operations teams might focus on optimizing processes that affect the **cost of goods sold (COGS)**. Robust financial metric tracking helps strengthen an organization's bottom line while also supporting strategic planning and resiliency.

This chapter covers numerous financial metrics and KPIs. Many financial KPIs are simple addition, division, and subtraction. In addition, the DAX language now contains over 50 dedicated financial functions for computing numerous advanced financial metrics. Therefore, this chapter seeks to explore some more uncommon financial scenarios as well as basic financial KPIs. Data and other files for this chapter are available in the GitHub repository for this book: https://github.com/gdeckler/DAX-For-Humans/tree/main/book.

Gross Margin, Revenue, and Cost

Gross margin is a simple calculation measuring the percentage of revenue a business retains after subtracting the direct costs of providing the goods and services associated with those sales. For example, in the professional services industry the direct costs are generally the fully loaded costs of the employee delivering the professional services. The formula for gross margin is as follows:

$$\% \ GM = \frac{(\ Revenue - Cost\ )}{Revenue} * 100$$

With a bit of algebra, we can rework this formula to solve for revenue when the desired % **GM** and **Cost** are known:

$$Revenue = \frac{Cost}{(\ 100 - \% \ GM\ )}$$

This is useful, for example, in cases where a professional services firm knows the fully loaded cost of an employee as well as the desired % **GM** they wish to achieve and need to know the hourly rate to charge.

We can also solve the formula for **Cost**:

$$Cost = Revenue * (\ 100 - \% \ GM\ )$$

This formula is useful in situations where there is a defined **Revenue** and a desired % **GM**. In this case you want to understand the maximum **Cost**. Situations like this can arise in circumstances such as professional services where a customer has specified a desired billable rate and you are trying to match suitable resources given a desired gross margin.

We can use this information to create a calculator of sorts for a professional services firm that allows us to determine the % **GM**, **Revenue**, or **Cost** based on knowing only two of the parameters. To do this, follow these steps:

1. In Power BI Desktop, select the **Modeling** tab.
2. In the ribbon, select **New Parameter**.
3. Select **Numeric Range**:

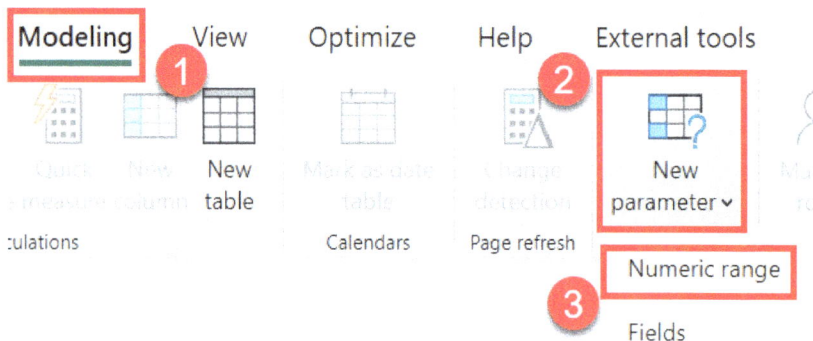

Figure 10.1: Creating a Numeric range parameter

4. For the **Name**, enter **Target Gross Margin**. Use a **Data type** of **Decimal number**, a **Minimum** of **.05**, a **Maximum** of **1**, an **Increment** of **.05**, and a **Default** of **.35**:

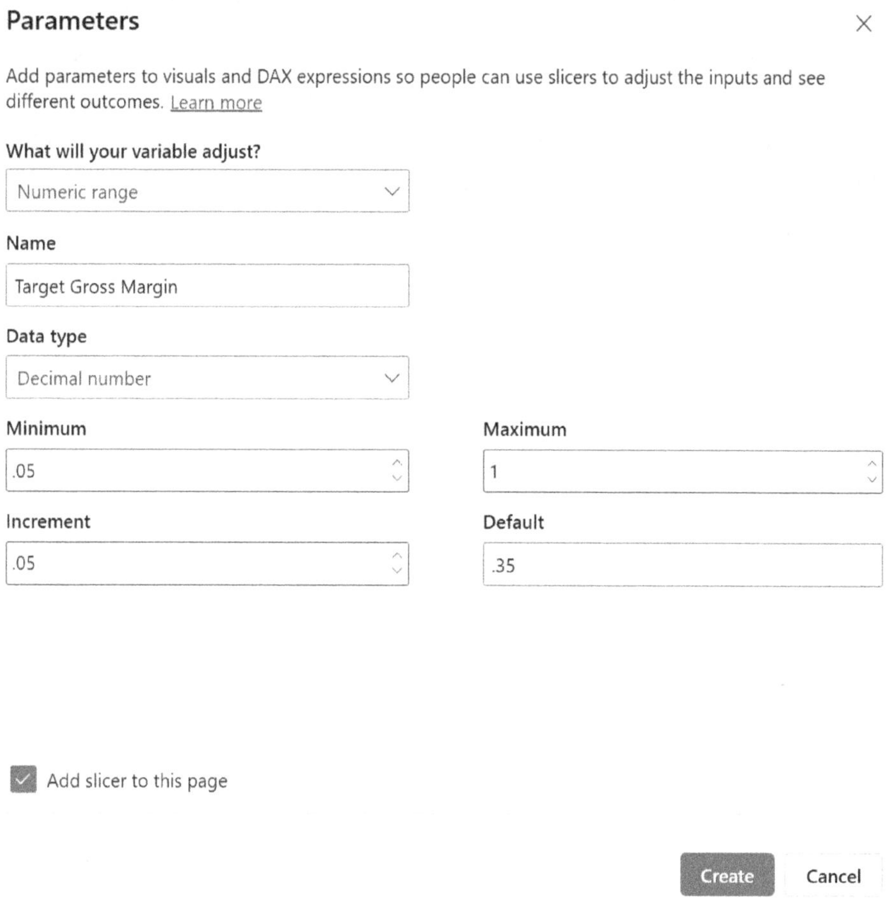

Figure 10.2: Gross Margin numeric range parameter

5. Click the **Create** button to create the numeric range parameter and add a single selection **Slicer** visual to the page.
6. Expand the **Target Gross Margin** table created in the **Data pane** and set the **Format** of the **Target Gross Margin** column to **Percentage** in the **Column** tools tab of the ribbon.
7. Repeat steps 1 through 5 to create a second numeric range parameter called **Target Hourly Rate**. Use a **Data type** of **Whole number**, a **Minimum** of **25**, a **Maximum** of **250**, an **Increment** of **5**, and a **Default** of **165**.
8. Repeat steps 1 through 5 to create a third numeric range parameter called **Target Hourly Cost** with the same parameters as the **Revenue** parameter.
9. Format the **Target Hourly Rate** and **Target Hourly Cost** columns as **Currency**.

Creating a numeric range parameter creates three items. First, a table is created that is named the same as the chosen parameter name. This table uses **GENERATESERIES** to create a single column table. The name of the column is the same as the parameter name.

Second, a measure is created. This measure is named the same as the parameter but is suffixed with "**Value**". This measure uses **SELECTEDVALUE** to retrieve the chosen value of the parameter from the table, using the optional second argument to implement the chosen default value. Finally, a single selection slicer is created on the page.

Next, create the following three measures:

```
% GM =
    VAR __Revenue = SELECTEDVALUE( 'Target Hourly Rate'[Target Hourly Rate] )
    VAR __Cost = SELECTEDVALUE( 'Target Hourly Cost'[Target Hourly Cost] )
    VAR __Result = MROUND( DIVIDE( __Revenue - __Cost, __Revenue, BLANK() ), .05 )
RETURN
    __Result
```

```
Revenue =
    VAR __GM = SELECTEDVALUE( 'Target Gross Margin'[Target Gross Margin] )
    VAR __Cost = SELECTEDVALUE( 'Target Hourly Cost'[Target Hourly Cost] )
    VAR __Result = MROUND( DIVIDE( __Cost, 1 - __GM, BLANK() ), 5 )
RETURN
    __Result
```

```
Cost =
    VAR __GM = SELECTEDVALUE( 'Target Gross Margin'[Target Gross Margin] )
    VAR __Revenue = SELECTEDVALUE( 'Target Hourly Rate'[Target Hourly Rate] )
    VAR __Result = MROUND( __Revenue * ( 1 - __GM ), 5 )
RETURN
    __Result
```

Format the **% GM** measure as a **Percentage** and the **Revenue** and **Cost measures** as **Currency** with **0** decimal places. Finally, add a **Card** visual to a report page for each measure.

You can now adjust the **Slicer** visuals to calculate the **% GM** for a given **Target Hourly Rate** and **Target Hourly Cost**, calculate the **Revenue** for a given **% GM** and **Target Hourly Cost**, or calculate the maximum **Cost** for a desired **% GM** and **Target Hourly Rate**.

All the measures are relatively simple using **SELECTEDVALUE** to retrieve the selected slicer value as appropriate. The **MROUND** function is used to round the results to the nearest **.05** (5%) for **% GM** and the nearest **$5** for **Revenue** and **Cost**. This is because we set our increments to be these same values when defining our numeric range parameters.

Let's now turn our attention to calculating currency exchange rates.

Currency Exchange Rates

Global organizations often conduct business in multiple currencies around the world. However, for reporting purposes, such organizations often wish to view reports on revenue and other financial metrics in a single currency. This naturally requires converting from one currency to another. To convert currencies in this manner requires a table of exchange rates.

To see how to use an exchange rates table to convert currencies, first use an **Enter data** query to create a **Currencies** table using the following data or alternatively load the **Currencies** sheet of the Excel file, **Chapter10_Data.xlsx**, available in the GitHub repository for this book.

Currency
USD
EUR
GBP

Table 10.1: Currencies data

Next, use another **Enter data** query to create an **Exchange Rates** table using the following data or alternatively load the **Exchange Rates** sheet of the Excel file, **Chapter10_Data.xlsx**, available in the GitHub repository for this book.

From	To	Date	Rate
USD	EUR	3-Dec-24	0.9026
USD	GBP	3-Dec-24	0.7706
EUR	USD	3-Dec-24	1.1078
EUR	GBP	3-Dec-24	0.8537

GBP	USD	3-Dec-24	1.2975
GBP	EUR	3-Dec-24	1.1711
USD	EUR	15-Dec-24	0.9014
USD	GBP	15-Dec-24	0.7685
EUR	USD	15-Dec-24	1.1065
EUR	GBP	15-Dec-24	0.8512
GBP	USD	15-Dec-24	1.293
GBP	EUR	15-Dec-24	1.1711
USD	EUR	27-Dec-24	0.9036
USD	GBP	27-Dec-24	0.7733
EUR	USD	27-Dec-24	1.1093
EUR	GBP	27-Dec-24	0.8564
GBP	USD	27-Dec-24	1.301
GBP	EUR	27-Dec-24	1.1711

Table 10.2: Exchange rates data

Now, use a third **Enter data** query to create a table called **Sales** using the following data or alternatively load the **Sales** sheet of the Excel file, **Chapter10_Data.xlsx**, available in the GitHub repository for this book.

Date	Currency	Amount
12/3/2024	USD	100.00
12/4/2024	EUR	100.00
12/5/2024	GBP	100.00

12/15/2024	USD	200.00
12/22/2024	EUR	200.00
12/24/2024	GBP	200.00
12/27/2024	USD	300.00
12/28/2024	EUR	300.00
12/29/2024	GBP	300.00

Table 10.3: Sales data

Ensure that there are no relationships between these three tables. Note that in the **Exchange Rates** table there are six lines for every date. This is because currency conversion rates between two currencies is not necessarily 100% reciprocal. Also note that there are not conversion rates for every day and thus we will use the last known exchange rate when performing our calculations.

Now create the following measure:

```
Converted Sales =
    VAR __TargetCurrency = SELECTEDVALUE( 'Currencies'[Currency], "USD" )
    VAR __Table =
        ADDCOLUMNS(
            ADDCOLUMNS(
                'Sales',
                "__ExchangeDate",
                    VAR __Date = [Date]
                    VAR __Currency = [Currency]
                    VAR __Result =
                        MAXX(
                            FILTER(
                                'Exchange Rates',
                                [Date] <= __Date && [From] = __Currency &&
```

```
                                        [To] = __TargetCurrency
                            ),
                            [Date]
                        )
                RETURN
                    __Result
            ),
            "__Rate",
                VAR __Currency = [Currency]
                VAR __Rate =
                    MAXX(
                        FILTER(
                            'Exchange Rates',
                            [Date] = [__ExchangeDate] && [From] = __Currency &&
                                [To] = __TargetCurrency
                        ),
                        [Rate]
                    )
                VAR __Result = COALESCE( __Rate, 1 )
            RETURN
                __Result
        )
    VAR __Result = SUMX( __Table, [__Rate] * [Amount] )
RETURN
    __Result
```

Note that this is a classic example of a semi-additive measure as covered in *Chapter 2, Measure Totals*.

Give this measure the following **Dynamic** format string:

```
SWITCH(

        MAX( 'Currencies'[Currency] ),

        "GBP",  "\£#,0.00;(\£#,0.00);\£#,0.00",

        "EUR",  "\€#,0.00;(\€#,0.00);\€#,0.00",

        "\$#,0.00;(\$#,0.00);\$#,0.00"

)
```

Add a **Slicer** visual for the **Currency** column in the **Currencies** table. In addition, create a **Table** visualization that includes the **Date**, **Currency**, and **Amount** columns from the **Sales** table along with the **Converted Sales** measure. Your visuals should look like the following:

Currency	Date	Currency	Sum of Amount	Converted Sales
☐ EUR	Tuesday, December 03, 2024	USD	100	$100.00
☐ GBP	Wednesday, December 04, 2024	EUR	100	$110.78
■ USD	Thursday, December 05, 2024	GBP	100	$129.75
	Sunday, December 15, 2024	USD	200	$200.00
	Sunday, December 22, 2024	EUR	200	$221.31
	Tuesday, December 24, 2024	GBP	200	$258.59
	Friday, December 27, 2024	USD	300	$300.00
	Saturday, December 28, 2024	EUR	300	$332.79
	Sunday, December 29, 2024	GBP	300	$390.31
	Total		**1,800**	**$2,043.52**

Figure 10.3: Exchange rate conversion

The **Converted Sales** measure starts by getting the selected target **Currency** using the **SELECTEDVALUE** function with a default of "**USD**" (**__TargetCurrency**). Next, we build a table using two nested **ADDCOLUMNS** statements targeting the **Sales** table. This is done so that the measure works correctly at the individual row level as well as in the total since this is a semi-additive measure.

The first column added, **__ExchangeDate**, determines the last known exchange rate date given the current row's **Currency** and the **__TargetCurrency**. This is done by using **MAXX** coupled with a **FILTER** statement that ensures that the **Date** in the **Exchange Rates** table is less than or equal to the current row's date and that the **From** and **To** currencies match the current row's **Currency** and **__TargetCurrency** respectively.

Once the **__ExchangeDate** for each row is determined, the next column is the **__Rate** column. This is calculated in a similar manner to **__ExchangeDate** with the added condition of using the

COALESCE function. The **COALESCE** function returns the first value that is not **BLANK** or **BLANK** if all values evaluate to **BLANK**. This is a fancy way of writing the following:

```
IF( __Rate = BLANK(), 1, __Rate )
```

An argument could be made to use this basic version for readability, and this would also be more in line with the No CALCULATE approach to using basic DAX functions and minimizing the DAX functions used. In any event, this additional check is required since our **Exchange Rates** table does not include rows for same currency conversions (for example, USD to USD). Therefore, when no exchange rate is found, this calculation assumes a same currency conversion is occurring.

Once the __**Table** variable is created, we can simply use **SUMX** to multiply each row's __**Rate** and **Amount** together and sum the result. The resulting measure works for both individual rows and the total row of the **Table** visual. If we had constructed a measure without considering the semi-additive nature of the calculation, we could easily have ended up with an incorrect total.

This concludes our exploration of exchange rates. Let's now take a look at periodic billing.

Periodic Billing

Subscription services have become all the rage with the advent of cloud computing models. Subscription services often have a specified commitment such as 12 months but are billed monthly. This can be true of services such as Microsoft 365 and Power BI Pro subscriptions. These services can be purchased on an annual commitment but billed monthly. The annual commitment provides a discount on the subscription price.

The following scenario involves a fact table that designates subscriptions for services with a start and end date as well as the monthly subscription cost. The desire is to create a calculation that provides the total monthly revenue for all subscriptions.

To demonstrate such a calculation, use an **Enter data** query to create a **Periodic Billing** table using the following data or alternatively load the **Periodic Billing** sheet of the Excel file, **Chapter10_Data.xlsx**, available in the GitHub repository for this book.

Customer	BeginDate	UntilDate	Amount
A	15-Jan-23	15-Jan-25	$35
B	30-Jan-24	30-Jan-25	$90
C	3-Feb-24	3-Feb-25	$35

Customer	BeginDate	UntilDate	Amount
D	6-Mar-24	6-Mar-25	$50
E	12-May-24	12-May-25	$35
F	24-May-24	24-May-25	$35
G	4-Jun-24	4-Jun-25	$90
H	1-Jul-24	1-Jul-25	$50
I	2-Aug-24	2-Aug-25	$90
J	15-Sep-24	15-Sep-25	$90

Table 10.4: Period billing data

Create a **Dates** table with the following formula:

```
Dates =

    ADDCOLUMNS(

        CALENDAR( DATE( 2023, 1, 1 ), DATE( 2025, 12, 31 ) ),

        "Year Month", FORMAT( [Date], "yyyy mmm" ),

        "YM Sort", YEAR( [Date] ) * 100 + MONTH( [Date] )

    )
```

Ensure that there is no relationship between the two tables. In addition, set the **Sort by** column for the **Year Month** column to the **YM Sort** column.

Now create the following measure:

```
Monthly Revenue =

    VAR __Billings =

        ADDCOLUMNS(

            'Periodic Billing',

            "__YMBegin", YEAR( [BeginDate] ) * 100 + MONTH( [BeginDate] ),

            "__YMEnd",   YEAR( [EndDate] ) * 100 + MONTH( [EndDate] )

        )
```

```
VAR __Table =

    SELECTCOLUMNS(

        GENERATE(

            __Billings,

            SUMMARIZE(

                FILTER(

                    'Dates',

                    [YM Sort] >= [__YMBegin] &&

                    [YM Sort] <= [__YMEnd]

                ),

                [YM Sort]

            )

        ),

        "Amount", [Amount]

    )

VAR __Result = SUMX( __Table, [Amount] )

RETURN

    __Result
```

The **Monthly Revenue** measure starts by adding **__YMBegin** and **__YMEnd** columns to the **Billings** table to create the table variable, **__Billings**. These columns create a numeric version of the combined year and month by multiplying the **YEAR** of the **Date** column multiplied by **100** and adding the **MONTH** of the **Date** column. Thus, for example, a **Date** of January 1st, 2024 produces a numeric value of 202401.

Next, the **__Table** table variable is computed using the **GENERATE** function. The **GENERATE** function constructs the Cartesian product of two tables by evaluating each row of the second table within the context of the first table. In this case, we use **SUMMARIZE** and **FILTER** to first filter the **Dates** table to only include dates that are between the beginning and ending year months and then summarize that filtered table by the **YM Sort** column.

We could have moved the **FILTER** outside the **SUMMARIZE** statement. However, this could possibly introduce inefficiency since some **Dates** that fall outside the desired filtered range would be computed as part of the **GENERATE** function and then subsequently be filtered. That said, it is likely the DAX query engine would automatically optimize the calculation regardless, but it's better to be safe and ensure this is the case.

Additional optimization is introduced by using the **SELECTCOLUMNS** statement to only return the **Amount** column for the generated table. This minimizes the memory storage consumed by the __Table variable. We can then simply use **SUMX** to sum the **Amount** column within the __Table variable.

Create a **Clustered column chart** with the **Year Month** column from the **Dates** table as the **X-axis** and the **Monthly Revenue** measure as the **Y-axis**. Use the ellipses (**...**) for the visual to ensure the visual is sorted by the **Year Month** column in **Ascending** order:

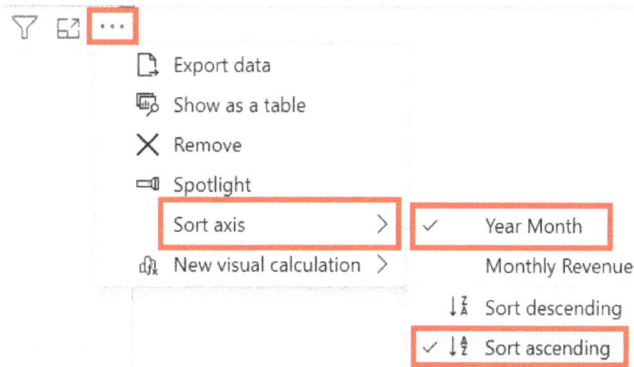

Figure 10.4: Specifying the sorting for a visual

Your visual should now look like the following:

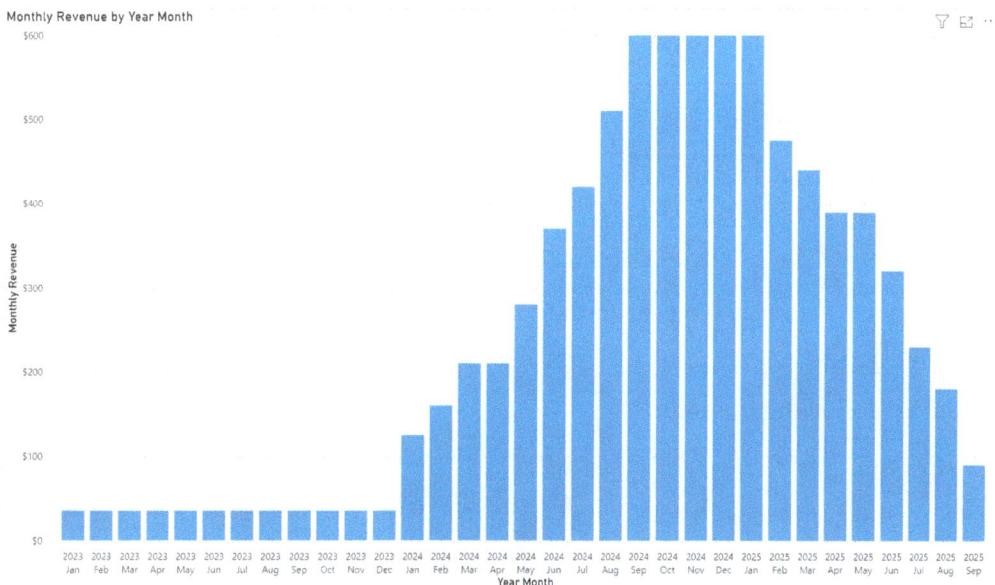

Figure 10.5: Monthly revenue for periodic billing

Our analysis of periodic billing is now complete. We now move on to dealing with reverse engineering year-to-date revenues.

Reverse Year-To-Date

Tracking monthly financial metrics such as revenue is common within many organizations. It is also fairly common to accumulate such monthly numbers via period to date calculations such as quarter-to-date and year-to-date as shown in *Chapter 3, Dates and Calendars.*

This calculation demonstrates how to reverse engineer monthly financial figures from accumulated year-to-date data. To demonstrate this technique, start by using an **Enter data** query to create a **Year To Date** table using the following data or alternatively load the **Year To Date** sheet of the Excel file, **Chapter10_Data.xlsx,** available in the GitHub repository for this book.

Year	Month	Revenue YTD
2024	10	$ 110,000,000.00
2024	11	$ 122,000,000.00
2024	12	$ 130,000,000.00
2025	1	$ 12,000,000.00
2025	2	$ 19,000,000.00
2025	3	$ 31,000,000.00
2025	4	$ 42,000,000.00

Table 10.5: Year to date data

This table tracks the cumulative year-to-date revenue for each month. Thus, the **Revenue YTD** resets in January 2025.

Now create the following measure:

```
Reverse YTD =
    VAR __Year = MAX( 'Year To Date'[Year] )
    VAR __Month = MAX( 'Year To Date'[Month] )
    VAR __CurrentYTD = MAX( 'Year To Date'[Revenue YTD] )
```

```
VAR __PreviousYTD =

    MAXX(

        FILTER(

            ALL( 'Year To Date' ),

            [Year] = __Year && [Month] = __Month - 1

        ),

        [Revenue YTD]

    )

VAR __Result = __CurrentYTD - __PreviousYTD

RETURN

    __Result
```

We start by getting the current **Year**, **Month**, and **Revenue YTD** in the **__Year**, **__Month**, and **__CurrentYTD** variables respectively. To get the previous row's **Revenue YTD**, **__PreviousYTD**, we use the **ALL** function to remove all filters from the **Year to Date** table. We then **FILTER** that table for the row where the **Year** equals the current year, **__Year**, and the **Month** equals the current month, **__Month**, minus one. We use **MAXX** to retrieve the **Revenue YTD** for that row. Finally, we simply subtract the two values, **__CurrentYTD** and **__PreviousYTD** to get the monthly revenue number.

> **Patron Recommendation**
>
> Alexis Olson notes that the **__PreviousYTD** calculation assumes that we have the **Revenue YTD** for every month with no gaps.

This calculation is rather simple but demonstrates a technique for comparing a current row to a previous row, which is a common requirement in various calculations.

Placing the **Reverse YTD** measure into a **Table** visual along with un-summarized **Year**, **Month**, and **Revenue YTD** columns from the **Year To Date** table produces the following visualization:

Year	Month	Revenue YTD	Reverse YTD
2024	10	$110,000,000	$110,000,000
2024	11	$122,000,000	$12,000,000
2024	12	$130,000,000	$8,000,000
2025	1	$12,000,000	$12,000,000
2025	2	$19,000,000	$7,000,000
2025	3	$31,000,000	$12,000,000
2025	4	$42,000,000	$11,000,000
Total			**$130,000,000**

Figure 10.6: Reverse YTD measure in a Table visualization

Let's next take a look at comparing budgets to actuals.

Comparing Budgets and Actuals

Comparing budgets to actuals is a common requirement for individuals involved in the financials of organizations. However, budgets and actuals are often tracked at different levels of granularity. For example, budgets are often tracked at the monthly level of granularity while actuals are often reported at the daily level of granularity. Because of the different levels of granularity, it can be challenging to compare the two sets of numbers.

This calculation demonstrates how to compare the budgets and actuals given two different levels of data granularity. To get started, use an **Enter data** query to create a **Budget** table using the following data or alternatively load the **Budget** sheet of the Excel file, **Chapter10_Data.xlsx**, available in the GitHub repository for this book.

Month Year	Moth Year Sort	Budget
Jan-24	1	$ 3,100,000.00
Feb-24	2	$ 2,800,000.00
Mar-24	3	$ 3,200,000.00
Apr-24	4	$ 3,000,000.00

May-24	5	$ 3,100,000.00
Jun-24	6	$ 2,900,000.00
Jul-24	7	$ 2,900,000.00
Aug-24	8	$ 2,800,000.00
Sep-24	9	$ 3,000,000.00
Oct-24	10	$ 3,200,000.00
Nov-24	11	$ 2,800,000.00
Dec-24	12	$ 2,500,000.00

Table 10.6: Budget data

Ensure that the **Month Year** column loads as **Text** and not a **Date** data type. Set the **Sort by** column for the **Month Year** column to the **Month Year Sort** column.

Next, create a **Revenue** table using an **Enter data** query with the following data or alternatively load the **Revenue** sheet of the Excel file, **Chapter10_Data.xlsx**, available in the GitHub repository for this book.

Date	Revenue
1-Jan-24	$ 100,000.00
2-Jan-24	$ 110,000.00
3-Jan-24	$ 110,000.00
4-Jan-24	$ 110,000.00
5-Jan-24	$ 115,000.00
6-Jan-24	$ 115,000.00
7-Jan-24	$ 115,000.00
8-Jan-24	$ 110,000.00

Date	Revenue
9-Jan-24	$ 110,000.00
10-Jan-24	$ 110,000.00
11-Jan-24	$ 100,000.00
12-Jan-24	$ 100,000.00
13-Jan-24	$ 100,000.00
14-Jan-24	$ 110,000.00
15-Jan-24	$ 110,000.00
16-Jan-24	$ 110,000.00
17-Jan-24	$ 115,000.00
18-Jan-24	$ 115,000.00
19-Jan-24	$ 115,000.00
20-Jan-24	$ 110,000.00
21-Jan-24	$ 110,000.00
22-Jan-24	$ 110,000.00
23-Jan-24	$ 100,000.00
24-Jan-24	$ 100,000.00
25-Jan-24	$ 100,000.00
26-Jan-24	$ 95,000.00
27-Jan-24	$ 95,000.00
28-Jan-24	$ 95,000.00

Date	Revenue
29-Jan-24	$ 90,000.00
30-Jan-24	$ 90,000.00
31-Jan-24	$ 90,000.00
1-Feb-24	$ 90,000.00
2-Feb-24	$ 90,000.00
3-Feb-24	$ 90,000.00
4-Feb-24	$ 90,000.00
5-Feb-24	$ 95,000.00
6-Feb-24	$ 95,000.00
7-Feb-24	$ 95,000.00
8-Feb-24	$ 95,000.00
9-Feb-24	$ 95,000.00
10-Feb-24	$ 100,000.00
11-Feb-24	$ 100,000.00
12-Feb-24	$ 110,000.00
13-Feb-24	$ 110,000.00
14-Feb-24	$ 115,000.00

Table 10.7: Revenue data

Ensure that the **Date** column loads as a **Date** data type.

We can now create a calculation that allows us to compare budgets and actuals at the monthly level as follows:

```
Revenue Per Month =
```

```
VAR __MonthYear = MAX( 'Budget'[Month Year] )

VAR __Table =

    FILTER(

        ADDCOLUMNS(

            'Revenue',

            "__MonthYear", FORMAT( [Date], "mmm-yyyy" )

        ),

        [__MonthYear] = __MonthYear

    )

VAR __Result = SUMX( __Table, [Revenue] )

RETURN

    __Result
```

We can use this measure to visually compare the budget versus actuals in a **Clustered column chart** by using the **Month Year** column from the **Budget** table as the **X-axis** along with the summed **Budget** column and **Revenue Per Month** measure as the **Y-axis**:

Sum of Budget and Revenue Per Month by Month Year

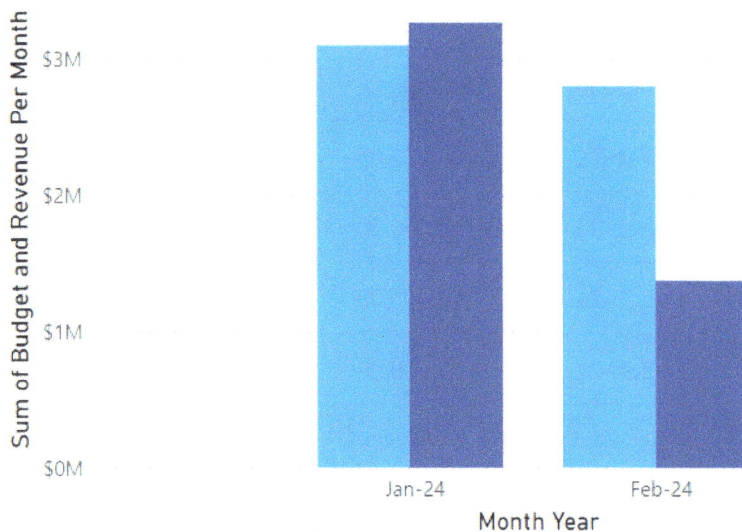

Figure 10.7: Comparing budget to actuals at the month level of granularity

The **Revenue Per Month** measure aggregates the **Revenue** column from the **Revenue** table at the month and year level of granularity so that we can compare with the budgeted revenue dollars. However, we can also go the other direction and break the budget down to the day level as follows:

```
Budget Per Day =
    VAR __Date = MAX( 'Revenue'[Date] )
    VAR __MonthYear = FORMAT( __Date, "mmm-yyyy" )
    VAR __Days = DAY( EOMONTH( __Date, 0 ) )
    VAR __Budget = MAXX( FILTER( 'Budget', [Month Year] = __MonthYear ), [Budget] )
    VAR __Result = DIVIDE( __Budget, __Days )
RETURN
    __Result
```

The **Budget Per Day** calculation gets the current **Date**, **__Date**, and uses that to construct the **__MonthYear** variable which uses the **FORMAT** function to format the date in the same manner as the **Budget** table stores its **Month Year** column. We then determine the number of days in the month using the **DAY** and **EOMONTH** functions. Using the **EOMONTH** function with a second parameter of **0** returns the day of the "current" end of month. We can then look up the correct **Budget** number from the **Budget** table and divide by the days in the month, **__Days**, to evenly allocate the month's budget across each day in the month.

We can create a **Clustered column chart** using the **Date** column from the **Revenue** table as the **X-axis** along with the summed **Revenue** column and **Budget Per Day** measure as the **Y-axis**:

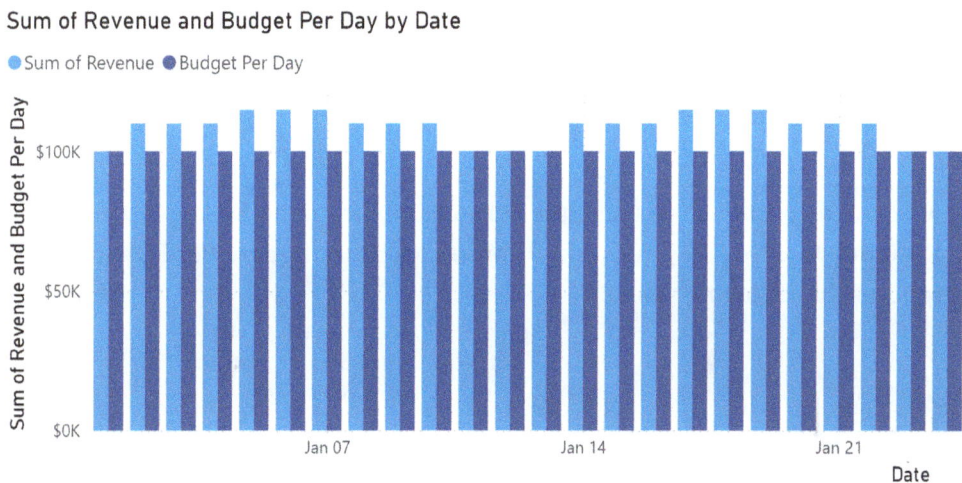

Figure 10.8: Comparing budget to actuals at the day level of granularity

We can take this concept a step further and create cumulative measures to compare budgets and actuals at the day level of granularity. To do this, create the following two measures:

```
Running Monthly Revenue =

    VAR __Date = MAX( 'Revenue'[Date] )

    VAR __MonthYear = YEAR( __Date ) * 100 + MONTH( __Date )

    VAR __Table =

        FILTER(

            ALL( 'Revenue' ),

            [Date] <= __Date &&

            YEAR( [Date] ) * 100 + MONTH( [Date] ) = __MonthYear

        )

    VAR __Result = SUMX( __Table, [Revenue] )

RETURN

    __Result
```

```
Running Monthly Budget Per Day =

    VAR __Date = MAX( 'Revenue'[Date] )

    VAR __MonthYear = FORMAT( __Date, "mmm-yyyy" )

    VAR __Days = DAY( EOMONTH( __Date, 0 ) )

    VAR __Day = DAY( __Date )

    VAR __Budget = MAXX( FILTER( 'Budget', [Month Year] = __MonthYear ), [Budget] )

    VAR __Result = DIVIDE( __Budget, __Days ) * __Day

RETURN

    __Result
```

Create a **Clustered column chart** using the **Date** column from the **Revenue** table as the **X-axis** and the **Running Monthly Revenue** and **Running Monthly Budget Per Day** measures as the **Y-axis** produces the following visual:

Running Monthly Revenue and Running Monthly Budget Per Day by Date

● Running Monthly Revenue ● Running Monthly Budget Per Day

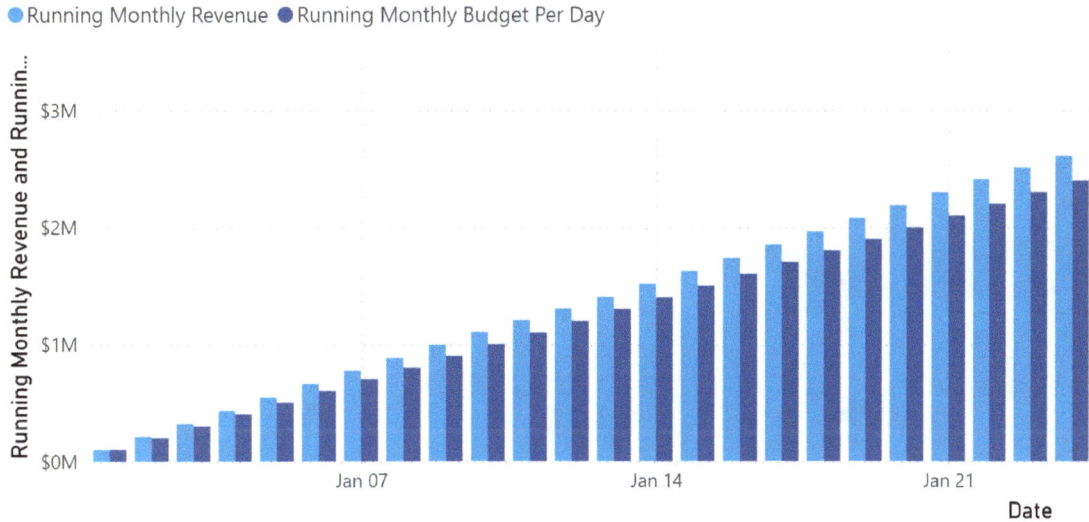

Figure 10.9: Comparing cumulative monthly budget to actuals at the day level of granularity

A final variation of this is creating measures that compare cumulative budget and actuals at the day level of granularity for an entire year which can be implemented using the following three measures:

```
Running Yearly Revenue =
    VAR __Date = MAX( 'Revenue'[Date] )
    VAR __Year = YEAR( __Date )
    VAR __Table =
        FILTER(
            ALL( 'Revenue' ),
            [Date] <= __Date &&
            YEAR( [Date] ) = __Year
        )
    VAR __Result = SUMX( __Table, [Revenue] )
RETURN
    __Result
Running Yearly Budget Per Day =
    VAR __Date = MAX( 'Revenue'[Date] )
```

```
    VAR __Year = YEAR( __Date )

    VAR __Table =

        ADDCOLUMNS(

            'Budget',

            "__Date", DATEVALUE( [Month Year] )

        )

    VAR __Budget =

        SUMX(

            FILTER(

                __Table,

                YEAR( [__Date] ) = __Year

            ),

            [Budget]

        )

    VAR __MinDate = DATE( __Year, 1, 1 )

    VAR __MaxDate =  DATE( __Year, 12, 31)

    VAR __Days = ( __MaxDate - __MinDate ) * 1. + 1

    VAR __Day = ( __Date - __MinDate ) * 1. + 1

    VAR __Result = DIVIDE( __Budget, __Days ) * __Day

RETURN

    __Result

Running Yearly Budget Per Day 1 =

    VAR __Date = MAX( 'Revenue'[Date] )

    VAR __Year = YEAR( __Date )

    VAR __Table =

        ADDCOLUMNS(

            'Budget',

            "__Date", DATEVALUE( [Month Year] )

        )
```

```
VAR __MinDate =
    MINX(
        FILTER(
            ALL( Revenue[Date] ),
            YEAR( [Date] = __Year )
        ),
        [Date]
    )
VAR __MaxDate =
    MAXX(
        FILTER(
            ALL( Revenue[Date] ),
            YEAR( [Date] = __Year )
        ),
        [Date]
    )
VAR __Budget =
    SUMX(
        FILTER(
            __Table,
            [__Date] <= __MaxDate && YEAR( [__Date] ) = __Year
        ),
        [Budget]
    )
VAR __Days = ( __MaxDate - __MinDate ) * 1. + 1
VAR __Day = ( __Date - __MinDate ) * 1. + 1
VAR __Result = DIVIDE( __Budget, __Days ) * __Day
RETURN
    __Result
```

The **Running Yearly Revenue** measure is identical to the **Running Monthly Revenue** measure except for removing the filter for the current month. The **Running Yearly Budget Per Day** measure calculates a daily budget with the entire year's budget allocated across every day of the year. Conversely, the **Running Yearly Budget Per Day 1** measure allocates the budget for only the months with revenue and allocates that budget across only the days that have revenue.

You should use caution when using the **DATEVALUE** function. The **DATEVALUE** function takes a text string that represents a date and converts that value to an actual date value. However, certain formats can cause problems. In our case, date text strings in the format "*mmm-yyyy*" such as "Jan-2024", for example, correctly convert to their equivalent date counterparts, January 1st, 2024. However, formats such as "*mmm-yy*" or Jan-24 do not translate to January 1st, 2024 but instead translate to January 24th, <Year>, where <Year> is the current year according to the system clock of the computer.

Creating a similar **Clustered column chart** for these measures as before produces the following visual:

Running Yearly Revenue, Running Yearly Budget Per Day and Running Yearly Budget Per Day 1 by Date

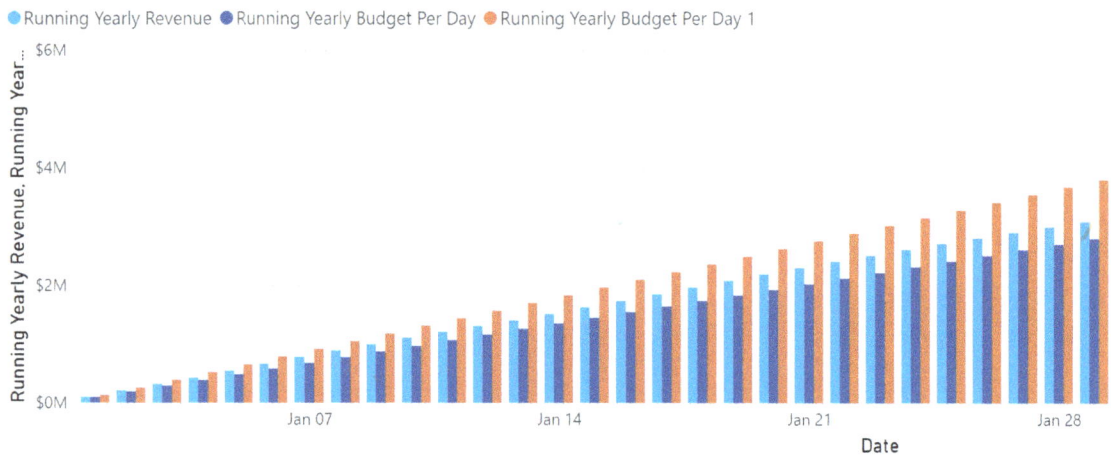

Figure 10.10: Comparing cumulative yearly budget to actuals at the day level of granularity

We are now finished exploring how to compare budgets and actuals. Next, we look at how to calculate an accounts payable turnover ratio.

Accounts Payable Turnover Ratio

The accounts payable turnover ratio is a metric that measures the short-term liquidity of a business. In short, the ratio indicates how many times a business can pay off its accounts payable within a set time period. Both investors and creditors can use the accounts payable turnover ratio to evaluate the health and strength of businesses in meeting their short-term obligations.

The formula for accounts payable turnover ratio or APTR is the following:

$$APTR = \frac{Total\ Supplier\ Purchases}{\left(\frac{(Beginning\ AP + Ending\ AP)}{2}\right)}$$

To get started, use an **Enter data** query to create an **AP Turnover Ratio** table using the following data or alternatively load the **AP Turnover Ratio** sheet of the Excel file, **Chapter10_Data.xlsx**, available in the GitHub repository for this book.

Date	Category	Amount	Year
1-Jan-24	Accounts Payable	$15,000,000	2024
31-Dec-24	Accounts Payable	$20,000,000	2024
1-Jan-25	Accounts Payable	$20,000,000	2025
31-Dec-25	Accounts Payable	$40,000,000	2025
31-Dec-24	Supplier Purchases	$110,000,000	2024
31-Dec-25	Supplier Purchases	$100,000,000	2025

Table 10.8: AP Turnover ratio data

Now create the following measure:

```
APTR =
    VAR __TSP =
        SUMX(
            FILTER( 'AP Turnover Ratio', [Category] = "Supplier Purchases" ),
            [Amount]
        )
    VAR __MinDate = MIN( 'AP Turnover Ratio'[Date] )
    VAR __BeginningAP =
        SUMX(
            FILTER(
```

```
            'AP Turnover Ratio',

                [Date] = __MinDate &&

                [Category] = "Accounts Payable"

            ),

            [Amount]

        )

    VAR __MaxDate = MAX( 'AP Turnover Ratio'[Date] )

    VAR __EndingAP =

        SUMX(

            FILTER(

                'AP Turnover Ratio',

                [Date] = __MaxDate &&

                [Category] = "Accounts Payable"

            ),

            [Amount]

        )

    VAR __AverageAP = ( __BeginningAP + __EndingAP ) / 2

    VAR __Result = DIVIDE( __TSP, __AverageAP )

RETURN

    __Result
```

A simple **Table** visual provides the following results:

Year	APTR
2024	6.29
2025	3.33

Figure 10.11: Accounts Payable Turnover Ratio

These results indicate that the company in question paid off their accounts payable 6.29 times during 2024 and 3.33 times during 2025. An ideal ratio is between 6 and 10. These results indicate that the company in question may be in financial distress considering that its accounts payable turnover ratio has fallen and is effectively half of what it was the prior year.

Now that we have covered calculating an accounts payable turnover ratio, let's next look at a calculation that leverages the modified Dietz method.

Modified Dietz Return

The modified Dietz method measures the historical performance of an investment portfolio with external flows. External flows are one-way transfers of money, securities, or other transactions into and out of an investment portfolio. Peter O. Dietz invented the method to simplify calculating the internal rate of return (IRR), which is computationally intensive.

The formula for a modified Dietz return is the following:

$$\frac{Investment\ Gain\ or\ Loss}{Average\ Capital} = \frac{(B - A - \sum_t^T F(t)}{A + \sum_t^T \left(\frac{(T - t)}{T} * F(t)\right)}$$

The variables in this equation are the following:

- A = Beginning investment balance
- B = Ending investment balance
- T = Total length of time of the investment
- t = Time of an individual transactional flow
- F(t) = Transactional flow at a particular time

The term $\frac{(T-t)}{T}$ is known as the weighting factor and is the proportion of the time between when the flow occurred and the end of the investment period.

To demonstrate calculating the modified Dietz return for an investment portfolio, use an **Enter data** query to create a **Portfolio** table using the following data or alternatively load the **Portfolio** sheet of the Excel file, **Chapter10_Data.xlsx**, available in the GitHub repository for this book.

Date	Category	Value
1/1/2024	Initial Value	$ 2,000.00
3/31/2024	Flow	$ 1,000.00
10/1/2024	Flow	$ (1,600.00)
12/31/2024	Ending Value	$ 2,400.00

Table 10.9: Portfolio data

This table represents an initial investment of $2,000. An additional $1,000 was added three months later, $1,600 was withdrawn after nine months and the portfolio had an ending value of $2,400.

Now create the following measure:

```
Modified Dietz Return =
    VAR __A = MAXX( FILTER( 'Portfolio', [Category] = "Initial Value" ), [Value] )

    VAR __B = MAXX( FILTER( 'Portfolio', [Category] = "Ending Value" ), [Value] )

    VAR __F = SUMX( FILTER( 'Portfolio', [Category] = "Flow" ), [Value] )

    VAR __InitDate =

        MAXX( FILTER( 'Portfolio', [Category] = "Initial Value" ), [Date] )

    VAR __EndDate =

        MAXX( FILTER( 'Portfolio', [Category] = "Ending Value" ), [Date] )

    VAR __T = ( __EndDate - __InitDate ) * 1. + 1

    VAR __Table =

        ADDCOLUMNS(

            FILTER( 'Portfolio', [Category] = "Flow" ),

            "__WF", DIVIDE( ( __EndDate - [Date] ) * 1. + 1, __T ) * [Value]

        )

    VAR __WF = SUMX( __Table, [__WF] )

    VAR __Return = DIVIDE( __B - __A - __F, __A + __WF, 0 )

RETURN

    __Return
```

The measure formula is relatively straight-forward based upon the stated equation for calculating the modified Dietz return. The most complex component is the creation of the table variable, __Table, which adds the __WF column that multiples the weight $\frac{(T-t)}{T}$ by the Value of the flow. In this case, the weight is calculated based upon the number of days.

Format the **Modified Dietz Return** as a **Percentage**. Next, create a **Card** visual to display the **Modified Dietz Return** measure and observe that the calculated value is **42.52%.**

As mentioned, the modified Dietz method has the advantage of not being as computationally intensive as IRR. In addition, the modified Dietz method's primary advantage over time-weight return calculations is that calculation of the modified Dietz return does not require known portfolio valuations for every instance of a flow.

For reference, here is a calculation for IRR using the **XIRR** DAX function for the same investment portfolio:

```
IRR =
    VAR __Table =
        DATATABLE(
            "Date", DATETIME, "Value", INTEGER,
            {
                { "1/1/2024", -2000 },
                { "3/31/2024", -1000 },
                { "10/1/2024", 1600 },
                { "12/31/2024", 2400 }
            }
        )
    VAR __Result = XIRR( __Table, [Value], [Date] )
RETURN
    __Result
```

This calculation returns a value of **42.16%**.

This completes our exploration of the modified Dietz method or modified Dietz return. We next examine calculating compound interest.

Compound Interest

Compound interest is the interest earned on a principal amount plus the accumulated interest over the length of the investment. This contrasts with simple interest which is simply the payout on a principal multiplied by an interest rate.

One can determine the future value of an investment with compound interest using the following formula:

$$FV = PV * \left(1 + \frac{r}{n} \right)^{nt}$$

The variables in this equation are the following:

- FV = Future value
- PV = Present value (initial value)
- r = Interest rate expressed as a decimal number
- n = Number of payments annually
- t = Number of years

Thus, for example, if an investor invests $10,000 at a rate of 5% for 5 years, the DAX formula for this would be:

```
FV Compound = 10000 * POWER( 1 + .05, 5 )
```

This produces a result of $12,762.82. Conversely, the following simple interest formula produces a result of $12,500.00:

```
FV Simple = 10000 + 10000 * .05 * 5
```

If we only want the actual interest earned instead of the full future value, we can instead use the following formulas:

```
Compound Interest = 10000 * ( POWER( 1 + .05, 5 ) - 1 )
```

```
Simple Interest = 10000 * .05 * 5
```

DAX's **FV** function can also be used to return the same amount as the **FY Compound** measure:

```
FV = FV( .05, 5, 0, -10000 )
```

In this version of the **FV** function, the third parameter is set to **0**, meaning that **$10,000** is invested and no further payments are made over the next **5** years. If we change the investment scenario slightly where additional **$7,500** investments are made each year:

```
FV Payments = FV( .05, 5, -7500, -10000 )
```

The **FV Payments** measure returns **$54,205.05**.

These are all rather simple investment scenarios. Unfortunately, not every investment scenario is so simple. In some cases, the annual interest rate and investment payments can vary over time.

To explore this scenario, use an **Enter data** query to create an **Investments** table using the following data or alternatively load the **Investments** sheet of the Excel file, **Chapter10_Data.xlsx**, available in the GitHub repository for this book.

Date	Investment
1/1/2021	$10,000
1/1/2022	$5,000
1/1/2023	$7,500
1/1/2024	$12,000
1/1/2025	$11,000

Table 10.10: Investments data

Use another **Enter data** query to create an **Interest Rates** table using the following data or alternatively load the **Interest Rates** sheet of the Excel file, **Chapter10_Data.xlsx**, available in the GitHub repository for this book.

Date	Rate
1/1/2021	0.05
1/1/2022	0.048
1/1/2023	0.051
1/1/2024	0.049
1/1/2025	0.047

Table 10.11: Interest rates data

Next, create the following table:

```
Calendar =
    ADDCOLUMNS(
        CALENDAR( DATE( 2021, 1, 1 ), DATE( 2025, 12, 31 ) ),
        "Year", YEAR( [Date] )
    )
```

Create relationships between the **Calendar** table and the **Investments** and **Interest Rates** tables using the **Date** columns. When you are finished, the semantic model should look like the following:

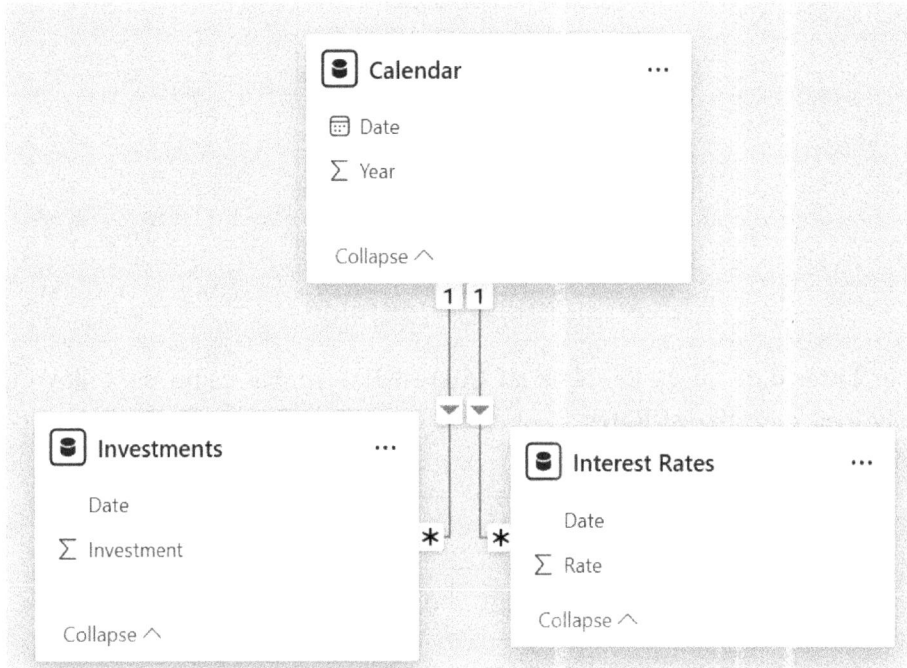

Figure 10.12: Compound interest semantic model

At first, the idea of calculating the future value seems daunting given that DAX does not support any type of recursion or previous value. For example, we cannot compute the future value at the end of the first year and then use that as input to the starting balance when computing the next year.

However, not every recursive type of problem must necessarily be solved via recursion. In this case, we can remove the recursive portion by instead performing the calculation where, for each year, we calculate each prior year's value plus the current year's current future value. Then, for any given year, we simply need to sum all the values.

To see this in action, create the following measure:

```
Future Value Complex =
    VAR __Year = MAX( 'Calendar'[Year] )
    VAR __Table =
        ADDCOLUMNS(
            SUMMARIZE(
```

```
                    FILTER( ALL( 'Calendar'[Year] ), [Year] <= __Year ),

                    [Year],

                    "__Amount", SUM( 'Investments'[Investment] )
                ),
        "__TotalAmount",

            VAR __CurrentYear = [Year]

            VAR __CompoundInterest =

                PRODUCTX(

                    FILTER(

                        ALL( 'Interest Rates' ),

                        YEAR( [Date] ) >= __CurrentYear && YEAR( [Date] ) <= __Year

                    ),

                    1 + [Rate]

                )

            RETURN

                [__Amount] * __CompoundInterest

        )

    VAR __Result = SUMX( __Table, [__TotalAmount] )

RETURN

    __Result
```

Create a **Table** visual using the **Year** column from the **Date** table, a summarized **Rate** column from the **Interest Rates** table, a summarized **Investment** column from the **Investments** table and the **Future Value Complex** measure.

Year	Sum of Rate	Sum of Investment	Future Value Complex
2021	5.00%	$10,000	$10,500
2022	4.80%	$5,000	$16,244
2023	5.10%	$7,500	$24,954.944
2024	4.90%	$12,000	$38,765.7363
2025	4.70%	$11,000	$52,104.7258
Total	**24.50%**	**$45,500**	**$52,104.7258**

Figure 10.13: Future value of a complex investment scenario

This completes our analysis of compound interest with DAX.

Summary

This chapter highlighted the calculation and tracking of a wide range of financial metrics and Key Performance Indicators (KPIs). We began with basic measures such as **Gross Margin**, **Revenue**, and **Cost**. We then then dove into more advanced calculations, such as converting revenue currencies using exchange rates, periodic billing, and reverse engineering year-to-date numbers.

Through the course of the chapter, we also covered comparing budgets to actuals from numerous perspectives such as different granularities and different time periods. Additional topics included specialized financial metrics and methods such as accounts payable turnover to assess short-term liquidity, and applying the modified Dietz method for calculating investment returns with external flows. Finally, we concluded with a thorough treatment of compound interest scenarios, including a scenario where investment payments and interest rates varied over time.

In the next chapter, we leave the world of finance behind and move on to scenarios involving operations.

CHAPTER 11

11

Operations

While financial KPIs and metrics are critical to the health and success of organizations, so too are operational KPIs and metrics. Operational KPIs and metrics are essential for organizations as these metrics provide timely insights about overall business performance, efficiency, and overall effectiveness. Operational metrics help track key aspects of daily operations, such as production rates, customer service response times, inventory turnover, and employee productivity. By monitoring such indicators, businesses can identify inefficiencies, detect potential problems, and make informed decisions to improve workflows. Operational KPIs also ensure that teams remain aligned with organizational goals, allowing leaders to drive performance improvements and maintain a competitive edge in the market.

Operational KPIs and metrics also contribute to accountability and strategic planning. When clear benchmarks are established, employees are better able to understand expectations and can thus work proactively to meet or exceed performance targets. In addition, using data-driven decision-making reduces reliance on guesswork which helps lead to more consistent and predictable outcomes. In short, well-defined and regularly monitored operational KPIs are critical for maintaining agility, ensuring sustainability, and fostering continuous improvement across organizations.

This chapter covers many different types of operational metrics and KPIs. Many of these metrics are quite complex and challenging to calculate and a few rank as some of the most difficult DAX problems to solve. Data and other files for this chapter are available in the GitHub repository for this book: https://github.com/gdeckler/DAX-For-Humans/tree/main/book.

On Time In Full

On time in full (OTIF) is a supply chain logistics KPI that measures whether orders were fulfilled with the full quantities, at the expected times, and in the desired locations. In other words, OTIF answers the question, *"Did our customers get what they wanted, when they wanted it?"*.

To examine calculating OTIF, first import the **OTIF** sheet of the Excel spreadsheet, **Chapter11_Data.xlsx** which can be found in the Github repository for this book: https://github.com/gdeckler/DAX-For-Humans/tree/main/book.

The OTIF table has data as follows:

Plant	Order	Shipment	Line	Ordered	Shipped	Customer	Segment	CustomerDueDate	DeliveredDate
Plant B	ORDB2724924	1	2	2	2	CUST00005885	Snowglobes	1/2/2025 0:00	1/2/2025 0:00
Plant B	ORDB2745890	1	2	1	1	CUST00007094	Snowglobes	1/4/2025 0:00	1/2/2025 0:00
Plant B	ORDC00522683	1	2	1	1	CUST00024527	Shot Glasses	1/2/2025 0:00	1/2/2025 0:00
Plant D	ORDB2688938	1	2	1	1	CUST00003701	Shot Glasses	1/5/2025 0:00	1/2/2025 0:00

Figure 11.1: On time in full data

This data is at the order line level of granularity. The data includes the **Plant** or warehouse where the item was fulfilled along with the **Order** identification (order level of granularity). There are also **Shipment** and **Line** columns as a single **Order** may have multiple order lines and require more than one shipment to fulfill.

The **Ordered** and **Shipped** columns reference the quantities that were ordered versus shipped. The **Customer** and **Segment** columns identify the customer and type of item respectively. Finally, the **CustomerDueDate** specifies when the customer requested the product be delivered while the **DeliveredDate** identifies when the customer received the product.

Now create the following OTIF measure:

```
OTIF =

    VAR __Table =

        ADDCOLUMNS(

            SELECTCOLUMNS( 'OTIF',

                "__Order", [Order], "__Ordered", [Ordered], "__Shipped", [Shipped],

                "__DueDate", [CustomerDueDate], "__DeliverDate", [DeliveredDate]

            ),

            "__OTIF",

                IF(

                    [__Ordered] = [__Shipped] && [__DeliverDate] <= [__DueDate],

                    1,

                    0

                )

            )
```

```
    VAR __Orders =

        GROUPBY(

            __Table,

            [__Order],

            "__Count", COUNTX( CURRENTGROUP(), [__Order] ),

            "__OTIF", SUMX( CURRENTGROUP(), [__OTIF] )

        )

    VAR __OnTime = COUNTROWS( FILTER( __Orders, [__Count] = [__OTIF] ) )

    VAR __All = COUNTROWS( __Orders )

    VAR __Result = DIVIDE( __OnTime, __All, 0 )

RETURN

    __Result
```

In the **OTIF** measure, a table variable is created, **__Table**, which uses **SELECTCOLUMNS** to only select the columns that are absolutely required by the calculation. This is a performance optimization feature that helps minimize memory usage.

The use of **SELECTCOLUMNS** is an optimization that can be done for just about any measure that we have largely ignored up until now since not using **SELECTCOLUMNS** results in shorter, less cluttered code. While such optimizations are rarely necessary with DAX the exception tends to be DAX calculations that operate against large fact tables. Operational data typically has such large fact tables and thus we introduce the optimization here.

An **__OTIF** column is added using **ADDCOLUMNS** which checks each row (order line level of granularity) to see if the amount ordered was the amount shipped and whether the shipment arrived on or before the customer's due date. If the correct number of items arrived on or before the due date then the column value is set to 1, otherwise the **__OTIF** column is set to 0.

A second table variable is created, **__Orders** which uses **GROUPBY** to summarize **__Table** by the **Order** column (**__Order**). The **__Orders** table variable summarizes the OTIF information at the **Order** level of granularity. Two aggregated columns are added, first a simple count of the number of order lines, **__Count**, and a second column, **__OTIF**, which sums the **__OTIF** column.

We can now determine the percentage of orders that were fulfilled on time and in full by first counting the number of rows in the **__Orders** table where the **__Count** and **__OTIF** columns are equal, meaning that all order lines were fulfilled on time and in full. This provides us with the number of orders that were fulfilled on time and in full. We can then simply divide that number by the total number of orders to arrive at our desired **OTIF** percentage.

You can create various visuals for breaking down the **OTIF** measure by **Segment**, **Plant**, or even **DeliveredDate**.

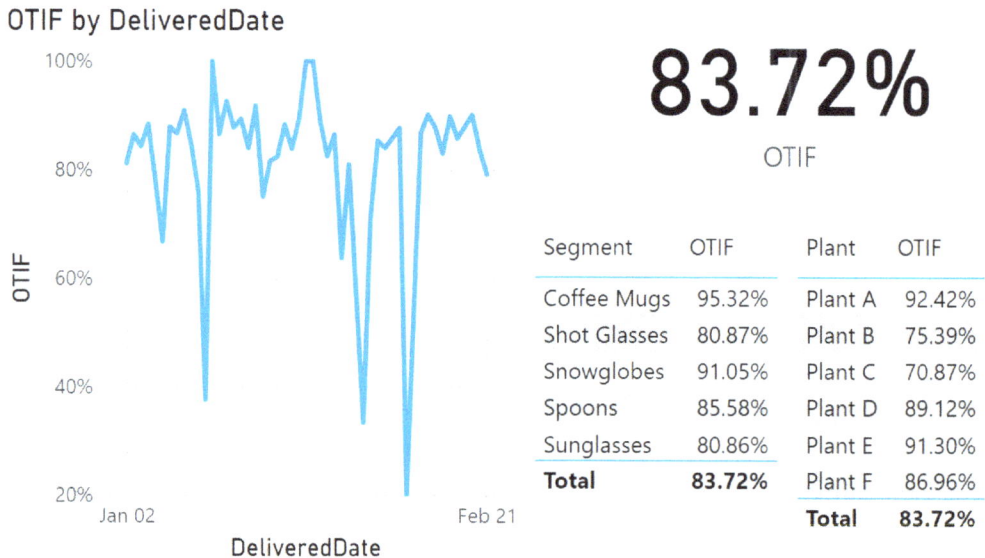

Segment	OTIF	Plant	OTIF
Coffee Mugs	95.32%	Plant A	92.42%
Shot Glasses	80.87%	Plant B	75.39%
Snowglobes	91.05%	Plant C	70.87%
Spoons	85.58%	Plant D	89.12%
Sunglasses	80.86%	Plant E	91.30%
Total	**83.72%**	Plant F	86.96%
		Total	**83.72%**

Figure 11.2: OTIF visuals

This completes our exploration of OTIF. We now look at another common supply chain and logistics KPI, order cycle time (OCT).

Order Cycle Time

Order cycle time (**OCT**) is the amount of time required to prepare orders for shipping. OCT specifically excludes shipping time, so this metric measures the internal business process efficiency in fulfilling orders. Depending upon the level of detail tracked, OCT can be broken down into different stages such as picking, packing, etc. A closely related metric is **order lead time** (**OLT**) which measures how long it takes customers to physically receive their orders once placed.

To examine calculating OCT, first import the **OCT** sheet of the Excel spreadsheet, **Chapter11_Data.xlsx** which can be found in the Github repository for this book: https://github.com/gdeckler/DAX-For-Humans/tree/main/book.

The OCT table has data as follows:

Plant	Order	Shipment	Line	Ordered	Shipped	Customer	Segment	ReceiveDate	ShippedDate
Plant B	ORDCORDF2754444	1	1	1	1	CUST00018993	Shot Glasses	1/19/2025 0:00	1/19/2025 0:00
Plant B	ORDCORDF2754436	1	1	1	1	CUST00018992	Shot Glasses	1/19/2025 0:00	1/19/2025 0:00
Plant B	ORDCORDF2754343	1	1	1	1	CUST00018981	Shot Glasses	1/19/2025 0:00	2/15/2025 0:00
Plant B	ORDCORDF2754012	1	1	1	1	CUST00018946	Shot Glasses	1/18/2025 0:00	1/30/2025 0:00

Figure 11.3: Order cycle time data

This data is at the order line level of granularity. The data includes the **Plant** or warehouse where the item was fulfilled along with the **Order** identification (order level of granularity). There are also **Shipment** and **Line** columns as a single **Order** may have multiple order lines and require more than one shipment to fulfill.

The **Ordered** and **Shipped** lines reference the quantities that were ordered versus shipped. The **Customer** and **Segment** columns identify the customer and type of item respectively. Finally, the **ReceiveDate** specifies when the customer's order was received while the **ShippedDate** identifies when the customer's order was shipped.

Now create the following **OCT** measure:

```
OCT =
    VAR __Table =
        ADDCOLUMNS(
            GROUPBY(
                SELECTCOLUMNS( 'OCT',
                    "__Order", [Order], "__Ordered", [Ordered],
                    "__Shipped", [Shipped], "__ReceiveDate", [ReceiveDate],
                    "__ShippedDate", [ShippedDate]
                ),
                [__Order],
                "__MinReceive", MINX( CURRENTGROUP(), [__ReceiveDate] ),
                "__MaxShipped", MAXX( CURRENTGROUP(), [__ShippedDate] )
            ),
            "__OCT", ( [__MaxShipped] - [__MinReceive] ) * 1. + 1
        )
    VAR __Result = AVERAGEX( __Table, [__OCT] )
```

RETURN

    __Result

In the **OCT** measure, a table variable is created, **__Table**, which uses **SELECTCOLUMNS** to only select the columns that are absolutely required by the calculation. This is a performance optimization feature that helps minimize memory usage.

Since the **OCT** table is at the order line level of granularity, and we wish to track OCT at the order level of granularity, we next use **GROUPBY** to group the table by the **Order** column. In addition, we add two columns, **__MinReceive** and **__MaxShipped**, which calculate the minimum receive date (**__ReceiveDate**) and maximum shipped date (**__ShippedDate**) respectively.

An **__OCT** column is added using **ADDCOLUMNS** which calculates the number of days between the **__MaxShipped** date and **__MinReceive** date. Shipments that are received and shipped on the same day are counted as having an OCT of 1 day. This is the purpose of the **+1** in the formula.

Now that we have our table, we can simply use **AVERAGEX** to calculate the average OCT for all orders. We can create various visuals for breaking down the **OCT** measure by **Segment**, **Plant**, or even **ShippedDate**.

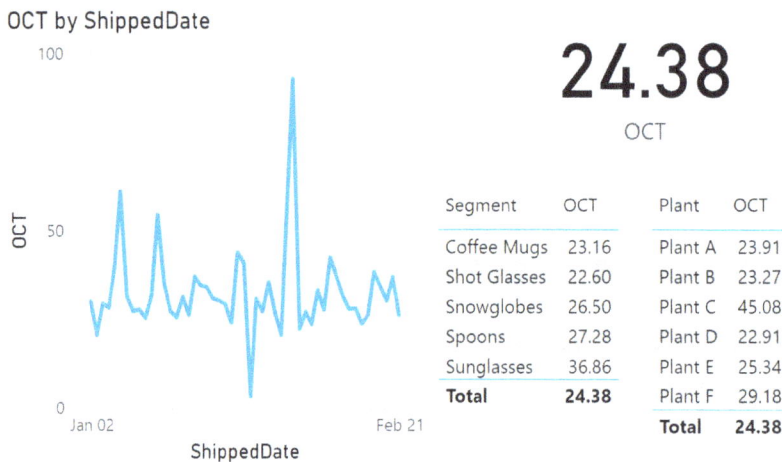

OCT by ShippedDate

24.38
OCT

Segment	OCT	Plant	OCT
Coffee Mugs	23.16	Plant A	23.91
Shot Glasses	22.60	Plant B	23.27
Snowglobes	26.50	Plant C	45.08
Spoons	27.28	Plant D	22.91
Sunglasses	36.86	Plant E	25.34
Total	**24.38**	Plant F	29.18
		Total	**24.38**

Figure 11.4: OCT visuals

This concludes our exploration of OCT. However, it should be noted that this same basic formula pattern can be used to calculate just about any cycle time. For example, if the data also included a "delivery date", and we wished to calculate **order lead time** (**OLT**) then we could simply substitute the delivery date column for the shipped date column in the OCT measure.

Let's now move on to a different type of metric, calculating delivery dates.

Delivery Dates

For this scenario, imagine an organization that works as a distributor selling different types of widgets from a variety of different manufacturers. When sales orders come in, those sales orders are fulfilled from the widgets kept in stock within their warehouses.

If there is an insufficient quantity to fulfill the sales order, a backorder entry is created that lists the type of widget and the quantity that must be fulfilled. Next, a purchase order is created to purchase more of the specified widget from the source manufacturer.

The organization desires to understand when backorders will be fulfilled. In addition, the organization wants to optimize the fulfillment of backorders according to particular business rules such as **first in first out (FIFO)**, **last in first out (LIFO)**, or even optimizing based upon the most backorders fulfilled.

To demonstrate this scenario and create the required measures, import the **Backorders** and **Purchase Orders** sheets from the Excel spreadsheet, **Chapter11_Data.xlsx** which can be found in the Github repository for this book: https://github.com/gdeckler/DAX-For-Humans/tree/main/book.

The **Backorders** table includes data such as the following:

Date	Sales Order #	Item #	Quantity
11/24/2025	SO00307834	12028	40
1/8/2024	SO00309390	12028	3500

Table 11.1: Backorders data

The **Date** column is when the backorder was created while the **Sales Order** # simply ties the backorder to the original sales order. The **Item** # column specifies the type of widget and the **Quantity** column holds the number of widgets.

The **Purchase Orders** table includes data such as the following:

Date	Order ID	Item #	ETA	Quantity
1/5/2024	230707	12028	1/5/2022	5490
1/5/2024	230707	12028	1/5/2022	126

Table 11.2: Purchase orders data

Here the **Date** column specifies the date the purchase order was created while the **Order ID** is used for tracking purposes. The **Item #** column specifies the type of widget ordered and the **Quantity** column holds the number of widgets ordered. Finally, the **ETA** column is the predicted fulfillment date for the purchase order (when the order will be fulfilled by the manufacturer/vendor).

Create an **Items** table using the following DAX code:

```
Items =
    DISTINCT(
        UNION(
            SELECTCOLUMNS( 'Backorders', "Item #", [Item #] ),
            SELECTCOLUMNS( 'Purchase Orders', "Item #", [Item #] )
        )
    )
```

This code ensures that we have a distinct list of **Item #**'s by using **UNION** to append the **Item #** columns from both tables together and then using **DISTINCT** to remove any duplicates. Now relate the **Items** table to both the **Backorders** and **Purchase Orders** tables using the common **Item #** columns. The semantic model should look like the following:

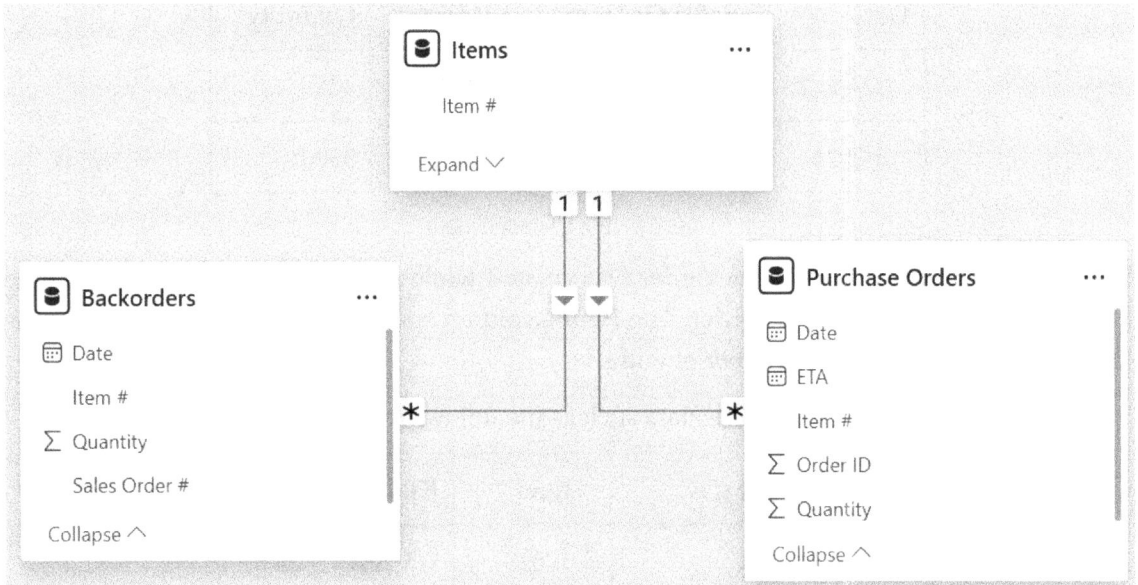

Figure 11.5: Data fulfillment semantic model

Now create the following measure:

```
FIFO Qty to Fulfill =

    VAR __Item = MAX( 'Backorders'[Item #] )

    VAR __Date = MAX( 'BackOrders'[Date] )

    VAR __Table =

        FILTER(

            ALL( 'BackOrders' ),

            [Item #] = __Item && [Date] <= __Date

        )

    VAR __Result = SUMX( __Table, [Quantity] )

RETURN

    __Result
```

This measure calculates the total quantity of widgets required to fulfill based upon the **Date** of the current backorder in context. Since the objective of this measure is a FIFO ordering then, for any particular backorder, the total quantity necessary to fulfill all orders up until the current backorder is **ALL** rows in the **Backorders** table that have a **Date** that is equal to or less than the current backorder's **Date**.

Next create the following measure:

```
FIFO Delivery Date =

    VAR __QtyToFulfill = [FIFO Qty to Fulfill]

    VAR __Table =

        ADDCOLUMNS(

            ADDCOLUMNS(

                SELECTCOLUMNS(

                    'Purchase Orders',

                    "ETA", [ETA], "Quantity", [Quantity]

                ),

                "__TotalQty",

                    SUMX(

                        FILTER( 'Purchase Orders', [ETA] <= EARLIER( [ETA] ) ),
```

```
                        [Quantity]

                    )

                ),

                "__LoopCounter", [__TotalQty] - __QtyToFulfill

            )

    VAR __TargetDate = MINX( FILTER( __Table, [__LoopCounter] >= 0 ), [ETA] )

    VAR __Result =

        IF(

            __QtyToFulfill = BLANK() || __TargetDate = BLANK(),

            BLANK(),

            __TargetDate

        )

RETURN

    __Result
```

This measure creates a DAX while loop. This may sound strange considering that DAX has no formal looping structures such as traditional for and while loops. However, while it is true that formal looping structures do not exist in DAX, we can still emulate such structures with a bit of creativity. Since DAX has no formal looping structures, we instead use the rows of a table to emulate the loops in a while loop. This is done within the __Table variable.

The __Table variable first uses **SELECTCOLUMNS** to select only the columns necessary for the rest of the calculation. This is a performance optimization feature that helps minimize memory usage. In addition, the use of **SELECTCOLUMNS** here provides benefits for the debug measure that is to follow.

Next, we add a column called __**TotalQty**. This column effectively does the same thing as our **FIFO Qty to Fulfill** measure but for the **Purchase Orders** table. This is accomplished using the **EARLIER** function. We could have used nested **VAR/RESULT** statements for this instead but using the **EARLIER** function results in cleaner code.

The name of the **EARLIER** function comes from referring to the "earlier" context of a particular column reference, in this case the **ETA** column. This is perhaps best explained with an image. We can visualize the __**Table** variable as the following for **Item # 1507**:

Purchase Orders

ETA	Item #	Sum of Quantity
2/1/2025	1507	6125
4/5/2025	1507	12500
4/13/2025	1507	17250
5/12/2025	1507	9000
Total		**44875**

EARLIER([ETA])

__Table

ETA	Quantity	__TotalQty
2/1/2025	6125	6125
4/5/2025	12500	18625
4/13/2025	17250	35875
5/12/2025	9000	44875
Total	**44875**	**44875**

Figure 11.6: Data fulfillment semantic model

As shown in *Figure 11.6*, when calculating the __TotalQty column for each row within the __Table variable, the **EARLIER([ETA])** code simply refers to the "current" row's **ETA** date. Thus, if calculating the total quantity of widgets purchased for the row where the **ETA** is **4/5/2025** then the code filters the **Purchase Orders** table to only those rows where the **Purchase Orders ETA** column is less than or equal to the current row's **ETA** date. In this case, the total is **18,625** which is **6,125 + 12,500**.

We can now implement our while loop. We do this by first adding an additional column, __LoopCounter. For each row, __LoopCounter is calculated by subtracting the **FIFO Qty to Fulfill** (_QtyToFulfill) from the __TotalQty column. We can then find the __TargetDate by finding the minimum **ETA** where the __LoopCounter column is greater than or equal to 0.

One can think of this as a while loop coded to exit once the __LoopCounter variable becomes **0** or less, such as "while x >= 0, do the following". In short, this sequence identifies the first **ETA** where the total of the current and all previous backorders can be fulfilled by the purchase orders. With a few additional checks, we can then return the __Result.

Add the **Item #** column from the **Items** table as a slicer and slice to item **1507**. Now add the **FIFO Qty to Fulfill** and **FIFO Delivery Date** measures to a **Table** visual along with the **Date, Sales Order #, Item #** and **Sum of Quantity** columns. Sort by **Date**. You can indeed see that the oldest backorders are fulfilled first.

Date	Sales Order #	Item #	Sum of Quantity	FIFO Delivery Date	FIFO Qty to Fulfill
10/21/2024	SO00306320	1507	1250	2/1/2025	1250
10/29/2024	SO00306637	1507	125	2/1/2025	1750
10/29/2024	SO00306642	1507	375	2/1/2025	1750
11/11/2024	SO00307164	1507	250	2/1/2025	2000
11/24/2024	SO00307826	1507	1500	2/1/2025	4000
11/24/2024	SO00307834	1507	500	2/1/2025	4000
12/1/2024	SO00308128	1507	1250	2/1/2025	5250
12/3/2024	SO00308293	1507	3000	4/5/2025	8250
12/20/2024	SO00309032	1507	1250	4/5/2025	9500
1/5/2025	SO00309292	1507	1250	4/5/2025	10750
1/8/2025	SO00309389	1507	2500	4/5/2025	13250

Figure 11.7: Data fulfillment semantic model

To gain a deeper understanding of how the **FIFO Delivery Date** measure works internally, create the following measure and add it to the **Table** visualization to expose the inner workings of the __**Table** variable.

```
FIFO Delivery Date Debug =
    VAR __QtyToFulfill = [FIFO Qty to Fulfill]
    VAR __Table =
        ADDCOLUMNS(
            ADDCOLUMNS(
                SELECTCOLUMNS(
                    'Purchase Orders',
                    "ETA", [ETA], "Quantity", [Quantity]
                ),
                "__TotalQty",
                    SUMX(
                        FILTER( 'Purchase Orders', [ETA] <= EARLIER( [ETA] ) ),
                        [Quantity]
                    )
            ),
            "__LoopCounter", [__TotalQty] - __QtyToFulfill
        )
    VAR __TargetDate = MINX( FILTER( __Table, [__LoopCounter] >= 0 ), [ETA] )
    VAR __Result =
```

```
    IF(

        __QtyToFulfill = BLANK() || __TargetDate = BLANK(),

        BLANK(),

        TOCSV( __Table )

    )

RETURN

    __Result
```

The only change in this measure is to return **TOCSV(__Table)** instead of the **__TargetDate**.

If we instead wish to use LIFO instead of FIFO to fulfill backorders, we can create the following LIFO measure and then substitute this measure for our **__QtyToFulfill** variable:

```
LIFO Qty to Fulfill =

    VAR __Item = MAX( 'Backorders'[Item #] )

    VAR __Date = MAX( 'BackOrders'[Date] )

    VAR __Table =

        FILTER(

            ALL( 'BackOrders' ),

            [Item #] = __Item && [Date] >= __Date

        )

    VAR __Result = SUMX( __Table, [Quantity] )

RETURN

    __Result
```

This scenario is meant to introduce the concept of looping in DAX and is therefore somewhat simplified which leads to potential issues with the approach. Notably, with the FIFO and LIFO calculations it is possible to have a large and small backorder on the same date, one of which could be fulfilled and one of which cannot based upon a particular purchase order ETA date. With this approach, both orders would be pushed to a future ETA date since two backorders for the same widget on the same date are effectively treated as a single backorder.

Ultimately, the issue stems from the fact that it is generally not possible to impose strict sorting within DAX. That said, there are potential mitigation strategies and there are more sophisticated techniques that will be demonstrated later in this chapter where sort order can be imposed; however, this comes with considerable complexity and introduces potential performance issues.

Before we move on to some of the more sophisticated techniques, there are other simple mitigation strategies that we can employ such as adjusting the calculation to accommodate other methods of fulfilling backorders. Two that come to mind are prioritizing fulfilling the greatest number of backorders and prioritizing fulfilling backorders with the most quantity. The first seeks to keep the most customers happy while the second seeks to prioritize large, important customers. The formula for these two methods are as follows:

```
Most Orders Qty to Fulfill =
    VAR __Item = MAX( 'Backorders'[Item #] )
    VAR __Qty = MAX( 'Backorders'[Quantity] )
    VAR __CurrOrder = RIGHT( MAX( 'Backorders'[Sales Order #] ), 8 )
    VAR __Table =
        FILTER(
            ALL( 'BackOrders' ),
            [Item #] = __Item &&
            ( [Quantity] & RIGHT( [Sales Order #], 8 ) ) * 1. <=
                ( __Qty & __CurrOrder ) * 1.
        )
    VAR __Result = SUMX( __Table, [Quantity] )
RETURN
    __Result
```

```
Most Qty to Fulfill =
    VAR __Item = MAX( 'Backorders'[Item #] )
    VAR __Qty = MAX( 'Backorders'[Quantity] )
    VAR __CurrOrder = RIGHT( MAX( 'Backorders'[Sales Order #] ), 8 )
    VAR __Table =
        FILTER(
            ALL( 'BackOrders' ),
            [Item #] = __Item &&
            ( [Quantity] & RIGHT( [Sales Order #], 8 ) ) * 1. >=
                ( __Qty & __CurrOrder ) * 1.
        )
    VAR __Result = SUMX( __Table, [Quantity] )
```

```
RETURN
    __Result
```

Here again, we can simply substitute one of these measures in our "Delivery Date" measure to modify the prioritization of backorder fulfillment. The notable difference between these measures and the FIFO and LIFO measures is the introduction of an element that prevents backorders from being grouped together. This is done by specifying an ordering that is based upon the **Quantity** of each backorder concatenated with the numeric portion of the **Sales Order** #. One could also use an index column or even a random number generated via the **RAND** function instead of the numeric portion of the **Sales Order** # column.

Let's now move on to looking at a topic relevant to maintenance, mean time between failure.

Mean Time Between Failure

Mean time between failure (**MTBF**) is a measure of the reliability of a component or system and is a critical KPI in manufacturing as MTBF measures the average time that a component or system will operate before failure. Thus, MTBF can be used to optimize maintenance schedules to maximize uptime. There is a simple formula for MTBF which is as follows:

$$MTBF = \frac{Total\ Operating\ Time}{Number\ of\ Failures}$$

There are also more advanced methods of calculating MTBF as well as a related metric, **mean time to repair** (**MTTR**) which we will also explore.

To begin exploring MTBF, first import the **MTBF** sheet of the Excel spreadsheet, **Chapter11_Data.xlsx** which can be found in the Github repository for this book: https://github.com/gdeckler/DAX-For-Humans/tree/main/book.

The MTBF table includes data such as the following:

MachineName	RepairStarted	RepairType	Cause	RepairCompleted
Machine1	1/7/2022 22:52	Repair	Other	1/7/2022 23:24
Machine5	1/11/2022 14:52	Repair	Failed Component	1/11/2022 14:53
Machine5	1/11/2022 15:08	Repair	Failed Component	1/11/2022 15:10
Machine5	1/13/2022 16:44	Repair	Failed Component	1/13/2022 17:19
Machine5	1/15/2022 15:00	Repair	Failed Component	1/15/2022 15:09
Machine5	1/18/2022 8:58	Repair	Failed Component	1/18/2022 9:58
Machine5	1/18/2022 11:43	Repair	Failed Component	1/18/2022 11:45
Machine5	1/22/2022 9:55	Repair	Misalignment	1/22/2022 11:42

Figure 11.8: Mean time between failure data

This data is at the machine failure level of granularity meaning that each row represents a failure of a particular machine. The data includes an identifier for the machine, **MachineName**, when the repair started (**RepairStarted**) and ended (**RepairCompleted**) as well as the type of repair (**RepairType**) and the cause of the failure (**Cause**).

It is important to note that the **RepairType** column includes preventative maintenance instances which are designated as "PM" and should not be included in the calculation of MTBF.

Now create the following simple MTBF measure:

```
Simple MTBF (Hours) =

    VAR __Start = DATE( 2022, 1, 1 )

    VAR __End = DATE( 2025, 12, 31 )

    VAR __OperatingHours = DATEDIFF( __Start, __End, HOUR )

    VAR __Table =

        SUMMARIZE(

            'MTBF',

            [MachineName],

            "__MTBF",

            DIVIDE(

                __OperatingHours,

                COUNTROWS( FILTER( 'MTBF', [RepairType] <> "PM" ) )

            )

        )

    VAR __Result = AVERAGEX( __Table, [__MTBF] )
RETURN

    __Result
```

This calculation makes some simplifying assumptions, particularly regarding the operating hours (**__OperatingHours**). In this case, all machines are assumed to have the same operating hours spanning the years from 2022 thru 2025. In reality, each machine may have its own operating hours depending on when the machine was originally installed. However, this can easily be handled by a separate table that identifies such information. In addition, continuous operation is also assumed, meaning that the machines are assumed to be constantly operating unless being repaired or having preventative maintenance performed.

The heart of the **Simple MTBF (Hours)** calculation is the creation of the __Table variable which uses **SUMMARIZE** to group the MTBF table by **MachineName** and then add the column __MTBF which divides the __OperatingHours by the total number of failures for the machine, which is calculated by simply counting the non-preventative maintenance rows.

We can then use **AVERAGEX** across the __Table variable to calculate the average of the __MTBF column. Thus, this calculation works at the individual machine level as well as across all machines. We can create different visualizations for displaying our **Simple MTBF (Hours)** measure:

	MachineName	Simple MTBF (Hours)
171	Machine1	143
	Machine10	81
	Machine11	49
Simple MTBF (Hours)	Machine2	96
	Machine3	60
	Machine4	216
	Machine5	121
	Machine6	258
	Machine7	263
	Machine8	66
	Machine9	523
	Total	**171**

Figure 11.9: Simple mean time between failure

Another method of calculating MTBF is to average the actual uptime between failures. This can be done with the following measure:

```
MTBF (Hours) =
    VAR __Today = DATE( 2026, 1, 1 )
    VAR __Table =
        ADDCOLUMNS(
            ADDCOLUMNS(
                FILTER( 'MTBF', [RepairType] <> "PM" ),
                "__Next",
```

```
            MINX(

                FILTER(

                    'MTBF',

                    [MachineName] = EARLIER( 'MTBF'[MachineName] ) &&

                        [RepairStarted] > EARLIER( MTBF[RepairStarted] )

                ),

                [RepairStarted]

            )

        ),

        "__Uptime",

            IF(

                [__Next] = BLANK(),

                DATEDIFF( [RepairCompleted], __Today, HOUR ),

                DATEDIFF( [RepairCompleted], [__Next], HOUR)

            )

        )

    VAR __Result = AVERAGEX( __Table, [__Uptime] )

RETURN

    __Result
```

This measure formula demonstrates an important technique for certain types of DAX calculations. It is quite common to need to calculate the difference between two rows of data. In this case, for each row, we wish to calculate the time between the current row's **RepairCompleted** date and time and the next failure's **RepairStarted** date and time. This provides the total amount of uptime (**__Uptime**) for the machine in between repairs.

We use the **EARLIER** function to create cleaner, more concise code. For an explanation of the **EARLIER** function, see the *Delivery Dates* section of this chapter. This version of the formula produces somewhat different results and has the advantage of not assuming anything about the total operating hours of each machine but instead simply averaging the uptime between failures

Again, we can create simple visualizations to display the MTBF measure:

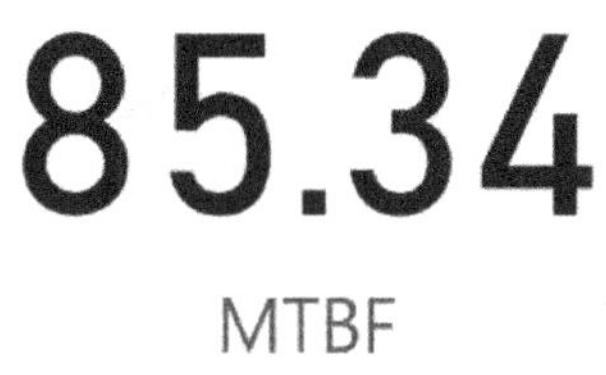

MachineName	MTBF
Machine1	126.81
Machine10	61.07
Machine11	30.95
Machine2	85.68
Machine3	53.92
Machine4	168.19
Machine5	115.26
Machine6	238.39
Machine7	238.28
Machine8	49.53
Machine9	284.30
Total	**85.34**

85.34

MTBF

Figure 11.10: Mean time between failure (MTBF)

As mentioned earlier, a related measure to MTBF is mean time to repair, MTTR. This can be calculated as follows:

```
MTTR =
    VAR __Table =
        ADDCOLUMNS(
            FILTER( 'MTBF', [RepairType] <> "PM" ),
            "__Hours", DATEDIFF( [RepairStarted], [RepairCompleted], HOUR )
        )
    VAR __Result = AVERAGEX( __Table, [__Hours] )
RETURN
    __Result
```

We can visualize MTTR as follows:

MachineName	MTTR
Machine1	1.78
Machine10	1.42
Machine11	1.19
Machine2	1.65
Machine3	1.32
Machine4	6.72
Machine5	3.18
Machine6	1.97
Machine7	1.38
Machine8	1.72
Machine9	4.54
Total	**1.90**

1.90
MTTR

Figure 11.11: Mean time to repair (MTTR)

Let's now move on to calculating overall equipment effectiveness (OEE).

Overall Equipment Effectiveness

Overall equipment effectiveness or **OEE** is a measure of how efficiently resources are being utilized compared with their maximum potential. Thus, OEE is important for maximizing the effectiveness and efficiency of resources such as manufacturing equipment.

OEE is actually a combination of three other KPIs, availability, performance, and quality. In a manufacturing scenario, availability is a measure of uptime while performance measures speed/capacity, and finally quality measures good parts produced versus bad parts. Each of these individual metrics, availability, performance, and quality are measured as percentages and OEE simply multiplies these percentages together.

To evaluate calculating OEE, start by completing the section *Mean Time Between Failure* if you have not already done in order to import the MTBF table. The MTBF table lists when machines were unavailable due to repairs or maintenance.

Next, create the following table:

```
Machines = DISTINCT( 'MTBF'[MachineName] )
```

This table simply lists the distinct machine names.

Now, import the **Production** sheet of the Excel spreadsheet, **Chapter11_Data.xlsx** which can be found in the GitHub repository for this book: https://github.com/gdeckler/DAX-For-Humans/tree/main/book.

The **Production** table has data as follows:

MachineName	Capacity	Date	Actual	Good
Machine1	1000	1/1/2022 0:00	828	778
Machine1	1000	1/2/2022 0:00	986	951
Machine1	1000	1/3/2022 0:00	886	830
Machine1	1000	1/4/2022 0:00	806	749

Figure 11.12: Production data

This table is at the date level of granularity. Here the **Capacity** column denotes the total daily capacity of the machine. The **Actual** column indicates how many "widgets" were produced while the **Good** column indicates how many of those widgets passed quality standards.

It may be interesting to note that the **Production** table was originally created using this DAX formula:

```
Production =

    VAR __Machines =

        { ( "Machine1", 1000 ),

          ( "Machine2", 800 ),

          ( "Machine3", 1200 ),

          ( "Machine4", 500 ),

          ( "Machine5", 1000 ),

          ( "Machine6", 800 ),

          ( "Machine7", 750 ),

          ( "Machine8", 1000 ),

          ( "Machine9", 120 ),

          ( "Machine10", 500 ),

          ( "Machine11", 750 ) }
    VAR __Calendar = CALENDAR( DATE( 2022,1,1 ), DATE( 2025,12,31 ) )

    VAR __Table =
```

```
ADDCOLUMNS(

    ADDCOLUMNS(

        SELECTCOLUMNS(

            GENERATE( __Machines, __Calendar ),

            "MachineName", [Value1],

            "Capacity", [Value2],

            "Date", [Date]

        ),

        "Actual", RANDBETWEEN( [Capacity] * .8, [Capacity] )

    ),

    "Good", RANDBETWEEN( [Actual] * .9, [Actual] )

)

RETURN

    __Table
```

Create relationships between the **Machines** table and the **MTBF** and **Production** tables using the common **MachineName** columns. Your semantic model should look like the following:

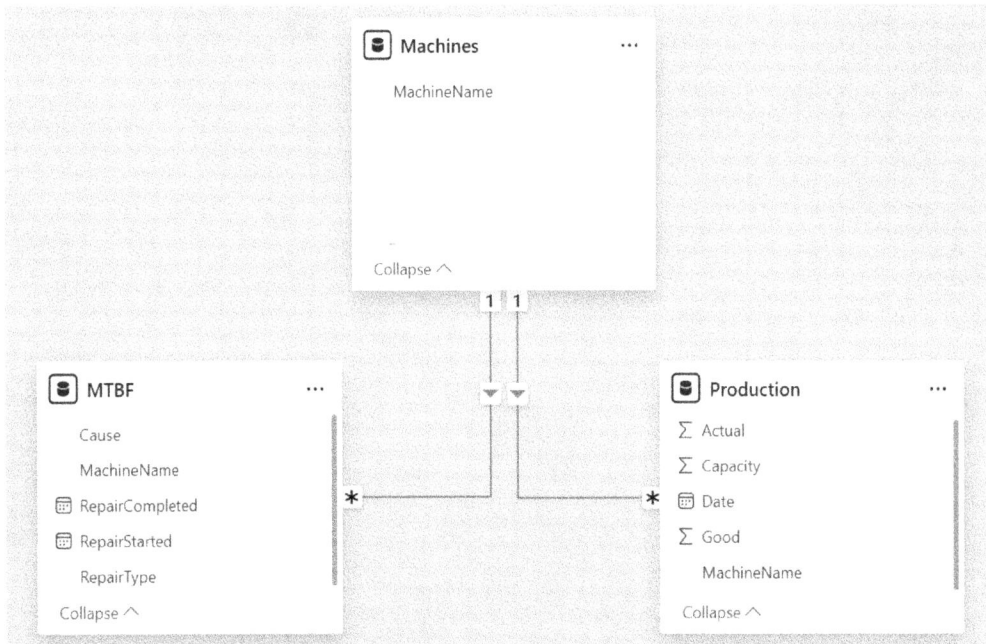

Figure 11.13: OEE semantic model

We can now construct our **Availability** measure as follows:

```
Availability =
    VAR __Start = DATE( 2022, 1, 1 )
    VAR __End = DATE( 2025, 12, 31 )
    VAR __OperatingHours = DATEDIFF( __Start, __End, HOUR )
    VAR __Machines = COUNTROWS( 'Machines' )
    VAR __Table =
        ADDCOLUMNS(
            'MTBF',
            "__Hours", DATEDIFF( [RepairStarted], [RepairCompleted], HOUR )
        )
    VAR __TotalDowntime = SUMX( __Table, [__Hours] )
    VAR __TotalOperatingHours = __OperatingHours * __Machines
    VAR __Result =
        DIVIDE( __TotalOperatingHours - __TotalDowntime, __TotalOperatingHours )
RETURN
    __Result
```

This measure is extremely similar to the **MTTR** measure from the section *Mean Time Between Failure*. Here we calculate the total downtime by not filtering preventative maintenance rows and summing the **__Hours** of repair time. We also make the same simplifying assumptions regarding operating hours as we did with the **Simple MTBF (Hours)** measure in the section *Mean Time Between Failure*.

To calculate performance, we use the following measure:

```
Performance =
    DIVIDE(
        SUMX('Production', [Actual] ),
        SUMX('Production', [Capacity] ),
        0
    )
```

Here we simply divide the **Actual** number of widgets produced by the total **Capacity** of the machines.

The **Quality** measure is similar:

```
Quality =
    DIVIDE(
        SUMX('Production', [Good] ),
        SUMX('Production', [Actual] ),
        0
    )
```

Here, we simply divide the number of **Good** widgets by the number of **Actual** widgets produced.

Finally, the OEE measure simply multiplies these three measures together:

```
OEE = [Availability] * [Performance] * [Quality]
```

We can visualize all of these measures as follows:

97.93%
Availability

95.01%
Quality

90.02%
Performance

83.76%
OEE

MachineName	Availability	Performance	Quality	OEE
Machine1	98.68%	90.05%	95.04%	84.45%
Machine10	97.77%	90.11%	94.82%	83.54%
Machine11	97.27%	89.83%	95.08%	83.08%
Machine2	98.13%	90.08%	95.01%	83.98%
Machine3	97.20%	90.06%	95.06%	83.22%
Machine4	96.63%	89.82%	95.01%	82.47%
Machine5	97.11%	89.96%	95.01%	83.00%
Machine6	99.07%	90.13%	95.12%	84.94%
Machine7	99.38%	90.08%	94.99%	85.04%
Machine8	97.18%	90.04%	94.87%	83.01%
Machine9	98.82%	90.01%	95.32%	84.78%
Total	**97.93%**	**90.02%**	**95.01%**	**83.76%**

Figure 11.14: OEE visualizations

This concludes our exploration of OEE. We now move on to Days of Supply.

Days of Supply

Days of Supply (DOS) is an inventory management metric that measures the average length of time that it takes for an organization to sell its entire inventory (**stockout**). This metric is also known as **Days in Inventory**, **Days Inventory Outstanding**, and **Inventory Period**. DOS is useful for a variety of purposes including optimizing inventory levels, improving cash flow, measuring supply chain efficiency, and risk mitigation to name just a few. The formula for DOS is straightforward:

$$DOS = \frac{Current\ Inventory\ Level}{Average\ Daily\ Demand}$$

To explore how to calculate days of supply, start by importing the **Days of Supply** sheet of the Excel spreadsheet, **Chapter11_Data.xlsx** which can be found in the Github repository for this book: https://github.com/gdeckler/DAX-For-Humans/tree/main/book.

The **Days of Supply** table has data as follows:

Week	Demand	Ending Inventory
3-Feb-25	0	49813
10-Feb-25	11360	36961
17-Feb-25	7952	37856
24-Feb-25	7485	32876
2-Mar-25	7131	24875
9-Mar-25	6785	76385
16-Mar-25	6854	73152

Figure 11.15: Days of Supply data

This table is at the week level of granularity. Here the **Demand** column denotes the total weekly demand (inventory sold). The **Ending Inventory** column indicates the current inventory level at the end of each week.

Now create the following measure:

```
DOS =

    VAR __Week = MAX( 'Days of Supply'[Week] )

    VAR __Inventory =

        MAXX(

            FILTER( 'Days of Supply', [Week] = __Week ),

            [Ending Inventory]
```

```
    )

    VAR __Table = FILTER( ALL( 'Days of Supply' ), [Week] <= __Week )

    VAR __AverageDemand = DIVIDE( AVERAGEX( __Table, [Demand] ), 7 )

    VAR __DaysOfSupply = DIVIDE( __Inventory, __AverageDemand, 0 )

    VAR __Result = IF( __DaysOfSupply = 0, BLANK(), __DaysOfSupply )

RETURN

    __Result
```

This formula is fairly simple. First, the maximum week (__**Week**) in context is found using the **MAX** function. Next, the **Ending Inventory** for this __**Week** is calculated using the **MAXX** and **FILTER** functions (__**Inventory**). We can then create a table, __**Table**, of all weeks that are less than or equal to the current week (__**Week**). To get the daily average demand, __**AverageDemand**, we use **AVERAGEX** to find the average demand per week and then divide this by 7 to get the average demand per day. The days of supply is then found by dividing the __**Inventory** by the __**AverageDemand**.

We can visualize **Days of Supply** in a **Line chart**:

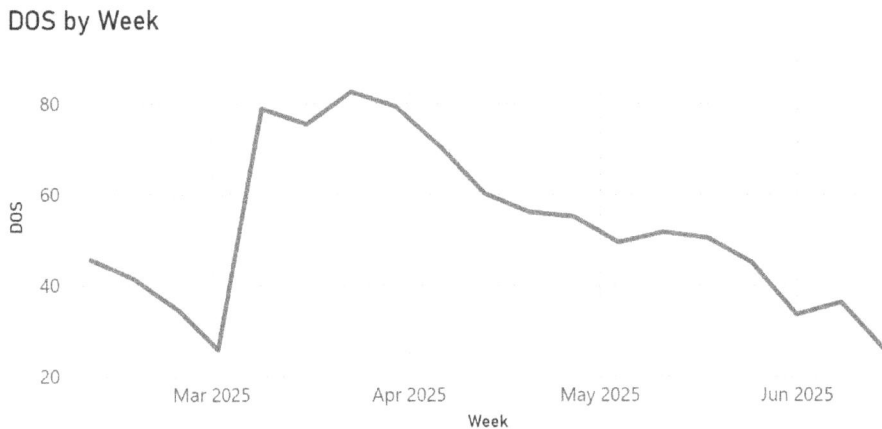

Figure 11.16: Days of Supply visualized as a line chart

With our exploration of Days of Supply complete, let's now look at Order Fulfillment.

Order Fulfillment

Optimizing supply chains, logistics, and operations can take many forms. One optimization that can be important is the efficient fulfillment of orders. Organizations may have multiple warehouses or locations within warehouses where orders can be fulfilled from existing inventory. This is generally referred to as "picking". Determining the most efficient manner or method of picking can be vitally important to optimizing the overall picking process.

To examine order fulfillment, first import the **Inventory** and **Sales Orders** sheets from the Excel spreadsheet, **Chapter11_Data.xlsx** which can be found in the Github repository for this book: https://github.com/gdeckler/DAX-For-Humans/tree/main/book.

The **Inventory** table has data as follows:

Location	ItemCode	Qty
L42	A3	6
L42	A10	6
L42	A16	6
L42	A19	6
L42	A30	6

Figure 11.17: Inventory data

The **Inventory** table includes the **Location**, **ItemCode**, and **Qty** columns which indicate the warehouse or bin, which item is stored in that warehouse or bin and the quantity of the item stored at that location respectively. This table was originally generated using the following DAX code:

```
Inventory =

    VAR __Locations =

        SELECTCOLUMNS(

            ADDCOLUMNS(

                GENERATESERIES( 1, 50, 1 ),

                "Location", "L" & [Value]

            ),

            "Location", [Location]

        )

    VAR __Products =
```

```
     SELECTCOLUMNS(

         GENERATE(

             GENERATESERIES( 1, 1000, 1 ),

             SELECTCOLUMNS(

                 { "A", "B", "C", "D", "E" },

                 "Item", [Value]

             )

         ),

         "ItemCode", [Item] & [Value]

     )

  VAR __Result =

     ADDCOLUMNS(

         GENERATE(

             __Locations,

             __Products

         ),

         "QtyStr", RANDBETWEEN( 2, 8 )

     )

RETURN

  __Result
```

The **Sales Orders** table is similar and contains data such as the following:

OrderNo	ItemCode	Qty
1	A3	39
1	A36	39
1	A64	39
1	A144	39
1	A148	39

Figure 11.18: Sales order data

The **OrderNo** column is assigned sequentially as orders are placed. The **ItemCode** identifies the item ordered and the **Qty** column indicates how many of the item was ordered.

This table was generated using the following DAX code:

```
SalesOrders =
    VAR __Orders =
        SELECTCOLUMNS(
            GENERATESERIES( 1, 10, 1 ),
            "OrderNo", [Value]
        )
    VAR __Products =
        DISTINCT(
            SELECTCOLUMNS(
                'Inventory',
                "ItemCode", [ItemCode]
            )
        )
    VAR __Result =
        ADDCOLUMNS(
            GENERATE( __Orders, __Products ),
            "QtyOrd", RANDBETWEEN( 20, 40 )
        )
RETURN
    __Result
```

Create a new table using the following DAX code:

```
ItemCodes = DISTINCT('Inventory'[ItemCode])
```

Create relationships between the **ItemCodes** table and the **Inventory** and **Sales Orders** tables using the common **ItemCode** columns. Your semantic model should look like the following:

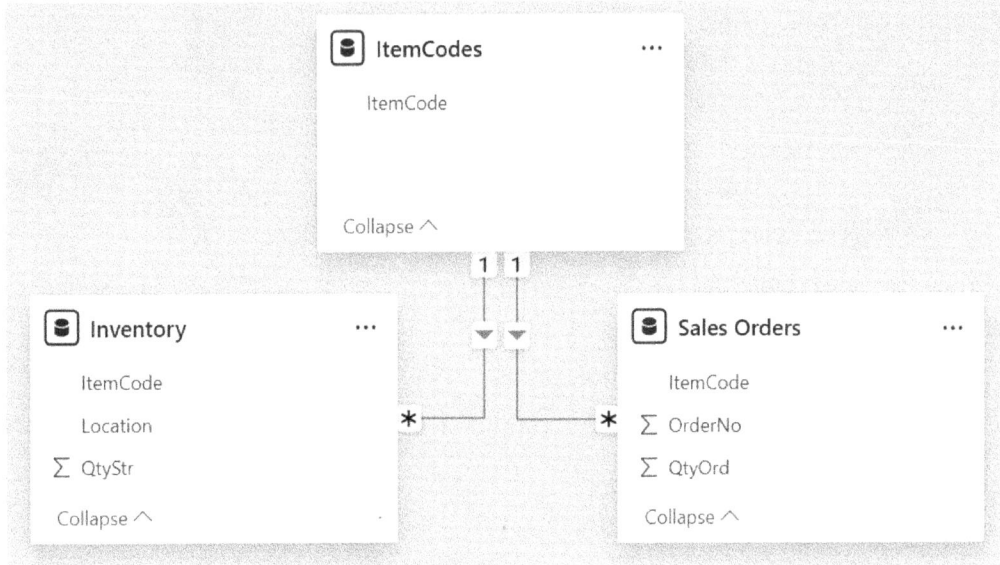

Figure 11.19: Order fulfillment semantic model

The goal is to identify the locations from which sales orders need to be picked with the following criteria:

- Sales orders should be fulfilled according to first in, first out (FIFO)
- Locations with the most inventory should be used to fulfill orders first to minimize the number of locations being picked for any particular order
- Locations with the most inventory should be used to fulfill orders first, including subsequent orders if the previous order(s) do not pick the entirety of its inventory

To fulfill these requirements, create the following measure:

```
FIFO Orders Locations =
    VAR __ItemCode = MAX( 'Sales Orders'[ItemCode] )
    VAR __OrderNo = MAX( 'Sales Orders'[OrderNo] )
    VAR __CurrentQty = MAXX( FILTER( 'Sales Orders', [OrderNo] = __OrderNo ), [Qty] )
    VAR __PreviousOrders =
            FILTER(
                ALL( 'Sales Orders' ),
                [OrderNo] < __OrderNo && [ItemCode] = __ItemCode
            )
    VAR __QtyOrdPrevious = SUMX( __PreviousOrders, [Qty] )
```

```
VAR __QtyOrd = __QtyOrdPrevious + __CurrentQty

VAR __LocText =

    CONCATENATEX(

        FILTER(

            'Inventory',

            'Inventory'[ItemCode] = __ItemCode

        ),

        [Location],

        "|",

        [Qty],

        DESC

    )

VAR __Count = PATHLENGTH( __LocText )

VAR __Table =

    ADDCOLUMNS(

        ADDCOLUMNS(

            GENERATESERIES( 1, __Count, 1 ),

            "__Loc", PATHITEM( __LocText, [Value], TEXT )

        ),

        "__Qty",

            MAXX(

                FILTER(

                    'Inventory',

                    [Location] = [__Loc] && [ItemCode] = __ItemCode

                ),

                [Qty]

            )

    )

VAR __Table1 =
```

```
        ADDCOLUMNS(

            ADDCOLUMNS(

                __Table,

                "__RunningTotal",

                SUMX(

                    FILTER( __Table, [Value] <= EARLIER( [Value] ) ),

                    [__Qty]

                )

            ),

            "__Decrement", [__RunningTotal] - __QtyOrd,

            "__Previous", [__RunningTotal] - __QtyOrdPrevious

        )

    VAR __Index = MINX( FILTER( __Table1, [__Decrement] >= 0), [Value] )

    VAR __IndexPrevious = MINX( FILTER( __Table1, [__Previous] >= 0 ), [Value] )

    VAR __LocCurrent = FILTER( __Table1, [Value] <= __Index )

    VAR __LocPrevious =

        FILTER( __Table1, [Value] <= __IndexPrevious && [__Previous] <= 0 )

    VAR __Locations = EXCEPT( __LocCurrent, __LocPrevious )

    VAR __Locations1 = CONCATENATEX( __Locations, [__Loc], ", ", [__Loc], ASC )

    VAR __Locations2 = CONCATENATEX( __LocCurrent, [__Loc], ", ", [__Loc], ASC )

    VAR __Result =

        SWITCH( TRUE(),

            __Index = BLANK(), "Insufficient inventory",

            __QtyOrdPrevious = BLANK(), __Locations2,

            __Locations1

        )

RETURN

    __Result
```

This is quite the long measure with more than its fair share of complexity. In fact, this problem was considered so difficult to solve that it was used to benchmark different AI models. Up until the release of ChatGPT's production 4o model, AI was generally unable to solve this problem.

The formula starts off simply enough, getting the current **ItemCode** (**_ItemCode**) and **OrderNo** (**_OrderNo**) in context. Next the current order's quantity (**_CurrentQty**) is looked up using the **_OrderNo** variable. After that, the previous order quantities, **_QtyOrdPrevious** is calculated by creating the table variable, **_PreviousOrders** which filters the **Sales Orders** table to all orders that are previous to the current order (in this case **OrderNo** is sequential with the lowest number being the first order). Finally, the **_QtyOrd** variable calculates the total amount ordered, which simply adds **_QtyOrdPrevious** and **_CurrentQty**.

The next task is to get the inventory locations in order, sorted by their inventory levels. This is the purpose of the **_LocText**, **_Count**, and **_Table** variables. Overall, this employs techniques covered in *Chapter 4, Text*. We first turn the **Inventory** table into a sorted text string using **CONCATENATEX**. Thus, the **_LocText** contains a sorted list of locations separated by the pipe (|) character which turns the string of text into a path recognized by the **PATH** family of DAX functions. Thus, the **_LocText** variable looks something like the following:

L15|L21|L3|L50|L42|L16|L39|L43

We now need to turn this sorted text path back into a table. We do this by first getting the number of items (**_Count**) in **_LocText** using the **PATHLENGTH** variable. Next, we can turn the **_LocText** string back into a table, **_Table**, using the **GENERATESERIES** function along with using **ADDCOLUMNS** to retrieve the **PATHITEM** from the **_LocText** string. We can then use **ADDCOLUMNS** again to add the quantity for each item in each location, **_Qty** by essentially looking up the **Qty** from the **Inventory** table. This then provides us with a table such as the following, which is a sorted list of locations and quantities for **ItemCode A1**.

Value	_Loc	_Qty
1	L21	8
2	L50	8
3	L15	8
4	L3	8
5	L42	8

Value	__Loc	__Qty
6	L39	7
7	L8	7
8	L16	7
9	L5	7

Table 11.3: __Table variable sample data

The next challenge is to implement a double while loop. For more about looping in DAX, see the *Delivery Dates* section of this chapter. This is the purpose of the __**Table1** variable. We start by adding a running total column (__**RunningTotal**) to the __**Table** variable. Thus, now our __**Table1** variable looks like the following:

Value	__Loc	__Qty	__RunningTotal
1	L21	8	8
2	L50	8	16
3	L15	8	24
4	L3	8	32
5	L42	8	40
6	L39	7	47
7	L8	7	54
8	L16	7	61
9	L5	7	68

Table 11.4: __Table1 variable sample data

The __**Decrement** and __**Previous** columns implement our while loop and might look similar to the following:

Value	__Loc	__Qty	__RunningTotal	__Decrement	__Previous
1	L21	8	8	-58	-18
2	L50	8	16	-50	-10
3	L15	8	24	-42	-2
4	L3	8	32	-34	6
5	L42	8	40	-26	14
6	L39	7	47	-19	21
7	L8	7	54	-12	28
8	L16	7	61	-5	35
9	L5	7	68	2	42

Table 11.5: __Table1 variable sample data with additional columns

Here, the __**Previous** column tracks when all previous orders have been fulfilled. The "exit" of the while loop is the lowest **Value** that has a positive __**Previous** column value. The __**Decrement** column does the same thing for all of the previous orders plus the current order. The "exits" for these while loops are stored in the __**PreviousIndex** and __**Index** variables respectively. For the example we have presented thus far, the __**PreviousIndex** would have a value of 4 and __**Index** would have a value of 9.

At this point, we can get a table of current locations that must be used to fulfill all previous orders as well as the current order, __**LocCurrent**. In addition, we can get a list of all locations required to fulfill previous orders but not the current order, __**LocPrevious**. Critically, __**LocPrevious** only includes locations where the full inventory of the location was used. The final list of locations, __**Locations**, is then created by using the **EXCEPT** function. The final bit of the calculation simply accounts for boundary cases, such as fulfilling the first order or when there is insufficient inventory to fulfill the order.

As mentioned, this is perhaps one of the most complex DAX calculations. The complexity comes from the specified business requirements as well as the need to enforce sorting, which DAX is not generally capable of doing outside of a function such as **CONCATENATEX**. We can create visualizations to display the **FIFO Orders Locations** measure:

ItemCode

A1   ⌄

ItemCode	Location	Sum of Qty		OrderNo	Sum of Qty	FIFO Orders Locations
A1	L15	8		1	26	L15, L21, L3, L50
A1	L21	8		2	40	L16, L3, L39, L42, L5, L8
A1	L3	8		3	37	L11, L27, L38, L40, L43, L46, L5
A1	L42	8		4	32	L12, L31, L35, L40, L44, L6, L7
A1	L50	8		5	34	L14, L2, L23, L24, L25, L26, L30, L47, L7
A1	L16	7		6	24	L10, L18, L20, L32, L34, L41, L47
A1	L39	7		7	38	L1, L13, L19, L22, L28, L29, L32, L33, L36, L37, L4, L45, L48, L49, L9
A1	L43	7		8	34	Insufficient inventory
A1	L5	7		9	28	Insufficient inventory
A1	L8	7		10	36	Insufficient inventory
A1	L11	6				
A1	L27	6				

Figure 11.20: Order fulfillment visuals

This concludes our exploration of operational metrics and KPIs.

Summary

This chapter explored several different operational metrics and KPIs. Operational metrics are important because they assist organizations with optimizing internal processes, which can lead to greater efficiency, effectiveness, and profitability as well as aid in customer service. We began with common metrics such as On Time in Full (OTIF) and Order Cycle Time (OCT) which are used throughout supply chains all over the globe. We then explored calculating Delivery Dates in the context of fulfilling backorders. Here we introduced the concept of DAX while loops as well as covered the use of the **EARLIER** function.

We used the knowledge gained to explore two different methods of calculating Mean Time Between Failure (MTBF) as well as Mean Time To Repair (MTTR) and the Overall Equipment Effectiveness (OEE). We then finished the chapter with a rather simple calculation for Days of Supply as well as an extremely complex metric for Order Fulfillment, which identified the locations from which to fulfill orders based upon some specific business rules.

Leaving the world of operations behind, we next take a look at calculations involving distance and space.

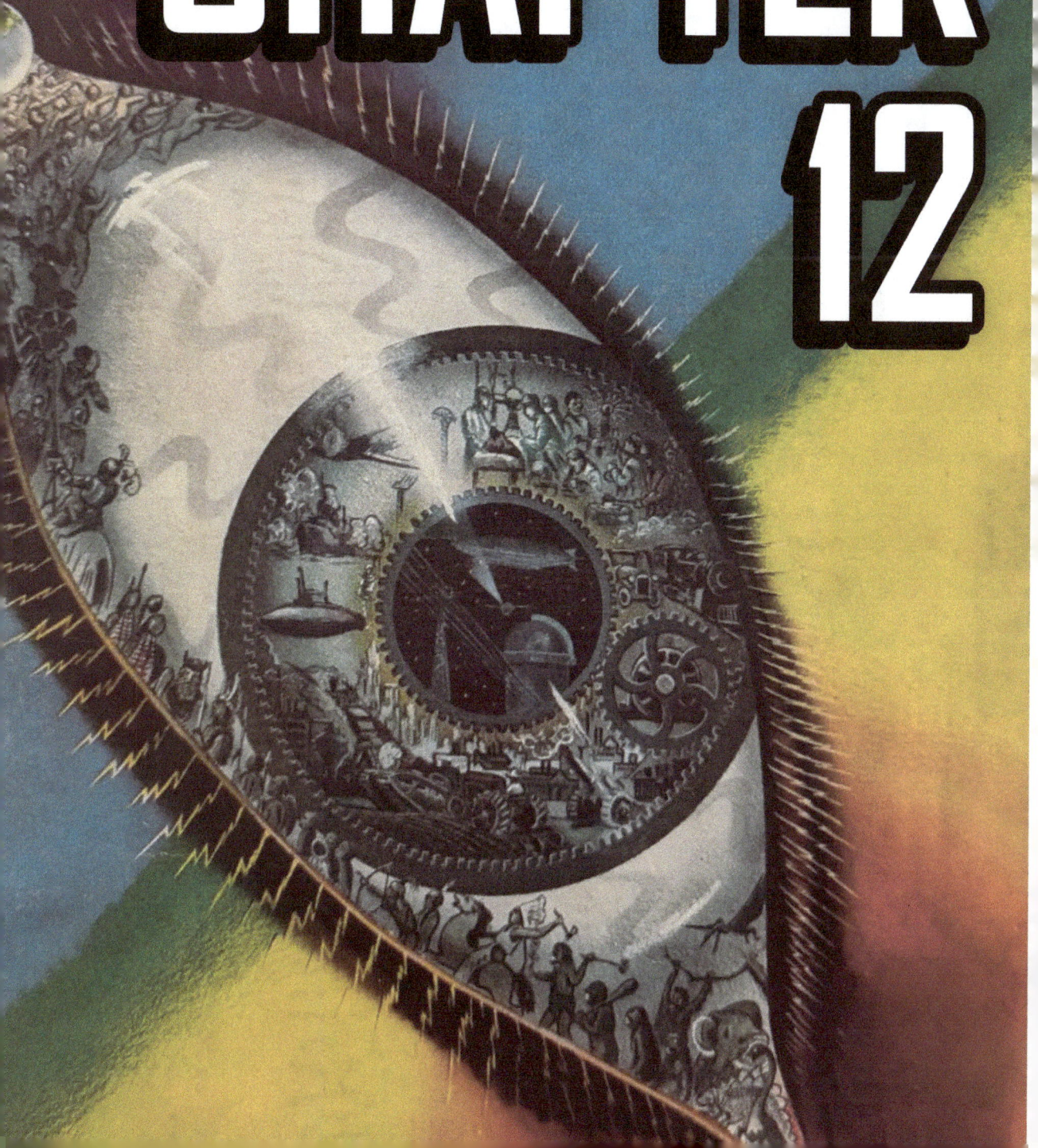

CHAPTER 12

Distance and Space

Distance and spatial calculations might not seem like a natural fit for a business intelligence tool, but in the age of geographic data and interactive maps, understanding how to perform distance and space calculations in Power BI has never been more relevant. From visualizing sales by region to analyzing supply routes and delivery coverage, spatial calculations help uncover relationships that are difficult to perceive in flat tables or standard charts.

This chapter introduces a powerful set of tools and techniques, starting with the essential ATAN2 function, to work effectively with spatial data, even in a formula language like DAX that lacks built-in spatial support. Throughout this chapter, we walk through practical scenarios including how to compute angles and distances between coordinates, convert between Cartesian and polar coordinates, calculate bearings for navigation, and work with grid-based systems like Eastings and Northings. We also dive into more advanced spatial logic such as identifying nearby points, computing transitive closures, and determining optimal box sizes for shipping. These techniques not only broaden what's possible in Power BI, but they also demonstrate how DAX can be extended far beyond traditional aggregations to solve real-world spatial problems.

ATAN2

The ATAN2 function has been a staple of many programming languages since early versions of FORTRAN in the 1960's. Unlike the ATAN function, which can only return values for angles between -90° and 90°, the ATAN2 function operates for all four Cartesian quadrants and returns angles from -180° to 180°. Given how critical the ATAN2 function is for areas such as game development, robotics, GPS, and navigation as well as its prevalence in coding languages; including the Excel formula language, the absence of the ATAN2 function from DAX is a bit of a head scratcher. Luckily, we can create our own ATAN2 function in DAX. To do so, start by creating the following table:

```
ATAN2 Table =

    VAR __x = SELECTCOLUMNS( GENERATESERIES( -1, 1, 1 ), "X", [Value] )
```

```
    VAR __y = SELECTCOLUMNS( __x, "Y", [x] )

    VAR __Result = CROSSJOIN( __x, __y )

RETURN

    __Result
```

This table creates points in all four quadrants of a Cartesian plane. Now create the following measure:

```
ATAN2 =

    VAR __x = MAX('ATAN2 Table'[X])

    VAR __y = MAX('ATAN2 Table'[Y])

    VAR __Result =

        SWITCH(

            TRUE(),

            __x > 0, ATAN(__y/__x),

            __x < 0 && __y >= 0, ATAN(__y/__x) + PI(),

            __x < 0 && __y < 0, ATAN(__y/__x) - PI(),

            __x = 0 && __y > 0, PI()/2,

            __x = 0 && __y < 0, PI()/2 * -1,

            BLANK()

        )

RETURN

    __Result
```

The **ATAN2** measure returns values in radians. We can convert this to degrees with the following measure:

```
ATAN2 Degrees =

    VAR __x = MAX('ATAN2 Table'[X])

    VAR __y = MAX('ATAN2 Table'[Y])

    VAR __Result =

        SWITCH(

            TRUE(),

            __x > 0, ATAN(__y/__x),
```

```
        __x < 0 && __y >= 0, ATAN(__y/__x) + PI(),

        __x < 0 && __y < 0, ATAN(__y/__x) - PI(),

       __x = 0 && __y > 0, PI()/2,

        __x = 0 && __y < 0, PI()/2 * -1,

       BLANK()

     ) * 180/PI()

RETURN

    __Result
```

Here we simply multiply the radians by **180/PI()** to convert to degrees. Alternatively, we could have used the **DEGREES** function such as **DEGREES([ATAN2])**.

Placing these measures into a **Table** visual, along with un-summarized **X** and **Y** columns, produces the following results:

X	Y	ATAN2	ATAN2 Degrees
-1	-1	-2.36	-135.00
-1	0	3.14	180.00
-1	1	2.36	135.00
0	-1	-1.57	-90.00
0	1	1.57	90.00
1	-1	-0.79	-45.00
1	0	0.00	0.00
1	1	0.79	45.00

Figure 12.1: ATAN2

As previously mentioned, **ATAN2** is a critical function with a wide array of applications because it can accurately return the correct angle from any of the four quadrants of a Cartesian plane.

Let's next demonstrate the utility of **ATAN2** by using **ATAN2** to convert Cartesian coordinates to polar coordinates and back again.

Polar

Polar coordinates are a way of representing points in a two-dimensional plane using a distance from a reference point (radius) and an angle from a reference direction. Unlike Cartesian coordinates (x, y) which define a point by horizontal and vertical distances, polar coordinates describe a point as a distance from an origin and an angle from the horizontal axis.

A point in polar coordinates is expressed as (r, θ) where:

- r (radius): The distance from the origin (0,0) to the point.
- θ (theta, angle): The counterclockwise angle from the positive x-axis, measured in degrees or radians.

To begin exploring the calculation for polar coordinates, please first complete the previous section on *ATAN2* in this chapter. Now, create these two measures:

```
r =
    VAR __x = MAX( 'ATAN2 Table'[X] )
    VAR __y = MAX( 'ATAN2 Table'[Y] )
    VAR __Result = SQRT( POWER( __x, 2 ) + POWER( __y, 2 ) )
RETURN
    __Result
```


```
theta =
    VAR __x = MAX('ATAN2 Table'[X])
    VAR __y = MAX('ATAN2 Table'[Y])
    VAR __theta =
        SWITCH(
            TRUE(),
            __x > 0, ATAN(__y/__x),
            __x < 0 && __y >= 0, ATAN(__y/__x) + PI(),
            __x < 0 && __y < 0, ATAN(__y/__x) - PI(),
            __x = 0 && __y > 0, PI()/2,
            __x = 0 && __y < 0, PI()/2 * -1,
```

```
            BLANK()

        )

    VAR __Result = DEGREES( __theta )

RETURN

    __Result
```

The formula for **r** is the standard formula for finding the hypotenuse of a triangle:

$$r = \sqrt{x^2 + y^2}$$

The formula for **theta** is simply an alternative to the **ATAN2 Degrees** measure from the *ATAN2* section of this chapter.

Placing these measures into a **Table** visual along with the **X** and **Y** columns from the **ATAN2 Table** creates the following:

X	Y	r	theta
-1	-1	1.41	-135.00
-1	0	1.00	180.00
-1	1	1.41	135.00
0	-1	1.00	-90.00
0	0	0.00	
0	1	1.00	90.00
1	-1	1.41	-45.00
1	0	1.00	0.00
1	1	1.41	45.00

Figure 12.2: r and theta polar coordinates

We could, of course, continue with this example and demonstrate converting the calculated polar coordinates back to Cartesian coordinates. However, instead, we will introduce something a little more fun visually to demonstrate this conversion. To get started, create the following table:

```
Polar =

    ADDCOLUMNS(

        SELECTCOLUMNS(
```

```
        GENERATESERIES(-100, 100, .2),

        "theta", [Value]

    ),

    "r", SIGN( [theta] ) * SQRT( ABS( [theta] ) ),

    "Color", SIGN( [theta] )

)
```

Now add the following two calculated columns:

$$x = [r] * COS([theta])$$

$$y = [r] * SIN([theta]) * SIGN([theta])$$

These two formulas convert polar coordinates to Cartesian coordinates. By plotting the **x** and **y** columns in a **Scatter chart** visualization and conditionally formatting the color of the markers based upon the **Color** column, we can achieve a rather fun and interesting spiral chart:

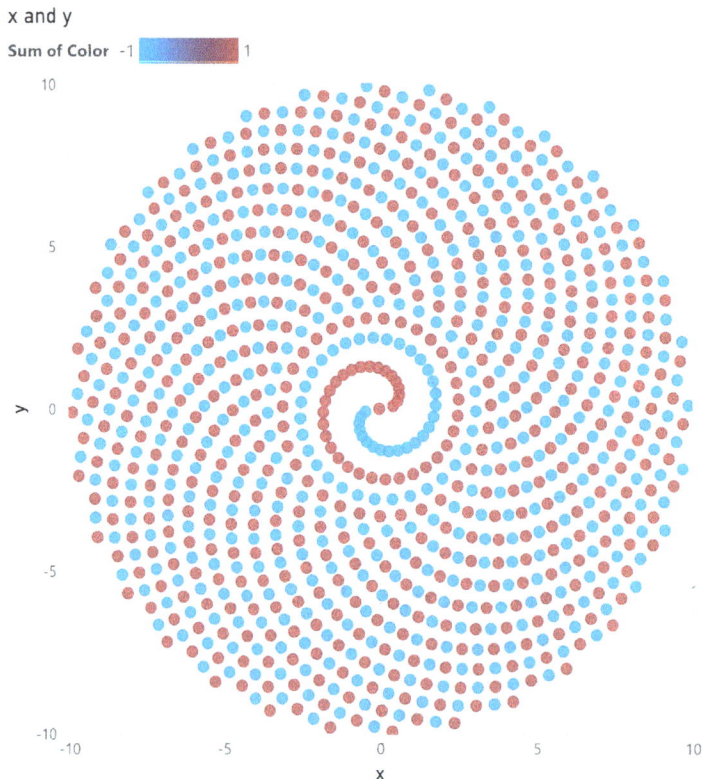

Figure 12.3: Spiral chart based upon converting polar coordinates to Cartesian coordinates

Let's next demonstrate the further utility of **ATAN2** in a more practical setting by demonstrating how to calculate the distance between two longitudes and latitudes.

Distance

Power BI Desktop includes no less than four different map visuals as default visuals. In addition, there are over 30 third-party map visuals for Power BI. Clearly, mapping is a critical feature in Power BI and that is because mapping in Power BI is essential for visualizing geographic data and uncovering spatial patterns that might be difficult to interpret in traditional tables or charts.

With Power BI's mapping capabilities, businesses can analyze sales performance by region, track supply chain logistics, or monitor customer distribution in real time. Maps help transform raw geographic data into actionable insights by highlighting trends such as high-performing areas, underserved markets, or regions requiring operational improvements.

With so much mapping going on, it is inevitable that the subject of distance between two points on a map would come up. However, none of the default map visuals provide any ability to compute distances between two points on a map. Luckily, there is a common formula for computing distances between points on a map, the **Haversine formula**.

The Haversine formula is a mathematical equation used to calculate the great-circle distance between two points on a sphere, given their **latitude** and **longitude** coordinates. It is particularly useful for calculating distances between locations on Earth, as it accounts for the planet's curvature.

The Haversine formula is as follows:

$$a = sin^2\left(\frac{\Delta\varphi}{2}\right) + \cos(\varphi_1) * \cos(\varphi_2) * sin^2\left(\frac{\Delta\lambda}{2}\right)$$

$$c = 2 * atan2(\sqrt{a}, \sqrt{1-a})$$

$$d = R * c$$

Where:

- φ_1, φ_2 are the latitudes of the two points (in radians).
- λ_1, λ_2 are the longitudes of the two points (in radians).
- $\Delta\varphi = \varphi_2 - \varphi_1$ is the difference in latitude.
- $\Delta\lambda = \lambda_2 - \lambda_1$ is the difference in longitude.
- R is the Earth's radius (commonly approximated as **6,371 km** or **3,959 miles**).
- d is the calculated great-circle distance between the two points.

To implement the Haversine formula for distance in DAX, first use an **Enter data** query to create a **Cities** table in Power BI or, alternatively, import the **Cities** sheet from the Excel spreadsheet, **Chapter12_Data.xlsx** which can be found in the Github repository for this book: https://github.com/gdeckler/DAX-For-Humans/tree/main/book.

City	Latitude	Longitude
Columbus, OH	39.961178	-82.998795
London, UK	51.507351	-0.127758
Kansas City	39.099728	-94.578568
St. Louis	38.627003	-90.199402

Table 12.1: Latitudes and longitudes

This table provides the latitudes and longitudes for four different cities in **decimal degrees** (DD) format. The latitudes and longitudes include six significant digits to the right of the decimal point which provide a high level of accuracy, about one meter of uncertainty at the equator.

Be sure to categorize (**Data category**) the **Latitude** and **Longitude** columns a **Latitude** and **Longitude** respectively. In addition, categorize the **City** column as **Place**.

Now create the following two tables:

```
From City = SELECTCOLUMNS( DISTINCT('Cities'[City]), "From City", [City] )

To City = SELECTCOLUMNS( DISTINCT('Cities'[City]), "To City", [City] )
```

Make sure that there are no relationships between any of the three tables. Now create the following two measures:

```
Radius of the Earth (km) = 6371

Radius of the Earth (Miles) = 3959
```

Next, create the following measure to compute c from the Haversine formula:

```
C =

    VAR __FromCity = MAX( 'From City'[From City] )

    VAR __ToCity = MAX('To City'[To City])

    VAR __FromLat = MAXX( FILTER( 'Cities', [City] = __FromCity ), [Latitude] )

    VAR __ToLat = MAXX( FILTER( 'Cities', [City] = __ToCity ), [Latitude] )
```

```
    VAR __FromLong = MAXX( FILTER( 'Cities', [City] = __FromCity ), [Longitude] )

    VAR __ToLong = MAXX( FILTER( 'Cities', [City] = __ToCity ), [Longitude] )

    VAR __distanceLong = RADIANS( __ToLong - __FromLong )

    VAR __distanceLat = RADIANS( __ToLat - __FromLat )

    VAR __a = ( SIN( __distanceLat / 2 ) )^2 + COS( RADIANS( __FromLat ) )

            * COS( RADIANS( __ToLat ) ) * SIN( (__distanceLong / 2) )^2

    VAR __y = SQRT( __a )

    VAR __x = SQRT( 1 - __a )

    VAR __atan2 =

        SWITCH(

            TRUE(),

            __x > 0, ATAN(__y/__x),

            __x < 0 && __y >= 0, ATAN(__y/__x) + PI(),

            __x < 0 && __y < 0, ATAN(__y/__x) - PI(),

            __x = 0 && __y > 0, PI()/2,

            __x = 0 && __y < 0, PI()/2 * -1,

            BLANK()

        )

    VAR __Result = 2 * __atan2

RETURN

    __Result
```

This formula is straightforward and simply implements the necessary calculations from the Haversine equation in DAX. We start by retrieving the selected **From City** and **To City** and then looking up both cities' latitude and longitude. At that point, we have everything we need to perform the calculation.

Because the latitude and longitude are given in degrees and the Haversine equation uses radians, we must use the **RADIANS** function to convert from degrees to radians. Also, note the presence of our **ATAN2** formula covered in the *ATAN2* section of this chapter.

We can finally create our two distance measures as follows:

$$\text{Distance (km)} = \text{[Radius of the Earth (km)]} * \text{[c]}$$

$$\text{Distance (Miles)} = \text{[Radius of the Earth (Miles)]} * \text{[c]}$$

We can construct two **Slicers** based upon our **From City** and **To City** tables. Two **Card** visualizations can be used to display our **Distance (km)** and **Distance (Miles)** measures. Finally, an **Azure map** visual can be used to display our **City** column from the **Cities** table.

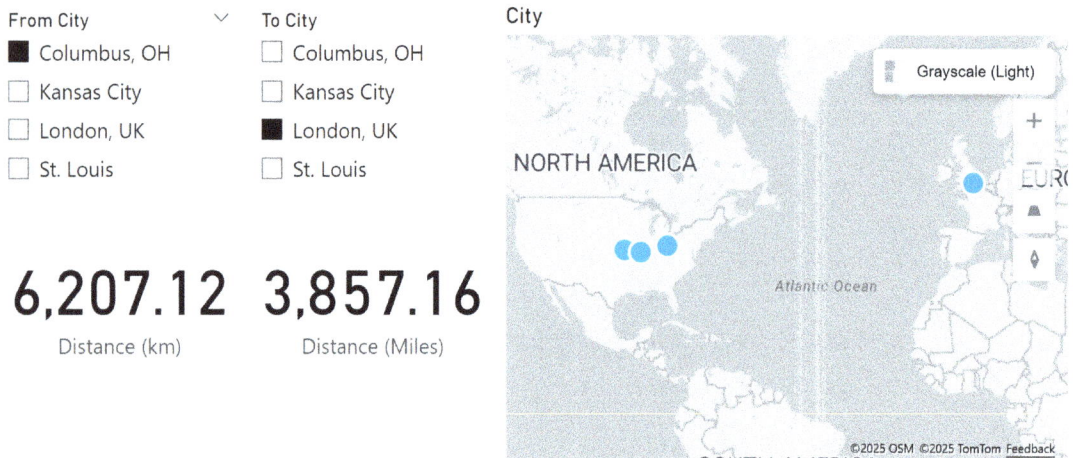

Figure 12.4: Distance measures

This completes our exercise in determining the distance between two points on a map. In the next section, we explore a related concept, bearing.

Bearing

In navigation, bearing refers to the direction of one point relative to another, measured in degrees from a reference direction, usually true north or magnetic north. Bearings help in determining the precise direction a traveler or vessel needs to follow to reach a destination.

There are different types of bearings including these three:

- **True Bearing** – Measured in degrees clockwise from true north (0°). Example: A bearing of 90° means due east.
- **Magnetic Bearing** – Measured relative to magnetic north, which shifts over time due to Earth's magnetic field changes.
- **Relative Bearing** – Measured from the current heading of the observer. Example: If a ship is moving north (0°) and another object is directly to the right, its relative bearing is 90°.

By combining the calculation for bearing with the calculation for distance from the previous section, one has all the information required to navigate from one point on a map to another.

We can compute a relative bearing using the following formula:

$$y = \sin(\Delta\lambda) * \cos(\varphi_2)$$

$$x = \cos(\varphi_1) * \sin(\varphi_2) - \sin(\varphi_1) * \cos(\varphi_2) * \cos(\Delta\lambda)$$

$$\theta = atan2(\,y, x\,)$$

Where:

- φ_1, φ_2 are the latitudes of the two points (in radians).
- λ_1, λ_2 are the longitudes of the two points (in radians).
- $\Delta\varphi = \varphi_2 - \varphi_1$ is the difference in latitude.
- $\Delta\lambda = \lambda_2 - \lambda_1$ is the difference in longitude.
- θ is the angle (bearing).

To begin exploring the calculation for bearing, please first complete the previous section on *Distance* in this chapter. Next, create the following measure:

```
Relative Bearing (Degrees) =

    VAR __FromCity = MAX( 'From City'[From City] )

    VAR __ToCity = MAX( 'To City'[To City] )

    VAR __FromLat =

        RADIANS( MAXX( FILTER( 'Cities', [City] = __FromCity ), [Latitude] ) )

    VAR __ToLat =

        RADIANS( MAXX( FILTER( 'Cities', [City] = __ToCity ), [Latitude] ) )

    VAR __FromLong =

        RADIANS( MAXX( FILTER( 'Cities', [City] = __FromCity ), [Longitude] ) )

    VAR __ToLong =

        RADIANS( MAXX( FILTER( 'Cities', [City] = __ToCity ), [Longitude] ) )

    VAR __deltaLong = ( __ToLong - __FromLong )

    VAR __y = COS( __ToLat ) * SIN( __deltaLong )

    VAR __x = COS( __FromLat ) * SIN( __ToLat ) - SIN( __FromLat )

            * COS( __ToLat ) * COS( __deltaLong )

    VAR __atan2 =
```

```
SWITCH(

    TRUE(),

    __x > 0, ATAN(__y/__x),

    __x < 0 && __y >= 0, ATAN(__y/__x) + PI(),

    __x < 0 && __y < 0, ATAN(__y/__x) - PI(),

    __x = 0 && __y > 0, PI()/2,

    __x = 0 && __y < 0, PI()/2 * (0-1),

    BLANK()

    )

VAR __Result = DEGREES( __atan2 )
RETURN

    __Result
```

We start by retrieving the selected **From City** and **To City** and then looking up both cities' latitude and longitude. At that point, we have everything we need to perform the calculation according to the relative bearing formula provided earlier.

DAX's **COS** and **SIN** functions require radians as input so we use the **RADIANS** function to convert the **Latitude** and **Longitude** which are given in degrees. However, for our final angle we desire this to be in degrees and thus use the **DEGREES** function to convert the radians back to degrees. Again, note the presence of our **ATAN2** formula covered in the *ATAN2* section of this chapter.

We can convert this relative bearing to a true bearing using the following DAX:

```
True Bearing (Degrees) = MOD( [Relative Bearing (Degrees)] + 360, 360 )
```

With the same slicers and other visuals as at the end of the *Distance* section of this chapter, we can add two additional **Card** visuals for our relative and true bearing measures:

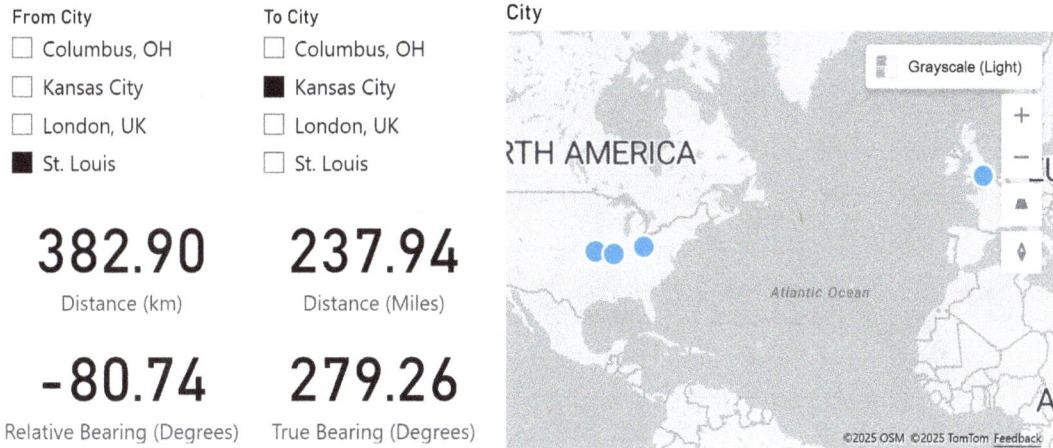

From City
☐ Columbus, OH
☐ Kansas City
☐ London, UK
■ St. Louis

To City
☐ Columbus, OH
■ Kansas City
☐ London, UK
☐ St. Louis

City

382.90
Distance (km)

237.94
Distance (Miles)

-80.74
Relative Bearing (Degrees)

279.26
True Bearing (Degrees)

Figure 12.5: Bearing measures

We are now done exploring the concept and calculation for bearing. Next up we tackle an alternative to latitude and longitude, eastings and northings.

Eastings and Northings

Eastings and **Northings** are coordinate values used in grid-based, projected coordinate mapping systems, such as the **Universal Transverse Mercator (UTM)** system or the **Ordnance Survey National Grid**. They represent distances measured in meters from a defined reference point, helping to locate positions on a flat, two-dimensional plane.

Eastings represent the horizontal (X) coordinate in the grid system, measuring the eastward distance from a defined origin such as a meridian. For example, an easting of 500,000 meters in UTM means the point is 500 km east of the zone's central meridian.

Northings represent the vertical (Y) coordinate in the grid system, measuring the distance northward from a reference point, often the equator or a false baseline. For example, a northing of 4,650,000 meters means the point is 4,650 km north of the equator (or a zone's baseline).

Eastings and Northings are used in land surveying, GPS systems, and mapping to provide precise location data. For small-scale navigation, eastings and northings are more practical than latitude and longitude and are used for engineering, military navigation and urban planning.

Given coordinates in eastings and northings, we wish to convert this to latitude and longitude coordinates since none of the native Power BI map visuals support projected coordinate systems such as eastings and northings.

To get started, use an **Enter data** query to create an **EastingsNorthings** table in Power BI or, alternatively, import the **EastingsNorthings** sheet from the Excel spreadsheet, **Chapter12_Data.xlsx** which can be found in the Github repository for this book: https://github.com/gdeckler/DAX-For-Humans/tree/main/book.

Location	Northing	Easting
Wieringerwaard, NL	348356	862582
London, UK	181031	530129

Table 12.2: Eastings and Northings

The following DAX code for converting from Eastings and Northings to latitude and longitude comes from porting the javascript function toLatLon (© Chris Veness 2005-2021) from the website, https://www.movable-type.co.uk/scripts/latlong-os-gridref.html.

Create a column in the **EastingsNorthings** table with the following DAX code:

```
Latitude Longitude =
    VAR northing = [Northing]
    VAR easting = [Easting]


    VAR radToDeg = 180 / PI()
    VAR degToRad = PI() / 180


    VAR a     = 6377563.396
    VAR b     = 6356256.909         // Airy 1830 major & minor semi-axes
    VAR f0    = 0.9996012717        // NatGrid scale factor on central meridian
    VAR lat0  = 49 * degToRad
    VAR lon0  = -2 * degToRad       // NatGrid true origin
    VAR n0    = -100000.0
    VAR e0    = 400000.0            // northing & easting of true origin, metres
    VAR e2    = 1 - (b*b)/(a*a)     // eccentricity squared
    VAR n     = (a - b) / (a + b)
    VAR n2    = n * n
```

```
VAR n3    = n * n * n


VAR m = 0

VAR lat1 = (northing-n0-m)/(a*f0) + lat0

VAR ma1 = (1 + n + (5/4)*n2 + (5/4)*n3) * (lat1 - lat0)

VAR mb1 = (3*n + 3*n*n + (21/8)*n3) * SIN(lat1-lat0) * COS(lat1+lat0)

VAR mc1 = ((15/8)*n2 + (15/8)*n3) * SIN(2*(lat1-lat0)) * COS(2*(lat1+lat0))

VAR md1 = (35 / 24) * n3 * SIN(3*(lat1-lat0)) * COS(3*(lat1+lat0))

VAR m1 = b * f0 * (ma1 - mb1 + mc1 - md1) // meridional arc


VAR lat2 = (northing-n0-m1)/(a*f0) + lat1

VAR ma2 = (1 + n + (5/4)*n2 + (5/4)*n3) * (lat2 - lat0)

VAR mb2 = (3*n + 3*n*n + (21/8)*n3) * SIN(lat2-lat0) * COS(lat2+lat0)

VAR mc2 = ((15/8)*n2 + (15/8)*n3) * SIN(2*(lat2-lat0)) * COS(2*(lat2+lat0))

VAR md2 = (35 / 24) * n3 * SIN(3*(lat2-lat0)) * COS(3*(lat2+lat0))

VAR m2 = b * f0 * (ma2 - mb2 + mc2 - md2) // meridional arc


VAR lat3 = (northing-n0-m2)/(a*f0) + lat2

VAR ma3 = (1 + n + (5/4)*n2 + (5/4)*n3) * (lat3 - lat0)

VAR mb3 = (3*n + 3*n*n + (21/8)*n3) * SIN(lat3-lat0) * COS(lat3+lat0)

VAR mc3 = ((15/8)*n2 + (15/8)*n3) * SIN(2*(lat3-lat0)) * COS(2*(lat3+lat0))

VAR md3 = (35 / 24) * n3 * SIN(3*(lat3-lat0)) * COS(3*(lat3+lat0))

VAR m3 = b * f0 * (ma3 - mb3 + mc3 - md3) // meridional arc


VAR lat4 = (northing-n0-m3)/(a*f0) + lat3

VAR ma4 = (1 + n + (5/4)*n2 + (5/4)*n3) * (lat4 - lat0)

VAR mb4 = (3*n + 3*n*n + (21/8)*n3) * SIN(lat4-lat0) * COS(lat4+lat0)

VAR mc4 = ((15/8)*n2 + (15/8)*n3) * SIN(2*(lat4-lat0)) * COS(2*(lat4+lat0))

VAR md4 = (35 / 24) * n3 * SIN(3*(lat4-lat0)) * COS(3*(lat4+lat0))
```

```
    VAR m4 = b * f0 * (ma4 - mb4 + mc4 - md4) // meridional arc


    VAR lat = (northing-n0-m4)/(a*f0) + lat4


    VAR cosLat = COS(lat)

    VAR sinLat = SIN(lat)

    VAR nu = a * f0 / SQRT(1-e2*sinLat*sinLat) // transverse radius of curvature

    VAR rho = a * f0 * (1 - e2) / POWER(1-e2*sinLat*sinLat, 1.5) //meridional radius
curvature

    VAR eta2 = nu/rho - 1

    VAR tanLat = TAN(lat)

    VAR tan2lat = tanLat * tanLat

    VAR tan4lat = tan2lat * tan2lat

    VAR tan6lat = tan4lat * tan2lat

    VAR secLat = 1 / cosLat

    VAR nu3 = nu * nu * nu

    VAR nu5 = nu3 * nu * nu

    VAR nu7 = nu5 * nu * nu

    VAR vii = tanLat / (2 * rho * nu)

    VAR viii = tanLat / (24 * rho * nu3) * (5 + 3*tan2lat + eta2 - 9*tan2lat*eta2)

    VAR ix = tanLat / (720 * rho * nu5) * (61 + 90*tan2lat + 45*tan4lat)

    VAR x = secLat / nu

    VAR xi = secLat / (6 * nu3) * (nu/rho + 2*tan2lat)

    VAR xii = secLat / (120 * nu5) * (5 + 28*tan2lat + 24*tan4lat)

    VAR xiia = secLat / (5040 * nu7) * (61 + 662*tan2lat + 1320*tan4lat + 720*tan6lat)

    VAR de = easting - e0

    VAR de2 = de * de

    VAR de3 = de2 * de

    VAR de4 = de2 * de2

    VAR de5 = de3 * de2
```

```
    VAR de6 = de4 * de2

    VAR de7 = de5 * de2

    VAR final_lat = lat - vii*de2 + viii*de4 - ix*de6

    VAR final_lon = lon0 + x*de - xi*de3 + xii*de5 - xiia*de7

    VAR result = final_lat * radToDeg & "," & final_lon * radToDeg
RETURN

    result
```

Due to the length of this formula, it is included as a text file **ToLatLong.txt** which can be found in the Github repository for this book: https://github.com/gdeckler/DAX-For-Humans/tree/main/book.

This DAX formula returns the latitude and longitude as a comma delimited text string. To separate the latitude and longitude into separate columns, create the following two additional calculated columns:

```
Latitude =
    LEFT(

        [Latitude Longitude],

        SEARCH( ",", [Latitude Longitude]) - 1

    )
```

```
Longitude =
    RIGHT(

        [Latitude Longitude],

        LEN( [Latitude Longitude] ) - SEARCH( ",", [Latitude Longitude] ) )
```

Set the **Latitude** and **Longitude** columns to have data categories of **Latitude** and **Longitude** respectively. In addition, set the **Location** column's data category to **Place**. You can then plot either the **Location** or the un-summarized **Latitude** and **Longitude** columns on an **Azure map** visual such as the following:

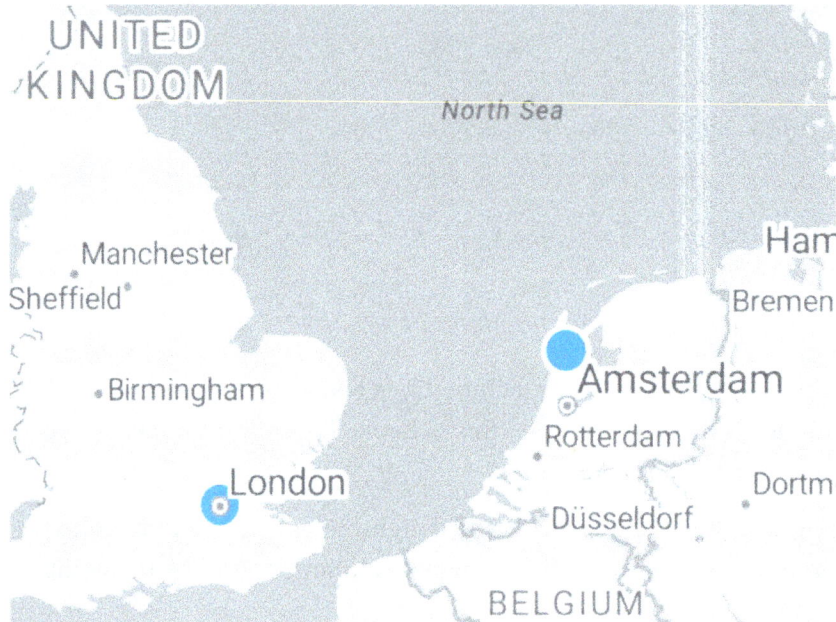

Figure 12.6: Eastings and Northings converted to Latitude and Longitude plotted on a map

The converted latitude and longitude coordinates for London correspond extremely well with the latitude and longitude used for London in the section on *Distance*. You can find more Eastings and Northings for the United Kingdom on the following website: https://gridreferencefinder.com/.

This completes our exploration of northings and eastings. Next, we will explore the relationship between multiple points.

Near

For clustering and other purposes, it is often convenient to understand which points are close to or near one another.

To implement the concept of "near" in DAX, first use an **Enter data** query to create a **Near** table in Power BI or, alternatively, import the **Near** sheet from the Excel spreadsheet, **Chapter12_Data.xlsx** which can be found in the Github repository for this book: https://github.com/gdeckler/DAX-For-Humans/tree/main/book.

ID	X	Y
1	5	5

ID	X	Y
2	0	0
3	9	9
4	100	100
5	105	105
6	95	95
7	10	10
8	15	15
9	10	15
10	15	10
11	200	200
12	300	300
13	50	200
14	53	202
15	48	199

Table 12.3: X and Y coordinates

Now create the following two measures:

```
Near Box =

    VAR __radius = 5

    VAR __x1 = MAX( 'Near'[X] )

    VAR __y1 = MAX( 'Near'[Y] )

    VAR __id = MAX( 'Near'[ID] )
```

```
    VAR __Table =
        FILTER(
            ALL( 'Near' ),
            [X] <= __x1 + __radius && [X] >= __x1 - __radius &&
            [Y] <= __y1 + __radius && [Y] >= __y1 - __radius


        )
    VAR __Result = COUNTROWS( __Table )
RETURN
    __Result

Near Radius =
    VAR __radius = 5
    VAR __x1 = MAX('Near'[X])
    VAR __y1 = MAX('Near'[Y])
    VAR __id = MAX('Near'[ID])
    VAR __Table =
        ADDCOLUMNS(
            FILTER(
                ALL( 'Near' ),
                [X] <= __x1 + __radius && [X] >= __x1 - __radius &&
                [Y] <= __y1 + __radius && [Y] >= __y1 - __radius
            ),
            "Distance", SQRT( ( __x1 - [X] )^2 + ( __y1 - [Y] )^2 )
        )
    VAR __Result = COUNTROWS( FILTER( __Table, [Distance] <= __radius ) )
RETURN
    __Result
```

Both of these measures are quite similar. The first, **Near Box** essentially draws a square around the given point whose sides are twice the value of __**radius** long. Any points that fall within this box are considered "near":

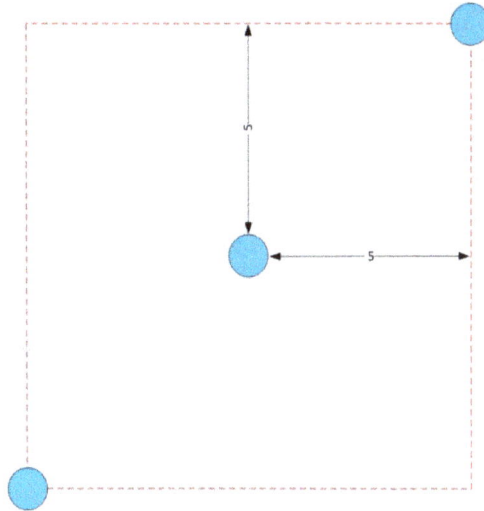

Figure 12.7: Visualizing the Near Box measure

Thus, for the **Near Box** measure, any points that fall on or inside the perimeter of this "box" are "near".

Conversely, the **Near Radius** measure adds an additional **Distance** calculation, which is the standard equation for finding the hypotenuse of a triangle. Visualizing the same set of points produces the following visual:

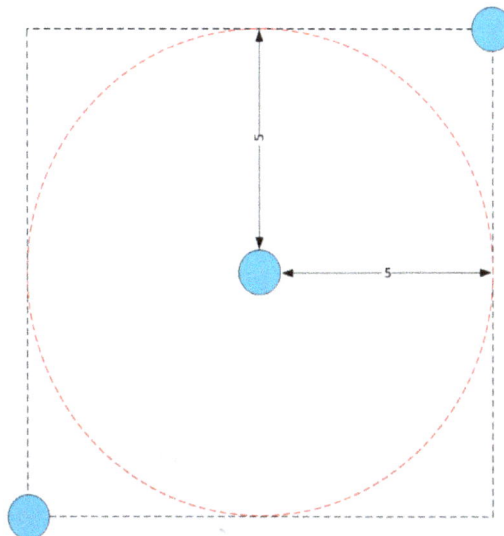

Figure 12.8: Visualizing the Near Radius measure

Here the other two points are not considered "near" because they do not fall within the circle, which has a radius of __radius.

You can observe this difference in the measures by creating two **Scatter chart** visuals using the un-summarized **X** and **Y** columns from the **Near** table. For one of the visuals, use the **Near Box** measure as the **Size** and for the other visual, use the **Near Radius** measure as the **Size**.

For the point at **100**, **100**, the **Near Box** measure produces the following visual:

X   100
Y   100
Near Box   3

100

Figure 12.9: Near Box measure produces the following visual

Here we can see that the **Near Box** measure produces a value of **3** for the point at 100, 100, which counts itself as well as the points at 95, 95 and 105, 105 as "near".

However, the **Near Radius** measure produces a value of 1 for the same point:

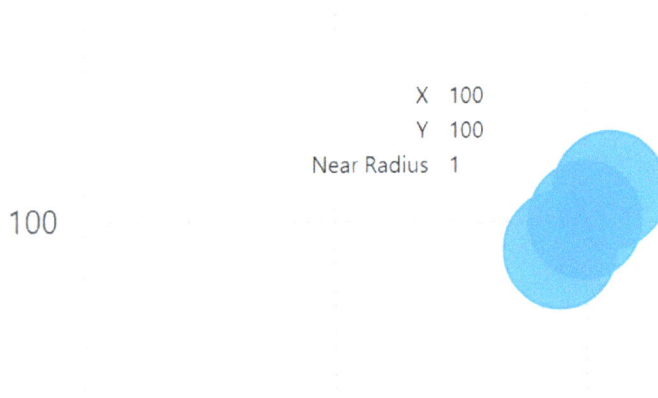

X   100
Y   100
Near Radius   1

100

Figure 12.10: Near Box measure produces the following visual

This concludes our exploration of the concept of "near" in DAX. We now move on to another interesting topic, transitive closure.

Transitive Closure

Succinctly, **transitive closure** describes how elements are indirectly related to one another through a series of direct relationships. The concept of transitive closure comes up in graph theory as well as relational databases but perhaps the easiest way to understand the concept is via a series of train stations. Imagine each train station has a direct connection to one or more other train stations. Transitive closure can be used to map out all the other train stations that can be reached from any particular train station by following the direct relationships between the individual train stations.

To better use an **Enter data** query to create a **Stations** table in Power BI or, alternatively, import the **Stations** sheet from the Excel spreadsheet, **Chapter12_Data.xlsx** which can be found in the Github repository for this book: https://github.com/gdeckler/DAX-For-Humans/tree/main/book.

From	To
1	2
1	3
2	4
3	8
5	6
6	7
6	8

Table 12.4: Station data

Here we can see that from station 1, we can travel to stations 2 and 3. From station 2 we can travel to station 4 and from station 3 we can travel to station 8. Thus, a proper transitive closure for station 1 would include 2, 3, 4, and 8.

We can create the measure for transitive closure in DAX as follows:

```
Destinations =

    VAR __Table = DISTINCT( SELECTCOLUMNS( 'Stations', "__to", [To] ) )
```

```
VAR __Table2 =

    DISTINCT(

        SELECTCOLUMNS(

            FILTER( ALL( 'Stations' ), [From] IN __Table ),

            "__to", [To]

        )

    )

VAR __Result = CONCATENATEX( DISTINCT( UNION( __Table, __Table2) ), [__to], "," )

RETURN

    __Result
```

This measure gets a **DISTINCT** list of **To** stations for the current station in context and holds these stations in the **__Table** variable. The **__Table2** variable is calculated by filtering **ALL** the **Stations** table for any **From** stations that are in **__Table1** and again collecting the **DISTINCT** list of **To** stations. We can then simply **UNION** these two tables together to return a concatenated list of the **To** destinations reachable from each station.

Visualizing the results gives us the following:

From	Destinations
1	2,3,4,8
2	4
3	8
5	6,7,8
6	7,8

Figure 12.11: The Destinations measure implements transitive closure

This DAX measure can only handle two levels of transitive closure. In other words, if we add an additional row to our table such as this:

From	To
8	9

Table 12.5: Additional Station data

In this case, the transitive closure calculation for station 1 would not catch station 9 destination because that station is 3 relationships removed from station 1.

However, we can reimplement the pattern as many times as we want. For example, the following measure handles all three levels of transitive closure:

```
Destinations 2 =
    VAR __Table = DISTINCT( SELECTCOLUMNS( 'Stations', "__to", [To] ) )
    VAR __Table2 =
        DISTINCT(
            SELECTCOLUMNS(
                FILTER( ALL( 'Stations' ), [From] IN __Table ),
                "__to", [To]
            )
        )
    VAR __Table2a = DISTINCT( UNION( __Table, __Table2) )
    VAR __Table3 =
        DISTINCT(
            SELECTCOLUMNS(
                FILTER( ALL( 'Stations' ), [From] IN __Table2a ),
                "__to", [To]
            )
        )
    VAR __Result = CONCATENATEX( DISTINCT( UNION( __Table2a, __Table3) ), [__to], "," )
RETURN
    __Result
```

Adding the **Destinations 2** measure to our existing visual produces the following result:

From	Destinations	Destinations 2
1	2,3,4,8	2,3,4,8,9
2	4	4
3	8,9	8,9
5	6,7,8	6,7,8,9
6	7,8,9	7,8,9
8	9	9

Figure 12.12: The Destinations 2 measure implements three levels of transitive closure

Now that we have covered the concept and calculation of transitive closure, we next explore the concept of box sizes.

Box Sizes

A common spatial problem in manufacturing and distribution organizations is determining the smallest appropriate box size for shipping goods. The issue is compounded by the sizes for boxes and goods are not always given in the same dimensions. In other words, while a box may consider its longest measurement its length, a certain good or item might have its longest measurement be width. Thus, it can prove challenging to determine which goods or items might fit within which predetermined box sizes.

To explore this topic in further detail, use an **Enter data** query to create a **Box Sizes** table in Power BI or, alternatively, import the **Box Sizes** sheet from the Excel spreadsheet, **Chapter12_Data.xlsx** which can be found in the Github repository for this book: https://github.com/gdeckler/DAX-For-Humans/tree/main/book.

Length	Width	Height	Size	Volume
9.5	6.5	3.00	F	185.25
15	10	4.00	G	600
8	8	4.00	H	256
12	8	4.00	I	384

Length	Width	Height	Size	Volume
12	8	8.00	J	768
19	14	4.00	L	1064
19	14	8.00	N	2128
19	14	12.00	P	3192
24	14	4.00	U	1344
24	16	16.00	S	6144

Table 12.6: Box size data

Now, use another **Enter data** query to create an **Orders** table in Power BI or, alternatively, import the **Orders** sheet from the Excel spreadsheet, **Chapter12_Data.xlsx** which can be found in the Github repository for this book: https://github.com/gdeckler/DAX-For-Humans/tree/main/book.

UOM_LENGTH	UOM_WIDTH	UOM_HEIGHT
1.27	13.97	19.05
12	4	9
6	13	22
5	6	7
7	5	6

Table 12.7: Orders data

Next, create the following measure:

```
Box Size =
    VAR __Height = MAX( 'Orders'[UOM_HEIGHT] )
    VAR __Width = MAX( 'Orders'[UOM_WIDTH] )
    VAR __Length = MAX( 'Orders'[UOM_LENGTH] )
```

```
VAR __Measure1 = MINX( {__Height, __Width, __Length }, [Value] )

VAR __Measure2 =

    IF(

        __Height = __Width && __Height = __Length,

        __Height,

        MINX(

            EXCEPT(

                { __Height, __Width, __Length },

                { __Measure1 }

            ),

            [Value]

        )

    )

VAR __Measure3 = MAXX( { __Height, __Width, __Length }, [Value] )

VAR __BoxTable =

    ADDCOLUMNS(

        ADDCOLUMNS(

            ADDCOLUMNS(

                'Box Sizes',

                "__Measure1", MINX( { [Height], [Width], [Length] }, [Value] )

            ),

            "__Measure2",

                IF(

                    [Height] = [Width] && [Height] = [Length],

                    [Height],

                    MINX(

                        EXCEPT(

                            { [Height], [Width], [Length] },

                            { [__Measure1] }
```

```
                ),

                    [Value]

                )

            )

        ),

        "__Measure3", MAXX( { [Height], [Width], [Length] }, [Value] )

    )

VAR __Table1 =

    ADDCOLUMNS(

        __BoxTable,

        "Fit1", IF( __Measure1 <= [__Measure1], 1, 0 ),

        "Fit2", IF( __Measure2 <= [__Measure2], 1, 0 ),

        "Fit3", IF( __Measure3 <= [__Measure3], 1, 0 )

    )

VAR __Table =

    FILTER(

        __Table1,

        [Fit1] = 1 && [Fit2] = 1 && [Fit3] = 1

    )

VAR __MinBoxVolume = MINX( __Table, [Volume] )

VAR __Result = MAXX( FILTER( __Table, [Volume] = __MinBoxVolume ), [Size] )

RETURN

    __Result
```

Due to the length of this formula, it is included as a text file **BoxSize.txt** which can be found in the Github repository for this book: https://github.com/gdeckler/DAX-For-Humans/tree/main/book.

The main trick to the **Box Size** measure is standardizing the dimensions of both the boxes and the item to be shipped. This is done in such a way that __**Measure1** will always contain the smallest dimension, __**Measure2** the next smallest, and __**Measure3** the largest. We then repeat this process using **ADDCOLUMNS** multiple times to similarly sort the box dimensions.

Once this process is complete, we can confidently compare the sorted dimensions of the item and the boxes to determine which boxes are able to fit the item being shipped. From this, we can then determine the minimum volume of all suitable boxes, **__MinBoxVolume**, and from there retrieve the **Size**.

We can visualize the results in a **Table** visual:

UOM_HEIGHT	UOM_LENGTH	UOM_WIDTH	Box Size
6.00	7.00	5.00	J
7.00	5.00	6.00	J
9.00	12.00	4.00	G
19.05	1.27	13.97	U
22.00	6.00	13.00	S

Figure 12.13: Box Size measure

This concludes our exploration of box sizes as well as our overall subject of distance and space calculations.

Summary

In this chapter, we explored a variety of distance and spatial calculations. Many of these calculations were dependent on the ATAN2 function, which DAX unfortunately lacks. Thus, we were forced to create our own ATAN2 function using other, base DAX functions. This then allowed us to tackle converting Cartesian coordinates to polar coordinates and back. In addition, the ATAN2 function proved critical in calculating the distances between points on a map using the Haversine formula as well as calculating the bearing for traveling from one location to another.

We then moved on to additional topics, such as an alternative to latitude and longitude, Eastings and Northings, a grid-based, projected coordinate mapping system and how to convert Eastings and Northings to latitude and longitude. We also explored the concept of "near" within DAX as well as the concept of transitive closure. Finally, we finished the chapter with a common spatial calculation problem, determining the smallest box size for shipping goods.

While some of the calculations in this chapter are not a direct fit for our No CALCULATE pattern, others were. However, in all cases, what was not needed was any explicit appearance of the CALCULATE function.

The next chapter begins the **Advanced** section of this book where we look at more advanced concepts and how to tackle their implementation using DAX.

CHAPTER 13

13

Advanced Scenarios

Thus far, we have progressed beyond the fundamentals of DAX to explore complex calculations across a wide variety of subject areas and scenarios. However, in almost all cases, the focus of each scenario was computing a particular metric or KPI. This chapter expands the types of problems that can be solved using DAX by exploring advanced scenarios that have wide application across a range of reporting needs. In some cases, this means changing the default behavior of Power BI itself such as with using inverse and AND slicers. In other cases, it is about expanding the range of visualizations by using scalable vector graphics (SVG). DAX even has the power to solve tricky visualization problems or even warp time.

Once you throw off the shackles of thinking that all data models must be star schemas and that all DAX code must use CALCULATE and be simple aggregations, an entire world of possibilities opens up. DAX can be a powerful ally in achieving unique reporting experiences where the focus is not so much about the calculation being performed but rather about making the report experience ideal for end users, or dynamically identifying insights and important information. By the end of this chapter, you will understand how DAX can extend beyond mere calculations to solve real-world business challenges in an innovative and efficient manner.

Disconnected Tables

Disconnected tables are tables in multi-table semantic models that are purposefully not connected (no relationships) to other tables within the model. While this may at first seem counterintuitive and decidedly against the "best practice" of using a star schema, disconnected tables are incredibly powerful, flexible, and useful in a wide variety of scenarios. The fact is, relationships between tables within Power BI are incredibly limited. Relationships in Power BI simply propagate filters from one table to another and these relationships only support exact matches between single columns.

One might be asking yourself, *"What in the world do disconnected tables have to do with DAX?"*. The answer is quite a lot. This is because DAX can be used to form the "relationships" between these disconnected tables and the rest of the semantic model. This is a surprisingly flexible and powerful approach that can solve a multitude of problems, particularly when it comes to how users interact with reports and dashboards. Because the relationships are formed via DAX, there are almost no limits to what report authors can do with these relationships.

It should be noted that there can be performance impacts when using DAX to relate disconnected tables to other tables in a semantic model. But, since using disconnected tables and DAX are the only ways to tackle certain problems, the performance impact is somewhat moot.

In this section, we start with a simplified example of using a disconnected table. We then present a much more complex example. In addition, several of the other sections in this chapter as well as previous chapters also use disconnected tables.

To understand how to use disconnected tables, start by using an **Enter data** query to create a table called **Table1** in Power BI or alternatively, import the **Table1** sheet from the Excel spreadsheet, **Chapter13_Data.xlsx** which can be found in the GitHub repository for this book: https://github.com/gdeckler/DAX-For-Humans/tree/main/book.

Item	Value
One	1
One	1
Two	2
Two	2
Three	3
Three	3

Table 13.1: Table1 data

Create a duplicate of this table using the following DAX:

```
Table2 = 'Table1'
```

Now create the following table:

```
Table = DISTINCT( 'Table1'[Item] )
```

Finally, create a relationship between **Table** and **Table1** based on the **Item** columns in each table. The final semantic model should look like the following:

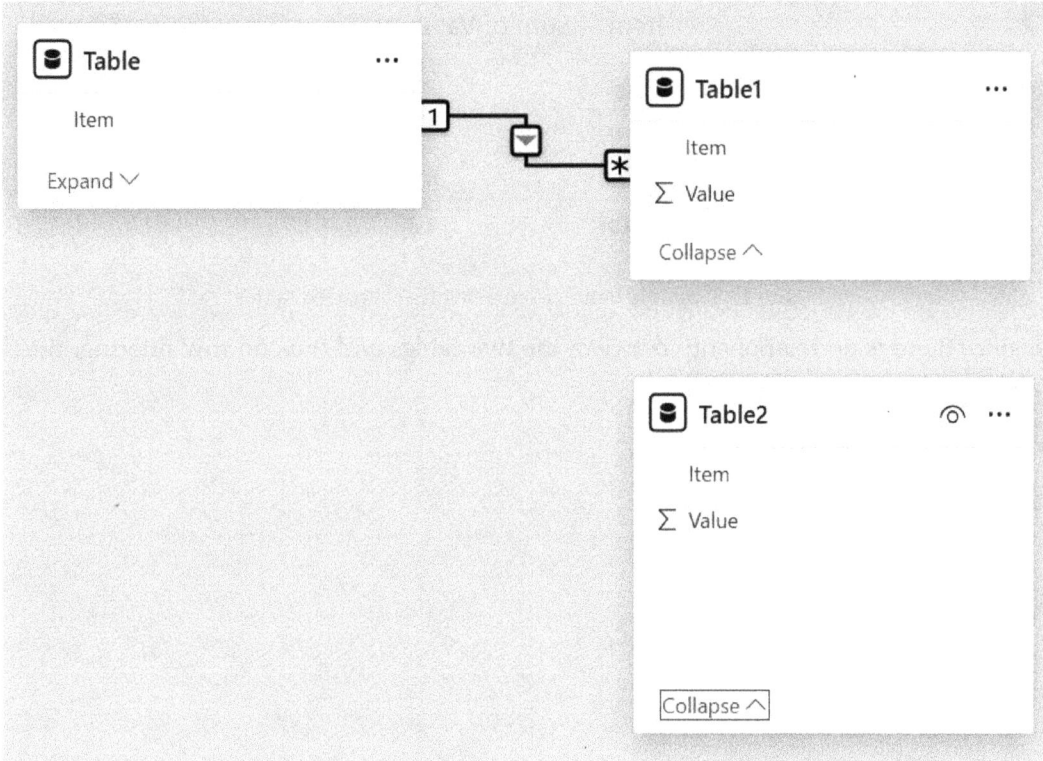

Figure 13.1: Simple disconnected table semantic model

In this semantic model, **Table2** is a disconnected table. Let's now see what we can do with connected tables such as **Table1** versus disconnected tables such as **Table2**.

Creating a simple **Table** visual using the **Item** column from **Table** and the **Sum of Value** from **Table1** produces the expected results:

Item	Sum of Value
One	2
Three	6
Two	4
Total	**12**

Figure 13.2: Simple table visual using connected tables

Similarly, creating a simple **Table** visual using the **Item** column from **Table** and the **Sum of Value** from **Table2** also produces the expected results:

Item	Sum of Value
One	12
Three	12
Two	12
Total	**12**

Figure 13.3: Simple table visual using disconnected tables

Here, since there is no relationship between the two tables and thus no row filtering, the **Sum of Value** is **12** for all values of **Item**.

Now create the following measure:

```
Measure =
    VAR __Item = MAX( 'Table'[Item] )
    VAR __Result =
        SWITCH( __Item,
            "One",
            SUMX(
                FILTER( 'Table2', [Item] = "One" || [Item] = "Three" ),
                [Value]
            ),
            "Two", SUMX( FILTER( 'Table2', [Item] = "Two" ), [Value] ),
            BLANK()
        )
RETURN
    __Result
```

Add this measure to the second table visualization:

Item	Sum of Value	Measure
One	12	8
Three	12	
Two	12	4
Total	**12**	**4**

Figure 13.4: Using a DAX measure to form a "relationship"

As you can see, the DAX measure itself defines the relationship between **Table** and **Table2**. According to the measure, when the **Item** from **Table** is "**One**", the rows in **Table2** that are for **One** and **Three** are summed while if the **Item** from **Table** is "**Two**" then the rows in **Table2** that are for **Two** are summed. Finally, if the **Item** from **Table** is "**Three**", then a **BLANK** is returned.

The preceding example is simply for demonstration purposes to show how measures can be used to define more complex relationships between tables than would otherwise be possible through standard table relationships. Let's next look at a more practical example involving employee training.

Use the following data in an **Enter data** query to create a table called **Training** in Power BI or alternatively, import the **Training** sheet from the Excel spreadsheet, **Chapter13_Data.xlsx** which can be found in the GitHub repository for this book: https://github.com/gdeckler/DAX-For-Humans/tree/main/book.

Employee	Training	Date
Greg	Training 1	9/19/2024
Brian	Training 1	9/19/2024
Dennis	Training 1	9/19/2024
Susan	Training 1	9/19/2024
Deron	Training 1	9/19/2024
Greg	Training 2	8/19/2024
Brian	Training 2	8/19/2024

Employee	Training	Date
Susan	Training 2	8/19/2024
Greg	Training 3	7/19/2024
Brian	Training 3	7/19/2024
Dennis	Training 3	7/19/2024
Susan	Training 3	7/19/2024

Table 13.2: Training data

Next, create a new table using the following DAX:

```
Employees = DISTINCT( 'Training'[Employee] )
```

Relate the two tables based upon the **Employee** columns:

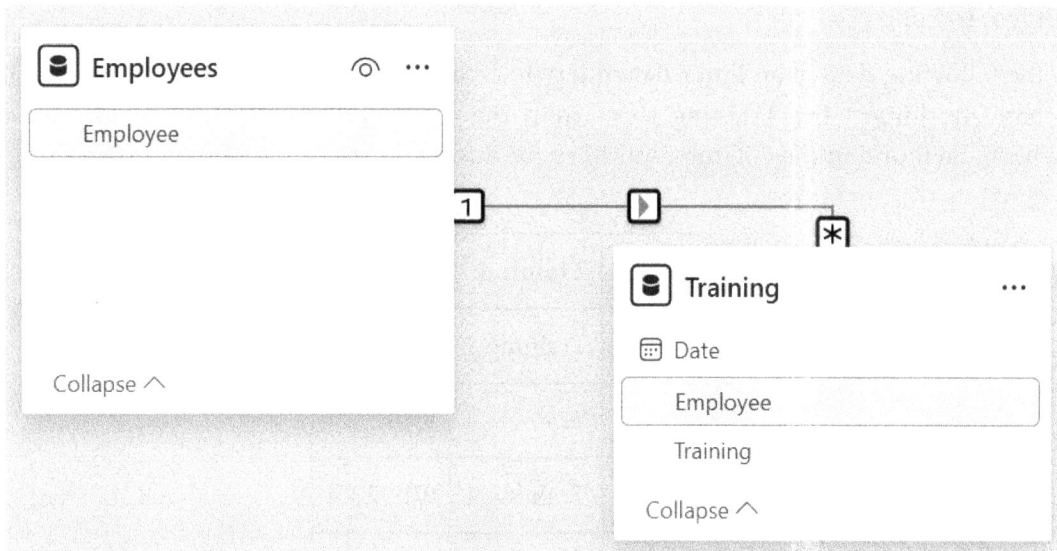

Figure 13.5: Employee and Training tables

Our goal is to easily identify which employees attended which training with a particular interest in employees that did not attend training. To accomplish this, we could create the following **Matrix** visual.

Employee	Training 1	Training 2	Training 3
Brian	9/19/2024	8/19/2024	7/19/2024
Dennis	9/19/2024		7/19/2024
Deron	9/19/2024		
Greg	9/19/2024	8/19/2024	7/19/2024
Susan	9/19/2024	8/19/2024	7/19/2024

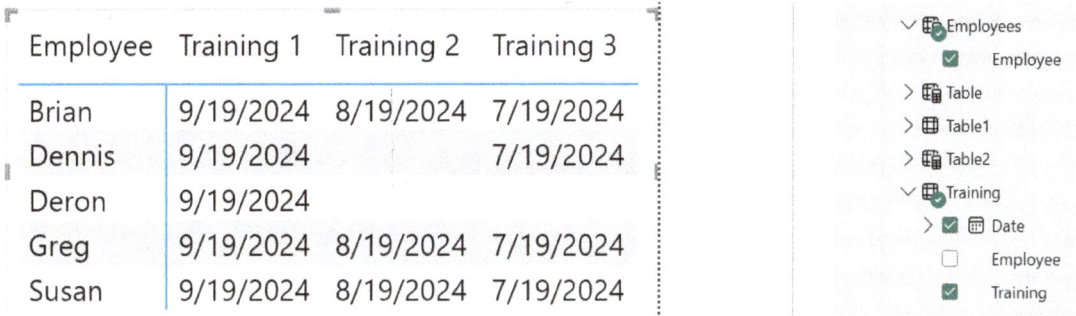

Figure 13.6: Matrix visual showing training dates for employees

We can improve on this visual by creating a measure that returns "Attended" or "Not Attended" respectively:

```
Attendance = IF( MAX( 'Training'[Date] ) = BLANK(), "Not Attended", "Attended" )
```

Using the **Attendance** measure instead of the **Date** column from the **Training** table, our **Matrix** visual now looks like the following:

Employee	Training 1	Training 2	Training 3
Brian	Attended	Attended	Attended
Dennis	Attended	Not Attended	Attended
Deron	Attended	Not Attended	Not Attended
Greg	Attended	Attended	Attended
Susan	Attended	Attended	Attended

Figure 13.7: Matrix visual using the Attendance measure

However, what would be ideal is if we could use a **Slicer** to filter the **Matrix** visual to just those who attended training and those who did not attend training. However, we cannot use measures in a **Slicer** visual. Thus instead, create the following **Attendance** disconnected table using an **Enter data** query:

Attendance
Attended
Not Attended

Table 13.3: Attendance data

Create a **Slicer** visual that uses the **Attendance** column from the **Attendance** table. Now, create the following measure:

```
Attendance 2 =
    VAR __Values = DISTINCT( 'Attendance'[Attendance] )
    VAR __Attendance = [Attendance]
    VAR __Result = IF( __Attendance IN __Values, __Attendance, BLANK() )
RETURN
    __Result
```

Replace the **Attendance** measure in the **Matrix** visual with the **Attendance 2** measure. You can now slice the **Matrix** visual using the **Attendance** slicer:

Attendance

☐ Attended

■ Not Attended

Employee	Training 2	Training 3
Dennis	Not Attended	
Deron	Not Attended	Not Attended

Figure 13.8: Disconnected table used as a slicer

Here the **Attendance 2** measure forms the relationship between the disconnected table, **Attendance**, used in the **Slicer** visual and the **Matrix** visual. This easily allows the user to focus on the most critical information, the employees who did not attend specific training events.

Hopefully, the utility of disconnected tables is now clear. Using DAX to form relationships between tables versus relying on standard relationships provides maximum flexibility and the ability to control the behavior of a report's user interface. We explore another example of this in the next section by creating a NOT slicer.

NOT Slicer

Ordinarily, selecting items in a slicer filters other visuals to just the values selected in the slicer. However, there may be times when the reverse behavior is desired where selections in the slicer filter out the selected values. This type of NOT slicer or inverse slicer can be built using disconnected tables and DAX measures.

To see how to create a NOT slicer, use the following data in an **Enter data** query to create a table called **Products** in Power BI or alternatively, import the **Products** sheet from the Excel spreadsheet, **Chapter13_Data.xlsx** which can be found in the GitHub repository for this book: https://github.com/gdeckler/DAX-For-Humans/tree/main/book.

Product	Category	Value
One	AA	20
Two	BB	30
Three	AB	25
Four	AA	20
Five	BB	30

Table 13.4: Products data

Now create the following disconnected table using DAX:

```
Categories = DISTINCT( 'Products'[Category] )
```

Next, create the following measure:

```
NOT Selector =
    VAR __Category = MAX( 'Products'[Category] )
    VAR __Categories = DISTINCT( 'Categories'[Category] )
    VAR __Result = IF( __Category IN __Categories, BLANK(), 1 )
RETURN
    __Result
```

This measure is quite simple; it first stores the current value of the **Category** column in the **Products** table in a variable called **__Category**. Then, the **DISTINCT** function is used to get the unique values for the **Category** column from the **Categories** table which are stored in a variable called **__Categories**. We can then determine whether the current **__Category** is in the table of distinct **__Categories** values and if it is return **BLANK**, otherwise return **1**.

We can now create a **Slicer** visual using the **Category** column from the **Categories** table. We can also create a **Table** visual to display the **Product** and **Category** columns from the **Products** table.

Finally, we can add the **NOT Selector** measure to the visual level filters for the **Table** visual and set the filter to **Show items when the value is 1**:

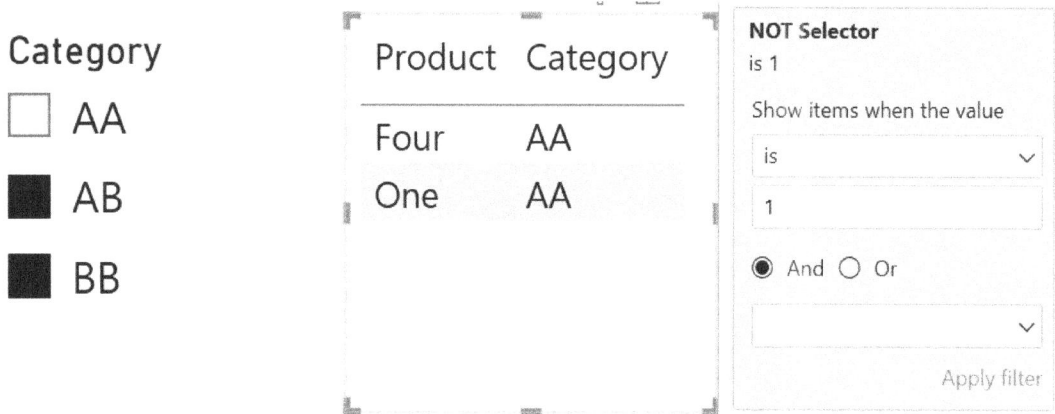

Figure 13.9: NOT slicer in action

As one can see, selecting **AB** and **BB** from the **Category** slicer filters out those values from the **Table** visual.

We can extend this concept of a NOT Slicer to a NOT Aggregator by using the following measure:

```
NOT Aggregator =
    VAR __Categories = DISTINCT( 'Categories'[Category] )
    VAR __Table = FILTER( 'Products', NOT( [Category] IN __Categories ) )
    VAR __Result = SUMX( __Table, [Value] )
RETURN
    __Result
```

Placing this measure into a **Card** visual displays the sum of the **Products** whose categories are not selected.

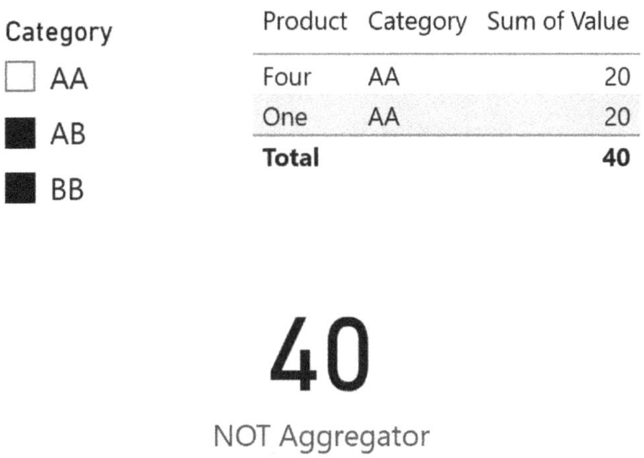

Category		Product	Category	Sum of Value
☐ AA		Four	AA	20
■ AB		One	AA	20
■ BB		**Total**		**40**

40

NOT Aggregator

Figure 13.10: NOT aggregator

This completes another example demonstrating the utility of disconnected tables. However, the **NOT Selector** measure is really just a specific implementation of a more general concept, the *Complex Selector*, which we explore next.

Complex Selector

The **NOT Selector** measure from the previous section uses a disconnected table along with a measure to invert the behavior of the standard **Slicer** visual. While useful, this concept can be generalized to handle any complex selection criteria for visuals. Measures that create complex criteria for filtering visuals are called complex selectors.

To explore the concept of complex selectors, start by creating the following **Sales** table using DAX:

```
Sales =
    ADDCOLUMNS(
        CALENDAR( DATE( 2024, 1, 1), DATE( 2024, 12, 31)),
        "Value", YEAR( [Date] ) + MONTH( [Date] ) + DAY( [Date] ),
        "WeekNum", WEEKNUM( [Date] )
    )
```

The goal is to allow users to select a week number (**WeekNum**) and then display that week's data plus the last four weeks of data in a column chart. To do this, we need to create a disconnected table first like so:

```
Weeks = DISTINCT( 'Sales'[WeekNum] )
```

We can then create the following measure:

```
Complex Selector =
    VAR __Week = MAX( 'Weeks'[Weeknum] )
    VAR __MinWeek= __Week - 4
    VAR __CurrentWeek = MAX( 'Sales'[Weeknum] )
    VAR __Result = IF( __CurrentWeek >= __MinWeek && __CurrentWeek <= __Week, 1, 0 )
RETURN
    __Result
```

This complex selector returns **1** if the week is within four weeks of the maximum week number in context.

Now create a **Slicer** visual using the **WeekNum** column from the **Weeks** table. Then create a **Clustered column chart** visual using the **WeekNum** column from the **Sales** table as the **X-axis** and the **Sum of Value** column as the **Y-axis**. Place the **Complex Selector** measure in the visual filters area for the **Clustered column chart** and set the filter to **Show items when the value is 1**.

Now, when selecting a **WeekNum** in the **Slicer** visual such as 7, weeks 3 through 7 are displayed in the column chart:

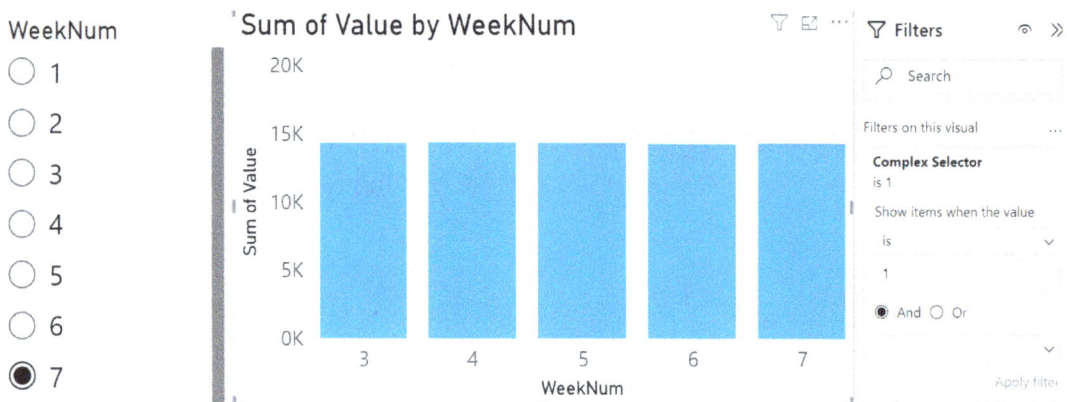

Figure 13.11: A complex selector filtering a Clustered column chart

It is important to realize that this is just a single example of using a complex selector. Again, because the relationship between the disconnected table and the other tables in the semantic model are formed via DAX, there are almost endless scenarios for using complex selectors.

This concludes our exploration of the complex selector. We now turn our attention to another DAX technique to manipulate the behavior of the **Slicer** visual, the AND slicer.

AND Slicer

By default, selecting multiple items within a slicer results in a logical OR. In other words, if you select the values "Red", "Green", and "Blue", then any related table is filtered to those rows that correspond to any of the three values. Thus, the more values in the slicer that you select, the more rows returned from related tables. While in most cases this behavior is what is desired, sometimes the opposite is true, we wish to be more selective as we select more values in the slicer.

Flipping the logical selection criteria for slicers results in an AND slicer. The AND slicer returns less and less results as more values are selected since rows must meet all the conditions selected in the slicer. A great example of this is when doctors and researchers select cohorts of patients for study. These individuals wish to create a collection of patients that all share the same diagnoses.

To explore this concept of the AND slicer, import the **Diagnoses** sheet from the Excel spreadsheet, **Chapter13_Data.xlsx** which can be found in the GitHub repository for this book: https://github.com/gdeckler/DAX-For-Humans/tree/main/book.

The resulting table contains two columns, an anonymized **Patient** column and a **Diagnosis** column. Our goal is to enable users to select various diagnosis codes and return any patients that have had all the diagnoses selected. To this end, create the following measure:

```
AND Slicer =

    VAR __Diagnoses = COUNTROWS( DISTINCT( 'Diagnoses'[Diagnosis] ) )

    VAR __Patients =

        SUMMARIZE(

            'Diagnoses',

            [Patient],

            "__Diagnoses",

            COUNTROWS( DISTINCT( 'Diagnoses'[Diagnosis] ) )

        )

    VAR __Table = FILTER( __Patients, [__Diagnoses] = __Diagnoses )

    VAR __Result = CONCATENATEX( __Table, [Patient], ", " )

RETURN

    __Result
```

Create a **Slicer** visual using the **Diagnosis** column from the **Diagnoses** table. Then, create a **Card** visual using the **AND Slicer** measure. In the slicer, select **F91** and **F92**. Only two patient ids are returned, **178758986** and **168947287**. These are the only two patients that have been diagnosed with both **F91** and **F92**.

Note that we could alternatively turn this into a complex selector measure for use in a **Table** visualization as follows by creating a disconnected table of the distinct **Diagnosis** values such as the following:

```
Diagnoses 2 = DISTINCT( 'Diagnoses'[Diagnosis] )
```

Now create the following measure:

```
AND Slicer Selector =
    VAR __Diagnoses = DISTINCT( 'Diagnoses 2'[Diagnosis] )
    VAR __NumDiagnoses = COUNTROWS( __Diagnoses )
    VAR __Patient = MAX( 'Diagnoses'[Patient] )
    VAR __PatientDiagnoses =
        COUNTROWS(
            DISTINCT(
                SELECTCOLUMNS(
                    FILTER( 'Diagnoses', [Patient] = __Patient &&
                        [Diagnosis] IN __Diagnoses
                    ),
                    "__Diagnosis", [Diagnosis]
                )
            )
        )
    VAR __Result = IF( __PatientDiagnoses = __NumDiagnoses, 1, BLANK() )
RETURN
    __Result
```

Note, if you intend to demonstrate both approaches on a single report page, use **Edit interactions** in the **Format** menu to ensure that the original **Diagnosis** slicer does not interact with the **Table** visual containing a list of **Patients** from the **Diagnosis** table.

While we are on the topic of AND slicers, let's explore one additional method of creating an AND slicer. To that end, create the following measure:

```
Cohort =
    VAR __Table =
        GENERATE(
            DISTINCT( 'Diagnoses'[Patient]),
            EXCEPT(
                DISTINCT( 'Diagnoses'[Diagnosis] ),
                CALCULATETABLE( DISTINCT( 'Diagnoses'[Diagnosis]) )
            )
        )
    VAR __Table2 = SUMMARIZE( __Table, 'Diagnoses'[Patient] )
    VAR __Table3 = EXCEPT( DISTINCT( 'Diagnoses'[Patient] ), __Table2 )
    VAR __Result = CONCATENATEX( __Table3, [Patient], ", " )
RETURN
    __Result
```

Placing the **Cohort** measure into a **Card** visual returns the same patients as the original **AND Slicer** measure.

At first glance, it is difficult to understand how exactly this DAX code results in an AND slicer and for good reason. To understand this DAX code fully, one must understand a great amount of nuance with the functions used, particularly **GENERATE, DISTINCT**, and **CALCULATETABLE**. Indeed, simply looking at the **EXCEPT** statement, one might expect this to always return a blank table, but this is not what happens.

First, we must understand a particular nuance of the **GENERATE** function. Many times, the **GENERATE** function is explained as creating the Cartesian product between two tables. This is true for unrelated tables but for related tables, what the **GENERATE** function actually does is create a Cartesian product between each row in the first table and each row in the second table that results from evaluating the second table in the context of each row of the first table. Thus, since the first table in the **GENERATE** function is a **DISTINCT** list of **Patient** values then the second table is evaluated within this context for each distinct **Patient**.

The second table is the result of an **EXCEPT** function. The first table of the **EXCEPT** function is a **DISTINCT** list of **Diagnosis** values. What is important to understand here is that the

DISTINCT function ignores row context. Thus, the **DISTINCT** list of **Diagnosis** values is not affected by being evaluated in the context of the first table used in the **GENERATE** function, the distinct list of **Patient** values. However, the **DISTINCT** function does preserve filter context and thus the table returned by the first table of the **EXCEPT** function is simply the list of **Diagnosis** codes selected in the slicer.

We now come to the second table in our **EXCEPT** function, which again is a **DISTINCT** list of **Diagnosis** codes but wrapped in a **CALCULATETABLE** function. It should be noted that the **CALCULATETABLE** function operates exactly like the **CALCULATE** function but returns a table instead of a scalar (single) value.

To keep the discussion short, the most important aspect of the **CALCULATETABLE** function is that it restores the original row context of the first table from our **GENERATE** function. Thus, the table of **DISTINCT** values returned by the second table in the **EXCEPT** function returns only the distinct **Diagnosis** codes for each **Patient**, which may be the same or less than the number of **Diagnosis** codes selected in the slicer.

Considering everything that has been explained thus far, the **EXCEPT** clause returns a **BLANK** table only when a patient has been diagnosed with all the selected **Diagnosis** codes and therefore the __Table variable contains all the patients that do *not* meet the desired conditions. We can then create __Table2, a single column table of **Patient** values in __Table. The __Table3 variable then performs another **EXCEPT** of all **Patient** values except those **Patient** values in __Table2. Since __Table and __Table2 contain all of the **Patient** values that do not meet the **AND** criteria, __Table3 contains only the **Patients** that do meet the **AND** criteria.

You may be wondering, what is the point of all this insane complexity of this alternative slicer measure? The answer is that we are again pointing out the radical differences between the No CALCULATE approach versus the **CALCULATE** approach. With the **CALCULATE** approach to DAX, you must fully understand and grasp the complex inner workings of the **CALCULATE** function just as, in order to understand the **Cohort** measure, you must understand all the nuances and inner workings of the **CALCULATETABLE** function. Why bother? And hence, the reason this book and the No CALCULATE method exist, to make the complex simple.

This concludes our analysis of the AND slicer. We now return to another use for disconnected tables, creating a custom matrix hierarchy.

Custom Matrix Hierarchy

In this chapter, we have thus far explored how disconnected tables and DAX can be used to change the default behavior of slicers, create custom filtering criteria for visuals, and create custom relationships between tables. But the techniques discussed thus far can do even more, even to the extent of being able to overcome the limitations in core Power BI visuals. One such visual is the **Matrix** visual.

To explore how DAX and disconnected tables can overcome the limitations of the **Matrix** visual, start by importing the **Online Sales** sheet from the Excel spreadsheet, **Chapter13_Data.xlsx** which can be found in the GitHub repository for this book: https://github.com/gdeckler/DAX-For-Humans/tree/main/book. The **Online Sales** data represents sales from an e-commerce website and has six columns, **Date**, **Product**, **Total**, **Year**, **Month**, and **MonthSort**. After importing the data, set the **Sort by column** for the **Month** column to be the **MonthSort** column. Ensure that the **MonthSort** column is a whole number, and that the **Year** column is **Text**.

We wish to visualize this data by **Product**, **Year**, and **Month** so create a **Matrix** visual with **Product** in the **Rows** field well, **Year** and **Month** in the **Columns** field well and **Sum of Total** in the **Values** field well. After using the expansion drilldown icon (see *Figure 13.12*) your visual should look similar to the following:

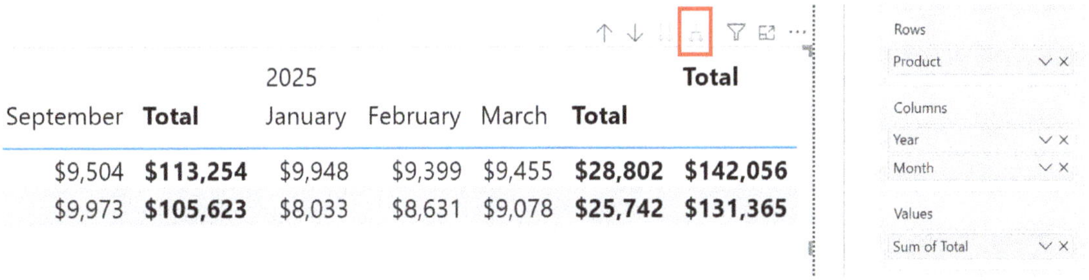

		2025					Total
September	**Total**	January	February	March	**Total**		
$9,504	**$113,254**	$9,948	$9,399	$9,455	**$28,802**	**$142,056**	
$9,973	**$105,623**	$8,033	$8,631	$9,078	**$25,742**	**$131,365**	

Rows
Product   ∨ ×

Columns
Year   ∨ ×
Month   ∨ ×

Values
Sum of Total   ∨ ×

Figure 13.12: Matrix visual of Online Sales

We now wish to add running totals for the current year and last year as overall totals so that we can easily compare the current year to the previous year. To this end, we create the following two measures:

```
CY =

    VAR __MaxDate = MAX( 'Online Sales'[Date] )

    VAR __CY = YEAR( __MaxDate )

    VAR __Product = MAX( 'Online Sales'[Product] )

    VAR __Table =

        SUMMARIZE(

            FILTER(

                ALL( 'Online Sales' ),

                YEAR( [Date] ) = __CY && [Date] <= __MaxDate
```

```
            ),

            [Product],

            "__Value", SUM( 'Online Sales'[Total] )

        )

    VAR __Result =

        IF(

            HASONEVALUE( 'Online Sales'[Product] ),

            SUMX( FILTER( __Table, [Product] = __Product ), [__Value] ),

            SUMX( __Table, [__Value] )

        )

RETURN

    __Result

LY =

    VAR __MaxDate = MAX( 'Online Sales'[Date] )

    VAR __LY = YEAR( __MaxDate ) - 1

    VAR __LYDate = EOMONTH( __MaxDate, -12 )

    VAR __Product = MAX( 'Online Sales'[Product] )

    VAR __Table =

        SUMMARIZE(

            FILTER(

                ALL( 'Online Sales' ),

                YEAR( [Date] ) = __LY && [Date] <= __LYDate

            ),

            [Product],

            "__Value", SUMX( 'Online Sales', [Total] )

        )

    VAR __Result =

        IF(

            HASONEVALUE( 'Online Sales'[Product] ),
```

```
        SUMX( FILTER( __Table, [Product] = __Product ), [__Value] ),

        SUMX( __Table, [__Value] )

    )

RETURN

    __Result
```

However, after adding these two measures to the **Values** field well, something unfortunate happens:

												Total		
February			March			Total								
Sum of Total	CY	LY	Sum of Total	CY	LY	Sum of Total	CY	LY				Sum of Total	CY	LY
$9,399	$19,347	$18,513	$9,455	$28,802	$27,617	**$28,802**	**$28,802**	**$27,617**				**$142,056**	**$28,802**	**$27,617**
$8,631	$16,664	$17,287	$9,078	$25,742	$25,625	**$25,742**	**$25,742**	**$25,625**				**$131,365**	**$25,742**	**$25,625**
$18,030	**$36,011**	**$35,800**	**$18,533**	**$54,544**	**$53,242**	**$54,544**	**$54,544**	**$53,242**				**$273,421**	**$54,544**	**$53,242**

Figure 13.13: Matrix visual with CY and LY measures

As shown, the **CY** and **LY** measures not only show up as totals but also for every individual month. This clutters up the **Matrix** visual and makes the visual impossibly wide.

While there are some rather manual, labor-intensive methods to solve this problem, one solution instead uses a disconnected table and DAX code. To see how this is done, create the following disconnected table:

```
Custom Hierarchy =

    {

        ("2024", "January", 1),

        ("2024", "February", 2),

        ("2024", "March", 3),

        ("2024", "April", 4),

        ("2024", "May", 5),

        ("2024", "June", 6),

        ("2024", "July", 7),

        ("2024", "August", 8),

        ("2024", "September", 9),

        ("2024", "October", 10),

        ("2024", "November", 11),
```

```
    ("2024", "December", 12),

    ("2025", "January", 1),

    ("2025", "February", 2),

    ("2025", "March", 3),

    ("2025", "April", 4),

    ("2025", "May", 5),

    ("2025", "June", 6),

    ("2025", "July", 7),

    ("2025", "August", 8),

    ("2025", "September", 9),

    ("2025", "October", 10),

    ("2025", "November", 11),

    ("2025", "December", 12),

    ("Total", "Total", 13 ),

    ("Total", "CY", 14),

    ("Total", "LY", 15)

}
```

This creates a table with three columns, **Value1**, **Value2**, and **Value3**. Set the **Sort by column** for the **Value2** column to the **Value3** column.

Next, create the following measure:

```
Value to Show =
    VAR __Level1 = MAX( 'Custom Hierarchy'[Value1] )
    VAR __Level2 = MAX( 'Custom Hierarchy'[Value2] )
    VAR __Order = MAX( 'Custom Hierarchy'[Value3] )
    VAR __Result =
        SWITCH( TRUE(),
            __Level2 = "LY", [LY],
            __Level2 = "CY", [CY],
            __Level1 = "Total", SUM( 'Online Sales'[Total] ),
```

```
            ISINSCOPE( 'Custom Hierarchy'[Value2] ),

                SUMX(

                    FILTER(

                        'Online Sales',

                        [MonthSort] = __Order && [Year] = __Level1

                    ),

                    [Total]

                ),

            ISINSCOPE( 'Custom Hierarchy'[Value1] ),

                SUMX( FILTER( 'Online Sales', [Year] = __Level1 ), [Total] ),

            BLANK()

        )

RETURN

    __Result
```

Now create a second **Matrix** visual using the **Product** column from the **Online Sales** table as the **Rows**, the **Value1** and **Value2** columns from the **Custom Hierarchy** table as the **Columns** and the **Value to Show** measure as the **Values**. Be sure to turn off **Column subtotals** for the **Matrix** visual. We now get a much cleaner looking **Matrix** visual where the **CY** and **LY** measures only show in the **Total** area:

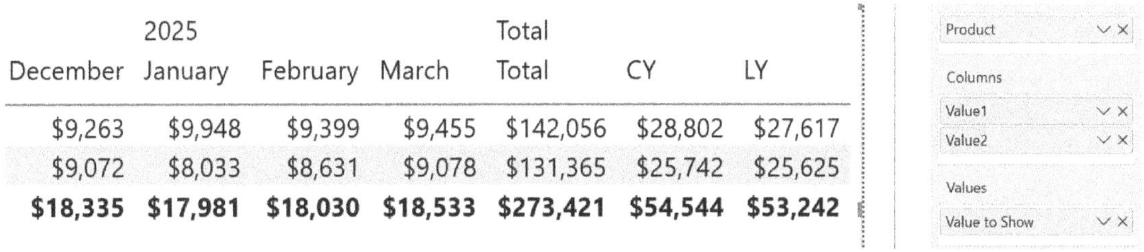

2025				Total			
December	January	February	March	Total	CY	LY	
$9,263	$9,948	$9,399	$9,455	$142,056	$28,802	$27,617	
$9,072	$8,033	$8,631	$9,078	$131,365	$25,742	$25,625	
$18,335	**$17,981**	**$18,030**	**$18,533**	**$273,421**	**$54,544**	**$53,242**	

Product
Columns
Value1
Value2
Values
Value to Show

Figure 13.14: Matrix visual using a custom hierarchy

By using a disconnected table for the columns of the matrix, the relationship between this custom hierarchy and the original fact table, **Online Sales**, is formed by the measure **Value to Show**. This allows us to override the default behavior of the **Matrix** visual and only show the **CY** and **LY** measures when desired.

It is important that the custom hierarchy contains enough information to provide the necessary context for calculations. In this case, the custom hierarchy contains the **Year** in the **Value1** column and a month number for **Value3** for non-totals. This allows the necessary context to calculate the monthly sums. The **Value3** column also serves to provide the sort order for the various values, including the total columns.

The power and flexibility of disconnected tables coupled with DAX should be obvious at this point as we can even use the technique to overcome crippling limitations with the core Power BI visuals. We next explore another way that DAX can be used to create visual elements via scalable vector graphics (SVG).

Scalable Vector Graphics (SVG)

Scalable Vector Graphics (**SVGs**) are two-dimensional vector graphics described using an XML-based markup language. SVG is a text-based, open standard specifically designed for use with other internet web standards including **Hypertext Markup Language** (**HTML**), **Cascading Style Sheets** (**CSS**), and **JavaScript**. Because SVGs are vector-based, the images described can be rendered at any size without the loss of quality associated with bitmap image formats such as **Joint Photographic Experts Group** (**JPEG**) and **Portable Network Graphics** (**PNG**).

While DAX is not the only way to use SVGs in Power BI, DAX provides a flexible, dynamic method of creating SVG graphics that incorporate the context of data being visualized. To explore how to use DAX to create SVG images, start by using an **Enter data** query with the following information to create a table called **Sales Targets**. Alternatively, import the **Sales Targets** sheet from the Excel spreadsheet, **Chapter13_Data.xlsx** which can be found in the GitHub repository for this book: https://github.com/gdeckler/DAX-For-Humans/tree/main/book.

Sales Person	Sales	Target
John Dages	200	100
Aske Laustsen	75	100
Tim Osborn	50	100
Rafiullah Shaheedullah	150	100
Henk-Jan van Well	125	100

Sales Person	Sales	Target
Henrik Vestergaard	80	100

Table 13.5: Sales Targets data

Next, create the following simple DAX measure:

```
Flag =
    VAR __Sales = SUM( 'Sales Targets'[Sales] )
    VAR __Target = SUM( 'Sales Targets'[Target] )
    VAR __Result = IF( __Sales < __Target, 1, 0 )
RETURN
    __Result
```

Create a **Table** visual using all of the columns from the **Sales Targets** table along with the **Flag** measure. Now create the following measure:

```
Red Dot =
    VAR __color = "Red"
    VAR __lineColor = "Black"
    VAR __lineThickness = 1
    VAR __radius = 4
    VAR __opacity = 1
    VAR __header = "data:image/svg+xml;utf8," &
            "<svg
                xmlns='http://www.w3.org/2000/svg'
                width='100%' height='100%'>"
    VAR __footer = "</svg>"
    VAR __shapeText =
        "<circle cx='10' cy='30' r='" & __radius & "' fill='" & __color &
        "' fill-opacity='" & __opacity & "' stroke='" & __lineColor &
        & "' stroke-width='" & __lineThickness & "'></circle>"
    VAR __Result = IF([Flag],__header & __shapeText & __footer, BLANK() )
```

```
RETURN
    __Result
```

Set the **Data category** for this measure to **Image URL** and then add this measure to the **Table** visual.

Marking important information on a report with a red dot was popularized by Stephen Few who advocated against the overuse of color in dashboard and reports. The thinking is that by minimizing the use of color and only using color for important information, the viewer's eyes are drawn to any elements that contain color making the highlighting more impactful.

The Red Dot measure breaks the SVG into three elements, the **__header**, **__footer**, and **__shapeText** variables. All SVG images start with a header that begins as:

```
data:image/svg+xml;utf8<svg …
```

It is important to note that SVG code pasted online, including the Fabric Community Site often replaces the colon with an HTML escape sequence as follows:

```
data&colon;image/svg+xml;utf8<svg …
```

The highlighted text must be replaced with an actual colon character (:) for the code to work properly.

We can even add animation to the SVGs. The following **Bounce** measure is identical to the **Red Dot** measure except for adding an **__animation** variable that is used when defining the **__shapeText**. This animation makes the red dot bounce continuously.

```
Bounce =
    VAR __color = "Red"
    VAR __lineColor = "Black"
    VAR __lineThickness = 1
    VAR __radius = 4
    VAR __opacity = 1
    VAR __header = "data:image/svg+xml;utf8," &
                "<svg
                    xmlns='http://www.w3.org/2000/svg'
                    width='100%' height='100%'>"
    VAR __footer = "</svg>"
    VAR __animation = "<animate attributeName='cy' from='30' to='9' " &
```

```
        "dur='.5s' begin='0s' repeatCount='indefinite'/>"

    VAR __shapeText =

        "<circle cx='10' cy='30' r='" & __radius & "' fill='" & __color &

        "' fill-opacity='" & __opacity & "' stroke='" & __lineColor

        & "' stroke-width='" & __lineThickness & "'> " &

        __animation & "</circle>"

    VAR __Result = IF([Flag],__header & __shapeText & __footer, BLANK() )
RETURN

    __Result
```

There is almost no end to the types and sophistication that can be achieved via SVGs. The following **Color Star Rating** measure creates a series of SVG stars based upon how close the salespeople came to meeting their targets:

```
Color Star Rating =

    VAR __MAX_STARS = 5

    VAR __Base = DIVIDE( SUM('Sales Targets'[Sales]), SUM('Sales Targets'[Target]) )

    VAR __Score = ROUND( __Base * __MAX_STARS, 0 )

    VAR __FinalScore = IF( __Score > __MAX_STARS, __MAX_STARS, __Score )

    VAR __color = "Red"

    VAR __backgroundColor = "White"

    VAR __header = "data:image/svg+xml;utf8," &

                "<svg

                    xmlns='http://www.w3.org/2000/svg'

                    x='0px' y='0px' width='" & 20*__MAX_STARS & "' height='20'>"

    VAR __footer = "</svg>"

    VAR __Star1 =

        "<polygon points=""10,0 12,9 20,8 13,13 16,20 10,15 4,20 7,13 0,9 8,9"" " &

            "style=""fill:" & __color & ";stroke:" & __color &

            ";stroke-width:0;fill-rule:evenodd;"" />"

    VAR __Star2 =

      "<polygon points=""30,0 32,9 40,8 33,13 36,20 30,15 24,20 27,13 20,9 28,9"" " &
```

```
            "style=""fill:" & __color & ";stroke:" & __color &
            ";stroke-width:0;fill-rule:evenodd;"" />"

    VAR __Star3 =
        "<polygon points=""50,0 52,9 60,8 53,13 56,20 50,15 44,20 47,13 40,9 48,9"" " &
            "style=""fill:" & __color & ";stroke:" & __color &
            ";stroke-width:0;fill-rule:evenodd;"" />"

    VAR __Star4 =
        "<polygon points=""70,0 72,9 80,8 73,13 76,20 70,15 64,20 67,13 60,9 68,9"" " &
            "style=""fill:" & __color & ";stroke:" & __color &
            ";stroke-width:0;fill-rule:evenodd;"" />"

    VAR __Star5 =
        "<polygon points=""90,0 92,9 100,8 93,13 96,20 90,15 84,20 87,13 80,9 88,9"" " &
            "style=""fill:" & __color & ";stroke:" & __color &
            ";stroke-width:0;fill-rule:evenodd;"" />"


    VAR __Star1a =
        "<polygon points=""10,0 12,9 20,8 13,13 16,20 10,15 4,20 7,13 0,9 8,9"" " &
            "style=""fill:" & __backgroundColor & ";stroke:" & __color &
            ";stroke-width:1;fill-rule:evenodd;"" />"

    VAR __Star2a =
        "<polygon points=""30,0 32,9 40,8 33,13 36,20 30,15 24,20 27,13 20,9 28,9"" " &
            "style=""fill:" & __backgroundColor & ";stroke:" & __color &
            ";stroke-width:1;fill-rule:evenodd;"" />"

    VAR __Star3a =
        "<polygon points=""50,0 52,9 60,8 53,13 56,20 50,15 44,20 47,13 40,9 48,9"" " &
            "style=""fill:" & __backgroundColor & ";stroke:" & __color &
            ";stroke-width:1;fill-rule:evenodd;"" />"

    VAR __Star4a =
        "<polygon points=""70,0 72,9 80,8 73,13 76,20 70,15 64,20 67,13 60,9 68,9"" " &
```

```
            "style=""fill:" & __backgroundColor & ";stroke:" & __color &

            ";stroke-width:1;fill-rule:evenodd;"" />"

    VAR __Star5a =

     "<polygon points=""90,0 92,9 100,8 93,13 96,20 90,15 84,20 87,13 80,9 88,9"" " &

            "style=""fill:" & __backgroundColor & ";stroke:" & __color &

            ";stroke-width:1;fill-rule:evenodd;"" />"

    VAR __rating =

        IF(

            __Base <> BLANK(),

            SWITCH( __FinalScore,

                0, __Star1a & __Star2a & __Star3a & __Star4a & __Star5a,

                1, __Star1 & __Star2a & __Star3a & __Star4a & __Star5a,

                2, __Star1 & __Star2 & __Star3a & __Star4a & __Star5a,

                3, __Star1 & __Star2 & __Star3 & __Star4a & __Star5a,

                4, __Star1 & __Star2 & __Star3 & __Star4 & __Star5a,

                5, __Star1 & __Star2 & __Star3 & __Star4 & __Star5,

                BLANK()

            )

        )

    VAR __Result = __header & __rating & __footer
RETURN

    __Result
```

Visualizing all these measures in the table visual is shown in *Figure 13.15*:

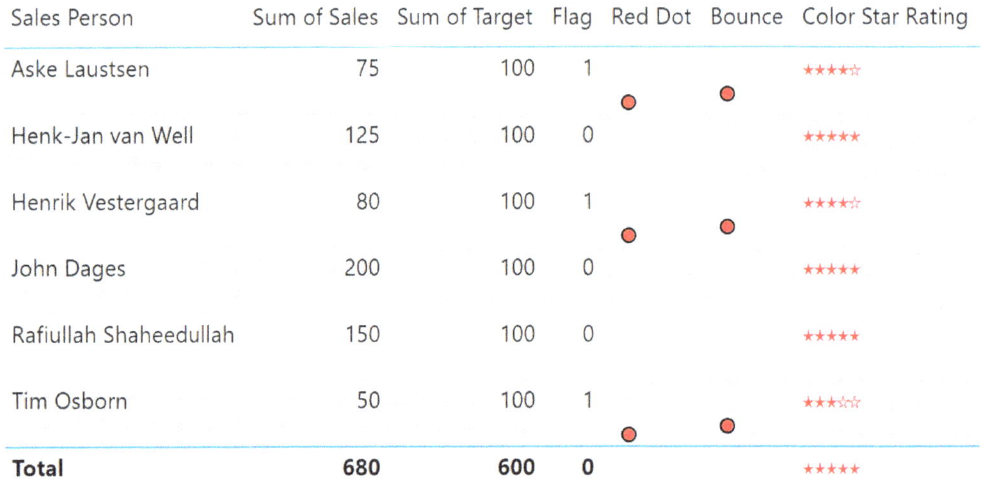

Sales Person	Sum of Sales	Sum of Target	Flag	Red Dot	Bounce	Color Star Rating
Aske Laustsen	75	100	1	●	●	★★★★☆
Henk-Jan van Well	125	100	0			★★★★★
Henrik Vestergaard	80	100	1	●	●	★★★★☆
John Dages	200	100	0			★★★★★
Rafiullah Shaheedullah	150	100	0			★★★★★
Tim Osborn	50	100	1	●	●	★★★☆☆
Total	**680**	**600**	**0**			★★★★★

Figure 13.15: Matrix visual using a custom hierarchy

SVG images are most often used in **Table** and **Matrix** visuals. You can control the overall height and width of the images in these visuals by using the **Image size** section of the **Visualizations'** **Format your visual** sub-pane:

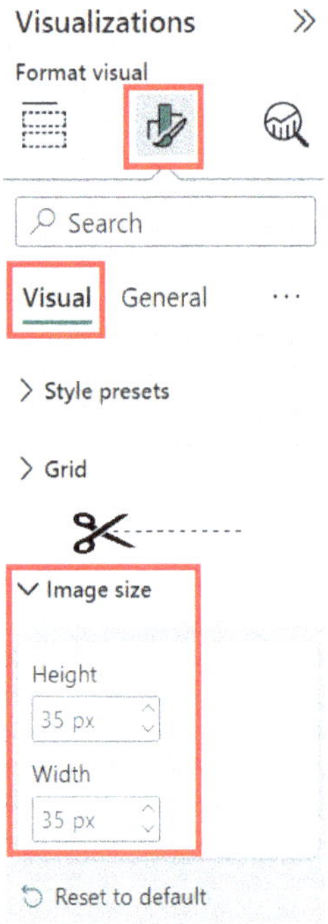

Figure 13.16: Matrix visual using a custom hierarchy

The completes our exploration of SVG images created using DAX. Our next topic explores an interesting way to view time.

Dynamic Granularity Scale

It is interesting how different organizations perceive the passage of time. In our daily lives, we all generally perceive the passage of time the same way, the passage of hours turns into days which turn into years. And for the most part, we all perceive this passage of time the same way. In contrast, organizations can vary wildly in their perceptions of time, which is perhaps best highlighted by the wide variety of different financial calendars used throughout the world.

However, financial calendars are not the only way in which organizations manipulate the passage of time. In some organizations, it is desirable to view data at different levels of granularity depending on the recency of the data. For example, the most recent quarter's data must be viewed at the week level of granularity while past quarters can be viewed at the quarter or even year level of granularity. This is the purpose of a dynamic granularity scale.

To see how to implement a dynamic granularity scale, create the following **Inventory** table:

```
Inventory =
    ADDCOLUMNS(
        CALENDAR( DATE( 2023, 1, 1 ), TODAY() ),
        "Inventory", RANDBETWEEN( 10000, 30000 )
    )
```

Now create the following **Calendar** table:

```
Calendar =
    VAR __Today = TODAY()
    VAR __CY = YEAR( __Today )
    VAR __CQ = QUARTER( __Today )
    VAR __Table =
        ADDCOLUMNS(
            ADDCOLUMNS(
                CALENDAR( DATE( 2023, 1, 1 ), TODAY() ),
                "IsCQ",
                IF( YEAR( [Date] ) = __CY && QUARTER( [Date] ) = __CQ, TRUE, FALSE )
```

```
                ),

            "DGS",

                SWITCH( TRUE(),

                    [IsCQ],

                        "W" & WEEKNUM( [Date] ) & " - " & YEAR( [Date] ),

                    YEAR( [Date] ) = __CY,

                        "Q" & QUARTER( [Date] ) & " - " & YEAR( [Date] ),

                    YEAR( [Date] ) & ""

                ),

            "DGS Sort",

                SWITCH( TRUE(),

                    [IsCQ],

                        YEAR( [Date] ) * 1000 + QUARTER( [Date] ) *

                            100 + WEEKNUM( [Date] ),

                    YEAR( [Date] ) = __CY,

                        YEAR( [Date] ) * 1000 + QUARTER( [Date] ),

                    YEAR( [Date] )

                )

        )

RETURN

    __Table
```

Set the **Sort by column** for the **DGS** column to **DGS Sort**. Create a relationship between the **Calendar** and **Inventory** tables using the **Date** columns.

Now create the following measure:

```
Weekly Inventory =
    VAR __Table =
        SUMMARIZE(
            ADDCOLUMNS(
                'Inventory',
```

```
            "__Year", YEAR( [Date] ),

            "__Quarter", QUARTER( [Date] ),

            "__Week", WEEKNUM( [Date] )

        ),

        [__Year],

        [__Quarter],

        [__Week],

        "__Value", SUM( 'Inventory'[Inventory] )

    )

  VAR __Result = AVERAGEX( __Table, [__Value] )
RETURN

    __Result
```

This measure has the effect of reporting on weekly data but also averaging the weeks from past quarters and years.

Create a **Clustered column chart** with the **DGS** column from the **Calendar** table as the **X-axis** and the **Weekly Inventory** measure as the **Y-axis**. Your visual will look similar to the following:

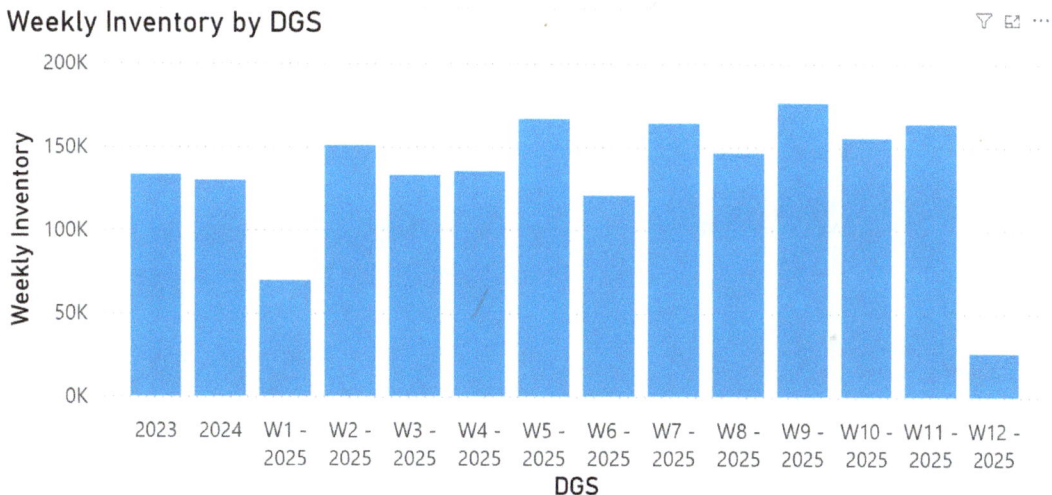

Figure 13.17: Viewing inventory at different granularities

With this visual, the most recent data is shown weekly while past quarters and years are easily comparable to the weekly data without the same level of detail cluttering up the visual.

This concludes our exploration of advanced scenarios in DAX.

Summary

This chapter has demonstrated that DAX is not only useful for performing calculations but can also change the default behavior of table relationships and core visuals within Power BI. Central to this ability is the concept of disconnected tables. By using disconnected tables, the relationships between these disconnected tables and other tables within the semantic model are determined by DAX measures. This technique can be used to modify the behavior of the core slicer visual, turning the slicer into a NOT slicer or an AND slicer for example. The same technique can also be used to impose advanced, complex filtering criteria on visuals, as shown with the *Complex Selector* section. Finally, disconnected tables and DAX can also provide the ability to modify how the core **Matrix** visual displays information by using a custom hierarchy.

In addition to using disconnected tables, we also demonstrated how DAX can be used to add visual elements via scalable vector graphics (SVG) to create both simple and complex visual elements that can even be animated. We also explored an advanced scenario of viewing data at different granularities within the same visual. In the next chapter, we continue to explore more advanced and complex scenarios and patterns.

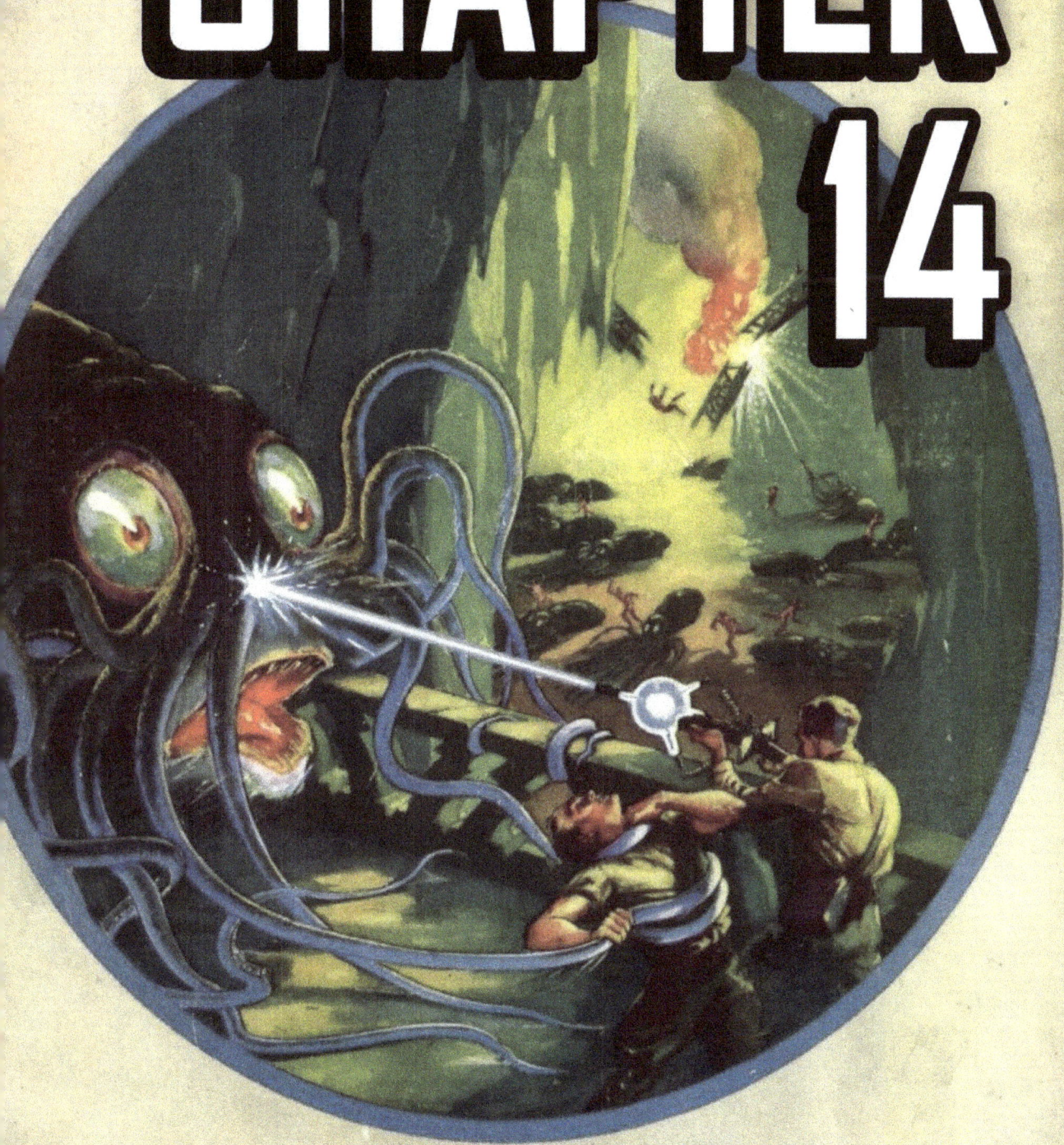

CHAPTER 14

14

Complex Patterns

As your DAX skills mature, you'll inevitably encounter scenarios that go beyond simple aggregations, date intelligence measures, or even some of the more advanced scenarios discussed throughout this book. These complex patterns often arise when real-world business logic doesn't fit neatly into traditional model structures or when relationships between data elements are indirect, conditional, or intentionally disconnected.

Similar to *Chapter 13, Advanced Scenarios*, this chapter focuses on identifying, deconstructing, and solving some of the more complex, reoccurring DAX patterns. These patterns include recreating some of the "forgotten" Excel functions that were never given a DAX equivalent. In addition, this chapter includes solving certain problems that were once considered impossible, like the DAX index. Finally, we tackle identifying streaks using DAX as well as aggregating across multiple columns.

GAMMA

While DAX has a wide variety of statistical functions; including those for beta distributions, chi-squared distribution, geometric means, normal distributions, t-distributions, Poisson distributions, and more, the DAX language curiously omits the gamma function, an important statistical function included in Excel. This is perhaps even more curious considering that the gamma function is included in the definition of the beta distribution and chi-squared distribution, which, as mentioned, are included in both Excel and DAX as the **BETA.DIST** and **CHISQ.DIST** functions.

In short, the gamma function is important because it extends the concept of factorials to non-integer numbers. The gamma function is used in statistics such as the gamma distribution, beta distribution, and chi-squared distribution as well as for computing continuous probability densities for non-integer values. The gamma function is also used in quantum mechanics, thermodynamics, fluid dynamics, and statistical mechanics. The formula for the gamma function is as follows:

$$\Gamma(x) = \int_0^\infty t^{x-1}e^{-t}dt$$

The challenging aspect of the gamma function is that it is recursive, and true recursion is not something that is possible in DAX. Fortunately, however, we can use **Lanczos approximation**, a numerical method for calculating the gamma function. To implement the gamma function in DAX, start by creating the following table:

```
z = UNION( { .4, .5 }, GENERATESERIES( 1, 6, .5 ) )
```

Next, create the following measure:

```
GAMMA =
    VAR __zInput = MAX( 'z'[Value] )
    VAR __Result =
        IF(
            __zInput = TRUNC( __zInput ),
            FACT( __zInput - 1 ),
                VAR __p =
                    {
                        ( 0, 676.5203681218851 ),
                        ( 1, -1259.1392167224028 ),
                        ( 2, 771.32342877765313 ),
                        ( 3, -176.61502916214059 ),
                        ( 4, 12.507343278686905 ),
                        ( 5, -0.13857109526572012 ),
                        ( 6, 9.9843695780195716e-6 ),
                        ( 7, 1.5056327351493116e-7 )
                    }
                VAR __EPSILON = 1e-7
                VAR __z = IF( __zInput < 0.5, 1 - __zInput - 1, __zInput - 1 )
                VAR __pTable =
                    ADDCOLUMNS(
                        __p,
```

```
                    "x", [Value2] / ( __z + [Value1] + 1 )
            )

    VAR __x = 0.99999999999980993 + SUMX( __pTable, [x] )

    VAR __t = __z + COUNTROWS( __pTable ) - .5

    VAR __y =
        IF(
            __zInput < 0.5,
            PI() / ( SIN( PI() * __zInput ) * SQRT( 2 * PI()) *
                POWER( __t, __z + 0.5 ) * EXP( -1 * __t ) * __x ),
            SQRT( 2 * PI() ) * POWER( __t, __z + 0.5 ) *
                EXP( -1 * __t ) * __x
        )
    RETURN
        __y
    )
RETURN
    __Result
```

This measure simply implements the Lanczos approximation which is accurate to within 12 or 13 decimal places. Some additional features are included. For example, the __**Result** variable checks if the __**zInput** is an integer using the following code:

```
    __zInput = TRUNC( __zInput )
```

If this is true, then we can simply return the factorial of the number and gamma is not needed. This results in a nested variable hierarchy which some might find unfortunate, but it is done to help ensure optimal performance.

Next, increase the decimal places for the **GAMMA** measure to **15** decimal places. Then, create a **Table** visualization using the **Value** column (not summarized) from the **z** table and the **GAMMA** measure.

Value	GAMMA
0.40	2.218159543757687
0.50	1.772453850905516
1.00	1.000000000000000
1.50	0.886226925452758
2.00	1.000000000000000
2.50	1.329340388179138
3.00	2.000000000000000
3.50	3.323350970447843
4.00	6.000000000000000
4.50	11.631728396567450
5.00	24.000000000000000
5.50	52.342777784553560
6.00	120.000000000000000

Figure 14.1: Results of the GAMMA measure

You can check the accuracy of these results compared to the **GAMMA** function in Excel using the **GAMMA** sheet from the Excel spreadsheet, **Chapter14_Data.xlsx** which can be found in the GitHub repository for this book: https://github.com/gdeckler/DAX-For-Humans/tree/main/book.

The key takeaway from this analysis of the gamma function is that when encountering calculations that involve recursion, you can sometimes implement numerical methods to achieve the same outcome, thus bypassing the recursive element. This is true with the gamma function as well as such things as differential equations which can be solved using Runge-Kutta.

Let's next look at another "forgotten" Excel function, TRIMMEAN.

TRIMMEAN

The **TRIMMEAN** function is another useful Excel function that is unfortunately excluded from the DAX language. The **TRIMMEAN** function calculates the mean (average) of a set of numbers after excluding a specified percentage of data points from the top and bottom (read largest and smallest). Thus, the **TRIMMEAN** function is useful for removing outliers within data.

To see how to create the **TRIMMEAN** function in DAX, use the following data in an **Enter data** query to create a table called **TM** in Power BI or alternatively, import the **TM** sheet from the Excel spreadsheet, **Chapter14_Data.xlsx** which can be found in the GitHub repository for this book: https://github.com/gdeckler/DAX-For-Humans/tree/main/book.

Value
4
5
6
7
2
3
4
5
1
2
3

Table 14.1: TM data

Also, create the following table:

Percents = GENERATESERIES(.1, 1.1, .1)

Ensure that there is no relationship between the **Percents** table and the **TM** table.

Now create the following measure:

```
TRIMMEAN =
    VAR __Table =
        ADDCOLUMNS(
```

```
            'TM',

            "Rank", RANKX( 'TM', [Value] )

        )

    VAR __Percent = MAX( 'Percents'[Value] )

    VAR __Result =

        IF(

            __Percent > 1,

            BLANK(),

                VAR __Count = COUNTROWS( __Table )

                VAR __Points = ROUNDDOWN( __Count * __Percent, 0 )

                VAR __Trim = IF( ISODD( __Points ), __Points - 1, __Points ) / 2

                VAR __MaxRank = MAXX( __Table, [Rank] )

                VAR __MinRank = MINX( __Table, [Rank] )

                VAR __RanksTable =

                    ADDCOLUMNS(

                        ADDCOLUMNS(

                            GROUPBY(

                                __Table,

                                [Rank],

                                "Count", COUNTX( CURRENTGROUP(), [Value] ),

                                "Value", MAXX( CURRENTGROUP(), [Value] )

                            ),

                            "CBCount",

                                COUNTROWS(

                                    FILTER( __Table, [Rank] >= EARLIER( [Rank] ) ) )

                                ),

                            "CTCount",

                                COUNTROWS(

                                    FILTER( __Table, [Rank] <= EARLIER( [Rank] ) )
```

```
                )
            ),
            "BWhile", __Trim - [CBCount],
            "TWhile", __Trim - [CTCount]
        )
    VAR __MinBottom =
        MAXX( FILTER( __RanksTable, [BWhile] <= 0 ), [BWhile] )
    VAR __MinTop =
        MAXX( FILTER( __RanksTable, [TWhile] <= 0 ), [TWhile] )
    VAR __FinalBottomRankTable =
        ADDCOLUMNS(
            FILTER( __RanksTable, [BWhile] >= __MinBottom ),
            "Product",
                IF(
                    [BWhile] >= 0,
                    [Count] * [Value],
                    ([Count] + [BWhile]) * [Value]
                )
        )
    VAR __FinalTopRankTable =
        ADDCOLUMNS(
            FILTER( __RanksTable, [TWhile] >= __MinTop ),
            "Product",
                IF(
                    [TWhile] >= 0,
                    [Count] * [Value],
                    ( [Count] + [TWhile] ) * [Value]
                )
        )
```

```
        VAR __Bottom = SUMX( __FinalBottomRankTable, [Product] )

        VAR __Top = SUMX( __FinalTopRankTable, [Product] )

        VAR __Result =

            DIVIDE(

                SUMX( __Table, [Value] ) - __Bottom - __Top,

                __Count - 2 * __Trim

            )

    RETURN

        __Result

    )

RETURN

    __Result
```

Obviously, this calculation is quite complex. Let's break down how this formula works. The first step is to rank the values in the data table. This is done using **RANKX** and produces the following table:

Value	Rank
1	11
2	9
2	9
3	7
3	7
4	5
4	5
5	3
5	3

Value	Rank
6	2
7	1

Table 14.2: Ranked TM data

Using **RANKX** allows us to define "top" and "bottom". We then get the desired percentage of points to exclude and store this value in the **__Percent** variable.

Like the **GAMMA** measure from the previous section, we next check if the percentage is greater than one and if it is, we simply return **BLANK** as the operation is invalid. Otherwise, we calculate the desired trimmed mean.

Calculating the trimmed mean starts by calculating how many points to trim off the top and bottom which is stored in the **__Trim** variable. This is a crucial operation as Excel's **TRIMMEAN** function is quite specific in how it determines this number. Excel's documentation states the following:

> *TRIMMEAN rounds the number of excluded data points down to the nearest multiple of 2. If percent = 0.1, 10 percent of 30 data points equals 3 points. For symmetry, TRIMMEAN excludes a single value from the top and bottom of the data set.*

It should be noted that **MROUND** cannot be used here because **MROUND** does not round numbers the same as Excel's **TRIMMEAN** function.

The next step is calculating the **__RanksTable** variable. This table sets up what is essentially a double, concurrent while loop. The resulting table looks like the following:

Rank	Count	Value	CBCount	CTCount	BWhile	TWhile
11	1	1	1	11	1	-9
9	2	2	3	10	-1	-8
7	2	3	5	8	-3	-6
5	2	4	7	6	-5	-4
3	2	5	9	4	-7	-2

Rank	Count	Value	CBCount	CTCount	BWhile	TWhile
2	1	6	10	2	-8	0
1	1	7	11	1	-9	1

Table 14.3: __RanksTable data

Note that this is the table returned for percentages of 40% and 50%.

The **Rank** and **Value** columns come from the __**Table** variable. The **Count** column holds the count of how many of the values appear in the original table. The **CBCount** (Cumulative Bottom Count) column is the total number of rows for all values that are less than or equal to the current **Value**. The **CTCount** (Cumulative Top Count) column is the opposite of the **CBCount** column, counting the total number of rows for all values that are greater than or equal to the current **Value**. Finally, the **BWhile** and **TWhile** columns implement while loop counters, subtracting the **CBCount** and **CTCount** values from the __**Trim** variable.

We can now calculate the "exits" to the while loops by getting the maximum value in the **BWhile** and **TWhile** columns respectively where the value is less than or equal to 0. In the continuing example this returns **-1** for the __**MinBottom** and 0 for the __**MinTop**.

It is now time to calculate the __**FinalBottomRankTable** and __**FinalTopRankTable** variables. Continuing our example, the __**FinalBottomRankTable** looks like the following:

Rank	Count	Value	CBCount	CTCount	BWhile	TWhile	Product
11	1	1	1	11	1	-9	1
9	2	2	3	10	-1	-8	2

Table 14.4: __FinalBottomRankTable data

While the __**FinalTopRankTable** looks like the following:

Rank	Count	Value	CBCount	CTCount	BWhile	TWhile	Product
2	1	6	10	2	-8	0	6
1	1	7	11	1	-9	1	7

Table 14.5: __ FinalTopRankTable data

Both of these tables are filtered by their respective "exits", __MinBottom and __MinTop respectively. The purpose of the **Product** column is to ensure that the correct number of points are removed from the data used to calculate the mean. This is necessary since the source data can contain duplicates of the same number. Looking at the __FinalBottomRankTable, one can see that while there are two rows in the original data with the value of 2, the **Product** column for this row contains 2 and not 4. This is because there are only 2 points being removed from both the top and bottom of the data and one point (Value = 1) has already been removed. This means that we only want to remove a single 2 and not both 2s.

At this point, we are essentially home free. We simply need to add up the values for **Product** in both tables, __**Bottom** and __**Top**. We can then subtract these values from the sum of the **Values** column and then divide by the total number of points minus those that we have trimmed to arrive at our desired mean.

Set the number of decimal points for the **TRIMMEAN** measure to **9** and then place the **TRIMMEAN** measure into a **Table** visual along with the **Value** column (not summarized):

Value	TRIMMEAN
0.10	3.818181818
0.20	3.777777778
0.30	3.777777778
0.40	3.714285714
0.50	3.714285714
0.60	3.800000000
0.70	3.800000000
0.80	3.666666667
0.90	3.666666667
1.00	4.000000000

Figure 14.2: Results of the TRIMMEAN measure

You can check the accuracy of these results compared to the **TRIMMEAN** function in Excel using the **TRIMMEAN** sheet from the Excel spreadsheet, **Chapter14_Data.xlsx** which can be found in the GitHub repository for this book: https://github.com/gdeckler/DAX-For-Humans/tree/main/book.

A key takeaway from the **TRIMMEAN** analysis is that not all problems can be solved simply by filtering a table and then aggregating over that table. Sometimes problems need to be broken down into their component parts. Instead of filtering to a table and then using **AVERAGEX**, we can realize that an average is simply a sum divided by a count. Realizing this, we can devise alternative methods of achieving the desired result.

This completes our recreation of Excel's **TRIMMEAN** function in DAX. If you are interested in how to replicate additional Excel functions in DAX, this author once endeavored to create DAX equivalents for all Excel functions and was able to achieve 96% coverage. You can find these equivalents at the following link: https://community.fabric.microsoft.com/t5/Power-BI-Community-Blog/Excel-to-DAX-Translation/ba-p/1060991.

Let's switch gears and this time recreate Power Query's fuzzy matching capabilities in DAX.

Fuzzy Matching

Fuzzy matching is a technique used to identify and compare text strings that are approximately, but not exactly, the same. Unlike exact matching, which requires two strings to be identical, fuzzy matching allows for differences such as typos, alternate spellings, abbreviations, or slight variations in formatting. This is particularly useful in situations where there are data inconsistencies (in other words, all situations), such as matching customer names across different databases or aligning product descriptions from multiple sources.

Fuzzy matching traditionally uses algorithms such as the **Levenshtein distance**, **Jaccard similarity**, or **soundex**. These algorithms quantify the similarity between two strings and help determine the best possible matches, even when data isn't perfectly clean or standardized.

While DAX includes numerous exact matching functions such as **SEARCH**, **FIND**, **EXACT**, **CONTAINSSTRING**, **CONTAINSTRINGEXACT**, or even the **FILTER** function, DAX does not include any fuzzy matching functions. One might question the need for such functions since Power Query includes fuzzy matching functions such as **Table.FuzzyGroup**, **Table.FuzzyJoin** and **Table.FuzzyNestedJoin**. However, Power Query cannot be used in all situations and there is a lack of exact control over the fuzzy matching algorithm. Thus, it can be useful to understand how to implement fuzzy matching within DAX.

To investigate how to implement fuzzy matching in DAX, import the **Clients** and **Projects** sheets from the Excel spreadsheet, **Chapter14_Data.xlsx** which can be found in the GitHub repository for this book: https://github.com/gdeckler/DAX-For-Humans/tree/main/book. Ensure that both tables promote the first row as headers. The **Clients** table has a single column called **Client Name** and the **Projects** table has two columns, **Project** and **Index**.

The goal is to use fuzzy matching to match the **Client Name** column in the **Clients** table with the **Project** column in the **Projects** table. To do so, create the following measure:

```
Fuzzy =

    VAR __MatchWord = MAX( 'Clients'[Client Name] )

    VAR __CleanMatchThreshold = 4

    VAR __KillThreshold = 3

    VAR __FuzzyThreshold1 = .4

    VAR __FuzzyThreshold2 = .8

    VAR __WordSearchTable =

        GENERATE(

            'Projects',

                VAR __Word = [Project]

                VAR __Result =

                    ADDCOLUMNS(

                        GENERATESERIES( 3, LEN( __Word ), 1 ),

                        "Search", LEFT( __Word, [Value] ),

                        "Original", __Word

                    )

            RETURN

                __Result

        )

    VAR __Table =

        FILTER(

            ADDCOLUMNS(

                __WordSearchTable,

                "Match", SEARCH( [Search], __MatchWord, , BLANK() )

            ),

            NOT(ISBLANK([Match]))

        )

    VAR __Max = MAXX( __Table, [Value] )
```

```
VAR __Match = MAXX( FILTER( __Table, [Value] = __Max ), [Search] )

VAR __Proposed =

    IF(

        LEN( __Match ) <= __CleanMatchThreshold,

        SWITCH(TRUE(),

            COUNTROWS( FILTER( __Table, [Value] = __Max ) ) > 1, "No Match 1",

            LEN( __Match ) <= __KillThreshold, "No Match 2",

            LEN( __Match ) = LEN( __MatchWord ), __Match,

            LEN( __Match ) / LEN( __MatchWord ) > __FuzzyThreshold1 &&

                SEARCH( __Match, __MatchWord, , 0 ) = 1, __Match,

            LEN( __Match ) / LEN( __MatchWord ) > __FuzzyThreshold2, __Match,

            "No Match 3"

        ),

        SWITCH( TRUE(),

            __Match = "Blue Cross" || __Match = "Blue Cross ", __Match,

            LEN( __Match ) / LEN( __MatchWord ) < __FuzzyThreshold2 &&

                SEARCH( __Match, __MatchWord, , 0 ) <> 1, "No Match 4",

            __Match

        )

    )

    VAR __Clean1 =

        IF(

            RIGHT( __Proposed, 1 ) = "(",

            LEFT( __Proposed, LEN( __Proposed ) - 1 ),

            __Proposed

        )

    VAR __Result =

        IF(

            RIGHT( __Clean1, 1 ) = " ",
```

```
            LEFT( __Clean1, LEN( __Clean1 ) - 1 ),

        __Clean1

    )
```

RETURN

```
    __Result
```

Obviously, this measure is quite large and complex with several custom tweaks for specific situations. However, the key components of this calculation are contained within the __WordSearchTable and __Table variables.

The __WordSearchTable blows out the **Projects** table such that each project name is expanded to additional rows where each row lists out the characters of the project name starting with the first three letters and then adding one letter per row. This is done in the **Search** column and is best explained in the following example snippet from the __WordSearchTable variable:

Project	Index	Value	Search	Original
Aaron's	1	3	Aar	Aaron's
Aaron's	1	4	Aaro	Aaron's
Aaron's	1	5	Aaron	Aaron's
Aaron's	1	6	Aaron'	Aaron's
Aaron's	1	7	Aaron's	Aaron's
ABB (CA VDA)	2	3	ABB	ABB (CA VDA)
ABB (CA VDA)	2	4	ABB	ABB (CA VDA)
ABB (CA VDA)	2	5	ABB (	ABB (CA VDA)
ABB (CA VDA)	2	6	ABB (C	ABB (CA VDA)
ABB (CA VDA)	2	7	ABB (CA	ABB (CA VDA)
ABB (CA VDA)	2	8	ABB (CA	ABB (CA VDA)
ABB (CA VDA)	2	9	ABB (CA V	ABB (CA VDA)

Project	Index	Value	Search	Original
ABB (CA VDA)	2	10	ABB (CA VD	ABB (CA VDA)
ABB (CA VDA)	2	11	ABB (CA VDA	ABB (CA VDA)
ABB (CA VDA)	2	12	ABB (CA VDA)	ABB (CA VDA)

Table 14.6: __ WordSearchTable data

The __**Match** table adds an additional column called **Match** using the **SEARCH** function which is case-insensitive and accent sensitive. This column returns **BLANK** if the **Client Name** (__**MatchWord**) is not found in the **Search** column and returns __**MatchWord** if the **Client Name** is found. The __**Match** table is then filtered to remove any rows where the **Match** column is blank.

Now that the __**Match** table is constructed, we can determine the best match by finding the maximum value of the **Value** column which is stored in the __**Max** variable. It is then a simple matter to look up the corresponding value of the **Search** column for that row. The rest of the code simply performs some customized tweaks to ensure the best match is found and returned as well as some formatting and text cleaning to remove the parenthesis portions of matches which are not desirable in this circumstance.

Creating a table visualization with the **Client Name** column from the **Clients** table and the **Fuzzy** measure allows us to check the accuracy of our matching. It is helpful to also have a table visual of the **Project** column from the **Projects** column when performing this check:

Client Name	Fuzzy		Project
# Administration #	No Match 2		A. Stucki
# Training #	No Match 2		Aaron's
*US150 - CHARGEABLE MISC	No Match 2		ABB (CA VDA)
A. STUCKI COMPANY	A. Stucki		Aflac
Aarons, Inc.	Aaron		Andersons (CARES)
ABB INC.	ABB		Aptiv
Acushnet NYC	No Match 2		Aramsco (CARES)
Administration	No Match 2		Array
Advanced Integration Technology, LP	No Match 2		ARRIS
Aegon USA, Inc	No Match 2		AstraZeneca (12-15)
Alticor, Inc	No Match 2		Axon
Altisource S.Ã r.l	No Match 2		Barclays (3Q estimates)
American Family Life Assurance Co Of Col	No Match 2		Barclays (current)
Andersons Inc, The	Andersons		Barclays (VDA)
APTIV PLC	Aptiv		Bicycle Therapeutics
Argo Group International Holdings, Ltd.	No Match 4		Blackrock
Array BioPharma Inc	Array		Blackrock (blockers)
Astrazeneca Pharmaceuticals LP	AstraZeneca		Blue Cross (CARES)

Figure 14.3: Fuzzy matching results

We can see in the table that our **Fuzzy** measure works quite well with few, if any false positives. However, you might be wondering about exactly which fuzzy matching algorithm the **Fuzzy** measure implements. Well, the answer is that it is essentially a custom algorithm that blends elements of more formalized fuzzy matching algorithms. To understand this, let's look at two formal fuzzy matching algorithms, the **Jaccard similarity** and **Levenshtein distance**.

The Jaccard similarity is relatively straightforward. You first convert the words to tables. You then compute the number of intersecting characters between the two tables and divide this number by the total number of rows after performing a union of the two tables. A DAX implementation of the Jaccard similarity is as follows:

```
Jaccard Similarity =

    VAR __FuzzyThreshold = .2

    VAR __MatchWord = MAX( 'Clients'[Client Name] )

    VAR __MatchTable =

        ADDCOLUMNS(

            GENERATESERIES( 1, LEN( __MatchWord ), 1 ),
```

```
                "__Char", MID( __MatchWord, [Value], 1 )
        )
    VAR __Table =
        ADDCOLUMNS(
            DISTINCT( 'Projects'[Project] ),
            "__JS",
                VAR __SearchWord = [Project]
                VAR __SearchTable =
                    ADDCOLUMNS(
                        GENERATESERIES( 1, LEN( __SearchWord ), 1 ),
                        "__Char", MID( __SearchWord, [Value], 1 )
                    )
                VAR __Intersect =
                    COUNTROWS( INTERSECT( __SearchTable, __MatchTable ) )
                VAR __Union = COUNTROWS( UNION( __SearchTable, __MatchTable ) )
                VAR __Result = DIVIDE( __Intersect, __Union, 0 )
            RETURN
                __Result
        )
    VAR __Max = MAXX( __Table, [__JS] )
    VAR __Result =
        IF(
            __Max >= __FuzzyThreshold,
            MAXX( FILTER( __Table, [__JS] = __Max ), [Project] ),
            BLANK()
        )
RETURN
    __Result
```

You can adjust the **__FuzzyThreshold** to make the matching more fuzzy or less fuzzy. Also, astute readers might complain that this implementation only counts intersecting characters in the same position within the strings, but practical testing found that this approach worked far better than simply ignoring the order of characters.

The Levenshtein distance is somewhat similar in approach. However, the Levenshtein distance computes the number of insertions, deletions, or substitutions required to transform one string into another string. A DAX implementation of the Levenshtein distance is as follows:

```
Levenshtein distance =
    VAR __FuzzyThreshold = 8
    VAR __MatchWord = MAX( 'Clients'[Client Name] )
    VAR __MatchTable =
        ADDCOLUMNS(
            GENERATESERIES( 1, LEN( __MatchWord ), 1 ),
            "__Char", MID( __MatchWord, [Value], 1 )
        )
    VAR __Table =
        ADDCOLUMNS(
            DISTINCT( 'Projects'[Project] ),
            "__JS",
                VAR __SearchWord = [Project]
                VAR __SearchTable =
                    ADDCOLUMNS(
                        GENERATESERIES( 1, LEN( __SearchWord ), 1 ),
                        "__Char", MID( __SearchWord, [Value], 1 )
                    )
                VAR __Result =
                    IF(
                        COUNTROWS( __SearchTable ) > COUNTROWS( __MatchTable ),
                        COUNTROWS( EXCEPT( __SearchTable, __MatchTable ) ),
                        COUNTROWS( EXCEPT( __MatchTable, __SearchTable ) )
```

```
                    )

            RETURN

                __Result

        )

    VAR __Max = MINX( __Table, [__JS] )

    VAR __Result =

        IF(

            __Max <= __FuzzyThreshold2,

            MAXX( FILTER( __Table, [__JS] = __Max ), [Project] ),

            BLANK()

        )

RETURN

    __Result
```

This is effectively the same DAX code as the **Jaccard similarity** measure except for how the fuzzy matching is performed between the two words converted to tables. Again, one can adjust the __**FuzzyThreshold**, which; in this case, designates the maximum number of insertions, deletions, and substitutions necessary to convert one string into the other string.

Placing both the **Jaccard similarity** and **Levenshtein distance** measures into the **Table** visualization we can compare the different fuzzy matching approaches:

Client Name	Fuzzy	Jaccard Similarity	Levenshtein distance
BlackRock Inc	Blackrock	Blackrock	Blackrock
Blue Cross of Idaho Care Plus	Blue Cross	Blue Cross (CARES)	
BLUE CROSS OF IDAHO CARE PLUS, INC	Blue Cross	Blue Cross (CARES)	
BNP PARIBAS SA	No Match 2		
BOSE CORPORATION	Bose		
BUNGE NORTH AMERICA, INC.	No Match 2		
California Steel Industries, Inc	California Steel	California Steel (review)	
Calpine Corporation	No Match 1		
Caseys General Stores, Inc	Casey		
CATERPILLAR INC.	No Match 2		
Charter Communications Inc.	No Match 3		
Circle Internet Financial, Inc.	Circle Internet	Circle Internet (CARES)	
COLLEGIUM PHARMACEUTICAL, INC.	Collegium	Collegium	
CommScope Holding Company, Inc.	No Match 3		
CommVault Systems Inc	CommVault	CommVault (FY15-19)	
Conagra Brands, Inc	No Match 1		
Conduent Incorporated	No Match 2		
CONSOLIDATED EDISON, INC.	No Match 2		
Covenant Logistics Group, Inc.	Covenant	Covenant Transportation	
Csw Industrials, Inc.	CSW Industrials	CSW Industrials	CSW Industrials
CUSHNET COMPANY	No Match 2		
DCG HOLDCO, INC.	No Match 2		
Dell Technologies Inc.	Dell		
Discover Financial Services	No Match 3		
DMC Power, Inc.	No Match 2		
DRIL-QUIP, INC.	No Match 2		
Duke Energy Corporation	No Match 2		
Education	No Match 2		Manitowoc

Figure 14.4: Fuzzy matching compared to Jaccard similarity and Levenshtein distance

The **Fuzzy** measure clearly performs the best with more matches and fewer false positives although it is possible that with enough tweaking, the other two approaches could potentially provide similar levels of accuracy. For example, one improvement to the **Levenshtein distance** measure might be to make the **__FuzzyThreshold** dynamic based upon a percentage of the overall length of the word being matched.

The key takeaway here is that DAX can be used to solve some rather gnarly problems and that sometimes a custom approach provides better results than standard algorithms.

This completes our analysis of fuzzy matching in DAX. We now move on to another problem that is traditionally solved in Power Query, creating a sorted table index.

DAX Index

While adding an index column to a table is generally done in Power Query or a source system, for the same reasons as fuzzy matching, there are situations where this is simply impossible or impractical. For years, adding an index in DAX was effectively considered impossible and particularly impossible if attempting to enforce a particular sort order for that index.

The reason for the supposed impossibility of a sorted index is that DAX functions are generally unable to guarantee sort order. This can be seen in the official DAX documentation regarding **TOPN** and other DAX functions. Yes, when writing DAX queries, the **ORDERBY** expression is available but the **ORDERBY** expression is not available when writing standard DAX. In addition, one can use a **Sort by** column, but this requires configuration outside of DAX itself.

Luckily, the solution to this dilemma is fairly simple and straightforward and is really a simple extension of a concept and technique that we have already covered numerous times throughout this book. To demonstrate this technique, first start by using an **Enter data** query to create a table called **Index** using the following data or import the **Index** sheet from the Excel spreadsheet, **Chapter14_Data.xlsx** which can be found in the GitHub repository for this book: https://github.com/gdeckler/DAX-For-Humans/tree/main/book.

Product
Orange
Banana
Apple
Grapes
Kiwi
Mango
Coconut
Pickle
Eggplant

Product
Jabuticaba

Table 14.7: Index data

Now create the following DAX table:

```
DAX Index Table =
    VAR __Table = 'Index'
    VAR __Path = CONCATENATEX( __Table, [Product], "|" )
    VAR __Result =
        ADDCOLUMNS(
            SELECTCOLUMNS(
                GENERATESERIES( 1, COUNTROWS( __Table ), 1 ),
                "Index", [Value]
            ),
            "Product", PATHITEM( __Path, [Index] )
        )
RETURN
    __Result
```

You may notice that this technique is effectively the same technique that we have used to convert strings of text into tables. We use **CONCATENATEX** to append elements together with the pipe character (|) turning the table into a string recognized as a path by the **PATH** family of functions. We can then use **GENERATESERIES** and pluck the desired path items from the path using the **PATHITEM** function. The output of this formula is the following table:

Index	Product
1	Orange
2	Banana
3	Apple

Index	Product
4	Grapes
5	Kiwi
6	Mango
7	Coconut
8	Pickle
9	Eggplant
10	Jabuticaba

Table 14.8: DAX Index Table data

Because **CONCATENATEX** supports sorting parameters, we can also sort the data as we please using this variation:

```
DAX Index Sorted Table =
    VAR __Table = 'Index'
    VAR __Path = CONCATENATEX( __Table, [Product], "|", [Product], ASC )
    VAR __Result =
        ADDCOLUMNS(
            SELECTCOLUMNS(
                GENERATESERIES( 1, COUNTROWS( __Table ), 1 ),
                "Index", [Value]
            ),
            "Product", PATHITEM( __Path, [Index] )
        )
RETURN
    __Result
```

Here we specify to sort the data alphabetically in ascending order which produces the following table:

Index	Product
1	Apple
2	Banana
3	Coconut
4	Eggplant
5	Grapes
6	Jabuticaba
7	Kiwi
8	Mango
9	Orange
10	Pickle

Table 14.9: DAX Index Sorted Table data

Duplicates can also be handled, and this technique has the advantage of being able to rank items without duplicating rank values:

```
DAX Index Duplicates Sorted Table =
    VAR __Table = UNION( 'Index', 'Index' )
    VAR __Path = CONCATENATEX( __Table, [Product], "|", [Product], ASC )
    VAR __Result =
        ADDCOLUMNS(
            SELECTCOLUMNS(
                GENERATESERIES( 1, COUNTROWS( __Table ), 1 ),
                "Index", [Value]
            ),
            "Product", PATHITEM( __Path, [Index] )
```

```
        )

RETURN

    __Result
```

This code produces results where the two Apple rows are index 1 and 2 respectively while the Banana rows are index 3 and 4. Finally, we can also handle multiple column tables with some extra text parsing such as the following:

```
DAX Index Table 2 =

    VAR __Table = ADDCOLUMNS( 'Index', "Value", RANDBETWEEN( 10, 100 ) )

    VAR __Path = CONCATENATEX( __Table, [Product] & "~" & [Value], "|", [Value], DESC )

    VAR __Result =

        ADDCOLUMNS(

            SELECTCOLUMNS(

                GENERATESERIES( 1, COUNTROWS( __Table ), 1 ),

                "Index", [Value]

            ),

            "Product",

                VAR __Item = PATHITEM( __Path, [Index] )

                VAR __Result = MID( __Item, 1, FIND( "~", __Item ) - 1 )

            RETURN

                __Result,

            "Value",

                VAR __Item = PATHITEM( __Path, [Index] )

                VAR __Result =

                    MID(

                        __Item,

                        FIND( "~", __Item ) + 1,

                        LEN( __Item ) - FIND( "~", __Item )

                    )

            RETURN

                __Result
```

```
        )

RETURN

    __Result
```

This code creates the following table:

Value	Index	Product
74	1	Mango
68	2	Banana
67	3	Jabuticaba
65	4	Orange
56	5	Pickle
42	6	Coconut
40	7	Grapes
38	8	Kiwi
23	9	Eggplant
10	10	Apple

Table 14.10: DAX Index Table 2 data

Your results will be different because of **RANDBETWEEN**.

While we have used DAX calculated tables to demonstrate this technique, you can also use this technique to create table variables as well inside of a DAX measure. The key lesson here is that just because the entire world doesn't think it is possible doesn't mean that you shouldn't try to do it anyway. Often, one simply needs to use some creativity or repurpose existing techniques to overcome a particular challenge.

This completes our exploration of creating a DAX index. Let's now move on to the subject of streaks.

Streaks

My original DAX for identifying streaks in data was written in 2018 and has since gone through several revisions and evolutions. The core problem is akin to a **DAX Index** but with a twist, the index must restart under certain conditions. In short, the need is for an index that increments by one for each consecutive row that is in the same "group" but restarts each time that group changes between consecutive rows. To pull this off, you need a column that defines "before" and "after" such as an index or date column which might come from Power Query or DAX, as demonstrated in the previous section.

To see how this can be done, use an **Enter data** query to create a table called **Streaks** using the following data or import the **Streaks** sheet from the Excel spreadsheet, **Chapter14_Data.xlsx** which can be found in the GitHub repository for this book: https://github.com/gdeckler/DAX-For-Humans/tree/main/book.

Animal	Index
Tiger	1
Tiger	2
Tiger	3
Tiger	4
Tiger	5
Lion	6
Lion	7
Lion	8
Tiger	9
Tiger	10
Elephant	11

Animal	Index
Elephant	12
Elephant	13
Tiger	14
Tiger	15
Tiger	16

Table 14.11: Streaks data

Now create the following measure:

```
Cthulhu =
    VAR __CurrentIndex = MAX( 'Streaks'[Index] )
    VAR __CurrentGroup = MAX( 'Streaks'[Animal] )
    VAR __InitialTable =
        FILTER(
            ALL( 'Streaks' ),
            [Animal] = __CurrentGroup && [Index] < __CurrentIndex
        )
    VAR __Table =
        ADDCOLUMNS(
            __InitialTable,
            "__Diff",
            (
                [Index] -
                MAXX(
                    FILTER(
                        ALL( 'Streaks' ),
                        [Index] < EARLIER( [Index] ) && [Animal] = EARLIER( [Animal] )
```

```
                    ),

                    [Index]

                )

            ) * 1.

        )

    VAR __Max = MAXX( __Table, [Index])

    VAR __MaxStart = MAXX( FILTER( __Table, [__Diff] > 1 ), [Index] )

    VAR __FinalTable = FILTER( __Table, [Index] >= __MaxStart)

    VAR __Result =

        SWITCH( TRUE(),

            ISBLANK( __Max ), 1,

            __Max = __CurrentIndex - 1, COUNTROWS( __FinalTable ) + 1,

            1

        )

RETURN

    __Result
```

You may be curious about the odd name chosen for the measure, **Cthulhu**. Cthulhu is a fictional cosmic entity created by American writer H.P. Lovecraft. First introduced in the short story "The Call of Cthulhu" (1928), Cthulhu is so vast, alien, and incomprehensible that trying to understand or even perceive it shatters the human mind, driving people insane. This is how I felt over seven years ago when creating this approach, albeit a time when I was far less proficient in DAX.

The Cthulhu measure presented here is effectively the same as the original measure created in 2018. The reasoning behind the measure was to calculate the difference in the **Index** column between rows for the same **Animal** or group, **__Diff**. The largest **Index** with a **__Diff** greater than **1** is therefore the start of the streak and thus with a bit of math, we can arrive at our desired index value.

Years later, patron *Alexis Olsen* improved upon **Cthulhu** with the following:

```
Local Group Index =

VAR _CurrIndex = MAX ( 'Streaks'[Index] )

VAR _CurrGroup = MAX ( 'Streaks'[Animal] )
```

```
VAR _LocalGroupStart =

    CALCULATE (

        MAX ( 'Streaks'[Index] ),

        ALLSELECTED ( 'Streaks' ),

        'Streaks'[Index] < _CurrIndex,

        'Streaks'[Animal] <> _CurrGroup

    )

VAR _LocalIndex = _CurrIndex - _LocalGroupStart

RETURN

    _LocalIndex
```

Obviously, this code is much more concise and cleaner than the original by maximizing the existence of a consecutive index column. However, both measures have the following issue, they rely on consecutive **Index** values between all rows. This means that neither measure works with nonconsecutive values for **Index**. This is an issue for sensor data or other types of data where a **Date** or **DateTime** value serves as the **Index** column. The other issue with the **Local Group Index** measure is that it uses the **CALCULATE** function. Kidding. Luckily, we can solve both problems with the following measure:

```
Bride of Cthulhu =

    VAR __CurrentIndex = MAX ( 'Streaks'[Index] )

    VAR __CurrentGroup = MAX ( 'STreaks'[Animal] )

    VAR __StreakStart =

        MAXX (

            FILTER(

                ALL( 'Streaks' ),

                [Index] < __CurrentIndex && [Animal] <> __CurrentGroup

            ),

            [Index]

        )

    VAR __LocalGroupCount =

        COUNTROWS(

            FILTER(
```

```
            ALL( 'Streaks' ),

            [Index] <= __CurrentIndex && [Index] > __StreakStart

        )

    )

    VAR __Result = __LocalGroupCount

RETURN

    __Result
```

This version does not rely on the **Index** column being consecutive and thus is the most general-purpose version of all the measures presented here. We can extend this concept of a repeating index to identify streaks within the data, such as the longest streak.

```
Longest Streak =

    VAR __Table =

        ADDCOLUMNS(

            'Streaks',

            "__Cthulhu",

                VAR __CurrentIndex = [Index]

                VAR __CurrentGroup = [Animal]

                VAR __StreakStart =

                    MAXX (

                        FILTER(

                            ALL( 'Streaks' ),

                            [Index] < __CurrentIndex && [Animal] <> __CurrentGroup

                        ),

                        [Index]

                    )

                VAR __LocalGroupCount =

                    COUNTROWS(

                        FILTER(

                            ALL( 'Streaks' ),

                            [Index] <= __CurrentIndex && [Index] > __StreakStart
```

```
                        )
                    )
                VAR __Result = __LocalGroupCount
            RETURN
                __Result
        )
    VAR __Result =
        IF(
            HASONEVALUE( 'Streaks'[Animal] ),
            MAXX( __Table, [__Cthulhu] ) & "",
            MAXX( FILTER( __Table, [__Cthulhu] = MAXX( __Table, [Cthulhu] ) ), [Animal]
)
        )
RETURN
    __Result
```

The majority of this measure is simply a column implementation of the **Bride of Cthulhu** measure as the **__Cthulhu** column. The code is identical other than **__CurrentIndex** and **__CurrentGroup**. The **__Result** returns either the longest streak number for individual animals or the animal that has the longest streak:

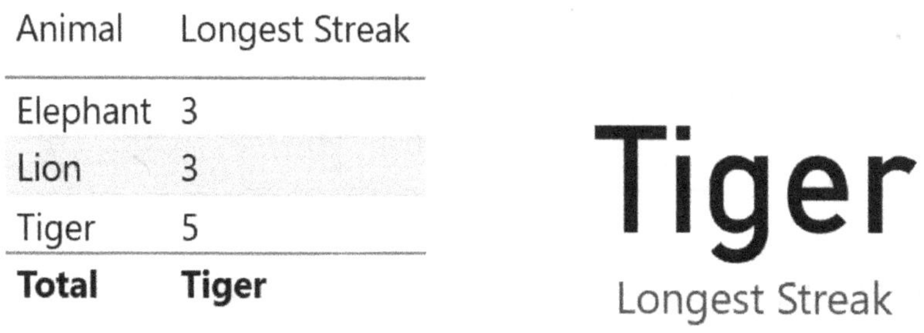

Animal	Longest Streak
Elephant	3
Lion	3
Tiger	5
Total	**Tiger**

Tiger

Longest Streak

Figure 14.5: Output of Longest Streak measure

When I created the original measure for **Cthulhu**, I honestly did not think it had much applicability or would prove useful. I was dead wrong. **Cthulhu** has proven to be extremely popular, and I have found uses for it time and time again.

Let's move on from streaks and next look at another scenario that can become quite complex, multi-column aggregations.

Multi-Column Aggregations

Aggregating data across multiple columns is not a natural or even recommended thing to do in Power BI and DAX. While data is often stored this way in Excel spreadsheets since it makes for a more natural user interface for entering data. Think a spreadsheet that stores monthly data with a column for each month. This data is normally unpivoted into two columns, a column storing the month name for example and a second column storing the value recorded for that month. However, situations can arise that make unpivoting the data impossible or otherwise difficult and hence the need for a DAX solution.

To explore multi-column aggregations, start by using an **Enter data** query to create a table called **MultiColumn** using the following data or import the **MultiColumn** sheet from the Excel spreadsheet, **Chapter14_Data.xlsx** which can be found in the GitHub repository for this book: https://github.com/gdeckler/DAX-For-Humans/tree/main/book.

Year	Jan	Feb	Mar	Apr
2025	1	2	3	4
2024	10	20	30	40
2023	100	200	300	400
2022	1000	2000	3000	4000
2021	10	10	10	10
2020	10	10	0	0

Table 14.12: Multicolumn data

We can create a multi-column aggregation such as a sum using this DAX measure:

```
Multi-Column Sum =
    VAR __Table =
        UNION(
            SELECTCOLUMNS( 'MultiColumn', "__Value", [Jan] ),
            SELECTCOLUMNS( 'MultiColumn', "__Value", [Feb] ),
            SELECTCOLUMNS( 'MultiColumn', "__Value", [Mar] ),
```

```
                    SELECTCOLUMNS( 'MultiColumn', "__Value", [Apr] )

        )

    VAR __Result = SUMX( __Table, [__Value] )
RETURN

    __Result
```

The solution is relatively straightforward, we simply use **SELECTCOLUMNS** to select each of the desired columns, use **UNION** to create a single table and then we can apply whatever X aggregator is necessary such as **SUMX, MAXX, MINX,** etc.

Interestingly, we can use a similar technique to perform a DAX unpivot such as with the following DAX table formula:

```
Unpivot =

    VAR __Table =

        UNION(

            SELECTCOLUMNS(

                'MultiColumn', "Year", [Year], "Month", "Jan", "Value", [Jan]

            ),

            SELECTCOLUMNS(

                'MultiColumn', "Year", [Year], "Month", "Feb", "Value", [Feb]

            ),

            SELECTCOLUMNS(

                'MultiColumn', "Year", [Year], "Month", "Mar", "Value", [Mar]

            ),

            SELECTCOLUMNS(

                'MultiColumn', "Year", [Year], "Month", "Apr", "Value", [Apr]

            )

        )

RETURN

    __Table
```

The obvious downside to this approach is that it is rather brute force and if your table is extremely wide there is quite a bit of typing involved. Thus, for large numbers of columns we need a more elegant solution. To see how this can be done, create a table called **Wide** by importing the **Wide.csv** file which can be found in the GitHub repository for this book: https://github.com/gdeckler/DAX-For-Humans/tree/main/book.

This file has 144 columns that we wish to aggregate across and is a real-world problem first proposed by patron *Tamer Juma*. In this case the data is meant to simulate streaming sensor data with readings every 10 minutes throughout the day. The data looks like the following:

Sensor Tag	Date	0:00	0:10	0:20	0:30
Sensor1	Monday, January 1, 2024	50	52	49	47
Sensor1	Tuesday, January 2, 2024	50	53	52	47
Sensor1	Wednesday, January 3, 2024	50	51	50	50
Sensor1	Thursday, January 4, 2024	50	52	47	48
Sensor1	Friday, January 5, 2024	50	52	52	52

Table 14.13: Wide data

These are just a few of the columns and rows from the data. The first two columns are non-numeric information columns while the rest of the columns are the numeric data columns we wish to aggregate over.

We could brute-force our way to victory here by hard-coding every column name as done previously with the **Multi-Column Sum** measure and **Unpivot** table calculation. However, we can instead make the calculation entirely dynamic using the following DAX formula:

```
Wide MC Average =
    VAR __TableWHeaders = SUBSTITUTE( TOCSV( 'Wide', , ",", 1 ), UNICHAR( 10 ) , "|")
    VAR __Headers = PATHITEM( __TableWHeaders, 1 )
    VAR __FirstColon = FIND( ":", __Headers )
    VAR __Left = LEFT( __Headers, __FirstColon )
    VAR __Commas = LEN( __Left ) - LEN( SUBSTITUTE( __Left, ",", "" ) )
    VAR __TableWOHeaders = SUBSTITUTE( TOCSV( 'Wide', , ",", 0 ), UNICHAR( 10 ), "|")
    VAR __Count = COUNTROWS( 'Wide' )
    VAR __Data =
```

```
    ADDCOLUMNS(

        GENERATESERIES( 1, __Count, 1 ),

        "__Data",

            VAR __Text = PATHITEM( __TableWOHeaders, [Value] )

            VAR __Path = SUBSTITUTE( __Text, ",", "|", __Commas )

            VAR __Result = PATHITEM( __Path, 2 )

        RETURN

            __Result

    )

VAR __DataText = CONCATENATEX( __Data, [__Data], "|" )

VAR __Path = SUBSTITUTE( __DataText, ",", "|" )

VAR __DataColumns = LEN( __DataText) - LEN( SUBSTITUTE( __DataText, ",", "" ) )

VAR __Table =

    ADDCOLUMNS(

        GENERATESERIES(1, __DataColumns, 1 ),

        "__Value", PATHITEM( __Path, [Value] ) + 0

    )

VAR __Result = AVERAGEX( __Table, [__Value] )

RETURN

    __Result
```

There is a lot going on with this formula so we will break it down line by line. However, keep in mind that the overall goal is to extract the 144 data columns and transform the data in such a way that we can find the average across all 144 data columns while also aggregated or segmented by the **Sensor Tag** and **Date** columns. In addition, we desire to have this formula work regardless of the number of data columns and additional columns. We want everything to be as dynamic as possible so that it is a general-purpose solution.

With these goals in mind, our first step is to collect information about the data that we are dealing with. We start by turning the data into a **PATH** by using **TOCSV** to convert the table into text and substituting line feed characters, **UNICHAR(10)**, with the pipe character. Each row of data is now a **PATHITEM**. We can thus retrieve the first **PATHITEM**, which are the column headers, **__Headers**.

The next line of code represents the only assumption we make, that the data columns have a colon in them while the other columns do not and that all non-numeric data columns come before any numeric data columns. Thus, to figure out how many "other", non-numeric information columns, exist we locate the first colon character in the __**Headers** variable. We can then retrieve the portion of the string to the **LEFT** of the first colon character and calculate the number of non-numeric information columns (__**Commas**) by using the simple **SUBSTITUTE** trick we learned back in *Chapter 4, Text*.

The next step is to retrieve only the data rows, turning these into a single **PATH** string where each row is a **PATHITEM**, __**TableWOHeaders**. We also determine the number of rows in our table which we store in the __**Count** variable. Note, we could have used **PATHLENGTH** instead of **COUNTROWS** to achieve this.

It is now time to turn our **PATH** string back into a table but only the numeric data columns we wish to aggregate. We do this via the standard text-to-table method we have used previously using **GENERATESERIES**. For each iteration through the loop, we retrieve the corresponding **PATHITEM**, which corresponds to an entire row of data with all columns. We then use **SUBSTITUTE** to replace the comma in the position calculated as the separation between non-numeric information columns and numeric data columns, which is our __**Commas** variable.

Recall, that the __**Commas** variable holds the number of non-information "pre" columns to our numeric data columns. Thus, if there are two such columns, the __**Path** variable code replaces the second comma with a pipe character. We can finally then retrieve the second **PATHITEM** from the __**Path** text, which returns only the numeric data columns and effectively drops the non-numeric information columns. Thus, the __**Data** column holds all numeric data columns in a comma separated text string and there is a row for each row of data.

Thus far, we have converted the table of data to a **PATH** and then back to a table again. It is now time to repeat this process. We start by using **CONCATENATEX** to turn each row of data in the __**Date** table variable into a **PATHITEM**. We then convert everything into a single **PATH** by replacing the commas with pipe characters. Thus, all rows and all columns in the __**Data** table variable are now effectively a single **PATH** string stored in the __**Path** variable.

Now we need to turn __**Path** back into a table so that we can aggregate across the table. We start by determining the total number of columns in our __**Path** variable by using the **SUBSTITUTE** trick once again. Thus, __**DataColumns** will be the number of numeric data columns multiplied by the number of rows in context. For each sensor, there is one row of data per date.

We now turn the __**Path** variable back into a table variable, __**Table**, using the standard text to table technique and we can then finally use an X aggregator function such as **AVERAGEX** to iterate over the table to obtain our desired result.

This is a rather lengthy explanation, but the code involved is quite complex, nuanced, and uses several techniques that have appeared in previous chapters. We can now create a visual such as the following **Line chart** visualization by placing the **Date** column from table **Wide** in the **X-axis** and the Wide MC Average measure in the **Y-axis**.

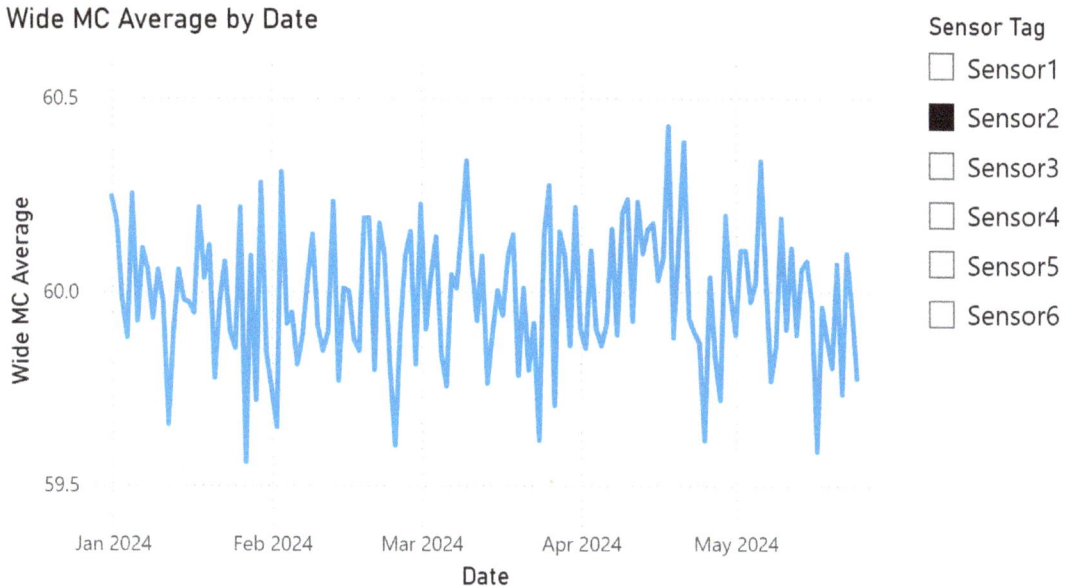

Figure 14.6: Line chart of Wide MC Average measure by Date

Note that with all sensors in context, the measure can take a long time to produce results so it can be helpful to include a **Slicer** visual for the **Sensor Tag** column.

This completes our exploration of complex patterns in DAX.

Summary

In this chapter, we created DAX equivalents for two functions that are found in Excel but not in DAX, **GAMMA** and **TRIMMEAN**. We also created DAX to perform fuzzy matching across text fields, and build a DAX-based index, something that once considered impossible. We also implemented logic for identifying and tracking streaks and executing complex multi-column aggregations. While these DAX solutions may seem rather fanciful, every single solution presented here comes from actual requirements identified by individuals within the business intelligence community.

This chapter should prove once and for all that the **CALCULATE** function is not required to solve incredibly difficult and challenging problems with DAX. Breaking complex problems down into the creation of table variables and X aggregation functions once again allows us to solve these problems, continuing the same basic pattern that has been used throughout this book.

In the next chapter, we switch gears and look at how to optimize DAX code as well as when and where the **CALCULATE** function can be useful.

15

Optimizing Performance

Generally, most DAX code runs within acceptable performance parameters. However, as semantic models grow in size and complexity it is possible to encounter measure calculations that grind to a halt at scale. In such cases, optimizing your DAX code becomes a necessity. While it is certainly true that optimizing your semantic model design can sometimes greatly simplify your DAX code and lead to better performing calculations, since this book is about DAX and not semantic modeling, we will be focusing on practical techniques for improving the performance of DAX calculations that do not involve semantic model changes and only focusing on how changes to your DAX code can improve performance.

Now, there are entire 800+ page books dedicated to optimizing DAX code that go into far greater detail than is possible in a single chapter. That said, it is our belief that you can learn the vast majority of what you will need in everyday situations within this chapter. Instead of focusing on theory and "how things really work", we instead focus on practical scenarios and techniques to improve the performance of your DAX code. To this end, we first explain what makes optimizing DAX such a difficult subject, provide an overview of the tools you can use to help optimize performance, and finally present different, real-world scenarios where we demonstrate various techniques for optimizing performance.

Why is Optimizing DAX a Difficult Subject?

The subject of optimizing DAX is a tricky subject to cover for a variety of reasons. One reason is that the optimization techniques required can vary depending on whether the semantic model is using import mode, **DirectQuery**, or is a **composite semantic model**. The second and perhaps more important reason is that there are two magical boxes that primarily determine if the DAX code you write performs optimally, the storage engine and the formula engine. You can visualize how your DAX code generates a result with the following visual:

```
Sum Total Cost No Pickle =
    VAR __ExcludeItem = "Pickle"
    VAR __Table = FILTER( 'Table',
'Table'[Item] <> __ExcludeItem )
    VAR __Result = SUMX( __Table,
[Total Cost] )
RETURN
    __Result
```

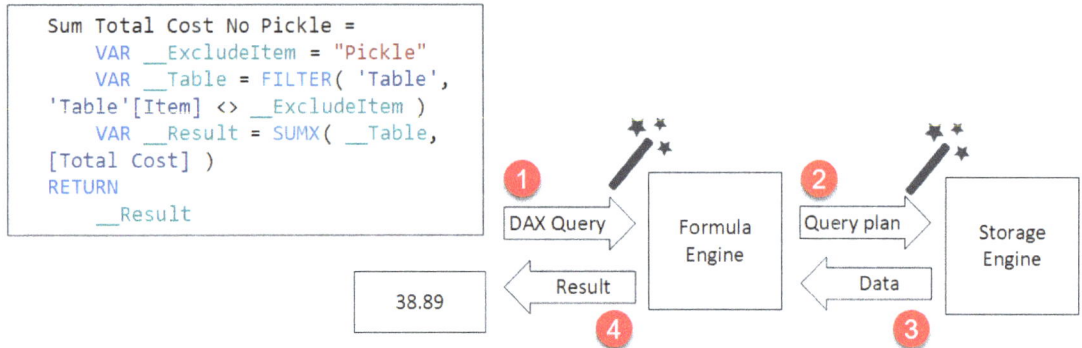

Figure 15.1: DAX execution pipeline

Without delving into the details, the **Formula Engine** (**FE**) analyzes your DAX code and attempts to create an efficient query plan for retrieving the required data from the semantic model via the **Storage Engine** (**SE**). This is exactly analogous to how SQL code works. Once the required data is retrieved by the storage engine, this data is then passed to the formula engine to complete the processing of the DAX code and finally return the result.

To be a bit more specific, the SE is responsible for retrieving data from the **VertiPaq** in-memory columnar store (or DirectQuery source, if applicable). It performs efficient scans, filtering, and aggregation operations over compressed data, typically using highly optimized, multi-threaded C++ routines. Specifically, here is what the SE does in more detail:

1. **Scans columns, not rows** – Because VertiPaq is a columnar store, the SE scans only the columns needed by the query, which minimizes memory and CPU usage.

2. **Applies filters** – The SE handles physical filtering (like **WHERE** clauses in SQL), returning only the data that meets specific conditions.

3. **Performs basic aggregations** – Operations such as **SUM**, **COUNT**, and **MIN/MAX** are handled natively by the SE when possible, without invoking the FE.

4. **Returns data tables** – After completing its scans and aggregations, the SE returns a result table (or a scalar if reduced) to the FE, which can then further process it or use it in nested expressions.

In an optimized DAX measure, most of the work should be offloaded to the SE because it's significantly faster than the FE. Writing DAX in a way that allows the SE to do more is a key principle of DAX optimization.

In contrast, the FE is responsible for parsing, interpreting, and executing the DAX expression logic. Unlike the SE, which deals with raw data retrieval and basic aggregation, the FE orchestrates the calculation flow, manages context transitions, and handles complex operations that require row-by-row logic or iterative evaluation. Specifically, here is what the FE does during measure evaluation:

1. **Parses and processes DAX expressions** – The FE reads the DAX syntax, builds an execution plan, and determines how to compute the final result based on dependencies, functions, and context.

2. **Manages evaluation context** – The FE sets up and maintains row context and **filter context**, ensuring the correct subset of data is used at each step of the calculation. It also applies context transitions when needed (e.g., in **CALCULATE**).

3. **Calls the Storage Engine** – When data is needed, the FE sends queries (usually in a simplified internal language called **XM SQL**) to the SE to retrieve filtered and aggregated tables or values.

4. **Handles complex and non-delegable operations** – Functions like **FILTER**, **ADDCOLUMNS**, iterators, and scalar expressions often require the FE to process data row by row in memory, which is slower than SE-based operations.

5. **Performs post-processing** – Once the raw data is retrieved and any intermediate logic is evaluated, the FE combines the results, performs any remaining calculations, and returns the final value for the measure.

In short, the FE is the "brains" of DAX evaluation, controlling the logic and flow, but it's slower than the SE because it processes data using a single-threaded .NET-based engine. Optimizing DAX often involves rewriting expressions so that more work is pushed down to the SE, minimizing what the FE must do.

This is as much "theory" that we are going to explore because knowing any more about the SE and FE is unlikely to be of much use. Even in 800+ page books solely about DAX optimization, the exact inner workings of the SE and FE are essentially chalked up as "unknowable".

As luck would have it, we don't actually need to know anything more about the SE and FE to understand how to make DAX more efficient. Even the level of detail provided here is complete overkill for all practical purposes. Instead, practical examples and experimentation are sufficient for laying out the basic principles of DAX optimization. But, before we get into the examples, let's cover the basic tools you will need when optimizing your DAX.

DAX Optimization Tools

When it comes to DAX optimization, it is helpful to have some tools to help you analyze how your DAX code is performing. There are three primary tools that you should consider:

- **Performance Analyzer** – This is a default pane built-in to Power BI Desktop that provides basic performance information.
- **DAX Studio** – This is the OG of DAX optimization tools and can provide extremely detailed information about what is going on within the storage and formula engines. DAX Studio is free and can be downloaded here: https://daxstudio.org/downloads/.
- **Power Optimizer by TruViz** – A newcomer to the DAX optimization world, this advanced tool uses AI and other cutting-edge techniques to recommend optimizations and best practices for your DAX code. When available, Power Optimizer can be downloaded from here: https://thepowertools.ai/. To a lesser extent, the **Powerops** tool from TruViz can also be useful for checking DAX code against best practices: https://powerops.app/.

Since the **Performance analyzer** pane is built-in to Power BI Desktop, let's take a look it first.

To access the **Performance analyzer** pane in Power BI Desktop, follow these steps:

1. In Power BI Desktop, click the **View** tab in the ribbon.
2. In the **Show panes** section, click the **Performance analyzer** button.

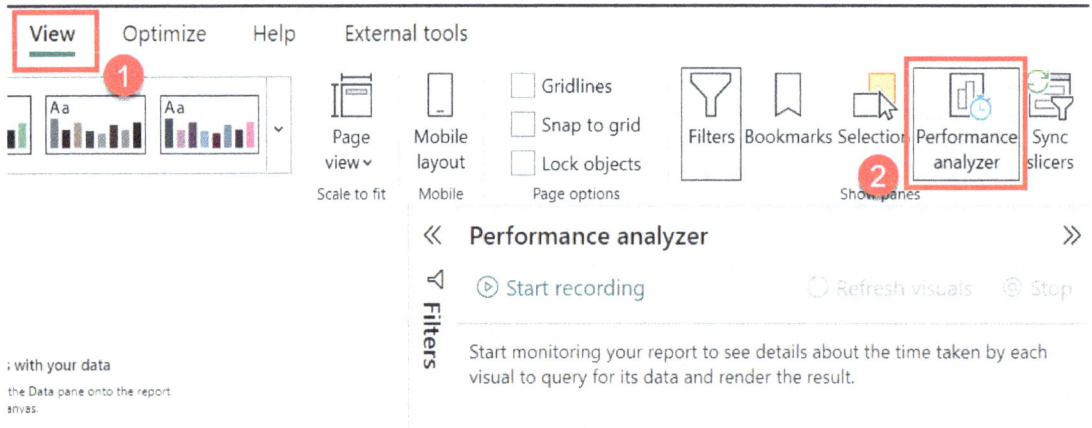

Figure 15.2: Performance analyzer pane

To explore how the **Performance analyzer** works, import the **Dates** sheet from the Excel spreadsheet, **Chapter15_Data.xlsx** which can be found in the GitHub repository for this book: https://github.com/gdeckler/DAX-For-Humans/tree/main/book.

Now, create the following measure:

```
Measure = COUNTROWS( 'Dates' )
```

Create a **Card** visual that uses this measure. In addition, create a **Table** visual with both the **Year** column from the **Dates** table and **Measure**.

Now click the **Start recording** button in the **Performance analyzer** pane and then click the **Refresh visuals** button. In the Performance analyzer pane, click the **+** icons next to **Card** and **Table** to display results like the following:

Performance analyzer »

▷ Start recording   ○ Refresh visuals   ◎ Stop

◇ Clear   ⬚ Export

Name	Duration (ms) ↓
⏱ *Recording started (4/11/2025 7:14:48 PM)*	-
○ *Refreshed visual*	-
⊟ Card	41
DAX query	4
Visual display	12
Other	25
⬚ Copy query	
⬚ Run in DAX query view	
⊟ Table	58
DAX query	4
Visual display	33
Other	21
⬚ Copy query	
⬚ Run in DAX query view	

Figure 15.3: Performance analyzer timings

The numbers displayed are the number of milliseconds required to complete the operations. In the image, the **Card** visual took a total of **41** milliseconds to display while the **Table** visual required **58** milliseconds to display. This total time is broken up into several categories as follows:

- **DAX query** – The time to execute the DAX query. Static visuals such as text boxes or shapes generally do not execute a DAX query and thus will not display this category.
- **Visual display** – How long to draw the visual. More complex visuals take longer to render, such as with the **Card** and **Table** visuals, the **Table** visual being more complex to render and thus takes longer.

- **Other** – The time required to prepare queries, waiting on other visuals, and performing background tasks. Only so many DAX queries can be executed at a time and thus when many visuals are displayed on a page, this number can grow quite large.
- **Evaluated parameters** – Only present if the field parameters preview feature is active, displays the time spent evaluating field parameters.

From a DAX perspective, all we can really impact is the **DAX query** category and thus, this is the number we will be looking to optimize in the scenarios presented in this chapter.

Clicking the **Run in DAX query view** presents the following queries respectively:

Card:

```
EVALUATE

    ROW(

    "Measure", 'Calculations'[Measure]

)
```

Table:

```
DEFINE

    VAR __DS0Core =

        SUMMARIZECOLUMNS(

            ROLLUPADDISSUBTOTAL('Dates'[Year], "IsGrandTotalRowTotal"),

            "Measure", 'Calculations'[Measure]

        )


    VAR __DS0PrimaryWindowed =

        TOPN(502, __DS0Core, [IsGrandTotalRowTotal], 0, 'Dates'[Year], 1)


EVALUATE

    __DS0PrimaryWindowed


ORDER BY

    [IsGrandTotalRowTotal] DESC, 'Dates'[Year]
```

You may be wondering why this looks nothing like the code for **Measure**. That's because you are looking at the actual DAX queries being executed. You can use these queries in DAX Studio to run a benchmark test to see how much time was spent in the SE versus the FE. In this case, the **Table** visual spends 100% of its time in the FE:

Figure 15.4: DAX Studio benchmark

While the ability to get detailed query information and timings are useful to a degree, they aren't necessarily helpful in actually improving the DAX code. This is where tools like TruViz's Power Optimizer really shine. Power Optimizer is built to help you optimize your entire semantic model including analyzing the performance of DAX calculations; identifying unused tables, columns, and measures; and visualizing relationships between measures, calculated columns, visuals, and pages. Even better, Power Optimizer identifies issues and suggests how to address and fix those issues:

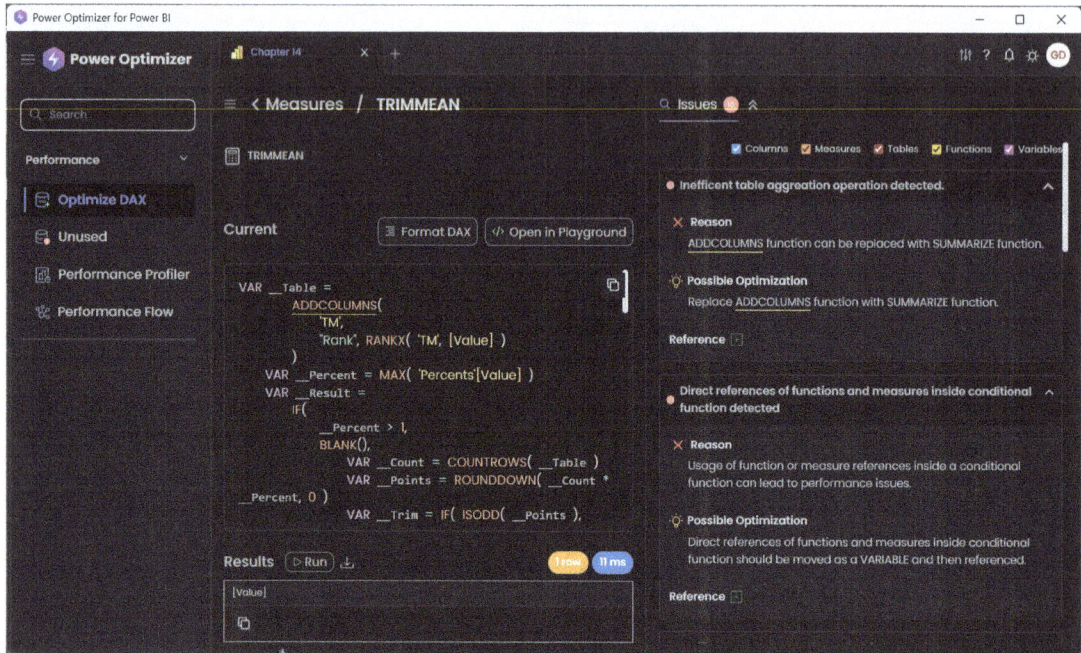

Figure 15.5: Performance Optimizer by TruViz

Now that you understand the basics of the tools used for DAX optimization, let's take a look at a real-world example of optimizing a DAX measure (query).

General Example

We have covered enough theory and introduced enough tools, so let's take a closer look at an example scenario based on á real-world question that appeared in the Power BI Community forums.

To explore this scenario, import the **DateTimeTable**, **Dim_Department**, and **Tracking_History** sheets from the Excel spreadsheet, **Chapter15_Data.xlsx** which can be found in the GitHub repository for this book: https://github.com/gdeckler/DAX-For-Humans/tree/main/book.

It is worth noting that the **DateTimeTable** consists of 1,776 rows of data containing a single column called **Date** with datetime values for each hour of the day between the dates of January 1st, 2020 and March 14th. The **Tracking_History** table is the main fact table and contains just over **59,000** rows.

Create a relationship between the **Dim_Department** and **Tracking_History** tables using the common **Department ID** columns in both tables. Your semantic model should look like the following:

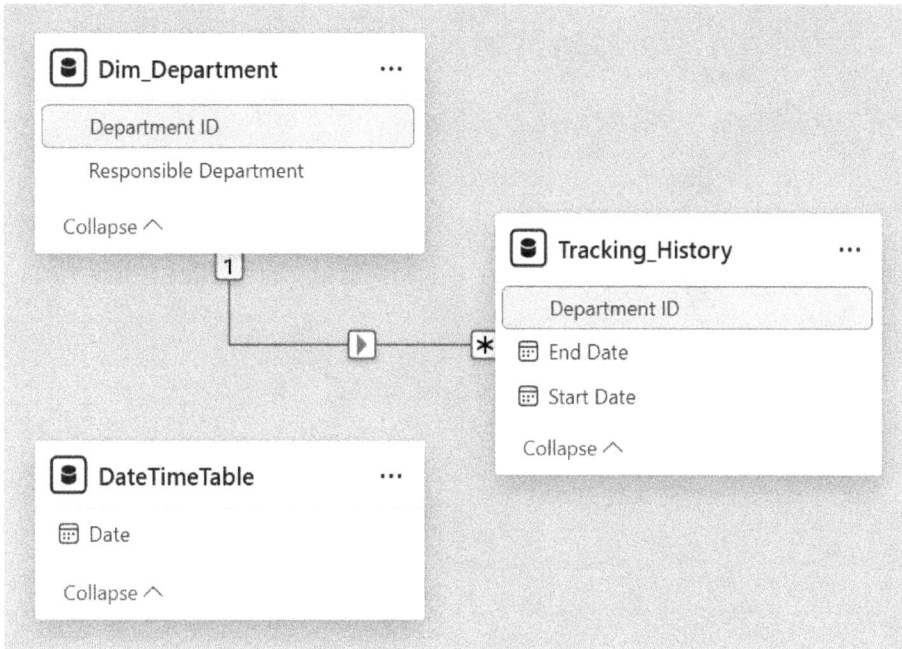

Figure 15.6: Scenario semantic model

Now create the following two measures:

```
No. of Orders =
    VAR __StartDate = VALUE ( SELECTEDVALUE ( 'Tracking_History'[Start Date] ) )
    VAR __EndDate = VALUE ( SELECTEDVALUE ( 'Tracking_History'[End Date] ) )
    VAR __MinDate = VALUE ( MIN ( 'DateTimeTable'[Date] ) )
    VAR __MaxDate = VALUE ( MAX ( 'DateTimeTable'[Date] ) )
    VAR __Result =
        IF(
            AND( __StartDate > __MinDate, __EndDate < __MaxDate ),
            1,
            IF (
                AND(
                    AND ( __StartDate > __MinDate, __EndDate > __MaxDate ),
                    __MaxDate > __StartDate
                ),
                1,
```

```
IF(
    AND(
        AND ( __StartDate < __MinDate, __EndDate < __MaxDate ),
        __EndDate > __MinDate
    ),
    1,
    IF(
        AND ( __StartDate < __MinDate, __EndDate > __MaxDate ),
        1,
        BLANK ()
    )
)
    )
)

RETURN
    __Result
```

```
Total Orders = SUMX( 'Tracking_History', [No. of Orders] )
```

Finally, create a **Line chart** visualization with the **Date** field (not the hierarchy) from the **DateTimeTable** as the **X-axis**, the **Responsible Department** column from the **Dim_Department** table as the **Legend** and the **Total Orders** measure as the **Y-axis**. Now get up and go grab some coffee, do some laundry, maybe weed the flower bed because the visual may very well take 10 minutes or more to render!

Total Orders by Date and Responsible Department

Responsible Department ● (Blank) ● Dept 1 ● Dept 2 ● Dept 3 ● Dept 5 ● Dept 6

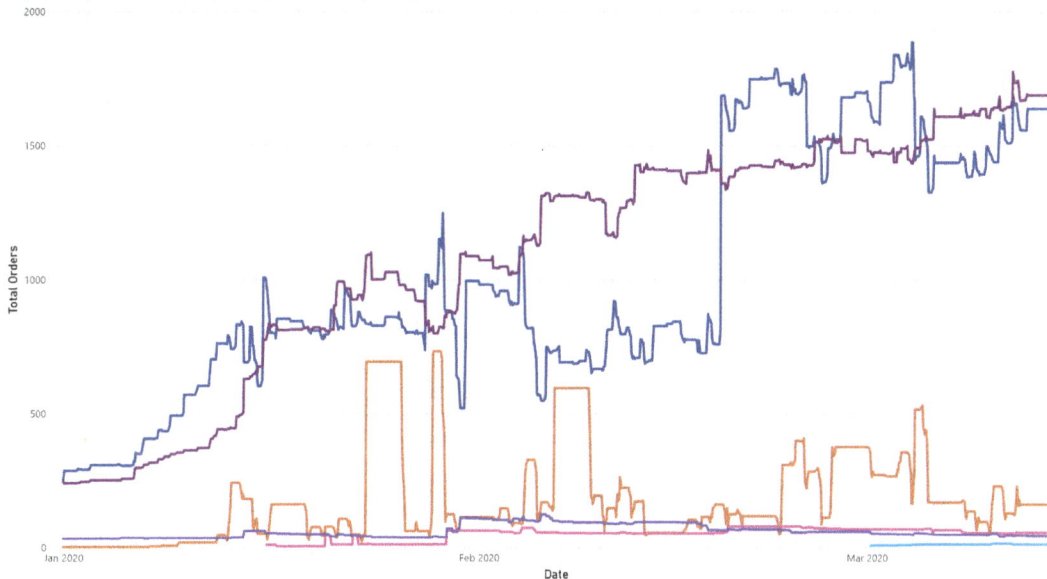

Figure 15.7: Total Orders over time

10 minutes is obviously a non-starter in terms of self-service reporting. To be more specific, on my test computer, the query runs for about **581,894 milliseconds** which is **9 minutes and 42 seconds**. Something is obviously very, very wrong.

Before doing anything else, create a new blank page. Otherwise, if you create a new measure while still on the page with the original visual on it, you will need to wait another 10 minutes before your measure is created while Power BI Desktop waits for the visual to render. Sigh.

In analyzing the visual and the measure, it is clear that the author was attempting to count the number of transactions that fell into defined one hour "buckets" of time, broken down by the transacting department.

As a first step towards optimization, let's get rid of the nested **IF** statements and instead use the **SWITCH** statement to help clean up the code and the logic. To this end, create the following two measures:

```
No. of Orders 2 =
    VAR __StartDate = VALUE ( SELECTEDVALUE ( 'Tracking_History'[Start Date] ) )
    VAR __EndDate = VALUE ( SELECTEDVALUE ( 'Tracking_History'[End Date] ) )
    VAR __MinDate = VALUE ( MIN ( 'DateTimeTable'[Date] ) )
    VAR __MaxDate = VALUE ( MAX ( 'DateTimeTable'[Date] ) )
```

```
VAR __Result =

    SWITCH(TRUE(),

        AND ( __StartDate > __MinDate, __EndDate < __MaxDate ),1,

        AND(

            AND ( __StartDate > __MinDate, __EndDate > __MaxDate),

            __MaxDate > __StartDate

        ),1,

        AND(

            AND ( __StartDate < __MinDate, __EndDate < __MaxDate ),

            __EndDate > __MinDate

        ),1,

        AND ( __StartDate < __MinDate, __EndDate > __MaxDate ),1,

        BLANK()

    )

RETURN

    __Result
```

```
                Total Orders 2 = SUMX( 'Tracking_History', [No. of Orders 2] )
```

Create the same graph as before but using **Total Orders 2** as the **Y-axis**. You should see significant performance improvements such as on the test machine the visual renders in about **58,175 milliseconds** which is **58 seconds**. This is an order of magnitude faster than the original measure, a **90%** improvement in the speed of the calculation. The practical lesson learned here is to avoid nested **IF** statements and instead use the **TRUE()** variant of the **SWITCH** statement.

We notice that we can improve/simplify the logic. The most likely scenario when evaluating any one-hour bucket of time is that the bucket only represents a small fraction of the rows within the semantic model. Therefore, it makes sense to include a check for whether the row falls outside of the bucket first as this eliminates the most rows with only a single logical test.

```
No. of Orders 3 =

    VAR __StartDate = VALUE ( SELECTEDVALUE ( 'Tracking_History'[Start Date]) )

    VAR __EndDate = VALUE ( SELECTEDVALUE ( 'Tracking_History'[End Date] ) )

    VAR __MinDate = VALUE ( MIN ( 'DateTimeTable'[Date] ) )

    VAR __MaxDate = VALUE ( MAX ( DateTimeTable[Date] ) )
```

```
VAR __Result =

    SWITCH(TRUE(),

        AND ( __StartDate > __MinDate, __EndDate > __MaxDate ),BLANK(),

        AND(

            AND ( __StartDate > __MinDate, __EndDate > __MaxDate ),

            __MaxDate < __StartDate

        ), BLANK(),

        AND(

            AND ( __StartDate < __MinDate, __EndDate < __MaxDate ),

            __EndDate < __MinDate

        ), BLANK(),

        AND ( __StartDate < __MinDate, __EndDate < __MaxDate ), BLANK(),

        1

    )

RETURN

    __Result
```

```
        Total Orders 3 = SUMX( 'Tracking_History', [No. of Orders 3] )
```

On the test machine, this measure returned after **27,424 milliseconds** or roughly **27 seconds**, which is about a **50%** improvement in speed. The lesson here is that you need to pay attention to how you structure your logical checks to either exclude or include the most rows possible depending on the situation.

One of the tenets of the No CALCULATE approach is to keep all your DAX code in a single measure versus separating the logic into multiple measures, so let's do that:

```
Total Orders 4 =

    VAR __MinDate = VALUE ( MIN ( 'DateTimeTable'[Date] ) )

    VAR __MaxDate = VALUE ( MAX ( DateTimeTable[Date] ) )

    VAR __Table =

        ADDCOLUMNS(

            'Tracking_History',

            "__No of Orders",
```

```
        SWITCH(TRUE(),
            AND (
                'Tracking_History'[Start Date] > __MinDate,
                'Tracking_History'[End Date] > __MaxDate
            ), BLANK(),
            AND(
                AND (
                    'Tracking_History'[Start Date] > __MinDate,
                    'Tracking_History'[End Date] > __MaxDate
                ),
                __MaxDate < 'Tracking_History'[Start Date]
            ), BLANK(),
            AND(
                AND (
                    'Tracking_History'[Start Date] < __MinDate,
                    'Tracking_History'[End Date] < __MaxDate
                ),
                'Tracking_History'[End Date] < __MinDate
            ), BLANK(),
            AND (
                'Tracking_History'[Start Date] < __MinDate,
                'Tracking_History'[End Date] < __MaxDate
            ), BLANK(),
            1
        )
    )
VAR __Result = SUMX(__Table,[__No of Orders])
RETURN
    __Result
```

This measure returned in approximately **25 seconds**, which is about a **7%** improvement. This performance improvement used to be much greater before Power BI implemented its measure fusion technology. Still, a nearly 10% improvement is nothing to sneeze at.

It's apparent that having dependent measures (measure branching) can hurt overall performance. Is this because the DAX query engine has more information to more accurately and effectively extract the information? Or is it because only a single DAX query is created versus multiple? Who can say really but consolidating multiple DAX measures into a single DAX measure is worth considering when optimizing your DAX performance.

We realize that instead of using the first clause of the **SWITCH** statement to filter out rows, we could instead implement an actual **FILTER** statement to initially filter the rows down to only the potential rows we care about.

```
Total Orders 5 =

    VAR __MinDate = VALUE ( MIN ( 'DateTimeTable'[Date] ) )

    VAR __MaxDate = VALUE ( MAX ( DateTimeTable[Date] ) )

    VAR __Table =

        ADDCOLUMNS(

            FILTER(

                'Tracking_History',

                OR (

                    'Tracking_History'[Start Date] > __MinDate,

                    'Tracking_History'[End Date] > __MaxDate

                )

            ),

            "__No of Orders",

            SWITCH(TRUE(),

                AND(

                    AND (

                        'Tracking_History'[Start Date] > __MinDate,

                        'Tracking_History'[End Date] > __MaxDate

                    ),

                    __MaxDate < 'Tracking_History'[Start Date]
```

```
            ),BLANK(),

            AND (

                'Tracking_History'[Start Date] < __MinDate,

                'Tracking_History'[End Date] < __MaxDate

            ),BLANK(),

            1

        )

    )

    VAR __Result = SUMX(__Table,[__No of Orders])
RETURN

    __Result
```

This generally returns within **16 seconds** which is a further **36%** improvement. It is critical to filter the rows of your table as early as possible to minimize the amount of data being retrieved by the SE and needing to be processed by the FE.

We now realize that the use of the **VALUE** function within this measure is not really doing anything of, well, actual *value*. So, let's get rid of them.

```
Total Orders 6 =
    VAR MinDateInContext = MIN ( 'DateTimeTable'[Date] )
    VAR MaxDateInContext = MAX ( DateTimeTable[Date] )
    VAR __Table =
        ADDCOLUMNS(
            FILTER(
                'Tracking_History',
                OR (
                    'Tracking_History'[Start Date] > MinDateInContext,
                    'Tracking_History'[End Date] > MaxDateInContext
                )
            ),
            "__No of Orders",
            SWITCH(TRUE(),
```

```
            AND(

                AND (

                    'Tracking_History'[Start Date] > MinDateInContext,

                    'Tracking_History'[End Date] > MaxDateInContext

                ),

                MaxDateInContext < 'Tracking_History'[Start Date]

            ),BLANK(),

            AND (

                'Tracking_History'[Start Date] < MinDateInContext,

                'Tracking_History'[End Date] < MaxDateInContext

            ),BLANK(),

            1

        )

    )

    VAR __Result = SUMX(__Table,[__No of Orders])

RETURN

    __Result
```

This time the measure returns in **14 seconds**, a **12%** improvement in speed. It is unfortunate that a lot of early DAX code used the **VALUES** function and, to a lesser extent, the **VALUE** function. In general, neither of these functions provides much actual value. In almost all cases you should favor **DISTINCT** over values and the **VALUE** function is almost never a good idea. Even the following would be preferred:

```
        VAR __MinDate = MIN ( 'DateTimeTable'[Date] ) * 1.
```

We now realize that perhaps eliminating the **SWITCH** statement altogether and simply using **FILTER** might be a better way to go:

```
Total Orders 7 =

    VAR __MinDate = MIN ( 'DateTimeTable'[Date] )

    VAR __MaxDate = MAX ( DateTimeTable[Date] )

    VAR __Result =

        COUNTROWS(
```

```
                FILTER(

                    FILTER(

                        FILTER (

                            'Tracking_History',

                                OR (

                                    'Tracking_History'[Start Date] > __MinDate,

                                    'Tracking_History'[End Date] > __MaxDate

                                )

                        ),

                            __MaxDate > 'Tracking_History'[Start Date]

                    ),

                    OR (

                        [Start Date] > __MinDate,

                        [End Date] > __MaxDate

                    )

                )

            )

RETURN

    __Result
```

We are now down to **10 seconds**, a further **28%** improvement. **FILTER** is quite possibly the king of all DAX optimization functions.

A final simplification of the logic brings the final result to only **6 seconds**, a further **40%** improvement.

```
Total Orders 8 =

    VAR __Date = MIN ( 'DateTimeTable'[Date] )

    VAR __Result =

        COUNTROWS(

            FILTER(

                'Tracking_History',

                'Tracking_History'[Start Date] < __Date &&
```

```
                    __Date < 'Tracking_History'[End Date]
        )

     )

RETURN

   __Result
```

Overall, the speed of the calculation improved by approximately **99%** over the original measure. To summarize the practical lessons here:

- Use **SWITCH(TRUE(), …)** versus nested **IF** statements.
- When structuring logical tests, put the logical tests that eliminate or include the greatest number of rows possible first.
- Consider putting all of your DAX code into a single measure versus having separate, dependent measures.
- The **FILTER** function is quite possibly the most powerful function in DAX when it comes to DAX optimization. Filter early and filter often.
- Don't use unnecessary functions, particularly functions like **VALUE** and **VALUES**.
- Nested **FILTER** functions perform better than **SWITCH(TRUE(), …)** statements.
- Simplify your filtering logic as much as possible.

It must be stressed that all these techniques were useful in this particular instance. In other circumstances, these techniques may not provide any benefit.

Let's now move on to a different scenario that highlights the performance difference between **CALCULATE** and the No CALCULATE approach.

CALCULATE vs No CALCULATE Act 1

To further explore DAX optimization techniques, let's compare the traditional **CALCULATE** approach to DAX with the No CALCULATE approach to determine if there are performance differences between the two methods. To this end, we will explore the subject using a classic business intelligence calculation, year-to-date sales.

To prepare for this scenario, if you have not already imported the **Dates** sheet from the Excel spreadsheet, **Chapter15_Data.xlsx** which can be found in the GitHub repository for this book: https://github.com/gdeckler/DAX-For-Humans/tree/main/book, please do so now. Also, import the **FactInternetSales** sheet. This is actually the AdventureWorks Internet Sales fact table.

Create a relationship between the **Date** column in the **Dates** table and the **OrderDate** column in the **FactInternetSales** table. Your data model should look like the following:

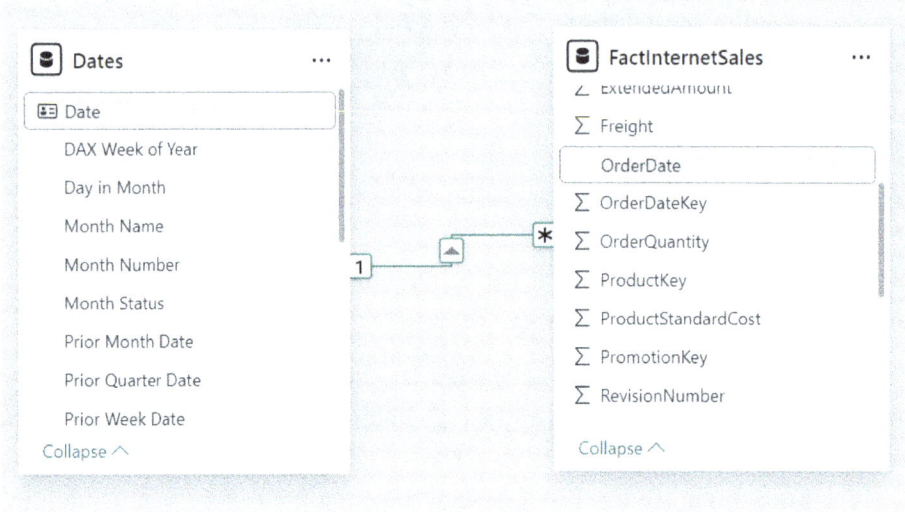

Figure 15.8: Simple two table semantic model

Next, right-click the **Dates** table in the **Data** pane and choose **Mark as date table**. In the **Mark as date table** dialog, toggle the **Mark as date table** to **On**, select the **Date** column for the **Choose a date column** and then click the **Save** button.

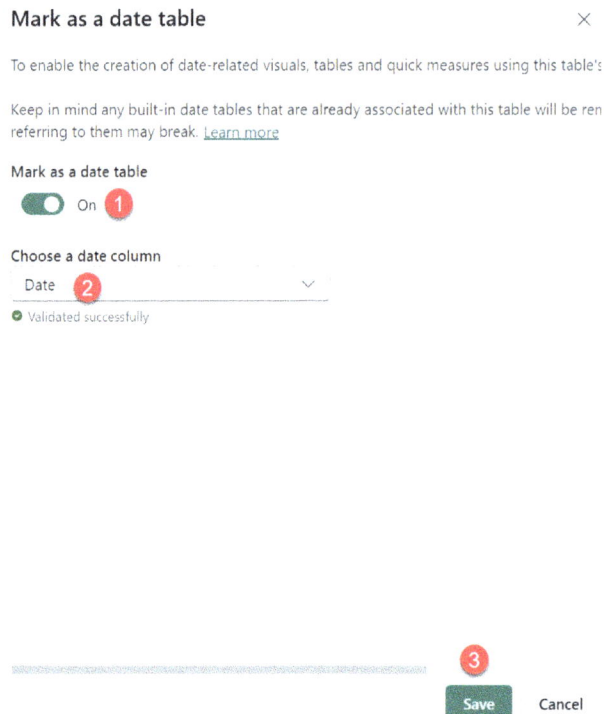

Figure 15.9: Mark as date table dialog

Marking the **Dates** table as a date table helps ensure that DAX time intelligence measures operate properly. Now create the following four measures:

```
                Internet Sales = SUM( 'FactInternetSales'[SalesAmount] )

Internet Sales (YTD) =

    CALCULATE(

        [Internet Sales],

        'Dates'[Year] = MAX( 'Dates'[Year] ) &&

        'Dates'[Date] <= MAX( 'Dates'[Date] )

    )

            Internet Sales (TOTALYTD) = TOTALYTD( [Internet Sales], 'Dates'[Date] )

NC Internet Sales (YTD) =

    VAR __Date = MAX( 'Dates'[Date] )

    VAR __Year = YEAR( __Date )

    VAR __Table =

        SUMMARIZE(

            ALL( 'FactInternetSales' ),

            'FactInternetSales'[OrderDate],

            "__Year", YEAR( [OrderDate] ),

            "__Sales", SUM( 'FactInternetSales'[SalesAmount] )

        )

    VAR __Result =

        SUMX(

            FILTER( __Table, [__Year] = __Year && [OrderDate] <= __Date ),

            [__Sales]

        )

RETURN

    __Result
```

The first two measures represent the traditional **CALCULATE** approach to DAX where a base measure is created, **Internet Sales**, and then **CALCULATE** is used to modify the context under which that measure is calculated. The third measure is the traditional time "intelligence" approach to DAX while the fourth measure is instantly recognizable as a classic No CALCULATE pattern.

Create three identical **Table** visuals that include the **Date** column from the **Dates** table. Place the **Internet Sales (YTD)** measure into one of these table visuals, the **Internet Sales (TOTALYTD)** measure into another of these table visuals and the **NC Internet Sales (YTD)** measure in the last table visual.

Open the **Selection** pane by clicking on the **View** tab in the ribbon and then clicking the **Selection** pane in the **Show panes** area. Rename the visuals in the **Selection** pane to help identify which measure is in which visual.

Now open the **Performance analyzer** pane and record the timings for the three visuals. The timings for the test machine are shown here:

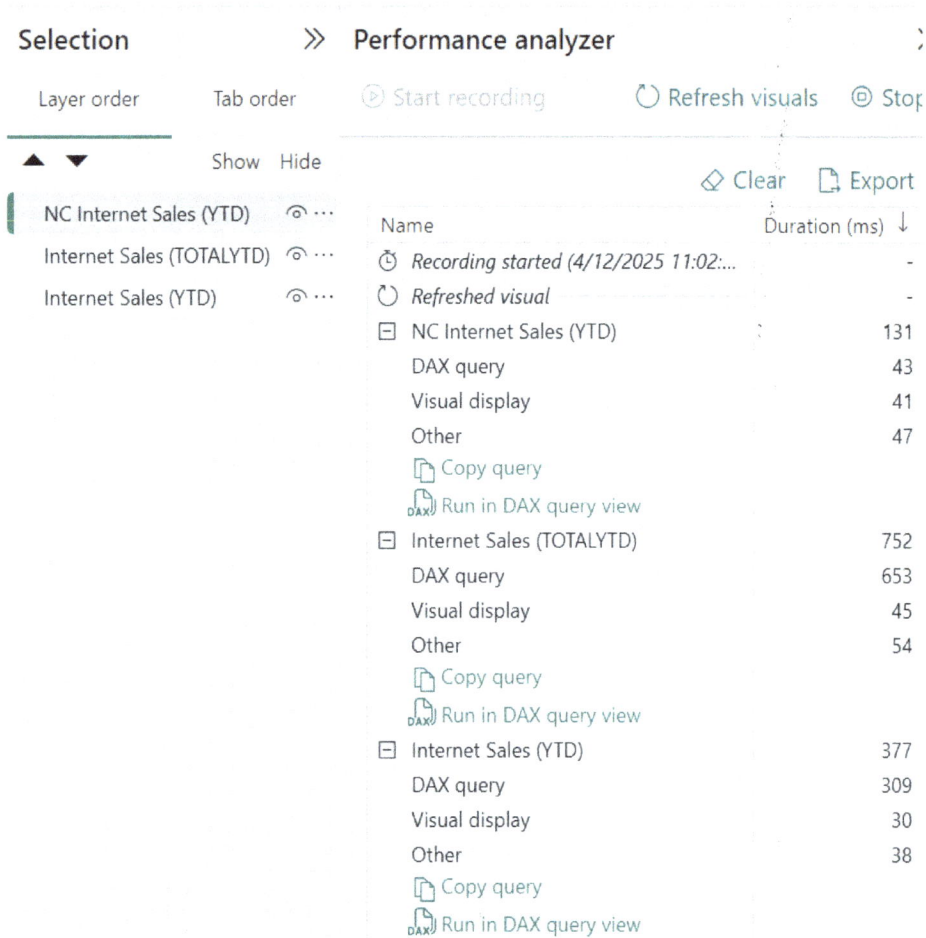

Figure 15.10: Performance analyzer timings

Looking at just the **DAX query** times, the **NC Internet Sales (YTD)** measure took **43 milliseconds** while the **Internet Sales (TOTALYTD)** measure took **653 milliseconds** and the **Internet Sales (YTD)** measure took **309 milliseconds**. Clearly, the No CALCULATE version of the measure is an order of magnitude faster than the traditional **CALCULATE** approach.

Perhaps even more surprising is the fact that the purpose-built function that literally has one job, **TOTALYTD**, was the slowest of the three measures by a wide margin. To put this a different way, the **NC Internet Sales (YTD)** measure is **89% faster** than the traditional **CALCULATE** approach and **94% faster** than using the **TOTALYTD** function.

It is perhaps worth mentioning that the No CALCULATE approach actually returns the same results within the same duration if the relationship between the **Dates** table and **FactInternetSales** table doesn't exist. The same is decidedly not true for either the traditional **CALCULATE** approach or the time intelligence approach which just return the total amount of the **SalesAmount** column across all years for all dates.

Obviously, the No CALCULATE approach is far superior in this specific case than either the traditional CALCULATE approach or traditional time intelligence approach. While this is not necessarily true in absolutely all cases, it is important to keep in mind that different approaches to DAX can lead to wildly different performance of your DAX measures.

In general, the No CALCULATE approach to DAX tends to lead the FE down a path where it can create an efficient query plan. It is worth noting that the **NC Internet Sales (YTD)** measure generates four SE queries while the **Internet Sales (TOTALYTD)** measure generates six. The **Internet Sales (YTD)** measure also generates four SE queries, but they are less efficient than those generated by the **NC Internet Sales (YTD)** measure.

It should be clear that even the most diehard **CALCULATE** and DAX time intelligence fan should keep the No CALCULATE approach in mind when troubleshooting DAX performance issues.

Let's next explore a second scenario where we compare the performance of the **CALCULATE** and No CALCULATE approaches.

CALCULATE vs No CALCULATE Act 2

For our next scenario, we will use another real-world scenario that is perhaps a bit less common. The basic problem is trying to determine which individuals attended events on one date but not another date. This may seem like a straightforward scenario but, trust me, it is anything but.

To prepare for this scenario, download the **Chapter 15.pbit** file which can be found in the GitHub repository for this book: https://github.com/gdeckler/DAX-For-Humans/tree/main/book. This file has been specifically prepared for this exact scenario.

Upon opening the Power BI template file, a data refresh will automatically occur. This refresh will create a fact table called **Table** that contains about 730 million rows. Each row consists of a **Date** column and an **ID** column. In addition, there are two tables called **Dates** and **Dates2**.

The fact table contains the Cartesian product between all dates in 2023 and 2024, and a list of sequential ids numbered from 1 to 1 million. However, the IDs 1,000,000 and 999,999 do not appear for any dates in 2024. Thus, if picking any date in 2023 and then any date in 2024, IDs 1,000,000 and 999,999 would appear as the IDs that attended on the date in 2023 but not on the date in 2024.

Once the refresh is completed, be sure to save the file. The total file size is approximately 1 GB, and the semantic model looks like the following:

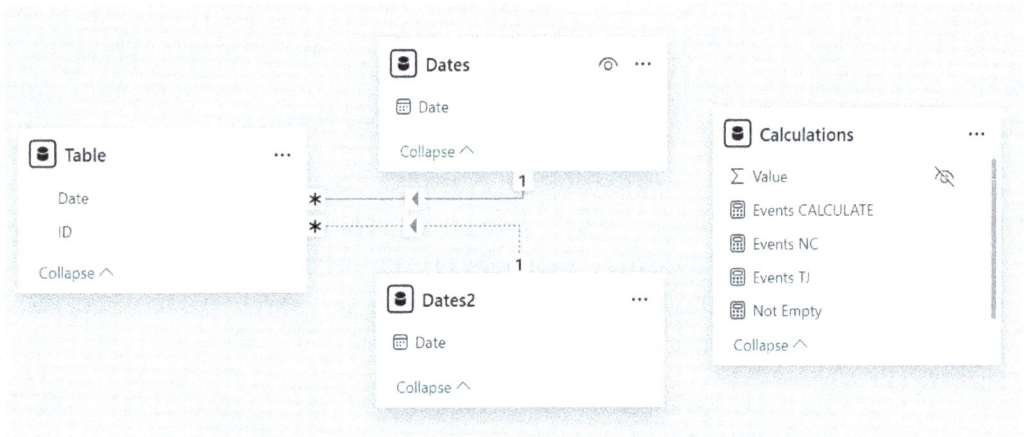

Figure 15.11: Events scenario semantic model

Once the report loads, you will see two slicers, one for dates in 2023 and one for dates in 2024. In addition, there are three table visuals. Each of the table visuals include the ID column from the table named **Table**. In addition, each table visual contains one of the following three measures:

```
Events CALCULATE =

    VAR __Table =

        CALCULATETABLE(

            DISTINCT( 'Table'[ID] ),

            ALL('Table'),
```

```
                    USERELATIONSHIP( Dates2[Date], 'Table'[Date] )

        )

    VAR __Result = COUNTROWS( EXCEPT( DISTINCT( 'Table'[ID] ), __Table ) )
RETURN

    __Result
```

The **Events CALCULATE** measure uses **CALCULATETABLE** as a surrogate for **CALCULATE**. Both functions are effectively identical except that **CALCULATETABLE** returns a table while **CALCULATE** returns a scalar.

The __**Table** variable contains all unique IDs from **Table** as filtered by the dates chosen in the **Dates2** table (2024 slicer). It then simply performs an **EXCEPT** between the IDs filtered by the **Dates** table (2023 slicer) and the calculated table __**Table**. The result is the IDs that were in 2023 that were not in 2024.

```
Events NC =
    VAR __ID = MAX( 'Table'[ID] )
    VAR __Dates2 = DISTINCT( 'Dates2'[Date] )
    VAR __Table1 = DISTINCT( 'Table'[ID] )
    VAR __Table2 =
        SELECTCOLUMNS( FILTER(ALL('Table'), [Date] IN __Dates2), "ID", [ID] )
    VAR __Table = EXCEPT( __Table1, __Table2 )
    VAR __Result = IF( __ID IN __Table, 1, 0 )
RETURN

    __Result
```

The **Events NC** measure effectively attempts to do the same thing as the **Events CALCULATE** measure except that it does not have the benefit of being able to use the **USERELATIONSHIP** function. Therefore, the method of getting the IDs associated with events in 2024 (Dates2 table) is more convoluted.

The final measure is one created by patron **Tamer Juma** as an alternate No CALCULATE method:

```
Events TJ =
    VAR __Result =
        COUNTROWS(
```

```
            FILTER(

                DISTINCT( 'Table'[ID] ),

                ISEMPTY(

                    FILTER(

                        TREATAS( ALLSELECTED( 'Dates2'[Date] ), Dates[Date] ),

                        [Not Empty]

                    )

                )

            )

        )

RETURN

    __Result
```

Here, since the **USERELATIONSHIP** function is not available, the **TREATAS** function is used instead.

Once the report is rendered, both the tables containing the **Events CALCULATE** measure and the **Events TJ** measure return 1 for IDs **1000000** and **999999**, correctly identifying the desired IDs. However, the table visual containing the **Events NC** measure likely errors out complaining that resources have been exceeded.

In short, while the **Events NC** measure performs with sub second response times when dealing with 1000 IDs, when the number of IDs is increased by two orders of magnitude, the query plan and storage engine queries quickly decline in performance. It should be stressed that this is not a common occurrence with the No CALCULATE approach but rather it is something specific to this scenario that causes the FE and SE to arrive at suboptimal solutions.

Ignoring the **Events NC** measure's performance when conducting performance tests using the **Performance analyzer** pane (because it errors out), we can test the performance of the **Events CALCULATE** and **Events TJ** measures. With a single date selected in each slicer, the **Events TJ** measure is notably slower than the **Events CALCULATE** measure but still performs within an acceptable range.

⊟ No CALCULATE TJ	1383
DAX query	1324
Visual display	13
Other	46
📄 Copy query	
⬛ Run in DAX query view	
⊞ No CALCULATE	1219
⊟ CALCULATE	1034
DAX query	970
Visual display	15
Other	49

Figure 15.12: Performance of Events CALCULATE and Events TJ measures

Here the **Events CALCULATE** measure represented by the visual named **CALCULATE** is a respectable 27% faster than the **Events TJ** measure represented by the visual named **No CALCULATE TJ**. However, as more dates are selected, this performance difference increases. For example, with nine dates selected in each slicer, the performance is as follows:

⊟ No CALCULATE TJ	2748
DAX query	2649
Visual display	18
Other	81
📄 Copy query	
⬛ Run in DAX query view	
⊞ No CALCULATE	1378
⊟ CALCULATE	1096
DAX query	985
Visual display	30
Other	81

Figure 15.13: Performance of Events CALCULATE and Events TJ measures

As you can see, while the **Events CALCULATE** measure keeps the same basic performance parameters, the **Events TJ** measure now takes twice as long with respect to its DAX query timing. The **Events CALCULATE** measure is now 63% faster than the **Events TJ** measure.

It should be clear now that there is no "one size fits all" when it comes to DAX performance optimization. Optimization techniques and methods must be adapted to the particular circumstances of the calculations and semantic model.

Summary

Optimizing DAX is both an art and a science. This chapter explored the practical side of improving DAX performance without altering the semantic model. While one can get mired in the complexity regarding the inner workings of the Formula Engine and Storage Engine, this chapter instead sought to distill the knowledge into actionable techniques. We introduced essential tools like Performance Analyzer, DAX Studio, and Power Optimizer, which help diagnose bottlenecks, pinpoint inefficiencies, and even recommend changes. Through a hands-on example involving performance analysis, this chapter demonstrated how refining logic structures, reducing nested **IF** statements, and applying techniques like row filtering and logic consolidation can reduce calculation times from nearly ten minutes to just six seconds—an astounding 99% performance improvement.

This chapter also contrasted the traditional CALCULATE-based DAX with the No CALCULATE approach, showing that in many cases, the latter can significantly outperform both standard DAX and time intelligence functions like **TOTALYTD**. However, edge cases are also highlighted to caution that not all optimization techniques are universally effective; performance gains depend on context, semantic model design, and query patterns. Ultimately, the key takeaway is to focus on writing efficient, context-aware DAX code that minimizes reliance on the slower Formula Engine, maximizes delegation to the high-speed Storage Engine, and emphasizes logical clarity and early row filtering wherever possible.

CHAPTER
16

16

AI, Debugging, and CALCULATE

In this chapter, we dive headfirst into the new frontier of writing DAX with the help of generative **artificial intelligence** (**AI**). Instead of relying on vague prompts and hoping for the best, we walk through a practical, structured process, pioneered by patron Brian Julius, that feeds a chatbot the information it actually needs, the BIM file from your semantic model. Armed with that, AI tools like ChatGPT can produce not just plausible DAX, but accurate, performant, and context-aware code that works within your specific semantic model. The real magic isn't just the AI; it's the context you give it. We also walk through a real-world example where AI goes from a wrong-but-reasonable guess to a spot-on solution in two iterations. And the best part? It's done in seconds.

From there, we jump into the murky world of DAX debugging. Context issues, circular dependencies, cryptic errors, yep, we tackle all of that. We show how to peel apart a DAX expression using variables, log what's happening with **TOCSV** and **EVALUATEANDLOG**, and even get the DAX engine to inform us what filters are in play. Finally, we talk about, yes, that function, **CALCULATE**. You've heard it's the most powerful function in DAX. Maybe. But it's also the most opaque, overhyped, and needlessly confusing one too. So, we tear it down, show you how it really works (or doesn't), and make the case that maybe, just maybe, you don't need it as much as you've been told.

Using Artificial Intelligence (AI) to Write DAX

As the complexity and scale of Power BI solutions grows, so too does the demand for faster, smarter ways to develop DAX (Data Analysis Expressions) code. Luckily, with the transformative technology of generative AI and **large language models** (**LLMs**), many mundane tasks can now be automated, including accelerating and democratizing DAX development. From generating first drafts of measures to debugging logic and optimizing performance, AI is becoming a valuable partner in the modern Power BI developer's toolkit. But while AI can suggest syntax and structures, it still requires a human expert to ensure business logic, context, and intent are correctly applied.

While DAX code can be generated using simple prompts to common AI chatbots such as **ChatGPT**, **Copilot**, **Claude Sonnet**, and **Gemini**, such DAX code is generally generic and must be adapted to work within a specific semantic model. However, there is a process that can provide much more accurate DAX code that works perfectly within specific semantic models. This process was pioneered by patron Brian Julius and is the process covered in this section.

The trick to this process is to provide the chatbot with more information about the semantic model so that the DAX measure works perfectly with that semantic model. We can use a **business intelligence model (.bim)** file for this purpose. A **BIM** file is a text file in JSON format that describes a Power BI semantic model. We can generate a BIM file quite easily in one of two ways.

One way to generate a BIM file is to use a preview feature in Power BI Desktop. This preview feature is the **Power BI Project (.pbip) save option**. This preview feature can be activated by going to **File | Options and settings | Options** in Power BI Desktop and then in the **Options** dialog, check the box for **Power BI Project (.pbip) save option**. Importantly, do NOT check the two checkboxes below this feature.

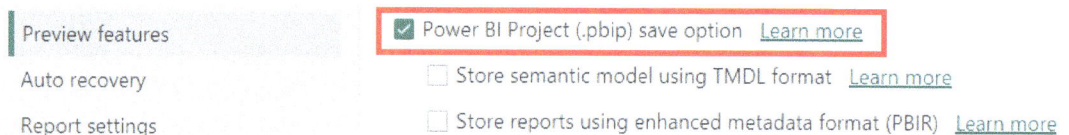

Figure 16.1: Power BI Project (.pbip) save option preview feature

After this feature is activated, you can use **File | Save as** to save the file as a Power BI Project (.pbip) file. Doing so creates the .pbip file as well as two folders, one ending in **.Report** and one ending in **.SemanticModel**. Inside the **.SemanticModel** folder you will find a **model.bim** file.

The second way to generate a BIM file is to use **Tabular Editor**. Even the free version of Tabular Editor (Tabular Editor 2.x) can generate a BIM file quite easily. Tabular Editor 2.x can be downloaded here: https://tabulareditor.github.io/TabularEditor/.

Once installed, simply connect Tabular Editor to the Power BI analysis services instance, or open your Power BI file in Power BI Desktop and choose **Tabular Editor** from the **External Tools** tab of the ribbon. Once connected, choose **File | Save As...** to save the .bim file.

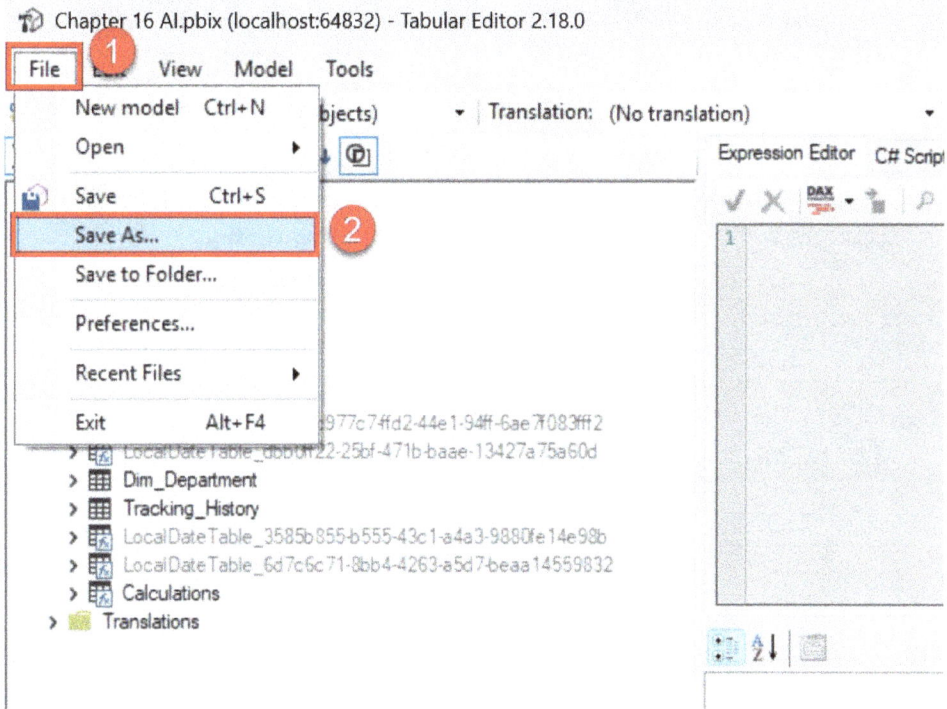

Figure 16.2: Creating a BIM file in Tabular Editor 2.x

Patron Recommendation

Alexis Olson finds that the BIM files can be bloated, so he runs a script in Tabular Editor to clean up much of the junk before saving it. You can often cut up to 80% of the file size by removing stuff like the linguistic metadata: https://gist.github.com/AlexisOlson/8cff91128d02d0b1857a93101309eb7b.

To explore a specific scenario of using AI to generate DAX code, import the **DateTimeTable**, **Dim_Department**, and **Tracking_History** sheets from the Excel spreadsheet, **Chapter16_Data.xlsx** which can be found in the GitHub repository for this book: https://github.com/gdeckler/DAX-For-Humans/tree/main/book.

Create a relationship between the **Dim_Department** and **Tracking_History** tables using the common **Department ID** columns in both tables. Your semantic model should look like the following:

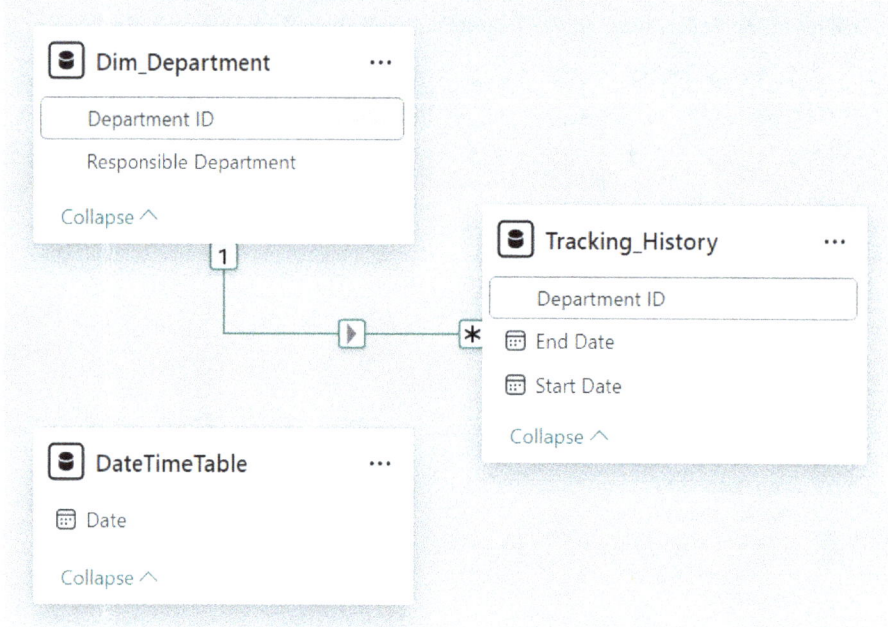

Figure 16.3: Scenario semantic model

You may recognize this model and scenario from *Chapter 15*. In fact, this is the exact same data and semantic model as used in the *General example* section of *Chapter 15*. Recall that there were nine iterations of improving the measure performance to go from a measure that took over 10 minutes to return to one that took mere seconds to return.

Save your work and then generate the BIM file for this model using one of the two techniques covered earlier in this section. Now that you have the BIM file, we can use this BIM file while prompting the chatbot. In our case, we are using ChatGPT 4o which supports multi-modal inputs. If the chatbot only supports text, you can copy the contents of the BIM file and paste these contents into the chatbot prompt.

To upload the BIM file in ChatGPT 4o, use the **+** icon and then choose **Upload from computer**:

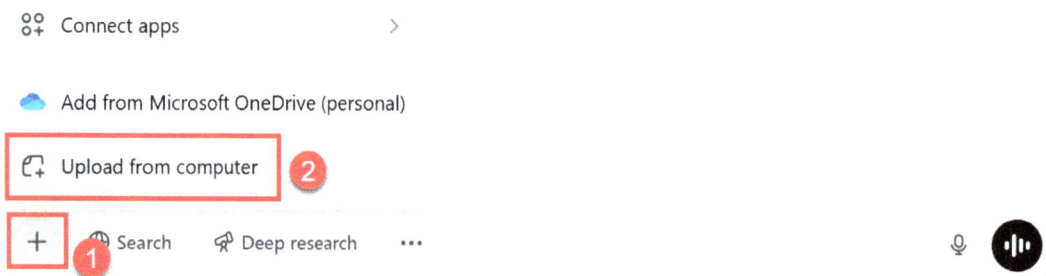

Figure 16.4: Uploading a file in ChatGPT 4o

The following is an actual chatbot conversation with ChatGPT 4o after uploading the specified BIM file:

Start of Chat

The attached BIM file contains the model information for a Power BI semantic model. For a visual containing the Date column from the DateTimeTable table as the x-axis and the Responsible Department column from the Dim_Department table as the legend, create a DAX measure that will be used as the y-axis. This measure should count the number of transactions in the Tracking_History table that were performed by each department during the hourly time interval specified in the x-axis.

ChatGPT said:

Based on the BIM model structure, we have the following:

- `DateTimeTable[Date]`: to be used as the x-axis (assumed to contain datetime values, down to hour level).

- `Dim_Department[Responsible Department]`: used as the legend.

- `Tracking_History` has:

    o `Start Date`: the datetime of each transaction.

    o `Department ID`: which links to `Dim_Department[Department ID]`.

To create a measure that counts the number of transactions per department and hour, we assume the following relationships:

- `Tracking_History[Department ID]` → `Dim_Department[Department ID]`

- `Tracking_History[Start Date]` → `DateTimeTable[Date]` (on datetime granularity)

Here is the DAX measure:

```
Transactions Per Hour =
CALCULATE (
    COUNTROWS (Tracking_History),
    TREATAS (
        VALUES (DateTimeTable[Date]),
        Tracking_History[Start Date]
    )
)
```

Explanation:

- TREATAS aligns the DateTimeTable[Date] context (from the x-axis) with Tracking_History[Start Date], enabling filtering by hour.

- COUNTROWS(Tracking_History) gives the count of transactions in that filtered context.

Would you like me to add this DAX measure directly into the BIM file and return the updated version?

You said:

That measure is not correct. The measure needs to return the count based on the Start Date and End Date must be less than the current x-axis time.

ChatGPT said:

Thanks for the clarification — you're looking to count transactions where:

- Tracking_History[Start Date] is on or before the current hour (from the x-axis),

- and Tracking_History[End Date] is after the current hour.

This suggests the goal is to count all active transactions at a given hour interval, filtered by department.

Here is the corrected DAX measure:

```
Active Transactions Per Hour =
VAR CurrentHour = SELECTEDVALUE(DateTimeTable[Date])
RETURN
CALCULATE(
    COUNTROWS(Tracking_History),
    FILTER(
        Tracking_History,
        Tracking_History[Start Date] <= CurrentHour &&
        Tracking_History[End Date] > CurrentHour
    )
)
```

What it does:

- SELECTEDVALUE(DateTimeTable[Date]) gets the current hour on the x-axis.

- The FILTER condition checks for active transactions during that exact hour.

- The visual must be sliced by both `DateTimeTable[Date]` and `Dim_Department[Responsible Department]`, which will handle grouping by department due to existing relationships.

Would you like me to inject this measure into the BIM model and provide the updated file?

You said:

That measure is exactly correct, can you create a version of the measure that does not use the CALCULATE function?

ChatGPT said:

Absolutely — here's a version of the same measure logic without using **CALCULATE**, using SUMX and FILTER instead:

```
Active Transactions Per Hour (No CALCULATE) =
VAR CurrentHour = SELECTEDVALUE(DateTimeTable[Date])
RETURN
SUMX(
    FILTER(
        Tracking_History,
        Tracking_History[Start Date] <= CurrentHour &&
        Tracking_History[End Date] > CurrentHour
    ),
    1
)
```

Explanation:

- SUMX iterates over the filtered rows of `Tracking_History`.

- Each matching row contributes 1, effectively counting them.

- The logic is exactly the same as before — this just avoids CALCULATE, which can be useful for debugging or experimenting with row context-based aggregations.

Let me know if you'd like this version or the original added to the BIM file, or both.

End of Chat

Recall that this same scenario from *Chapter 15, Optimizing Performance* took us nine iterations to arrive at a truly performant solution. The last two measures created by ChatGPT both returned in about 3 seconds on the same test machine used previously. And, bonus, we can simply copy the code and paste it into Power BI when creating a measure and the measure works flawlessly! Obviously, ChatGPT and other LLMs can write some impressive DAX code!

What is perhaps most impressive about this chat session however is that the second prompt isn't even very clear, but the AI was able to reason out what was intended and return the desired result. While AI may or may not take over the world one day, today AI tools like ChatGPT 4o and other similar models are extremely good at writing code and, given adequate information, are able to generate accurate and performant DAX code. The key, however, is providing the AI models with as much information as possible and including the BIM file is a great shortcut for doing exactly that.

Let's now move on to the subject of debugging DAX code.

Debugging DAX

When writing any kind of code, one will inevitably need to fix problems (debug) and DAX is no exception. Luckily, if you are following the No CALCULATE approach to DAX, you are already ahead of the curve when it comes to debugging your DAX code. The reason is that the No CALCLULATE approach breaks problems down into steps, using a variable (**VAR**) for each step. Thus, you can easily modify the **RETURN** statement to return any of the intermediate steps in your DAX calculation. This is invaluable because the results of DAX calculations are dependent upon context and thus being able to see intermediate steps in context is critical to debugging efforts.

As covered in *Chapter 2, More Core Concepts* in the section *Visualizing Your DAX*, you can use **TOCSV** to return variables that contain tables. Prior to the existence of the **TOCSV** function, we used to use the **CONCATENATEX** function to achieve similar results. While the combination of variables and the **TOCSV** function will likely solve 90% of the debugging situations you find yourself handling, this section delves even deeper into DAX debugging to demonstrate several additional, more advanced debugging techniques as well as how to handle errors and other specific topics such as circular dependencies.

To start this debugging section, however, let's see how we can use artificial intelligence to help us debug DAX.

Debugging with AI

If you have not completed the section, *Using Artificial Intelligence (AI) to Write DAX*, please do so now as the techniques used in that section are required for this section. Debugging using AI is effectively the same basic process as writing DAX using AI. We still want to convey as much information to the AI as possible so we will still want to upload the BIM file before prompting the AI further.

In this scenario, instead of creating the DAX code from scratch via prompting, we instead start by asking ChatGPT 4o to improve the performance of the original **No. of Orders** measure and then use ChatGTP 4o to fix issues in the resulting DAX code. Consider the following chat session initiated after uploading the same BIM file as before:

Start of Chat

Using the BIM file for reference, the following DAX code is running extremely slowly, can you improve and optimize this measure for performance?

```
No. of Orders =
    VAR __StartDate = VALUE ( SELECTEDVALUE ( 'Tracking_History'[Start Date] ) )
    VAR __EndDate = VALUE ( SELECTEDVALUE ( 'Tracking_History'[End Date] ) )
    VAR __MinDate = VALUE ( MIN ( 'DateTimeTable'[Date] ) )
    VAR __MaxDate = VALUE ( MAX ( 'DateTimeTable'[Date] ) )
    VAR __Result =
        IF(
            AND( __StartDate > __MinDate, __EndDate < __MaxDate ),
            1,
            IF (
                AND(
                    AND ( __StartDate > __MinDate, __EndDate > __MaxDate ),
                    __MaxDate > __StartDate
                ),
                1,
                IF(
                    AND(
                        AND ( __StartDate < __MinDate, __EndDate < __MaxDate ),
                        __EndDate > __MinDate
                    ),
                    1,
                    IF(
                        AND ( __StartDate < __MinDate, __EndDate > __MaxDate ),
                        1,
```

```
                            BLANK ()

                    )

                )

            )

        )

RETURN

    __Result
```

ChatGPT said:

Yes — that measure is inefficient primarily because it's trying to evaluate a complex branching logic row-by-row, using scalar values and multiple nested IF statements, all within a visual context. Additionally:

- SELECTEDVALUE(Tracking_History[Start Date]) and SELECTEDVALUE(Tracking_History[End Date]) return scalars — not row context aware inside visuals.
- The current logic is trying to manually simulate overlap logic using scalar comparisons, which results in poor performance especially on large datasets.

Optimized Version of the Measure:

Here's a much faster and scalable version using COUNTROWS + FILTER — this computes how many Tracking_History records overlap with the visual's x-axis range, using vectorized filtering:

```
No. of Orders (Optimized) =

VAR MinDate = MIN('DateTimeTable'[Date])

VAR MaxDate = MAX('DateTimeTable'[Date])

RETURN

COUNTROWS(

    FILTER(

        ALL('Tracking_History'),

        Tracking_History[Start Date] < MaxDate &&

        Tracking_History[End Date] > MinDate

    )

)
```

Performance Improvements

1. Uses table filters instead of row-by-row logic — this leverages the VertiPaq engine's strength.
2. Avoids SELECTEDVALUE for Tracking_History columns, which doesn't work well in a row context.
3. Uses ALL(Tracking_History) to ignore filters that would otherwise restrict the scope unexpectedly.
4. Overlap logic simplified to one expression:
    *   Start < MaxDate && End > MinDate correctly captures any overlap with the interval.

Optional Filter Preservation

If you don't want to ignore slicers on Tracking_History, remove the ALL:

```
No. of Orders (Optimized with Filters) =

VAR MinDate = MIN('DateTimeTable'[Date])

VAR MaxDate = MAX('DateTimeTable'[Date])

RETURN

COUNTROWS(

    FILTER(

        Tracking_History,

        Tracking_History[Start Date] < MaxDate &&

        Tracking_History[End Date] > MinDate

    )

)
```

Let me know if you'd like this rewritten into your BIM file as a new measure, or integrated into a visual-specific calculation.

End of Chat

While this scenario primarily highlights performance improvements, which is a type of debugging, AI can similarly solve other debugging issues just by describing the problem and providing enough information for the AI to diagnose the issue. What is remarkable about this chat session is that the **Total Orders** measure was not included in the chat, only the original **No. of Orders** measure. However, the AI was able to diagnose the overall intent when creating the measure for improved performance. Furthermore, the AI anticipated a potential issue with using the **ALL** function and provided an alternative measure that preserved filters. The above measures return in approximately 6-7 seconds on the same test machine as used in *Chapter 15, Optimizing Performance,* so the performance improvement is substantial although not the absolute best we have seen.

Clearly, using AI is not a bad first choice when it comes to debugging measures. However, let's explore some more manual methods of debugging starting with error handling.

Handling Errors

Handling errors in DAX is both a necessity and a skill that separates resilient models from brittle ones. DAX does not fail silently. When something goes wrong, DAX usually throws a visible error that often breaks the display of visuals. These messages, while sometimes cryptic, are signals that the logic or calculation needs refinement. Common causes of DAX errors include type mismatches, incorrect use of context-modifying functions, or referencing columns or measures that return incompatible structures. Understanding the source of these issues requires familiarity with evaluation context, function categories, and the semantic model's relationships.

To manage and prevent errors proactively, DAX offers functions like **ERROR**, **IFERROR**, and **ISERROR**. These functions can generate and catch errors and return alternative values or fallback logic to maintain a smooth user experience. For example, IFERROR([Measure], 0) ensures that a blank or erroneous calculation doesn't disrupt a report visual with an error message. When used thoughtfully, error handling in DAX not only safeguards your report and model from breaking but also improves interpretability, especially in dynamic reporting environments where data changes frequently or user inputs vary.

The **ERROR** function allows you to raise your own custom errors. To demonstrate this, create the following measure:

```
Error = ERROR( "Something bad happened" )
```

Placing this measure into a **Card** visual predictably breaks the visual. Clicking on the **See details** link displays the custom error message:

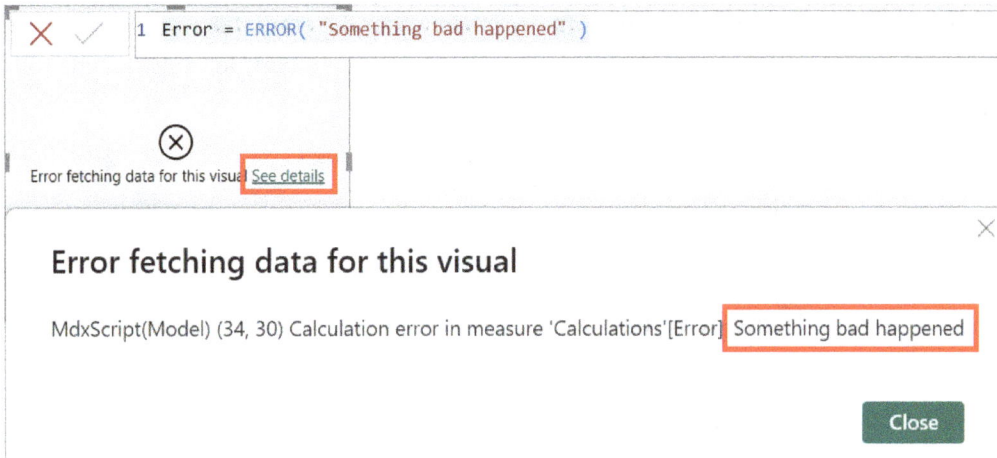

Figure 16.5: Generating a custom error message

To prevent the visual from breaking, we can use **ISERROR** or **IFERROR**. For example, create the following two measures:

```
IsError =
    IF(
        ISERROR(
            ERROR( "Something bad happened" )
        ),
        "Something bad happened",
        "Everything is good"
    )
IfError =
    IFERROR(
        ERROR( "Something bad happened" ),
        "Something bad happened"
    )
```

Placing each of these measures into their own **Card** visuals displays "Something bad happened" for both visuals.

Obviously, simply repeating the error message as text is likely not an effective solution for most situations and neither is simply using the **ERROR** function to generate an error. Both are used simply as examples. Instead, one can use the **IFERROR** function like a try/catch block in other programming languages. In the event of an error, the second parameter can instead attempt to perform a different calculation or return an alternate value. For example, consider the following measure:

```
IfError 2 = IFERROR( 100 / 1, 0 )
```

This measure returns the value **100**. However, this next measure:

```
IfError 3 = IFERROR( 100 / 0, 0 )
```

This measure returns **0** since dividing by zero generates an error. Note that it is possible to nest **IFERROR** statements.

IFERROR and **ISERROR** statements should be used sparingly in production calculations because both functions can negatively impact the performance of a measure in a significant way. In the case of the **IfError2** and **IfError3** measures, a better solution would be to use the error tolerant function, **DIVIDE**. Other error tolerant functions include **SELECTEDVALUE**, **LOOKUPVALUE**, **FIND**, and **SEARCH**.

Now that we understand error handling in DAX, let's next look at debugging context.

Debugging Context

One of the somewhat novel aspects of the DAX language is the concept of context where the same code can produce different results depending on the context in which the formula is evaluated. In fact, debugging context in DAX is one of the most crucial, and often most challenging, aspects of mastering the language.

Unlike traditional programming languages, DAX operates within two types of contexts, row context and filter context, both of which influence how a measure or calculated column behaves. Most errors in DAX logic aren't syntax-related but stem from misunderstandings about which context is active during evaluation.

For example, a measure may return unexpected results because a filter from a slicer is silently overriding a column filter in **CALCULATE**, or because context transition (such as using a measure inside **ROW** or **SUMX**) introduced a filter unexpectedly. Understanding what context exists when your code runs is essential for interpreting why your measure behaves the way it does.

The No CALCULATE approach is specifically designed to minimize issues with context and make debugging context issues easier. This is done using variables as well as avoiding the **CALCULATE** function since the obtuse internal workings and context transitions of the **CALCULATE** function make debugging rather difficult, if not impossible.

Despite how important content is to DAX, the actual DAX language has a dearth of DAX functions for dealing with context. In fact, the first place to look regarding understanding context is at the visual level. Each visual includes a filters icon that reports on the active filters affecting a visual as shown here:

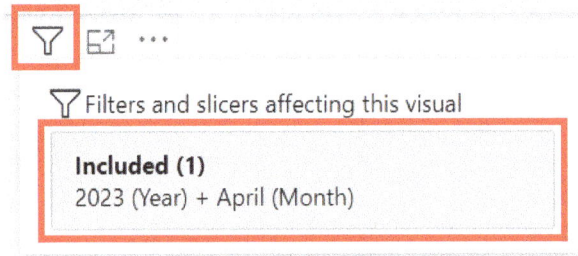

Figure 16.6: Filters icon showing active filters (context) for a visual

Within DAX itself, there are three functions that can report information about context, **FILTERS**, **ISFILTERED**, and **ISCROSSFILTERED**. To see how we can use these functions, create the following table:

```
Dates =
    ADDCOLUMNS(
        CALENDAR( DATE( 2023, 1, 1 ), DATE( 2025, 12, 31 ) ),
        "Year", YEAR( [Date] ),
        "Month", FORMAT( [Date], "mmmm" ),
        "MonthSort", MONTH( [Date] ),
        "Weekday", FORMAT( [Date], "dddd" )
    )
```

Now set the **MonthSort** column as the **Sort by column** for the **Month** column. Next, create a **Table** visual containing an un-summarized **Year** column as well as the **Month** column.

The **FILTERS** function takes a column reference as its only input and returns a table of values that are directly applied as filters to that column. For example, we can create the following measure:

```
Filters = TOCSV( FILTERS( 'Dates'[Month] ) )
```

Adding this measure to our **Table** visual displays the filter values for the **Month** column for each row.

The **ISFILTERED** function takes a table or column reference as its only parameter and returns true if the table or column is directly filtered while the **ISCROSSFILTERD** function returns true if the table or column is directly filtered or a column from a related table is filtered.

We can create a measure to report on the various filters active within the context of a visual and use this measure in a tooltip. For example, we can create the following measure:

```
All Filters =
    VAR __YearFilters = FILTERS( 'Dates'[Year] )

    VAR __MonthFilters = FILTERS( 'Dates'[Month] )

    VAR __MonthSortFilters = FILTERS( 'Dates'[MonthSort] )

    VAR __WeekdayFilters = FILTERS( 'Dates'[Weekday] )


    VAR __YearTable = TOCSV( __YearFilters )

    VAR __MonthTable = TOCSV( __MonthFilters )

    VAR __MonthSortTable = TOCSV( __MonthSortFilters )

    VAR __WeekdayTable = TOCSV( __WeekdayFilters )


    VAR __YearText = SUBSTITUTE( __YearTable, UNICHAR( 10 ), "|" )

    VAR __MonthText = SUBSTITUTE( __MonthTable, UNICHAR( 10 ), "|" )

    VAR __MonthSortText = SUBSTITUTE( __MonthSortTable, UNICHAR( 10 ), "|" )

    VAR __WeekdayText = SUBSTITUTE( __WeekdayTable, UNICHAR( 10 ), "|" )


    VAR __YearValue = PATHITEM( __YearText, 1 ) & ": " &
                        CONCATENATEX( __YearFilters, 'Dates'[Year], ", " )
    VAR __MonthValue = PATHITEM( __MonthText, 1 ) & ": " &
                        CONCATENATEX( __MonthFilters, 'Dates'[Month], ", " )
    VAR __MonthSortValue = PATHITEM( __MonthSortText, 1 ) & ": " &
                        CONCATENATEX(__MonthSortFilters,'Dates'[MonthSort],", ")
    VAR __WeekdayValue = PATHITEM( __WeekdayText, 1 ) & ": " &
                        CONCATENATEX( __WeekdayFilters, 'Dates'[Weekday], ", " )
```

```
VAR __Table =
    {
        IF( ISFILTERED( 'Dates'[Year] ), __YearValue ),
        IF( ISFILTERED( 'Dates'[Month] ), __MonthValue ),
        IF( ISFILTERED( 'Dates'[MonthSort] ), __MonthSortValue ),
        IF( ISFILTERED( 'Dates'[Weekday] ), __WeekdayValue )
    }
VAR __Result = CONCATENATEX( __Table, [Value], UNICHAR( 10 ) & UNICHAR( 13 ) )
RETURN
    __Result
```

We can create a tooltip report page, add this measure to a table visualization and then activate a report page tooltip for our **Table** visual. The result is as follows:

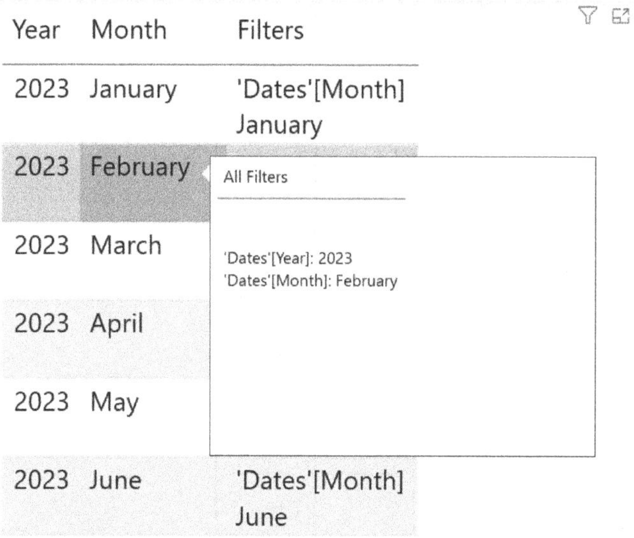

Year	Month	Filters
2023	January	'Dates'[Month] January
2023	February	
2023	March	
2023	April	
2023	May	
2023	June	'Dates'[Month] June

All Filters

'Dates'[Year]: 2023
'Dates'[Month]: February

Figure 16.7: Filters icon showing active filters (context) for a visual

This completes our discussion regarding debugging context in DAX. Let's now look at circular dependencies.

Circular Dependencies

A **circular dependency** in Power BI occurs when two or more calculated columns or measures depend on each other either directly or indirectly, creating a loop that the calculation engine cannot resolve. For example, if Column1 references Column2, and Column2 references

Column1, the model enters a state where it doesn't know which calculation to evaluate first. This results in an error because DAX calculations require a clear, acyclic order of operations.

Circular dependencies can also arise when using calculated columns for relationships, creating relationships involving calculated tables, or when using the **CALCULATE** function in calculated columns. Avoiding or resolving circular dependencies typically involves redesigning the logic to break the cycle, simplifying dependencies, or shifting calculations to a different layer such as Power Query.

To explore circular dependencies, use an **Enter data** query to create the following table called **Table**:

Index	Value
1	One
2	Two
3	Three
4	Four
5	One
6	Two
7	Three
8	Four
9	One
10	Two

Table 16.1: Table data

Now create the following two identical columns:

```
Val1 = CALCULATE( MAX( 'Table'[Value] ), 'Table'[Index] > 1 )

Val2 = CALCULATE( MAX( 'Table'[Value] ), 'Table'[Index] > 1 )
```

Unexpectedly, you receive a circular dependency error creating the second column.

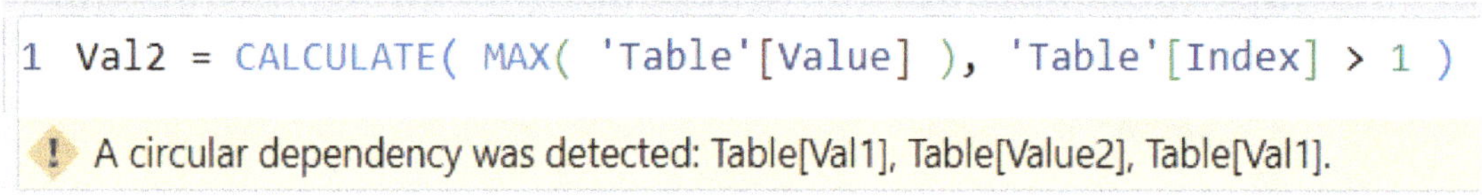

```
1  Val2 = CALCULATE( MAX( 'Table'[Value] ), 'Table'[Index] > 1 )
```

> ⚠ A circular dependency was detected: Table[Val1], Table[Value2], Table[Val1].

Figure 16.8: Circular dependency error

There are long-winded explanations for exactly why this occurs, but the easy solution is to just not use the **CALCULATE** function. Creating the following identical columns returns no errors.

```
Val3 = MAXX( FILTER( 'Table', [Index] > 1 && [Index] = EARLIER( 'Table'[Index] ) ),
                                 [Value] )

Val4 = MAXX( FILTER( 'Table', [Index] > 1 && [Index] = EARLIER( 'Table'[Index] ) ),
                                 [Value] )
```

This is not to say that using the **CALCULATE** function in calculated columns will always produce circular dependency errors. Indeed, the following two identical columns produce no circular dependency errors:

```
Val5 = CALCULATE( MAX( 'Table'[Value] ), ALL( 'Table' ), 'Table'[Index] > 1 )

Val6 = CALCULATE( MAX( 'Table'[Value] ), ALL( 'Table' ), 'Table'[Index] > 1 )
```

Again, you may be interested in the specific details of why and there are plenty of articles available on the internet to explain those specifics. But the easy answer is, don't use the **CALCULATE** function in calculated columns and you won't run into this issue.

Let's now turn our attention to the DAX query view.

Using DAX Query View

For all the hype that **DAX query view** received upon launch, the reality is that the **DAX query view** is not exactly super useful when it comes to debugging, or much of anything else. The interface is unintuitive and heavily dependent on memorizing keyboard shortcuts. You can use **DAX query view** similar to using **DAX Studio** by using the **Copy query** option in the **Performance analyzer** pane and pasting the query into **DAX query view**. Clicking the **Run** button evaluates the query and returns the results:

```
        ▷ Run        ↑ Update model with changes (0)

  1     // DAX Query
  2     DEFINE
  3         VAR __DS0Core =
  4             SUMMARIZECOLUMNS(
  5                 ROLLUPADDISSUBTOTAL(
  6                     ROLLUPGROUP('Dates'[Year], 'Dates'[Month], 'Dates'[MonthSort]), "IsGrandTotalRowTotal"
  7                 ),
  8                 "C", 'Calculations'[C]
  9             )
 10         VAR __DS0PrimaryWindowed =
 11             TOPN( 502, __DS0Core, [IsGrandTotalRowTotal], 0, 'Dates'[Year], 1, 'Dates'[MonthSort], 1,
 12                 'Dates'[Month],
 13                 1
 14             )
 15     EVALUATE
 16         __DS0PrimaryWindowed
 17     ORDER BY
 18         [IsGrandTotalRowTotal] DESC, 'Dates'[Year], 'Dates'[MonthSort], 'Dates'[Month]
```

Results   Result 1 of 1 ∨   📋 Copy ∨

⊞	Dates[Year]	Dates[Month]	Dates[MonthSort]	[IsGrandTotalRowTotal]	[C]
1				True	1096
2	2023	January	1	False	93
3	2023	February	2	False	85
4	2023	March	3	False	93
5	2023	April	4	False	90
6	2023	May	5	False	93
7	2023	June	6	False	90
8	2023	July	7	False	93
9	2023	August	8	False	93

Figure 16.9: DAX query view

Unfortunately, unlike **DAX Studio**, **DAX query view** lacks any kind of performance data or much else in the way of debugging or anything particularly useful.

You can also use the **Quick queries** option in the **Data** pane by right clicking a column, table, or measure, selecting **Quick queries** and then choosing an option. The options vary by object type and include **Show top 100 rows** for tables, **Show column statistics** for tables and columns, and **Define and evaluate** for measures.

Most of the options are informational in nature, and this is perhaps the best use of DAX query view since this is the only place, bizarrely, that you can run the **INFO** family of functions. The **INFO** family of functions return information based upon the **Dynamic Management Views** (**DMVs**) in **Analysis Services**. DMVs have long been a useful method of documenting the semantic model. That said, there are numerous third-party tools that make documenting the semantic model far easier than using DAX **INFO** functions and **DAX query view**.

Let's now look at an interesting DAX function, **EVALUATEANDLOG**.

EVALUATEANDLOG

The DAX function **EVALUATEANDLOG** is a diagnostic and debugging function introduced to help developers inspect intermediate results in DAX expressions. The **EVALUATEANDLOG** function logs the result of an expression while still returning its value. Think of it like inserting a "debug print" into your DAX code, like how console.log works in JavaScript or print() in Python. It doesn't change the calculation outcome but gives visibility into what's being evaluated, making it easier to trace logic and validate assumptions.

The "log" part of the **EVALUATEANDLOG** function refers to logging within Analysis Services and in particular traces performed via **SQL Profiler**. Thus, to utilize the **EVALUATEANDLOG** function as intended, you must have SQL Profiler installed or some other third-party tool. SQL Profiler can be installed when installing **SQL Server Management Studio** (**SSMS**).

An easy way to use **EVALUATEANDLOG** is to install SQL Profiler and then create a quick text file that allows you to open the SQL Profiler tool as an external tool in Power BI. This way SQL Profiler is automatically connected to your semantic model. To do this, create the following text file:

SQLProfiler.pbitool.json

```
{
  "version": "1.0",
  "name": "SQL Profiler",
  "description": "SQL Profiler",
  "path": "C:\\Program Files (x86)\\Microsoft SQL Server Management Studio
18\\Common7\\PROFILER.exe",
  "arguments": "/A \"%server%\" /D \"%database%\"",
  "iconData": "image/png;base64,…"
}
```

The text shown here does not include the full **iconData** value. The full version of this file is available in the GitHub repository for this book: https://github.com/gdeckler/DAX-For-Humans/tree/main/book.

Place this file in the following directory:

```
C:\Program Files (x86)\Common Files\Microsoft Shared\Power BI
Desktop\External Tools
```

After restarting Power BI Desktop, the **SQL Profiler** tool shows up in the **External tools** tab of the ribbon:

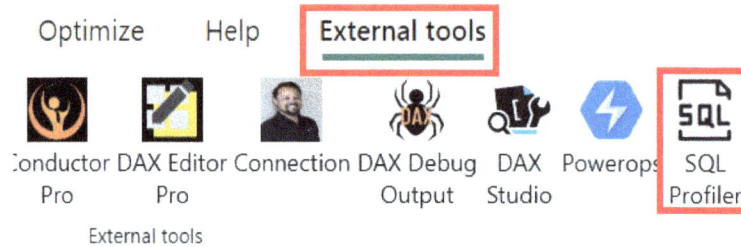

Figure 16.10: SQL Profiler in External tools tab

Clicking **SQL Profiler** in the **External tools** tab of the ribbon opens SQL Server Profiler and initiates a trace:

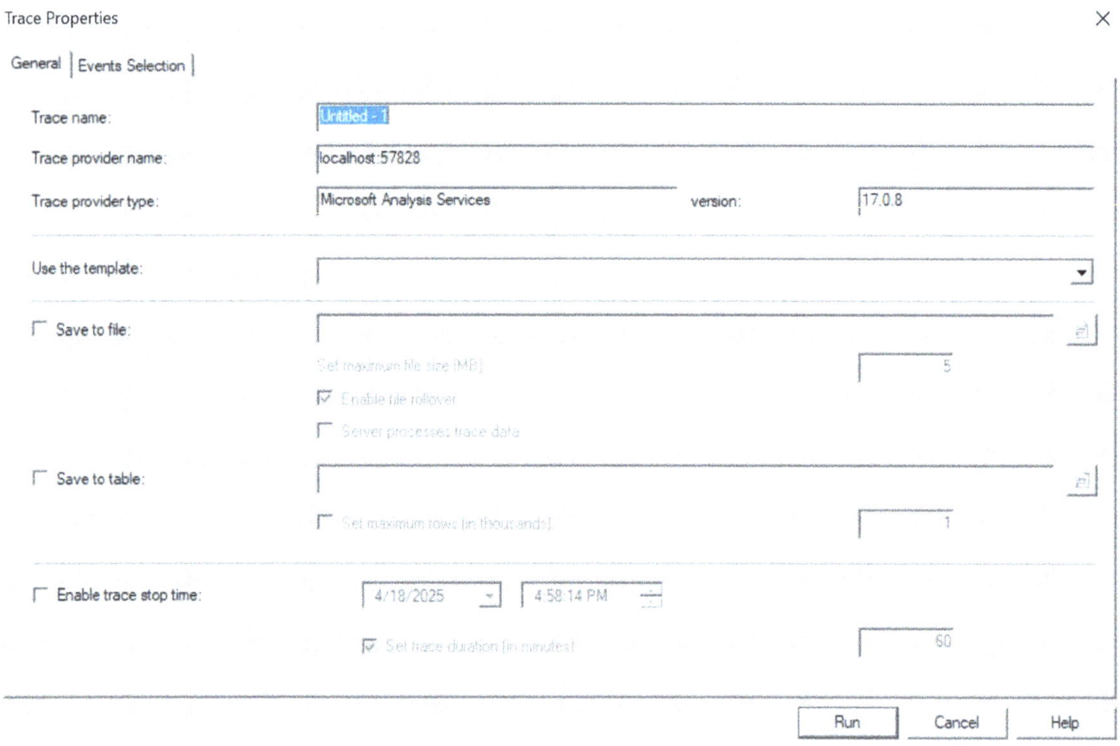

Figure 16.11: SQL Server Profiler trace

Switch to the **Events Selection** tab, expand the **Query Processing** section of the **Events** column and select the DAX-related events:

Trace Properties

General   Events Selection

Review selected events and event columns to trace. To see a complete list, select the "Show all events" and "Show a

Events	ActivityID	ApplicationContext	ApplicationName	CPUTime
☐ Calculation Evaluation	☐	☐	☐	☐
☐ Calculation Evaluation Detailed Infor...	☐	☐	☐	☐
☑ DAX Evaluation Log	☑	☑	☑	☑
☑ DAX Extension Execution Begin	☑	☑		
☑ DAX Extension Execution End	☑	☑		☑
☑ DAX Extension Trace Error	☑	☑		
☑ DAX Extension Trace Info	☑	☑		
☑ DAX Extension Trace Verbose	☑	☑		
☑ DAX Query Plan	☑	☑	☑	☑
☑ DAX Query Shape	☑	☑	☑	
☐ DirectQuery Begin	☐	☐		☐
☐ DirectQuery End	☐	☐		☐

Figure 16.12: DAX query trace events

Select the **Run** button to initiate the trace. Now, back in Power BI Desktop, you can create visuals, interact with visuals or use the **Performance Analyzer** to refresh the visuals on a page. The query events of any measure using **EVALUATEANDLOG** are then displayed in the SQL Server Profiler trace:

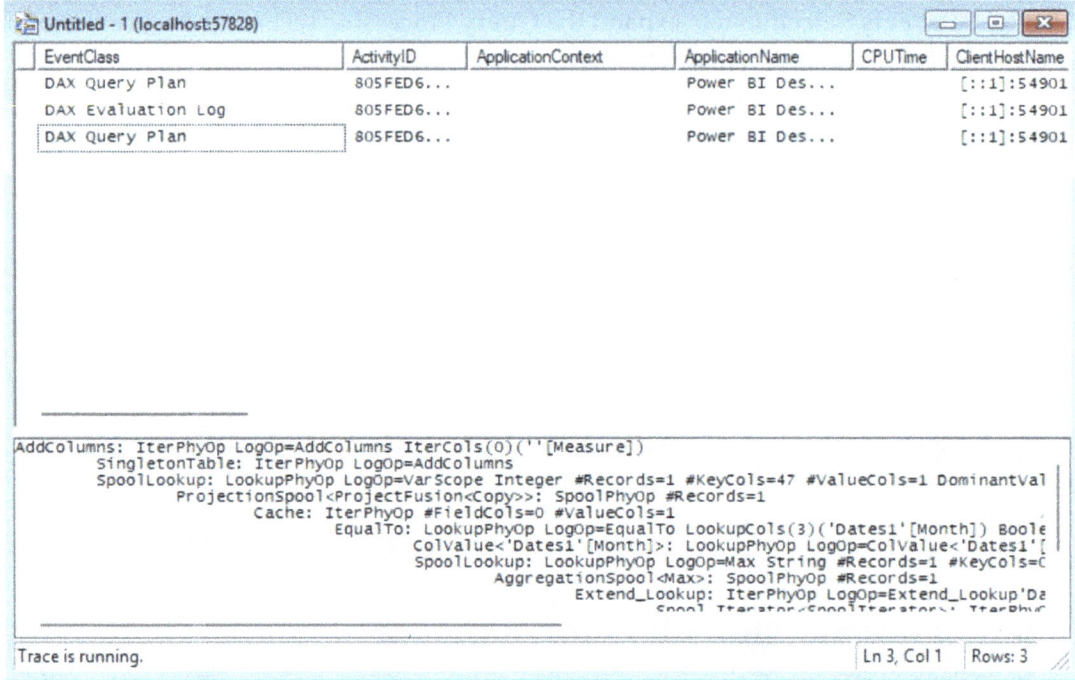

Figure 16.13: SQL Server Profiler trace

Note that **EVALULATEANDLOG** is not intended for use in production but rather only as a debugging tool. Thus, it is generally the case that measures are created and then a separate measure is created that uses **EVALUATEANDLOG([Measure])** in order to debug the measure. Once the measure is debugged, the **EVALUATEANDLOG** measure is removed and replaced with the original measure in the report.

This completes our analysis of the **EVALUATEANDLOG** function. As our final topic, let's address the **CALCULATE** function head on.

Let's Talk About CALCULATE

Throughout this book, we have made mention of the **CALCULATE** function numerous times, mostly in the context of avoiding it. While we did briefly cover the **CALCULATE** function in *Chapter 2, More Core Concepts*, it is now time to revisit the subject and provide some closure.

If you are utterly new to DAX, you may be wondering what this mysterious function, **CALCULATE**, is. However, if you have any experience with DAX at all, it is likely that you have seen or used the **CALCULATE** function in most of your DAX code. Finally, if you are an old school DAX coder, it is quite likely that you use **CALCULATE** all the time and have been told repeatedly that it is *"the most powerful function in DAX"*.

However, throughout this book you have seen how **CALCULATE** is not required for the vast majority of calculations. In fact, we have been able to solve incredibly complex and difficult problems without using the **CALCULATE** function. But the question may still remain in the minds of many readers, why is the **CALCULATE** function considered important and why not use the **CALCULATE** function? If you are one of these readers, let us explore what the **CALCULATE** function does and, in detail, the primary issue(s) with the **CALCULATE** function that originally inspired the search for a better method of learning and understanding DAX.

What is CALCULATE?

For all the praise and superlatives heaped upon the **CALCULATE** function, the **CALCULATE** function is really nothing more than a rather "fancy" filter function. To understand this, create the following table:

```
Dates1 =
    ADDCOLUMNS(
        CALENDAR( DATE( 2023, 1, 1 ), DATE( 2025, 12, 31 ) ),
        "Year", YEAR( [Date] ),
        "Month", FORMAT( [Date], "mmmm" ),
        "MonthSort", MONTH( [Date] ),
        "Weekday", FORMAT( [Date], "dddd" )
    )
```

Now set the **MonthSort** column as the **Sort by column** for the **Month** column. Next, create a **Table** visual containing an un-summarized **Year** column as well as the **Month** column. Now create the following two measures:

```
NC =
    VAR __Month = MAX( 'Dates1'[Month] )
    VAR __Table = FILTER( ALL( 'Dates1' ), [Month] = __Month )
    VAR __Result =
        IF(
            HASONEVALUE( 'Dates1'[Month] ),
            COUNTROWS( __Table ),
            COUNTROWS( 'Dates1' )
        )
```

```
RETURN

    __Result

C =

    CALCULATE(

        COUNTROWS( 'Dates1' ),

        ALLEXCEPT( 'Dates1', 'Dates1'[Month] )

    )
```

Add these measures to the **Table** visualization. Both of these measures do the same thing within the context of the **Table visual**. They both ignore all other filters, filter the table by the current row's **Month** value, and then count the number of rows in the table. Thus, January for all years returns **93** which is 31 + 31 + 31 = 93 since January has **31** days and the **Dates** table covers three years, 2023, 2024, and 2025.

If you have done any kind of coding, know a bit of Excel, or especially after reading this book, what the **NC** measure is doing is obvious. However, even if you have coded before but are new to DAX, what exactly the **C** measure is doing is not entirely clear without knowing much more about the functions involved.

The **CALCULATE** function takes two parameters or arguments. The first is a DAX expression to be evaluated. The second is an optional filter expression. This filter expression can be multi-part and can include logical (Boolean) filter expressions, table filter expressions as well as filter modifying functions such as **ALLEXCEPT**. In other words, the **CALCULATE** function filters something and then performs a calculation over that filtered something, essentially short-hand and syntax sugar for the No CALCULATE approach to DAX. As bizarre as it might sound, the **CACULATE** function was originally designed to make DAX "easy".

What **CALCULATE** proponents insist on promoting is that **CALCULATE** is the only function in DAX that can *replace* filter context. In other words, the claim is that because the **NC** measure uses the **ALL** function, it effectively brings the entire table back into context sucking up huge amounts of memory and retrieving more data than needed from the storage engine until then subsequently filtering down to the desired information while instead the **CALCULATE** function performs black magic wizardry to not do any of that. The problem with this argument is that it is utterly false.

Think back to the last chapter when we explained the Formula Engine and the Storage Engine. Recall that in terms of speed and performance, the DAX you write really just needs to lead the Formula Engine down a correct path to create as optimal a query plan as possible. The actual DAX that you write is of less consequence in this than you might otherwise believe. The Formula

Engine just needs to be able understand the gist of what you are trying to achieve in order to create the optimized query plan. Therefore, it is entirely possible that two measures, one written with **CALCULATE** and another written without **CALCULATE** could generate the same exact query plan.

CALCULATE proponents often also cite that DAX is *written* for **CALCULATE**. And thus, all measures that use the **CALCULATE** function are somehow better or easier for the Formula Engine to optimize. This is obviously not the case considering that sometimes like in *Chapter 15, CALCULATE vs. No CALCULATE Scenario 1* that the Formula Engine cannot find an optimal query plan for even incredibly simple formulas.

Now, is **CACULATE** used behind the scenes when evaluating measures? It sure is, and that's exactly where the **CALCULATE** function should largely stay. Just like we don't interact with a computer in ones and zeros, there is no real need to see the **CALCULATE** function out in the wild when it comes to modern DAX, with only a few possible exceptions.

Thus, the **CALCULATE** function at first glance is a rather innocuous looking "fancy" filter function with perhaps some dubious "advantages". In fact, Microsoft classifies the **CALCULATE** function as a filter function in its *Data Expressions Analysis (DAX) Reference*. However, let's take a closer look at the **CALCULATE** function to uncover some of the troubling aspects of the function.

The Trouble with CALCULATE

Now that you understand the basics of the **CALCULATE** function, let's dig a little deeper to uncover its true nature. To begin getting to the bottom of the CALCULATE function's true nature, create the following measure:

```
Days in February ? =
    CALCULATE(
        CALCULATE(
            COUNTROWS( 'Dates1' ),
            'Dates1'[Month] = "February"
        ),
        'Dates1'[Month] = "January"
    )
```

Considering what we learned in the last section, that the **CALCULATE** function's filter expression replaces context, we might reasonably expect one of two outcomes from the **Days in**

February ? measure. One possibility is that the two filters are mutually exclusive and thus blank is returned. The other reasonable outcome is that the outer **CALCULATE** function's filter clause replaces the context of the inner **CALCULATE** function's filter clause.

Sadly, both of these outcomes are incorrect. Placing the **Days in February ?** measure into a **Card** visual returns **85**, the number of days in February for the years 2023, 2024, and 2025. You see, **CALCULATE** has an arbitrary rule that when considering nested **CALCULATE** functions that the innermost **CALCULATE** function's filter overrides the outer. And thus, we uncover part of the true nature of the **CALCULATE** function. The "fancy" part of **CACLULATE** being a filter function is that it is a magical black box that follows a bunch of arbitrarily decided "rules".

But, let's dig deeper, there is more to discover. Now create the following measure:

```
Days in February ?? =
    CALCULATE(
        CALCULATE(
            COUNTROWS( 'Dates1' ),
            KEEPFILTERS(
                'Dates1'[Month] = "January" || 'Dates1'[Month] = "February"
            )
        ),
        'Dates1'[Month] = "April" || 'Dates1'[Month] = "February"
    )
```

Considering what we just learned, one might reasonably expect that the **Days in February ??** measure would return 178 which is the number of days in January for all years (93) plus the number of days in February for all years (85). You would again be disappointed. Placing the **Days in February ??** measure into a **Card** visual again returns 85, the number of days in February for the years 2023, 2024, and 2025.

What is going on here is the use of the **KEEPFILTERS** function. The **KEEPFILTERS** function modifies the modified behavior of the **CALCULATE** function to make the final filter clause an intersection of the two filter clauses versus the inner **CALCULATE** function's filter clause completely overriding the outer **CALCULATE** function's filter clause. Since **'Dates'[Month] = "February"** is the only common filter between the two filters, the final filter only considers dates in the month of February when counting the rows of the **Dates** table.

If we then consider that no less than seven filter modifier functions exist:

- **REMOVEFILTERS**
- **ALL**
- **ALLEXCEPT**
- **ALLNOBLANKROW**
- **KEEPFILTERS**
- **USERELATIONSHIP**
- **CROSSFILTER**

And then further consider the immeasurable possible ways in which those filter modifier functions might interact. This is 5,040+ (n!) when considering nesting where order matters but not allowing repetition. If we allow repetition, then the number is n^r where n is the number of filter modifier functions (7) and r is the number of times we use a filter function. We thus quickly come to realize that the **CALCULATE** function is not only a magical black box that follows a bunch of arbitrarily decided "rules", but also is a magical black box that follows a bunch of arbitrarily decided "rules" with its own mini-formula language.

In all respects, the **CALCULATE** function is a mini-formula language within the overall DAX language. Most of the filter modifier functions cannot be used outside of the **CALCULATE** function. These filter modifier functions form a syntactical language that is unique to the **CALCULATE** function. And this is why there are innumerable blog posts about the secret inner workings of this mini-formula language.

Thus, I never understood the focus on **CALCULATE** when attempting to teach people DAX. It's like trying to teach people how to fly before they can walk or trying to understand the full scope of an entire video game from some random mini game within the game.

But, with all of this said, the truly troubling aspect of the **CALCULATE** function is its impenetrability. In other words, how does one debug what is going on inside the **CALCULATE** function? We cannot break the two nested **CALCUATE** functions into separate expressions because the results would be entirely different. And thus, one has no way of really knowing which arbitrary rules are being enforced and how the filter expressions and filter modifier functions are really interacting with one another. One just simply has to "know". *This, above all else, is what makes DAX hard for people to learn and understand.*

When to Use CALCULATE?

Now that you understand the No CALCULATE method as well as the basics of the **CALCULATE** function, you might be wondering when it might be appropriate to use the

CALCULATE function. And the answer is, use it whenever and wherever you want. There is no such thing as the No CALCULATE police that are going to stop you from using it.

If you can learn the many nuances and inner complexities of the **CALCULATE** function then, by all means, use **CALCULATE** to your heart's content. There are certainly times when it can be convenient such as when you have a base No CALCULATE or other measure and you simply need that measure to be calculated in a slightly modified context. Instead of repeating a bunch of DAX code from the original measure and modifying it, it's certainly convenient to use the **CALCULATE** function instead. That said, it's easy to get wonky results, especially when using the filter modifying functions.

Summary

This chapter had three main topic areas, using artificial intelligence to write DAX code, advanced techniques for debugging DAX, and finally a look at the **CALCULATE** function. For the first topic, we learned a process of working with generative artificial intelligence chatbots that can dramatically increase the accuracy and useability of generated DAX code. In addition, we learned several different debugging techniques for debugging DAX code. Finally, we covered the **CALCULATE** function including what the **CALCULATE** function is as well as the various issues with the **CALCULATE** function.

It is poetic that we end our DAX journey here, talking about the **CALCULATE** function since this is exactly where the **CALCULATE** function should be in everyone's DAX journey, at the end. **CALCULATE** is perhaps the most complex function to master in DAX and, as demonstrated throughout this book, is largely unneeded. If you would like to continue your DAX journey and learn more about the **CALCULATE** function, simply pick up any other book on DAX, literally any other DAX book.

We hope you have enjoyed this exploration of the DAX language and that you can leverage the techniques and patterns explored within this book in your own practical, real-world scenarios. This book has been a labor of love for myself and many of my patrons so on behalf of myself and my patrons, we sincerely appreciate your support and wish you the best on your continuing journey in business intelligence, Power BI, and DAX.

It has been said that the road to hell is paved with good intentions and good intentions are exactly why the **CALCUATE** function exists. Unfortunately, the road to hell is paved with good intentions…

Index

C

www.ingramcontent.com/pod-product-compliance
Lightning Source LLC
Chambersburg PA
CBHW081214220326
41598CB00037B/6771